ENGLISH
SANTALI DICTIONARY

ENGLISH
SANTALI DICTIONARY

Published by

Gyan Publishing House
5, Ansari Road
Daryaganj, New Delhi-110002
Phone: 011-47034999, 9811692060
E-mail: books@gyanbooks.com

Distribution Network
gyanbooks.com
India, USA, Canada, UK, Australia, France

ISBN : 978-81-212-2686-8 (HB)

2nd Impression 2021

Printed at: Gyan Press, Delhi.

English Santali Dictionary

ENGLISH–SANTALI DICTIONARY.

N. B. Abbreviations Used.

(M) and (F) refer not only to the genders of words but also to words used by, and of, men and women respectively.

(2) Signifies that the word immediately preceding is reduplicated, e. g. *bhọc (2)* means *bhọc bhọc.*

A.

A (*the indefinite article*)—miť, miťțeč, miťțən, miťțaň.
Aback, to be taken—haka caka.
Abandon, to—bągi, pąc, teag.
Abandoned, to be—bhǫdǫr.
Abated—hin.
Abatement—ghąți.
Abdicate, to—teag.
Abdomen, the—lač.
Aberrant—apa bąrią, aprąr.
Abge bonga, place for worship of—kulkhi.
Abhor, to—hirkhą.
Abhorrent—hirkhą parkha.
Abide, to—bęrel, thąwi, thǫl.
Ability—bhas, butląk, dare, dhęj, khęmǫta, kut, lor, lordhej, lur, sąddi, sądhi, sąkti ; (*full*) bharsak.
Able—lǫhąni ; (*to be*) dare, lęțęč, sęțęč ; (*to do*) dhęj ; (*to run,-of leverets*) țela ; (*bodied*) lekman, pakța.
Abode—thǫl ; (*to take up*) bęrel, mąriąu.
Abolish, to—mąhkup, mąuta, uțhąu.
Abomination, indicating—chią, chiąre.
Aboriginal—buniądi.
Aborigines, castes and tribes of—Bąuri, Beldar, Chamar, Dhunią, Dhusąt, Ḍǫm, Dusąd, Ghațwal, Hądi, Käekũi, Kẽrẽkõrẽ, Kherwar, Ḳoda, Kol, Kurmbi, Mushąr, Nąiyą, Suṇḍi, Turi, Urão.
Abortion, to cause—hamal khũn, hemal khũn.
Abounding—anęč dhanęč, dhurpąu ; (*to be*) cąrhi, phar.
About—(*of number, time, etc.*) abe tabe, gan, laga lągi, lega ligi, leha lihi, lǫgbhǫg, nąhi nindhąn ; (*concerning*) babǫtre, reaǩ, reaň ; (*the present time*) teheń gapa ; (*here*) neman ; (*to on the point of*) dąkhil, lagať, lągiť, mãrã ; (*one*) țek.
Above—cetan, cǫț, upąr, upǫr.
Abrade, to—bender.
Abraded—hadra hądri, hadrao, hudriť.
Abridged—sanchep.
Abrogate, to—lǫțǫm.
Abscess—(*a kind of*) nąrgi ghao ; (*over scapula*) dąbi bebeǩ ; (*on the back*) paląnią ghao ; (*perineal*) andhärgąṇḍ ; (*of scalp*) uru eṅga.
Absence—pharak ; (*of, in the*) gupti mar ; (*of blemish*) napae.
Absent—(*to be*) bąnuǩ ; (*oneself, to*) aṅkher.
Absolutely—nirdae, țhae, utąr ; (*none*) niti.
Absorb, to—cusąu.
Absorbed in, to be—raktao, raṅgao, rosao.
Abstinence—net.
Abstract anything other than by proper method, to—puțuč.
Abstract nouns, particle for—teť.
Abundance—acel pacel, borket, rane bane.
Abundant—amela, ąmilą, asambhęr, asęč tasęč, bąląi, gargadlaǩ, hamram, hela, jhane jhapane, sahta, sasta, sorpha, teretese, udhiã.
Abuse—(*to*) barǫ bakhan, bis bakhan, ęgęr, lese, sǫṇḍa, țhanka țhąnki ; (*self, to*) hejęr, pisiṛ ; (*a term of*) condho, cudi, eṅgam doṅgam, eṅgraň, gabhri, gąṇḍi, gaṇḍke, hagal gąṇḍią.
Abusively—sidraǩ badraǩ.
Accede to, to—dąhin, muńjur, rębęn.
Accent, difference in—garmaǩ.
Accept, to—ąṅgikar, aňrąu, ąṅgrąu, gatao, hatao, mąńjur, muńjur ; (*by placing hand on*) hat capra ; (*as true*) jǫm ; (*a reason*) kar maṅgao.
Acceptable—murji ; (*to become*) sarthi.
Access, a narrow way of—ghaț.
Accident—(*an*) apce, beora, dąb, dob ; (*absence of*) napae ; (*by*) bęjan, dąbte, khęn leka.
Acclaim, to—sarhao.
Accomodated, to be—sahǫp.
Accompaniment—satalaǩ, sętęlaǩ.
Accompany, to—galsal, gǫrǫ, jumąu, loe, sohga, sǫṅgę.
Accomplice, an—jąsu ; (*to become*) lapțao.
Accomplish, to—dhęj, purąu ; (*sarcastic*) nehal, nepra.
Accomplished—sid, sidbid, sidho ; (*to be*) harap, harrap, sid ataň, ti bąisąu.
Accordance with, in—hisabte, jake jęmǫn, jęmǫn...tęmǫn, leka.
Accost, to—țokao.

ACCOUNT,—bil, hisab, lekha jokha; (*statement*) katha, khesa; (*book*) bahi, buhi, nathi; (*to make up*) ganda guti, nikas, nikas baki; (*to give*) jabab dahi emok; (*to demand*) kutau.

ACCOUNT OF, ON—babotre, badalte, badat, dae, eron, iate, kar, karaite, khatirte, lasanga, lasarhe, losoñ, sabab, satate, teron, tese.

ACCUMULATE, TO—juktau, (*of water*) tombao.

ACCUMULATION—(*of drift-wood*) hadi; (*of thread on spindle*) kukurhi.

ACCURATE—bhede bhed, khape khap, khapkhap, sudh, thik, thik thak, uju.

ACCUSATION—kalak, kali, sabab; (*a false*) phasad, phesad; (*to keep back part of*) jibka; (*to bring an*) lalis, nalis; (*to bring up an old*) jojna; (*against each other, to bring*) nalsa nalsi; (*fear of*) kalak.

ACCUSE, TO—ardas, bad, bohok, darao, khoca, khota, latak; (*falsely*) dohmot, duhmot, khõca khũci, khocao, phand, phond, phorphond,; (*each other*) bada badi, hura huri, khaua khawi.

ACCUSED—asami, kadi, mudali; (*to be*) ghotao; (*and complainant*) kadi badi.

ACCUSER, AN—badi, phiriadi.

ACCUSTOM, TO—bhãoar, bhãwãr, catiau, curau, hewa, rigdau, sadhao, teñjao, tiñjau; (*to work*) eto.

ACCUSTOMED TO—bhetro, bohon, copao, hitau; (*to be*) baisau, lindar, lindor; (*to become*) katao, parkau.

ACHING—kankanao; (*in neck*) hadi. *Cf.* STOMACH.

ACID—jhal, jojo, jojo moroć, kãć kãć, moroć; (*slightly*) comkoroć, coromokoć; (*of stomach*) amol.

ACKNOWLEDGE, TO—añgachao, añgoc, gachao, gatao, godao, kabul, mañgao, sikar; (*gratefully*) gun manao; (*by placing hand on*) hat capra.

ACKNOWLEDGEMENT—(*deed of*) ikrar nama; (*by plaintiff*) raji nama; (*of money paid*) roka, uslat.

ACNA—topot.

ACQUAINT, TO—janti, lai.

ACQUAINTANCES—cinha parca, jana suna, jan pahcan, ñepel oprom pera, paribs, parijan, pera parbha.

ACQUAINTED WITH—heto, hitu, jana jani, parcha.

ACQUIESCE, TO—kabul, reben, sikar.

ACQUIRE, TO—arjao, birgau; (*merit*) danpun.

ACQUIT, TO—khalas.

ACQUITTAL—rihai.

ACRIMONIOUS—aĩtaha, cauchalia, khara, titi, tito.

ACROSS—gandgand, par, parom; (*to put or go*) parom; (*country straight*) sodok rodok, sopok rodok.

ACT, AN—kami; (*to see in the*) tebak.

ACT, TO—kami; (*together*) jog; (*secretly*) bhidi.

ACTED UPON, TO BE—dhamsao.

ACTION, DENOTES SUDDEN OR FORCIBLE—pacpacao.

ACTIVE—cogor, halhal, hat chut, hath chuti, kasmi, kharañ khacañ, ragi, ragragia, usrau.

ACTUALLY—bañse, thae.

ACUTE—lag.

ADAM'S APPLE—hor okot.

ADD, TO—(*to*) agad, gortoroć, gotoć, jutić, jutuć, lahkao; (*up*) jorao, lekha gut.

ADDICTED TO—copao; (*gañja*) gañjeri; (*liquor*) matal, matla, piak, reñka.

ADDITION TO, IN—artet, uprand; (*length of house*) tonor; (*rent*) bheja.

ADDLED EGG, AN—dhokok bele.

ADDRESS—nãogão, não thikan.

ADDRESS, TO—(*as pleader*) sawal; (*one able to*) sawalia.

ADDRESS, FORMS OF—(*respectful*) baba, bap dhon, hajur; (*between inlaws*) samdhi, sangat, sari, sumdhi; (*to young females*) biti, boe, mai, na; (*to males*) maya, mayo, meya; (*to young persons*) ja, na, ya; (*to boys*) babu, babu rae, beta; (*between children and women*) bau; (*to girls when scolding*) bhũsndi, bhũsri; (*by female returning salutation*) cipciryop; (*abusive*) cudi; (*between husband and wife*) tiri; (*to inferiors*) ea.

ADEPT—kharkaha, kharkhari; (*at the flute*) baskaria.

ADHERE TO, TO—jalať, jaṭaǩ, jileť, lata, laṭkao, lẹṭkọm, ṭhẹkọm; (*of clay to feet*) thọkṛe, thubṛe, tokṛe; (*together*) cẹpṭhẹ, jimṭau.

ADHESIVE—jaṭaň, jẹkṛẹ, jẹmṭhẹ, jẹnṭhe, jẹṭkẹ, jewen, jewer, laṭha, laṭlaṭ, leṭko; (*non-*) kharkasaha.

ADHIBIT SIGNATURE, TO—dọskhọt.

ADIEU, TO BID—bidạ.

ADJECTIVAL SUFFIX—ten.

ADJUTANT BIRD, THE—garuṛ.

ADMINISTER, TO—calao, laṛcaṛ, lọrcọṛ.

ADMIRABLE—cakmak.

ADMIRATION—(*exclm. of*) dekja; (*to excite*) cakmak.

ADMIT, TO—aňgọc, gachao, godao, hẽ, himạn, humạn, mạnjur.

ADMIXTURE, WITHOUT—nichora, nirola, sada, tartạrịạ.

ADMONISH, TO—mana, samjhao.

ADMONITION, EXCLM. OF—mẹn!

ADOLESCENT—cẹṇḍa, juạn, sẽṛã.

ADOPT, TO—badha.

ADORN, TO—husnạk, saj, sajao, sobha, thạṭbond.

ADORNED—jhiki miki.

ADROIT—caher, sarghạrịạ; (*of young persons*) saṛphạrịạ.

ADULT—ḍaṭha ḍuṭhu, dhạṭha ḍuṭhu, goṭa guṭi, hara jarjo, haraṭạl, maṭha muṭhu, sean, sẽṛã.

ADULTERATE, TO—bheňjan, mesal.

ADULTERY—(*to commit*) latghat, lọtghuṭi, (*one who commits*) bhanḍ (M), bhạṇḍin (F).

ADVANCE, AN—(*of money*) baena, dạdni; (*without interest*) hạulạt; (*of payment, to force*) cacao. *Cf.* PAY.

ADVANCE, TO—badhao, calao, caṛhao, sọhọr; (*money or grain*) bilat.

ADVANCED IN YEARS—cipoč copoč.

ADVANTAGE—bapha, mulạpha, parapạt, phaeda, pọrhọ.

ADVERSE—(*supernatural influence*) bẹd, bẹr, bidịạ; (*unaffected by*) obidhan; (*fortune, to meet with*) jarkhar.

ADVERSITY—durdosa, jala.

ADVERTISEMENT—istihar.

ADVICE—budbhorsa; (*to take*) tạdbir.

ADVISE, TO—lại bujhạu, poramẹs, salha, sikạu, sikhạu, sọlhọ.

ADVOCATE, AN—ukil, wạkil.

ADZE, A SMALL—bạslạ; (*to dress wood with*) laǩ.

AERIAL ROOTS OF BANYAN &C., TREES—jọrọ.

AERIOLITE, AN—cẹṭẹr dhiri.

AFFABILITY—sohag; (*with*) soloman.

AFFAIRS—bọndọbọs.

AFFECT, TO—bhijạu, ṭasak, ṭhasak.

AFFECTED—(*to be*) dhamsao; (*not well*) bẹraji.

AFFECTION—hĩt pirit, mãya, mel, mil, milụạ; (*by force of*) mãyã jalate, ṭhonk; (*with demonstration of*) cehor behor; (*to think of with*) uihạr.

AFFECTIONATE—helmel, hilmil, hitmiṭạr, humur (2), muri (2), pirit.

AFFINITY—sombond.

AFFIRMATION, A SOLEMN—halap, kiriạ.

AFFIX (*to from adverbs signifying sudden action*)—marte, mẹnte.

AFFLICT, TO—santao.

AFFLICTED—harkhetiạ, jarkhar, nara dhura.

AFFLICTION—bhuk duk, dukdukuạs, dusko, harkhet, jala, kọclọn, kọndọl, mar muhim, muhim, pajet, santap; (*bodily*) nara dhura; (*from supernatural influence*) laṭu bhạnḍu.

AFFLUENT—bạrião.

AFGHAN, AN—Kabalịạ, Kạbulịạ.

AFLOAT, TO SET—bhasan.

AFRAID—ḍorokiạ; (*to be*) bhilki, bọrọ, bọtọr, dalkao, lẹwẹ.

AFTER—ạṭre, bad, kur, mahre, re, tayọm; (*that*) inạkate, kate, (*a long time*) asãe sawãe; (*math*) doja.

AFTERBIRTH, THE—baha, ãowãr.

AFTERGLOW OF SUNSET—jholphol.

AFTERNOON—dhinạň, tarasiň, ulṭi ghạṇṭa; (*to-day*) dhinạň tarasiň.

AGAIN—arhõ, aro, eṭaǩ garte, ghurịã, ghurikaete, ghurkaete, pher, sạni; (*of again*) ghurại ulṭại, ghurịã (2), ghuri phiri, huč (2), huluč (2), jãoṛe (2), kane (2), rigiṛ, thetmet, uṭiuṭi; (*and again without success*) orgo pọrgo.

AGAINST—birud, upạrre; (*one's will*) dhara bandha, mọsọkusi; (*the hair*) sirgạt.

AGE—bas, jug, tur, turiạ, umạr, umạriạ, umer, umor, umur ; (*of*) sẽrã ; (*of equal*) ek turiạ, juạri, mit̕ tur, ọpọr jọpọr ; (*of full*) hara jarjo, hapamun (F), haratạl ; (*under*) adãt, kãca umer, nabalọk ; (*of tender*) liear ; (*the present*) nahak̕ jug ; (*not looking one's*) bagar gạthiạ ; (*little difference in*) lẹdẹ pọtẹ ; (*varying in*) lẹdẹ̕ thẹkrẹ̕ ; (*upon age*) jug cetan jug. *Cf.* OLD.

AGED—ạdharo budharo, budi (F), burhạ (M), burhi (F), umạriạ.

AGENT, AN—gạriạ, gọmọsta, gumạsta, lọndbọnd.

AGGRAVATING—carcapar, isbis.

AGGREGATE NUMBER, AN—(1280)-khạri.

AGGRIEVE, TO—bạtul.

AGILE—perel.

AGITATE, TO—dahlao, dalmalao ; (*water*) hudgạr, leoda.

AGITATED—ḍamaḍol, khuṭkhuṭ ; (*of liquid*) cawak̕ cawak̕ ; (*to be*) biklạ bikli, caṭpaṭao ; (*in mind*) beakul.

AGOING, TO SET—calao, parsao.

AGONY—alajhala.

AGREE, TO—ạṅgikar, banao, banọt, katha jọm, ṅapam, suhi; (*to*) ạṅgrạu, ạṅkus, aoda, ekrar, gacao, hẽ, ikrar, kạbul, kar manao, rẹbẹn, sạhi, sipi ; (*as food*) jirạu ; (*to a forfeit*) akhaji.

AGREEABLE—murji.

AGREEMENT—bọnọt, girmiṭ, mel, mil, milạp, milijili, milimisi ; (*an*) mocolka ; (*to come to an*) rap dhap, rẹṭ, riạ, rikit, riạu rajọṭ ; (*to establish*) paka pạki ; (*a written*) ekrar nama, ikrar nama, karar nama.

AGRICULTURAL—(*produce*) arjon, cij, durib ; (*property*) on cun ; (*holding*) jot ; (*holding, occupier of*) jotadar ; (*implement, an*) baksa, karha ; (*year, end of*) Dinmas, Mag ; (*operations, to begin*) puhnạ. *Cf.* SERVANT.

AGROUND, TO BE—dhañ.

AHA !—hallạ bhại !

AHEM, TO—ẹhẹm, ẹthẹm.

AID, TO—gọrọ, sạhai, sạhaita, sahas, saṅgarhe, torao.

AILING—ạtruṅ, dormad, dọrmọ̕c, dọrọñ sọrọñ, dọrọsọrọ, robojholo.

AILMENT—kạrni, karọn, kạsur, kusur ; (*without*) khilkam, nirogi.

AIM—as, asãe sawãe ; (*to*) ghatghatao ; (*to take*) as ; (*with gun*) cak ; (*with bow and arrow*) habak̕.

AIMLESSLY—ajlạtiạ, alak balak, alak ḍiḍi, alaklạṇḍi, alañ pholañ, aṅgot baṅgot, asok̕ ṭayok̕, jarmak̕ tormak̕, kalañ ḍolañ, kulạñ, liṛọ̕c lọṛọ̕c, liṛọñ lọṛọñ, tormak̕ ; (*to go*) aṇḍa maṇḍa, culuñ bhuṭuñ.

AIR—họe, họyọñ ; (*to suffer from want of*) ghulghul ; (*to take the*) ṭahalao, ṭahlao.

AIR, AN—(*tune*) khọd, rar ; (*name of*) manọt rar, Sohrae rar.

AIRS, TO PUT ON—alak jhalak, bạdagiri, bilit̕, chamak damak (F), mecka micki.

AKIN—sanam.

ALARM—bhãe ; (*shout for*) guhạr, kulkuli ; (*rat-tat on drum*) guhriạ ; (*exclm. of*) mẹn ; (*to take*) ṭạtka birki.

ALAS !—aha, hae, haere, jahre, jare (2), uh.

ALCOHOL—mạhur.

ALERT—(*to be*) cahak mahak, sọntọr ; (*to be on the*) birlañ, caṅke, cehao, jagao, jagarna, jagrọn, jagwar, jạigir, johjohao, tahtahao, uạkep, wakhep ; (*to put on the*) bargao.

ALGA, A FRESH WATER—sealom.

ALIEN—algẹl.

ALIGHT, TO—(*on branch, &c.*) ap ; (*on ground*) tạpuk̕.

ALIKE—ẹk jọntọr, saman, soman, somasom.

ALIVE—(*to become*) jiwẹt̕ ; (*to keep*) bañcao, jiạu, teweñ jiwẹt̕.

ALL—atom, bebak, bhor, caba, cạr, cạtur, chinci punci, chuchạ, gạyum, harẹk, irci gurci, irti̕c garti̕c, istọk, jọtọ, khaṇḍe khaṇḍ, lae, liti birsi, mọmblọt, ṅam ṅam, ọstọk, pạcuk̕, sagor, sanam, sara, sobbo ; (*to take*) hameṭ ; (*in*) moṭh ; (*at*) kọkhọno ; (*directions, in*) ạlmạl, ãonda ãundi, bera biri, beṛhae, bhasbhus, bidlại, bọnẹ badarẹ, cạrio kọṇḍ, cạtur, cạtur dig, cạukhũṭ, dahades, dhamdhaser, hạlmạl, hiḍo hoḍo, kọṇḍ (2), phac phuc, pon kọṇḍ, tahãr bihãr, tereṅ goreṅ (*kinds of*) barọ bakhan, chạtik, emanteak̕, emanten, ghaser, hoṭak picạk, hunạr, laṭbalaṅ, ligiṛ sigiṛ, liṭi birsi, parkar, tẹgẹć masak ; *(together)* jhamajhum, jhamjhum, jhapjhup, jhumblạı mẹnte, jomka jumki, jomkao, miṫte, miṫ jomkao ; *(without exception)* ṅam ṅam ; *(as it occured)* khaṇḍe khaṇḍ ; *(day)* asṭo ghạri, bajar kuṛi din, cạupọhọr din, din bhor, sara din, siṅ sạṭup ; *(night)* cạupọhọr rat, jaḍam (2), ṅindạ bhor, rọḍọk (2), sara rạt ; *(day and night)* miṫ siṅ miṫ ṅindạ, siṅ lae ṅindạ lae ; *(the year)* barọmas, tiris bạris ; *(times)* sobbo kal ; *(one's life)* tire juge, ṭuṇḍaṅ bhor.

ALLAY EXCITEMENT, TO—suć.

ALLAYED, TO BE—nẹmbroṫ.

ALLEVIATION—salsāt.

ALLIGATOR, AN—maṅgaṛ.

ALLOW, TO—aṛak, oco.

ALLOWABLE—chạḍ.

ALLOWANCE—mojra ; *(for subsistence)* nankar.

ALLURE, TO—bahka bạhki, bahkae, jhakrao, lobdhao, ulạr, urạl.

ALLURED, TO BE—ṭanao.

ALLURES, ONE WHO—urạliạ.

ALLY, AN—modet.

ALMANACK, AN—pạṅji, patra.

ALMOND, AN—badam jọ.

ALMOST—abga, baṛić, lihạlahe, lọgbhọg, palek, prae : *(of darkness)* popolhoṫ.

ALOE, THE AMERICAN—koṅga, morsba, ọguru.

ALONE—eka, eka chinạ, ekaha, eka jibạ, ekan, ekarha, ekāt, ekla, eknạr, ekōt, eskar, eskar toskar, tala taṇḍi ; *(and silent)* gusuṅ (2).

ALONG WITH—lagae, lekate, loe, niyō, sạhit, salak, samet, sāo, satalak, sẹlẹṫ, sẹtẹlak, sọṅ, sọṅgọ, sudhạ, tahẽ tuluć, tuluć ; *(to take)* ḍuriạu ; *(companions)* gate ora uri.

ALONG THE EDGE—paṭhe.

ALPHABET, A LETTER OF—akhọr, harọp.

ALSO—ar, hõ, pọrjọnt, sudhạ.

ALTAR, AN—kaṇḍ, piṇḍ.

ALTER, TO—bạdli, pheṭ ; *(appearance or form)* bẹ-rup.

ALTERATION—dọlbadọl.

ALTERCATE, TO—apṭha apṭhi, bakhoṛ, contha cunthi, dhukạ dhuki, ḍiḍhi bạḍhi, hạrka hạrki, ipicak, jigrạ jigri, kẹṅmẹṅ, kọckọcọ, lakṭha, leṭha, rẹgẹṅ tẹgẹṅ, rẹpẹć, rẹtẹ pẹtẹ, reṭha riṭhi, rọpọr rọpọk, rọpọr, tẹgẹṅ, tekhraṛ, tokraṛ.

ALTERCATION, AN—jhaka jhạki, kạjiạ.

ALTERNATE—*(to)* erpher, phera phiri ; *(days, on)* pạsri.

ALTERNATELY—olapạlite, orapạlite, pạri (2) ; *(high & low tone)* ṭikọr ṭọkọr.

ALTHOUGH—ẹnrehõ, rehõ.

ALTOGETHER—caṅ cuṅ, hoṫ husiṫ, nikạṛkhaṛ, nirdae, nitantọ, sanam lekate.

ALUM—phiṭkiri.

ALWAYS—asṭo ghạri, barabar, barọmas, gisić (2), haighạri, here gese, here phere, hisir (2), holo (2), jaejug, jaoge, jao jaote, jugạjug, modam, mondam, ọsṭọ ghuṛi, sadae, sanam ghuṛi, sodae, tire juge, tiris jug, tiris bạris ; *(on the move)* bhacaṅ bhucuṅ.

AMALGAMATE, TO—johṛa.

AMASS, TO—halaṅ, juktạu, samṭạo, saṅgrạu.

AMAZE, TO—ṭhak.

AMAZED, TO BE—bharọ, hae moe, mọgọn, mọṅgọn, tharbasao.

AMAZING—bẹhaj.

AMBIGUOUSLY—dandha mandha, ṭhare ṭhore.

AMBLING TROT OF HORSES—kadam, kọdọm.

AMBUSH—*(an)* aṭa, kanas ; *(to lie in)* oḍao, ograo, tãrāk.

AMEN—amin.

AMIDST—ghasen, mod, mọtẹre, mud.

AMITY—sapo.

AMOK, TO RUN—muhā.

AMONG—gasen, ghasen, madhe, mandhe, mod, modhe, mud, talare ; *(the villagers)* gãya ghọre ; *(themselves)* ghọre (2).

AMOROUS DALLIANCE, TO INDULGE IN—khilḍu.

AMOUNT—*(reasonable)* ọj ; *(of rice put in dhinki, &c)* ghạni ; *(of thread put on winder)* phola ; *(to let off part of)* khesaroṭ.

AMPLE—ajhal pajhal, phael, phaela ; *(of food)* thele (2).

AMUSE, TO—bulau, laboj, lobhao, lubhau ; (*a child*) cereć.

AMUSEMENT—roń rij ; (*fond of*) irić cikić ; (*seeking*) itra itri.

AMUSING—laphua.

AN (*indef. article*)—mić, tań, teć, ten.

ANAEMIA—had hamus, hamus, har hamus.

ANALOGOUSLY—ona sikte.

ANCESTORS—aja purkha, bap dada, bapa purkha, hapramko, jaro, purkha.

ANCHORED, AS IF—jekre, jerpēreć.

ANCIENT—agari, jug, kahtuk, mare; (*times*) sedae.

ANCIENTS, THE—mare hapramko.

AND—ar, kate.

ANGEL OF DEATH—hudul raj, jom hudar, jom raja.

ANGER—corcotań, edre, kan, kanas, khunus, kurud, kuskusi, pit, rag, surbań ; (*to show*) kurkur ; (*to feel*) lahraok ; (*restless from*) siki (2) ; (*to be excited with*) kunkunau, sarńgao, surma, tamao, tamtamao ; (*exclm. of*) o !

ANGERED, EASILY—bisaha, bispitaha, coenda, khāisaha.

ANGLE, AT AN—hoyań, koce, perta, tarcha, tircha.

ANGRILY—dere (2), karra, kharań khuruń, sidwak badwak ; (*to speak*) corcotań, dhuńgrau, etrań, regeń (2), tarań tirań, tiriń tarań.

ANGRY—birodhi, coń bai, khāisā khāisī, kuskusau ; (*to be*) agar karar, bhutau, bikhar, birgha, edre, endre, kadrao, kāisāu, kope bacre, kurkur, kurkurau, pit capar, rag uprak, rańgao, saniau, taoa tawi, uprak ; (*to get*) etrań, khāisā, tiriń tarań ; (*to move as one*) gidgidau ; (*to speak as one*) ror halań ; (*and awaiting revenge*) kuskusau.

ANGUISH—bhāuri, dhoros.

ANIMAL, AN—jan janwar, janwar, pasu, posu ; (*wild*) bir janwar, bir pasu ; (*domesticated*) ato janwar, ato posu, pos ; (*grazing*) carapia ; (*the young of any*) hon, hopon ; (*appetites, under the sway of*) umas, umbrau, umkau, umra, umta, umtau, umuk ; (*to train*) bolao.

ANIMOSITY—badi, badisti, bairi ; (*to harbour*) kisiau, kunkunau.

ANISE SEED—muhri, panmuhri.

ANKLE—(*bone, the*) kutha, thōrē ; (*to twist the*) hureć.

ANKLET, AN—bāk, bańki, kara, kharu, khila bańki, lipur, paińgan.

ANNA, AN—ana ; (*2 or 4*) sika, suki ; (¼) khańca, paesa, poesa ; (*1/12*) pae.

ANNIHILATE, TO—nasao, nasti, uchad.

ANNIHILATED, TO BE—marao.

ANNIVERSARY, AN—porob.

ANNOY, TO—alkau, ansao, aris, dhik, dik, dikiau, diksik, gańjan, handkao, hantao, heteć, hudgu dugur, hujat, hujut, jhik jhikau, kahīs, kondoli, paniau, phajhet, takać tukuć, tamardak, tita titi ; (*by making a din*) kalkalao.

ANNOYANCE—dik, gańjan, haran, haron, kahīs, khirri, upan jhapan ; (*exclm. of*) aigu, aiyo, chia, dhirhak, dhirkara, dhit, dhokran (F), dhurhak, dhurkara, dhut, dhuthak, durkarak, durya, dut (2), duthak, i, is, jah, ũhũk, uhu uhu ; (*with the purpose of causing*) halwani, harwani ; (*to cause*) khirri, torlad.

ANNOYED—kondolia ; (*to be*) berosta, kalsau, khīs, kickic, titau, tomol dak ; (*easily*) arisia.

ANNOYING—isbis, kackac, khalkhal, nepran, uichau, uichnaha.

ANNUALLY—bachri (2), bochor ke bochor, salsal, salesal, serma ke serma, sonesen, tiris baris.

ANOINT, TO—kalgat, ojod, ojok ; (*with oil and turmeric*) tere.

ANOINTERS—tetre.

ANOTHER—dosar, dosra, etak, porek, porer, uai ; (*belonging to*) uai ; (*time*) etak garte, ghurikaete.

ANSWER—(*an*) jabab, jobab, juab, utar ; (*to give*) jobab, ror ruar, utar emok.

ANSWER, TO—(*a shout by a shout*) tokar ; (*when called*) goń ; (*when another is called*) ańjom gãore.

ANT, AN—ciũti, muć; (*species of*) copre m., coto m., gundiari m., rol m. ; (*white*) bhuku, bhuska, buku, ńindir ; (*queen white*) bunum eńga ; (*black*) hende m., sunum m., uṗ m., ḍoḍa m., ḍonḍa m., cuṭuń m, kolhe m.; (*red*) arak̇ m., hao m., khonṭa m., sadọm m., (*flour*) lobok̇ m.; (*oil*) sunum m.; (*English*) saheb m.; (*stinking*) sọ m.; (*winged at one stage*) upi kalgaṫ; (*nest of*) hao pọṭọm, muċ chatta; (*hill of white*) bunum, bunum ḍhopo.

ANT-EATER, THE INDIAN SCALY—arba, harba, suruj mukhi.

ANTAGONISTIC, TO BE—ṭher.

ANTELOPE, A SPECIES OF—bhãoṭia.

ANTICIPATE, TO—tebak̇.

ANTIPATHY—sikiṛ.

ANTS AND BUTTERFLIES—ciũṭi pipri.

ANUS, THE—bhanḍar, linḍhi, linḍhi bhuk̇.

ANVIL, AN—nehae, nihai.

ANXIETY—bhab, cinta, dandagiri, dandha, hadọs, jala, jańjal, jhańjhaṭ, jońjal, porbhae, saset, sọc; (*to be in*) dandha, dhãe khãe, hadọs, saset; (*to cause*) saset; (*to be relieved from*) khaṭir jọma; (*great*) maha jala, mahakal; (*without*) khulasa, mẹkẹċ, mọstọram, nicind, nidanḍi, niṛai, nirdand, phạria phạṭi, rehãṛ, susṭob.

ANXIOUS, TO BE—akham dukham, ande sale, dand, guni bhạbik̇, haelaċ (2), reńkao, thartharao, thurthurạu, titikhạk̇, uṭu puṭu.

ANXIOUSLY—dandra dạndri, dhãoṛa dhạuṛi; (*to search for*) dhãosa dhạusi.

ANY—jãhã, jahan.

ANYHOW—andhe mandhe, ańgot bańgot, cạcuṛ mạcuṛ, dhọńgọl phọsọl, ghẹjẹ bẹjẹ, jande mande, jane tane, jhoto poto, khedar bedar, khẹjẹ bẹjẹ, kherbejer, lọdọr bọdọr, luḍur buḍur, luṛuń buṛuń, sitoċ sọṭọċ, soto poto.

ANYONE—jãhãe, jãhãe kãhãe, jãhãeṭak̇, jãhaniċ, jãhãṭak̇, konho.

ANYTHING—jãhã, jãhãk̇, jahanak̇, jãhãnak̇, konho; (*and everything*) hạr ghạser, sẹrẹ gore.

ANY TIME, AT—jahãn, sobbo kal.

ANYWAY—jãhã leka, jãhã kãhã, keceṭ meceṭ, sadga bidiṛ, teṛeń goreń.

ANYWHERE—anthạri, jãhã ṭhen, jãhã man tãhã, jande mande, jane tane, teṛeń goreń.

APART, WIDE—alag balag, bẹgbẹge, cań (2), lelhar, phandṛa, ṭapṭapa.

APARTMENT, AN—hudṛa, kandha, khauḍ, khurpi, kuṭhri; (*inner*) bhitạr.

APATHETIC—haruṛ.

APERTURE, AN—phukạr; (*to close*) mohṇḍa marao.

APOSTLE, AN—prerit.

APPARATUS—sanaphana; (*for raising beams*) ciguṛi.

APPAREL—ahran paharand.

APPARENT, TO BE—lahkao.

APPARITION, AN—bheona.

APPEAL FOR JUSTICE, AN—aphil, dohae, rae dohae.

APPEAR, TO—dekhaok̇, janam, ńẹl, rakaṗ; (*of apparition*) upel; (*for first time*) molok̇.

APPEARANCE—bhẹs, caher, chin, ḍọgọr, rup; (*careless of*) gạnduk̇ sạnduk̇; (*unprepossessing in*) kạbḍuċ, kador, kenderpeċ; (*of fat person sitting*) lẹpẹḍhẹr.

APPEARING—(*and disappearing, of light*) dagar dugur; (*just*) mẹrẹċ.

APPEASE—(*to*) dạhnao, kudrạu, nembroṫ; (*to give to*) em lạbuk̇; (*the appetite, to*) lọcọr bhańgao.

APPETITE—daris; (*to lose*) bhoṭko, pít mara; (*having voracious*) dhebra (M), ḍhibri (F); (*without*) licań picań, ọgọroj, ọrọc, ricań picań.

APPLE—(*tree*) kaṭ bel, sẹo dare; (*wood*) kõc bel; (*of the eye*) kharen.

APPLIANCE—bandheċ.

APPLICATION, TO MAKE—ujur, ujur mujur.

APPLY, TO—laga, lagao; (*medicine externally*) bokram, ileṫ, lep, makhan, mohlon, ọjọk̇; (*oneself to*) cesṭa, ṭesṭa; (*ball of rice flour to person*) lunḍa.

APPOINT, TO—badao, bahal, banal, ṭahrao, ṭạmil, teńgo; (*time, &c*) nenḍa.

APPOINTED—(*time*) lagan; (*to, to be*) motaen, motean.

APPOINTMENT, AN—bahạli, tọndạri.

APPORTION, TO—bakhra, bẹbọsa, bhag, bibri, citil bitil; (*fairly*) solo sońjok.

APPRAISEMENT—anman.

APPRECIATE, TO—sebel.

APPREHEND, TO—dharao, doelao; *(by warrant)* giripdar; *(and imprison)* leglao.

APPREHENSION—bhorok, comol; *(absence of)* khatir, khulasa, rehar.

APPRISE, TO—hakao, janti.

APPROACH, TO—cahtao, hijuk.

APPROBATION—rij roṅ.

APPROPRIATE, TO—aoda, badha, meteam, motiao, mutiau.

APPROVE, TO—parpasind, pasind; *(of)* basut, manjur.

APPROXIMATELY—amdaj, gan, macha.

APRIL-MAY—Baisak.

APTITUDE—hẽt; *(to shew)* laker.

ARBITRATE, TO—chindau, salis.

ARBITRATORS—mõrẽ hor, salisdar.

ARCH THE BACK, TO—kutkutuć.

ARCHED—kabua.

AREA—*(a large)* jagesar, lapondaṅ, leplep, mander, mela; *(of village)* nager caker, dih dandi.

ARECA NUT, the—gua.

ARGUE, TO—takrar; *(in Court)* sowal; *(hotly)* rapta rapti.

ARGUMENT—*(to meet in)* epeseť; *(to fence in)* ghawar, ghorna.

ARISE, TO—upel; *(from sleep)* bereť; *(of smells)* phutau.

ARK OF THE COVENENT—an sunduk.

ARM—*(the upper)* bãhi, sopo; *(the lower)* ti; *(from shouder to finger-tips)* sop; *(of a balance)* dandić, dandiť; *(stretched out, with the)* giria; *(full stretch of)* eora; *(to stretch)* beg, laphao; *(to raise)* awil; *(to put under)* hermeť; *(to break)* lokaṅ; *(stiff)* luṅkar; *(disabled)* lokore, loṅki (F); *(marks burnt on lower)* sikha.

ARMED WITH A SWORD, TO BE—gadiau.

ARMLET, AN—baju, jhabu, tabij, tad; *(of lac)* lahti; *(of bell metal)* sekra sakom.

ARMOUR-BEARER, AN—dhal sikaria.

ARMPIT, THE—hatlak; *(a sore in)* kãkh bilar ghao.

ARMS—*(gun, sword, &c)* hatiar, larhai sanaphana, sapaṗ.

ARMS—*(in)* heneo; *(to keep moving the)* halobalo; *(to encircle with)* haruṗ; *(to swing)* biť bikoć, hurla; *(crossed over chest)* kutu.

ARMY, AN—ara, laskar, palton, phad.

AROMATIC POWDER, A—nokhi.

ARRANGE, TO—bandhao, bondobos, khaṅj bhaṅj, mili guti, pontha, rika; *(for)* dagao; *(in order)* gutiau.

ARRANGEMENTS—*(to make preparatory)* sarsor; *(without)* khedar bedar, kheje beje, kherbejer.

ARREARS—baki, baki dhike, kasar; *(to make up)* phujau.

ARREST—*(to)* dharao, hat; *(by warrant)* giripdar; *(warrant of)* waront.

ARRESTED DEVELOPMENT—boroć.

ARRIVE, TO—dakhil, dakhilau, habrao, pohncao, seter, tiok.

ARROGANCE—dhomok.

ARROGANT—bahali, bariau, budrag, dhomokia; *(to be)* adai badai, badagiri.

ARROW, AN—sar; *(blunt)* tuti sar; *(unfeathered)* laṅta sar; *(pointless)* thotha; *(iron headed)* apari sar; *(poisoned)* bisal apari; *(nock of)* phõk; *(tube of cross-bow)* sar thoṅga; *(kind of head)* sogoť lutur apari; *(tang of head)* baraṅgi; *(straight, as)* jomkao; *(grass used for shafts)* gundri mẽť sar, sar, sari sar; *(to shoot with bow &c)* tuń; *(to shoot straight up)* khutla; *(to shoot a blunt)* tuti; *(to fit on bowstring)* tuniau; *(to draw to head)* hambuć; *(to pierce with)* harar, tuń janjanao, sar.

ARROWS—*(method of fixing feathers on)* hari tol, sikri tol; *(poison for)* dakra, jahar mahra; *(magazine for)* thoṅga sar.

ART—hunar.

ARTAGOM, THE CRY OF—kandrać kondroć.

ARTFUL—natkhat, sean.

ARTICLE, AN—cij, jinis, tij.

ARTIFICE—chol; *(to attract males' attention)* cindar candar; *(to send away by)* tarkao.

ARTISTIC—dhob.

ARTISAN AN—karigar, karigol.

ARTLESS—modhu, sora.

AS—ceť leka, jaesan, je jemon, je leka, jemon, jesan, te; *(much as)* bhor, jatna, jotna; *(much as this)* nin habić, nun habić, nin tiriť, nun tiriť, tiriť, titiť; *(much as that)* un habić, un tiriť, un titiť; *(much as possible)* remhe regoť; *(many as)* jotna ; (*far as*) bhor, dhạbić, hạbić ; (*soon as*) bithag bithạk ; (*long as*) dhạbić; (*big as that*) un marań ; (*large as of beasts and birds*) jọpọr ; (*often as*) pichạ, piche ; (*you say*) bọtẹ ; (*they say*) enkathae ; (*...as*) iyo ; (*...so*) jẹmọn...tẹmọn ; (*that*) enka, onka, onkan ; (*one*) jhumblại mẹnte; (*a rule*) asokaete, ḍherkaete ; (*best one can*) labre, lọḍọr bọḍọr, luḍur buḍur; (*formerly*) tẹsnẹk, se ke se.

ASCEND, TO—rakap̣.

ASCENDING AND DESCENDING—ḍọyọl (2), ghaṭać ghuṭuć.

ASCENT, AN—ranakap̣ ; (*from river bed*) gạḍa ranakap̣.

ASCERTAIN, TO—nirọpọn, ọj, ṭhekan, ṭhikạn.

ASCETIC, AN—ạtit, jugi, tit, utit ; (*naked*) nańga jugi ; (*wandering*) nańgar jugi.

ASH TREE, THE—oren dare.

ASHAMED—bẹạbruk, harea garea, kakṛa kokṛo, kokṛo ; (*to be*) kirdhum, lajao, lajbij, usum suruć ; (*as if*) cudi ; (*after defeat*) hạriã busiã.

ASHES—ḍigir, tọrọć ; (*burnt on ground for manure*) ḍạhi ; (*to reduce to*) bhasam.

ASHY-CROWNED FINCH-LARK, THE—sirloć cẽrẽ.

ASIDE—ẹkdhar, kanas ; (*to set*) ańgao, pandol ; (*to go*) sa, sah, ghajẹr ; (*to put*) kehna, sa, sah.

ASK, TO—jigạs, kuli, ohge, pucạu, puce ; (*for*) aleť, bab, khọj, kọe ; (*with threats*) damae dundrại ; (*importunately*) khodao ; (*to see if it can be had*) kọe gelaǩ ; (*altho one knows*) kothe, kuthni ; (*for querulously*) ńarań ńuruń ; (*a question repeatedly*) thetha.

ASKING, FOR THE—mạgni, mańgnite.

ASLEEP, ALL—gitić sarasạtiń.

ASPERSE, TO—jojogna, mundi.

ASS, AN—gadha (M), gạdhi (F).

ASSAULT, TO—dańga, marpiṭ, ńẽť.

ASSEMBLE, TO—cumkaǩ, dumha, jamkao, jaora, jarwa, jhomble, jomkao, juṭạu, ṭhaurạ, thopro, tobṛe, tombṛe ; (*gradually*) sẹn jaora ; (*in large numbers*) jạuhar ; (*together*) lẹothẹ, tudrạ.

ASSEMBLY, AN—bhiṛ, dọrbar, mańjlis, mońjlis, muńjlis, pańc, sabha ; (*to break up*) bhińgṛạu.

ASSENT—mạrji, murji ; (*to*) ańgọe, hẽ, sikạr ; (*to express*) hẹ̃hũ, hũ ; (*to refuse*) mạhrạu, nakạbul ; (*to, to*) hũ, kạblạu, nẹ ; (*deed of*) ikrar nama.

ASSESS, TO—tolao.

ASSESSMENT ON RENT, ADDITIONAL—bheja.

ASSIDUOUS—jạri jạnti, jidạhi, jidạjid ; (*to be*) cahak mahak, jạkir, jid, markaṭ ; (*in attending to*) jọtọn.

ASSIMILATED, TO BE—bijạu.

ASSIST, TO—algao, buk, dạhin, gọrọ, le calao, loe, luṭhu, modet, modod, sambṛao, sap̣ dap̣, sẹrọm, sohga, sọhoť, tala, torao, upgạr, upkạr, usas ; (*by giving*) em calao, em gọrọ, pạlike pasa ; (*by speaking*) rọṛ sọhoť ; (*by taking hold of*) sańgarhe.

ASSISTANCE—modod, sạhạita, upgạr, upkạr ; (*to call for*) garja barja ; (*to give in emergency*) gạrsusar calao ; (*of another, by the*) parepore.

ASSISTANT, AN—modet, sohoda, sota ; (*of village headman*) parạnik.

ASSISTING GENERALLY—jabar jubạr.

ASSUAGE, TO—nẹmbroť, ṭạndha.

ASSURANCE—(*of reliability*) sạkhiyạt, sat, sot ; (*without*) dharma korma, dhorma korma.

ASSURED, TO BE—ikọṭ, khạṭi, khạtir.

ASSUREDLY—bańsẹ, bẹ-sok.

ASTHMA—dama, dhõk, hạpsi duk.

ASTONISH, TO—mạluń, ṭhak.

ASTONISHED, TO BE—ande sale, bharọ, haemoekaṭ, hahara, hạimuikaṭ, mạluń, mọgọn, mọńgọn, tharbasao.

ASTONISHING—bẹhaj, ẹk jọntọr, hahạra, kạṭhin.

ASTRAY, TO LEAD—ạnḍić, bhańḍao, bhańṭao, bhińgṛạu, bigrạ bigṛi, bulạu.

ASTRIDE THE HIP, TO CARRY—hẹo, ṭọṭẹ.

ASTRINGENT—kasa, kasať.

ASTRONOMER, AN—gọnọǩ.

AT ALL—nirọt.

AT ONCE—bidlại, bidnaǩ, burbudluǩ, cạbhruǩ, char, culuń, dhãk, ẹkkalte, ẹkbar, ẹkdam, hatepate, batọkaete, họtọkkaete, jạraǩ marte, jạrap̣ mẹnte, jạtaǩ, jhak marte, jhap jhup, kalaǩ, kaloǩ marte, khaṭ, sanaǩ, tạrak marte, ṭạtkamạr, turãt, turte. *Cf.* TIME & TIMES.

ATHLETE, AN—mal.

ATMOSPHERE, THE UPPER—serma.

ATOM, AN—khudri, rukhi.

ATOMS, TO BREAK INTO—chakacun, chiti chaṅ, ciri biri, gẹjẹr.

ATTACH, TO—jabọd; *(under a warrant)* jạbid, jọbọd, jọbọt, korok, koroṭ, kuṛki, kuṛak; *(land)* bāsgạḍi; *(oneself to another for charity)* henḍkok̓.

ATTACHED, TO BE—lata.

ATTACK, TO—dhawa, mũhạ̃; *(suddenly)* jhapṭao; *(from all sides)* kacṭa kạcṭi.

ATTEMPT, TO—aesan, cesṭa, ẹṭẹć, ẹṭẹ cẹṭẹ, gela, lega, rikạ, ṭesṭa; *(again & again)* amaṛ omoṛ.

ATTEND TO MANY THINGS, TO—leṭaṅ ḷeṭaṛ.

ATTENDANCE—hạjri; *(to be in)* hạjir, hạjur; *(register)* hạjri bạhi; *(careful)* cikisạ.

ATTENDANT TO MASTER'S PIPE—hukạ bardar.

ATTENDING TO DUTY, NOT—cerka bherka.

ATTENTION—*(to draw)* utkut̓; *(-by touching)* cukuć, gạduć, godak̓; *(-by coughing)* ẹthẹm; *(to slacken)* ḍhilạu; *(to pay)* aodhan, hetao; *(many things requiring)* daṛae dhampae.

ATTENTION, USED TO CALL—arr, ehe, eho; ei, hai, hẽho, heho, henda, ho, iạ, iyo, *(to boys)* ehe re, eya; *(to girls)* ehe ge, ena.

ATTENTIVE, TO BE—ucit.

ATTENUATED—jalpa.

ATTEST, TO—suhi.

ATTIRE—*(a piece of male)* bhagwa, dhuti, kupni, sirpuć, tọlọṅ; *(method of wearing)* dhabṛe ḍeṅga; *(careless of)* bodre, dindir sit̓.

ATTIRED—*(to attract)* jhalak malak; *(immodestly)* lọṛọć (2).

ATTITUDE, TO ASSUME A HUMBLE—gola gamcha.

ATTORNEY, POWER OF—ukilạtnama.

ATTRACT, TO—ạnijok̓, bạsut, gạhi, jhakao, jhakrao, jhokao, lobdhao, ọr; *(notice)* chamak.

ATTRACTED, TO BE—ạnijok̓, ṭanao; *(& held)* laṭha; *(by seeing others)* uṛạle patale.

AUCTION—*(to)* lilạm, nilạm; *(to bid at an)* hakao; *(against each other)* haka hạki.

AUDIBLE, SCARCELY—ńẹrẹ̃ (2).

AUGUR, TO—paetar.

AUGUST-SEPTEMBER—Bhadọr.

AUNT—hatọm, kạki, mạmi, nana; *(& nephew or neice)* kạkiạ.

AUSPICIOUS—paetara.

AUTHOR OF BEING—jạk̓namić, janam data.

AUTHORITY—adọl, ạidari, ạmạli, bọs, ẹktiạri, iktiạr, mạliki, sạd, sọdra, umuk; *(to have)* cạtiạu; *(to exercise)* mạliki calao; *(under)* tabere; *(without)* rạwić.

AUTUMN—pat jhaṛa.

AVARICE—lọb, lọb lalọc; *(full of)* lobhatiạ, lubhi, lubhiạ.

AVAUNT!—dur.

AVERAGE—ghũṭ, mańjla ras.

AVERRUNCATE, TO—taṛao.

AVERSION—*(with)* ẹskõs; *(to have)* hirkhạ.

AVOID, TO—eṛan, ẹrẹr.

AWAKE—*(to)* bẹṅgẹt̓, ẹbhẹn; *(not fully)* andha ondho, asam usum, daraṅ duruṅ; *(to keep)* jagao, jagrọn, jagwar, jạigir; *(to appear not)* torlo morlo.

AWARE OF, TO BE—disạ.

AWAY—*(from each other)* aparek̓; *(over there)* hanạ; *(far)* sạṅgiṅ.

AWED, TO BE—dabkao.

AWKWARD—aldhundhạ, dundhạ, leṛwa laṛwe.

AWN, AN—*(of grain or grass)* suṅgạ; *(of pricking grass)* sagak̓.

AWRY—ghọcẹ.

AXE—*(small)* potam cupi ṭẹṅgọć, tabla, ṭẹṅgọć; *(large)* ṭaṅga; *(middle-sized)* tala ṭaṅga; *(kind of)* gudiạ ṭẹṅgọć; *(cut made by)* ṭaṅgadar; *(to dress with)* lak̓; *(to cut deeply with)* sigi; *(handle)* ṭẹṅgọć daṇḍọm. *Cf.* BATTLE AXE.

AXLE OF CART—niṅghạ; *(pin of)* anole; *(noise made by)* heṇḍroṅ (2), hinḍroṅ hoṇḍroṅ, hoṇḍrọṅ.

B

Babble, to—bakhnao, bọkbọk, khọdọr (2).

Babbler, a—cạuchạł.

Baboon, a species of—birsindić.

Baby, a—bale bẹṭkẹć, bale gidrạ.

Bachelor, a—ḍạṅguạ korạ; *(an old)* aṛharo baṛharo.

Bachelorhood—ḍạṅguạ, ḍiṅgạ ḍạṅguạ.

Back, the—dea, sạmbir; *(to bend)* kojo; *(to arch)* kuṭkuṭuć; *(to carry on)* gugu; *(to turn on)* sara; *(to turn)* dea, thot; *(on)* sạmbir; *(of the hand)* lulhạ.

Back—*(to give)* ạdại, em ruạṛ, phirạu, phirot; *(to turn)* cikić, lạuṭạu; *(too far—of a load)* pạchil, pichạr; *(of house, etc.)* kuḍạm; *(part, the)* pạchil; *(ground, to put in)* khọṭ.

Backbite, to—cugli, phecaṅ, sulạ; *(given to)* cugliạ.

Backbone, the—bisi jaṅ.

Backwards—cikić, pạchlạ, sirgạt, taenọm sẹć; *(to go)* cudi, pạchlạ, pạcoǩ; *(and forwards)* ạcur bihur, ulṭi pulṭi; *(—to walk)* ṭahlao.

Bad—bạṛić, bọd, coṛtha, kharao, kharap, khokṇḍo, liloj, papisṭa, rạḍin, ubạṛ khabạṛ; *(of stangnant water)* bọkọl (2); *(to go)* ahnaoǩ, gajwaǩ, lambao, mạndhuạ, monda, palpał, pelpel, phaṭao; *(gone)* liṭi; *(repute)* ọpjọs; *(smell)* ạĩs; *(habit)* lachan; *(name)* bodnam; *(tempered)* coenda, khecraha (M), khecṛạhi (F); *(humour, to be in)* ạruṅ pạruṅ. *Cf.* BEHAVIOUR, LUCK, OMEN.

Badge, a—capras.

Badger, the Indian—parkọm bana.

Badger, to—ạris, dạbṛi maṅgal.

Badly—*(clad)* gayur gạpur; *(executed)* dopca; *(cooked)* capos (2); *(off, to be)* ṭan, ṭanaṭạni.

Bael fruit and tree—siṅjo.

Bag, a—bẹg, bora, bosta, thạilaǩ, thạili; *(money)* toṛa; *(small)* bạṭu, bugli, dhukṛi, gubli; *(leaf)* khuli; *(for silk moths)* khuṅgi; *(cloth)* khuti; *(pack)* gõṛẽ; *(not even shakings of)* orop̓ koṭop̓.

Bag in the centre, to—ghaṅjloṅ.

Baggage—ḍạḍha ḍumbạṛ, sạmṭi umṭi.

Baggy—jhạlur, khoṅja, gãhjur; *(as clothes)* gudui (2).

Bail—jạmindar; *(to go)* ḍạrmạl, jạmin.

Bait—cara, cạri.

Bait, to *(badger)*—dạbṛi maṅgal, khackhacao.

Baked, under *(of pottery)*—bhiro bhoro.

Baker, a—pik̓ṭhạrić.

Balance *(surplus)*—bạki, bạki dhike, kasar, sarẹć barẹć; *(to hold the)* luṭhu.

Balance *(for weighing)*—mikti, tạrju tulạ, tulạ; *(arm of)* ḍạṇḍić, ḍạṇḍiǩ; *(scales of)* ḍalwaǩ, tulạ; *(notches on)* ank oṛaǩ.

Balanced, unequally—jhiṅko jhạkur, jhiṅkạ taṛe, jhiṅkạ jhokor, jhiṅko toṛo.

Bald—ḍuṇḍge (M), ḍuṇḍgi (F), cạdra (M), cạdri (F), ṭhuṇḍguṭ; *(on the crown)* cạdra (M), cẹḍe (M); *(head)* ḍuṇḍge, ḍuṇḍi.

Bale, a—bhiṇḍ.

Bale out water, to—arẹć.

Ball, a—ḍhumbaǩ, gẹnd, guli; *(small)* buṛi; *(of twine)* luṇḍi; *(of thread)* luṭi, guli suṭạm; *(of dried clay)* gorkha guli; *(of the foot)* panaska; *(of bread)* ḍomboǩ; *(to make into)* gulu mulu; *(to roll as)* daṛdarao, ghargharao; *(in the air, to strike)* phoṭao.

Bamboo, a—maṭ; *(species of)* des m., kaṭaṅ m., khaṭaṅ m., khol m., ropa m., ṭhiṅgi m., *(immature)* kạrlạ; *(young shoot)* helta, jạli, kạril; *(branch from node of)* kạnại; *(husked seed of)* m. caole; *(food prepd. from shoots)* hạṇḍuạ; *(strip of)* bata; *(pointed piece of)* hạiạr; *(pipe)* coṅga; *(lime box)* cun ṭhoṅga; *(piece of hollow)* ṭhoṅga; *(hooked)* ạkhạini; *(fixed on attached land)* bãsgạḍi; *(cart)* bagi; *(horizontal)* anak; *(by which men swing)* ḍhiluạ; *(ware)* mahle bhajan. *Cf.* BASKET, MAT, UMBRELLA.

Bamboos—*(a clump of)* maṭ dạṛdhi; *(tied to rafters)* andhạriạ bata; *(a tribe of workers in)* mahle.

BAN, AS IF UNDER A—hae phoe.

BAND, A (*company*)—dọl, phạd, thak, thọk; (*in a*) gạdea gudiạ, jhargae jhurgui, jharak jhuruk, juṅgur (2).

BAND, A—(*plaited*) jạmki; (*to tie a sheaf*) chõṇṭ, chõṭ; (*of wheel, iron*) bandh; (*for the hair*) bheṭuaḱ, phitạ; (*round ankle*) lipur.

BANDAGE, TO—bạdhi.

BANDICOOT RAT, THE—bhus, bhus goḍo.

BANDS, IN—thake thak, thọke thọk, thọk thak.

BANDY WORDS, TO—loka, rẹpẹć, rẹṭẹ pẹṭẹ.

BANG—harạs; (*with a*) liṭhir marte, rihiṛ marte, rihṛaḱ marte.

BANGHY LOAD—(*to prepare a*) arrao; (*to swing in time with*) lujuḱ.

BANGING—ḍhae, diṛim, rihiṛ, rihṛaḱ; (*as of gun*) liṭhir, luṭhur.

BANGLE, A—curi.

BANK OF A RIVER—ḍhip, ghuṭu.

BANTER, TO—nisṛau.

BANYAN TREE, A—bare dare, pẹṭẹr bare.

BAPTISE, TO—bạptis, um.

BAR—(*a horizontal*) jaṅge; (*of door*) huṛkạ; (*to*) ṭekao.

BARBAROUS—arna, bẹsọbbọk.

BARBER, A—lapit, napit, nạu.

BARBETS, TWO SPECIES OF—gutruť.

BARBS ON ARROW HEAD—kanari.

BARE—cẹṇḍẹń, heṇḍer, heṇḍra, hutur, khaḍ, khaḍea, khaḍge, khaḍra, oṭań polań, ṭạṇḍi; (*as tree*) ḍheṇḍra, ṭhaṇḍga, ṭhaṇḍgaṭ, ṭhuṇḍga, ṭhuṇḍguṭ; (*as head*) ṭhuṇḍgạ; (*of hair*) heṇḍra (M), hiṇḍri (F), henṛa (M), hinṛi (F); (*of leaves*) hutur; (*in parts*) heṇḍer (2); (*necked*) koeḍoḱ; (*to make*) khalkhalao, poṭaḱ.

BARGAIN—(*to*) dam daṛi, dọrdar; (*proof of*) dubdan, dubdhan; (*a man who makes a*) koyal; (*into the*) unkạ.

BARK, TO—bhoḱ, hạu (2), jhạu (2), jhão (2); (*in heat*) kãskãs.

BARK OF TREE—baklaḱ, chal; (*of sapling*) pataṅgeť; (*of Ebony tree*) cẹṭẹteť; (*to be rubbed off*) hadra hạdri, hadrao.

BARLEY—jao.

BARNDOOR FOWL, THE—*Cf.* FOWL.

BARREL, A—pipạ; (*of gun*) nạli, nuli.

BARREN—aṭkuṛạ, bạhlạ, bańjha (M), bạńjhi (F), bạhạla, ṭhãṭ; (*of soil*) kańkhar, khańkhar, kharań, kharkhaṇḍ, malọṭ, narca; (*as tree*) ḍạṅguạ.

BARS, HORIZONTAL—ganaḍe; (*of door*) karhaṛ; (*to fence with*) jaṅge.

BARTER, TO—dọlbadọl, utiń.

BASE—(*foot*) peṇda, phẹḍ, phẹḍat; (*mean*) harmad, kuṭnạ, mạriã piṭiạ, nichok, paji, rạd (M), rạdin (F).

BASHFUL—harea garea, soromiạ.

BASIN, A—(*metal*) bạṭi; (*leaf*) dolkha.

BASKET, A—bhajan, duhṛi, duhuṛi, khaclaḱ; (*small*) nạcu ṭuplaḱ, khaci, phạṭiaḱ, piṭari, piri; (*bamboo*) ṭukri, udiạ; (*large bamboo*) harka, ṭheka; (*small bamboo*) nạcu, ṭuńki, ṭuplaḱ, ṭupliḱ, uḍhi; (*round bamboo*) peṭara; (*small round flat*) ḍalić; (*large*) ḍala, dhaki, khańca; (*large flat*) ḍalwaḱ, ḍaura; (*shallow flat*) ḍauṛić; (*to catch fish*) khạlai, khaloe, kholoe, mucu; (*for carrying earth*) jhaba; (*for raising water*) ḍobka, ḍopka, sẽrẽ; (*for storing grain*) ḍili, ḍimki, ḍiṛmi; (*for measuring grain*) umãṛ khaclaḱ; (*hen-coop*) ṭapa; (*ware*) mahle bhajan; (*to pour out of*) uṗ.

BAST FIBRE—laṛ.

BASTARD, A—bidhuạ.

BASTE, TO—jalai.

BAT, A—bardũṛũć; (*species of*) họn b.; poṭọm b.; (*small*) coha, cuṭiạ b.; (*large fox*) kạhu b.

BATCH, A—calan.

BATHE, TO—jọbẹ, um; (*& tidy oneself*) siṅgar.

BATHED IN PERSPIRATION—jhaḱ jhaḍur.

BATHING-CLOTH—gamcha.

BATTLE-AXE—kạpi; (*kinds of*) bhaluạ k., hoedoḱ k., khupạ k., potam cupi ṭẹṅgọć; (*small*) kherco k.; (*with broad blade*) gudiạ k.

BAYONET—kirić, saṅgin.

BAZAAR—bajar, sahar bajar.

BE, TO—hẽnaḱ, hoe, hoyoḱ, mena, pạṛao; (*about to*) lagaṭ, lạgiṭ; (*at its height*) bamka bạmki, sạrdi; (*done with it*) atar, dapoṛ, doroḱ, napoṛ.

BEGONE!—dhurdhur, dur, durya.

BEAD, A—mala, jurul mala; (*with wide hole*) budhi mala.

BEADS—mala; (*coral*) muṅgạ m., pãola m., sãk m.; (*like birds' eggs*) jihu m.; (*praying*) udrạṅ m; (*fruit*) bhãuri m., (*rock-crystal*) dhiri m.; (*like mustard-seed*) tuṛi m., (*made from bael*) belwạri m.; (*a string of*) lar, mit̓ lar m.; (*double necklace of*) barlar m.; (*threaded in hair*) sili m.

BEAK (*of bird*)—ṭhonṭa, ṭhonṭha.

BEAM—(*of sugar-cane press*) kạtri; (*of scales*) tulạ ḍạṇḍit̓; (*of roof*) dharen, koale, pạṛ, satepạṛ, mutul pạṛ, kupipạṛ, saṅga; (*apparatus for rassing*) ciguṛi; (*wooden cushion for*) piṛhi.

BEAN, A LONG WHIP-LIKE—muṅgạ suṭi.

BEAR, TO—bhọg, lahao, sahao, sombhrao, sumbhrạu, uput̓; (*tales*) bajhao, cokhna, cugli; (*hunger*) sahao; (*ill-will*) akhaṭ, badọt; (*love to*) bạsut; (*the consequences*) sẹn hamạlok̓; (*witness*) gohak̓; (*up*) sepeń; (*with*) sọmbhori.

BEAR, THE BLACK—bana; (*hunting-term*) rata sukri; (*species of*) boyo b., dhạlgum b., kit̓ b.; (*scrotum of*) duṛe; (*to make noise like*) huhkạu.

BEARD, A—goco, kewa goco, sodro; (*man with*) sodro; (*to pull the*) cọkọć; (*and whiskers, long flowing*) gọdọr.

BEARING, AS AN UNSTAMPED LETTER—biriń.

BEARING, TRUE ON (*as an axle*)—kalgar.

BEAST, A—janwar, posu.

BEAT, TO—dal, dhạtiń, domao, humạk̓, kạṛai, kehnao, khenhao, piṭạu, ru; (*a drum*) bajna, ru; (*for game*) chuḍạ, jhora; (*with a stick*) ṭạṭhe; (*with a cane*) camkạu; (*lightly*) thapa; (*into small pieces*) dal gasmạṇḍao; (*conquer*) harao, hẽṭ; (*up—as an egg*) phẹṭao.

BEATEN, TO BE (*conquered*)—alao, ala ạli, elao, hạrit, pạhuṛ.

BEATING—(*to punish by*) kạṛai; (*of drums, sound of*) gubuḍ (2).

BEAUTIFUL—cakmak, chuk (2), cọhõk, dikhnor, husnạk, jhile mile, khulạ, khulạn, lọgnọ, mọńj, nạnuạr, ńõhõr (2), ńọrọm (2), sajọntar, sobha, soghoṛ, sohan, sughoṛ, sundạr, sundor mukhi, suthạr, ṭhonọk, ṭosgor; (*of young leaves*) lẹgẹć labak̓; (*with coloured patterns*) lilibici; (*& soft as fruit*) lẹṛẹm (2); (*to make*) ṭhạṭbond.

BEAUTIFULLY—ḍhab ḍhọb, ḍhabẹ ḍhọbẹ, rẹṅglẹć.

BECAUSE—cedak̓ je, ẹnte, te, tẹrọń; (*of*) badat.

BECKON, TO—gạwić.

BECOME, TO—hoe, hoyok̓, utrạu; (*of necessity acceptable after being refused*) sạrthi.

BECOMING—lek, saja; (*as is*) lek lekate.

BED, A—aṭẹt̓, parkọm; (*small*) khaṭlak̓; (*closely woven*) palak parkọm; (*cross-lines in mattress*) eṅga; (*framework of*) pariaṛe; (*twine at foot of*) uphãṇḍ; (*leg of*) kuṭhe; (*cross-bars of*) gạnạḍe; (*of water-course*) gạṛha; (*word used in testing*) ind; (*to place for use*) bel; (*time for*) gitić pọhọr; (*ridden*) jạṛao.

BEDECKED—jhane jhapane, jiki miki.

BEE, SPECIES OF HONEY—dumur, kuḍạm luti, luti, ńẹlẹ, terom.

BEE-EATER, THE INDIAN—ṭirom cẽṛẽ.

BEEF—ḍaṅgra jel, gại jel; (*witted*) urbhuṅgạ.

BEER, RICE—*Cf.* LIQUOR.

BEE'S WAX—sitet̓, sithạt̓, sithet̓.

BEETLE, A—uru; (*kind of*) deńca aọsrọć, ić uru, kạṭ uru, sansuniạ, sunsuni; (*small*) cạpri; (*stinging*) kạṭ sereń; (*red and black*) caroṛiń; (*larvae of some*) gạṇḍar.

BEFALL, TO—hoe, hoyok̓, paṛao.

BEFITTING—sãohạ; (*to be*) saja.

BEFORE—ạuri, laha, mạṛań, matrań, pạhil, samańre; (*just*) dela dili; (*and after*) utạhuli; (*one's eyes*) dikhitte.

BEG, TO—alet̓, bakhẽṛ, bhạṭ, ḍhạṇḍkao, jhẹńjle, kọe, ujur mujur; (*earnestly*) jacao, kãwari; (*hard*) ajak̓, ạri, jari, jẹńjle, jhiki, jigir, juṅgi, ńuruń (2); (*whiningly*) ńarań ńuruń, ńuruń (2).

BEGET, TO—gidrạjoń, họpọn, janam.

BEGGAR, A—bhikhari ; (*religious*) bhaṭ ; (*wallet of*) dhukṛi, dukhṛi, gubli.

BEGGING—ḍeheṭ ḍuṇḍheṭ ; (*persistent in*) haṭi ; (*for food*) khao (2).

BEGIN, TO—bahal, chuṭau, ḍhorao, dhundhaṛbeṭ, dhurau, egar, ehop, eṭeć, gatao, gotao, keṛe, laga, munai, nandhao, oram, osrao, parsao, pasante, phuṭau, porton, sirjau, sirjon, taltul, ṭhekao ; (*to move*) calcul ; (*to grow*) biṛhau ; (*to wither*) tolmoć ; (*rice-planting*) pacaṭi ; (*to germinate*) poṭe.

BEGINNING—ad, buṭa, eṭohop, oṛ, oṛaṭ, oṛphed ; (*just*) mereć ; (*from the*) oṛe oṛ, oṛphed khon ; (*in the*) porthomre, pahil porthomre ; (*or end, without*) oṛna soṛ.

BEGOTTEN, ONLY—ekaput, eskar janam.

BEGUILE, TO—bakao, bhabrao, caçki, ramjau, mońj.

BEGUILED—ora uri.

BEHALF OF, IN—babotre.

BEHAVE, TO—bebohar, beohar.

BEHAVIOUR—bebohar, beohar, caecolon, calcolon ; (*bad*) becol, corṭha, lacan, lochon ; (*of good*) benao, soghoṛ.

BEHEAD, TO—khatlak, khetlok.

BEHIND—kudam, taenom, tayom, tayomre, tayomte ; (*-hand*) aber, diri, kubela ; (*to fall*) lambri, larkao.

BEING—(*pres. part.*) hũiya ; (*a human*) hoṛ, manwa ; (*author of*) jaknamić, janam data ; (*the supreme*) ṭhakur ; (*to come into*) uptau.

BELCH, TO—dhekar, hekoc.

BELCHING—(*sound of*) ḍhep (2) ; (*a fit of*) hekoc bai.

BELIEF—biswas.

BELIEVE, TO—paṭiaṛ, paṭiau ; (*make*) jhuṭa muṭha, jhuṭh pus, jhuṭo puso, phẽs phãs.

BELIKE—mena.

BELITTLE, TO—dusau, por monda.

BELL, A—(*large*) ghanṭa ; (*small*) ghanṭi ; (*cow's*) dunda ghanṭi, dundha ; (*wooden*) ṭhekra, ṭoṭko ; (*tongue of*) laṛu ; (*to sway as tongue of*) luṛuń (2) ; (*metal*) kãs, kasa, kaskasa.

BELL, SOUND OF—dharań (2), luruń (2), phoṭo (2), riṛań raṛań, riṛiń, ṭeker, ṭharań ṭhuruń, ṭhiriń, ṭiriń ; (*wooden*) ṭeke (2), ṭopor ; (*cattle*) phoṭo (2), ṭimpi ṭiriń ; (*small*) ṭipiń (2).

BELLIED—*Cf.* BIG, POT.

BELLOW, TO—adrao, arra arri, arrao, bhokrao ; (*in pl.*) adra adri.

BELLOWS—bini, capua, phukni ; (*to blow*) dhukau ; (*sound of*) bugur (2), capos (2), gadar gudur, pagae pugui.

BELLS, MORRIS—ghugra ; (*worn on loins*) urmal ; (*sound of*) hanar (2), hanar jhanar ; (*of different tone*) dharań dhuruń.

BELLY—dojok, lać, marań gada, peṭ ; (*a pendulous*) gahnju, obra (M), ubri (F) ; (*one whose god is*) peṭdandia ; (*to become big*) putriṭ (F) ; (*to stuff the*) lai puṭi.

BELONGING TO—(*government*) sarkari ; (*different castes*) bitoń botoń.

BELONGINGS—dadha dumbar.

BELOVED—dulaṛ (M), dulaṛi (F), dularia, sohagi (F).

BELOW—latar, phed.

BELT, CLASP OF—bakuk.

BEMOAN, TO—hae hiatiń, haelać (2).

BENCH, A—beńc.

BENCH-MARK, A (*in earth*)—sakhi.

BEND, TO—kubkubu, kuca, kućkuć, kukuć, laṭić, leweṭ, liweṭ, nawan ; (*slightly*) lewe (2) ; (*a bow*) tiak ; (*ears of grain*) ludludu, tulkup ; (*hand at wrist*) luṛkuć ; (*the back*) kojo ; (*the body*) sara ; (*backwards or down*) liṛwa ; (*a limb*) laṛkuć ; (*down*) kaba kobo, kada kodo, ladgui, lakuć, leṛwe, tãṛkuć ; (*over*) ladur, ladwir, lawer, leṛwe, liṛwa ; (*& twist*) kacra kacri ; (*forwards, kneeling*) ombak.

BEND IN A RIVER, A—kucel.

BENEFIT—bapha, barphai, bhalai, parapat, phaeda, porho.

BENEVOLENCE—bũihar, girhar, sil.

BENGAL BABBLER, THE—bhonda jihu.

BENGAL KITE, THE—kuṛiṭ, ganga kuṛiṭ ; (*cry of*) ci hõ hõ.

BEN NUT TREE, THE—munga ; (*fruit of*) suṭi.

BENT—baka, dhọkṛẹ, ghõ̤rce, haṛbaṅ huṛbaṅ, kabea, kobea, kạbnũć, kạbuạ, kaca kucạ, kạṭwić (F), kẹbẹkẹbẹ, khẽṛẽ khõ̤ṛẽ, kobe, kobjo, kobṛẹ, koṇḍe, koṇḍeṫ, kọṛbẹṫ, kõ̤ṛmbeṫ, koṭba, kubạ, kubjạ, kubkubu, kubrạ, kukuć, kuṛbạṅ, ladea, nawan ; (*easily*) lạbus (2), libhrạ ; (*down*) ladgur ; (*to keep fingers*) lọk lọkọ ; (*& slightly broken*) meckao ; (*& stiff*) lukṛe ; (*over, as stalks of grain*) jhạrguaḱ.

BENT OF MIND—dhae.

BENUMBED, TO BE—oṛososo ; (*with fear*) cokao.

BERYL—boidurjọ.

BESEECH, TO—ajaḱ, ạjij, ạri, gọdhẹ, gọḍ pạri, lạriạ pạriạ, nẹhõ̤r, raḱ ; (*humbly*) hatiare.

BESHREW, TO—lese.

BESIDE—bẹgọr, chaḍa, chaḍakate, chọṛkate, hõ̤, upṛạnd.

BESMEAR ONESELF WITH ASHES, TO—bhoṭa.

BESPATTERED WITH MUD, TO BE—jobḍao, jọbẹ, jụdọ bọdọ, lọsọṫ.

BESPEAK, TO—dagao, phorman.

BEST—aol ; (*to be past the*) jhakaṇḍ, mạruṛ ; (*man at marriage*) babṛẽić.

BESTIR ONESELF, TO—jạhīt, upại.

BET—(*a*) bạrjid ; (*to*) akhaji, bạji.

BETEL—(*palm*) guạ ; (*nut*) kạsạili.

BETRAY TRUST, TO—ameṭ, hameṭ.

BETROTH, TO—họrọḱ cikhnạ, sạhi juhi.

BETTER—sir ; (*of one, to get the*) jọjọ, oṛ.

BETWEEN—talare.

BEWAIL, TO—geraṅ huruṅ, haecọḱ, haeḍhae, haehiạtiń, haelać (2).

BEWARE !—bãhaḱ, mẹn.

BEWILDER, TO—ạulạu.

BEWILDERED—alaṫ bakaṫ, ạndhup, anduḱ manduḱ, ayaḱ oyoḱ, cahaṗ cạṭur.

BEWITCH, TO—aha, nẽ̤ṫ, pạthri, pạtihar.

BEWITCHED, TO BE—aha, mạlun.

BEYOND—bahar, baher, bahre, hana, ọntẹ, ọn parọm, parọm ; (*one's means*) ẽ̤ć kõ̤ć ; (*measure*) asambheṛ.

BHANGY POLE, A—marāṛ.

BHUIYA CASTE, A SECTION OF—ghaṭwar.

BIBACIOUS—piạḱ.

BICKER, TO—rẹgẹń tẹgẹń, rego peto, tẹgẹń.

BID, TO—(*adieu*) bidạ ; (*at auction*) hakao ; (*against each other*) haka hạki.

BIDDING—bulahaṭ.

BIESTINGS—pīrũs.

BIFURCATED—caṅga, caṅgra.

BIG—ạsin daṛin, baṛhantar, dama domo, dạpṭhu, dạrgu (2), daṛhaṗ, daṛu, dhabaṛ dhubuṛ, dhạrgu (2), dhạrgu sạrgu, ḍobo, ghogo, hahadaṅ, hapṛaḱ, huduṛaḱ, jahbaj, jọbdọ, lạṭu, maraṅ, mọstọ, muṭhu, napṛaḱ, raeka, sẽṛã, ṭhabu ; (*of things on ground*) tẽṛẽjhaḱ ; (*so*) in maraṅ, isko maraṅ, nimin, nun maraṅ, un maraṅ ; (*to make*) lạṭu, maraṅ ; (*& broad*) lẹgẹsaḱ, lạpickaḱ ; (*& fat*) cakendaḱ, gạbḍulaṅ, habela, ohdar, ramdhu ; (*& unsightly*) badaḱ ; (*but slim*) sõ̤rga ; (*& little*) ḍamka ḍumkạ, ḍamkạ ḍurạ, dhạlać dhạluć, dhuluć dhupuć, phuckạ phucki, rayal ruyul, sẹgẹć pẹṭẹć, sele ṭoke, ṭhaṅgar ṭhuṅgur, tulić tupuć, ṭurạ ṭuri ; (*bellied*) bhuṭ bhuṭiạ, bhuṭiạ, ḍhẹb ḍhẹbẹ, ḍhọbḍhọbọ, ḍubu (2), jạhurae, joho (2), lọbọjhọr, obra (M), ohjar, pạṭra poṭra, pạṭraṫ poṭreṫ, poṭea, poṭma, poṭra (M), puṭri (F), raboskaḱ, robea, roboskaḱ, roden, ubri (F) ; (*bodied*) lodga (M), ludgi (F), lodhea ; (*head*) dạṭhu bọhọḱ, ḍapṭhu bọhọḱ, dạru bọhọḱ ; (*head and eyes*) banḍoḱ ; (*mouthed*) boaḱ moca.

BIGHA—(*half a*) bhaṅga muri ; (*twentieth part of*) kaṭha.

BIHARI DIALECT—gãowạri buli.

BILL, A—(*account*) bil, hisạb ; (*to run up*) dhar ; (*of a bird*) ṭhọṇṭa.

BILTONG—rọhọṛ jel.

BIND, TO—bandhọn, tọl ; (*round the loins*) bande (F), paṭhẹ (M).

BIRD, A—cẽṛẽ ; (*species of*) bak, bakoli, bana c., bhorṅga, ere, huć bir, hukes, jihu, kạli boṛbodoć, kãṛī c., karkor, kẹrkeṭa, kherguńjạ, laṇḍha galoć, machreṅka, phoṫ c., sahraj, sugi c., ṭuri c., urić ; (*small*) biń c., ḍẹrẹṫ, ḍhena c., gại cańcir, hạthi urić, jeć jewer, jugi suć, khoṫ c., kumbạ lipi, laṅtiti, lapre haṭak c., ṅokor c., phuci c., pirthi c., ruirui c. tude, tuṫ c., (*forest*) jejewer ; (*with small beak*) kuṭis ; (*large migratory*) artagom ; (*jungle*) askal ; (*wading*) mạnikjoṛ, samkhol ; (*sun*) sakwa suć, suć, ṭirioṅ ; (*note of*) rak. *Cf.* PADDY-BIRD, KITE, FOWL, etc.

BIRDLIME—laṭha ; (*bamboo box for*) laṭha ṭhoṅga ; (*twigs with*) bichṛi.

BIRDS IN GENERAL—cẽṛẽ cipruṫ, phạkrạ̃kanko ; (*small*) phuci c., (2 *mythical*) hãs hạ̃sil.

BIRTH—biạn, bihãṛ, jọnọm ; (*ceremony 5 days after*) nahan, narta ; (*of premature*) adpakolia ; (*next in order of*) sotok ; (*immediately following in*) soptok ; (*to travail in*) bedan, bijhạuk ; (*to give*) janam, paeda, uyuk ; (*place*) bukạ topa, jọnọm than, phẹdat.

BISCUIT, A KIND OF—jhinuk piṭhạ.

BISHOP'S WEED—ạjuạ.

BISON, THE FEMALE—kạpil gại.

BIT, A (*horse's*)—bag, lagam.

BITCH, A—seta eṅga.

BITE, A—cakoṗ ; (*to take*) haṗ.

BITE, TO—cabać cubuć, cạblạu, ger, lasok, lese, pohak, satok ; (*of dogs*) losak ; (*of snakes*) sogak, thagal ; (*with front teeth*) hạmbuṛ ; (*each other*) lẹpẹse, thagla thagli ; (*off a bit*) pohak ; (*the under lip*) haṗ ikṛum.

BITS—ṭukrạ ṭukri ; (*of fallen food*) sạkhṛi ; (*to cut into*) hubạg.

BITTER—ạ̃ṭaha, gargaṫ, harhaṫ, kạ̃ć-kạ̃ć, kasa, kasaṫ, titi, tito ; (*& sweet*) tito miṭho.

BITTERLY—awapapa, bẹbạrić, ṅarak (2); (*of weeping*) hũk hũk.

BIVALVE, A—jhinuk.

BLAB, TO—bạṭa, bayaṫ buyuṫ, buyuṫ mẹnte, labak cabak.

BLACK—baṅgorae, hẹndẹ, kajar, kạri, kạrya, khạurạ, ṅaṅgal ṅiṭe, roṭha, roṭhaha ; (*very*) ṅaṅgoyak, ṅolhaṫ ; (*almost*) kạrya ; (*of a person*) kuilạ (M), kuili (F) ; (*of clouds*) kạridaṅ, ṅạ̃ṛạ̃daṅ ; (*smutted with*) kuyạ ; (*and bulky*) ṅạhum dạrum ; (*dirty*) kạ̃ṭh, roṭha, roṭhaha ; (*& heavy-cloud*) gara jala, unạu ; (*arts, skilled in*) kaṭkuṭ ; (*to be*) koya.

BLACKGUARDLY—lucạ (M), luci (F).

BLACKISH—hẹndẹ macha.

BLACKSMITH, A—kamar mistri, lohar mistri ; (*work or pay of*) kamari ; (*to work as*) pasra ; (*a caste of*) kamar ; (*a tool of*) bhalwa.

BLADDER AFFECTION, A—koḍra. *Cf.* STONE.

BLAME, TO—bejha, bọhọk, dhusạu, dudrạu, dusạu, indiṫ, khoṭa, ọjọk jalaṫ, subha ; (*another*) bejha.

BLAMELESS—miridọs, nirdọs.

BLAMEWORTHY—dusạu, dusi.

BLANK, A—phãk.

BLANKET, A—kambra.

BLASTED—copa, copra, coroeṭho, kạ̃rạ.

BLASTING—(*powder*) bạrud ; (*to bore hole for*) suruṅ.

BLAZE, TO—dãhgao, dahṅgao, dhandha, durdurạu, hudgu dugur, phorophoro phorphor.

BLAZING—dahṅga dạhṅgi, daraṅ, ḍẹć ḍẹć, dhandha, dhạu (2), sạusạu.

BLEAT, TO—bẹbhaok, bhebhao, bhẽ (2) ; (*as goat*) bhek (2), mek (2).

BLEED, TO—mayam ; (*from gums*) dãtrisạ.

BLEMISH, A—dag, kusur ; (*without*) napae, niphuṭ.

BLEMISHED—dạgi, darpoṭ ; (*in character*) dạgi mara, hurạ.

BLESS, TO—ạsirbad, bhọr.

BLESSED—bhạgan ; (*to be*) barket.

BLESSING—ạsirbad, barket, bhọr, borket.

BLIGHT AFFECTING RICE-PLANT, A—ṭaku.

BLIGHTED—agṛa, coroeṭbo, mạndhuạ.

BLIND—andhra (M), ạndhri (F), kạ̃rạ (M), kạ̃rĩ (F) ; (*when scolding*) kọrdhọć ; (*half*) ạndhuạ, perla (M), perli (F) ; (*of one eye*) ṭesra (M), ṭisri (F), ṭhesra (M), ṭhisri (F) ; (*night*) andheṫ dundheṫ, ạndhuạ, ratạ̃ode, ratkana ; (*to*) bạuli, najer bọnd ; (*and lame*) kạ̃rạ̃ khoṛhe.

BLINDERS OF AN OILMAN'S BULLOCK—tili ṭopar.

BLINDFOLD, TO—bẹṫ, ṭopar.

BLINK, TO—andha ondho, jalaṭ julut, jilpiṭ (2), jilu milu, jipa (M), jipi (F), jirip (2), jirit (2); (*when drowsy*) jolo japit, jolo (2).

BLISTER—(*to*) phoka; (*raised as*) lut-luṭu; (*which becomes a sore*) gargadi.

BLISTERING PLANT, A—kedar.

BLOCK, TO—tepeṭ, ṭoktoko; (*a way*) ọseṭ, paṭeṭ; (*with thorns*) ram, rampha.

BLOCKHEAD—akorma.

BLOOD—khūn, māyām, rokot; (*from womb passages*) arak pordhol; (*an offering of*) bul māyām; (*passing of*) arak sul, pond risa; (*to track by*) māyām pañja; (*thirsty*) mūhā, rokot mūhā.

BLOT OUT, TO—kaṭiṭ, meṭao; (*entirely*) mobor meṭao.

BLOTCHES ON THE SKIN—surhi.

BLOTTED—jabre.

BLOW, A—(*with one*) khaṭ marte; (*with a stick*) ṭheṅga; (*with hammer*) kuṭam.

BLOW, TO—phaph, phũ, phuphuau; (*out of mouth*) phū, phur; (*as breath*) oñ; (*as wind*) bohao, sagae; (*a wind instrument*) oroñ; (*a blast on a horn*) tutu (2); (*hard—as wind*) sayar; (*bellows*) dhukau; (*out smoke*) odoe padoe.

BLOWPIPE, A HOLLOW BAMBOO—phukni.

BLOWN AWAY, TO BE—otañ.

BLUBBERING—beñbeñ, sombe suruć.

BLUDGEON, A—mutak ṭheṅga.

BLUE—lil; (*stone*) tutiya.

BLUNDER—(*a*) bhul, cuk; (*to*) andha, bata, cukau.

BLUNDERING—aldhundha, alhua, alua basua, phanda phondo, sio soyo.

BLUNT—bheṭro, bhondo; (*to*) bhoṭko, bondo.

BLUNTED, TO BE—korga, kõrẽ.

BLUSH, TO—dharcir.

BLUSTER, TO—dhamae dhurai, dham dhur, dhum dham, hurum durum, hutma hutmi, jhik jhok, jhok jhokao, ṭher.

BLUSTERING—adopia, dhora dhuri.

BOAR, A—bhator sukri, datela, kudu, rata sukri, sukri kudu; (*castrated*) badhia.

BOARD, A—takta.

BOAST, TO—bakha, bhaka, bhakha, eren beten, gal, hākao, hẽko, phaph, suhu, taras, tawić, uć, usić; (*of insignificant people*) ṭereṭere.

BOASTER, A—galkaṭua, galua, phaphuda.

BOASTING—bakhara, bakhera, bhakara, galkaṭua, katha bajoria, ṭhaṭarbaj.

BOAT, A—kishti, lauka, nao; (*small*) duṅgi; (*of hollow tree*) dhoṅga; (*pole used to propel*) cihiri dañ.

BOB, TO—(*the head*) kayar; (*up and down*) bhandul, dhacal dhucul, dole, kayar, lawar (2), lawić, liwić, rayul, royol, ruirui, ruyu, ruyul, ṭuyul (2); (*to & fro*) dhacal dhucul, rayul.

BOBBIN, A—chuci; (*to wind*) beṭhaon.

BODE ILL, TO—digić.

BODILY—(*affliction*) nara dhura; (*representation*) chin.

BODY—camraṅga, cola, deh, hormo, kaya; (*dead*) lahas; (*mortal*) hasa hormo; (*of one breadth*) bhuila; (*trunk only*) gund; (*the members of*) hormo haṭiñ; (*the side of*) sorta; (*to exercise the*) teñjao.

BODY, IN A—gor, jhumblaimente, jomka jumki, jomkao, jomok, miṭ jomkao, pal bhiñjan.

BOGGY—lubur.

BOIL, A—bisphor, ojo; (*blind*) gañ; (*core of*) tuka.

BOIL, TO—dabkao, dahalao, dapkao, hedeć, khicir (2), lokphokao, teke; (*over*) se, udhiau, utlau; (*down*) cachi; (*leguminous fruits whole*) puṭhuć; (*sound of*) godo (2), khudu (2), lede phede, phokok.

BOILER, A—bhaṭhi.

BOISTEROUS—(*of laughter*) haha (2), khak (2).

BOLD—dhidrik, dilgar; (*from immunity*) laghar.

BOLDLY—muk dorho, sahasae.

BOLE OF A TREE—kunda.

BOLT, A THUNDER—ceṭer.

BOLT, TO (*swallow*)—kuryuṭ (2).

BOMB, A—bom.

BOND, A—bandhon, dalis, ikrar nama, mocolka, mucalka, tamasuk, tomosuk.

BONE, A—haḍ, jaṅ ; (*the collar*) hās.

BONES—(*pain in*) haḍ hạmus ; (*only*) royot ; (*projecting at joints*) ḍopṭho ; (*appearing under skin*) khaḍra (M), khaḍri (F) ; (*rescued from funeral pyre*) jaṅ baha, usti.

BONY—coeta.

BOOBY OF THE CLASS, THE—lenda.

BOOK, A—ketab, kitạb, pustạk, puthi ; (*account*) bạhi.

BOOM, TO—ṭher (2) ; (*sound of*) sarsar.

BOOR, A—cạtrạrią.

BOOTH, A—camḍa, capcamḍa, jhạpri, jhupri, kumbạ ; (*low*) chepra kumbạ ; (*marriage*) manḍha, manḍhwa.

BOOTLESS—bertha.

BOOTS—panahi ; (*sole of*) tala.

BORAX—sohaga, sohga.

BORDER OF CLOTH—sọhọr ; (*lengthwise*) macho ; (*breadth-wise*) añcar ; (*of double thread*) pacan ; (*coloured*) pạṛ, sọhọr ; (*corner of*) ṭep.

BORE, TO—gharṛa, pạṭi ; (*with hot iron*) bal ; (*a bullock's nose*) nat ; (*in rock for blasting*) suruṅ ; (*bother*) ạris, jọdhe.

BORING, AN INSTRUMENT FOR—gharṛa.

BORN—(*to be*) busạ̃r, hoe, janam, uyuk ; (*out of wedlock*) bidhwạ ; (*when raining or cloudy*) badoli.

BORROW, TO—pañca, rin ; (*& lend*) em capal, pạlike pasa.

BORROWER, A—dharuạ.

BORROWING—rin dharkate ; (*a system of*) sak.

BOSOM—họbọr ; (*to rend the*) chạti jarao ; (*friends, to be*) ọṅsọṅ, sọtasọṅ.

BOSSED—uṭ uṭu.

BOTH—banar, dẹnẹ banar ; (*parties*) duyokul.

BOTHER—ajar, dik, harọn, pajet ; (*to*) ạlkạu, ạris, dik dikạu, diksik, hạkup cạkup, hantao, hujạt, pajet.

BOTHERED, TO BE—berosta, tọmọl dak.

BOTHERSOME—nepran, nichạn, nichnạha (M), nichnạhi (F).

BOTTLE, A—(*earthen*) ḍumdhukak ; (*ink*) dawat, doat ; (*small*) sisi ; (*water*) surạhi, tumbạ ; (*half-full, as*) paṭ ; (*filler, a*) coṅga.

BOTTOM, THE—penda, phẹḍ, thah ; (*having flaw in*) penda ḍọpọt.

BOTTOMLESS—athanthar, bẹthah, patạṛphọṛ.

BOUGH, A—ḍar, kahle.

BOUND, TO—dhạmcuk, jhạruk (2), kẹrẹp (2), lẹp, padak, pạrdak, rạyul, rọyọl ; (*of creatures without legs*) pẹresaṅ.

BOUND, CARELESSLY—bhiso bhoso.

BOUNDARY—ḍạnḍi, sarhad, simạ, simạ ḍạnḍi, simạna ; (*limit*) simạtbaṛ ; (*the whole*) cạtur simạ ; (*between 2 villages*) dosimạ ; (*to fix a*) khap kạṭi, simạ ; (*godlet, the*) simạ boṅga ; (*mark, a*) ḍhui, gurji, tehara, thum ; (*where 3 villages meet*) ḍhipi, gurji tehạṛa.

BOUNDING—dhạmcuk, pạrdak (2), piḍgạ pidgi.

BOUNTIFUL—diwạya.

BOW, A—ak ; (*large*) bag dhinuk ; (*pliant*) libhrạ ak, lipsạ ak, lubhrạ ak ; (*notch at end of*) kạnại ; (*sharp ends of*) sursạ ; (*fiddle*) ak ; (*& arrows*) ak sar ; (*string-bamboo*) pạnichạ, pọ̃rcha ; (*-hemp*) ghũṛa ; (*shot*) teraṅ ; (*crack shot with*) dhinkią ; (*to unstring*) ạsiṭ ; (*to string*) dak ; (*to aim with*) hạbak ; (*to shoot with*) tuṅ ; (*to draw the long*) lahna ; (*one who draws the long*) batkunda.

BOW THE HEAD, TO—ḍọbọk, ḍọnḍọbot, ḍubuk, ḍubuk (2), kọkọrbọk, kudbur, kuḍuṅ (2), kuluṅ ḍubuṅ, kuṛbur, kuyuṅ, tirup, tumbuṭ ; (*of children*) lumu.

BOW-BILLED CORBY, THE—bhọnḍa kạhu.

BOWED DOWN—hẹrwẹć, kobo.

BOWELS—(*any complaint of*) lać haso ; (*looseness of*) ḍhisọḍhọrọ, lać ọḍok, pọdrọć.

BOWL, A BRASS—(*large*) khora ; (*small*) bạṭi, ḍubhi ; (*metal*) ḍubhạ.

BOWWOW—hạuhạu, jhạu jhạu.

BOX, A—sạnduk, sinduk, sunduk ; (*for lime*) cunạiṭi.

BOY, A—bạbu, chọnḍa, kọṛa ; (*10 to 12*) chọnḍ kọṛa ; (*12 to 14*) chọnḍaṭią ; (*dancing*) ras dhạrią.

BOYS—(*when calling*) ehe re ; hoeja, hoja, (*when addressing*) ja, ya.

BRACE—(*for boring*) bhãora; (*a drum, to*) caṛhao; (*up spirits, to*) ṭhukạu.

BRACELET, A—barphaṛa sakom, cuṛi, kạtri, khilạ sakom, lạhṭi, sakom.

BRAG, TO—bakha, bhaka, gal, hĕko, ṭher.

BRAGGING—bakhara, bakhera, bhakara, galkạṭuạ, gạluạ, katha bajoṛiạ.

BRAHMAN, A—babrẽ; (*resident in a temple*) paṇḍa; (*a title of*) ṭhạkur.

BRAID—phitạ; (*to*) galaṅ, pạṭeṭ; (*the hair, to*) up galaṅ.

BRAIN, THE—hataṅ, mogoj.

BRAINLESS—urbhuṅga.

BRANCH OF TREE—ḍar; (*small, with leaves*) ḍharwạk; (*main*) mutul ḍar.

BRANCHES—(*& leaves*) patpala; (*thin*) jhuri; (*for fencing*) jhạnṭi; (*stakes*) jhaṭa; (*laid on rafters*) sirhi; (*for firewood*) koṭaṅ sahan; (*a shelter of*) jhupri; (*having*) thopnak; (*without*) ṭhuṇḍgạ, ṭhuṇḍguṭ.

BRANCHING OFF—caṅga, caṅga cạṅgi.

BRAND, TO—dag; (*with a hot iron*) tobak.

BRANDED—dạgi.

BRANDING-IRON, A—dạgni.

BRANDISH, TO—epel.

BRASS—pitạl, pitol; (*a wo ker in*) ṭhaṭera, ṭhaṭori; (*household utensils*) loṭa luṭi; (*castes who work in*) kãe kũi, kẽrẽ kõrẽ, sekra. *Cf.* BOWL, PLATE, VESSEL, WATER-POT, ETC.

BRAVADO—ḍhadnas.

BRAVE—bagrạsiạu, ḍhaḍos, ḍharos, dil, dilgạr, dilman, sahas, sahạsiạ.

BRAVO !—bah, bahware, hạllạ bhại.

BRAWL, A—kaṇḍo.

BRAWNY—kuṭeṭ paṅjar, rotho.

BRAZEN-FACED—kẹṭẹc cạndi.

BRAZIER, A—ṭhaṭera.

BREACHED, TO BE—phoṛ.

BREAD—piṭhạ, roṭi, ruṭi; (*kind of sweet*) kacauṛi, (*balls of*) dombok; (*kneaded with feet*) pao piṭhạ; (*thin cakes of*) lapar (2) piṭhạ; (*to make by frying in oil*) karao; (*other kinds of*) *Cf.* piṭhạ.

BREADTH, THE—onosarteṭ, osarteṭ; (*a finger's*) kạṭuṗ, tạsu.

BREAK, TO—bhaṅga, bhaṅgabhaṭ, bhaṅgao, bhaṅlabhaṭ, bhaṅj, boskao, cewak, cẹwẹc, chachak, chakachun, coak, cowak, darkao, haṛhe, kecak, kẹcẹṭ, khucrạ, kucạ, posak, poseṭ, rạpuṭ, ricoṭ, rọcọṭ, topak; (*earthen vessels*) pohaṅ; (*the arm*) lokaṅ; (*a law*) lạṇḍhu, talao; (*a holy day*) bhaṇḍ; (*harmony*) bhaṅga; (*faith*) arkhao, harkhao; (*a long fast*) ahaṅ; (*as the morning*) pahpahao; (*by striking*) kọṭẹc; (*up, as water falling*) pạsir; (*into a house*) sind; (*a part off*) coak, kecak; (*a smooth surface*) poṭak; (*down*) bhaṅlabhaṭ, ghoṅrao, mambṛao; (*half through*) caṭkao; (*in cattle*) bhãoar, bhãwar, caṭiạu, eto, hewa, sạl; (*to pieces*) chikican, chiticḥaṅ, chitrạ phuṭạu, citil bitil, gaṇḍra guṇḍrạ, gẹjẹr, ghasmaṇḍao, kẹcẹṭ, khaiạ khudri, khaya khudri, khaya khutri, khẹcẹṭ, khidibidi, khucrạ, ṭakrạ ṭukrạ, talga tạuak; (*into two*) coak; (*off from*) phuṭ; (*off*) cagar, coak, huceć, hulạk, kẹcẹṭ; (*off with fingers*) hucạk, huleć, pẹṭẹć, ṭuṅgạu; (*out, as sore*) phadphadao; (*out, as epidemic*) ạcur sorta; (*out afresh*) dohlao; (*up*) bhaṅgao, bhiṅgoṛ, bhiṛ bhaṅgao, budạk, phuṭ phaṭ, uṭhi bạisi; (*up camp*) uṭhạu; (*up, to cause to*) bhiṅgrạu; (*up & mix*) gaṅja gaṅji, lẹhẹ (2); (*wind*) gasić, ghasić.

BREAK—(*of day*) pahapoho, piạṅ payaṅ; (*without a*) sadamạd, sodamod.

BREAKFAST—maṅjan.

BREAKING—(*up an assembly*) cạlcul; (*water falling*) chirić (2); (*to destroy by*) haṛhe; (*out in one place after another*) gohla guhli; (*stones with hammer, sound of*) ṭheć (2).

BREAST, THE—chạti, koṛam; (*female*) bạs, nunu, thanel, toa; (*to give*) nunu; (*suppurating*) toa bele; (*bone, top of*) kondoram.

BREATH—bao, nisạs, satahẹṭ; (*a long*) baraṅ buruṅ, phukur, pukus; (*from one, to take*) hẹk.

BREATHE, TO—pukus, sahẹṭ; (*through the month*) phũ; (*on*) ọṅ; (*heavily*) baṭak, dọmẹdọm, hapho, hẽsrao, khẽs (2), lakọphọkọ, phakar phukur, phẽs (2), phọphọ, phuk, phukur, sāsũ, sẽphõ, sop̓ ; (*as a bear*) pudruk̓ ; (*and move*) ukus pukus ; (*only able to*) leṭep̓ (2).

BREATHING—(*heavily*) phaphu, sõsõ, upardom ; (*with difficulty, sound of*) khẽs (2), sẽsẽ, ṭhẽs (2) ; (*hole made by rats*) sinin̓.

BREATHLESS—dọmẹdọm, nirdọm, sakardọm, sokordom ; (*to be*) sẹṅgẹt̓, sop̓ ; (*from fear*) lẹṅgẹt̓ sopot̓.

BREED—tur ; (*to*) họpọn.

BREEZE—họyọn̓ ; (*to blow a*) sagae ; (*without*) nijhum, nirot.

BREVITY, WITH—sanchep.

BREW, SECOND—doja.

BRIBE, A—ghus, jhāp, ŕisbod̓.

BRICK, A—iṭạ ; (*layer*) raj mistri.

BRICKS—(*ground for mortar*) surki ; (*to set in mortar*) gatao.

BRIDE, A—bạhu ; (*price paid for*) conda ṭaka, gọnọn̓ pọn ; (*father's gift to*) jạituk ; (*to accompany*) baretok̓, lumti ; (*to mark brow of*) bundi.

BRIDEGROOM—jāwāe ; (*party of*) bạriạt ; (*party meeting*) sạriạt.

BRIDGE A—pul, sakhọ, sakọ ; (*of nose*) nak ḍạṇḍi ; (*broken*) hurwan̓, khaipić, khaptak̓, nakṭa (M), nạkṭi (F).

BRIDLE, A—bag, jhin baber, lagam, ras jhin.

BRIGHT—chik chok, chuk (2), ḍig (2), jhak (2), phini phik̓ ; (*of atmosphere*) phiriphan̓ ; (*red*) jẹṅgẹt̓ (2), jọrọn̓ (2) ; (*& clean*) jhalmal ; (*& cheery*) khasa, susulṭak̓ ; (*to make*) sikil.

BRIGHTLY—dhạu, dugur (2).

BRILLIANT—baran̓ (2), dag (2).

BRIM—(*full to the*) cebel (2), cebel cepel, cẹmcẹrẹm, cepel (2), cẹrẹm (2), cuhlạ cuhli, curu buru, ṭẹmṭẹrẹm, ṭẹrẹm (2), ṭomṭombao, ṭulṭulạu, ṭuṅgạu ; (*to fill to the*) cuhlạu ; (*with tears, to*) pẽpẽrkat̓.

BRIMSTONE—gandhak, gondhọk.

BRING, TO—ạgu ; (*in*) ader ; (*up as child*) palao, pokhao ; (*up delicately*) barmạṇḍ ; (*out*) oḍok, tot̓ ; (*forward*) ukti, upusti ; (*forward again*) ghurạiulṭạì ; (*through as illness*) nimbhạ, nimbhẹu ; (*round*) sāorao ; (*under*) kabja ; (*along with*) ạgu dara, sap̓ dara ; (*anything undesirable on oneself*) jhokrao ; (*up an old matter*) ṭhokao ; (*together materials*) sapsor ; (*as rain*) paghrao ; (*forth young, of cow*) dhirũ ; (*forth dead offspring*) gabḍhao.

BRINJAL, THE—bẹṅgar.

BRISTLY—ḍundun, karcap̓, paṭocak̓, rạgumcak̓, ramcam, rape, sạdgum bạdgum ; (*of face*) bạdgocak̓.

BRITTLE—rucup̓, ṭhasaha ; (*breaking, sound of*) ṭhas.

BROAD—cakendar, capṛa, ḍabdaba, ḍapdapa, dhab dhaba, dhạblu, ḍhalka, dhalpa, ḥakurpak̓, lablab, lạpickak̓, (F), lapockak̓ (M), lẹgẹsak̓, lẹplẹpe, osar, phael, phaela, phạṇḍ ; (*of face*) badgok̓ (2), bedbede, pạkursak̓ ; (*faced & black*) baṅgorae ; (*of feet*) dhabṛa. dhạblu ; (*of cloth*) cindạr condọr ; (*and thick*) dhạbṛu ; (*& horizontal*) laplapa.

BROADEN, TO—osar, phaelao.

BROKEN—baher, cacak̓, dalsin̓ ṭalsin̓, dhaṅgladhas, hara hurạ, jhaṅga jhuṭạ, kaca kucạ, khẹkre, ṭuṭạ bhaṅga, ṭuṭạu ; (*as limb*) lukṛe ; (*in places*) odra udri, phọnphọn̓ ; (*to pieces*) kaca kucạ ; (*easily*) ṭhasaha ; (*in*) bọhọn ; (*into holes*) badak̓, budạk̓ ; (*up, as soil by plough*) phodlo ; (*to work, not*) abọṭ ; (*pieces*) guṇḍạ guṇḍi ; (*in estate*) bhaṅtao, bhaṅga suli ; (*into pieces*) gaṇḍa guṇḍạ ; (*to be*) bhaṅgaṭ, ṭuṭạu.

BROKER, A—dalal.

BROKERAGE—dalali, dallạli, ḍạsturi, keali.

BRONCHITIS—kạsi dhõk ; (*wheezing sound of*) hākār (2), sẽsẽ.

BRONZE—kas kasa.

BROOD, THE SMALLEST OF A—lenda, lendaṭuriạ.

BROOM, A—jọnọk̓ ; (*worn*) ṭuṭki jọnọk̓ ; (*bamboo*) mat̓ j. ; (*grass*) lukui j., kharan̓ j., sirom j. ; (*to plait grass for*) j. galan̓ ; (*noise made by stiff*) khẹrẹć (2).

BROTHER—baret, bhại, bhạyạ, boeha, mit̓ lać boeha ; (*elder*) dada ;

(*younger*) **bọkọt koṛa**; (*used in addressing young*) **ja, ya**; (*in-law*) **bahọṅhar, erwel koṛa, teṅa, teṅaea, teṅa era, tiṅyạṅ**; (*wife of elder*) **hili**; (*children of elder*) **họmọn**; (*wife of younger*) **erwel.**

BROTHERHOOD, A CEREMONY OF—bā̃ihā̃.

BROTHERS—bhạiạdi, bọkọ boeha; (*wives of*) **ṅamea**; (*children of young*) **goṅgo**; (*children of elder*) **bhạicạ**; (*in-law-address between*) **marde.**

BROUGHT INTO THE WORLD, TO BE—busā̃ṛ.

BROW, THE—kopal; (*of hill*) **kaṅkha.**

BROWBEAT, TO—humdhum.

BROWN—gola (M), guli (F), kạiri, khaera (M), khạiri (F); (*earth*) **mạṭiol**; (*of fowls*) **herạk**; (*of bullocks*) **kaera.**

BROWNISH—kạiri; (*as thread*) **podgoe.**

BROWSE, TO—ạtiṅ.

BRUIZE, TO—chẹo, gasmaṇḍao, talga tạuạk, tuạṅ.

BRUIZED—lọṭọc; (*slightly*) **hudrič.**

BRUSH, A—buruj, burus; (*tooth*) **datạni, ṭuṭki jọnọk**; (*weaver's*) **jọṭọč.**

BRUSH, TO—(*off*) **koṭa**; (*with hand*) **jọč, urlạ urli**; (*slightly against*) **jak, jọhọt, ṅọhọč.**

BRUSHWOOD, A LARGE AREA OF—hela.

BUBBLE, TO—badač buḍuč, bambkao, bamkao, bhak, bhakaṛ (2), bhukuṛ (2), bhumbuk, bhurbhurạu, buḍuč (2), bukuṛ (2), burbuḍuč, hẹḍẹč, khadkhad, leke pheke, lakphak, phakphak, phẹkẹ (2), phud (2); (*with a*) **bhọkọṛ marte.**

BUBBLING—bhọkọṛ, gaṛgaṛ, goḍogoḍo, khadkhad, khadkhadao, khẹḍẹč (2), khẹḍẹ khẹd, khudu (2), kiciṛ (2), lakọphọkọ, lẹḍẹphẹḍẹ, phọk (2), sarsar; (*suppressed sound of*) **sẹṭẹ.**

BUBBLES, TO RISE AS—barač buruč, bhurbhurạu, biḍič (2), bukuṛ (2).

BUCK, A—(*of ravine deer*) **badaṛ selep, mẹṭrẹč jel**; (*of spotted deer*) **jhaṅkar.**

BUCKET, A—balti; (*iron*) **dol.**

BUCKLE, A—bạkuk.

BUCKLER, A—dhal.

BUD—(*a*) **ṭusạ**; (*a leaf*) **ḍọg**; (*to*) **mọhō, sagẹn, sarhe.**

BUFFALO, A—(*bull*) **kaḍa, kaṛa**; (*breeding bull*) **bayar**; (*cow*) **bitkil**; (*milking*) **mār bitkil**; (*calf*) **kạḍru (M), kạḍi (F)**; (*F, till she calves*) **saṇḍharụ**; (*with 6 teeth*) **ṭẹṇḍa bayar**; (*short-legged*) **suạr jạṅghiạ**; (*to tie horns of*) **siṅghaoṭi.**

BUFFALO, LOW OF—ā ā, ọ̃č ọ̃č, oṇḍroč; (*young*) **ẽč ẽč**; (*excited*) **aṇḍrač oṇḍrọč.**

BUFFALOES, A CALL TO—bạr (2), ḍrui (2), hạriak, hạrjạk (2), ihet; (*young*) **ḍuru (2)**; (*to lie down*) **bạrbạr.**

BUFFOONERY—nạbhuạ.

BUG, A—ọrmọč; (*small*) **topoč**; (*stink*) **caya.**

BUGLE, SOUND OF—pẽpẽ.

BUILD, TO—(*a wall*) **bhit, kāt**; (*with bricks or stones*) **tọl.**

BULB, A—da.

BULBUL, THE—(*green*) **barọmạsia**; (*Indian*) **ṭič ṭọrọk.**

BULGE, TO—gāhjur, lẹḍẹ (2), lẹḍlẹḍẹ, ludludu, puipui; (*on both sides*) **lẹgọe pẹgọe.**

BULKY—asāt osōt, goho (2), lẹgẹsak.

BULL, A—saṇḍ, saṇḍ ḍaṅgra, sāṛ; (*breeding*) **adar, adar urič, rạsiā̃u ḍaṅgra**; (*calf*) **bacha, damkọm**; (*snort of excited*) **hukạ**; (*coughing sound of*) **hudrak (2)**; (*having propensities of*) **chandgar (F), saṇḍgar (M).**

BULL-NECKED—kondo, okroč, thom thorok, tombroč.

BULLET-HEADED—darmaṅ, ḍạṭhu.

BULLOCK, A—ḍaṅgra, urič; (*young*) **damkọm urič**; (*pack*) **lade ḍ., chala badla, ladhna ḍ., paghạiạ**; (*long-horned*) **rạukạ ḍ.**, (*loose-horned*) **lurkạ ḍ.**; (*hired for season*) **kạnd-hi ḍ.**; (*on left of row*) **meh ḍ.**; (*with white forehead*) **dusi**; (*wood tied round neck of*) **ghū̃rā̃**; (*killed for sacrifice*) **kuṭạm ḍ.**; (*to bore nose of*) **nat.**

BULLOCKS, A CALL TO—pawetar, ṭhāo ghurghur; (*to turn*) **ṭhōṭhō.**

BULLOCK'S HEART, THE—(*a cultivated tree*)**—amsophori, gom.**

BULLY, TO—ạruk dhạruk, dhamkhum, dhara dhurạ, dharamara, humdhum, jhik jhọk, jhik jhọr, jhọk jhokao.

BUMP, TO—dhampol, dhaṛkuć; (*with nose*) dhunạu; (*against*) ṭhapa ṭhuk'; (*to fall with a*) lẹthẹć; (*sound of*) dharae.

BUMPTIOUS—ạḍại bạḍại, bạḍại.

BUMPY—uṭ uṭu.

BUNCH, A—ẹdẹ ṭhompe, thopa; (*to make into*) jhomble; (*to become*) candheṛ; (*of red cotton fixed on hair*) amba gạuṛạ.

BUNCHES—(*to hang in*) ṭamka ṭạkur; (*not tied into*) gaṇḍra guṇḍṛạ.

BUNDLE, A—ạṭi, bhiṇḍiạ, biṇḍạ, moṭ, moṭra; (*small*) bạniạ potòle, guchi; (*to make into*) koṗ (2), moṭ, moṭra.

BUNDLES—jhoṭra moṭra, moṭ jhoṭ, moṭra jhoṭra; (*several tied together*) lacha; (*to make into*) biṇḍạ.

BUNGLE, TO—bọsẹrṭạk, loro (2), loṛo thoṛo.

BUNKUM—ḍhaḍnas.

BUOY, FLOATING AND STATIONARY AS A—ḍọmkọl.

BURDEN, A—ajgaṛ, bhari, boj, bojha; (*moving under a*) ṭimbạ ṭambe.

BURDENSOME—hamal.

BURLY—rạmdhu, rotho.

BURN, TO—atar, chuć, ẹrẹć (2), jalao, jaljalao, jạri jarao, jẹrẹt', jol, junḍi, lọ; (*in cooking*) kharao; (*a corpse*) dag, dahọn, gọk' sahan; (*brightly*) parpao; (*feebly*) ńũṛũ (2), sọć (2), dhũṛsạu; (*in a kiln*) rapak'; (*incense*) dhup, dhudhup; (*with glowing wood*) jhola; (*up*) ḍahao; (*to cause to*) salgao, sulgạu.

BURNED, TO BE—(*food when cooking*) ọk'; (*alive*) sạti; (*to death*) lọ gọć; (*up*) jạri jarao.

BURNING—(*sensation*) arae oroe, caraṭ (2), chan (2), chẹk, chuć, ẹrẹć (2); (*& itching*) sikiṛ; (*of throat*) gargat'; (*mark of*) ḍạhni dag; (*heat*) jhańj; (*of green wood, sound of*) soro (2); (*to tell, &c.*) ukut' bukut'.

BURNISH, TO—molao, sikil.

BURNISHED—jhile mile; (*to be*) jhalkao.

BURNT, TO BE—rọṅgọ; (*up*) ḍahon; (*food*) jạri poḍa, ọk', rọṅgọ cọṅgọ.

BURR, STICKY AS A—laṭlaṭiạ.

BURST, TO—bhirobhoro, bhoskao, ọṭẹć, phuṭạu, posak', poset'; (*open*) bhaskao; (*the heart*) chati jarao.

BURSTING, SOUND OF—ṭhu; (*roasted grain*) cẹrẹ pẹṭẹ; (*semi-liquid*) pọdrọć, poroporo; (*seed germinating*) beker beṇḍań.

BURY, TO—gạḍiạu, hasa, rọhọe, topa; (*treasure*) topa goṅjao.

BUSH, A—jhaṛ, jhạuạ; (*low*) por; (*of wheel*) ulạ; (*a kind of*) ḍaṅgra sea, gaḍa hund baha, gaḍa sigrik', gote, khaṇḍerae, por, sarjọm, sindwạri dare; (*climbing*) pańjot nạ̃ṛi; (*thorny*) ẹdhẹ jạnum, ẹdhẹ raṅgaini, jọm jạnum, kendro jạnum, kurit' rama, sega jạnum; (*small*) bạ̃riạ̃ kạṇḍhum, berdoṛ, bhabri, maṭhasuṛạ, maṭha arak', mihindi dare, nanha bạ̃riạ̃ kạṇḍhum, nicak', peṭcamṛa, seta ạndiṛ, sọl, sũṛũkuć, tarse koṭap, tilại dare; (*hedging*) mehndi dare; (*jungle*) aṭhel, nạ̃ṛi siris, rama kurit', roṛa.

BUSH AND BRAKE—bir pakaṛ, jhaṇṭe jhaṛe, jhaṛe pataṛe, muṇḍu pakaṛ, pakaṛ.

BUSH CHAT, THE—jạnum jihu.

BUSHY, AS HAIR—ḍaḍuṛham, hạdui (2).

BUSIEST SEASON, THE—dhurpạu.

BUSINESS—beoṛa, kaj, kam, kamkaj, karsaj, rajkaj; (*to transact*) kaj jug, kạmi jạri, karbar, lanban; (*one who transacts*) karbạri, karbạriạ; (*pressure of*) beoṛa, dhõ̤nj, gạhul.

BUSTLING—cạṇḍuć.

BUSY—ạhi bạhi, ạujhaṛ, daṛaedhampae, jõ̤hoṭ, lajhar, najhar; (*as a road*) rohpoṭ; (*body, a*) ạbuń sẹlẹdokić; (*to be*) bhiṛ, ambaṛ omboṛ, lagao.

BUT—ạikạ, bickọm, bọrọń, mẹnẹk, mẹnkhan; (*just then*) taṅgaṭ; (*rather*) bickọm, bọrọń; (*certainly*) ạikạ.

BUTCHER, A—bhucaṛ, kạsại.

BUTT, TO—dhunạ dhuni, rọk'.

BUTTER—nạinu; (*clarified*) gọtõ̤m, sọ sunum; (*milk*) ghẹr.

BUTTERFLY, A—pipṛiań.

BUTTOCK, THE—bituć, picạ; (*small in*) phuciạ, phuckạ (M), phucki (F).

BUY, TO—kharid, kirin', saoda; (*at a market*) haṭ baṭ; (*on credit*) dhar; (*& sell*) bạnij bepar, bepar, lanban, pher bepar.

BUYER, A—gãhak, gaharak, gạhki, kiǩriṅič, ; (*and seller*) paikạr.

BUZZ, TO—(*as flies*) bhan ; (*round about*) ḍhaṇḍhanao.

BUZZING—dão (2), dhẽṛẽ (2) ; (*as mosquitoes*) dhão (2) ; (*round about*) ḍhan (2), ḍhanman.

BY—hoṭeṭe, kate, ke, te, toroṗte ; (*& by*) dina, hapen ; (*chance*) oka bhagte ; (*degrees*) dhire suste, enka enkate ; (*fits & starts*) chada mela ; (*force of*) dhomosṭe, kakhante, tese ; (*means of*) butel, butlak, dara, dhomos, hoṭeṭe, iaṭe, niaṭe, locna, parsadte, toroṗte ; (*way of*) lekate ; (*oneself*) nijgut, nijut ; (*littles*) nare jore ; (*tnrus*) pali palite, pali pasari ; (*mistake*) ajante ; (*the dozen*) baro bakhan.

BYGONES IN ONE'S TEETH, TO CAST—khoṭa.

BY-NAME, TO GIVE A—gokhna.

BYRE, A—goṛa oṛaǩ ; (*worship*) goṛa puja.

C

CABBAGE PLANT, THE—kubi aṛaǩ.

CABULEE, A—kabalia, kabulia, mogol.

CACKLE, TO—khaṭkhaṭao, khoṭ (2), khoṭkhoṭao, kimboť koroť, kiroť koroť, koroǩ, koro (2), koroť (2), koṭ, koṭeť, koṭkoṭeť.

CACKLING—(*of a cock*) ghogo gho, koko (2) ; (*of hens*) korkor.

CACTUS, A SPECIES OF—ghi kuar.

CAGE, A—khaṅca, padra.

CAIRN, A—dhiri gada.

CAJOLE, TO—bãosao, ghãose, lai puṭi, lalkar, lol, muhni, phusalau.

CAKE, A—cakti, thapra ; (*flat*) caki ; (*thin*) puri ; (*of raw sugar*) caki guṛ, cakti guṛ ; (*fried in oil*) sunum piṭha ; (*of bread, thin*) lapar (2) piṭha ; (*oil*) kaṛe.

CALAMITY—aphoti, bao, beoṛa, mar, uphad, uphar ; (*impending*) khen ; (*to meet with*) jarkhar, landuhandao.

CALCULATE, TO—ae ; (*roughly*) amdaj.

CALCULATION—hisab, surik.

CALENDAR, A—paṅji.

CALF, A—mihũ, bacha m. (M), damkom (M), bachi m. (F) ; (*call of*) ombe ; (*of leg*) coṭo jel, ṭhiṭrãǩ.

CALL, A—bolahaṭ, ḍak, dhok, phukar ; (*of beasts*) raǩ ; (*to call attention*) arr ; (*reply to*) oi ; (*on, to make a*) hiri.

CALL, TO—ḍoḍe, hoho, tolob ; (*by name*) ńum ; (*to each other while watching crops*) hãkar ṭokar ; (*one to attend*) banij, barmaṅgao ; (*name*) bahna, kahlao, men ; (*attention*) eho ; (*atteution by touching*) gaduč ; (*names*) baro bakhan, dhuṅgra dhuṅgri ; (*out*) dae (2), hakao ; (*to give alarm*) kulkuli ; (*as chaukiaar*) ron ; (*upon a deity*) ḍakao, ḍakrao, hakrao ; (*for assistance, from pain or fear*) garja barja.

CALLS OF BEASTS, &C.—(*bear*) huh (2), khoṭo (2), dhok (2) ; (*wild-cat*) boas ; (*leopard*) hãkãr (2), haṇḍruṅ (2), haṇḍkur, hõkõr (2) ; (*jackal*) hua (2), huke (2), karaj, kheo (2) ; (*striped squirrel*) cudruč (2) ; (*tiger*) ãoão, hãkur (2) ; (*dog when chasing*) hakar (2) ; (*calf*) ombe ; (*partridge*) cedo (2), cercer, cero (2), ceť ceret cepreť, kedo (2), kirkir ; (*some birds*) cẽč, cẽǩ, cicuri cipi curi, cirioń (2), cĩaṗ, cĩuṗ, ṭeṭeč ; (*peacock*) dhekoč (2), hẽyo, niyõr (2) ; (*pea fowl*) hẽohẽo ; (*Scops owlet*) cerkoť (2) ; (*cuckoo*) koho (2) ; (*kari bird*) hakopako ; (*parokeet*) ṭereč, ṭirioť ṭorioť ; (*quail*) ; cehor behor, ghurauǩ, kẽṛẽ (2), uu ; (*shrike*) ṭẽṭẽ ; (*artagom*) andrač ondroč. *Cf.* CRY OF.

CALLS TO BEASTS, &C.—(*pea fowl*) curu (2) ; (*partridge when hunting*) biṅja biṅji ; (*pigs*) drudru, durdur ; (*sheep*) druheť (2), durheť (2) ; (*elephant*) caicai ; (*to drive away cat*) pusič ; (*to drive away jackal*) labhaeč lublaič ; *Cf.* DOG, BUFFALO, CATTLE, FOWL, GOAT.

CALL OF NATURE, TO FEEL A—osor.

CALLED, TO BE (*named*)—bikau, kahao.

CALLING—bulahaṭ ; (*profession*) birit.

CALLOUS—kaṭhor, kaṭjiba ; (*to become*) ṭhela.

CALLOW—belteń, beṭkeč.

CALM—ḍelḍel, guṭum, nijhum, nirot.
CALMLY—sanegumane.
CALUMNIATE, TO—cugli capạṭi, phareb, phond, phorphond.
CALUMNY—kalak, kạli.
CALVE, TO—dhirū, khalas.
CALVES, A PLACE TO KEEP—gudṛi, gujhi.
CALYX OF SOME FRUITS, THE—bẹnẹt́.
CAMEL, A—ũṭ; (to walk as) dạeyok̇ (2); (hump of) ḍoho.
CAMP, A—ḍera; (ground of) thạnit; (to break up) uṭhạu.
CAMPHOR—kạpur.
CANAL, A—nahar.
CANCEL, TO—bhiṅgoṛ.
CANCER OF FACE, OR CANCRUM ORIS—bandor gạli.
CANDOUR—khulạsa.
CANE, A—bẹt. *Cf.* SUGARCANE.
CANISTER, A—ṭin.
CANNON, A—top; (to fire) t. aṛak̇, t. jẹrẹt́; (pin of axle) khep khunṭi.
CANTANKEROUS—ṭhẹṭham, thethṛamu.
CAP, A—ṭupri; (percussion) ṭupi.
CAPABLE—kabel, kạbil, lek; (to be) harap̣, harrap̣.
CAPARISON, TO—jabrao.
CAPE, A (promontory)—lọcọṅ.
CAPITAL, (stock)—puṅji, puṅji paṭa.
CAPON, A—gaya; (with long feathers) lọbọe gaya.
CAPTIVATING—liṭhur.
CAR, A—rāt; (festival) rāt pọrọb.
CARAVANSERAI, A—sạrại.
CARBUNCLE, A—kherkhone, marań ojo.
CARCASE, TO CUT UP A—dạulạdauli, khaṇḍa huṇḍi.
CARCASE, PARTS OF—(eaten by elderly people) tinik likiṛ; (his who cuts it up) kaṭnaso; (the killer's) mandal; (the officials's) ḍuṇḍe.
CARD, TO (cotton)—phidli, piteś.
CARDS—(playing) juạ, tas; (to play) juạ ẹnẹć, tas ẹnẹć.
CARE—dandha, jogas, porbhae, porbosti; (take) hāhāk̇, khaberda, mẹn; (without) anthạri, hub, khulạsa, mẹkẹć, nicind, nidạndi, nirại, nirdand; (with) jate jute, nana bond; (weighted with) dhāe khāe.
CARE FOR, TO—(affection) bạsut; (look after) hạr sāohā; (not) bẹhephajot.
CARE OF, TO TAKE—goras sāohā, hebajọt, hepajot, jaṅge, jogao, jogaṛ, jogaṛsan, jọtọn, ruhuṭuhu, sotok̇, susạr, tae tolas, tạhkiạt, tạlik, tạnkhi, tapos, tạtbir.
CAREFUL—jogaṛiạ; (nursing) chikisa, cikisạ; (to be) guni bhạbik̇, jid, sọntọr.
CAREFULNESS—jugut.
CAREFULLY—bhage sạhīte, bisi suṭuć, dolo (2), gangante, horo (2), jate jute, kajak, kiḍakaḍe, koṅkorobot́, lahke (2), lake (2), lọhke, ọstẹ, race bacete, race pace, ramo (2), sạhīte.
CARELESS—ḍhemạli, ḍhil, ḍhilisili, gạphil, gọsṛẹ, lạṇḍur bhạṇḍur, lọṇḍhea; (as to caste) lạṭae ghoṭae; (as to propriety) garsa gale; (of attire) bodre, dindir sit́, ojra; (of appearance) gạnduk̇ sạnduk̇; (of consequences) mọstọram; (to be) ḍhilisili.
CARELESSLY—adhkhẹcṛa, akhaṭ bakhaṭ, andhe pạthạuṛi, aṅgot baṅgot, aṛi ḍhaṛi, aṭsaṭ, auṛi, bẹhudis, bijọbọjọ, cạcuṛ mạcuṛ, chidgạ chidgi, chiṇḍel, ciṇḍạl, ciṇḍel, dhọṅgọl phọsọl, dọṅgọl phọsọl, gaphlạti, habak̇ cubak̇, hạṭọkaete, hela, helapela, herań petań, họṭọkkaete, huṛạ huṛi, jẹmọn tẹmọn, lạdur bạdur, lẹḍẹr bẹḍẹr, lẹṇḍẹr bẹṇḍẹr, lọrọṅ phọcọṅ, pạthạuṛi, sede bede, sẹdgẹ bẹdgẹ, sidi bidi, sitoć sọṭọć; (tied) bhiso bhoso; (dressed) bojra (M), bujri (F), dindirsić (F).
CARELESSNESS—gaphlat.
CARESS, TO—dulạṛ.
CARNALLY, TO KNOW—pap.
CARPENTER, A—bạḍhi, baḍhoe, baḍohi, bạṛhi mistri, chutạr, cuthạr, kaṭ baḍhoe, kaṭ mistri; (plane of) rạundạ; (chisel of) rukạ; (workshop of) kaṭ sal.
CARPET, A—daṛi.
CARRAWAY SEED—jirạ.
CARRIAGE, A—gạḍi, (4 wheeled) rāt; (pushed by men) ṭhela gạḍi; (to enter a) dẹć; (shafts of) bom.

CARRIED, TO BE—*(as a bride)* doṅgak̕ ; *(as dust)* ḍiglạu ; *(by the wind)* oṭaṅ, uḍiạ uḍi, uḍiạu ; *(by water)* bhasao.

CARRY, TO—bohao, dhoao, gẹmẹr ; *(on shoulder)* bhariạ, bohao, gọk̕ ; *(astride on shoulder)* ghõṛã ; *(astride hip)* hẹo, ṭuṭẹ ; *(on head)* dipil ; *(on back)* gugu ; *(slung on pole)* ṭạḍa ; *(on hands)* sepeṅ ; *(suspended in hand)* teweṅ ; *(pressing to stomach)* horo (2) ; *(headlong)* dhọtpọt ; *(a sword, &c.)* gạdiạu ; *(small things tied in cloth)* gopca ; *(heavy load)* kere (2) ; *(about)* asẹn ; *(off)* leglam ; *(on-conduct)* calao.

CARRY AWAY, TO—hondoṛ ; *(as water)* odhrao, odrao, siḍgir ; *(as wind)* uper khaper ; *(by percolation)* lẹḍlẹḍẹ.

CARRYING, DANGLING, DRIVING, &C.—ṭikọr ṭọkọr.

CART, A—gạḍi ; *(bamboo)* bạgi ; *(with solid wheels)* sagaṛ ; *(with 2-spoked wheels)* sagaṛ gạḍi ; *(driving)* sagaṛ jhagaṛ ; *(cannon pin of)* khep khunṭi ; *(bars uniting shafts of)* gạḍi pạṅjri ; *(part behind axle)* pạchlạ ; *(shaft of)* hudaṛ ; *(track)* ḍahar, rasta, soran ; *(to)* sagaṛ.

CART WHEEL, A—sagaṛ cak ; *(solid)* sagaṛ ; *(centre piece)* putlạ ; *(wooden rim)* puṭhiạ ; *(part of)* bandh.

CARTRIDGE, A—ṭoṭa.

CARVE, TO—garhao, gọṛhọn, khodao, khokrao, kundạu.

CARVING, A—likhọn gọṛhọn.

CASCADE, A—hud hudi.

CASE—*(condition)* hal ; *(court)* makordama ; *(records)* misil ; *(in that)* ẹnḍẹrema, rema.

CASH—nagad, nogda, roka, ṭaka poesa ; *(a cheque, &c., to,)* bhaṅjao.

CASHMERE CLOTH—kạsmir lugṛi.

CASSIA—kiddạ.

CAST, TO—*(a spell)* pạthri ; *(into the shade)* pandol ; *(longing eyes on)* celhe, elhe celhe ; *(metal in a mould)* dul ; *(off)* bạḍra, giḍi ; *(the skin)* ur ; *(about in one's mind)* nạndi gundi.

CAST—*(iron)* dul mẽṛhẽṭ; *(net, a)* lebda jal.

CASTE—jạt ; *(to lose)* jạt calak̕ ; *(to readmit to)* jọm jạti, jọmjạt ; *(low)* nic jạt ; *(of one)* kạri hạnḍi sal pat ; *(to break another's)* jạt ạgu ; *(to put out of)* ajạt, jọl ghuṭi barọn, ọjạt ; *(without any)* nijạt ; *(belonging to the)* jạtiạ ; *(of another)* parjạt, pọrjạt, pọr jạtiạ ; *(& customs)*, jạtpạt, pạt.

CASTE OF HINDUS, A—Bãṛiã, Cão, Camar, Chạtri, Dhubi, Goala, Gaṅjhu, Ghạsi, Gosãe, Halwae, Jugi, Kahar, Kạithạ, Kạt, Kẽoṭ, Khạtri, Kuiri, Kulhu, Kuṅkạl, Lala, Mahara, Mahra, Mạnḍwạri, Muci, Mudi, Nạpit, Pạsi, Sekra, Tãṭi, Teli, Ṭhaṭera, Tili ; *(whose women are prostitutes when young)* Khelḍa, (M), Khilḍi (F) ; *(who deal in charms)* Jadọpạṭiạ ; *(traders & pedlars)* Moera ; *(workers in iron & wood)* Bạḍhi. *Cf.* ABORIGINES.

CASTING LOTS, A METHOD OF—gulibãṭ.

CASTOR OIL—eranḍọm sunum, julạp ; *(tree)* eranḍọm dare.

CASTRATE, TO—kạsi, khạsi ; *(by rupturing seminal ducts)* kọṭẹc̕.

CASTRATED—*(swine, a)* sukri bạdhiạ ; *(inefficiently)* ạndra.

CASUARINA TREE, THE—sãe sũi dare.

CAT, A—pusi ; *(kind of wild)* badaṛ runḍạ, boak̕, boas r., kabra r., koṭal, koṭas, runḍạ, sagak̕ r., togoṭ, ṭoṭok̕ ; *(the palm)* mạhạlạ, mạhlạ, maṅgo ; *(mew of)* mão, meoṅ ; *(call to)* gunu (2) ; *(to drive away)* pusic̕ ; *(out of the bag, to let)* bayaṭ buyuṭ.

CATAMENIA, THE—sotra.

CATARACT, *(disease)*—chale.

CATCH, A *(hook &c.)*—ṭaghẹn, ṭhegan.

CATCH, TO—hatwa, pakaṛ, pakoṛ, pakrao, sap̕ ; *(in hands)* loka ; *(with both hands)* lạp̕, lạp̕ lạp̕ ; *(in mouth as dog)* loka ; *(on a thorn)* bak̕ ; *(fire)* sẹṅgẹl lagao, sẹṅgẹl sap̕.

CATECHU THREE, THE—khayar.

CATERPILLAR, A—tejo ; *(kind of)* pakaṛe t. ; *(hairy)* pạṭạicak̕, suạpukạ ; *(large)* bhạṛuạ.

CATGUT—tãt.

CATTLE—ḍaṅgri, gai ḍaṅgra, gai urić, guru bachur, jeleń caṇḍbol, lachmi, mihṭ merom, mowasi, pasu, posu ; (*white*) kaila (M), kaili (F) ; (*draught*) dhur, hatiar ; (*plough*) guṇḍhi baṇḍhi, guṇḍi, orokko, urić arar ; (*a small breed of*) jura, jurga ; (*with loose horns*) lurka ; (*grazing at a distance*) cara ḍaṅgra, cari ; (*to drive*) bahkao ; (*a disease of*) boṅga sobok, bosonto, gola kanṭa, ḍhena, pilhoe, poca pilhoe, simbra, sursa ; (*worm attacking teeth of*) kasai ; (*a tender of*) gupiić, gupi kuri ; (*a herd of*) gai pal ; (*a way of fastening*) kurnḍa ; (*careful attendance to*) kasni ; (*having no*) nidaṅgiria ; (*shed, a*) char, gora, gudri ; (*divinity of shed*) goroeya ; (*place of mid-day rest*) aḍa, goṭ, goṭh ; (*to collect for rest*) goṭao, goṭhao ; (*a system of hiring*) caro.

CATTLE, A CALL TO—bihet (2), ghur (2), hak, hija, khar ; (*when ploughing*) as ghur (2), ghur (2), goḍetar, hum.

CAUGHT, TO BE—(*entangled*) laskao ; (*in a trap*) dharap.

CAUSATIVE INFLECTION, A—a-, oco.

CAUSE—dae, karne, karon, sabab.

CAUSELESSLY—akha makha, benahak, binhok, ḍhorḍhosaha, hak nahak, hoknak, kanakha, khomokha, micha michi, nahak.

CAUSTIC—cauchalia.

CAUTERISE, TO—dag, tobak.

CAUTION, AN EXCLM. OF—men.

CAUTIOUS—cirgal, husiar ; (*to be*) cehao, sontor, uṇkep, wakhep.

CAVALRY, MUSSULMAN—Turuk.

CAVE, A—bhugak, dander, dhiri ḍonḍhor, khorlon ; (*in a bank*) konḍha ; (*under a bank*) kandar, kandhar, kandor.

CAVITY, A— ḍoḍhor, gonghor ; (*in an upright object*, lopak.

CAWCAW OF CROW—kak kak.

CEASE, TO—bond, chuṭau, domkao, mesoṭ, mucaṭ, tambhao, tham, ṭhankao, thir ; (*raining*) asor, dharun.

CEASING, WITHOUT—darak (2).

CEDAR TREE, THE—deb daru dare, eroj.

CEILING, A—koṭha.

CELEBRITY—sabasi.

CEMENT, TO—jorao.

CENSURE, TO—dhusau.

CENTIPEDE, A—kidiń marmar, mahle kidiń ; (*poisonous*) seṅgel marmar ; (*very large*) lenḍoń, raimal lenḍoń.

CENTRE—(*the*) bhog, gabha, madhe, mańj, munai, tala, tala mala ; (*of river &c.*) ghag ; (*in the*) mańja mańjhi, mańjha mań hi, tala malare ; (*post of roof*) kham khunṭi.

CEREMONIAL SANCTIFICATION—nẽo dhorom, um amiń.

CEREMONIAL UNCLEANLINESS—chut, chuṭaha ; (*to remove*) puruchun.

CEREMONIALLY—(*to pollute*) bhonḍa ; (*to purify*) amiń.

CEREMONY—(*at marriage, sohrae, and rice-planting*) cumaura ; (*by youths at Sohrae*) gadoe ; (*of friendship*) phul patao, karam ḍar ; (*on first day of some festivals*) sańjot ; (*after death*) bhanḍan ; (*in silk-spinning*) bhaṅga puja ; (*after defilement*) chaṭiar ; (*5 days after bi th*) nahan, narta. *Cf.* DEATH, MARRIAGE, &C.

CERTAIN—(*sure*) khaṭi, paka ; (*person, a*) phalna (M), phalni (F), tuska, umuk.

CERTAINLY—arse tãhã, asokaete, bańkhan, besok, bisbiswas, boṭe, dharle, dhitho, dhorage, haike boṭe, haske boṭe, jarur, kaje, khaṭi, maruk, nijgut, nijut, niscae, obeso, sake, sarige, sarinak, soebot, taha ; (*not*) bańteṭ ; (*thus*) sege thor.

CERTAINTY—(*a moral*) hena ; (*without*) aṭ toṭ, bethikan, dhãk jiba, konṭhekan.

CESS, A—(*zemindary*) bab, kar, kheja, saina ; (*forest*) bonkor ; (*silkworm*) patkar ; (*road*) rod ses ; (*public works*) pabli ; (*paid in oil*) telhan ; (*to collect a*) kar uṭhau.

CESSATION—talbhań ; (*without*) ruyu.

CEYLON—Loṅka.

CHAFE, TO—(*rub*) har, ragrao ; (*fret*) bitlau, puṭu.

CHAFF—bhusa ; (*to*) nisrau.

CHAIN, A—sikol, sikri ; (*necklace*) sikri mala ; (*worn on head or waist*) gunsi ; (*to measure land with*) jurip.

CHAIR, A—meo, mej ; (*with back*) ṭeṇdar maci ; (*framework of*) paria-ṛe ; (*leg of*) kuṭhe.

CHALK—khaṛi maṭi.

CHALLENGE—(*a*) jhãp ; (*to*) apṭhao, hakao, jhap em, ṭawić, ṭokao.

CHAMELEON, THE—raekakaṛbak.

CHANA—buṭ.

CHANCE—bhag, lisi, sinić ; (*a good*) dao ghao ; (*by*) bhagte, dabte, khon leka, oka bhag ; (*on*) dhāk jiba, dharma korma, dhok jiba, dhorma korma, labṛe.

CHANCRE—chuchandar, cuchundar ghao.

CHANGE—pher ; (*of garments*) jarge palaṭ, palaṭ ; (*a*) jota ; (*without*) barabar, tal, ṭesnok ; (*given to*) dupiṭhia, ispat.

CHANGE, TO—bodla, bodol, orpher, pherao, phera phiri, pheṭ ; (*money*) bhaṅgao, khucra ; (*clothes*) bhandur (F), palaṭ ; (*appearance*) bərup ; (*colour*) palo ; (*from place to place*) ucaṛ nacaṛ, upan jhapan ; (*one's mind*) mosoť ; (*residence*) daṛ, gendher ; (*from civility to impertinence*) silpher.

CHANNEL, A WATER—bulan, duni gada, khorloṅ, nali gada, pagar ; (*overflow of tank*) pãeṛẽ ; (*of a river*) ṛet ; (*to construct a*) pagrao.

CHAPLET WORN BY BRIDE AND GROOM—maṛ.

CHAPPED—gandrao.

CHAPTER, A—haṭiṅ.

CHARACTER—cae colon, cal, cal colon ; (*of bad*) bəc ,l.

CHARCOAL—koela, kuila ; (*for pipe*) ṭikia ; (*to become*) khaura ; (*to prepare*) keṛe.

CHARGE—bhar, jima ; (*to give in*) jima, sompao, soprot, sumjhau, saprud ; (*to be in*) tamil ; (*to make a false*) phareb, phasad, phesad.

CHARGE, TO—(*exact*) agu ; (*rush at*) ghisghisau ; (*with powder*) bojao ; (*legally*) lalis, nalis ; (*with*) ardas, indiť ; (*strictly*) jāk, junjunau, kajiãu, sakti.

CHARIOT, A—rāt gaḍi.

CHARITY—(*to travellers, giving*) rahdani ; (*to throw oneself on*) hendkok.

CHARM, A—jinṭhi pathri, lagu ; (*holder*) madoli ; (*doctor*) ahṛi, jhajharić, jharni, kambru guru, matri, ojha.

CHARM, TO—(*exorcise*) bandhon, jhaṛ, paṭihar ; (*attract*) lobdhao, lobhao, lubhau, sohan.

CHASE, TO—ḍiglau, khadkhadao, khidkhidau, khuda khudi, khudau, laga ; (*closely*) ragdao ; (*carve*) kundau.

CHASM, A—bhuĩphoṛ.

CHASTISE, TO—cheṅchao, curau, ilaj, karai, oṛ, sorad, uriau.

CHATTELS—dadha dumbaṛ, dhon durib, ghorkorna, jalmal, maljal.

CHATTER, TO—bakaṭ bokoť, bakbakaok, bakhnao, bara (2), bhac (2) bhackao, bhaknao, bhede (2), bheder (2), bhejor (2), bhoc (2), bhocbhocao, bokoť (2), boktaok, hẽko, labar (2) (F), lacar, phadphadao, phar (2), phedar (2), phedo (2), phodor (2), pokoť (2) ; (*incessantly*) leber (2) ; (*of children*) ceṛo beṛo.

CHAUKIDAR, A—khamdar, rondar ; (*call of*) ron.

CHEAP—andhoṅ, odhoṅ, owara, sahta, sasta, sorpha, ṭhos.

CHEAT, A—naṭkhaṭ, ṭhakna (M), ṭhakni (F).

CHEAT, TO—garib mara, hahi dudi, hordodo, ṭhak, ṭhakua ; (*in a game*) ero suruć ; (*in measuring*) khãoja.

CHECK—(*a*) ṭeghan ; (*to*) aṭkao, dabao, dabri, dubnao, dobon, eseť, sambrao.

CHECKERED—khand (2).

CHEEK, THE—cauhaṛi, joha ; (*bones, high*) loṭoak.

CHEEPING OF CHICKENS—ciap̣ (2).

CHEERFUL—dhados, sohbod.

CHERISH, TO—sostop.

CHERISHING—porbosti, pos.

CHEROOT, A—cuṭi.

CHEST—(*box*) sinduk, sunduk ; (*breast*) koram.

CHESTNUT TREE, THE—cinaṛ.

CHEW, TO—lakum, togoć, togoć lahuť ; (*of toothless person*) lagui pagui ; (*of old people*) legoe pegoe ; (*the cud*) pagur.

CHICKEN, A—gendlaṅ sim, sim hopon ; (*cheep of*) caé cũć, ciap̣ (2).

CHICKEN-POX—milmilia̦.

CHIDE, TO—dabao, d̦anțao, dhamka dhamki, dhamkao, dhomkao, dobnao, domkao, hantao, nisr̦au, tərgeń.

CHIEF—asol, marań, mukhia̦, mul, pordhan; (*wife, the*) bar̦ki.

CHIEF, A—babu rae, calaua; (*village*) ato mańjhi; (*district*) des mańjhi, pargana; (*social*) hand̦i mańjhi.

CHIGNON, A—d̦uria̦.

CHILD, A—butru, gidra̦, hon, hopon, lerka; (*veiled name*) amka (M), amki (F); (*small*) dət́ dətić g., dhena g., lirić; (*young*) bale g.; rak̉ g.; (*newly born*) nawa pera; (*4-6 weeks old*) belteń; (*2 months*) sidup̉ g; (*able to walk*) caco g., caco kətəć g.; (*9-10 years*) ceńra (M), ciǹri (F); (*only*) ekaput; (*by former husband*) dewer potom; (*healthy*) bolman g., chalchalia; (*to amuse*) cerəć, kan kanțu, labhae lubhai; (*to walk as*) caco, d̦uluń (2); (*to be with*) bharti hormo, d̦um, gabd̦ulań, gabd̦uyak̉; (*bearing, past*) țhaekok̉.

CHILDBIRTH—(*to travail in*) bedan; (*defilement from*) janam chut.

CHILDLESS—ațkura̦, bańjha (M), bańjhi (F), char hatua̦ (F), nirbõs, țhãț.

CHILDREN—bõs, ceńcuria̦, gadar, gələ bale, gidar bandar, gidra̦ pidra̦, labeko, letka; (*very little*) d̦eləm (2), lirić pitić; (*troop of performing*) kurum; (*of a sister*) bhagna̦, deo bhagin; (*of sisters, relationship between*) maemasi, mamasi; (*of same parents*) dud bhai boeha, mit́ lać boeha; (*& such belongings*) larka parka.

CHILL—țand̦ha.

CHILLED TO THE MARROW—kațh, kațhnau, kațhua̦.

CHIMNEY OPENING, A—phukar.

CHIN, THE—kewa; (*projecting*) bador sațok̉.

CHINA—Chin, Chin disom.

CHINK, TO—sahrak̉, sohrəć, sokrəć.

CHIP—(*of wood, a*) chailak̉; (*to*) khecə, odhrao, odrao; (*off, to*) khand̦.

CHIPPED—dorpot́, khecro, khendwań, kherco; (*here & there*) odra udri; (*to be*) khecə, khendo.

CHIRP OF BIRDS—cirioń (2), ciup̉; (*sparrow*) cirić (2); (*chickens*) cać cũć.

CHISEL, A—ruka̦; (*cold*) chini; (*small*) chimni r.; (*round*) kund r.

CHIT-CHAT—golpo.

CHITTAK, A—choțak.

CHITTER, TO—susua̦, susu (2).

CHOCKFULL—rət́ təpət́.

CHOICE,—aprug, ektiar, kusal, rij roń.

CHOKE, TO—chur, dić, kanțet́; (*sound of*) khić khəć, kić kəć; (*spell for*) chuchukut́.

CHOLERA—arhaia̦, bao, bosonto, hawa duk, hoe duk, marań duk, mari, mururi, namhaui.

CHOOSE, TO—bacao, bachao, badao, banal, hat bacha, ńam cet́, nolao, noljol, parpasind, pasind, torajut; (*a bride for another*) leao.

CHOP, TO—cewak̉, hubag, mak̉, samak̉; (*with blunt instrument*) thugul.

CHORUS TO A SONG—corań; (*sung at Sohrae*) leobhak̉.

CHRIST—Isa̦, Masi.

CHRISTIAN—Isai, Iswi.

CHRONIC—gahri, guhi; (*to become*) jariau.

CHRYSALIS—(*to become a*) gurhak̉; (*to kill in cocoon*) jiau.

CHUBBY—hakurpak̉, lesker, lodro, lusku lundur, luțkum, pikopuko; (*of children*) lədgəć; (*cheeked*) pakursak̉, peke poko; (*of girls*) pheknok̉, puknət́; (*faced*) pukrot́.

CHUM, A—sotasoń.

CHURCH—(*a*) girja̦ orak̉; (*the*) Kalisia̦.

CHURL, A—catraria̦.

CHURN, THE STIRRER IN A—mondhaeni.

CICADA, A COMMON—rərəń.

CIGAR OR CIGARETTE, A—cuți.

CINDERS—khaura̦; (*glowing*) hurum (2).

CINNAMON—dar chini.

CIRCLES, IN EVER WIDENING—bohol (2).

CIRCUITOUS—ghuranț.

CIRCUMCISE, TO—khatna, țosea̦.

CIRCUMCISION—sunat, sunat.

CIRCUMFERENCE—pher.

CIRCUMSPECT, TO BE—cehao.

CIRCUMSPECTION—jugut; (*without*) hatọkaete, họtọkkaete.

CIRCUMSTANCES—hal, halat, hal hawal; (*in the*) hale; (*easy*) cạlti, culti, suk; (*reduced in*) alatoka, hạrsuṛ.

CITRON, THE—jambir dare.

CITY, A—nagar, nagraha, nańgar, nańgraha, sọhọr.

CIVET, THE SMALL—sọgoť.

CIVIL—(*as opposed to criminal*) dewani; (*suit, time limit of*) tamadi.

CIVILITY—sil; (*to force, to change from*) silpher.

CLAD—(*ill*) bẹbọstọr, bhaṭań bhuṭuń, bhoelo (M), bhuili (F), caekop̀, gaṇḍheť muṇḍheť, gạndur gạpur, garluń, garọć gapọć, gạyur gạpur, lẹdẹr pẹdẹr (F); (*stout & heavily*) lidgoe lọdgọe; (*immodestly*) lọṛọć (2).

CLAIM, A—dạbi, sat, sot; (*to prefer or prosecute*) pecha, pichạ.

CLAIM, TO—amda, aoda, aphoti, dạbi, dawa, lakṭha; (*protection or justice*) dạrsạu.

CLAIMANT—mudoe, oaris.

CLAMANT—ḍạṭhi.

CLAMBERING—ragọṛ pagọṛ.

CLAMOROUS—dawahi, hạṭhi.

CLAMOUR FOR, TO—ajaǩ, bestoǩ, hạṭi, jạri.

CLANG—(*to*) raṛań, riṛań raṛań, ṭheń; (*with a*) raṛań marte, tapań marte, ṭhań marte, ṭheń marte.

CLANGING SOUND—ṭheń; (*of gong*) ṭrań (2); (*of different tones*) ṭhae ṭhui.

CLANKING SOUND—daṛae daṛae.

CLAP—(*in a*) haṛas; (*with a*) ṭhap̀ marte.

CLAP, TO—(*hands*) tayo, tayo sarap̀, thayo; (*wings*) ḍhap̀ (2), phadphad.

CLAPPER-TOUNGED—caego.

CLARIFIED BUTTER—gọtọm.

CLASP—(*of belt*) bạkuǩ; (*knife*) cạku.

CLASS—hudạ; (*leader of*) paṭh cela.

CLAW, A—rama; (*of crabs*) dạṭo, diṭom; (*to seize with*) dạtọm.

CLAW, TO—gạdur, jadgo, rabọṛ.

CLAY—(*red*) jaṭań hasa; (*burned*) eṭko hasa; (*used as mortar*) gara; (*pellet of burned*) gorkha guli; (*to spread soft*) pạliạu.

CLAYEY—ciṭạha, lẹhẹ guhe; (*soil*) kharna, kharnaha, kharnạtiạ, rehḍa.

CLEAN—ạrik pạrik, barať boroť, cẹmkẹć, chuk chuk, cikạ̃ṛ, pạrchạ, parhaṛ, ralaǩ, ralaǩ masaǩ, rili phili, riṛim (2), sada, sapha, sidho, tartạriạ; (*as water*) jiri (2); (*& bright*) jhalmal; (*sweep, to make a*) hora; (*to be*) jhalmalao.

CLEAN, TO—pharcha, ralaǩ, saphạ; (*the teeth*) datạni; (*out, as house*) jhalao, uriạu sapha; (*grain by pounding*) sọǩ; (*entrails*) lać duhạu.

CLEANSE, TO—ạrup̀, sudh; (*ceremonially*) chut meṭao, um ạmiń; (*the hair*) naṛka gidi.

CLEANSED—(*to be*) sọlthọnoǩ; (*imperfectly*) heńjlań peńjlań.

CLEAR—isposṭo, pạrchạ, phariạ, phariạ phạṭi, phini phiǩ, phiṛipań, phiṛphoń, poriskar, puṛcha, purṭhạ, rili phili, riṛim (2), ruńruń, ruṛuń (2), sapha, tartạriạ; (*as sky*) phiṛphoń, rilạ mala; (*as water*) pharcha, phĩṛĩphić, ṭiń ṭiń; (*space, a*) phiṛphoń.

CLEAR, TO—(*as debt*) sọd, poriskar; (*of obstruction*) chitrạ phuṭạu, ṭạndi, maǩ ṭạndi; (*as water*) phariạ, phinạu; (*up*) bhańj, pạrchạ; (*up a dispute*) sapha, sạphại; (*after rain*) asoṛ, dharun, pharcha, phiṛipan, piṛioń, uber; (*away by breaking*) toṛao; (*of mist*) pahak, phahak, phohok, pohok.

CLEARANCE, A—calan.

CLEARING NUT TREE, THE—khucilạ, kucilạ.

CLEARLY—bharaṛ, khulạsa, niṭhur, pọsṭọ, pusṭạu, rilạ mala, sposṭo, ṭahaka, taṛṭariạ.

CLEAVE TO, TO—lata, lọoṭhẹ.

CLEM, TO—kańdoṛ.

CLERK, A—muhri.

CLEVER—budgariạ, bujhạntar, calak, cạtur, cọlọnti, gakhur, gansud, kabel, kabil, kharkhạri, lọhạni, nipun, sarghạriạ; (*of young persons*) saṛphạriạ.

CLEVERNESS—hikmat.

CLICK, TO—ṭak ṭak.

CLICKING SOUND—poṭes, ṭes, ṭhak, ṭhes; *(of hoofs)* karap (2); *(of sandals)* ciṭeṭ caṭeṭ.

CLIENT, A—asami.

CLIMATE—dak, hoe.

CLIMB, TO—deć; *(up into or on)* coga, coghe; *(a tree)* aple; *(with hands & feet)* ragoṛ pagoṛ; *(sound of)* khiriṛ.

CLING TO, TO—lata; *(house)* loṭopuṭo.

CLINK, TO—sahrak, sekeć, sekṛeć, sikṛić, simpasaṛe, siṛip, sohṛoć, sokṛoć, ṭheń.

CLIP, TO—chāṭ, tope; *(with scissors)* kapci.

CLIQUE, A—khūṭ.

CLOCK, A—ghanṭa, ghaṛi; *(that strikes hours)* dhorom ghaṛi.

CLOD OF EARTH—ḍhelak, ḍhelka, helṭa; *(large)* jaṛdhe (2).

CLOD CRUSHER—āṛgom; *(with one yoke of oxen)* eka ṭaṛia āṛgom, haṛia.

CLOSE—*(oppressive)* gajgaj, gamgam, ghulghul, gijgij, huṭ huṭ, khulkhul, olkopolko; *(near)* laga lagi, logbhog, phed, sor; *(reserved)* buktan, gaḍia; *(resemblance)* chanban, chonbon; *(after each other)* oloegotoe; *(not)* siṭo soṭo; *(to come go or make)* sor, sōrboṭ, sōrmboṭ; *(to put)* bhiṛau, ṭesao, ṭhesao, tomboń.

CLOSE TOGETHER—gajaṛ, gajeṛ, gańjeṛ, ghacpac, ibil, jabṛe, kuca kuci, repe ciriṭ, saṭasaṭ, sopor, ṭãohẽ, ṭãuhẽ, ṭesaṭes, ṭhãi ṭhãi, ṭhaohe, ṭheke ṭheke, ṭhekom, ṭherethepe, ṭhesa ṭhes; *(very)* aṭhe aṭhoń; *(to be)* jopok, repe ciriṭ; *(to put)* sapṭa, saṭao.

CLOSE, TO—sikup, siń; *(an aperture)* mohnda marao, munda; *(firmly)* kaṭkaṭao; *(suddenly)* siṭap; *(the hand)* cupuṭ; *(up)* paṭaṛ, tepeṭ; *(to)* liḍak; *(the eyes)* janapiṭ, japiṭ.

CLOSED, TO BE—bond.

CLOSELY—ragda ragdi, rogda rugdi, ṭaohẽ, ṭãuhẽ; *(following)* daradaṛi; *(packed)* renṭe penṭe, segebege.

CLOT, TO—sakiṭ.

CLOTH—gendṛak, khanḍuak, kicrić, lijak, luga, lugṛi; *(woollen)* dhus; *(drill)* jin; *(cotton)* cadoṛ; *(coarse)* jeljelia; *(fine)* malmal, mihī kicrić, musna; *(loosely woven)* ghangri; *(old & worn)* bhańka bhakur, cethra; *(with coloured border)* paṛlak kicrić; *(an asortment of)* aṭal gonḍal. *Cf.* BORDER.

CLOTH, A PIECE OF—khanḍuak, kicrić than; *(folded round waist)* kanso; *(old)* gendreć; *(for F. dress)* gonok, khanḍi; *(for M. dress]* bhagwa, dhuti, kaca; *(short quilted)* dalpuń; *(one cubit broad)* gaji; *(less than usual width)* pańci; *(of extra width)* halwan; *(worn on head)* bhanḍan daḥṛi; *(double)* dohar; *(used when bathing)* gamcha; *(3 cubits long)* paṛhanḍ.

CLOTH GIVEN AS A PRESENT—siripa, siropa; *(by bridegroom)* mamosalaka, eńga itaṭ, gońgo salaka, sara daḥṛi.

CLOTHE, TO—arao, bande (F), ḍeńga (M), horok, sajao.

CLOTHED, SLIGHTLY—bhoelo (M), bhuili (F), jhapṛe.

CLOTHES—ahran paharand, bostor, horok bandenak (F), horok ḍeńganak (M), ladenak, lijak, lugṛi; *(to change)* bhanduṛ (F), palaṭ; *(to take off)* bhuṛi (F), bhūṛūć (M), boć, lańṭa (M), lańṭi (F); *(to wash)* dhubi; *(wrapped up in)* gaboć (2), gaelo (2), gaha goho, golop (2); *(in need of)* bebostor, dende, lańgaṭ. *Cf.* CLAD, TATTERED.

CLOUD, A—rimil; *(without)* phini phik.

CLOUDS, FLYING—lahra.

CLOUDY—dondho, ḍonḍrok, ḍopḍop, gholao, jhopso, jopso.

CLOYED, TO BE—tobo.

CLUB, A—ḍanṭa, muṭak, ṭheńga; *(thick)* mungа muṭak; *(to beat rice bandis)* gudna.

CLUCK, TO—koṭ koṭ.

CLUE, A—bomal, loṭ pańj momal, suṛag; *(to search for)* bhidi.

CLUMP, A—buda, ḍanḍhi, dhumbak, dumcak, ede thompe, jhaṛ; *(of trees)* cumkak dare; *(to become a)* candheṛ.

CLUMSY—boserṭāk, dhoḍoṛ poḍoṛ, katha kothe, lerwa laṛwe, moṭa; *(of carpentry)* gadha godho; *(& heavy)* jaṛdhe, jeṛdhe, joṛdhe.

CLUSTER, A—ẹdẹ ṭhompe, thobla, thopa; *(in a)* haṭabuṭ, ṭhaba ṭhube, ṭhube; *(of fruit)* ṭhaba ṭhobo; *(of cobwebs)* lateṛ.

CLUSTER, TO—tudrạ; *(of large fruits)* daṛa duṛuć.

CLUSTERS, IN—ḍaṇṭha ḍoṇṭho, jhamka jhạkur, jhaṅka jhạkur, ludguḿ, ṭamka ṭạkur, ṭhạkumṭhaḱ; *(large)* lạdgu pạdgu, lapa dhopa, lapha dopha.

CLUTCH, TO—khablao, racaḱ; *(repeatedly)* khabla khabli.

CLUTCHING—rẹpẹć ipicạḱ.

COAGULATE, TO—jamao, sạkiṫ.

COAL—koela, kuilạ; *(a live)* aṅgra; *(tar)* alkatra sunum, kuilạ sunum; *(mine, a)* koela khad; *(open mine)* gaḍa; *(miner, a)* malkaṭa.

COARSE—badaḱ, moṭa, paṭka, paṭo, raṭko; *(hair)* paṭa, paṭocaḱ; *(meal)* sege sege; *(rice)* roḍga roḍgo; *(herbs)* paḍga; *(cloth)* jeljelia.

COAST—ḍhip; *(till clear, waiting)* elem celem.

COAT, A—kurtạ; *(ong quilted)* aṅga; *(long-sleeved)* aṅgrọp.

COAX, TO—bāosao, bhāosāo, chuchkạr, ghaose, goras, lalkao, lalkar, lại libuḱ, lilkạu, lulu bạchu, mọsọkusi, nehra jebra, phusalạu.

COB, A CORN—phọṭ.

COBRA—ayaṅ biṅ, kabra ayaṅ, kārā ayaṅ, paṇḍu biṅ; *(noise of)* ghuraụḱ.

COCK—murgạ, sạṇḍi, sim sạṇḍi; *(kept for breeding)* bayar sạṇḍi; *(its comb)* docoṫ; *(steel spur for)* kạt; *(note of loud-voiced)* ghogo gho; *(cackling of)* kọkọkọkọ; *(offered to maraṅ buru)* buru sim.

COCK, TO—*(the ears)* biṫ; *(a gun)* caṛhao.

COCK-CROW—sim raḱ.

COCK-EYED—ṭera (M), ṭiri (F).

COCK-PIT, A—paṛa.

COCKROACH—capṛa.

COCOANUT—nạrkol, nạrkoṛ.

COCOON—diṇḍi, koa; *(of Tassar worm)* jạdui, lumạm, muṅgạ; *(with one end cut off)* ṭhuiạḱ; *(pedicle of)* bõk; *(to emerge from)* kaṭao.

COERCION—jaejulum.

COG PUT BEFORE A CART-WHEEL—bạndhi, cak bạndhi.

COGNIZANT OF, TO BE—baḍae, baṛae, cạrit.

COGNOMEN, A—hudạ.

COHESIVE, NON—pharhar, phạṛphạṛiạ, pisạṛ pasạṛ.

COIL, TO—ghurci, piṭi; *(& uncoil)* khiṛiạ paṭe.

COIN, A—*(1/12 anna)* pae; *(¼ pice)* dokṛa; *(small silver)* rejki, rijki, sikạ, siki, suki; *(gold)* asạṛphi, mọhọr.

COINCIDE, TO—ṅapam.

COLD—bẹrẹl, kalha, rabaṅ, reaṛ, rabon raj, sitol, ṭaṇḍha, ṭhaṇḍha; *(icy)* kankan; *(water)* bẹrẹl daḱ; *(numbness from)* sitlo; *(weather)* rabaṅ din; *(weather crops)* rabi cas; *(clothes)* dhus; *(in the head)* manda; *(in the head, suffering from)* sẹrẹṅ (2).

COLD, TO BE—rabaṅ, reaṛ, sitạṅ, sitlạu, sitlo; *(drawing oneself together)* ḍuḍurguć; *(shivering)* kaṇṭa koṇṭo; *(very)* kaṭh, kaṭhnạu, kaṭhnao, kaṭhuạ.

COLIC—cẹṅ bai, cẹṅga paṭha, paṭhok.

COLLAPSE, TO—bhaskao, bhindaṛ, bhoskao, bindaṛ, boskao, dasao, dhasao, dhaskao, lạnduḿ, lạnduṛ, ọbọr, raḿ ruḿ, ruḿ; *(as wall)* lenduṛ; *(in illness)* labejan; *(from fatigue)* lorao.

COLLAR-BONE, THE—hās jaṅ; *(a sore on the)* hạsli ghao.

COLLECT, TO—jaora, jarwa, tulạu; *(as money)* sạṅgṛạu, tolao, uṭhạu; *(dues)* ạdai, sidi, taḥsil; *(by littles)* juhṛạu, jumạu, juṛạu; *(necessaries)* johṛao, mohjut, utjog; *(outstandings)* dhaṛa; *(in lumps)* ḍhumbaḱ; *(cattle for midday rest)* goṭao; *(perquisites)* arpa; *(as water in hollow)* ḍobhaḱ; *(together)* dumhe, hạr, jhạuạ, moṭiao, muṭiạu, samṭao, thopro.

COLLECTOR, A *(of rents, &c.)*—tạhsildar.

COLLUDE, TO—jog, rẹt, sajọt.

COLOUR,—bọrọn, raṅ, rọṅ; *(to)* gabao, raṅ, rọṅ; *(over, to)* aga; *(without)* beraṅ, bẹrọṅ.

COLOURED—chĩṭ, raṅga, rǫsanjǫn; (*dark*) kuila (M), kuili (F); (*fair*) gǫl, garlae, raṅgia, telsãoar; (*many*) cand bagar, kabrak kobrok, raṅ bi raṅ; (*border on cloth*) paṛ, paṛlak, paṛlak sǫhǫk.

COLOURING—(*used by potters*) gabis; (*lac*) hiṅgu.

COLT, A—bachra sadǫm.

COLZA OIL PLANT, THE—tuṛi.

COMA—jhapni bai, sugam bai.

COMB, A—nakić; (*bamboo*) sar n., kundar n.; (*small-toothed*) kakri n.; (*worn by men*) kundag n.; (*of a cock*) docot; (*of loom*) rac; (*teeth of*) bakhoṛ.

COMB THE HAIR, TO—nakić; (*& tie it up*) rǫt nakić.

COMBINE, TO—(*as herds of cattle*)—pal bhiṅjan.

COME—dela, deloi; (*to say*) doat.

COME, TO—dara, hec, hijuk; (*near*) cahaṭao, habṛao, hobǫ (2), sor, sõrbot, sõrmbot; (*short*) atra; (*out*) odok, tot; (*as a spirit*) suman; (*to pass*) hoe; (*to oneself*) apnao; (*& go*) ragrao; (*again & again*) heder (2), hidir (2); (*together*) pakpakao.

COME INTO CONTACT WITH, TO—ṭhapa ṭhuk, thukrau; (*slightly*) thapre; (*anything sharp*) khoca; (*& be stopped*) ṭhakẹt; (*repeatedly*) ṭhakẹt (2).

COMELY—carba, dhob, dikhnor, khulan, nakhe mukhe, reṅgleć.

COMET—candbol ipil, jǫnok ipil.

COMFORT, TO—bahalao, bãhnok, jiwi raṛeć, ṭhandha.

COMFORT, IN—phusuć (2) sukraj; (*brought up in*) sukhi.

COMFORTED, TO BE—khatir jǫma, ṭandha.

COMICAL FELLOW—phokṭia.

COMING & GOING—ana gona, asa jawa, ghura ghuri.

COMMAND—(*authority*) bǫs; (*an order*) hukum.

COMMEND ONESELF BY WORD ONLY, TO—luṭhu.

COMMISERATE, TO—sir ṭaṭao; (*exclm. of*) hae hae.

COMMISSION—(*discount*) baṭa, dalali, dallali, dasturi, keali.

COMMIT, TO—(*a fault*) baṛić, bhul, cukau; (*to*) dalao, jima. *Cf.* MEMORY.

COMMON—canke; (*in*) sajha; (*to partners in estate*) sarkari.

COMMONLY—bastǫbik.

COMMONPLACE—aprẽ, sadharǫn.

COMMOTION—kando.

COMMUNITY, A—khũṭ, ṭhǫk.

COMPACT (*close*)—rẹṭẹpẹṭẹ, rẹt ṭẹpẹt, sumurguć; (*village*) cumkak ato.

COMPACT, TO—riau rajǫt.

COMPANIES, BY—khaṭa khaṭi.

COMPANION, A—gate, saṅ bhai, saṅga, saṅti, saṅwar, sãotenić, sǫṅ bhai, sǫṅgẹ, sǫṅgetenić, sǫtasǫṅ.

COMPANIONS, CLOSE—jǫpǫrjole, ǫṅsǫṅ; (*along with*) gate ora uri.

COMPANY—(*a*) dǫl, dǫṅgǫl, gahandi, gahndi, khata, pal bhiṅjan, thak, thǫk, torphan; (*in*) gate ora uri, gudia gudyi, jamka jumki, sǫlgǫl, tara toro; (*with, in*) lekate, são, sǫṅ, sǫṅgẹ, tuluć; (*to keep*) galsal, gate, sẹlẹt.

COMPARE, TO—bheaṛ, juri, tulau.

COMPARTMENT—hudra.

COMPASS—(*a surveying*) kampas, oṭkoe; (*points of the*) caukhũṭ, ponon kõṛ, nakha; (*to*) sarbharao; (*within*) in gan.

COMPASSION—mãya, moh; (*to feel*) sir ṭaṭao.

COMPEL, TO—jhotra jhutri, mǫsǫkusi.

COMPETE, TO—apṭhao, haparao, hapṭao, hara hari, haṭha badi, haṭha baji, odabad.

COMPETITION—hara hari.

COMPLAIN, TO—ardas, lalis, nalis, phedar (2), roṅ khoṅ; (*whiningly*) pheṅ pheṅ; (*against each other*) lalsa lalsi, nalsa nalsi.

COMPLAINANT, A—badi, phiriadi.

COMPLAINING—dhodya (M), dhodyo (F), kadra kadri.

COMPLAINT, A—nalis, lalis; (*to lay*) candiau, lǫmbǫr, pes.

COMPLETE—paka, pura, sabit, samthul, tear, thul; (*to*) caba, caṅcuṅ, dharkao, dursut, jhal jhalao, jhaṅjhaṭ, kamal, mạr, marot, mạr pạsir, nimbhạu, niṅghạr, niṅghrạu, pạṭ, purạnti, purạpuri, purạu, sabaṛ, sạkim, sarao, sạt, saṭsuṭ, sid ẹm, sikim, sumạr, thul, thur.

COMPLETED, TO HAVE—cukạu.

COMPLETELY—caṅ cuṅ, ẹkkalte, ẹkbar, họṭhusiṭ, jhaṅjhaṭ, mọmblọt, nirdae, pạcuk, paka pạki, purạpuri, rẹnd bẹnd, rukrạbon, sae, sạmuṅ, saprum, utạr.

COMPLICATE, TO—lạṭku pạṭku.

COMPLICATED—ẹdẹbẹdẹ, ẹdhẹ bẹdhẹ, enbend, jama.

COMPLY WITH, TO—rẹbẹn.

COMPORT ONESELF, TO—bebohar, beohar.

COMPOSE A SONG, TO—sereń joṛao.

COMPOUND, A (*enclosure*)—hata.

COMPREHEND, TO—bujhạu, samńjhao, suj buj.

COMPRESS, TO—samṭao.

COMPROMISE—rạji nama, rap dhap, rọp dhọp.

COMPULSION—hucuk.

COMPULSORY—jhakmạr, mạruk.

COMRADE, A—*Cf.* COMPANION.

CONCAVE, SLIGHTLY—khupạ.

CONCEAL, TO—danań, dapal, gupạṭ, gupti, pheṅkao ; (*nothing*) khulạu, phaṅka phayaṛ.

CONCEDE PRECEDENCE, TO—apaj, henda hindi.

CONCEITED—alak jhalak, bạḍagiri, gọrọb, gọrọbiạ.

CONCEIVE, TO—rakhao.

CONCERN—cintạ, dhak, garaj, gọrọj.

CONCERNING—babọt, bisoe, cetan, daṛun, reak, reaṅ.

CONCERT, TO—rẹṭ.

CONCH, A—kạuḍi eṅga, sãk, sãk ghoṅga, sãk rọkọć, sãnk.

CONCILIATE, TO—ḍhar ḍhur.

CONCISELY—sanchepte.

CONCLAVE, A—darbar.

CONCLUDE, TO—akasok, niptạu.

CONCOCT, TO—turtạ.

CONCOCTED—cạmpur.

CONCORD—mel, milạp, milijili, milimisi, salsãt ; (*to cause*) jut jat, milạu, milijili.

CONCUBINE—ḍhemni, lạuṇḍi era.

CONCUSSION—dildil.

CONDITION—dasa, dob, dosa, gutik, hal, halat, hal hawal, hawal, jinis, ọbọsta ; (*in good*) awala, baṛhọntar, batar, cerṭha, ehel (2), jiṅgạṛ, kuṭmel, maṅgar, pakṭa, salsal, sulsulṭak, susurṭak, telgar. *Cf.* ILL.

CONDITIONAL SENTENCES, USED IN—honań, hutkạm, hutkẹć.

CONDOLENCE, A VISIT OF—bhẽṭ.

CONDUCT—acar beohar, bebohar, beohar, cae cọlọn, cal, calcọlọn.

CONDUCT, TO—asẹn, ạyur, calao ; (*water for irrigation*) baelao.

CONDUIT, A—bulạn.

CONE, IN FORM OF A—cuicui ; (*to make*) puṅgi.

CONFEDERATES—satasọṅ, sọtasọṅ.

CONFERENCE, A—mạjlis, mojlis, mõṛẽ họṛ, muńjlis ; (*of neighbours*) cạurạsi bạisi ; (*of relatives*) bạisi kuṭum.

CONFESS, TO—aṅgachao, aṅgọc, ekraṛ, gacao, goḍao, himạn, humạn, kạbul, sikạr ; (*to cause to*) kạblạu.

CONFIDE IN, TO—hirlạ.

CONFIDENCE—barsa, bhorsa, bud bhorsa ; (*to gain*) khạtir jọma ; (*to give*) buk ; (*without*) lạpa lopo.

CONFIDENT—arõṭ, khạtiran ; (*to become*) pạrkạu.

CONFINE, TO—kohṛao.

CONFINED (*narrow*)—kucit, sakyaṛ.

CONFIRM, TO—nisṭạ.

CONFIRMATION—nisṭạn.

CONFIRMED, TO BE—hewa giḍi.

CONFLICTING—hạlmạl.

CONFLUENCE OF TWO RIVERS—dul miṭ.

CONFORMITY WITH, IN—je jẹmọn.

CONFOUNDED—akul bạkul, awaṭapa, cạkṛi ghum ; (*to be*) aral koral.

CONFRONT, TO—hajrao, mokabilạ, mukhạ mukhi, samkasạṭi, sạnmuk, sọnmuk.

CONFRONTING—samna sạmni, sạnmuk, sọnmuk.

CONFUSE, TO—aṛgoṅgaṛ, ạulạu, ḍagmagao, dọlbadọl, gạbuć sạbuć, gaelo saelo, gaṛbaṛao, ghẽj mẹj, gheńj mẹńj, gulmal, mesa misi, phadgal, ukạṭ pakaṭ, ulạṭ palạṭ.

CONFUSED—abhu cabhu, akbakao, akul bakul, alač bakač, albaṭ salbaṭ, ạlmạl, ạlmạlao, anakup, aṇḍa maṇḍa, andhe paṭhauṛi, ạndhup, andmand, anduk manduk, asbas, asbasao, aṭ nạ sạṭ, aṭ sạṭ, ạulạ ạuli, bagaṛ, baj, beñjañ binjiñ, cạkṛi ghum, eṅgel peṅgel, gaḍbaḍ, galoč saloč, garbaṛ, hara hurạ, hạlmạl, oṛna pathan, oṛna sạṭ, oṛna soṛ, paṭhauṛi, sal mesal, saluč bakuč, sigič bigič, sodgoro, solok bokok, targal ; (*noise*) chạu (2).

CONFUSEDLY—saguč baguč, ulṭạ palṭa, ulṭi pulṭi.

CONFUSION—golmal, goṇḍogol, gulmal, tagatusạ, targal ; (*of mind*) haran, haron.

CONFUTE, TO—kạhil, ṭewet.

CONGEAL, TO—jamao, kaṛkaṛao, sạkič.

CONGESTED, TO BE—ṭilṭilạu.

CONICAL—bucbucu.

CONJECTURE, TO—amdaj.

CONJOINTLY—ejmạli.

CONJUNCTIVITIS—mendok.

CONJURER, A—ṭaṭak, ṭaṭokdar.

CONJURING—jạdu.

CONNECTION—leñjhar, pas, sombond.

CONQUER, TO—bhagao, daṛe, harao, jitạu, lahao, lahat, hoṭak pạsir, pesṛao, phoṭao, ṭhasiạu.

CONQUERED, TO BE—harna, pạhuṛ.

CONSCIENCE, THE—akaṭkarak, são-bakdaeak.

CONSCIENTIOUS—iman, imandar.

CONSCIOUS, TO BE—cetao ; (*of*) aṭkar, disạ.

CONSCIOUSNESS—hos, hus ; (*to regain*) cetao.

CONSECRATE, TO—dhorom.

CONSENT, TO—aṅkus, kạbul, reben, sikạr.

CONSEQUENCE OF, IN—dhoros, taṛaste, uthumte.

CONSEQUENCES—(*to bear the*) sen hamalok ; (*of evil action*) pee.

CONSIDER, TO—bicaṛ, dạnại, dandagiri, dandha, daṛiạp, gaṇḍon, gundi, imtam, khañjao, khondrond, mejas, meñjas, nandi gundi, onman, sõc, tạjbij, ṭhohor, tohor, tojbij, uakep, wakhep ; (*carefully*) ạri bạndhi.

CONSIDERATION—jugut, phikir ; (*without*) haṭokaete, hoṭokkaete.

CONSIGNMENT, A—calan.

CONSOLE, TO—jiwi raṛeč.

CONSOLED, TO BE—khạtir joma.

CONSOLIDATE, TO—paṭao.

CONSPIRE, TO—jog, meñjas, mis, ret, sajot, sipi.

CONSTABLE, A—kanasṭabal ; (*head*) doroga, jamadar, jamedar.

CONSTANCY—muruk.

CONSTANTLY—hergoe (2), hole (2), holo (2).

CONSTELLATION, A—ãrgom, kaemạiyạ, potam bele ; (*yoke*) arãṛ ; (*great bear*) budhi parkom ; (*pleiades*) sorenko, (*milky way*) haṭ ḍahar, pañjar ḍahar.

CONSTERNATION—hãhãkar.

CONSTRAIN, TO—taltalao, toltolao, tultulạu ; (*to go*) jhotrao.

CONSTRAINT, WITHOUT—khulạsa, khusi khos.

CONSTRINGE, TO—samṭao.

CONSULT, TO—bujhạu, galsal, jigạs, kedrao, khañj, kheñjer meñjer, khoj puchar, lạpại, mepen, mili guṭi, mili misi, parames, porames, pucạu, salha, sipi, solho ; (*together*) bujhạ bujhi, mejas, meñjas, mis.

CONSUME, TO—hulạr, jom.

CONSUMMATED, ALL BUT—hoclo.

CONSUMPTION,—(*phthisis*) raj rog ; (*intended for*) khạdiạn.

CONTACT WITH, TO COME IN—laga, tạkič, thaket, ṭhapa ṭhuk ; (*something behind*) cikič ; (*slightly*) thapa, thapre.

CONTAGIOUS, TO BE—ucạr.

CONTAINED, TO BE—sahop, samao.

CONTEMN, TO—henosta, posṛa.

CONTEMPLATE, TO—bicạr.

CONTEMPORARIES—pạriạrenko.

CONTEMPT FOR, TO FEEL—chiak, chibañ, posṛa.

CONTEMPTUOUSLY—algạsi.

CONTEND, TO—akhaji, apṭhao, aṭã ãṭi, bada bạdi, bajha bạjhi, hapṭao, haṭa bạdi, haṭha bạdi, haṭha bạji, odabạd, ṭanaṭani ; (*about precedence*) apaj.

CONTENTED—bahal, dhirpur, raji, ropha, suk; (*looking*) kharsala.

CONTENTIOUS—conda cundi, tendos, tendosia, kando, turphi.

CONTENTMENT—dhirja.

CONTEST, TO—apthao, haparao, hata badi, hatha badi.

CONTIGUOUS—ropok.

CONTINUALLY—bara, barabar, baromas, bare (2), gisić (2), here gese, hisir (2), jao jaote, modam, mondam, osto ghuri, sadae, siń satup, mit talao.

CONTINUE, TO—idi.

CONTINUOUS—jõhot, ladlad, ruyu; (*as rain*) jhomor (2).

CONTINUOUSLY—bharar, bhodor (2), dinam, garak (2), jadam (2), jamar, karakar, kobot (2), kombet (2), kombot (2), rengos, rikir, rodok (2), rogor, rogot (2), sadamad, sodamod, taletal.

CONTORT, TO—mocra mucri, mocrao.

CONTRACT, A—bandhon, ikrar nama, thika; (*to give on*) kutau.

CONTRACT, TO—(*shrivel*) cacalkat, khasao, ojhrao, uń, tenten; (*as wet rope*) puti; (*as fruit*) jolkhot, cupuikut, (*as insects*) kokorbok; (*undertake*) añrau, bandhok, rikit.

CONTRACTED—atgate.

CONTRACTOR, A—thikadar, thikedar.

CONTRADICT, TO—katha katao, ror parom, ther.

CONTRADICTORY—albat salbat, at sat, birud, ẽrga.

CONTRARY—ẽrga, ulta, ultau, (*on the*) reset, taha reset; (*to be*) gajhao.

CONTRIBUTION—canda, puri; (*to impose*) bab.

CONTNIVARCE—bandheć, phikir; (*with much*) nana bond.

CONTRIVE, TO—monsuba, pontha.

CONTROL—adol; (*to*) kabja, kaboj, kabu; (*out of*) obos; (*lacking*) ulkhania.

CONTUMACIOUS—adopia, pephra, phephra; (*to be*) adop.

CONTUMACY—bhuc bhuci.

CONTUMELY ON, TO BRING—bokobhond, lende.

CONTUSE, TO—gań, tuań.

CONVALESCENT—certha, tamak tumuk, tanak tunuk.

CONVENIENCE—dhok.

CONVENIENT—subita; (*place or time*) ghai.

CONVERSATION—(*casual*) phalu; (*humorous*) kap.

CONVERSE, TO—galmarao, galsal.

CONVEYANCE, A CLOSED—kirachi gadi.

CONVICT—(*a*) kaidi; (*to*) hal kahil, kahil, kal; (*to transport*) damul.

CONVINCE, TO—bujhau, kahil, kal, samjhao.

CONVINCED, TO BE—le.

CONVOY, TO—ńel got.

CONVULSIONS—bahir bai, bandor bai, camek bai, dhanuk bai, harna bai, hicki bai, jhanak bai, jhapni bai, katkatao, suruj bai; (*to be seized with*) bai, bayok, bai capar.

COO, TO—bak bakur, kuhũr (2), kuku, kuku ku, kuku (2).

COOK, TO—aro, daka, dapkao, isin, jambo; (*food*) isin aro; (*over-*) isin laha; (*hastily*) tuku (2); (*by boiling*) teke; (*by steaming*) baphao, bhaphao; (*with rice*) sure; (*on slow fire*) goso isin.

COOK—(*a female*) randhoni; (*house*), datka orak, dakka orak.

COOKED, BADLY—capos (2), soroć poteć; (*not enough*) kacur (2), kadro, kecer, kharuas, maruas, kutuć, latać lutuć, lutuć, mańja, poho, radgo padgo, tara tapra; (*over*) gajwak, lasak pasak.

COOKED RICE—daka, mandi; (*well*) bidir (2); (*left on plate*) itat daka.

COOKING—dadka; (*vessel*) laki, luiha, luki, patloe, tasla; (*trench*) jhuli bhathi; (*preparations for*) satka sutku; (*earthen pot*) celań; (*to use up moisture in*) suras.

COOKING, A METHOD OF—(*meat*) korhe; (*vegs.*) hondak; (*grain*) lapsi; (*fish, &c.*) bharta.

COOL—jud, juda judi, rear.

COOL, TO—jud, judas, judasi, judau, rareć, rear, thanda; (*food*) haheć; (*after anger*) apnao.

COOLY, A—kuli; (*depot*) ḍhipu; (*recruiter*) aṛkaṭhia.

COOT, THE—ḍubạ cẽṛẽ, panḍubạ, paniḍubạ.

COPIOUS—hamram, hiḍir (2).

COPPER—tamba; (*money*) anaphana, phuṭia; (*sulphate*) tutiyạ; (*a*) bhạṭhi.

COPSE, A—munḍu.

COPULATE, TO—dẹr, dhạkuć, jerkeć, kamḍa; (*as dogs*) lẹnṭhẹ.

COPY, TO—nọkọl, tulạu, utrạu.

COQUETRY—aṅgra (M), aṅgri (F), jhalka (M), jhạlki (F).

CORAL—pọrbal; (*large*) muṅgạ mala; (*seller of*) sãk. *Cf.* BEADS.

CORBY, THE BOW-BILLED—bhoṇḍa kạhu.

CORD—baber; (*fastened to loins at narta*) sasaṅ ḍora.

CORE THE—(*of a boil*) munại, tukạ; (*of trees*) maṅj; (*of corn-cob*) khaḍi.

CORIANDER-SEED—dhạnia, dhũnia.

CORK, A—kāk, ṭhipi.

CORMORANT, THE LITTLE—dak̓ sim.

CORN ON SOLE OF FOOT—koraeṭhi, korāṭ.

CORNER—koca, kona, konac, kọnḍ, kõṛ, kundạu, kundhi, sirạ; (*of cloth*) ṭẹp.

CORNERS, THE—kana kona, kona kuni, pon kọnḍ, pon sirạ.

CORPORAL—nạk.

CORPSE—lahas, mạ̃ṛi, mạ̃ṛi murdạ, murdạr; (*to burn*) ḍahon; (*disposal rites*) kandkạṭhi; (*to allow to remain in house*) bạsi mara, mara.

CORPULENT—ahal ẹhẹl, amoṭ, ạsrāṭ, bagrum, bhạtkuṛa, bhitkuṛ, bhõḍa, bhogao, bhọnḍa, bhunḍa (M), bhunḍi (F), bhuṭel, bidgoe bodgoe, bigọbẹgọ, dhamdhusạr, ḍheke, dhọdlọ, dhumạ (M), dhumi (F), dhumrạ (M), dhumṛī (F), kạriḍaṅ, lạpiokak̓ (F), lapockak̓ (M), lọdhọr (2), lodhrok̓, lodo dhorok̓, madhãs, mandhas, odrok̓, rondho, thom thorok̓, uduṛ dhumạ; (*very*) lobo dhorok̓, lokom dọrok̓, luduṛyuć, tumsaṅ.

CORPULENT, GAIT OF—ladać luduć, ladak luduk, lẹdọṛ pẹdọṛ, luduk (2).

CORRECT—bọṭẹ, jothat, jut, sudh, ṭhik, ṭhik ṭhak.

CORRECT, TO—jujut, ṭhik ṭhak; (*faults*) sudhrạu.

CORRODE, TO—murcạ.

CORRUPT—cọrpọṭ; (*to*) bhanḍ, bhanḍ.

CORYZA—manda.

COSTIVE—ḍubḍubi, guṛhak̓, khilạ.

COTTON—(*raw*) kaskọm; (*of tree*) rui; (*poetical*) kapasạra; (*ginned*) tulạm, rić tulạm; (*species of*) *Cf.* kaskọm; (*twist*) markha; (*dried pods*) kārā; (*seed*) baṅgaura; (*carded*) piteć tulạm; (*to card*) phidli, piteć; (*amount carded*) paha; (*to separate seeds*) rić; (*machine for separating seed*) cạrkhi; (*European cloth*) mạrkin; (*pin for*) khuili; (*to make rolls of*) piũri; (*bunch fixed to hair*) amba gạurạ.

COTTON PLANT, THE—bhoga kaskọm, jeṭhwa, jurguḍạ, kaskọm; (*pod*) dinḍi.

COTTON TREE, THE—edel; (*traditional name*) soho doho.

COUCH, TO—(*as beast of prey*)—lambẹć.

COUGH, TO—ẹhẹm, khok̓; (*to call attention*) ẹthẹm; (*as bull*) hudrạk̓ (2).

COUGH—(*a dry*) ṭhại (2); (*& cold*) khok̓ manda.

COUNCIL, A—bạisi, dọs, kulhi duṛup̓, mõṛẽ họṛ, panć, sabha, sobha.

COUNCILLOR, A—dataram.

COUNSEL—rae; (*to keep one's own*) bhidi; (*to take*) bujhạu, parames, porames, tạdbir; (*together, to*) bujhạ bujhi, mejas, meṅjas, mis.

COUNT, TO—gạnti, ginti, gunti, lekha, tạlikạ; (*up*) munjrạ.

COUNTENANCE, THE—cehra, mẽṭāhã; (*cheerful*) kharsala, khasa; (*of a good*) nakhe mukhe; (*out of*) orloporlo.

COUNTER (*contrary*)—ẽṛga.

COUNTERFEIT—phosol.

COUNTERFOIL, HAVING A—cẹ̃k.

COUNTERPART—bạnki; (*of lease*) kabuliạt.

COUNTING—likhwạtia.

COUNTLESS—alekha, bẹsumạr.

COUNTRY—des, disom, duniạ; (*round a village*) dihạli; (*division of*) pargana, tạluk; (*all kinds of*) rọḍọk̓; (*native*) des; (*distant*) birạn; (*large*) kaṅjela; (*a traditional*) Kaenḍe,

Sat disom; (*one after another*) des bides; (*belonging to*) disi, gãoali; (*of another*) pordesi; (*king of the*) desapạti raj.

COUPLE, TO—sẹleṭ; (*names of marriageable couple*) leao.

COURAGE—dil, partap, sahas.

COURAGEOUS—jhũk, jhũkel, sahas, sahạsiạ; (*as tiger*) bagrạsiãu.

COURSE—(*of bricks, &c.*) rada; (*water*) lala, nala; (*one of*) akhaṛ, akhṛa; (*to direct one's*) mohlao, mohṇḍa.

COURSE, OF—bhạtić, sẹ bhạtić.

COURT, A—(*of justice*) adalot, ejlas, kacahari, korãṭ, koroṭ, misil; (*criminal*) phaddạri adalot; (*at national hunt*) lọ bir bạisi; (*head clerk of*) dewan; (*bailiff*) peada; (*records of*) saristha; (*recordkeeper*) sirishtadar; (*conversant with*) karbạria; (*hangers-on*) kapla.

COURTYARD OF HOUSE—baṭe, raca; (*about the*) andaṛe pandaṛe.

COUSINS—kaka khuṛa boehako; (*by F. side*) maemạsi, mamạsi.

COVENANT—niạm; (*ark of the*) ạn sunduk.

COVER, TO—aḍon, bẹt́, dalop̆, ḍambrao, ḍap̆, dapal, ḍhakao, gạrim sạrim, hạrup̆, jhampa, jhạpni, jhapṛe, jhompa, kapok̆, ṭopar; (*the eyes*) bẹt́; (*the head*) ṭuṭuri bạṭuri (F); (*over*) jalop, lọṭọm, topa; (*anything objectionable*) lunḍạ; (*with blanket*) oyo, oyo pọṭọm; (*with lid or basket*) jhạpni, jhapon; (*as a book*) pẹṭọm; (*as water*) ḍubạ, ḍubạu, ḍublạu; (*with cloth, wings, or body*) gunguṭ; (*by placing something on top*) dọhọ lọṭọm.

COVERED, TO BE—dabao; (*with leaves*) ladọp̆, ruhuṛ. *Cf.* ORNAMENTS.

COVERING, A—danapal, ẹnẹsẹt; (*thin*) jạlại; (*of leaves for head*) gungu; (*to remove*) khaḍra, oṭak̆.

COVERT, A—aotan.

COVET, TO—arkha, celhe, elhe celhe, halkhao, harhao, harkhao, jiwi jọm, lalọc, lilkạ lilki, lilkạu, lọb.

COVETOUS—lacaṅ locaṅ, lalca (M), lạlci (F), lalca lạlci, lalọciạ, lobhatiạ, lobhi, lubhi, lubhiạ, olaṅ mocaṅ.

COVETOUSNESS—lalọc, lọb lalọc.

COVEY, IN A—jhumblại mẹnte.

COW, TO—sursuṇḍuć.

COW, A—ḍaṅgri, gạiı; (*black*) kari gại; (*brown*) guli gại, (*white*) kạili gại; (*the Blue*) murum jel; (*with calf*) dhirũ gại, pal gại; (*broken to plough*) gunḍi; (*present to bridegroom*) salakagại; (*with horns bent forward*) kubi gại; (*with loose horns*) lurki gại; (*lowing of*) hudur (2); (*call to*) seṭ́, sudheṭ́; (*first milk of*) pĩrũs; (*shed*) goṛa, goṛa oṛak̆; (*tick, the*) cạmki, camokan.

COWARDLY—poçra (M), pucri (F).

COW-DUNG—gurić; (*dry*) gõeṭha; (*to smear with*) gẹć gurić, gurić, kukạr, lunḍạ.

COWED & SPEECHLESS—sugubugu.

COWERING—dondkoṛo.

COWHERD, A—goala, gupi; (*Hindu caste*) Goala, Mahara, Mahra.

CO-WIFE, A—hirom; (*younger sister as*) unkạ.

COWS—(*large drove of*) gại gadel; (*& calves*) guru bạchur; (*up-country*) bạini gại; (*broken to plough*) gunḍhi bạnḍhi; (*to milk*) duhạu.

COZEN, TO—bhulạu, cạcki, cạmpur, hordodo.

CRAB, A—kaṭkọm; (*species of*) rẹṭhẹ k., ṭoklak̆ hoṛo. *Cf.* kaṭkọm; (*pincers of*) ḍaṭo,, ḍiṭom; (*sound of*) sẹṭẹ.

CRACK, TO—bhirobhoro, catkao, cirkạu, dardarao, darkao, paṛak̆, paṭpaṭao, raṭpaṭ, raṭruṭ, ruṭuk̆ (2), taraṛ, ṭhas; (*as roasted grain*) paṭapuṭu; (*joints*) ciṭeṭ́ caṭeṭ́, ṭhọć.

CRACK, WITH A—rẹc marte, phaṭ m., poć m., ṭhas m., ṭhuṅ m., ṭhus m., ṭuṅ m.

CRACK SHOT WITH BOW & ARROW, A—dhiṅkiạ.

CRACKED—caṭcaṭ, dhọrọṭ́ (2), ganḍrao, khiyo khoyo, mackao, ṭuṭạ bhaṅga, dorpoṭ́; (*& worn*) dhọrọṭ́ (2); (*crazy*) bạulạha (M), bạulạhi (F), bạulạu.

CRACKED DRUM, SOUND OF—dhoḍọr (2).

CRACKING SOUND—caṭ caṭao, cẹṭcẹṭ, dharaṛ, haṛas, (2) mạṭruk̆, paṭpaṭ, pẹṭẹs, phaṭ phuṭ, raṭruṭ, rẹć, rẹcẹć, ṭhus; (*of brittle things*) ṭhus (2); (*to cause a*) ṭhu.

CRACKLE, TO—caṭa cuṭu, jhan jhanao.

CRACKLING—jhan (2), khaṛ khoṛ; (*of dry leaves*) racap̣ rucup̣, ricoṭ ṛocoṭ.

CRAFT—porkar, prokar.

CRAFTILY—bondhokte, pherkaṭite.

CRAFTY—sean.

CRAM IN, TO—tubeṭ, tuheṭ, tuweṭ.

CRAMMED—geje pete, pete (2), reṭ tepeṭ, segebege.

CRAMP, TO BE SEIZED WITH—ṭaṭao; (*in the stomach*) berõṭi.

CRAMPED—aṭgaṭe, pete (2).

CRANE, A SPECIES OF—ḍak, ḍheṅka.

CRASH, WITH A—haṛas marte, rạhṛuk m., rihiṛ m., ruhuṛ m.; (*thunder*) liṭhir m., luṭhur m.

CRASHING SOUND—bhaṛ bhuṛ, liṭhir, luṭhur, rạhṛuk, rihiṛ, ruhuṛ.

CRAVE, TO—nehõr; (*for*) cuṭcuṭ, larlarao, lolao, uṛuṭ (2); (*food or drink*) hạdiạu, hirohi, laklakao, locor.

CRAVINGLY—erem (2), merel.

CRAW OF A BIRD, THE—okoṭ.

CRAWL, TO—leń; (*as caterpillars*) kibiṛ (2); (*of children*) kaḍa.

CRAYFISH, A—bãunḍi.

CRAZY—baul (M), bạulạ bauli, bạulạha (M), bạulạhi (F), bạulạu, bạwil (F), bạuṛan.

CREAK, TO—kĩṛĩc kõṛõc, raṭ, raṭraṭ saḍe; (*as shoes*) macmac, ropoṭ, ropoṭ.

CREAK, WITH A—kĩṛĩc marte, poc m., rec m., ropoṭ m., ropoṭ m.

CREAKING SOUND—dhararaṛ, kĩṛĩc kõṛõc, poc, raṭraṭ, recec, recrec; (*of shoes*) ricoṭ rocoṭ, roprop.

CREAM—toa chale.

CREASE, TO—cokṛo, joṅgrao, korcoṭ, run.

CREASED—cakṛa cokṛo, kircoṭ korcoṭ, kokorcoṭ, korcoṭ, kukuṛbań, run.

CREATE, TO—sirjạu, sirjon; (*disturbance*) andka ạndki, londphond.

CREATOR, THE—janam data.

CREATURES—jan janwar, jib jontu, podartho, porani, sirjon; (*small*) bele botke; (*horned*) dereńauko; (*crawling*) leńokko.

CREDIT, TO—(*believe*) pạtiạr, pạtiạu; (*in an account*) minạ, uslạt, usul.

CREDIT, TO BUY ON—dhar, udhar; (*in another's name*) ḍhal.

CREEP, TO—leń; (*gently*) rugum (2).

CREEPER, A (*plant*)—jo sań, kidiń baha, lat, nạṛi.

CREEPING INSECT, A—tejo.

CREEPING SENSATION—ragabaga, ragam (2), rumuń (2).

CREMATE, TO—dag, jalao, kạṭhạuṛi, porao, rapak; (*to help to*) gok sahan.

CRESS—hạlim.

CREST—cuṛạ.

CRICKET, A—suạni; (*spec. of*) sõạriń.

CRIME, A—dos, ghạṭ, gunạ, gunạgar, gunhạ, kại, khõc, laṭak, oprad, phasad.

CRIMINAL—opradi; (*case*) phaddạri mamla; (*court*) phaddạri adalot.

CRINGE, TO—harea garea.

CRIPPLED—kondha, lokṛe, nason.

CRISIS—lagan, logon, somsom, tak.

CRISP—caṭa cuṭu, jhanjhan, kạrcup̣, kecer, rucup̣, ṭaṭao.

CROAK OF FROGS—bebe, ṭorṭor; (*young*) ṭuryuṭ (2), teretere; (*bull*) ão ão; (*tree*) ṭoroṭ.

CROCODILE, A—tayan.

CROOK, A—bakuk.

CROOKED—ạkuṭ, badhoṛ, bajhaṛ, baka, bak bheṅkoṛ, dhokṛe, ghõṛce, haṛbań huṛbań, honḍeal, kabea kobea, kabja kubjạ, kanḍeṭ, karbań kuṛbań, kaṛcań, kaṭac kuṭuc, kaṭbac kuṭbuc, kebekebe, khẽṛẽ khõṛẽ, khĩṛjõń khõṛjõń, kiṛboń korboń, kobe, kobṛe, konḍe, korbeṭ, kõṛmbeṭ, koṭba, kuṭbe, kuba, kubjạ, kubrạ, kukuc, kukuṛbań, kuṛbań, laḍea, laṭea, laṭhea, liṛuań, panṭeṭ, paṭea, piṭuạ paṭwe, ṭerha, tirchạ tirchi; (*of trees*) laṛea.

CROP—(*a cultivated*) alpalua, raheṛ; (*the full*) samphola; (*of bird*) okoṭ; (*a garden*) boḍa ghaṅgra.

CROP, TO—(*the ears*) bucạ (M), buci (F); (*the hair*) munḍlạ (M), munḍli (F), munḍrạ (M), munḍri (F).

CROPPED BARE—ḍunḍgạ; (*of the hair*) ṭhunḍgạ (M), ṭhunḍgi (F).

CROPPING, SOUND OF— rusuk' (2).

CROPS—arjon, ọrjọn, phasal, phọsọl, upjạ, upjạn ; *(growing)* cas; *(cold weather)* khạdiạṛ, rạbi ; *(depending on dew)* sisir cas ; *(ripening in Bhador)* bhadra.

CROSS—*(ill-tempered)* thetha ; *(transverse)* gạṇḍe ; *(ridge)* gạṇḍ ; *(roads)* dọbạṭiạ ; *(the)* kurus ; *(purposes, at)* haṛka hạṛki.

CROSS, TO—baj ; *(over)* makargạti ; *(in front of)* eṇḍak' ; *(a thread, &c)* hạṛi ; *(the legs)* paṭẹt' ; *(legs when walking)* ciṭet' paṭet', haṛak' paṭak', haṛẹt' paṭẹt' ; *(question)* jera, sowal.

CROSS-GRAINED—badhọṛ, bedha, bedha bidhi, bẹdhọṛ, edhoṛ bedhoṛ.

CROSS-LEGGED, TO SIT—paṭgạṇḍo.

CROSSLY—kosle.

CROSS-WISE—ẹprẹ, gạṇḍ.

CROUCH, TO—chapkao, chapka chapki, coko, dabṛao, lambẹt', lọplọpọ ; *(down)* dabkao, dapkao.

CROUP—bandor kokhi.

CROW, A—kạhu ; *(the King)* ḍhipcui, ḍipṭuć.

CROW, TO—kukṛu ; *(learning)* kekrecet'.

CROWBAR, AN IRON—sabọl.

CROWD, A—aṛa, bhiṛ, dọṅgọl, gạd, gadel, gahạṇḍi, jhuṇḍ, laskar, phạd ; *(noise of)* hạuhạu ; *(in a)* jhargae jhurgui, jhama jhum, jham jhum, jharak jhuruk ; *(to break up)* bhiṛ bhaṅgao, phuṭ phaṭ.

CROWD, TO—ganganao, gańja gạńji, lẹsẹn, pakpakao, rẹpẹ ciriť ; *(together)* gadgadao, gạjgajao, hader, ṭhạuṛạ, tudrạ ; *(upon)* ghaṭghaṭao.

CROWDED—barjao, dọlọp' (2), gadel, gahagạd, gańja gạńji, ghańja ghạńji, gujguj, kucạ kuci, pẽnc, rẹṇṭẹ pẹṇṭẹ, rẹpẹ ciriť, rẹṭẹpẹṭẹ, sakṛa sạkṛi, ṭhela ṭhili ; *(together)* pẹṭẹ (2), ṭhẹkọm, ṭhube.

CROWDS, IN—ạṭuṭ, bujuk (2), chạu (2), dão (2), duṅgel, duṅguť (2), durum (2), gadagạd, gadal piṭạl, gadgad, gahamgạd, gaja guju, hẹńjẹt' (2), hujuk (2), jhaṛa jhạṛ, jhaṛ (2), jhạu (2), ladladao, laskar, mele (2).

CROWN, A—jit ṭupri, raj ṭupri.

CRUEL—cọrcọṭa, corṭha (M), curṭhi (F), kaṭhor, kaṭ jiba, khaṛa, kumaya, sọć bọdrọć.

CRUELLY, TO ACT—hane mar.

CRUMBLE DOWN, TO—dasao.

CRUMPLE, TO—cokṛo, kọrcọt'.

CRUMPLED—cakṛa cokṛo, kircọt' kọrcọt', kọkọrcọt', kọrcọt', kukurbań ; *(as a horn)* meṛha (M), miṛhi (F).

CRUNCH—*(to)* masrao, rạṭuk', rẹṭẹć (2), ruṭuk' (2), ṭọgọć ; *(with a)* rạsuk' marte, rạṭuk' marte.

CRUNCHING SOUND—kạcur (2), khaeyar (2), khaṭar (2), khaṭọr (2), khaṭrok' (2), khạṭruk', khayar khuyur, khẹcẹt', khuṭur, kucur (2), kuyur (2), mạkur, masar (2), maṭar muṭur, mạṭruk' (2), mucur, mukur (2), muṭur (2), rege cege, sarak' (2), suṭur ; *(of anything crisp & juicy)* rạsuk'.

CRUPPER, A—dimci, dumchi.

CRUSH, TO—lạhuť, lẹsẹn, rẹsẹt', rẹṭẹt', rideť, rideť ciriť, talga ṭạuạk' ; *(to atoms)* gẹjẹr ; *(to deaths)* ṭẹn gọć ; *(into a lump)* koṭeam ; *(to pieces)* rọcọt' ; *(each other)* lẹpẹn ṭẹpẹn.

CRUSHED OUT OF SHAPE—cakṛa cokṛo, cokṛo.

CRUSHING SOUND—sarak' (2) ; *(crisp)* rucup'.

CRUTCH, TO WALK WITH A—dhạṛuk' (2).

CRY, A—aṛań ; *(of infant)* koha (2), ṭẽṭẽ ; *(from pain or cold)* ahh uhh, ih, ish, uh ; *(of bird or beast)* rak'.

CRY, TO—abaṛ, kando, kikiạ kikiyi, rak' ; *(of infants)* ṭẹhõ, ṭehõ, ṭehõ ṭĩhĩ ; *(of children)* ńẹrẹ (2), sarać soroć, sẹrẹć ; *(peevishly)* abaṛ, tiriń goriń ; *(loudly)* cancan ; *(for justice)* dohae, rae dohae ; *(poverty, tho' well off)* ninyạ̃u, ninyạ̃ ninyĩ ; *(cause to)* kandao.

CRY OF BEASTS, &C.—*(some birds)* aṇḍrać ọṇḍrọć, cẹk', ṭẹṭẹć ; *(birds on seeing tiger)* khẹkhẹ (2) ; *(pigeon)* bakbakur, sas ghạṭi; *(crow pheasant)* duhup' (2) ; *(fowls)* cọrcọr ; *(chickens)* ciạ̃p' (2) ; *(crow)* kak' kak' ; *(hạpuk')* capo (2), cẹwẹć (2), cọt' cọt' cọdọr ;

(*kokor*) cerkoṭ (2); (*kite*) ci hõ hõ; (*ghardidi*) piaṅ (2); (*sauri*) piriaṅ (2); (*he-goat*) bobobok; (*goat whose head is severed*) bhek; (*wildcat*) boas; (*young buffalo*) ẽc ẽc. *Cf.* CALL OF.

CRYING—hũhũ, jhãora jhãuri, raona jhaona; (*for little*) askandni (F), askandnu (M); (*of infant*) ẽhõ; (*of petulant child*) jenephene, jhẽjhõ; (*daily, of children*) kandin bai.

CRYSTAL, A—amsam, hisir.

CRYSTALIZED RAW SUGAR—bali gur, gitil gur.

CUBIT, A—moka; (*rod of 2*) gaj.

CUCKOO, THE—takmas; (*hawk*) galoc cẽrẽ, galua c.; (*pied crested*) jhomojhoc, jhorojhoc; (*shrike*) kalaiya; (*Indian*) kol.

CUCUMBER, A KIND OF—taher.

CUD, TO CHEW THE—pagur.

CUDGEL, A—ṭheṅga.

CULL, TO—hucec.

CULMINATING POINT, TO BE AT—dhurpau, sardi.

CULTIVATE, TO—cas, jot.

CULTIVATING—(*rights, price of*) pon; (*tenant*) raeot.

CULTIVATION—abad, cas, kheti bari, khiti; (*a system of*) aedhor, aṅgwar, bhag jat, bhañj, hal batoria, kurãu, kut bhag, mela bhag.

CULTIVATOR, A—girosto, kirsand; (*non-resident*) boha casa.

CULVERT, A—khorloṅ.

CUMBERED, TO BE—tebe (2).

CUNNING—khar, porkar, sean, thakai.

CUNNINGLY—pherkutite.

CUP—basna; (*metal*) bati; (*leaf*) bhãutic, cokorhaṭ, cukrũc, dhondra khalak, dhondra phuruk, khalak, phuruk, sorha; (*large leaf*) dolkha, sorwa; (*of double leaves*) atal phuruk; (*large earthen*) hatha; (*for oil*) kathli, katli, mali.

CUP, TO—mali.

CUPIDITY—rogor; (*full of*) rogoria.

CURB, TO—dabao, dobnao.

CURDED MILK—dahe.

CURDLE, TO (*of milk*)—gijri, jamao, phatao.

CURE, TO—bes, pharia; (*snake-bite by charms*) jhar.

CURED, TO BE—pharnao.

CURL UP, TO—cacalkaṭ, cokro, ghurci, ĩrci ghũrci, kurcup, piṭi, uṅ.

CURLED UP—dhokre, dhombok, hurbaṅ, karcup, kurbuṅ.

CURLY (*as hair*)—kirooṭ korcoṭ, piṭi.

CURRENCY NOTE—loṭ, noṭ.

CURRENT—calit, colit, colon; (*story*) udau; (*to be*) bikau.

CURSE—asis, sarap; (*under*) hae phoe.

CURSER, A—sarapia.

CURTAIN, TO—jhabrao, orwal, parda, porda.

CURVE, TO—nawan, tarcha.

CURVED—baka, kabnũc, kabua, kõrmbeṭ, kubja, kubkubu, kukurbaṅ, nawan.

CURVET, TO—kecmecao.

CUSHION—gadi; (*wooden, beam rest*) pirhi.

CUSTARD APPLE—mandargom.

CUSTODY, SAFE—jabid; (*to give in*) saprot, soprot; (*to keep in*) kaidau, mormorao.

CUSTOM—bebohar, beohar, bhasi, bidha, cali, car, colit, dastur, kader, legcar, nathi, rae, rewaj, rit; (*at sohrae*) jale.

CUSTOMARY—calit, car, culti, ligi bhagi; (*to make*) legcar.

CUSTOMS—acar, acar beohar, targhar; (*to institute*) acar bicar; (*of caste*) jat pat. *Cf.* SOCIAL.

CUT, TO—geṭ, katao, khodrao, kobak, laher, lahur, lak, tope; (*as with sword*) heter, hetrao, katop, mak khundlaṅ; (*down*) mak goc, mak gitic; (*out*) khokrao; (*off*) geṭ gidi, hatar, hejer, mak pasir; (*off goat's head*) bhek; (*off ears of grain*) chopao; (*off a piece*) bandia; (*evenly*) murchau; (*deeply*) aogar, dhaṅglao, lamak; (*by scraping*) khotrao; (*cloth*) orec; (*quickly*) dhaṅgla dhaṅgli; (*with difficulty*) khete (2); (*the hair or tail of fowl*) tope; (*the hair*) dunda, kapcao, katrop; (*the breath from one*) hẽk; (*a figure*) lolok; (*through water*) chalchalao; (*up a carcase*) dauladauli; (*into pieces*) gandra gundrą, kuṭi; (*the throat*) jaba, jabe, jąbu; (*a dam*) phor; (*into lengths*) ṭhuni, ṭona, ṭona ṭuni; (*into pieces*) dhanglao, gẹt kuṭrą, gaṇḍra guṇḍrą, giṇḍrą, guṇḍrą, hubąg, khucri, kuṭi, ṭana ṭukrą, ṭona ṭuni.

CUT, A—gẹt; (*deep*) bhongar; (*with axe*) ṭangadar; (*with sword &c.*) ghao; (*with one*) khaṭ marte.

CUT THROUGH, TO—bhuṅgrąu, hẹsẹ, mak topak; (*by chopping*) cewak; (*with axe &c.*) giri; (*with a stroke*) hẹlẹć, hẹtẹr; (*with a swish*) khẹc; (*deeply with axe*) sigi.

CUTTING, A—ṭhuni; (*in earthwork*) kąṭin; (*of plant*) kọlọm; (*of sugarcane*) ḍoga.

CUTTING—(*speech*) irą, irsą; (*sound of*) khar khar, rusuk (2).

CUTTING WEAPON—kaṭaha; (*folding up*) piṭi khaṇḍa.

CYCLONE—birbao.

CYMBALS—bajna, kortal; (*large*) chań.

CYPRESS TREE—tąsur dare, tirsą.

CYSTIC TUMOUR—batori, bąturi.

D

DAGGERS—(*looking*) kurkuṇḍuć; (*drawn, to be at*) akhaṭ.

DAILY—din hilok, dinąm, diṇṭa, jaoke jao, roj, sadae; (*wants, one who provides for*) rojgarią.

DAINTY—bąḍarią, bądgarią, cunu munu, kakosią.

DAL MASHER—ghuṭni.

DAM, TO—aṛe, paṭẹt; (*to cut a*) phoṛ.

DAMAGE—khatra, khuti, loksan, mara, ṭuṭi; (*to suffer*) hą̃si hanao, khatra, khotra, ṭuṭ, ṭuṭi.

DAMAGE, TO—hondwań, huąń, huloṛ, hurwań, uper khaper.

DAMAGED—bẹhal, hara hurą, hurą, ṭuṭą bhanga.

DAMP—ḍola, ḍolao, gajgaj, galgalao, gẹjẹć (2), gilą, hemal, jabjab, jẹgẹć jągum, jẹgẹć (2), jọbọ (2), jọć jọć, lọhọt, mẹhao, oda, oda moda, olahẹt, olhan, purmu, rosaṛ, rosgaṛ, roskar, sirpiṭiąk, tąbuć; (*very*) jọhọ jọbọ; (*soil*) jobho, jọbjọb; (*to*) moao, purmu.

DAMUDA RIVER—nąi; (*direction of*) mora muhą̃.

DANCE, TO—ẹnẹć, khel; (*to cause*) nacao; (*& wheel round*) uḍmalao.

DANCE, A KIND OF—jąṭur ẹnẹć; (*by men*) ḍaṇṭa e., jhalka e., lampọṭ e. *Cf.* ẹnẹć; (*a step in*) khanḍ, khọḍ; (*sword & shield*) pąk dọn.

DANCER, A—nącnią; (*boy*) ras dhąrią; (*Dom*) naṭuą.

DANCING STANCE, A—akhṛa.

DANDIFIED—alak jhalak.

DANDLE, TO—ẹnẹć; (*in the hands*) loka.

DANDRUFF—upią̃s.

DANGER—dąb, gąr, gara, muhim; (*supernatural*) ląṭu bhąṇḍu; (*time of*) mahakal; (*fearful of*) bhọrọk, comol; (*to save from*) rąhąu; (*of, in*) dayik.

DANGEROUS—bagahi, khatra khotra; (*from spirits*) kotaha; (*from wild beasts*) ąukhąu, bagher; (*from illness*) japao.

DANGLE, TO—dhąlui (2), jhąlui (2), ląkuć, ląrkuć, ląruń, lawak, lawań, tawar (2).

DANGLING—doloe (2), liwar lawar, ṭikọr ṭọkọr, tiwąr tawar.

DARBARS, ONE IN HABIT OF ATTENDING—dọrbarią.

DARE, TO—samsao.

DARK—galam, ńũt; (*very*) karąń (2); (*clouds*) ńą̃rą̃dąń; (*colour*) karya; (*person*) kuilą (M), kuili (F); (*grey*) kajra (M), kąjri (F); (*in the*) kaḍam (2); (*after sunset*) lupąk.

DARKEN, TO—ńũt.

DARKNESS—aląundhą, andhar, ńũt; (*pitch*) karąń (2), ńũt; (*before storm*) guńj.

DARN, TO—jąląi.

DART, TO—sọhọr, sursur; (*the head, as snake*) ąwil; (*the tongue*) mẹlọt.

DART, WITH A—hurgus marte, sur m.; (*out*) puyul m., puyuṛ m.

DASH DOWN, TO—lebda, tawak.

DATA—sąkhiyąt.

DATE—tąrikh; (*to fix*) barte; (*to put back*) ṭhelao.

DATE PALM, SPECIES OF—kindeṭ; (*tree, Chinese*) jąnum.

DATIVE CASE, SIGN OF—te, ṭheć, ṭhen.

DAUB, TO—chõc, jeṛeṛ, lasrao, lesrao; (*on the person*) kalhaṫ; (*with the hand*) joṭ; (*with soot*) goyaḱ.

DAUGHTER, A—biṭi, hopoṇera, kuṛi gidra, kuṛi hopon, mãi; (*eldest*) maraṅ hopoṇera; (*3rd.*) saṅjli kuṛi; (*4th.*) maṅjhli kuṛi; (*& her husband*) dhi damad; (*veiled name*) thuria ukhuṛ; (*in-law*) kimin; (*in marriage, to give*) goṅ; (*of young brother or sister*) goṅgo kuṛi.

DAUGHTERS' PREQUISITES BEFORE MARRIAGE—khenha.

DAUNT, TO—sursunduć.

DAWDLE, TO—loroṅ phocoṅ, tehe mẽhẽ.

DAWN—aṅga, ṅaham ṅahum, palaḱ poloḱ, payaṅ; (*first signs*) pahpaha.

DAY, A—din, hiloḱ, mãhã, roj; (*sunrise to sunset*) siṅ; (*the same*) on hiloḱ, roka, roka ruki; (*previous part of same*) enaṅ; (*future part of same*) dhinaṅ; (*late in*) kubela; (*break of*) piaṅ payaṅ, paha poho; (*after tomorrow*) meaṅ; (*before yesterday*) mahnder; (*of death*) harna morna hiloḱ; (*or two*) arsiṅ barsiṅ, mursiṅ barsiṅ, musiṅ, ursiṅ barsiṅ. *Cf.* ALL, UNLUCKY.

DAY, EVERY—din hiloḱ, dinam, dinam hiloḱ, din ke din, hergoe (2), jao hiloḱ, hole (2), holo (2), jaoge, jao ke jao, jao jaote, modam, mondam, sodae.

DAY-HORSE, THE—siṅ sadom.

DAY-LIGHT—siṅ marsal; (*before*) hadam hudum, hugui (2).

DAYS—(*a few*) arsiṅ barsiṅ, ursiṅ barsiṅ; (*2 or 3*) barsiṅ pe mahã, barpe mãhã; (*many*) mahakal; (*on alternate*) pasri; (*a few ago*) hali sali; (*3 ago*) on mahnder; (*2 ago*) mahnder; (*3 hence*) endrae; (*4 hence*) pher endrae.

DAY'S JOURNEY, A—jojon, muṅjil.

DAZZLING—piriṫ.

DEAD—mora; (*as if*) mora mohnda leka; (*nearly*) gujuḱ napit, mora muri; (*calm*) deldel, nijhum; (*body*) lahas, mari; (*to dispose of*) kaṭhauṛi; (*last rites of*) bhandan, gaṅga gaya, gaya gaṅga, kaj korom, kaṭhoria; (*offspring, bearing*) gabdha gabdhi, gabdhao.

DEAF—bahra, kala (M), kali (F); (*& dumb*) kala guṅga.

DEAFENING—andakul, tiṅgiṫ.

DEAFNESS—bahir bai.

DEAL, A GOOD—thoren.

DEAR—(*beloved*) dular, dularo (M), dulari, dularini (F), sohag (M), sohagi (F); (*high-priced*) akra, mahaṅga, maharog, mahṅga, mahrog; (*from buyer's point of view*) andhoṅ.

DEAR ME!—babure, dur karahaḱ, duṭhaḱ, haehae, mor, morhaḱ.

DEARTH—akal, ṭan, ṭanaṭani.

DEATH—gujuḱ, mirtika, morna, moron; (*at point of*) abe tabe, aṅgaṗ (2), gujuḱ marae, gujuḱ dakhil, kukuṫ (2), moron soman, labejan; (*angel of*) hudul raj, jom hudar, jom raja; (*ceremony 3 days after*) tel khar; (*5 days after*) tel nahan; (*to feign*) gampatao; (*to die a natural*) harna morna. *Cf.* RITES.

DEBATE, TO—ridkhid, rond kond, ronkhon.

DEBT—karja, korja, koroj, rin, rinpan; (*to incur*) dharao, dharua, karja, rin; (*deep in*) gad, garad; (*free from*) nidharua; (*to clear off*) poriskar; (*to seize goods to pay*) berband; (*mode of extorting payment*) dharna; (*to give property in payment*) bharna, hari bhari, harna bharna, molao.

DEBTOR, A—asami, dharua, khatok.

DECAY—(*to*) jarkhar, lambao, landbhandao, maruṛ; (*senile*) ṭan paṫgla.

DECAYED—phoska, poca, pocla, podra; (*of timber*) phophra; (*in centre of fruits*) phora.

DECEIT—chol kopoṭ, dokha, ulbul; (*without*) niskapaṭ.

DECEITFUL—calak, copa kuṭa, dagabaj, dombaj, jadu, kopoṭ, labar, labhra (M), labhri (F), labori, laboria, labra (M), labri (F), lai labar, paṭweṫ, pend, pendla, phakua, phaṅga, phasiara, ṭhakna (M), ṭhakni (F.)

DECEIVE, TO—audha, andić, arkhao, badohi, bahkao, bahka bahki, bauli, beda, bhulau, bulau, daga, dhoka, dhokha, ere, ere monj, ere lipuḱ, hoṛ beda, labhae lubhai, laboṛ, lai puṭi, libuk, lipuk, phaki, phareb, phēkphāk, phoṭao, ṭapi, ṭhag, ṭhak, ṭhakna, ṭhakua, ṭhar, ṭhok.

DECEIVED, TO BE—bhakṇḍao.

DECEIVER, A—bhataha, bhiṅgoṛa, ekre hoṛ, galua.

DECEMBER-JANUARY—Pus.

DECENT—khara khari.

DECEPTION—calaki, chol.

DECEPTIVE—bhulania, bhulauni.

DECIDE, TO—bicar, danai, goṭa, ikoṭ, meṭmaṭ, neae, neao, niruk, niṭ, ṭahrao, ṭarhao; (*a dispute*) phaṇḍao, phariau; (*upon*) baca; (*without full investigation*) ārgom laga.

DECIMATE, TO—bhaṇḍaṅ bhuṇḍuṅ, kaṅkhar.

DECIPHER, TO—bhoṅ.

DECKED OUT FOR SHOW—abhran, jhalak malak, jhala mala, saj, sajao.

DECLINE, TO—(*lessen*) dambrao, domkao, khasao, niṅjhau, norma, norom; (*refuse*) mahrau.

DECLIVITY—anargo.

DECOMPOSE, TO—barao, galao, liṭi, sea; (*of moist vegetables*) ol.

DECORATE, TO—saj.

DECOY, TO—bajhao, gahi, muhni.

DECOYED, TO BE—bajbajhi.

DECREASE, TO—ghaṭao, ghaṭi, hin, khagao, khento, kom, komao, madhua, norma, norom, ohra, ohṭao, ṭhankao; (*& increase*) ghaṭal barhal, ghaṭi barhi.

DECREE, A—digri.

DEDUCE, TO—ohman.

DEDUCT, TO—mina.

DEDUCTION—mojra; (*returned*) phirot.

DEED, A (*document*)—nama.

DEEP—atha, gahir, kandraṅ, khāiduk, khal, khandaraṅ, khandri, khāyuk, khondoṛ khocak, patal; (*as blow with axe*) bodgak bidgak, bodgak (2), gad; (*& narrow*) khulkhuli; (*of ploughing*) gargarao; (*pool in river*) darha; (*sound*) hudur (2); (*as a forest*) kandraṅ; (*mud*) dal; (*as a man's height*) unum sumuṅ; (*seated*) jariau; (*sleep*) ghumghor, osoc (2), ōsōs; (*in debt*) rin gaḍ; (*very*) bethah; (*of foot-marks*) padgak.

DEEPLY—gabgab, gab marte, gad; (*to insert or sink*) gabgab.

DEER, A—harna, jel; (*Ravine*) badar selep, metrec jel, kurmbi selep; (*that has shed horns*) gutruṭ; (*part sent by slayer to his sisters*) k nda jel; (*cry of*) khau (2); (*mythical*) boi bindi jel; (*hind of Ravine*) ghotreṭ jel, merom jel; (*spotted*) jhaṅkar (M), posta (F); (*small*) muṇḍghos; (*species of*) bhauṇṭia jel, iar jel, icak saram, jola jhaṅkar, mirgi jel. *Cf.* jel.

DEFAME, TO—khoṭ.

DEFEAT—harjit; (*to*) harao, harwani, siṭhau, siṭhwao, ṭhasiau; (*ashamed after*) haria busia; (*running away from*) picom podroc.

DEFEATED, TO BE—haṭkao.

DEFECT, A—rog, toṅcok; (*having*) roga, rugi; (*without*) niphuṭ, sajontar, susṭok, tartaria *Cf.* SPEECH.

DEFECTIVE—darpoṭ, dusau, phi, phiṭ.

DEFEND, TO—hebajoṭ.

DEFENDANT, A—asami, kaḍi, mudali; (*& plaintiff*) dae mudoe.

DEFER, TO—agdhao.

DEFERENCE—sohag, tamai.

DEFERRED, TO BE—mahkup, makup, mukup.

DEFIANCE—(*term of*) land (M), landi (F); (*exclm. of*) o; (*to show thumb in*) katup uduk, ṭhepo.

DEFIANT—ṭendos, ṭendosia.

DEFICIENCY—baki, ghaṭi, han, hane, hani; (*to cause*) hanao; (*to make up*) phujau.

DEFICIENT—hin, khaṭo badho, kom, komao, komti, kumti, raya royo; (*in intellect*) alhasua; (*in stamina*) thosoṭ morgoṭ, tosot morgot.

DEFILE, TO—bhand, bhaṇḍao, bhosṭo, bosṭo, laṇḍbhand, loṇḍbhoṇḍ.

DEFILED—bhōṇḍa, nakara, nekra, siluṅ pituṅ; (*of food leavings*) āiṭha jūiṭha; (*ceremonially*) chuṭaha; (*by outsiders*) baher; (*ceremony to cleanse those*) chaṭiar; (*from childbirth*) janam chut.

DEFLECT, TO—ṭarao.

DEFLECTED, TO BE—phencoṛ.

Deflower, to—bhaṇḍao.

Deformed—dhạpuạ, lọkrẹ; (*in feet*) koṇḍha, kuḍạ. *Cf.* nose.

Deformity, a—(*protuberant*) ḍẽhẽ, jo; (*physical*) leḍha khoṛha; (*without*) napae.

Defraud, to—aṛgoṅgaṛ, ạṛič, hajam, hẫuṇḍi, jog, mara, pacao; (*by keeping to oneself*) bạṭiạu.

Defy, to—ṭhepo.

Degree—amdaj, darja; (*in a high*) ọkọč; (*inferior in*) nirọs.

Degrees—(*by*) dhire suste; (*various*) uṇu unu.

Deity, a—bhokta, ṭhạkur; (*Hindu*) bhidata; (*Santal lesser*) bạghut boṅga, gạṇḍo guru, kambru buru; (*a female*) gosãe era, jahẹr era; (*of Ms. of family*) abge boṅga, barhet; (*to invoke*) hakrao; (*residence of*) than.

Dejected, to be—aṅjhluṅ, ạtruṅ, dolomolo, hulạs bhaṅga, kolok̕ (2), lạbruk̕, merlañ mirliṅ, mirluṅ, mọč-mọč, momoyot̕, mulin, orloporlo.

Delay—harakat; (*accidental*) beoṛa; (*without*) catpat, culuṅ, daṛae dhampae, dhaoṛa dhẫuṛi, dhatpat, doro (2), ekep̕ sekep̕, mit̕ ghạṛite, harephare, họt̕, kạcuṛ mạcuṛ, khaṛe khaṛ, khuḍạ khudi, marge, ṅire hojore, phucuč, pucuč, tạhbi, ṭạtka mạr, torko morko, turãt, turte, usạra.

Delay, to—agdhao, ạhil mạhil, akọt̕, bidhaura, bilom, dera diri, diri, dom, gạhul, hemkhem, jama, jọhọt̕ mọhọt̕, lọhọr, lọhọr pọhọr, nemor, okoṭ, oṭkao, polom.

Delayed, to be—mạhkup, mạkup, mukup.

Delegated authority—umuk.

Deliberate, to—bicạr, nani gạndi, ọnman, tạdbir.

Deliberately—chio choko, dekhit, galaṅ guluṅ, gangante.

Deliberation—jugut.

Delicate (*of food*)—ciknạr.

Delicately—bhọrmẹ bhọrmete; (*to bring up*) barmãṇḍ.

Delicious—hẹrẹm, ńuṭuk̕ (2), sọrọm, sọstọk, tọrọp.

Delight—hẫs.

Delighted, to be—rijhạu, rijhuạ, riṅgi ṭiṅgi.

Delinquency—tuskil.

Delirious, to speak as one—akhaṭ bakhaṭ, bhasa bharṛa.

Delirium—bạì.

Deliver, to—bac, chaḍao, dạkhilạu, gatao, hạjir, hạjur, jimạ, oar, rạhạì sạhạì, rạhạu, rạkhiạ, rukhiạ; (*over*) saprot, sompao, soprot, sumjhạu, sạprud.

Deliverance—rạkhiạ, rihạì, rukhiạ, salsãt.

Delivered, to be—khalas; (*of young*) biạn, bihẫṛ.

Deliverer, a—dhatkaha, ok̕warič; (*present given to*) sumjhạuni.

Delivery, near the time of—lẹhẹdẹhẹ.

Delude, to—bahka bạhki, bahkao.

Deluder, a—bhataha.

Deluge, a—bayaban.

Demand, to—bab; (*dues*) oghe, sidi; (*with bluster*) dabae dundrạì, dham dhur.

Demand, to meet a—calao, purạnti.

Demented—pagal, pagla (M), pagli (F), pagol.

Demerit—gunạk̕.

Demolish, to—otor.

Demon, a—bhut, boṅga, gosãe, rakas; (*one-legged*) eka guriạ; (*possessed with*) boṅga cạpaṛ; (*haunted by*) bhutạha.

Demoniac—bhutel, rakasiạ.

Demonstrate, to—sodọr, uduk̕.

Demur, to—mạhrạu.

Den, a—aotan, dander, khọrloṅ.

Denial—(*emphatic*) bulte; (*to take no*) dhora bandha.

Denounce, to—naṭ.

Dense—akaṭ, ạkuṭ, arna, arõṭ, ạṭuk̕ jhạruk̕, ạṭuṭ, dọlọp̕ (2), gajaṛ, gajeṛ, gaṅjeṛ, ibil, jholaṇḍ, jhopro, jhuṇḍ, kandrañ, lateṛ; (*to become*) sạkit̕; (*foliaged*) jhạrpạ;

Dent, to—cokro, lẹckẹ.

Denticulated—regra.

Denude, to—poṭor.

DENY, TO—bañ, chi bań, dh tk , dodao, dudrạu, nakạbul, naka ar, nạsti, nindạu ; (*knowing a person*) erka ; (*repeatedly*) dundur muhạ̃

DEPART, TO—(*this life*) beṇḍao, danań, goć calao, jatra, nọsṭọ ; (*give permission to*) bidạ.

DEPARTMENT—mahal.

DEPARTURE, IN CONJUNCTION WITH VERBS IMPLIES—aṭo, oṭo.

DEPEND ON, TO—baclao, ṭebaḍ.

DEPENDED ON, NOT TO BE—lọcọr pọcọr.

DEPENDENCE—barsa, bhorosa, tabeteḱ, ̂udhin.

DEPENDENT—par ạdhin, tabe, tabedar.

DEPENDING (*hanging*)—ḍawań (2), ḍiạñ (2).

DEPONE, TO—gohaḱ, goha gujrạu, porman, sạkhi ẹm, sạkhi gujrạu.

DEPORT ONESELF PROPERLY, TO—sulạń.

DEPOSIT—jạpti ; (*money in court, to*) amanọt.

DEPOSITION—ejahar, ijạhar.

DEPOT FOR EMIGRANTS—ḍipu.

DEPRECIATE, TO—bhades, dhusạu, dusạu, mańgal, okta.

DEPRECIATORY TERM—gạnḍi (F), mara, mordha, morgoť, mudguć, muiguć.

DEPRESSED—(*sad*) ańjhluń, ạtruń, cirmoḱ, dolomolo, hulạs bhańga, jeṭloḱ (M), jipuť, jirluñ, jirmoḱ, jiṭluḱ (F), mańga murạ, nirghin ; (*sunken*) khaepaḱ khoepoḱ, khaepoḱ, khaploḱ, khạpuạ, lạṭkić.

DEPRESSED, TO BE—(*sad*) maraḱ moroḱ, mayaḱ moyoḱ, ọlọń ; (*hollow*) lọndọć.

DEPRESSED, TO LOOK—dholomolo.

DEPRESSION, A—gaḍa, gadlaḱ godloḱ, khaepaḱ khoepoḱ, khaepoḱ, khoepaḱ, lạṭkić, lọndọć.

DEPRIVE, TO—ạgu ; (*of freedom*) gurgur.

DEPUTY, A—naib.

DERANGED, TO BE—ugni monda.

DERIDE, TO—cirhạu, nisrạu.

DERIVE AS A CONSEQUENCE, TO—ehman.

DESCEND, TO—ãrgo ; (*with a jolt*) dharkaḱ dhorkoḱ.

DESCENDANTS—ãosa bãosa, bõs ; (*without*) nirbõs.

DESCENT, A—anạrgo.

DESCRIBED, THAT CANNOT BE—bẹsumạr.

DESERT—(*merit*) gunạḱ ; (*wilderness*) hahakar.

DESERT, TO—bạgi, teag ; (*one's side*) beńparsi, buruć

DESERTED—nicol, nisun, ujạr, ulạg.

DESIGN,—joh ; (*without*) khẹjẹ bẹjẹ, kherbejer.

DESIGN, TO—ańgao, aoda, ghatghatao.

DESIGNING—kọpọṭ.

DESIRABLE, TO BECOME—sarthi.

DESIRE—daris, gagọj, hīchạ, hurso, miluạ, rij rọń, sad, sadh, sana, sõk, sonk, ṭok ; (*strong*) bhuc bhuci, rọgọr ; (*of eating*) rọc ; (*objects of*) asãe sawãe ; (*having no*) ọgọrọj.

DESIRE, TO—ạnijoḱ, barmańgao, cahao, haya, hurso, lilkạu, lomosoro, sana, sasnao, sọke ; (*eagerly*) lalkao, ruhu ṭuhu, thurthurạu.

DESIROUS—humur (2) ; (*to be*) thartharao.

DESIST, TO—sumạn.

DESOLATE—kańkhar, khańkhar, kharań, nisun, sunạ, sunsạn, susạñ, ṭaḱṭaḱ, udạs, ujạr, ulạg, urạn ; (*to be*) bhańgọr, jarkhar.

DESPAIR—(*to*) as chuṭạu, hae nisạs, surma ; (*in sheer*) dhọk jibạ.

DESPARAGE, TO—dhusạu.

DESPATCH, TO—rawana.

DESPICABLE—chiạḱ, hirkhạ parkha.

DESPISE, TO—acbic, dạbri, dhaṭ dhuṭ, ẹrgejaḱ, garẹć, hẹnọsta, hirkha, leṇḍe, linḍiḱ, nandan, nehat, nemor, neńghao, nihạ̃t, nindạ, nindhạn, posra, ṭhaṭa.

DESPONDENT—kalań ḍolań.

DESTINATION, SHORT OF—thaproḱ.

DESTITUTE—awaṭapa, dhaṇḍhania, kańgla, kańla, lamṭa, laṇḍha phuciạ, laṭlaha, lendaṭuriạ, nandan, nikhạr, nindhạn, phạkir ; (*to be*) awañ ewer, halak, hale ḍale, kalor, lalao, lala lạli, lolao.

DESTROY, TO—bagḍao, bạrić, beṇḍao, bhańḍao, bhańgabhaṭ, bhańgaṭ, bhańlabhaṭ, bhańṭao, bharabhaṭ, bhosṭo, bistur, bosṭo, dhańdhaser, durathan, gọbọr mạṭi, gucạu, haler, hulạr, josao, kadhaṛ, kaṅkhar, khane karap, khaṅkhar, lạṇḍur bhạṇḍur, leglam, loksan, mạuṭạ, mulạhạn, mulehabad, muṛạ̃hạu, nas, noksan, nọsṭọ, ọbọsṭa, sọrbọnas, uchạḍ, uchet, upạr khapar, urạn; *(by forcing way)* mambṛao.

DESTROYED, TO BE—bạbiloṇḍ, baṛić, bebiloṇḍ, bẹhal, berbad, bhaṅgaṭ, bhoṭ, borborao, halak, hasa, kheanat, khotra.

DETACH, TO—cagaṛ, cagaṫ, codaǩ.

DETACHED, TO BE—bọsoǩ coṭaǩ, odhrao, odrao, pharhaṛ, phạṛphaṛia.

DETACHMENT, A—aṛa, dọl, dọṅgọl, phạd.

DETAIL, IN—bhẹdẹ bhẹd, khape khap, khode khod, oṛe oṛ.

DETAIN, TO—mormorao, rokao.

DETAINED, TO BE—diri.

DETECT, TO—ṭhekan, ṭhikạn.

DETECTIVE, A—jạsu.

DETERIORATE, TO—monda, ọbọsta; *(physically)* marca.

DETERIORATED—mọrọt sọrọt, ulạg.

DETERMINATION—muruk; *(with)* umạr sumar; *(of one)* sạṭ, saṭọp.

DETERMINE, TO—aṅgao, barmaṅgao, nirọpọn, nirukh, niṭ, ṭahrao, ṭarhao, ṭhanao.

DETERMINED, TO BE—ọktiạr, sạniạu, ṭarhao, ṭhukạu.

DETRACTINGLY—hẹj.

DETRIMENT—*(to cause)* huạṅ, hurwaṅ; *(without)* napae, tẹsnẹk.

DEVASTATE, TO—kadhaṛ, uchạd, ujaṛ, urạn.

DEVELOP, TO—curti, utrạu; *(fully)* benao; *(of an insect's wings)* siṅgaṛ.

DEVELOPED—*(well)* barhọn; *(fully)* nawatur; *(not fully)* khõṛẽ.

DEVIATE, TO—sere.

DEVICE—bandheć.

DEVIL, THE—sọetan.

DEVIL MEAT WITHOUT SAUCE, TO—khuṛkhuria.

DEVISE, TO—kạrkhana, pontha.

DEVOID OF—bẹgọr, bin, binạ.

DEVOTE, TO—*(attention, &c.)* bicar; *(for sacrifice)* dãṛẽ.

DEVOTEE, A—ạtit, utit.

DEVOUR, TO—cabhao, tạhuṛ; *(as tiger)* pohaǩ; *(as locusts)* murhuć; *(in large mouthfulls)* ṅahum daṛum.

DEW—sisir daǩ.

DEWAN, A—montri.

DEW-CLAW OF A DOG—saba.

DEWLAP OF A BULLOCK—lapoṫ.

DEXTEROUS—cọlọnti.

ḌHINKI—*(sound of)* dampol (2), ḍhạkuṛ, dhampuṛ (2); *(pestle of)* dhusra, musrạ.

DIABETES—bạhumut, ṭan korra.

DIAGNOSE, TO—barnao, gamao.

DIALECT—bhaka, boli, buli; *(difference in)* garmaǩ; *(Bihari)* gaowari buli.

DIAMOND—hirạ.

DIARRHOEA—cidir, cidrạ, lać oḍok, lacpac, pọdrọć; *(autumn)* pat jhaṛa; *(slight)* ḍhisọḍhọrọ, picọr pọcọr.

DIBBLE, A—khuci.

DICE—juạ.

DICTIONARY—mane kitạb, obidhạn.

DIDDLE, TO—phạki, phoṭao.

DIE, TO—añjẹṫ, beṇḍao, caba, dọ̃rsẹć, durũć, gọć, gọć gur, gujuǩ, gur, harna morna, japao, jatra, jiwi calaǩ, jobab, khaṅkhar, kharap, khatam, khọtọm, khotra, loksan, marao, mohṇḍa, sọć, ṭẹpṭẹpẹ; *(used by angry women)* lohom; *(to give oneself up to)* jiwi alae; *(about to)* gujuǩ dạkhil, mọrọn soman; *(as plants in winter)* ạsiṫ.

DIFFERENCE—pharak, taphat, tophad.

DIFFERENT—ạnu ạnu, ạegar, bẹlọk, judạ, pharak, pọrẹ, ulṭạu, unu unu.

DIFFICULT—ajhạṭ, ạṭ, bajhaṛ, bẹjhọṛ, bẹhọṛ, bhar, bhọjọkọṭọ, ciriṫ, gạhri, gohlao, had, hod, jạk, kackac, kạṭhin, mọh jọr, mọsọkọt, muskil; *(as a road)* akọṛ; *(very)* maha muskil.

DIFFICULTIES—*(to raise)* rọkṭọk; *(to get into)* bajha bajhi.

DIFFICULTY—aṛgaṛha, baj, gạr, gara jala, gạrkugạr, gạrsạr, garsusạr, ghạr, gọr, gorsor, halak, jala, jañjal, jọñjal, khal, kugạr, mahre, mọsọkọt, mostẹ, muhim, muskil, pẽc, pẽnc, phạṇḍo, phasad, phesad, siniṫ, sondhe, sọṅkọṭ; *(time of)* gạr ghuṛi ; (*in a*) ọsusạr ; (*to be in a*) ạsusạr, chaċ chuċ, sakṛa sạkṛi, tạkiċ ; (*to cause*) cipạ, kosola ; (*to put in a*) ecepẽce, ẽcpẽc ; (*with*) baṛia, ẹskọ̃s, jẹrẹ mẹtẹ, jhako jhoko, jhikạ jhake, jhikọ jhọkọ, kat mọhñjọrte, kẹrẹ mẹtẹ, kikọkọkọ, kọstọ mọstọ, riạt̓ (2).

DIFFIDENCE—sọrọm ; (*with*) kiḍạ kaḍe.

DIFFIDENT—kakṛa kokṛo, kokṛo, soromiạ.

DIFFUSE THROUGHOUT, TO—ada.

DIG, TO—la, po ; (*out*) taṛao ; (*quickly*) dhaṅgla dhạṅgli ; (*elbow into*) ucuṅ.

DIGEST, TO—hajam, pacao.

DIGGING IMPLEMENT, A—kuḍi, ṭamna.

DIGITS—kạṭup̓ ; (*supernumerary, of horse, &c.*) bọnkhuṛạ.

DIGNIFIED—mọstọram.

DILAPIDATED—bhaṅlabhaṭ, dhaṅgladhas, dhẹdrẹ, dhọdọr pọdọr, dhọrọṅ pọrọṅ, dhum dharkaṭ, dhum dharkaṛ, jhadọr padọr, jhaṅga jhuṭạ, jharọċ jhapọċ, jharoeak̓, khẹkre.

DILATORY—jahat johot, jape tope, jhahat jhohot, jhọhọt mọhọt, jọhọt mọhọt, pọhọṭ, rahan rohon, rahaṭ pahaṭ, rọhọṭ pọhọṭ.

DILIGENCE—dandagiri ; (*to use*) jạkir, jid.

DILIGENT, TO BE—chaṭ paṭ, kạsmi, kẹṛẹċ mẹṭẹċ, kurumuṭu, markaṭ.

DILIGENTLY—ajhaṭ, amar omoṛ, ambaṛ omboṛ, bhage sahĩtte, bisi muṭi, bisi suṭuċ, cure mare, dandra dạndri, dạṛae dhampae, dhamdhaser, dhạmkạu, dhampa dhuṛe, dhãora dhạ̃uṛi, huṛum suṛum, jida,id, rapeṭ, rikiṛ, rusuk̓ (2), sạhĩtte.

DILLY DALLY, TO—alae phulạe, lọhọr, lọhọr pọhọr.

DIM—dhund ; (*sighted*) perla (M), pirli (F), popolhet̓ ; (*twilight*) ṅaham ṅạhum ; (*outline*) bọ̃họ̃k.

DIMINISH, TO—bhạṇḍaṅ bhuṇḍuṅ, ghaṭao, ghaṭi.

DIMINUTIVE—galae, jeneċ, jorgel, junuċ, kạpṭiċ, puṭuryut̓, reme ṭele, ṭuryut̓.

DIMLY—apalhet̓, palak̓ polok̓.

DIN—gabaṛ guñj, gajaṛ, galgal, galgul, gọndọgọl, ragạu (?) ; (*to make a*) andka ạndki, andkao, galgalao, gul, gulmal, hạuarạua, hạu hạu, hạurạu, kalkalao.

DING-DONG OF A BELL—ḍhaṛaṅ (2).

DINGHI, A—lạukạ.

DINGLE IN THE EARS, TO—cao.

DIP INTO, TO—cạbuk̓, ṭuḍạk̓ ; (*water*) lo ; (*vessel in water*) bhuṛạk̓.

DIRECT—sojhe mojhe.

DIRECT, TO—calao ; (*one's course*) mohlao ; (*prayer, &c*) oḍe.

DIRECTION—jọk, kanas, kọnḍ, kọ̃r, mohṇḍa, muhạ̃r, nakha, pahṭa, pọhọṭ, sẹċ, sẹn, tọrọp, dara, pahaṭ ; (*of that*) ọntẹn ; (*in that*) enka enkate, ẹnte, ọntẹ ; (*in this*) neman. *Cf.* ALL, WHICH.

DIRT—gạdrum, mailạ ; (*in house or yard*) hur gundur.

DIRTY—arọ̃ṭ, bajrạhi, baṭur saṭur, bhạsuḍaṅ, bhosḍoṅ, bhosṇḍo, bhoso, boḍe, bọkọl (2), cacarhat̓, dạlsiń ṭạlsiń, dapat̓, ḍhiso ḍhoro, dhoro dhoso, dhosodhoro, garlaṅ gurluṅ, garluṅ, gesoṭiạ, gesṭaha (M), gesṭahi (F), ghesṭaha (M), ghesṭahi (F), gosoċ, hagal gạndiạ, hẹjlẹċ, hẹjlẹċ pẹjlẹċ, hẹndẹ riṭhạ, heńjlaṅ peńjlaṅ, hidrạ gisrạ, hiraṅ petaṅ, hiraṛ gareṛ, kacar, kackac, kacọr, kadrok̓, kạrạ̃iṭha, kạ̃ṭh, khariaṭ, kharkhaṇḍ, laṭae ghoṭae, lejraha (M),lejrạhi (F),leńjraha (M),leńjrạhi (F), lijrạha, losopoṇḍo, mailạ, maṅga murạ, margạiṭha, mudguċ, muiguċ, musrạ (M), musri (F), nakara, ńaṅgal ńiṭe, nekra, nekraha, niṭe, ọdọr thọpọr, pẹjlẹċ, riṭhạ, serẹ sibuċ, silmoċ, siluṅ piṭuṅ, thọkọbọkọ, thọkọr bọkọr, thọrọbọkọ, urum bhusum ; (*very*) ńaṅgal (2) ; (*to be*) aptar ; (*of water*) bọdọr (2), gạrsilom, khidor, sẹdẹ bẹdẹ, sẹdẹr bẹdẹr, sẹdgẹ bẹdgẹ ; (*face & hands*) sọdọr bọdọr, thọrọṅ thọpọṅ ; (*as used pot*) basiạ ; (*as ploughed field*) gạdrum sadrum ; (*as unswept room*) kadar kapar ; (*of large sores*) galak̓ (2) ; (*of plates &c.*) sạkhṛi ; (*of habits*) dhẹjraha (M), dhẹjrạhi (F), gesṭahi, gọsọċ, gosrẹ ; (*& ill-condi-*

tioned) jurpuć, morgoṭ, murguć, nekraha; (*& untidy*) dhum dharkar, hedge hesak; (*& ragged*) gadroć sadroć; (*& miry*) kacor.

DIRTY, TO—ghend guhend; (*of water*) sede bede; (*by stirring*) sedge bedge.

DISADVANTAGE, AT A—ghai, ghar, siniť.

DISAGREE, TO—bhina, didhi badhi, dirbi barhi, kadha kadhi, rete pete.

DISAGREEMENT—laelotha, lag.

DISAPPEAR, TO—adger, angen, banwas, bayaban, bhaondao, biltau, bonwaṭ, chan, danań; (*as the moon*) ńir.

DISAPPOINT, TO—arkhao, daga, harkhao, sithau, sithwao, thakdama.

DISAPPOINTED, TO BE—bebhorsa, hae nisas, hemeryǒk, huceć, jiwi lorao, marak morok, niras, sithal mithal.

DISAPPOINTMENT—dokha.

DISAPPROVE, TO—be-basut.

DISARRANGE, TO—ghend guhend, gaelo saelo, gańjao, phadgal, phidli.

DISARRANGED—dhimsi punsi, pasar, sadga bidir, sadgayak, saguć baguć, sarsadle, sigić bigić, sodgoro, solok bokok, ukaṭ pakaṭ; (*as clothes*) orlo-porlo.

DISASTER—uphad, uphar; (*to meet with*), hońjań, huńjań, jarkhar.

DISAVOW TO—dhatka, dodao.

DISC MADE OF TWIGS, A—jhora.

DISCERN, TO—bicbnau, pohom.

DISCHARGE, TO—(*of pus*) bele, sere; (*an obligation*) puranti; (*from a sore*) garań dak; (*urethral*) garmi, gurmi; (*from eyes*) sereć, suluć.

DISCIPLE, A—catia, cela, paiha.

DISCIPLINE, TO—catiau, curau, sadhao.

DISCOLOURED—(*burnt food*) dapaṭ; (*anything stored damp*) madhua.

DISCONCERTED, TO BE—usum suruć.

DISCONNECTEDLY—habak cubak.

DISCONSOLATE—anduk canduk, cirmok, jirmok, olon.

DISCONTENTED, TO BE—bhanga, birasali, kadra kadri, kadrao, kǎuca kǎuci, mon bhangak.

DISCORD—kando; (*sowing*) batar; (*a sower of*) bajhani; (*absence of*) napae; (*to create*) lundphond.

DISCORDANT—cereń.

DISCOUNT—baṭa, dasturi.

DISCREDITABLE—nico.

DISCRIMINATE, TO—cinhau.

DISCRIMINATION—(*with*) lahke (2), lake (2), race bacete, race pace; (*without*) alam galam.

DISCUSS, TO—binti, khańj, kheńjer meńjer, lapai, ridkhid, rond khond, ronkhon; (*angrily*) kaha kahi; (*for settlement*) phandao.

DISDAIN, TO—halka.

DISEASE—jańruli, karon, rog; (*any unknown*) berǒṭ duk; (*a*) patria; (*infantile*) khala; (*menstrual*) pordhol; (*of children*) gah; (*of the old*) ṭan pańgla; (*a horse*) kurkuri; (*of silk-worm*) ańgari; (*chronic, as*) jariau; (*without*) napae; (*to suffer from*) nason, ringor rongor, roga, rugi; (*to weaken from*) jarao. *Cf.* CATTLE, RENAL, SKIN.

DISENGAGAED, TO BE—aodhan, chuṭa, chuṭalia, phada, phalti.

DISENTANGLE, TO—phariau.

DISESTEEM, TO—apuc, halka.

DISFIGURE, TO—berup.

DISFIGURED—jirmok; (*by grief, &c.*) nirghin.

DISGRACE—apjos, opoman; (*to be conscious of*) lajao, lajao para.

DISGRACE, TO—badnam, banda, bebhar, bebhorom, behurmat, bemurwad, bibhorom, bodnam, bokobhond, mańgal, mũ goṭ, nakkaṭa.

DISGRACED—beabron; (*to feel*) lajbij.

DISGRACEFUL—dhedre.

DISGUISE—chin.

DISGUST—ghin, ghirna; (*to feel*) chi bań, chi tho, cihrau; (*exclm. of*) chi.

DISGUSTED—atruń.

DISGUSTING—aris, arǒṭ, bador saṭok, bejelgak, bekar, bhirik, dhirik, ghin, hirkha parkha.

DISH, A—*(round flat)* karahi; *(of pumpkin)* laụa; *(small earthen)* dạbri, rojha; *(of meat & flour)* ạriyạn.

DESHABILLE, IN—orloporlo.

DISHEARTENING—dayak (2).

DISHEVELLED—damcak (M), dạmci (F), dhạrpilak (F), lạṭae ghoṭ̣ae; *(& out of sorts)* dondorkole; *(of hair)* dalcaṅ (M), dulcuṅ (F), darkadale, darkal markal, rạguisạk.

DISHONEST—lubhiạ.

DISHONOUR, TO—bẹmanọt, nakkaṭa, ọpọman.

DISINCLINATION—ẹskõs.

DISINCLINED—ạtruṅ; *(to effort)* muṇḍ mọrọn.

DISINTEGRATE, TO—ghoṅrao, talgataụak.

DISINTERESTED—algel.

DISJOINTLEDY—ṭhạhri.

DISLIKE—bạdisṭi, bẹbạsut, sikiṛ.

DISLOCATED, TO BE—pasaṛ, pọṭọċ.

DISLOYAL—nimạk haram.

DISMANTLE, TO—otoṛ, upạr khapar.

DISMISS, TO—bạgi, bạtul, bidạ, borkas, bọrkhas, jobab; *(legally)* ḍhismis, ḍismis, kharij.

DISMISSAL—chuṭạu, chuṭi, jabab, jobab.

DISOBEDIENT—bat kạṭi, bẹsrọm, cechoṛ, chẹchọṛ, coaṛ, copa kuṭạ, corṭha (M), curṭhi (F), dharkaṭ, gạḍọr, gẹdut, leṭho, liloj, loṇḍhea, nimạk haram, papisṭạ, pạtit, raḍ (M), rạḍin (F).

DISOBEY, TO—bẹbatao, katha kaṭao, nọhẽ, rọd, sãrgọm.

DISOBLIGING—paṭea, paṭweċ.

DISORDER—kạrni, karọn, kạsur, rọg; *(having a)* roga, rugi; *(in)* ạkuṭ, ạulạ ạuli, dhum dharkaṛ, dhunsi punsi, gaḍbaḍ, ganjha gạnjhi, pasaṛ, sadga bidiṛ, sadgaeak, sadgayak, sạguċ bạguċ, sạluċ bạkuċ, sarsadle, sẹgẹċ pẹṭẹċ, sigiċ bigiċ, sọdgọrọ, solok bokok, tagatusạ, tasṛa tạsṛi, ulbul, ulṭạ palṭa, ulṭi pulṭi, ukạṭ pakạṭ.

DISORDER, TO—ạlmạlao, argoṅgaṛ, gaelo saelo, gạṛbaṛao, gasmạṇḍao, phadgal, ukạṭ pakaṭ, ulạṭ palaṭ.

DISORGANISED—ḍamaḍol.

DISPARAGE, TO—hẹj, nihạ̃t; *(a term)* cucạ, cudi.

DISPARITY—taphat, tophad.

DISPEL, TO—gucạu.

DISPENSARY, A—ran oṛak.

DISPERSE, TO—bhaṅgao, chiriạ chit, chiriạu, chirbitir, cirbitir, pasnao, phaṭ phuṭ, phuṭạ phuṭi, phuṭ phaṭ, tamtase, tarak birạk, uḍạr; *(as clouds)* piṛioṅ.

DISPERSED—chitir bitir, tamtase, taral basal.

DISPIRITED, TO BE—jiwi ọlọṅ, jiwi loṛao, nirghin.

DISPLACE, TO—dọlbadọl, ucạṛ.

DISPLACENCY—bẹbạsut.

DISPLAY—*(with grand)* biyol boyol; *(without)* bhorma.

DISPLEASE, TO—bẽocao.

DISPLEASED, TO BE—agar karaṛ, ạtruṅ, bẹbạsut, bẹṛaji, bẹrọs, besõk, gajha gạjhi, gajhao, kadra kạdri, kadrao, naraj, raṅgao, roṅkhoṅ, uruṅ (2).

DISPOSE OF, TO—ạkriṅ.

DISPOSITION—bhạsi, jọntọr, mejaj, rãwã, sọbhab, swabhab; *(favourable)* kusạl; *(of a like)* ẹk jọntọr.

DISPOSSESS, TO—bẹdọkhọl.

DISPROPORTION, TO—lalhar.

DISPROVE, TO—bhoṭ, darao.

DISPUTATIOUS—bakhạṛiạ, bakheṛa, kuṭeċ.

DISPUTE, A—bibạd, kạjiạ, lạuạ lagṭa, ragaṛ jhagaṛ, rego peto, ṭhạicạ; *(to settle)* mọndọt, neae, phaṇḍao, phariạu.

DISPUTE, TO—akhaṭ, apṭha ạpṭhi, apṭhao, aṭã ạ̃ṭi, bakhaṛ, eper heṇḍe, huputeċ, ipicak, kẹṅmẹṅ, kọckọcọ, laelokṭha, lakṭha, laolokṭa, lekṭha, leṭha, rapṭa rạpṭi, rẹgẹṅ tẹgẹṅ, rẹpẹċ, rẹṭẹ pẹṭẹ, reṭha riṭhi, rọpọṛ rọpọk, takraṛ, tẹgẹṅ, tekhraṛ, tekhra tikhri, tekra tikri, ṭhona ṭhuni, tokraṛ; *(about land &c)* lokṭạ; *(violently)* bakhoṛ, dhukạ dhuki, raga rạgi, raṅga rạṅgi.

DISQUIET, TO—ạris pạris.

DISQUIETED, TO BE—chaṭpaṭạo.

DISREGARD, TO—bebatao, neṅghao, nọhẽ, sãrgọm; *(an order)* adoli.

DISREPAIR, IN—bhaṅlabhaṭ, dhọdọr pọdọr; *(to fall)* bhọdọr, dhaṅgladhas, dhargoċ, jhadgoċ.

DISREPUTABLE—ḍiṅgạr, lucạ (M), luci (F); (*looking*) dhẹdrẹ.

DISRESPECT—bẹmanọt; (*to show*) bẹgadnao, bẹman, maṅgal, ṭhẹnṭa.

DISRESPECTFULLY—algạsi, hẹj.

DISSATISFIED, TO BE—gajhao, hẹmọñ gọrọñ, kadra kạdri, kadrao, khãs khũs, uruñ (2).

DISSEMBLE, TO—erka, pephṛa, phephṛa.

DISSENSION—laeloṭha, lag; (*sowing*) bataṛ, durạha.

DISSIPATE, TO—uḍạu.

DISSOLUTE—lamọṭ, lampọṭ, lampọṭia, umrạ (M), umri (F), umtạ (M), umti (F).

DISSOLVE, TO—lẹ, sabsab, sobsob.

DISTANCE—jọjọn, pharak, taphat, tophad; (*a great*) ạki laṅka, jọjọn; (*following at a*) jope thope; (*to what*) oka utạr; (*to go to a*) sah, sahaṛ; (*to keep at a*) dhurmạr, durmar; (*to put to a*) dur, pharak, sa, sahaṛ; (*between sun & horizon*) ber; (*between elbow & knuckle*) muṇḍrạ.

DISTANT—ạki laṅka, durạnta, laṅka, loṅka, pharak, sạṅgiñ, taphat, tophad; (*relative*) dak pera; (*place or country*) birạn.

DISTEND, TO—pasar, phulạu.

DISTENDED, TO BE—bhara, bharao, ṭilṭilạu; (*of stomach*) rẹbrẹbẹ.

DISTIL, TO—cuạ, cuwạ, sẹrẹ.

DISTILLED LIQUOR—mod.

DISTINCT—bitoṅ (2), pharak, sapha.

DISTINCTION—(*glory*) sabasi; (*difference*) taphat, tophad.

DISTINCTLY—ispoṣṭo, niṭhur, phaṛphaṛiạ, pọsṭọ, purchạ, purṭhạ, pusṭạu, rilạ mala, sposṭo, ṭahaka, tartạria, ṭohok; (*to see*) pohom; (*to speak*) pusṭạu.

DISTINGUISH, TO—bichnạu, pachan, pacnao, pọrọk.

DISTRACTED—calcalwa, jerbar, kalaṅ ḍolaṅ, kọlọṅ ḍụbọṅ, uduṛ dhupuṛ, ulmạl.

DISTRAIN, TO—jạbid, jabọd.

DISTRESS—alajhala, aphoti, bao, bẹḍọn, bhuk duk, bipod, dorloe, dusko, haora, harọn, jala, jhaṅjhaṭ, khal, kọsṭọ, mạr muhim, muhim, muskil, pajet, phaṇḍo, santap, saset, uphad; (*great*) maha jala, mahakal; (*causing*) harwạni; (*to be in*) kacal, kacar; (*to cause*) pajet, santao, saset, torlad, tin torlad; (*exclm. of*) jare (2).

DISTRESSED—aka baka, akham dukham, akul bạkul, ande sale, ạndhup, aṅkha ạṅkhi, ạṭ paṭ, awaṭapa, bẹhal, cãwãok, ḍamaḍol, halụa harọn, lọṭọpọṭọ, paṭpạṭao, torlo morlo, udạs; (*from hunger, &c.*) ahal (2); (*looking*) mọčmọč.

DISTRESSING—paṭpaṭ.

DISTRESSINGLY—kalkal, khalkhal.

DISTRIBUTE, TO—bilhạu, bilo, bimạs; (*food*) parsao.

DISTRICT, A—elaka, ilạka, jilạ, jirlạ, mahal; (*of another*) pordesi; (*subdivision of*) muhukumạ.

DISTURB, TO—ạris, ạlkạu, bhusku, dalmal, heola; (*water*) humṭạk.

DISTURBANCE—gabaṛ guñj, golmal, gọnḍọgol, gulmal, hulmạl, kaṇḍo; (*to make a*) andka ạndki, andoṛ, ansa, gul, hạurạu; (*without*) sạhbit, sasot.

DISTURBED, TO BE—biklạ bikli, bikol; (*in mind*) aṅkha ạṅkhi, cọncọl.

DISTURBING THE PEACE—pilhoe, uphạdiạ.

DISUNITED—hirạk (2).

DITCH, A—lala, nala, nạli, nạli gaḍa.

DIVER BIRD, THE—ḍubạ cẹrẹ.

DIVERGE FROM DIRECT COURSE, TO—aere.

DIVERSE—ạnu ạnu, emanteak, emanten.

DIVERT, TO—bulạu, lobhao, lubhạu.

DIVIDE, TO—bakhra, bãṭ, bẹbọsa, bhag, bhinạ, chirbiṭir, cirbiṭir, ciro, citil bitil, gạṇḍa guṭi, hạṭiñ, joro, khaṇḍao, kuṭrạ, laowao, lawao, misri bãṭ, sora; (*into pieces*) bhạgao, kiṭrạ; (*into small pieces*) khẹṇḍẹč bẹkrẹč, khẹñjẹr meñjẹr; (*a carcase*) buṇḍạ; (*justly*) solo sonjok; (*inheritance*) begar; (*remainder*) cala culạ.

DIVINATION—(*a method of*) hatkhaṛi, sunum paṛhao; (*to foretell by*) paetar; (*possessed with spirit of*) bharao.

DIVINE, TO—bhao, khaṛi; *(by oil & leaves)* sunum pañja.

DIVINER, A—mạtri, ojha, phaphu hoṛ.

DIVINITY, A—*(of cattle shed)* goroeya *(of ojhas)* saket.

DIVISION—gaṇḍ, haṭiń, hĩs, hisạ, khaṇḍ, khata, khũṭ, kitạ, thak, thok, torphan; *(of country)* jilạ, jirlạ; *(of village)* cok kaṭi; *(of village lands)* khicṛi bãṭ; *(as a stripe or spot)* koṭha.

DIVISIONS—dọla dọli; *(in)* khaṭa khaṭi, remeć (2); *(to make into)* khaṇḍao; *(having)* khaṇḍ (2).

DIVORCE, TO—bapag, sakam ọṛẹć; *(solatium on)* chaḍaoḍi.

DIVORCED—chuṭạ chuṭi; *(man)* doja kora; *(woman)* doja kuṛi, penda ḍopoć.

DIVULGE A SECRET, TO—buyuć mẹnte.

DIZZY, TO BE—cạkṛi ghum, caṭo, ḍagmagao, jinjin, thaṅgal thuṅgul, thuṅgul muṅgul, tirmirạu.

DO, TO—cedaḱ, ceka, cewaḱ, ịạ, kạmi, kạrkhana, karsaj, khaṭuạ, rikạ; *(sarcastic)* cothao, nehal, nepṛa; *(in chaff)* lọpọć; *(again)* dohṛa; *(away with)* mauṭạ; *(for)* baṅgam, luṭuć, ṭhasao; *(one out of)* phus caṭao; *(one's best)* ẹṭẹ cẹṭẹ; *(quickly)* tara taṛi, taṛi ghaṛi; *(inefficiently)* laṭku paṭku, lorbo sorbo; *(enough to bar others' claims)* ṭanḍao.

DO *(pleading)*—baṛe

DOCILE—soghoṛ, subod, sujat; *(to be)* rọhọm dọhọe.

DOCK, TO—tope.

DOCKED—baṇḍa (M), bạṇḍi (F), bạṇḍiạ (M).

DOCTOR—ḍagdọr, ḍakṭar; *(Indian)* bạida, kubrạj; *(charm)* ojha.

DOCUMENT—dalel, dạlil, dolel, kagoj, potor; *(written)* khat, khot; *(of lease)* ijạra paṭṭa; *(rolled up)* sọdra.

DODGE,—TO—cakla coklo, eran, ẹrẹr, khẹńcẹr, lạṭić; *(about)* gaṛpać guṛpuć, phẹnṭẹ phẹrẹ.

DOER, A—gạriạ.

DOG—kutru, seta, ạndiạ seta; *(wild)* ḍahal, koya, tan; *(hunting)* jarnaha seta; *(mad)* bhaloḱ s.; *(snarl of)* ghãi (2); *(call of, when chasing)* hakar (2). *Cf.* BARK.

DOG, CALL TO A—*(to come)* leh; *(to drive away)* haṛi; *(to set on)* hale bhạć, khuć (2), labhaeć lubhạić, lebhạć, lehaha, lele (2), lubhạị; *(to lie down)* bạsbạs.

DOGGED RESOLUTION—bhuc bhuci.

DOGMATIC—pephṛa, phephṛa.

DOLDRUMS, TO BE IN THE—ạruń pạruń, deona diuni, gampatao, usạć.

DOLL, A PERFORMING—ṭhap.

DOMESTICATE, TO—ạsul.

DOMESTICATED ANIMAL—ato posu.

DOMINEER, TO—jaejulum.

DONKEY—gadha.

DON'T—alo, hahã.

DOOLIE, A KIND OF—rạhi.

DOOR, A—kapaṭ, phiṛki, silpiń, siniń; *(double)* kaoaṛ; *(large)* phaṭọk; *(matting)* ṭaṭi; *(from court to street)* chaṭka; *(sliding bars of)* karhaṛ; *(bar of)* huṛkạ; *(leaf of)* kapaṭ, kopaṭ; *(frame)* cạukaṭha; *(socket of)* bhurni; *(keeper)* ardạli, darban, darwan.

DOOR, TO SHUT A—japaḱ, laḍaḱ, siń; *(partly)* laḍọṕ.

DORSAL SURFACE OF FOOT, THE—suptić.

DOSE, TO *(snooze)*—hũṛũ (2).

DOTAGE, TO BE IN—kalobalo, utuć tumbuć.

DOUBLE—dọbọr, dohṛa, duhṛi; *(cloth)* dohar; *(meaning)* bhenta; *(minded)* barmọn.

DOUBLE, TO—*(up)* hẹrwẹć, kućkuć, kukuć; *(without cutting)* tak.

DOUBT—digdhạ, dokha, toṅcọk; *(particle signifying)* cọ, cọń, na; *(without)* ayã, bẹsok, bisbiswạs, dharle, hạike bọṭẹ, hena, kaje, khulạsa, mạruk, nirdae, niscae, sake, soebot, tãhã; *(to be relieved from)* ikoṭ.

DOUBT, TO—dhoka, dhokha, digaḱ, dighi, digić, olocolo, sọndhọ.

DOUBTFUL—dhowa bhowa, dhuwạ bhuạ, digaḱ, kajak, kẹcẹć (2).

DOUBTFULLY—dandha mandha, hucku cukur.

DOUGH—(*to roll*) belna ; (*like*) jeber (2).

DOVE—(*brown*) saṇḍi karkar potam, ṭhekro p., ṭhikri p. ; (*Ring*) tilại p.

DOVECOT, A—ṭaṅgi, ṭaoge.

DOWDY—darań duruń, garsa gale.

DOWN—(*below*) tạri ; (*feathers*) lopotiań il ; (*to fall*) bindạr ; (*to put*) dhurmạr.

DOWNHEARTED—cirmok̇, heholok̇, hẹmẹṛyok̇ ; (*to look*) jiput̆, orloporlo.

DOWNY—lopioń.

DOWRY OF A COW—jọm daka.

DOZEN, BY THE—barọ bakhan.

DRAG, A—badha ; (*net*) ọr jal.

DRAG, TO—ghac ghacao, ghẹcẹ (2), gọhọr, họdọr (2), ṭanao ; (*into*) leṭha, lapṭao ; (*along ground*) dhadrao, gasrao, gharao, ghasghasao ; (*the feet*) cirhoṫ cọrhọṫ, cọrhọṫ, lapaṭ lupuṭ.

DRAGGING & CARRYNG—ore ṭikur.

DRAGGLED, TO BECOME—garsa gale.

DRAGOON, TO—ạruk̇ dhạruk̇, cilcilạu, dhamkhum, dhara dhurạ, dharamara, durduri, habka dubkạ, hacpacao, hapka dupkạ, humdhum, huṛum duṛum, taltalao, toltolao, tultulạu.

DRAIN, A—lala, nạli gaḍa ; (*surface*) pogaṛ ; (*large*) cumas, nahar ; (*pipe*) magra, mogra, moṅgra ; (*small*) pãoci ; (*to*) reńjeṫ.

DRAUGHT—(*air*) họyọń ; (*cattle*) dhur.

DRAW, TO—(*attract*) jhakao, jhakrao ; (*pull*) ọr ; (*figures, &c*) ọl ; (*back*) pạc ; (*out*) ṭanao ; (*through*) ọr taṗ ; (*towards*) gạri, hạr ; (*from sheath*) bọċ ; (*along ground*) gọhọr ; (*blood by pricking*) pạṭi ; (*oneself together from cold*) duḍurguċ ; (*on*) họbọ (2) ; (*water*) lo ; (*an arrow to the head*) hạmbuċ. *Cf.* LEGS.

DRAWN, TO BE—ṭanao ; (*together*) murculu, rọmọọlọk̇ ; (*up*) beṭiạr.

DREAD, TO—bọr, bọṭọr, dhupuċ, dhupuc, hickạu.

DREADFUL—bhọyọn.

DREAM, A—kukmu ; (*representation seen in*) samek.

DREARY—susạń.

DREGS—lenda, res ; (*of disease*) kaser.

DRENCHED—chọbchọb, cọbcọb, jabar jubur, jebe jobe, jẹhẹ jọbẹ, jhabar jhubar, jhọrọjhọċ, jọbjọb, jọbọ jọbọ, jọr bọdeak̇.

DRESS—saj ; (*F.*) khaṇḍa, khaṇḍi, saṛi ; (*of girl*) putli ; (*very short*) dapań (2) ; (*a striped*) doal.

DRESS, TO—họrọk̇, bande (F.) ; (*up*) coṭok ; (*the hair*) cerkoṫ, suṫ ; (*by paring*) lak̇, murchạu.

DRESSED—(*well*) cikon cokon ; (*carelessly*) ojra.

DRESSER IN A HOSPITAL, A—susạria.

DRIBBLING—ciroċ cọrọċ.

DRIED UP—ḍọḍọ (M), ḍhạdri (F), surạs ; (*of soil*) khangọṭ.

DRILL—gnẹċ, pareṭ gnẹċ ; (*cloth*) jhin kieriė, jin.

DRINK, TO—họṅgọr, jẹmbẹṫ, ńũ ; (*cause to*) ạńu ; (*to excess*) họṅgọr ; (*to satiety*) ńũ ṭuilạ ; (*by putting mouth to water*) jẹmbẹṫ ; (*an acid or sour*) kạńji.

DRINKING VESSEL, A BRASS—gilạs ; (*large*) jam bạṭi.

DRIP—(*to*) liṅgi, phec, suḍsuḍạu, suḍusuḍu, ṭọpọk̇ ; (*with a*) suṭuk̇ marte.

DRIPPING—ciroċ cọrọċ, jabar jubur, jebe jobe, jẹhẹ jọbẹ, jhabar jhubar, jhọrọjhọċ, jọċ jọċ, ṭipok̇ ṭọpọk̇ ; (*sound of*) cọrọċ (2), coro (2), cuḍu (2), jhoṛo (2), saṭak̇ suṭuk̇, suḍur (2), ṭorok̇ (2).

DRIVE, TO—caḷao, lạga, taltalao, toltolao, tultulạu, turburạu ; (*off*) dur ; (*out*) lurgạ ; (*in*) helao ; (*home*) ohjao ; (*away*) dhurmạr, durmạr, khadkhadao, khed, khidkhidạu, phadgal ; (*fish in pool*) umjhạu ; (*game*) chuḍạ, dak jhạli, jhọra ; (*cattle*) bahkao ; (*into a heap*) laga jhạuạ ; (*in with hammer*) kuṭạm ; (*to head, as nail*) janjanao ; (*a number of children*) ṭikọr ṭọkọr.

DRIVEN—(*at work*) jhak (2) ; (*back*) hạṭkao ; (*by wind*) jhaṭạs.

DRIVER—(*of a ca t*) sagaṛiạ ; (*elephant*) mahut.

DRIZZLE, A—paḍar poḍor, ribiċ, rubuċ ; (*continuous*) jhipir (2) jhupur (2).

DRIZZLE, TO—burui (2), jhuṭuċ (2), jipir (2), phuḷi, poḍor (2), porce, rabaċ ribiċ, sipir (2).

DROMEDARY, A—ũṭ.

DRONE, TO (*as beetles*)—bhanbhan.

DROOP, TO—labṛaṅ, leṛwak̕, leweṭ, liweṭ.

DROOPING—jhaṛguak̕, jhaṛpa; (*branches*) jhapṛu; (*horns*) laṛa (M), laṛi (F).

DROP, A—bund, ṭhop̕, ṭipak̕, ṭop.

DROP, TO—joro, lorok̕ torok̕, phec, ṭop, ṭopok̕; (*as rain*) ṭipak̕.

DROPPING, SOUND OF—coroc̕ (2), saṭak̕ suṭuk̕.

DROPPINGS, A GOAT'S—bhelṭundi, ladauri.

DROPS, IN—ṭipok̕ ṭopok̕.

DROPSY—udri rog; (*slight*) ḍhopsa (M), ḍhupsi (F); (*swollen by*) bharao, dama domo.

DROSS—ic̕.

DROVE OF COWS, A LARGE—gai gadel.

DROWNED, TO BE—aṭu goc̕, unum goc̕.

DROWSINESS—nidra.

DROWSY—asam usum, ḍudṛum, jhap (2), umdhi; (*looking*) dholomolo.

DRUG—(*a*) murgan, ran; (*to*) bul.

DRUM, A—ḍhak, ḍhol, ḍhulki, ḍumdhukak̕, kirtan tumdak̕, tumdak̕; (*kettle*) ḍhak, ṭamak; (*large*) damana, rahaṛ; (*small*) ḍedger, khanjri, tabla, tumbri; (*lacing of*) maoṛa; (*stick*) ṭamak ḍanḍom; (*music*) bajna, (*to brace*) caṛhao; (*to beat*) bajna, ru.

DRUM, SOUND OF A—capoṭ (2), huḍuk (2), ḍhoḍo (2), gubuḍ (2), kurum (2), jhagaṛ (2); (*tamak*) kuruḍubu; (*ḍhak*) ḍeḍeṅ, ḍheḍheṅ, reḍeṅ; (*dedger*) reberr (2); (*cracked*) dhoḍor (2); (*with-hole*) ḍhop̕ (2); (*with varnish worn*) dhoroṭ dhopoṭ; (*rolling*) taraṅ; (*left-hand stroke*) capoṭ (2). *Cf.* RAT-TAT.

DRUMMER, A—bajni, bajondar, mandaṛi, mandṛia; (*adept*) ṭamkia; (*caste*) turi.

DRUNK, TO BE—bhek̕ bhok̕, bul, matal, matla, matua.

DRUNKARD, A—piak̕.

DRY—caṭcaṭ, hiṅjiṭ, jhunjhun, jhunjhuni, joko, kaṛcup̕, karkaṛ, nisoṭ, podor, raḍhua, roroc̕, rukaṛ, sitha, sukhle, than ṭhania, ṭhonko; (*absolutely*) jhunjhun; (*over*) siṭkoc̕; (*not quite*) ṭabuc̕; (*soil*) kuṭhaṛ; (*mouth*) laṭak̕ paṭak̕; (*cough*) ṭhai (2); (*weather*) dharun; (*land*) ṭondaṅ.

DRY, TO—goso, haweṭ, lohor, rohor, sakiṭ; (*as by towel*) joṭ haweṭ; (*hard*) kaṛkarao; (*before ripening*) moroc̕; (*up*) aṅjeṭ, horao, haweṭ, heṅjeṭ, rohor hinjidok̕, sokhao, sukau; (*to spread out to*) tase; (*be very*) kharṅgao, siṭkoc̕, ṭaṭao.

DUAL, SIGN OF THE—kin.

DUB, A—ḍabra.

DUBIOUS—kecet̕ (2).

DUCK, A—gede.

DUCTILE—cemoṛ.

DUDGEON, TO BE IN HIGH—kãuca kãuci.

DUE—(*to be*) lag; (*paying what is*) khara khari; (*to fail to pay*) khilap.

DUES—damkam, lagna; (*to collect*) sidi, tahsil; (*to demand*) oghe.

DUG (*teat*)—cuṅci.

DUG-OUT, A—ḍhoṅga.

DULL—(*of mind*) behoḍ, dimak, galta golaṭ, godhra, gosre, jiṛmok̕, torko morlo; (*of hearing*) bahra; (*cloudy*) ḍonḍrok̕; (*feeling in head*) thuṅgul muṅgul; (*sound*) thugul, thuluk̕.

DULL-WITTED—alaṭ bakaṭ, albakaha, albasua, bandha (M), bandhi (F), bhõḍa, bhonḍa, galak̕ salak̕, galaṭ solaṭ, joḍo, salaṭ, thotho.

DUMB—abola, gaṅguṅ, goṅga, guṅga (M), guṅgi (F).

DUMP, TO—kacao.

DUMPING WET CLOTHES, SOUND OF—phecek (2).

DUMPS, TO BE IN THE—aruṅ paruṅ, uruṅ (2), usaṭ.

DUMPY—agar ogor, bhuṭra, buṭra (M), buṭri (F), khedra, pedle (M), pidli (F), thothma (M), thuthmi (F); (*pice*) golokpuri poesa.

DUN, TO—dhara, dhara dhura, ghigya, hakup̕ cakup̕, khodao.

DUNCE, A—akorma, alua, bhoto.

DUNG—ic̕, sahar; (*cow*) guric̕; (*dry cow*) gõeṭha; (*hill, a*) mande.

DUPE, TO—andic̕, ṭhar.

DUPLICITY, WITHOUT—sojha, sojhe.

DUSK—ṅaham ṅaḥum.

DUST—dhuṛi, ḍigir, gaṛda ; *(fine)* lopoč ; *(to)* phaṭkao ; *(covered with)* laploṇḍe, leṭa, orloporlo ; *(in the)* ọrtọgọrẽ ; *(to make into)* ḍiglạu, lọṭọr, podor ; *(to fly off as* podoe ; *(to roll in)* gholṭa ; *(to raise)* lọṭọk̇, uḍiạu ; *(to transfer to cloth)* ọn, enelngol ; *(to throw in the eyes)* ọr tẹpẹč ; *(like)* guḍ guḍạu.

DUSTY—bhoso, bhoṭa, leṭa, leṭao, losopoṇḍo, musrạ (M), musri (F), orloporlo, urum bhusum.

DUTY—*(an omission of)* bhisor, bhosor ; *(not attending to)* cerka bherka.

DWARF, A—bãoṛa (M), bãuṛi (F), bọrọč dọdọč, ghuṭlạ (M), ghuṭli (F), gudra (M), gudri (F), gũṭhlạ (M), guṭhli (F), ṭhikri (F), ṭhuṛkạ (M), ṭhuṛki (F) ; *(in scolding)* khemṭok ; *(small as)* gaḍar guḍur.

DWARFISH—bhuṭkạ (M), bhuṭki (F), buṭrạ (F), duč, gidri (F), jẹrẹ bẹḍhẹ, koṭlo (M), kuṭli (F), pedgo (M), pedle (M), piḍgi (F), piḍli (F), rega, regaṭhiạ, ṭemel, ṭhẽṛbok̇ (F), ṭhõṛbok̇ (M).

DWELL, TO—bẹrẹl, tham gạḍi.

DWELLER, A—nibasi.

DWELLING PLACE, A— bas, bẹrẹl ṭhão, bọskọt, oṛak̇.

DYE, TO—gabao, raṅ, rọṅ ; *(red or scarlet)* ṅeč.

DYED—raṅga.

DYEING, TO PREPARE THREAD FOR—garcha.

DYING—mora muri ; *(time of)* harna morna hilok̇, gujuk̇ jokhač.

DYING WORLD, THE—mọrọt bhũi.

DYSENTERY—mãyãm oḍokok̇, poṇḍ sul, risạ, sul ; *(a kind of)* kuthạ duk ; *(chronic)* amsam, garhạni, gorhoni ; *(bloody)* arak̇ sul.

DYSPEPSIA—amọl.

E

EACH—aṅge (2), koḍa ke koḍa, ke, mič, parti, pichạ, piche, proti ; *(man)* họrọ (2), mạnsi, mimič họr ; *(for himself)* jạni jạti, joṇa joti ; *(in succession)* họr proti ; *(his own)* aṅga ạṅgi ; *(ordering, the other)* hẽsã hĩsi.

EAGER, TO BE—cahak mahak, dhipạu, kẹre, larlarao, tahtahao, ṭhak (2), ṭhanṭhanao, thartharao, thurthurạu.

EAGERLY—ekẹp sekẹp, mẹrẹl, rumbuč cumbuč.

EAGERNESS—rọgọr.

EAGLE—*(a species of)* buru pajhaṛ ; *(Harrier)* kuhi besra.

EAR, THE—lutur ; *(large-lobed)* loṛpe ; *(face in front of)* kan jạṛi, luṭkuṛi ; *(hollow below)* kan hupạ, lutur hupạ ; *(ornament)* jhim jhimi, jhiṅgur, jhurjhuri, kanphul, nara ; *(ring)* cẹprẹ, makoṛi, pagra ; *(of dhan)* sis ; *(of grain)* gẹlẹ ; *(formed within sheath)* gabhãṇḍ ; *(to put oil in)* arjo.

EAR-SPLITTING—tiṅgič.

EARLY—ãrgat ; *(in morning)* hadam hudum.

EARN, TO—arjao, birjạu, kamao, rojgar ; *(easily)* jọm suk.

EARNER, AN—ọrjọniạ, rojgariạ.

EARNEST—*(money)* baena ; *(to take in)* sạri ; *(not in)* ẹrẹ ẹrẹte.

EARNESTLY—dirạ muṇḍte, jạri jạnti, jãore (2), kanekane ; *(to charge)* kạjiãu.

EARNINGS—kamại, khaṭạli.

EARS—*(broad)* ḍhalka lutur ; *(hanging)* lạprạ (M), lạpri (F) ; *(small)* piṭu ; *(with all your)* kanekane ; *(to cock)* birlạṅ, bič ; *(to crop)* bucạ (M), buci (F).

EARTH—has, hasa ; *(the)* dhạrti, ọt, pirthimi, pirthi ; *(fuller's)* sạji hasa ; *(for dyeing)* gamcha hasa ; *(for washing hair)* nakra hasa, narkan hasa ; *(a friable)* ṭirom hasa ; *(well manured)* kuṇḍạ maṭiạ ; *(a clod of)* ḍhelak ; *(in bowels of)* patal ; *(a tremor of)* bhui cạl ; *(a disc to carry)* jhoṛa ; *(to raise up)* bhurkạk̇.

EARTHENWARE—kuṅkạl bhaṛan ; *(piece of)* bursi, khapra, ọhọč. *Cf.* CUP, DISH, POT, VESSEL.

EARTHQUAKE—bhucampa, bhui cạl, bhũi ḍol, bhumcampa, dhạrti dalkaok, ọt laṛaok.

EARTHWORK, A MEASURE OF—cạukạ.

EARTHWORM, THE—lẹṇḍẹt; (*a traditional*) gicho rạni.

EARWAX—ẽṛgot.

EARWIG, AN—kankaṭra, kankoṭra.

EASE—aosan, suk; (*used to*) sukhi, sukhwạr, sukwạr; (*at*) khạtir, sạhbit, sukraj; (*with*) ṭhas marte; (*to*) bahalao, khalsa.

EASEMENT—salsat.

EASILY—chaṭ, haṭọkaete, hoṭọkkaete, ruyu (2), ṭahaka, ṭhas marte; (*broken*) ṭhasaha; (*wakened*) torkal. *Cf.* ANGERED, OFFENDED.

EAST, THE—ber rakap̣ sẹc̣, purạb, purub, puruạ; (*of the*) purbi.

EASY—alga, aṛẹc̣ gaṛẹc̣, sahaj, sohij, sọhọj; (*circumstances*) cạlti, culti, suk; (*minded*) khạtiran.

EAT, TO—bukạ lọlọ, cạblạu, caṭao, hap̣, huạk, jọm, leṛ, leṛgo, lilạm, maceṛ, mạruk, mocṛao; (*gradually*) jọm jaora; (*over*) abgun, sạruạ, sẹṛẹ gore; (*greedily*) ạhum tạhum, habadiạ, kudhạ, lẹpẹkọpẹ, ṅạhum dạrum, sọgọr, sograo, sogra sugri; (*in big mouthfulls*) tạgum, tạhuṛ; (*quickly*) lembe tumbe, masra mạsri; (*with gusto*) tọkọp̣; (*up*) cạrpaṭ, mạcuk, mạcur, mecoṛ, jọm pạsir, mạr pasir; (*one up*) jọm rẹṅgẹc̣; (*a little*) hap̣; (*pretend to*) hap̣ iṅgul; (*seeking something*) jaṭal koṭal; (*with paurạ*) cakhna; (*noisily*) takap̣ (2); (*one who can do nothing but*) jọmer aṅgra, jọm poḍa.

EATABLES, GIVEN TO STEALING—locra (M), lucri (F).

EATEN AWAY—gaṇḍrao; (*as by leprosy*) jẹṛẹt.

EATER, A—khạuạ, khạwạiạ.

EATING—(*always*) melaṅ cẹṭaṅ, mẹlọt cẹṭọt; (*anything*) achọk, olaṅ mocaṅ; (*desire of*) rọc; (*each other*) khạuạ khạwi; (*noise of*) chọkchọk, takap̣ (2).

EAVES—sate; (*at back*) kuḍạm s.; (*at ends*) mutul s.

EAVESDROP, TO—atẹn, kandheṛ.

EBB AND FLOW—gheola.

EBONY—terel mańj; (*tree*) terel; (*firewood*) ceṭe sahan; (*bark*) ceṭetet.

ECHO, AN—guṅgwạok.

ECLIPSE, AN—(*of sun or moon*) gahana, gahna.

ECONOMISE, TO—rạkhi jogao, ramo (2), rukhi jogao.

ECZEMA—bisphoṛ, uru ghao.

EDGE—aṛe, dhar, dhara dhạri, dhạri, ẹkdhar, kạni, mache, sa, sah, sindir, sir, sirạ; (*breadthwise*) aṅcar; (*lengthwise*) mache; (*at the*) dhar dhur, ẹk sirtạl; (*along the*) mache (2), paṭhe; (*to lose*) bhoṭko; (*to turn back*) kõṛẽ; (*to put on*) molaṭ, silạu.

EDIBLE—(*leaves*) aṛak; (*jungle products*) jae jupạtiṅ.

EDUCATE, TO—rigṛạu, sikhnạu.

EDUCATED—pạḍhuạ, pạṛhuạ; (*well*) kagjia.

EEL, AN—bạmbi; (*spec. of*) kuclạ, lituṛ hako.

EFFECT—dhọmọs; (*to have—as medicine*) sunạn.

EFFECT, TO—dhunạu; (*a compromise*) rọp dhọp, ropha.

EFFECTED—sid.

EFFECTIVE—usrạu; (*to be*) batao.

EFFECTIVELY—bes ọkọc̣te, bhage sạhĩtte, sãohã.

EFFETS—mal, maljal.

EFFICIENT—cọlọnti, gạkhuṛ, harap̣, harrap̣, khạrkạhi, laker, paka, pakṭa, paṭioṛ; (*to become*) liṇḍạr, liṇḍor.

EFFICIENTLY—bes ọkọc̣te, khub leka, majbut, mańjgut.

EFFLUVIUM—sọ.

EFFORT—butel, butlạk; (*to make*) jạhĩt, jid, upại; (*without apparent*) labhaṅ lubhuṅ, lubuṅ (2).

EGG, AN—bele; (*addled*) ḍhokok b.; (*to incubate*) ghorao, ghurni; (*to lay*) bele; (*plant*) beṅgaṛ; (*yolk*) botke; (*film under shell*) ganthar; (*of green-fly*) asãe.

EGG ON, TO—bargao, cạṛhiạu, cạṛiạu, liliạu, udgạu.

EGGS—(*sitting on*) bubrum, burum ; (*to hatch*) busaḱ.

EGOTISTICAL— dhomokię.

EGRESS, PLACE OF—onodoṅ ; (*& ingress*) duar.

EIGHT—iral ; (*anna piece*) adhuli.

EIGHTEEN—gel iral.

EIGHTY—iral gel.

EITHER—ba ; (...*or*) hoe...hoe, hoeto... hoeto.

EJECT, TO—bahar, baher, bahre ; (*from mouth*) budur, phur, ula ; (*from basket*) up.

ELABORATE—dhob.

ELAPSE, TO (*as time*)—bitau.

ELASTIC—taogar ; (*non-*) rabać rubuć.

ELATED, TO BE—tilki bilki, tiṅgi.

ELBOW, THE—bãhĩ, moka ; (*joint*) moka ghaṭi ; (*bone*) ṭhõrẽ ; (*to tip of middle finger*) moka ; (*to nudge with*) ucuṅ, ṭhelepaese.

ELDER—jheṭ ; (*an*) morubi, mukhia, murubi, purkha. *Cf.* BROTHER, SISTER.

ELDEST—jheṭ, maraṅić.

ELEGANT—reṅgleć, ṭhonok.

ELEMENTS—samagiri ; (*in marriages, &c.*) sarajan.

ELEPHANT, AN—hathi ; (*trunk*) sunḍ ; (*tusk*) hathi sonḍa ; (*goad*) aṅkus ; (*cushion*) gadi ; (*driver*) mahut ; (*pad*) sar ; (*call to drive*) cai (2).

ELEPHANTIASIS—goda.

ELEVEN—garo, gel miť.

ELFIN LOCKS, WITH—dhandri.

ELIDE, TO—lop.

ELONGATE, TO—tić.

ELOPE, TO—aṅgir, sipi.

ELSE—baṅkhan.

ELUDE, TO—kheṅcer.

EMACIATED—cuikup, dẽrẽć dẽpẽć, dhẽrẽpeṭe, dhõya dhape, hadgẽra, hahalpać, haṭya, jhaṅjaṭi, jirluṅ, kabaṅ (2), khad, khadea, khadra (M), khadri (F), khikrĩ (F), kiboṅ koboṅ, koboṅ (2), laṭlaha, leṭeć peṭeć, rẽhẽ, riboṅ koboṅ, roṅjo, roroć, royoť, ruhuṅ rupuṅ, ṭhaṭra (M), ṭhaṭri (F), ṭhoekoḱ ; (*of children*) jiṅjri (F), ṅuruć ; (*& weak*) daibuṅ, hidaṅ ṭhapaṅ, hinḍaṅ ṭhapaṅ, jhõnẽa, jhõrẽ, leraṅ peṭaṅ, liṭir piṭir, mora, mora muri, mora jora, mornaha, rapaṅ rupuṅ ; (*& big-bellied*) dubea ; (*from indigestion*) rohor naṅjom ; (*to become*) dublau, jhulau, kakra jambe, ooḱ, rohdoć, rohor, sukau.

EMANATION—ahla.

EMBANKMENT, AN— band, pinḍha ; (*to raise an old*) tulau ; (*a cross*) ganḍ.

EMBARGO ON, TO LAY AN—dob, jabid, jakao, jubod, rakha, rokao.

EMBARK, TO—deć.

EMBARRASMENT—jaṅjal, joṅjal, somsom.

EMBEDDED FIRMLY, TO BE—jankao.

EMBELLISH, TO—coṭok, saj, torahẽć.

EMBERS—aṅgra ; (*to put in a vessel*) eć.

EMBRACE, TO—harup, hober ; (*the neck*) koke.

EMERGE, TO (*from cocoon*)—kaṭao.

EMERGENCY—gar ghuri, gar kugar, garsar, garsusar, ghaṭal saṅj, gorsor, somsom, susar.

EMETIC, AN—phaḱṭkaraḱ.

EMIT, TO—khalas.

EMPEROR, AN—maharaj.

EMPHATIC PARTICLE, AN—co, coṅ, do, do, ge, teť, tho, thor, thoya, to ; (*negative*) ẽheḱ, jug, oho.

EMPLOY, TO—acu, larcar, lorcor.

EMPLOYED, FULLY—oloṅ (2).

EMPLOYER, AN—aḱcu hor, gola, kirsand, kisãr, munib.

EMPLOYMENT—kami.

EMPRESS, AN—maharani.

EMPTY—ajauri, oken, hiṅjiť, khali, nicol, nikhar, nisun, otaṅ polaṅ, phuki, sĩrĩć soboť, sirik taham, sudhe, sun, suna, sunsan ; (*to become*) heṅjeť ; (*to sound*) raṅruṅ ; (*house*) mela oraḱ ; (*of liquid, to*) sokhao ; (*handed*) bhuṭuṅ (2), lirok lorok, lorkaeni, lorok (2), sukhle.

EMULATE, TO—badabadi.

ENACTMENT, AN—an.

ENCAMP, TO—daba mara, deraḱ.

ENCAMPMENT, AN— chauni.

ENCIENTE—*Cf.* PREGNANT.

ENCHANTMENT—jạdu, jiṇṭhi pạthri, lạgu.

ENCIRCLE, TO—beṛhae, gherao; (*with arms*) hạṛup̌, kọkọ.

ENCOURAGE, TO—bãh, bãhńok̓, buk, sahas; (*particle*) sẹ.

ENCOURAGEMENT—bud bhorsa, ḍhaṛọs; (*exclm. of*) bah, hạllạ.

ENCROACH UPON, TO—capao.

ENCUMBER, TO—ạsiạṛ.

ENCUMBERED, TO BE—abjoṛ.

END, THE—ạkhir, munucạt̓, mucạt̓, muṇḍạ, sạmuń, sẹs, sẹs kal; (*about*) sesa sisi; (*in*) atar, dapoṛ, napoṛ, sesantire; (*to bring to*) akasok̓, khatam, marao, sẹs, sesanti, sesao; (*to come to*) hoe; (*to make*) bańgám; (*to set on*) dọṛọm; (*without*) barọ bakhan.

END, TO—kecak̓, khatam, khọṭọm, mucạt̓, pạṭ, sumạr.

ENDEARMENT, A TERM OF—baba, bacha, dhạni, dhona, hirạ, khere, kuĩṇḍi miru, mạiri, mạku.

ENDEAVOUR, TO—phikir, sondhe; (*to*) cesṭa, jid, kuṛpaṛ, lomosoro, rikạ, ṭesṭa, upại, utjog.

ENDURANCE, BEYOND—asambheṛ, sahao khon bahre.

ENDURE, TO—bhọg, bhuńjạu, sạbur, sahao.

ENDURING—sạburi, sobori.

ENEMY—bạiri, benea, dusman, kal, mudoe, sạtru.

ENERGETIC—hat chuṭ, hath chuṭi, jiddhi, kạsmi, khacaṛ, khackhaciạ, khara, kharań khacań, khạrkhạṛi, tạji, taṛbaṛiạ, toṛ, tuṛbuṛiạ, uṛum suṛum.

ENERGISE, TO—muruk, tatao, uskur.

ENERGY—aṭha saṭha, muruk, rag, tạpis.

ENFEEBLED, TO BE—hiwel hawal, jakan jukun, kokhọdo, sõrmbot̓, ṭapać ṭupuć, tirmirạu.

ENGAGE, TO—(*in*) dhorao, dhurạu, gotao, nandhao, ṭhekao; (*appoint*) ạcu, bahal, bharti, nạcu; (*promise*) karaṛ; (*sarcastic*) huṛ.

ENGAGED IN, TO BE—khạṭuạ.

ENGLAND—bilạt.

ENGLISH—bilạti; (*language*) añgrạji, raj bhasa; (*people*) añgrej.

ENGRAFT, TO—kọlọm mit̓.

ENGRAVE, TO—gọṛhọn.

ENGROSSED IN, TO BE—ayak̓ oyok̓, raktao, rosao.

ENGULF, TO—ḍubạ, ḍubạu.

ENJOY, TO—bhọg, bhuńjạu; (*oneself*) hẹsẹć sẹkrẹć, sẹkrẹć, sulạń; (*food*) tarkao.

ENJOYMENT—hub.

ENLARGE, TO—badhao, cakrao.

ENLARGED GLAND—gaṇḍ.

ENLIST, TO— bharti.

ENMITY—adwati, badabạdi, badarot, bạdi, bạdisṭi, bạiri, bibạd, ḍah, kadha kạdhi, kun; (*to be at*) ạḍa ạdi, badọt, bẹnẹ, bikhạṛ, biroṭ, era iri, irạ iri, lage lorẽ, rerad.

ENORMOUS—aṛañga, ased marań; (*of tigers*) ãṛdu, atha.

ENOUGH— (*to have*) alao, ale, elao; (*not*) ọkulạn.

ENQUIRE INTO, TO—bhańj, carcao, dạriạp̌, jigạs, kedrao, khuṛiạu, kuli, puche, siṛi, soṭik, suṭik, sutrạu, tadarat, tagada, tạjbij, tạpus, todarot, tọjbij, tondehi, tondori; (*privately*) suikạr; (*in detail*) rukhi pańja; (*at an oracle*) rumjhum; (*for someone lost*) sug; (*definitely*) kuli puṛcho.

ENQUIRY—surạg; (*one who makes private*) suikạriạ; (*to pursue an*) pacha, pecha, tolas.

ENRAGED, TO BE—kuṛkuṛ, kuṛkuṛạu, tamao.

ENROLLED, TO BE—bhạrti.

ENSNARE, TO—bajhao, lajbajhi, phand, phạsi.

ENTANGLE, TO—ạrjhạu, ạujhaṛ, baj, bajhao, bạjhuạ, lobdhao.

ENTANGLED, TO BE—ajbajhao, bajha bạjhi, ḍhań, ẹprẹ, lajbajhi, laskao, phạsi.

ENTANGLEMENT—aṛgaṛha.

ENTER, TO—bọl, bọlọ, cahaṭao, dạkhil, huṛet̓, sandhaoṛe, sodṛe; (*as air*) pogoe; (*carriage &c.*) dẹć; (*humbly*) ghusiạu; (*without invitation*) sodre; (*for hiding*) sọndẹ; (*craftily*) soṛlok̓.

ENTERTAIN, TO—laboj, man, marjad, merjad, morji; (*hospitably*) chaklachak.

ENTERTAINING—laphua.

ENTERTAINMENT, AN—lila, tamasa.

ENTHUSIASM—latkar; (*to raise*) jhulkau.

ENTHUSIASTICALLY—sekep sekep; (*to do*) lahkao, thankao, thonkao.

ENTICE, TO—ere libuk, ghãose, lobdhao, lobhao, lubhau, ora uri.

ENTICING—lithur.

ENTIRE—pura, purau, thul.

ENTIRELY—ekbar, jhañjhat, nari thuri, nichora, nikarkhar, pacuk, rend bend, rukrabon, sae, saprum.

ENTRAILS—mota lač, nanha lač, lačlič, lič; (*to clean*) lač duhau; (*of fowl, part of*) mundu lač.

ENTRANCE, THE—botolo.

ENTRANCINGLY (*of sound*)—ńõhõr (2).

ENTRAP, TO—bajhao, lajbajhi, phand.

ENTREAT, TO—ajij, bestok, dehet dundhet, god pari, jorhat, kãoari, nehõr, ujur mujur.

ENTREATY—(*with much*) dedhet; (*exclm. of*) de, den, denya, dese, dini; (*to assume attitude of*) gola gamcha.

ENTROPIUM—lapatič.

ENTRUST, TO—alae, saprot, saprud; (*to*) sompao, soprot, sumjhau; (*for nourishing*) tehad.

ENVELOPE, A—laphap.

ENVIOUS—dahgoria, hẽsalia, hisalia, lalca (M), lalci (F), singhin; (*to be*) mẽt jolok, iolo.

ENVY—dah, dahok, hiska, hiska huluń, kurud; (*to*) huluń, kurud.

EPILEPSY—bai, hanak gujuk, mirgi.

EPISTLE, AN—cithi.

EPSILON LYRAE—potam bele.

EQUAL—barabar, eklayek, hala hali, mič barabari, ora sora, saman, soman, somasom, tal, tesnek; (*size—beasts and birds*) jopor; (*rotunidty*) sondmond; (*to*) johok, tulni; (*in value*) sordor; (*to, to be*) lindar, lindor, tič. *Cf.* AGN, PARTS, PROPORTIONS.

EQUALLY—hala hali, ora sora, rodbodol, sarasar, soka suki, soloman, somujos.

EQUIPMENT—sajbaj, sanaphana.

EQUITABLE—hike, oj maphik, solo sońjok.

EQUITY—hak, hok.

EQUIVOCALLY—thare thore.

ERADICATE, TO—ukhrau.

ERECT—demcok, dondon, sidup; (*a fence, to*) jhanti panti; (*a hut, to*) kumba; (*an idol, to*) thapna.

ERECTION, A TEMPORARY—camda, chamda.

ERR, TO—bhakundao, kai; (*cause to*) bhińgrau.

ERRONEOUS—bhulauni.

ERROR, AN—bhisor, bhosor, bhul bhisor, cuk, bhulcuk; (*to bring up an old*) cokhna.

ERUCTATE, TO—amol.

ERUPTION, AN—(*on legs*) kar; (*on body*) milmilia.

ESCAPE—bacol, par, rihai.

ESCAPE, TO—baclao, bańcao, chutau, ńirphor, paskao, phasur; (*through an opening*) puyul.

ESCONCE, TO—hombo.

ESCORT, TO—habrao.

ESPECIALY—asokaete, dherkaete.

ESSAY, TO—upai.

ESTABLISH, TO—baisau, bandhao, bel, dirho, khara, tahrao, tarhao; (*an agreement*) paka paki.

ESTATE—(*paternal*) bapoti dhon; (*division of*) pargana; (*belonging to*) sarkari; (*broken in*) bhańtao; (*to increase in*) hor hara, hor harta.

ESTEEM, TO—manot, ugur.

ESTIMATE, TO—hisab, barae, imtam, kut, onman, orad, pasind, tajbij, tojbij; (*to exceed*) algel.

ESTIMATED—kuta.

ESTIMATING—(*roughly*) nindan; (*how much work he should do*) likhwatia; (*carefully*) auman; (*to fix by*) ja.

ET CETERA—emanteak, emanten.

ETERNALLY—jaejug.

EUNUCH, AN—cakra, mayo.

EUROPEAN, AN—saheb; (*soldier*) gora.

EVAPORATE, TO—ọr, sạkiṫ; *(by boiling)* cạchi.

EVEN—*(level)* barabar, cạuthoṙ, soka suki; *(handed)* soloman, solo soṅjoǩ; *(surface)* sotel; *(also)* hō̤, parjat, pọrjọnt.

EVENING—ạyuṗ, sañjholi; *(meal)* kedoǩ; *(star-Vanus)* sukạr.

EVENT, AN—ghotna, lạṭak, lọṭọk.

EVENTIDE—ạyuṗ payar, ạyuṗ pọhọr.

EVENTUALLY—atar, dapoṛ, napoṛ.

EVER—tis hō̤.

EVERY—istọk, jao, ke, miṫ ke miṫ, ọstọk, sobbo; *(one)* atom, harẹk, jhaṅgae poṭae, jhạṭiạ pạṭiạ; *(thing)* chinci punci, hoṭaǩ picaǩ, iṛci guṛci, iṛtiċ gaṛtiċ, jhaṅgae poṭae, jhạṭiạ pạṭiạ, rạṭi kuṭi; *(particle)* gẹċ gạyum, ralaǩ masaǩ; *(where)* aṇḍroǩ saṇḍroǩ, aonda ā̤undi, ạruǩ dhạruǩ, bọnẹ badaṛẹ, cario dig, cạukhũṭ, goṭa ṭạṇḍi, hoṭaǩ picaǩ, sanam ṭhen, tereń goreń; *(time)* pichạ, piche; *(little while)* ghane (2). khane (2) *Cf.* DAY, NIGHT, YEAR.

EVICT, TO—bẹdọkhọl, bẹjaega.

EVIDENCE—ejahar, porman, sạkhiyạt, sat, sọt; *(in court)* ijạhar; *(to give)* goha gujrạu, sạkhi ẹm; *(to call)* darao, dorao; *(to keep back part of)* jibkạ.

EVIL—bọd, dusṭama, dhutại, dusṭu, kharap; *(courses)* lachan, lochon; *(case, in)* durdosa, hạluạ harọn, hā̤si hanao, thalhalao; *(action, consequences of)* poe; *(to do)* baṛiċ. *Cf.* OMEN, SPELL.

EWE, A—bhiḍi; *(lamb)* bạkri.

EXACT—niṭsahī, purạ, purạu, ṭhik, ṭhik ṭhak; *(likeness)* chanban, chonbon; *(measurement)* moka ḍaṭoṗ.

EXACT, TO—ạdại, ạgu, bab, tolao; *(by threats)* durduri.

EXACTLY—nipaṭ, sinạm, taman, tanman; *(right)* bes ṭhik; *(so)* ẹrọń, hē̃hō̃.

EXAGGERATE, TO—aga, baḍohi, lah̃na, lapaǩ capaǩ, toṛah̃ẽṭ.

EXAGGERATING—katha bajoṛiạ, labhra (M), lạbhri (F), lapco, phaṅga; *(given to)* batkunda, labaṛ, lạbuǩ cạbuǩ, lahra (M), lạhri (F), lạpuǩ cạbuǩ, phaph.

EXAMINE, TO—ajmao, barnao, bheaṛ, bidạu, imtihạn, pacnao, parikha, tạjbij, tọjbij; *(carefully)* ạri bạndhi; *(by questions)* kạblạ kạbli.

EXAMINATION—imtihạn.

EXAMPLE—nạmunạ.

EXASPERATE, TO—busku, carhao, ciṛhạu.

EXASPERATED—kondoliạ.

EXASPERATING—caṛ capaṛ, ciṛhạ ciṛhi.

EXCAVATE, TO *(as tank)*—gẹlẹċ.

EXCAVATION FOR FOUNDATION—dargaḍa.

EXCEED, TO—baṛti, sarẹċ; *(present need)* bạtil; *(estimate)* algel.

EXCEEDINGLY—andha dhund, anẹċ dhanẹċ, baṛti, bejā̤e, dhā̤e khā̤e, tiriṫ leka; *(of darkness)* karań (2); *(of corpulence)* mạsurdań; *(of height)* rakḍań; *(of weight)* rọhọċ (2).

EXCEL, TO—jind, lahāt.

EXCELLENT—aprug, khub, ọsnẹ (2), sạbit, subita, sughoṛ, supoṭ; *(to cause to be)* supṭạu.

EXCELLENTLY—ḍhab ḍhọb, ḍhabẹ ḍhọbẹ; *(well)* sọsṭọk.

EXCEPT—baṅkhan, bẹgọr, bin, bina, chadakate, choṛkate, eskar.

EXCEPTION—*(without)* bebak; *(with few)* abga.

EXCESS—bạki, bạtil, satarẹċ; *(in)* phadel, sarẹċ; *(to)* bhuceṛ, bhuteṛ, buceṛ.

EXCESSIVE—akaṛdhak, aṛwạidha, bhạri, bharkhar, ḍher, nirdhọk, jạsti, sadasuk.

EXCESSIVELY—kandoṛ, kańdoṛ; *(of corpulence)* kondoṛkeṫ, liṇḍbhiṇḍ, mạsurdań, obhoǩ (2); *(of cold)* kaṅkiṛiṫ, kankiṛiṫ.

EXCHANGE—badla, bạṭa, dọlbadọl, oja; *(in)* bạdli, bodla, hala hạli, kar; *(to give in)* utiń; *(of daughters in marriage)* golāṭ.

EXCHANGE, TO—badla bạdli, bạdli, bọdọl, dọlbadọl, erpher, orpher, phera phiri; *(flowers)* patao.

EXCITABLE—khanṭaha (M), khanṭahi (F), kharañ khacañ.

EXCITE, TO—dalmal, jhulkau, uskur.

EXCITED—andak tawak, cahap caṭur, cañmañgao, coñcol; (*of buffaloes*) arra arri; (*from fear or joy*) bilbilau; *with anger*) tamao; (*to move as when*) sansanao.

EXCITED, TO BE—andhi candhi, chilbilau, jhũkau, kharbarao, kickicau, saniau, sansanao, surma, tao, umtau; (*with anger*) sarngao.

EXCITEDLY—ampa ompo, bhas bhus.

EXCITEMENT—rag, sur; (*shaking with*) lodo dhoro.

EXCITER TO REBELLION, AN—huhulić.

EXCLAMATION, AN—(*commiseration*) hae hae; (*grief*) dure, durhak; (*prohibition*) hãhã; (*defiance*) o; (*fear*) aege; (*encouragement*) bah, halla; (*scorn*) chi; (*to call attention*) hai; (*anger*) o; (*pleasure*) ah. *Cf.* ANNOYANCE, SURPRISE, ENTREATY, &c.

EXCLUDE, TO—atrom, bahre.

EXCLUSIVE OF—bin, bina.

EXCREMENT—ić, jija, norok; (*of horse, &c.*) led; (*passed in small quantities*) gundué; (*of goat*) bhelãundi, ladauri.

EXCRESENCE, AN—dhonṭho, doho, dombe.

EXCRESENCES COVERED WITH—danṭha donṭho, dhampa dhompo, domba dombe.

EXCRUCIATING—darun.

EXCUSE—arja arji, aroj, arsa, dhẽs, lisi, sinić, susi, ujur; (*to plead*) andun, arsa arsi, dhẽs, ujur.

EXCUSE, TO—map, maph, ujur mujur; (*oneself & blame another*) dhẽsa dhĩsi.

EXECRATE, TO—lese.

EXECUTE A WARRANT, TO—aronṭ jari.

EXEMPT—akar, chad, chada, chadakate, elak chada.

EXERCISE, TO—(*a horse*) cakar, rol; *as an athlete*) bhañjao, bhãoar, bhawãr, sara bhañjao, teñjao.

EXERT ONESELF, TO—garmao, ghamao, jahĩt, jid, kere mete, kurumuṭu, lagiã parao, larao, lomosoro, mehnot, ruhuṭuhu, ṭesṭa.

EXERTION—ghamaoṭa, mehnot; (*with great*) laria paria; (*to cause*) dahlao; (*with apparent*) lubhuñ (2).

EXHALATION—so.

EXHAUST, TO—cañ cuñ, dharkao, niñghar, niñghrau, nipat, reñjeṭ.

EXHAUSTED—alap (2), aloć paloć, asiṭ, cothra, jirmok, lerwa larwe, narca, siṭ, usṭaha; (*by fatigue*) ṭhopoñ; (*by illness*) thakao; (*used by children*) papuk; (*as soil*) hirhaṭ, khokndo, kokhodo, marca, siṭha, usaṭ; (*as a store*) jhakaṭ; (*to be*) tobo.

EXHORT, TO—binti, udgau.

EXIGENCY—rogor.

EXIST, TO—bahao, gujrau, hẽna, mena, mõhjam, mohñjam; (*not to*) banu, banuk.

EXISTENCE—(*to come into*) hoe, hoyok, upel; (*to pass*) jojao, khemao.

EXIT, AT EACH WAY OF—ghaṭe ghaṭ.

EXORCISE, TO—bandhon, bulau.

EXORCIST, AN—ojha, phaphu hor.

EXPAND, TO—lablab, pasar; (*a statement*) torahẽṭ; (*ready to*) bhoṭok.

EXPANSE, A WIDE—(*land*) bilan, biland, phael, phaela; (*water*) leṭ leṭ.

EX-PARTE—ek torphi.

EXPECT, TO—as, baṭ cahao, bãṭ ñel; (*to cause to*) joban.

EXPECTATION—barsa, bharsa, bharosa, bhorsa, khuṭu; (*having*) jethe.

EXPECTORATE, TO—tho.

EXPEDIENT, AN—aṭ, bandheć; (*to try several*) kurpar.

EXPEDITE, TO—calao, canda candi, candaki, hako phare, usara.

EXPEDITION—jhak.

EXPEL, TO—khed, odok.

EXPENSE—khoroc; (*a place invloving*) jom duar; (*of another, at the*) pare pore, por caṭa, porchaṭi, porepare.

EXPENSES, MISCELLANEOUS—baibi.

EXPERIENCE, TO—sumbhrau; (*to gain*) hewa jaora, ñel her.

EXPERIENCED—ñel herer, uakep, wakhep.

EXPERT—bhãoar, bhawãr, calak, chuṭau, colonti, kabel, kabil, kharkahi, kharkhari, kheas, kheasi, lohanĩ, nipun, pagol, paṭior, sargharia; (*in wood-work*) baḍhoria, kaṭkuṭ; (*in hunting*) jalim sar, jarnaha; (*to become*) ti baisau.

EXPIRATION—(*with a long*) phū marte; (*sound of*) sāe sūi.

EXPIRE, TO (*breathe*)—sahet odok, sahet giḍi.

EXPLAIN, TO—barnan, bayan, bean, beyan, bhao, bhoṅ, bornon, bujhau, lai bujhau, ohjao, samjhao, suċ.

EXPLANATION—beyan, birtant, pariau.

EXPLETIVE, AN—eṅgam.

EXPLOSION, AN—gola jambra; (*noise of*) liṭhir, ṭhu.

EXPOSE, TO—sodor, sudri, ughrau.

EXPOSED—bead, phada, ughar.

EXPOSTULATE, TO—ram ror.

EXPRESS, TO—len.

EXPRESSION, OF FACE—cehra.

EXTEND, TO—phaela, tiriau; (*to*) ṭuṅgau; (*horizontally*) laplapa.

EXTENDED—capcapa; (*to full length*) boṅboṅ; (*in one direction*) bonto-botoċ.

EXTENSIVE—phael, phaela.

EXTENUATE, TO—aṇḍuṅ.

EXTERMINATED, TO BE—marao.

EXTERNAL—bahar, bahre.

EXTINCT—siroṅ soroṅ.

EXTINGUISH, TO—iṛiċ.

EXTORTING PAYMENT, MODE OF—dharna.

EXTRA—phalti, phauti, unka; (*work as punishment*) dalil.

EXTRACT, TO—odok, toṫ; (*as teeth*) boċ.

EXTRAORDINARY—had.

EXTREMELY—aḍi bariċ, bebariċ, heran, kandor, kaṅdor; (*of blackness*) ṅaṅgoyak; (*of whiteness*) tehe (2); (*of fatness*) ahal ehel, liṅdbhiṅd, lobo dhorok, luduryuṫ, obhok (2), padgurae (M), pidgurae (F), thothomthorok; (*of cold*) kaṅkiriṫ, kankiriṫ; (*of fear*) puyul; (*of hunger*) phakphak, phokphok; (*of weight*) rohoċ (2).

EXTRICATE, TO—rahau, rakhia, rukhia.

EXUDATION FROM CERTAIN TREES—jer.

EXUDE, TO—sere; (*in small quantity*) sio soyo.

EXULT, TO—riṅgi ṭiṅgi.

EYE, THE—meṫ; (*pupil of*) kharen, rajas; (*having mote in*) cubak; (*inflammation of*) mendok, meṫ, tirsul; (*blind of one*) ṭesra (M), ṭhesra (M), ṭhisri (F), ṭisri (F); (*brows*) kuṭi; (*lashes*) pipni.

EYELIDS—jhapni, meṫ sarim; (*stye on*) ṭoke; (*inversion of*) lapaṭiċ; (*drooping*) jipa.

EYES, THE—(*to open*) beṅgeṫ; (*to close*) janapiṫ, japiṫ; (*unable to open*) jilpiṫ, jilu milu; (*with open*) dekhit, dikhitte; (*wide open*) ripripi; (*fixed & staring*) dhere (2); (*to rub*) itkiṫ, tirhol; (*standing out*) jaral jurul, laṇḍa loṇḍo, loṇḍkoṫ; (*nipping*) aral koral, chek; (*to cover*) beṫ; (*to fill with tears*) biriṅ (2), ḍabḍabao, dhar (2), peperkaṫ; (*discharge from*) sereċ; (*hollow*) horok; (*rivetted on*) morol (2), muṭur (2); (*to cast longing*) elhe celhe; (*salve for*) ajan; (*to throw dust in*) er tepeṫ; (*oblique*) pelka (M), pilki (F), ṭera (M), ṭiri (F).

F

FABLE, AN OLD WIVES'—pocla gam.

FABRICATE, TO—jorao, turta.

FACE—(*the*) metāhā; (*part in front of ear*) kan jari, luṭkuri; (*side of*) lutpuri; (*before one's*) samuk; (*downwards*) taber; (*swollen*) komkom; (*broad*) bed bede, boak, pakursak; (*expression of*) cehra; (*to turn away*) koṇḍe kose, kose (2); (*to harden*) ṭheṭhamū; (*to stare one in*) ahirkuhir; (*to face*) muhā muhī, mukha mukhi, samka saṭi, samna samni; (*to face, to bring*) hajrao, mokabila; (*to*) samaṅ.

FACT, IN—arse tāhā.

FACTIOUS—kuṭeṫ.

FACTOTUM—dewan; (*to act as*) lanbaṅ.

FADE, TO—larua, moseṫ.

FADED—usaṭa, ustāhā.

FAGGOT, A—bhiṇḍ, bhiṇḍia.

FAIL—(*to*) atra, cukau, ḍigau, ḍigoha, harna, kacokam, phel; (*sarcastic*) lopoṅ thopa; (*in purpose, to*) pasur;

(*without*) bisbiswas, jarur; (*to cause to*) harwani; (*to pay when due*) khilap, kilap.

FAILING, HAVING ANY PARTICULAR—emon semon.

FAINT—alap (2), ankha ankhi, apalhet, atrun, jham (2), jhin (2), kath, kathnua, latwak, tewelgat; (*from hunger*) hapak (2), janje; (*hearted*) pocra (M), pucri (F); (*to*) jhãe, jhin, hinau, jinjin, jinjinau; (*to be*) cato, kathua; (*to become*) karigham, lorao.

FAIR, A—mela, parab.

FAIR—(*equitable*) oj maphik; (*colour*) esel, garlae, rangia, telsãoar; (*very*) selsel.

FAIRLY—(*equally*) soloman, solo sonjok.

FAITH—barsa, bhorosa, biswas, net, sacai; (*to break*) arkhao.

FAITHFUL—iman, imandar, patiar, saca, suca (M), suci (F).

FAITHLESS—obiswas, olan mocan.

FAKEER, A HINDU—babaji, phakir.

FALL, TO—dasao; (*from a height*) nũr; (*from standing &c.*) gur, ujuk; (*backwards*) bindran, sandan, sombot; (*headlong*) tupuc; (*on the knees*) sombot; (*down*) barao, bhindar, bindar, dhaskao, landur, lendur, obor, rap rup, rup, thasrao; (*in*) dhasao, landup; (*into*) khanjo, parao; (*short*) atra; (*to ground*) bhindran; (*into a pit*) khãri, khonja; (*with a flop*) lethec, lodop marte; (*in price*) monda, rakap.

FALLEN—(*in*) copot londoc; (*leaves*) pataulak.

FALLING SICKNESS, THE—bai, mirgi.

FALLOW—arda, arthi parthi, khil, khil khũt, khil khunt, parti, patit

FALSE—asarthi, asat, asathi, auri, bhua, bhulania, binhok, jhuta, labar, labhra (M), labhri (F), lai labar, matha, micha, nase, nisarthi, osot; (*report*) bhakara; (*charge*) phareb, phasad, phesad; (*pretences, to lead by*) bhabrao; (*to play one*) thar; (*witness, to cause to bear*) kan phuka. *Cf.* ACCUSE.

FALSIFIED, TO BE—jhuta, matha.

FALTER, TO—(*in speech*) that thot; (*in steps*) dhoyot dhopot, kidma kadme.

FAME—daksari, jos, sabasi.

FAMILIAR WITH—ghesa, heto, hitau, hitu, khand akhar; (*to be*) gãwao, hera ghesa, jak jotet, jodhe, letho.

FAMILIARIZE, TO—hewa.

FAMILIARIZTD WITH—bhetro; (*to be*) laghar; (*to become*) parkau.

FAMILY—bos, dahgi, gabndi, garosti, ghar gusti, gharonj, grostali, gusti, gutri, era hopon, orak renko, satar gatar; (*all the*) dhia puta, ghar gusti, jhingae potae; (*of one*) gharaia; (*not of the*) algel; (*having no*) datha dutbu; (*head or*) morubi, murubi; (*4th. of*) manjhla (M), manjhli (F); (*5th. of*) ganjliic; (*the only remaining one of*) sotok sumun; (*of an old*) taliau. *Cf.* OLDEST, YOUNGEST.

FAMINE—akal, dorloe, haora, kandor, lukhi palon, malot, palon.

FAMISHING—akalia, atwasi patwasi, kandor, kãokão, khaknha khankhi; (*cry of*) kãokão.

FAMOUS—daksaria, lohani, namdak, namjadi.

FAN—(*a winnowing*) suptic; (*a bamboo*) bini; (*to*) ewer.

FANCY—sok, sonk; (*to*) kheal; (*to tickle the*) laboj; (*to take a*) soke.

FAR—sangin; (very) aki lanka; (*away*) duranta, lanka, lonka, taphat, tophad; (*as eye can reach*) tiyal (2); (*how*) oka dhabic, oka utar.

FARE—(*rent*) bhara, keraya, mahsul; (*daily*) nirbah.

FAREWELL, TO BID—bida.

FARM, A—jaega, jagah, jot; (*& stock*) cas bari. *Cf.* SERVANT, PRODUCE.

FARMER, A—casa; (*well-to-do*) girosto; (*of land or revenue*) ijardar.

FARMING LEASE, A—ijara.

FASCIANTE, TO—malun.

FASHION—rewaj; (*to*) banao, benao, garhao.

FAST—at, cogor, curamar, cure mare, curmar, hakopako, hotak picak, ribir (2).

FAST, TO—bar, barao, dhean, nayar, songar, upas; (*to break*) ahan;

(*to cause to*) **khorkhorao, kohrao, pokhao.**

FASTEN TO—**tol** ; (*garment round waist*) **benden.**

FASTENING, A—**tonol.**

FASTIDIOUS—**badai, badaria, badgaria, gorob, gorobia.**

FAT—**ahal ohol, bagrum, bhatkura, bhitkur, bhõda, bhogao, bhogdo, bhonda, bhosonga (M), bhosongi (F), bhuger, bhunda (M), bhundi (F), bhutel, bhutia, bidgoe bodgoe, bigaboge, dheke, dhulki, dhuma (M), dhumi (F), dhumra (M), dhumri (F), dudhma, ehel (2), gabdulan, itil, karidan, kotho, kutmel, lendker, lobhok, lobo dhorok, lodhea, lodhor (2), lodhrok, lodo dhorok, lodro, lothro (M), luthri (F), lusku lundur, lutkum, madhas, mandhak, mandhas, mosto, mota, musra (M), musri (F), odrok, pedgor (M), pidgur (F), peke poko, rindiol, rondho, seret beret, sirak barak, soroc, taj, tear, telgar** ; (*of cattle*) **salsal** ; (*of children*) **lesker, ludgup, phodle (M), phudli (F), pedgor (M), pidgur (F)** ; (*of women*) **bodgoe** ; (*moderately*) **udguc** ; (*very*) **cakendak, kondorket, latumpak, ludgup, luduryut, obobo, tumsan** ; (*to unsightliness*) **dhambosak jobodhon (F)** ; (*& big-bellied*) **lobojhor** ; (*& big-buttocked*) **pedorae (M), pidgurae (F)** ; (*& dumpy*) **agar ogor, lapir jadir, matku, padgurae (M), pidgurae (F), thothma (M), thuthmi (F)** ; (*& lazy*) **bhundin (F), dholo (F), dhuma (M), dhumi (F)** ; (*& unweildy*) **adhac udhuc, bigobogo, dhomsol** ; (*& naked*) **adar odor, odor (2)** ; (*cheeked*) **pheknok (F), pikopoko** ; (*to become*) **umbrau**; (*to be come again*) **phandgar** ; (*animals, running of*) **bhandal bhundul** ; (*person, movements of*) **isot esot, lepedher, luduk.**

FATE—**bhag, bidhanta, danai, kapar, kopal, korom, larbhad, likha, likhal, likhal badal, molon, nasib** ; (*by what*) **oka bhag.**

FATED—**olsit atet sit.**

FATHER—**apa, ba, baba, bap** ; (*his*) **apat** ; (*& child*) **apa hon** ; (*& brothers*) **apa bare** ; (*in-law*) **honhar** ; (*in law's house*) **sasrar** ; (*elder brother of*) **gongo** ; (*elder sister of*) **nana** ; (*sister of*) **hatom** ; (*sister's husband of*) **kuma** ; (*younger brothers of*) **kaka, kakabala** ; (*relatives of*) **hadkur** ; (*in-law, salutation of*) **saheb, samdhi** ; (*soul of deceased*) **porodhol** ;

FATHOM, A—**arpa, purus** ; (*to*) **thah.**

FATHOMLESS—**patarphor.**

FATIGUE—**dhõk** ; (*& worry*) **langa haron.**

FATIGUED, TO BE—**akar kukar, alap (2), lakar phakar, lakar thakar, langa, larbuk, lecer pecer, lere there, lokor phokor, nison, tharrao, thorrao, timba tambe.**

FATTEN, TO—**posao.**

FAUCET, A—**tontoroc.**

FAULT, A—**apai, apco, bhisor, bhosor, dos, galti, gaphlat, ghat, ghati, guna, gunha, kai, kalak, kasur, khõc, kusur, latak, oprad, toncok, tuskil** ; (*to commit a*) **bhul, cukau, ghati, ghat guna, kai, kasur** ; (*to find*) **dhodya (M), dhodyo (F), dhusau, dusau, khacraha (M), khacrahi (F), soda, tergen, terges** ; (*with food, to find*) **jom tanao** ; (*continually finding*) **kheckhecao, khijau, khockhoc** ; (*one who has commited a*) **kaidar.**

FAULTLESS—**miridos, nichora, nirdos, suca (M), suci (F).**

FAULTS—**bhul bisor, ghat guna, kai kasur** ; (*to correct*) **sudhrau.**

FAULTY—**bẽrbak, bethik, dusau, loron phocon.**

FAVOUR, TO—**sahai, sahaita** ; (*to give to win*) **em libuk.**

FAVOURABLE—(*disposition*) **kusal** ; (*time*) **ãrgat, at ghat.**

FAVOURABLY, TAKING,—**marji, murji.**

FAWN, TO—**gadea gudia, gudiauk.**

FEAR—**bao, bhoe, bhorok, bhoyon, bor, botor, dhoros, dhupuc, dhupuc, porbhae** ; (*superstitious*) **bhãe** ; (*to*) **boro, hickau, tatka birki** ; (*to be in*) **dhupuc dhupucok, lenget sopot, sopot** ; (*to be relieved from*) **ikot** ; (*to hide through*) **picpic** ; (*exclm. of*) **aege** ; (*without*) **asam usum, khula-**

sa; (*in abject*) luṭuk' (2), luyut' cupu t'; (*numbed with*) cokao, dhak-cakao, haemoekaṭ, kẹklẹsẹt', ṭaṭka; (*to lose*) paṛkau.

Fearful (*timid*)—bhọyọn, bọtọr, ḍoro-kiạ.

Fearless—arọ̃ṭ, bagṛasiạ̃u, bẹporbhae, ḍhaḍọs, dhidrik, ẹk jiba, nirbhọe, sahas, sahạsiạ.

Fearlessly—sahasae, sọhọka, sọhọsae, ṭhak' ṭhok', ṭhaṅka ṭhoraṅ.

Fearsome—bọtọr, camal cọmọl.

Feast, a—bhọj, khelọd, pọrọb; (*to attend*) pạhnạ; (*to give*) mạn mar-jạd.

Feasting, given up to—agamgạr.

Feather—il; (*ornament*) ṭoya dhaca.

Feathers—(*very young*) sui il, tabẹn il; (*half-grown*) tabẹn il; (*first 3 quil*) kanso il; (*tuft on head of bird*) duci.

Featured, broad—badgok' (2).

Febrifuge, a fruit used as—pipol.

February-March—phạgun.

Feckless—gayo gapo, gunduc' gusuc', haja hojo, lạṇḍur bhạṇḍur, poca, sotyot'.

Fee—(*to priest who offers his blood*) bạlkạṭi; (*to witch-finder &c*) bundạ; (*of midwife*) narkaṭaoni.

Feeble—adpakoliạ, ḍhanman, hạlso, lạkṛuc', lerosiạ, leṛwa laṛwe, lesoṛiạ, licaṛ, momomoc', mordha, morjha, mornaha, nijhuliạ, nisok', ọsad, paṛao, rẽhẽ, ruṅku juduṅ, tewelgat', thorio; (*& lean*) lẹṭẹc' pẹṭẹc', lẹṭẹr pẹṭẹr; (*& carelessly attired*) jhitoc' jhọṭọc'; (*minded*) utut' tumbut'; (*to become*) labṛaṅ, lạbṛuk', lạbṛuṅ, lạṛbuṅ, libṛuk', lorao, nijọr; (*& old*) tukup' (2).

Feebly—liṛwa saṛwe, thạluk' thạpuk', ṭapạc' ṭupuc'.

Feed, to—ạtiṅ, khawao, khiạu, khilạu; (*another*) ajọ; (*a bride & groom with sugar*) guṛdak'.

Feeder, a—khạuạ.

Feeding at night—raṭcora.

Feel, to—aikạu, aṭkar; (*for*) hatṛao; (*with hand*) tunum; (*with hands or feet*) ṭamḍao; (*here & there*) ṭamḍa ṭạmḍi; (*pulse*) ti tunum; (*a call of nature*) tọlọb; (*pleasure*) bhọg; (*scorn*) chi tho, chiak', chi baṅ, posṛa; (*an impulse to*) sarbharao, uriạu

Feeling—(*everywhere*) hatra hạṭri, sandra sondṛe; (*the way*) tahao; (*with feet*) tharsat' thorsot', thirsot' thorsot'; (*of sympathy*) mãyã; (*an eerie*) cũicũi. *Cf.* sensation, ill.

Feelings, to hurt the—chorwaṅ, kandao.

Feet, the—amba, jaṅga, pao; (*a sore of*) paeṭhan, ras; (*cracked*) dhọrọt' (2); (*deformed in*) koṇḍha, kuḍạ; (*tender in*) dhaṛak' dhorok'; (*to drag*) carhat' cọrhọt', cirhọt' cọrhọt', lapaṭ luput; (*to cross, when walking*) ciṭẹt' paṭẹt'; *peculiar way of lifting*) kaṭaṅ kuṭuṅ; (*wide apart*) hiḍhiḍi, higạ hage; (*in the air*) birṭuṅ; (*reaching to*) cindạr cọndọr, jhọlṅga, jhọlọṅ, jihor jọhọr; (*feeling with*) thirsot' thorsot'; (*pressing down alternately*) capae cupui.

Feign, to—baṛkac', eṅgol; (*death*) gampatao.

Feigning—ḍhaḍnạsiạ, ḍhọrḍhosaha.

Fell, to (*as an ox*)—kuṭạm.

Fellow—bạnki, bataṛic', jọṭ, jọṭic', jukur, juri, juridar; (*a lazy*) kam bhak'ṇḍuric'; (*a stout*) pahalwan.

Female, a—eṅga, era, kuṛi họpọn, maejiu jạt, mạ̃i. *Cf.* organ.

Females—aimai jạt, maejiu jạt.

Feminine appearance, of—mayo.

Fence, a—ghorṇa; (*of branches*) jhạṇṭi; (*of wooden bars*) bindhaṛ; (*of thorns*) jạnum jhạṇṭi; (*uprights for*) khuci; (*to trap hares*) pacan.

Fence, to—aḍon, ẹṭẹt', ghawaṛ, ghorṇa, jhạṇṭi pạṇṭi; (*round*) gaṛ guṛhạ, ghorṇa berna; (*with thorns*) rampha; (*with horizontal bars*) jaṅge.

Fennel seed—kạliạ jirạ.

Ferment, to—bidic' (2) caoão, cawãok'.

Ferment used to make rice beer—rạnu.

Fermentation—(*completion of*) isin; (*to steep till*) jawa.

Fern, a—badgocak', dodhari, nanha bodhạri; (*small water*) ọt poraeni.

FEROCIOUS—rokot muhạ̃.

FERRET—ghirri.

FERRULE—sambhe.

FERRY, A—ghat.

FERTILE—lag, sokra sendeḱ; (*soil*) bolgaria, bolman, sargat, sebel ot.

FERVENTLY—rumbuć cumbuć.

FESTER, TO—bele.

FESTIVAL—parab, porbas, porob; (*Hindu*) amal gañjal, bandna, barwari, chat, chata, dol, polhar, ras, sakrat; (*Bhuiya*) buru; (*Santal*) buru beret, got, karam, karma, sahar lunda, sohrae; (*at seed-sowing*) eroḱ sim; (*after reaping thatching grass*) mag sim; (*at rice-planting*) hariar sim, karma; (*5-yearly*) maḱ mõrẽ; (*sun*) jom sim; (*in January*) jatra; (*in Phagun*) phagua; (*flower*) baha porob; (*2nd. day of Sakrat*) bãundi; (*to Mahadeo*) pata.

FESTOONS, IN—jhañka jhakur.

FETICH, TO SET UP A—than baisau.

FETID—moroć.

FETTERS—biri, hari.

FEUD, TO BE AT—larhai.

FEVER—rua; (*a kind of*) askandua, bhalki rua, pit rua, sagaḱ rua; (*to have*) bejar, rua; (*first symptoms of*) masmas; (*long-continued*) gahri; (*onset of*) katkatao, rasras; (*slight*) dãrã sõrẽ; (*to increase*) dundiḱ.

FEVERISH—dahdahao; (*to be*) dahao.

FEW, A—eka duka, eskar toskar, thora gan; (*days*) ursiń barsiń; (*days ago*) halisali.

FIBRE—jãrĩ; (*bast*) lar; (*of Palmyra palm*) bagra, baja; (*yielding plant a*) dare kudrum, jãrĩ, kudrum, miru baha, narca, sãci son, san, son; (*mixed with clay*) baja; (*animal*) tãt.

FICKLE—barmon, coñcol, khatpat.

FICTION, A—udacal.

FIDDLE, A—banam; (*kind of*) huka b., kat b., kindiri b., sarañga, sarngi; (*bow*) aḱ; (*string*) tãt; (*brass string*) tar; (*to*) reta.

FIDDLE ABOUT, TO—kaituk.

FIDELITY—net.

FIDGETTY—bandhej, cañmañgao, catpatao, erce perce, halbal, halbalia, kharbarao, khut khut.

FIE !—chi.

FIELD, A—barge. *Cf.* RICE-FIELD.

FIERCE—cañke, kataha, khãc, khacar; (*of sun*) jharla jharli, uruć putuć.

FIERCELY—rañga rañgi; (*of quarrel*) ragra ragri, rogra rugri.

FIERY—khacar, khantaha (M), khantahi (F), kharań khacań; (*of tiger's eyes*) jorol (2), jurul (2); (*cross of Santals*) dharwaḱ.

FIFTEEN—gel mõrẽ.

FIFTH OF A FAMILY—gañjliić.

FIFTY—mõrẽ gel, pońcas; (*each*) mõmõr gelkate; (% *interest*) derhi sud.

FIG TREE, A SPECIES OF—añjir, capakia bare, gada podo, loa, madhur lata, pakare, podo, seta podo, sunum jor.

FIGHT, TO—dañga, dapal, larhai, markat; (*in the air*) lapka; (*with heel or fists*) kudra kudri.

FIGHTING—larañkar.

FIGURE, A—ak; (*to cut*) lalak; (*to draw*) ol.

FILCH THROUGH GREED, TO—lubhi.

FILE—(*a*) ret; (*in single*) otoń tayom.

FILL, TO—gabao, pepreć, pereć, turuń; (*in*) bhorao, bhuraḱ, dhapao, sajao, sambao; (*up*) bhara, bhatao, bhurti; (*full*) cepel, cuhlau, tuheć, tuñgau, umãr; (*& heap up*) curu; (*up again*) kope.

FILLED FULL—ambao, lajhar, najhar; (*to satiety*) tobo.

FILLIP, TO GIVE A—puchla puchli.

FILM—(*a thin*) jalai; (*under egg-shell*) ganthar; (*on baby's tongue*) gitaḱ; (*produced by insects*) sutam.

FILTERING, TO SEPARATE BY—chakao.

FILTH—gadrum, maila, norok; (*liquid*) bejeḱ (2); (*pit of*) norok kund.

FILTHY—aroṭ, dhudor podor, dhoroń poroń, gesotia, gestaha (M), gestahi (F), hedge hesaḱ, hende ritha, maila, ńagal (2), nite.

FIN OF FISH—il.

FINALLY—akhir.

FIND, TO—bachao ńam, jokha, juṭạu, khọrọ, ńam, ṭewan; (*out*) baca, ṭhekan, ṭhikạn; (*fault*) dhusạu, dusạu, soḍa, terges; (*something ownerless*) rimi.

FINE—(*beautiful*) dharahara, suthạr, tolgoyam; (*of dust*) lẹmẹń, lomoń, podoe; (*thin*) lubui, mĩhĩ, phinphiniạ, piliń; (*of houses*) darahara; (*rain*) padar podor, podor (2), poroe, rabać ribić, ribić, rubuć; (*very*) ḍigir, luhui, mĩhĩ (2), piliń; (*to make*) guṇḍrạ, lạhuť, lẹmẹń, lopoť; (*as spray*) bijir (2).

FINE, A—ḍaṇḍ, ḍaṇḍọm, jạribana; (*for social offence*) kuṭum ḍaṇḍ; (*to impose*) ḍać ḍuć, daṛ, phurạn.

FINGER, A—kaṭup̕; (*fore*) uk̕duk̕ kaṭup̕; (*middle*) mutul k., tala k; (*little*) sić k.; (*4th.*) mundạm k.; (*breadth*) k. tạsu; (*nails*) ti rama; (*ring*) mundạm; (*to mark with tip*) ṭikạk̕; (*to dip in*) ṭudạk̕.

FINGERS—(*having extra*) caṅgra (M), caṅgri (F); (*kept bent till stiff*) lọk lọkọ; (*to snap the*) cuṭki.

FINISH—(*to*) alse, baṅgam, caba, cạrpạṭ, dharkao, dursut, gạyum, gọbọr maṭi, gucạu, hoe, hora, jhańjhaṭ, kamal, khatam, khọṭọm, mạcur, mạr, marọṭ, mạr pasir, mọhọr meṭao, mọkọń, mọsọť, mucạť, nimbhạu, niṅghạr, niṅghrạu, niptạu, pạcuk̕, pạṭ, pharcha, purạpuri, sabaṛ, sạkim, sariạu, sạrpạṭ, sạṭ, saṭsuṭ, sẹs, sesanti, sesao, sid em, sikim, sumạr, surạs; (*the*) sạmuń.

FINISHED—sidbid, tear; (*to be*) kecak̕, siť; (*used by children*) pạpuk̕; (*to have*) cukạu.

FINISHING TOUCHES, TO PUT THE—mohṇḍa marao, sabaṛ.

FIRE—sẹṅgẹl, sokol; (*pan*) s. bursi; (*in a pit*) kere s.; (*rain*) s. dak̕; (*to light a*) jẹrẹť, s. jol, salgao, sulgạu, tiṅgi; (*to put out a*) iṛić; (*to go out*) iṛić, sọć (2); (*to catch*) s. lagao, s. sap̕; (*to push into a*) ṭhekao; (*to put fuel on a*) tiṅgi; (*to spread*) gọṭọr; (*to become low*) hạrsuṛ; (*to warm oneself at*) jadwạhi, jorok̕; (*to kindle form embers*) s. salgao; (*to reduce to ashes by*) bhasam; (*to put on a*) conda. *Cf.* FLAME, TO SET.

FIREBRAND, TO WAVE A—ḍuṇḍuk.

FIREFLY, THE—bakjunu.

FIREPLACE, A—culhạ; (*opening for pot*) ạchiạ; (*a rude*) iṭhulạk̕, uṭhulak̕; (*trench as*) jhili gaḍa, khandha; (*part of*) culhạ ocoť; (*back of*) c. kuḍạm; (*front of*) c. koṛam.

FIREWOOD—sahan; (*plenty of*) bela s.; (*long pieces of*) laṛga s.; (*thin pieces of*) jhuri; (*& leaves*) kaṭpat; (*a heap of*) koṭhauṛi, kuṭhauṛi; (*branches for*) koṭań s.

FIREWORKS—bhuicampa, bom.

FIRM—cera (2), cerda (2) kajak, urić; (*to be*) thambhao; (*to remain*) diṛ.

FIRMAMENT, THE—cọṭ, serma.

FIRMLY—canḍ, diṛamuṇḍte; (*in comp.*) raṭpaṭao.

FIRMNESS OF MIND—dharọs.

FIRST—buniạdi, pạhil, pordhan, porthọm, sirạ; (*in time or place*) maṛań; (*time*) asãe sawãe, pahla pạhli, salas; (*wife*) bạṛki, bạṭki; (*born*) jhẹṭ, marańić, pạhilạuṭhạ; (*man*) kakaṛ, pilchu haṛam; (*woman*) pilchu budhi; (*hand, at*) nijgut, nijut; (*sale of day for cash*) pạhnạ; (*seed sown*) muṭh; (*class*) aol, awạl; (*fruits, to offer*) loban, luban, nạũwai.

FISH—hako; (*to catch*) bạ̃rsi, huṇḍạ, ṭipkạ; (*to drive about*) umjhạu; (*to poison*) rup̕; (*swim of*) ḍuldul; (*scales*) ạs, cũiạk̕; (*tail*) cupi; (*fin*) il; (*gleanings of*) baṛạudha; (*hairs on mouth of*) goco; (*method of cooking*) bhartạ, lať hako; (*hook*) bạ̃rsi; (*spear*) kạhli, ṭẹṇṭa; (*intoxicants*) haṛ; (*method of catching*) bạhĩj, bẹr. *Cf.* BASKET, NET, TRAP.

FISH, SPECIES OF—badhoṛ, bạslạ, bheḍa h., boaṛ, bumbuć h., calka, caole ghure, chiṛ h., citol, coḍa, cọdgọć, ḍaṇḍkạ, daṛkạ, ḍhaṇḍkạ, dũrĩ, gaḍa coḍa, gadjal, gajal, gendlań, ilsa, jhõea, jiol h., kakṛa h., kalbokos, kara ghakor, kãrã h., katla, khucilạ, koṭro, liṇḍa, maṅgri h., mať sakam h., matkọm h., mirik h., paṅgas h., poṭea gaṛai, poṭha h., ragho boaṛ h., rereť h., ruhi h., rui, siṅghịn h., sirhọć h., siriń h., sisiń h, siṭkạ bowar, sọrọć h., sũ h., tale h., ṭeṅgra h., ṭirom h., (*river*) calhạ.

FISHERMAN, A—kẽoṭ, kẽoṭa; (*expert*) machreṅka.

FISSURE, A—dar, hạndṛuṅ; (*that must be jumped*) dọn gaḍa.

FIST, THE—cupuć; (*to close*) cupuć, muṭhiạu; (*to strike with heel of*) guḍạ guḍi, guḍạu, kedra kidri, kilạu, kuḍṛau, kuhạu, thegṛao; (*the closed*) muṭh.

FISTULA DUE TO DECAYED TEETH—sonpat.

FIT—lek, sọmbhọb; (*to be weaned*) bakarna, bakorna, gutruć; (*to be*) jowao; (*a*) bạị, suruj bạị; (*to be seized with a*) bhẹn (2), ripi (2); (*a convulsive*) dhạmuk bạị.

FIT, TO—bạisạu, khaṭao; (*closely*) jẹmbẹć, milạn, piạ; (*into*) haṛọṕ; (*together*) milạṭ; (*arrow to bowstring*) ṭuniạu.

FITFUL—olocolo.

FITTING—lek; (*as is*) lek lekate; (*accurately*) jẹpẹć, khap (2); (*ill*) dhọdlọ, jhadeć (2), jhadọć (2), jhaṇḍel (2), siṭar paṭar, siṭbasaṛe.

FIVE—mọṇẹ, mõṛẽ, pāc, panc; (*each*) mọ̃mõṛkate; (p. m.) huḍiń daḱ lo ber; (*seers*) pasari.

FIX, TO—bạisạu, bandhao, ja, laga, motaen, niṭ, rikit, ṭahrao, ṭarhao, ṭhekan, ṭhikạn; (*horizontally*) bindhạṛ; (*time or place*) neṇḍa, neṇḍa goṇḍa; (*rent*) rek bạndhi; (*a word in writing*) caṇḍiạu; (*eyes on*) ạhirkuhir; (*upright in ground*) biť; (*teeth into*) cạblạu; (*date of hunt*) barte, ḍahur bulạu. *Cf.* RATE.

FIXED—dondorcoć, motean; (*stare*) morel (2); (*to be*) sidho.

FIXTURE, A—jam; (*to make*) ṭahrao, ṭarhao.

FIZZING SOUND, A—chọr, chọr marte, sẹrẹ (2), soro (2).

FLABBY—copsaha, labas lubus, lẹjẹr (2), lejraha, phoksaha.

FLAG, A—cir, jhaṇḍa; (*staff*) cir ḍaṅ.

FLAKES, TO COME OFF IN—cạṭić, rọć.

FLAME—ac, dhak, elaṅ, jharka jharki; (*sound of*) phoro (2), phor (2).

FLAMING—dhandha, dhạu dhạu.

FLANK, THE—hawań.

FLAP, TO—dulup̕ (2), phud (2); (*the wings*), lablab, lep̕, lẹpẹ (2), liplap, phadaphud, phada phodo, phad (2), ripi (2); (*of large birds*) lạṕ (2); (*while sitting*) piḍil (2); (*while hovering*) ripi (2).

FLAPPING—ḍhapaṛ, ḍhaṕ (2), leṕ (2), pharphur, phẹṭẹ (2), phẹṭẹḱ (2); (*of long garments*) tilmạń talmań; (*as strips*) ṭiyạl ṭapal.

FLARE UP, TO—bambkao, bamka bạmki, dãhgao, dahṅgao, tiṛiń.

FLARING—bilis (2), dahṅga dạhṅgi, dugur (2).

FLASH—(*a*) jhalak; (*with a*) jhak marte; (*to*) bilik balań, biliť, camkao, comkao, ḍig ḍigauḱ, dulup̕ (2), jalać julut́, jhalkao, malkao; (*when shaken*) jhipir (2), jipir (2).

FLASHING—bilis (2), jaral (2), jeleṕ (2), jiliṕ (2), julut́ (2); (*as tiger's eyes*) jọrọl (2), jurul (2); (*in the sun*) jiṛiṕ (2).

FLASHY—jhiki miki, jiki miki.

FLAT—capṛa, celcekeć, cẹpẹ, cepel, cepṛa, cẹpṛẹ, ceprot, lapondań, lẹplẹpẹ, thapṛa; (*as opposed to steep*) laclaca, lẹclẹcẹ; (*& board*) cakta, laclacạ, lẹclẹcẹ; (*& small*) cạkti; (*of fruitpods*) laṛpa; (*as beer*) ḍemba; (*cake*) cạki; (*earthen dish*) tawa; (*nosed*) cẹpṛẹ, cẹpṛẹć, khenderpeć; (*on back of head*) khonta bọhọḱ.

FLATTEN, TO—lapaḱ capaḱ, lẹp lẹpe.

FLATTER, TO—luhu cuhu, phusalạu.

FLATULENCE—gum bạị; (*suffering from*) padna (M), pạdni (F).

FLAVOUR—mahatom, sọṛọmtẹć.

FLAW, A—dọpọć, dorpaṭ, kạsur; (*with*) darpoṭ, dopca, dorpoć; (*without*) napae, nimon, niphuṭ, nisạṇḍ; (*in bottom*) penda dọpọć.

FLAX—musnạ; (*plant*) cikno.

FLAY, TO—khal, khalkhalao.

FLEA, A—mẹr mẹṭẹć.

FLEE, TO—daṛ, ńir, paṇḍuć, pharkao, pọlọć; (*at full speed*) biṛampạṭ.

FLESH—jel; (*to gain*) moṭa jaora; (*to recover*) pheṭ; (*to lose*) jhaṭkao, ojhṛao, osmao, pajhrao; (*to become rough*) run tukun, sim jel; (*proud*) toloke; (*hanging in folds*) ladać luduć, ladhar lodhor; (*never putting* *on*) patranga (M), patrangi (F); (*beside back-bone*) bhuṇḍạ jel ; (*of fat woman*) lidur pidur.

FLESH MEAT—jel ; (*method of cooking*) lat jel, kohra jel, leto ; (*cooked with rice*) jel sure ; (*cut into strips & dried*) rohor jel ; (*method of keeping*) run ; (*greedy for*) lemeture ; (*inferior quality of*) leran petan ; (*given to officials*) ḍuṇḍe ; (*to neighbours*) porsad.

FLEXED, TO BE—(*as a limb*)—kucạ.

FLEXIBLE, TOO (*as a bow*)—labus (2), lubus (2).

FLICKER, TO—dagar dugur, dulup (2), julut (2).

FLIES FOUND IN FIGS—hạrũ.

FLIGHT, A (*as of locusts*)—kanbol.

FLIMSILY TIED—ḍhiusi.

FLINCH, TO—bhẽrcak, latić.

FLINT, A—chakmak, cokmạki ; (*& steel gun*) pathor kala bạnduk.

FLIPPANT—caego.

FLIRT, TO—khamda, khamda khạmdi, khel, kheldu, khildu.

FLIRTING—ạngra (M), ạngri (F), candoro, celko melko, hihi koko, ikil sikil, jhalka (M), jhạlki (F).

FLOAT, TO—ạtu, cape, payar, uphlạu, uphlạ uphli ; (*away*) bohao, buhel, hehel ; (*on surface*) cạmdhul, caple.

FLOAT FOR FISHING-LINE—puhi, ṭipkạ.

FLOATING & STATIONARY—ḍomkol.

FLOCK, A—ara, gadel, gahạndi, gạhndi, jhunḍ, kanbol, khar, pal.

FLOG, TO—carnao, chenchao, curạu ; (*with a cane*) bẽt.

FLOOD, A—bạd, bạḍi, ban, banbạsi, bayaban, ḍubạ ; (*to be carried by*) banbạsi, bhasao.

FLOOD, TO—cape, chạpilman, chạplạu, ḍubạ, ḍubạu, taloi, ṭạpu.

FLOOR—ot ; (*threshing*) kharai ; (*cloth*) dari.

FLOP, A—lapak (2), lopok ; (*with a*) lapak mente, larbhad m., lethẽć m., lijrak m., lopok m., rihir m.

FLOP, TO—ladbad ; (*down*) lijrak ; (*fall with a*) lethẽć, lodop marte ; (*throw down with a*) lethẽć.

FLOUNDERINGLY—tahap ṭaṭup, tawak ṭaṭuk.

FLOUR—aṭa, holon, lobok, maeda, moeda, talsa ; (*finely ground*) lemen holon, luhui ; (*kinds of*) Cf. lobok ; (*ant*) lobok muć.

FLOURISH, TO—ḍagḍag, ḍagḍagao, ḍogḍogao ; (*as plants*) susurṭak ; (*in music*) laboj.

FLOW, TO—ạtu, buhel, chạpilman, dahadahi ; (*as blood*) jiro joro, sira soro, siro soro ; (*as tears*) hidir (2) ; (*gently*) lingi ; (*freely*) suḍrạu ; (*out*) bhulkạu ; (*into*) dul midok.

FLOWER, A—baha, phul ; (*kind of*) atal b., bir surạj mukhi, ḍunḍun b., kạpur mạli b., kukrucut b., kusmbi b., larka b., mạli b., modor muli b., surạj mukhi, toa b. ; (*to*) baha, gele ; (*to pass along dancers*) baha bas ; (*an edible*) kaenai b., matkom. *Cf.* PLANT.

FLOWERS—(*which remain on tree*) jama ; (*garland of*) baha mala ; (*to deck with*) baha ; (*of Matkom tree*) jara.

FLOWING—bạhi, bohi, cohol bohol ; (*in full flood*) cehel (2), cehel cepel ; (*quickly, as blood*) chir (2) ; (*to cease*) ṭhamkao ; (*water*) gadgadao ; (*as a beard*) godor.

FLUENT—badohi, batkạti, cogor, colonti, kahbajia, lecer (2), leser (2).

FLUID—(*a little*) sebẽć ; (*to thicken by evaporation*) cạchi.

FLUSTERED—aksak, ạndhi cạndhi, ạndhup, armarao, ạṭpaṭ, cahap caṭur, cạnda cạnḍi, caṭpaṭao, gạni sạni, khuṭkhuṭ.

FLUTE, A—tirio ; (*bamboo*) bẽrẽ t. ; (*part of*) dhạpi ; (*to play*) t. oron ; (*an adept at*) baskạri, baskạria ; (*sound of*) hudur (2).

FLUTTER, TO—dhak (2), dhuk (2), phadaphud, phada phodo, phede (2), ripi (2), tirmirạu ; (*as garments*) lindlạpur ; (*noise of*) phete (2).

FLY, A—ro ; (*small*) basạndi, bhũsạndi, busạndi ; (*cattle*) loṭoć, kada l. ; (*dog*) seta loṭoć ; (*dragon*) bakdulu ; (*flisk*) kapil gai cãoar ; (*sand*) cucumhuć, jujuhũć ; (*eggs of green*) asãe.

FLY, TO—pharkao, udau; (*up & down*) apir; (*as chips from axe*) phantil, phicir, picir; (*of sparks*) bijir (2), cercetec, pasir, phentor; (*at*) jhũkau; (*off*) chontal, podoe; (*at a tangent*) phencor; (*slowly*) lipa lape; (*back by force of contact*) thikrau; (*into a rage*) tirin; (*away*) udia udi.

FLY-CATCHER, THE—(*Indian paradise*) lantiti; (*Grey-headed*) sasan cẽrẽ.

FLYING-FOX, THE—kahu barduruc.

FLYING FROM PLACE TO PLACE—dacan (2).

FOAM—phẽr; (*a mass of*) dondha.

FODDER—adhar, cara, cari. *Cf.* GRASS.

FOETUS, THE—gorob.

FOG, A—ron kuhra.

FOLD—(*a*) haria, latum; (*cattle*) bathan; (*times*) dabol, dobor, dobra, guna; (*two*) duna, mit latum.

FOLD, UP TO—samtao; (*into a lump*) koteam.

FOLDS, HANGING IN—liwar lawar; (*of flesh*) obobo.

FOLK-LORE—gam.

FOLLOW, TO—duyun (2), gohnao, oton, panja; (*to give assistance*) sotok; (*after*) goson, goyon; (*suit*) besao, bhesao; (*up*) pacha, pecha; (*interstices, as water*) soro.

FOLLOWER, A—paiha, tabedar.

FOLLOWING—(*at a distance*) jepe thope, jope thope; (*closely*) daradari, godoe godae; (*each other*) oloe gotoe, oton tayom, pacha pache; (*in a line*) giroe gorge; (*in birth*) sotok.

FOMENT, TO—sekao; (*quarrels*) lond-phond.

FONDLE, TO—dular, gudiauk; (*legs or feet*) godhe.

FONDLED, TO WISH TO BE—alaria, alarok.

FONDNESS—his, mel, mil, milua.

FOOD—adhar, ata sata, ata talsa, cara, cari, dal daka, dana, dogoj, jomak, khana, khorag, khorca, khurag, lobok, mandi, lac mandi, on, on cun, on muk, udkhud; (*uncooked*) kharca; (*a helping of*) paras; (*advance of pay for*) khorag, khurag; (*without*) khankhaila; (*forbidden*) ais amol, as amol; (*abstinence from forbidden*) net; (*unrestricted as to*) khaji; (*sand in*) rege cege; (*searching for*) khau (2), lalejanje, patar cata; (*offered to deities*) porsad; (*of bamboo shoots*) handua; (*for an emergency*) solo sanjok, sonjok; (*given to induce sleep*) janapitak; (*exhausted*) ghatal sanj; (*to prepare*) aro; (*to give*) khawao, khiau, khilau; (*to help to*) harta, parsao; (*to give 2nd. helping of*) ãrti; (*to partake of*) onjolok; (*to withhold*) erao, pokhao; (*to retain*) jirau; (*to be burnt in cooking*) jari poda, ok, rongo congo; (*to find fault with*) jom tanao; (*to loathe*) doyok; (*not to give at proper time*) kharkharao, khorkhorao; (*to stuff in*) kopet, lepekope, masra masri, masrao. *Cf.* LEAVINGS.

FOOD & DRINK—dak daka, dana pani, khana, jom nũiak, oljol, onjol, on pani; (*to give*) khiau piau, khilau pilau; (*to partake of*) buka lolo, oljol; (*given to bridegroom's party*) toraoni.

FOOL, A—bemblaha, bhucun, gabhri; (*blind*) kordhoc mara herel.

FOOLISH—akil gawar, anta, bandha (M), bandhi (F), baura, bebuj, bekup, bhembha (M), bhembhi (F), bhoco, bhuc, boka, bondo, dhundha (M), dhundhi (F), dundha (M), dundhi (F), gãowar, gãwar, hoto budhi, jambhua, khaowar, khepa, kõka (M), kũki (F), konka (M), kunki (F), lelha (M), lelha melha, lilhi (F), murkho, nirbak, nirbodh, olkobaha, olo, ondiot, orlo, phariabaj, thulau, urbhun; (*ness*) nabhua

FOOT, THE—janga, kata, pao; (*base*) penda, phed; (*ball of*) panuska; (*dorsal surface of*) suptic; (*sole of*) talka; (*to hold up*) kakac kukuc, kocon; (*rest for*) lenebet; (*to stamp*) dhap (2); (*to strike against*) tohot, torot; (*marks*) lebet gada, khaida baida, khaeda khaidi, odgak bidgak, padgak, panja; (*rule*) gaj; (*sore*) dhorot (2), lipoc lopoc.

FOOTSTEPS, SOUND OF—dahap (2), karap kurup, kudup (2), kudur (2); (*rushing*) dhar dhur.

FOPPISH & DISSOLUTE—lancan.

FOR—ced**a**kje, ente, khon, mente; (*the purpose of*) lagat, lagit, mente; (*ever*) hot husit, jaejug, jug cetan jug, jugajug, tiris jug; (*the present*) barsin ursin; (*nothing*) moste, omnete, muphut; (*that reason*) tobe eron.

FORAGE—cara, cari.

FORBEAR, TO—sombhori, uput.

FORBEARS—hapramko.

FORBID, TO—baron, dabot, dapkao, jabod, jakao, mana, nised.

FORBIDDEN—manahi, palon; (*food*) ais amol, as amol.

FORCE—ajhat, dhamas, jala, jobor, jobrani, jormot, jor, julum, moth, tap, tapis, tor; (*by*) jor bajor, jor bandhi, jor bojor, kajiau, moth maria, muruk; (*with great*) andha dhund, badrak, barat, bardak, bharsak, hujlak marte, ringau; (*of habit*) thonk; (*to put or come into*) jari, kayem, tamil; (*to use*) dhorao, jhotra jhutri, jobran, jobrani, jor julum; (*to take by*) reć.

FORCE, TO—dharkau, joborjos, mosokusi; (*a way in*) gusuć, kokcao, lale, sandhaore (F); (*onself on another*) jodhe; (*to go*) ghac ghacao; (*by bullying*) dhamkhum, dhara dhura, dharamara, jhik jhor; (*down from perpendicular*) patuć; (*advance payment*) cacao.

FORCED LABOUR—begar, beth begar, bigria, bithi; (*like*) bithiahi.

FORCEFUL—hadrap, jobori.

FORCIBLE—at. khara.

FORCIBLY—dhara bandha, dhora bandha, dhora dhori, garda gardi, garte, jorâe, jor bajor, jor bandhi, jor bojor, jormot, moth, meth maria, tarkha.

FORD, A—ghat; (*on Damuda river*) Barni ghat.

FOREFINGER, THE—uduk katup.

FOREFATHERS—bap dada, hapramko.

FOREHEAD, THE—candi, matha, molon; (*white blaze on*) candla (M), candli (F), tikla (M), tikli (F); (*to mark*) tika, tilak; (*to knock*) tapin; (*ill-shaped*) doemon; (*mark on women's*) kedar.

FOREIGN—bidas, bides, bilati, biran.

FOREIGNER—bidesia, pordesi, pordesia.

FOREKNOW, TO—badae daram.

FORELOCK—dhacri.

FOREMAN—sardar, sordar.

FOREMOST—pahil, sira.

FOREORDAIN, TO—atet sit.

FORERUNNER—aguadar.

FORESKIN,—lomor; (*to turn back*) hejer, pisir.

FOREST—bir; (*dense*) akut bir, atut bir, arna bir, urni bir; (*to live in*) banwas; (*to clear*) chitra phutau; (*marriage*) mundu bapla; (*a traditional*) khanderae bir, manbir; (*cess*) bonkor. *Cf.* TREE.

FORESTALL, TO—tebak.

FORETELL, TO—paetar; (*by oil & incantations*) patra.

FORETHOUGHT—danda giri.

FORFEIT—barjid; (*to agree to*) akhaji.

FORGET, TO—bhul, hirin, kacokam; (*cause to*) anman.

FORGETFUL—behos, gandać gunduć, gani sani.

FORGIVE, TO—ika, katit, map, maph, rahai sahai.

FORKED—canga, canga cangi; (*to place on anything*) harop.

FORLORN—anduk canduk, anjhlun, jarmak jormok, jarmak tormak, kalan dolan, tormak.

FORM—bhes, chand, chin, chond, cond, dhob, dol, muthan, rup; (*bench*) benc.

FORM, TO—benao; (*as ear of grain*) gele; (*as fruit*) cinćić.

FORMERLY—agari, indara, nindara, sabik, sedae, sei; (*as*) sei ke sei.

FORNICATION—lat ghut, lotghuti.

FORSAKE, TO—bagi, teag, tiag.

FORT, A—gar, garh, kila; (*traditional*) khaira. koenda gar, sim gar.

FORTHWITH—sat mente.

FORTUNATE—bhagan, lakhi (M), lukhi (F), nasiban, sahar.

FORTUNE—bhag, danai, khariat, lachmi, larbhad, molon, nasib; (*good*) asae sawae, borket, khariat, maha bhag, sahar; (*ill*) abjos, latu bhandu; (*by what*) oka bhag; (*to meet with ill*) landbhandao.

FORTY—bar isi, pon gel.

FORWARD—ḍhīṭ; (*to*) calao, huḍą; (*to be*) cahak mahak; (*to go straight*) haṛbaṅ haṛbuṅ, hureć paṭeć, soror; (*to put oneself*) lęhę (2).

FORWARDNESS, NOT IN THE SAME STATE OF—mama bhągną.

FOUL—(*as a sore*) bęjęk (2); (*as abuse*) siṭ bhāṇḍ, siṭh bhāṇḍ.

FOUND, TO—baisąu.

FOUNDATION—buniąd, neo, rębęć, tąli, tuli; (*excavation for*) dargaḍa.

FOUNDERS OF A VILLAGE—buniądi hoṛko.

FOUR—car, pon, ponea; (*all the*) ponon; (*a set of*) gaṇḍa, goṇḍa, hąli; (*corners*) ponkoṇḍ, pon sirą; (*days ago*) on mahnder; (*days hence*) pher endrae; (*each*) popon goṭaṅ; (*fold*) pon guną; (*& a half*) saṛhe car; (*p. m.*) maraṅ dak lo ber; (*quarters of the heavens*) cario dig; (*points of compass*) cąukhūṭ.

FOURTH, THE—ponak, poneaṭak; (*son*) maṅjlą koṛa; (*daughter*) maṅjli kuṛi; (*son's wife*) maṅjli bąhu; (*one*) pao; (*more, one*) sawa.

FOWL, A—(*barndoor*) sim; (*black*) karanath sim; (*small*) hopon sim; (*Guinea*) chinsim, sęṅgel ṭiṭi; (*sacrificial*) goṭ sim, maṇḍwa sim, tiąk; (*large*) kikokoko, kuląm sim; (*jungle*) bir sim; (*water*) bęć bedręć, bonbayar, dhẽkjoṛ, ḍholkaṭa, ḍom ṭuṅki, ḍubą cẽįẽ, gaṇḍar cẽrẽ, panserali, serali; (*with reversed f athers*) risą sim; (*with scanty feathers*) ḍeṇḍka; (*with feathered legs*) jhaṅga sim; (*entrails of*) muṇḍu laċ; (*house*) sim khundṛi, kole, kuli, sim gaṛ; (*call to drive away*) soć; (*call to warn*) cikkur; (*scream of*) corcor, keryõṭ.

FOX, A—loyoṅ jalo; (*the Indian*) khikṛī; (*flying*) kąhu barduṛūć; (*cry of*) khāo (2) khąu (2), peṭkhāo-khāo.

FRACTION, A—cuṭki, ṭukrą.

FRACTURED, TO BE—ṭuṭąu.

FRAGMENTS—gaṇḍa guṇḍa, khaea khucra, khae khudri, ṭakra ṭukrą, ṭuṭą bhaṅga; (*small*) khaya khudri; (*to make into*) khiciṅ bidrić, khutri, kiciṅ bidrić; (*to tear into*) khaią khudri, khaią kucrą, khaya khudri, khaya kucrą.

FRAGRANT—mahka mąhki, mahkao, sondgond.

FRAILTY, HAVING ANY PARTICULAR—emon semon.

FRAME—(*well-knit*) jhabrąhi, jhabrąli; (*door or window*) cąukaṭha.

FRAMEWORK—saj; (*for thatch*) chaṭāṛ; (*of bed, chair, &c.*) pariaṛe.

FRANK—khulą, khuląsa; (*to be*) khuląu.

FRANKINCENSE—kunduru, loban.

FRANKLY—khulą khuli, phaṅka phayaṛ.

FRANTIC—rokoṭ muhą̃.

FRAUD—caląki, chol; (*full of*) calak, harrap; (*to take by*) ręć.

FRAYED, TO BE—phodlo.

FREE—akar, bahbah, bahbąhią, bętabe, chaḍ, chuṭa, chuṭąlią, elak chaḍa, iląk chaḍa, mophoṭ, muphuṭ, omneṭe, parhaṛ, phaḍa, sądhin, udhmą; (*of earth*) burui (2); (*space*) phāk; (*to set*) arak, chadao, khalas; (*from anxiety &c.*) phaṛią phąṭi.

FREEDOM—khuląsa, rihai; (*from ca e*) hub; (*from fear*) salsāt; (*to deprive of*) gurgur.

FREELY—bęphao, dan, khos, khulą khuli, khusi khos, luhum suhum, mostę, phaṅka phayaṛ, sahasae, sohoka, sohosae.

FREEZE, TO—karkarao.

FREIGHT—bhara, mąhsul.

FRENZIED—bhalok; (*to be*) rokoṭ muhą̃, sansanao, sarngao, surma.

FRENZY—sur.

FREQUENTED—(*of a road*) rohpoṭ, rosoḍ.

FREQUENTLY—canke, darak (2), here phere; (*in comp.*) bara; (*of diarrhoea*) lacpac.

FRESH—bale, balebõs, beręl, labaṅ dohaṅ, lęgęć labak, nawa, taj, ṭaṭka, tartąrią; (*of pot-herbs*) kanḍer; (*leaves*) bolkoṅ.

FRESHNESS, TO LOSE—ḍola, ḍolao; (*of meat*) moroṭ soroṭ.

FRET, TO—ąktąu, arsa, bitlą bi[illegible] jaljalao, uṭu puṭu; (*at delay*) puṭu.

FRETFUL—askandnu (M), askandni (F); (*of children*) naṭkhaṭ.

FRIABLE—bhud bhudia; (*earth*) ṭirom hasa.

FRICTION, TO APPLY—ragṛao.

FRIDAY—sukar, sukol, sukor, sukulbar, sukur.

FRIEND—gate, hĩt mitar, saṅga.

FRIENDLESS—alag, anthaṛi, awaṭapa, tala ṭaṇḍi.

FRIENDLY—aiso baiso, ghesa, helmel, hilmil, hĩt, luhum suhum, pirit; (*to be*) banot, dahin, gate, ǫñsoñ, risbod, rosbot, sahai, same game; (*to become*) samge; (*hand, a*) hat bai.

FRIENDS & RELATIVES—gate peṛa, peṛa parbha.

FRIENDSHIP—bhab, haobhao, hĩt, mil, suloñ; (*to be in close*) pia; (*ceremony of*) karam daṛ, patao, phul, saika.

FRIGHTEN, TO—borkao, cilcilau, haba duba, hama homo; (*by threats*) habka dubka, hapka dupka.

FRIGHTENED—ḍurukia, keklseṭ, liki phiki, lucpucia; (*away*) caukau; (*to be*) bharao, bhiṛkau, bidṛau, bilbilau, biraj, biṛkau, biṛki, botor, dhuk (2), dhupuć, leṅgeṭ, liṅgiṭ, lucpuc, toras; (*anything that makes children*) bibi.

FRIGHTFUL—bhoyon, botor.

FRILL—kanaso, kaso.

FRINGE—dasi, duria.

FRISK, TO—don, kamsa kamai, piḍgak, pidga piḍgi.

FRITTER AWAY, TO—riai khiai, riyai khiyai, ubla dubla, udai padae; (*time*) alae phulae.

FRIVOLOUS—lamkamaria, loṅgor coṅgor, mirsitar, ṭum.

FRIVOLOUSLY—pathauri; (*to work*) kaituk.

FRIZZLE, TO—caṭa cuṭu, choñ, gadgad, gadgadao; (*sound*) choñ godo (2).

FROG—roṭe; (*buried deeply in earth*) patal r.; (*species of*) *Cf.* roṭe. *Cf.* CROAK.

FROLIC—hãsae khelae, hãsi, hãsi khelae, hãsi tamasa, sihan; (*to*) makmak; (*given to*) sihania.

FROM—khoć, khon; (*all directions*) almal, almalao, amiñ, ulmal; (*among*) madhe, mandhe, mod, modhe, motore, mud; (*here & there*) joro joṭo.

FRONT—samañ; (*the*) samañ seć; (*to push to the*) thare mare; (*always to the*) lahar cahar, lahe cahe; (*in*) mohṇḍa, samañre, samna samni; (*rank, in*) sira.

FRONT OF, IN—laha, matrañ, muhã muhĩ, samuk; (*to cross*) endak.

FROST—borop; (*hoar*) pala, ratañ.

FROTH—phẽr, phoṭo; (*mouth*) patahañ, patohañ; (*to*) cãwãok.

FROWARD—bheroṭ, chutṛari, dhĩṭ, dhocor, khacaṛ.

FROWN, TO—binduć satok, kurkunduć, kuṛkuṛ, kuṛkuṛau; (*with a*) kosle.

FRUGAL—jogaria; (*to be*) rakhi jogao.

FRUGALLY—ramo (2).

FRUIT—bapha, jo, phal, phol; (*a*) aṛa; (*all kinds of*) phal dol; (*forming*) ciñcić; (*young*) jali; (*nearly ripe*) kasrać; (*not fully developed*) khõrẽ; (*of leguminous plants*) jañ; (*of a jungle climber*) bando, lamak; *forming after rains*) sisir jali; (*a kind of*) bandor lauri, juṅgi; (*remaining on tree when ripe*) jama; (*used to clear water*) nirmoli; (*a medicinal*) pipol; (*rind of*) baklak, cokak; (*inner skin of*) ganthar; (*pulp of*) gabe; (*stone of*) jañ; (*to bear*) jo, jojao, pholao; (*to be loaded with*) jhabrao; (*to pluck*) goć; (*to knock down with a pole*) hunda.

FRUITLESSLY—bonahak, bertha, bhandur, micha, nahak.

FRUITS OF ANYTHING, ONE WHO ENJOYS—bhogdar.

FRY, SMALL—chiṛ hako, jhõea, jiṛyañ miṛyañ; (*poṭha*) puṭhi hako.

FRY IN OIL, TO—curcuria.

FUEL, TO PILE ON—orop, tiṅgi.

FUGITIVE, A—udacal.

FULFILLED, TO BE—ghoṭao, pura puri, purau.

FULL—asãt osõt, bhor, cemcerem, curu buru, paka, pepreć, pereć, pura, samthul, saprum, seksẽke, ṭomba; (*quite*) cepel; (*of F. breasts*) kenel

(2); (*to be*) andkao, tuhel; (*the*) sagor; (*to the*) chẹ̌ć bẹ̌ć; (*not to the*) hạn, odgel, pat; (*in*) nikạrkhar, purạ (2); (*filled*) lajhar; (*cheeked*) pọknẹt (F), pọkrọť; (*faced*) hạkurpak; (*length, at*) boňboń; (*measure*) ḍiṭọp; (*fledged*) il saprum; (*return of crops*) rạsi puńji; (*force*) bharsak, dare bhor; (*tilt*) umdhum; (*to overflowing*) dorobotolo, sarer; (*& gliding, as river*) lẹmlẹm; (*requirements for marriage*) solo sańjok. *Cf.* BRIM

FULL-GROWN—barhọn, goṭa guṭi, hara jarjo, hara juạn, hara kańjela, haratal, jargo, jhamaṭ, bhar juạn, kańjela, lekman, moṭa muṭi, pakṭa, purạn, rata; (*of unmarried women*) jhaka; (*of women*) hapamum, hara jhamaṭ; (*of men*) hara rata; (*of bulls*) matao; (*almost, of M. buffaloes*) cẹṇḍa bayar; (*just*) nawatur; (*not*) aedhọn, chaoṛa, licạr.

FULLER'S EARTH, A KIND OF—saji hasa; (*for washing hair*) naṛkan hasa.

FULLY—gan, saprum, sumuń; (*of ripeness*) har; *developed*) barhọntar; (*occupied*) bhir, lajhar, najhar, ọlọń (2).

FUME, TO—seke (2).

FUN—hãsae khelae, hạ̃si, hạ̃si khelae, hạ̃si tamasa, hạ̃si ṭhaṭha, phulạ khạsiạ; (*with*) gudiạ gudyi; (*to make*) gokhna, hasna, hạ̃snua, isir siṭkoć, khelọḍ, phalu, phulạị, ṭhaṭha; (*given to*) phulạniạ.

FUNCTION (*marriage, funeral, &c.*)—kajẹ bhọjẹ.

FUNDAMENT, TO BE IMPALED THROUGH THE—cigi.

FUNDAMENTAL—asọl, mul.

FUNERAL PYRE—sara; (*unconsumed wood of*) murdạr sahan; (*corner post of*) torre khuṇṭi; (*wood on corpse*) danapal; (*bones from*) jań baha.

FUNGI—oť; (*a genus of*) puṭkạ, kaṭ oť. *Cf.* oť.

FUNK, TO BE IN A—pucpuc.

FUNNY—gal bajoriạ, kạsiạ, khạsiạ, lambhuạ, lamkambạri, nạbhuạ, pagal, phukṭi, phulạniạ.

FUR—uṗ.

FURIOUS—cańke; (*to be*) kisiạu.

FURIOUSLY—andha dhund, dandanao, ghaṭamạr, raṅga rạṅgi.

FURNACE—bhaṭa, bhaṭha, kaṇḍ; (*smelting*) kuṭhi; (*roar of*) gudur (2).

FURNITURE—sanaphana.

FURROW—nahẹl gaḍa; (*length of*) ḍuṇḍak; (*distance between*) bhili.

FURTHER—(*to go a little*) sẹn ạ̃ṛti; (*side*) ọn parọm.

FURY—ṭapis; (*a fit of*) surmạ.

FUSE, TO—torlao.

FUSIONLESS—adpakoliạ, asań poḍa, gayo gapo, gunduć gusuć, loṛdho, mạdhuạ, mạndhuạ, modhu, poca, sotyoť; (*& slovenly*) thosoť morgoť, tosot morgot.

FUSSILY—ampa ompo.

FUSTY—bạsi, baske.

FUTILE—bertha.

FUTURE—(*the*) agam, tayọm daram; (*in the*) hapẹn, miť din kalre; (*part of day*) dhinạń.

G

GABBLE, TO—alok bakok, bakbakaok, barạ (2), bhac (2), bhacbhacao, bhẹk (2), bhọcọr (2) kuṭnạsiṭ, lacar (2), phadphadao, phedar (2), phẹḍẹ (2), pọkoť (2).

GABLE OF A HOUSE—mutul; (*a house without*) gudi oṛak.

GAIN—ae upạị, barphạị, bhạlạị, pọrhọ; (*to*) arjao, birjạu.

GAIT—(*of tall person*) lạhuć (2); (*hesitating in*) leḍga (M), liḍgi (F); (*of stout female*) lisoe losoe, losoe (2); (*of one with stiff joint*) heṛcań, hutlań; (*of fat person*) isoť osoť, lẹḍọr pẹḍọr; (*waddling*) idhoć ọdhọć, ladać luduć, ladak luduk, udhuć (2); (*peculiar*) kaṭań kuṭuń.

GALE, SOUND OF A STIFF—hadaṛ (2).

GALL—haṛhaṭ sisir, pit.

GALLANT—aṅgra (M), ạṅgri (F), jhalka (M), jhạlki (F).

GALLED, TO BE—berosta, isbis.

GALLOP, TO—kamsa kạmsi, pidgạk; (*to cause*) kamsao, khamsao; (*sound of*) kardaṗ, kaṭaṗ (2).

GAMBOL, TO—kẹrẹp (2), khaṇḍa, pidgąk.

GAME—(*a trapper of*) sikạri ; (*to drive*) chuḍạ, dal jhạli, jhora ; (*killing much*) jarnaha ; (*killed at hunt*) mạr ; (*small*) jiryaṅ miryaṅ.

GAME, A—bhelguḍạ, diga ẹnẹć, lobde e., saj, sim gọyọr, thạiạ, thạiyo hạruṕ, thum ; (*children's*) ṣ̃iṭạ̃u pạ̃iṭạ̃u, bẹť bẹť, bhạluk luka, bhelwa ṭaṕ ṭuṕ, bhiṛkạ, bhiṛkạí (2), bukạ cur cuṭuć, bukạ curṛuć, calao guṭi, cạliạ, chạliạ, cumcumbạ, gạbḍi, guḍạu, gur tawaḱ, hedel guḍạ, họn gujur, iḍi duḍi, jhagwar, jhā̃mpa, jhankar mankar, kaera sarae sapae, kaṇṭhar dare, kitkitạ, kuḍi, kulkul, loka guṭi, maraḱ bele, mā̃yā̃m paṅja, muṭhu, oko e., pusi (2), raja paṭa, rẹrẹ̃ć pẹṭẹć, sikrịć (2), simić (2), sui topa, sui gutu, sutạm ọrọk, tayo (2), thapo (2), ṭhọć, ṭhuṭhukur, ṭir e. ; (*of men & boys*) gurguri ; (*of herd boys*) guṭi e. ; (*like pitch & toss*) kạti ; (*to play*) ẹnẹć ; (*to be put out of*) pọnḍe ; (*lines in*) gạḍi.

GANG, IN A—jamka jumki.

GANGES RIVER, THE—gaṅga, gaṅ nại.

GANJA—gaṅja, maraṅ thamakur ; (*addicted to*) gaṅjeṛi.

GAP, A—hạndṛuḋ, phąk ; (*in a row, &c.*) khaṇḍọ.

GAPE, TO—cahaṕ ; (*as ripe pod*) ọṭẹć.

GAPING—baṅbaṅ, caehaṕ (M), caeliṕ (F).

GARDEN—bagan, bạgica, bagwan, barge ; (*out-lying*) bahẹr barge ; (*flower*) phulbariạ.

GARDENER—mạli.

GARGLE, TO—gargarao.

GARLAND—(*of flowers*) baha mala ; (*to weave*) baha gutu galaṅ ; (*for cows at Sohrae*) dhā̃oa.

GARLIC—rasun.

GARMENT—(*to take off*) bọć ; (*to wear carelessly*) jhadeć (2) ; (*of rags*) gadle.

GARMENTS—ladenaḱ ; (*flowing*) gadae gudui ; (*soiled*) gạnduḱ sạnduḱ, gendrạḱ cethṛaḱ ; (*shorter than usual*) dalpaṅ.

GARNER, TO—samṭao.

GARRULOUS—bẹjẹ (2), labar (2) (F), lasar (2) (F), lasra (M), lạsri (F), lece cere (F).

GAS TAR—koela sunum.

GASH, TO—lạhur, lamaḱ.

GASP FOR BREATH, TO—ukbuk, aṅgaṕ (2) ; (*to be at last*) baṭaḱ.

GATE—phaṭọk.

GATHER, TO—jaora ; (*as an abscess*) bele ; (*fruit*) gụť ; (*pot-herbs*) siť ; (*by littles*) arpa, korpa ; (*together*) cumkạḱ, gaṛha gurhe, hạr samṭao, jomkao, juṛau, ṭhạurạ, tobre, ṭombrẹ ; (*& put back in dhiḋki*) tele ; (*weeds*) hẹrhẹť, kokoṭ, korkoṭ.

GATHERING, A—(*tuck*) kanaso ; (*meeting*) bạisi, kulhi duṛuṕ ; (*religious*) mela ; (*sores*) copsa.

GAUNT—hadgẽra.

GAUR, THE INDIAN—sạl.

GAZE, TO—bẹngẹť, naṅjer, nọjọr ; (*intently*) aṇḍir kuṇḍir, ḍhoro (2).

GAZELLE, HIND OF INDIAN—ghoṭreť jel.

GAZETTE, A—gejeṭ.

GEAR—sapaṕ.

GELD, TO—kạsi, khạsi.

GEM, A—(*Himalayan*) go medak ; (*found in snakes' head*) mạnik.

GENDER—jạt.

GENEALOGY—bõs buḍạ.

GENERAL—mela.

GENERALLY—aṅgọm, asokaete, ḍherkaete.

GENERATION—hiborọn, bidạl, pirhi, purus, pusṭi ; (*after generation*) usti pusti.

GENEROSITY—sil ; (*to give with*) ogor.

GENEROUS—dạni, dini, lahe cahe.

GENETIVE, SIGN OF—reaḱ, reaṅ, ren.

GENTLE—bẹhũṭ, gaemae, khinur, mạhĩr, sapoť, sopoť, sora, subod, supotia, supud, ṭạnḍha ; (*of wind*) hugui, siạḋ sayaṅ.

GENTLEMAN, ACTING THE—ọlọm jhọlọm.

GENTLY—barạṅ buruṅ, dolodolo, gẹmẹń (2), jute (2), kẹrmẹ kẹrmẹte, khanaḱ khunuḱ, lahke (2), lake (2), lọhke, mẹhẽť (2), misiť, phusur (2), rabać rubuć, rase (2), raste, riṅji, rokme (2), rose (2), rosme, rosom, ruyu (2), ṭahari, ṭahri, ṭhahri; (*of rain*) ribić, siṭić (2); (*of wind*) hisić (2), luhui (2), ruili, sugui (2); (*of laughing or crying*) khunũ (2), khunus.

GENUINE—asol, niṅjam.

GENUS—jinis.

GEOGRAPHY—bhugol.

GERMINATE, TO—aṅkur, batrao, omon, potkoć; (*to begin*) poṭo; (*of steeped grain*) barbar, jawa.

GET, TO—hasil, jokha, jurta, juṭau, milan, milau, ńam; (*up*) bereć; (*over*) sarao, torao.

GET OUT!—dhur (2), dur, durya.

GHOST, A—bhut, jin; (*of a father*) porodhol; (*of pregnant woman*) curin.

GHEE—goṭom, so sunum.

GIANT—birbanṭa.

GIFT—dan, ńoṅjor.

GIG—ghor bagi.

GIGGLE, TO—khete (2).

GILD, TO—aṅu.

GILLS—(*of fish*) harrak; (*of turkey*) lapoć.

GINGELLY OIL PLANT, THE—til, tilmiń; (*wild*) kaṭ tilmiń.

GINGER—ada; (*dry*) sũṭ.

GINGERLY, TO WALK—cipa cape, dharak dhorok.

GINNED COTTON—tulam, rić tulam.

GIRDLE—patarohar.

GIRL—chundi, kuri, kuri gidra; (*metaph.*) erba; (*little*) kendle; (*not yet wearing clothes*) bhuili; (*2-6 years*) putli bande; (*8-10*) chend kuri; (*10*) misi juan; (*6-12*) panci bande; (*marriageable*) hira; (*who wears full sari*) khandi bande; (*hood*) ãora bas.

GIRTH, A—berband, patarohar.

GIST—ṭep; (*to give the*) bhoṅ.

GIVE (*imperative*)—den, denya, dese, dini.

GIVE, TO—cal, em, hajir, ne, ni, tela; (*way*) arak, bheńcok, boskao; (*in*) alao, elao; (*up*) alae, dabinas, mosoć, teag, tiag; (*back*) adai, em ruar, phirau, phirot; (*mind to*) bhage sahitte; (*in small quantity*) churuć, curuć; (*a large quantity*) badhi; (*gradually*) em jaora; (*liberally*) ogor, umar; (*to win favour*) em libuk; (*the go-by*) eran, erer; (*more*) juṭić; (*in trust*) amanot, jima; (*in marriage*) ṭehad, ṭhai; (*up work without reason*) bhut kilau; (*away secretly*) pãerẽ; (*properly to pay debt*) bharna, hari bhari, harna bharna, molao.

GIVER, A RELUCTANT—kokoć, papi kokoć.

GIZZARD—kundi.

GLADNESS—hulas.

GLANCE OFF, TO—arap, caric, corań, hoyań, khencer, phencor.

GLANDS, SWELLING OF—gand, piṭiri.

GLARE—rãt.

GLASS—kãc; (*looking*) arsi.

GLAZED—cikar, phiripbić.

GLEAM, TO—camkao, jhak (2).

GLEAN, TO—tumal, tumal tasań; (*matkom*) kondel, kondol; (*to leave grain to*) nara.

GLEANINGS OF FISH—baraudha.

GLEE—hãs; (*full of*) hãsao khelae, keco bedro.

GLEEFULLY—habhab, heseć sekreć, riri (2), ritia riti, sekreć.

GLIB—bhacko, lasar (2) (F), pharhar, pharpharia, ragar cagar, thuthi kuta.

GLIBLY—lecer (2), pharphar.

GLIDE, TO—atu; (*over surface*) horior; (*as water*) legem (2).

GLIMMER, TO—jalać juluć.

GLIMPSE, A—jhalak; (*to catch*) alam galam, apalbeć.

GLISTEN, TO—bilik balań, camkao, jhak (2), jirić (2), pirić.

GLOBULAR— dudumdhukak, duldul, dumka, ṭhal (2), ṭhol (2).

GLOOM, TO—kosoć, kurkur.

GLOOMY—anduk canduk.

GLORY—mahima, sabasi, ṭhonok, ṭhosok.

GLOSSY—chik chok, chuk(2), cikan, galgaeatiń, jirip (2), liplip, lumuń.

GLOWING—darań.

GLOW-WORM, THE—kidiń.

GLUM—aruń paruń, khãs khũs.

GLUTINOUS—tiṛotoṛo, toṛtoṛ, tokoṛ (2).

GLUTTED—dane sane, tobo.

GLUTTON, A—ḍalidar, daṛdaha, daṛidar, habadia, hahut, khauka (M), khauki (F), peṭ posa, peṭdandia, piṭuk, rakas, rẽkh.

GLUTTONOUS—akalia, aklaha, asur, bhojpuria, khae poda, khãk, khãk poda, khaua khawi, lebra (M), libri (F), peṭlaha, piṭukia ; (*& lazy*) khae bhuska (M), khae bhuski (F).

GNARLED—dhampa dhompo.

GNASH THE TEETH, TO—togoć daṭa, maṭmaṭ.

GNAW, TO—togoć.

GNAWING PAIN—kalkal, khalkhal.

GO, TO—calak', dãṛã, dhamsao, dukan, rãodão, raundau, rawana, sańgar, sen ; (*among*) suruć ; (*in*) bol, bolo ; (*under*) unum ; (*aside*) ghajer, sa, sah ; (*after*) duyuń (2) ; (*out*) odok ; (*over*) parom ; (*out as a fire*) iṛić, soć (2) ; (*through*) sumbhrau ; (*away*) samak' (F) ; (*off*) adger ; (*here & there*) ambak' ombok', asok' ṭayok', bhac bhuc, bhaṭau, chalchalao, dhanman, huṛa huṛi, phacak phucuk, phaṭak phuṭuk, pidić (2) ; (*angrily*) ghus ghusau ; (*about*) baṛać buṛuć, dãṛã baṛa ; (*from house to house*) bomboń, nagar bhuli ; (*on impulse of seeing others*) udra udri, udrau ; (*smash at a thing*) aruć paṭuć, aruć taruć ; (*& come again*) ghuri phiri ; (*out of the way*) ayak', banwas, dulkau, ghusau ; (*round about*) girgirau ; (*to & fro*) payar ; (*in head first*) sunduć ; (*a little further*) sen ãrti ; (*straight forward*) hureṭ' paṭeṭ', soror ; (*near*) sõrboṭ', sõrmboṭ'.

GOAD, A—(*buffalow*) arjan ; (*elephant*) ańkus ; (*wooden*) pãerã ; (*mark of*) topond.

GOAT, A—boda merom (M), merom, sakam okṛećić ; (*large flap-eared*) paeda m. ; (*hermaphrodite*) ram khasi m. ; (*young M.*) paṭha, boda paṭha ; (*castrated*) kasi ; (*not properly castrated*) bod khasi ; (*in children's language*) memek' ; (*sacrificial*) caḍi, saket m. ; (*brown*) gola boda (M), guli m. (F) ; (*droppings*) bhelãundi, laḍauri ; (*call to*) ḍorae (2), hedok' ; (*cry of*) bhek', bhek' (2), bobonok' ; (*beard*) goco ; (*house*) gudri, guhi.

GOBBLE, TO—ahur ṭabur, lasok', lembe tumbe, macuk' ; (*up*) kudha, macer ; (*quickly*) masar (2) ; (*sound of*) cak' (2), cakop' (2), chak' (2), chok (2).

GO-BETWEEN, A—raebar goco, raebarić ; (*to act as*) raebar.

GOBLIN, A—bhut.

GOD—Isor ; (*my father*) bapu ṭhakur ; (*of the chase*) rongo ruji ; (*Sun*) surjahi bońga.

GODDESS—(*of sal grove*) gosãe era, jaher era ; (*a Hindu*) kali.

GODLET, A Santal—kaṛi dano bońga, końko buru, kudra, kudra dano b., kudri (F), kuńku buru, lele b., lepe leńgoṛ (F), mahadano, mõṛẽko turuiko, rańga haṛi, rongo era, saṛi caṇḍi b., sima b., sura nańgin b. ; (*of medicine*) kambru buru.

GOING—(*here & there*) caṭna (M), caṭni (F), cundul bhuṭul, dhanka dhanki, doema duimi, ghura ghuri, hoboń (2), hucku cukur ; (*from house to house*) dhosma dhusmi ; (*about continually*) kadae (2) ; (*away, in comp.*) tora ; (*at once, in comp.*) okoe tora ; (*about*) chanań nandań.

GOLD—sona ; (*obs. name*) samanom ; (*genuine*) asol sona ; (*spurious*) phosol sona ; (*coin, a*) asarphi, mohor.

GOLDEN ORIOLE, THE—pio, sasań pio.

GOLDSMITH—sonhar, thaṭori.

GONG, QUICK STROKES ON—gadjal.

GONORRHOEA, &C—garmi, gurmi.

GOOD—awal, bes, bhage, bhal, bhala, bhalai, bhal (2), bhale (2), boge, khub, lasgar, osno (2), sebel, sorom, sosṭok, suca (M), suci (F), sughoṛ, sundar, supoṭ, susṭok, torop, ṭosgor ; (*of food*) taribos ; (*name*) lohani, mahatom ; (*will*) bũihar, baobhao, sonmot ; (*natured*) bapuić, gambhir, nemor ; (*tempered*) dhima, sujat ; (*humouredly*) riri (2) ; (*looking*) cehra, ceṭha, chakmakia, cikon cokon, konekoć, nakhe mukhe, sundor mukhi; *(soil)* hasawan ǫt; *(moderately)* mǫlcǫ; *(& bad)* niki bạdi; *(to be, of crops)* supṭau. *Cf.* FORTUNE, LUCK, OMEN, CONDITION.

GOODS—dhǫn, ghǫrkǫrna, jinis, mal, maljal, saoda, sǫmpǫt; *(& chattels buy)* cij bạsut, dhǫn durib, jalmal, cij sǫmpǫt, tij, tij durib; *(to buy)* saoda; *(a seller of)* hạtwek.

GOOSE, A—hãs, sãk.

GORE, TO—rǫk̇.

GORGED WITH FOOD—dane sane.

GORGEOUS—ṭhǫnǫk.

GOSPEL, THE—boge hukigot, bhage sombat.

GOSSAMER—sutạm, toṛe sutạm.

GOSSIP—*(to)* bạḍohi, gal gǫppǫ; *(of girls)* koboe (2); *(a)* lạṛu caboṛi.

GOSSIPING—bạjnia (F), labak̇ cabak̇; *(to go about)* ajaṛe, kubui (2 F).

GOUGE—*(a)* kuni ruka; *(to)* khokrao, *(cut, to)* khaḍrao, koḍrao.

GOURD, A—*(drinking)* ṭoṭe, tumbạ; *(as drum)* tumbṛi.

GOVERNMENT, WORK OF—raj paṭ, sarkar.

GOVERNOR—cạlạua, cak̇laoić; *(provincial)* hudiń laṭ saheb; *(of nether world)* hudul raj.

GRAB, TO—kamcao, kamṭao, kapṭao, khablao, khamcao; *(at)* conthao; *(repeatedly)* khabla khạbli; *(several at once)* luṛạ luṛi.

GRACE—sạbai.

GRACEFUL—cǫhǫ̃k, rẹṅglẹć.

GRADUALLY—bạibại, dhire suste, hore (2), jaora, kẹrmẹ kẹrmẹte, kǫrmẹ (2), ǫstẹ, rạhi rạhite, rosme.

GRAIN—an, anaj, anja, dana, ǫn, phosol; *(a cultivated)* bajṛa, erba, rukhi, siswa bajṛa, sitạ, suthni; *(ripe)* bele jaṅ, gẹlẹ bale; *(husked)* caole; *(small & shrivelled)* copa cupi; *(an ear of)* gẹlẹ; *(blighted)* pẹṭẹć lipić; *(broken)* khode; *(malted)* mera; *(found in husking refuse)* markhu; *(from shaking wrappings)* jhala jhulạ; *(for consumption)* khạdiạn; *(removed by winnowing)* lipić pẹṭẹć, pẹṭẹć; *(borrowed on interest)* rin cal anaj; *(lender, to act as)* lanban; *(given as wages)* dạhnạ; *(given to recent bride)* jhanauri. *Cf.* STOLE, THRESH, HUSK, BASKET.

GRAINED, CROSS—badhoṛ, bedha.

GRAM—but, dana.

GRAMMAR—beyakaran.

GRAND—jhikimiki, sughoṛ, suthạr, ṭhạṭbond; *(father)* gǫrǫm, jiạ.

GRANDCHILD—koṛạṛ, nati, gǫrǫm koṛa (M), gǫrǫm kuṛi (F), nạtkạr; *(great)* jae koṛaṛ.

GRANDCHILDREN—nạti nạtkạr, nạti natkoṛ, nạti puti.

GRANDEUR—ṭhǫsǫk.

GRANDFATHER—aja, buḍạ, gǫrǫm baba, gǫrǫm haṛam, tata; *(relationship)* tataea; *(great)* jae dada; *(to name child after)* ńum cẹṅgẹṭ.

GRANDLY—suthrại; *(attired)* jhiki miki.

GRANDMOTHER—ạji, buḍhi ayo, gǫrǫm ayo, jiạ buḍhi; *(paternal)* boṅga jiạ; *(maternal)* hẹṛe jiạ.

GRANDPARENTS—jiạ tata.

GRANULATIONS, LARGE *(of flesh)*—toloke.

GRAPE, A—aṅgur, dak jǫ; *(a cluster of)* dak thopa.

GRASP, TO—kamcao, kamṭao, kapṭao, tǫhǫp̣; *(tightly)* muṭhiau; *(moving thing)* hatwa; *(repeatedly at)* hatwa hạtwi.

GRASS—ghãs; *(a species of)* adagaṭhiạ, backǫm, bare baḍwarak̇, baṛi baḍwak̇, bena, boṅga carẹć, dǫl, dhubi g., dhubi tasak̇, gaḍa khạsi g., gạṇḍiari, garạḍi, jab, jebkhoć, jhurjhuri, jolha ḍeṅga, jurguḍạ, kaḍa cạndi, kạsi, kaṭkǫm carẹć, lapoć, nanha ḍuḍhi, nạṛi g., seta sagak̇, sitań, toṛ caṇḍbǫl; *(an edible)* jera janhe, kukrạ; *(a fodder)* dub g., ickoć, lǫbǫe, lopotiań, lubui, sama g., suntu bukuć; *(sun)* cero; *(a tall swamp)* kakeṛ; *(a tall)* duṛhi, karsaṛ, kharsaṛ, khạsi, kũs, lukui, sirom; *(thatching)* dak̇ dakramak̇, ḍhoḍhiạ sauri, sauri; *(withered)* marheṛ; *(for arrow-shafts)* jhańkaṛi sar; *(for brooms)* kharań, lǫbǫe kharań; *(cutter)* ghạsiạṛa; *(awns of some)* sagak̇.

GRASSHOPPER—sǫsrǫć; *(kind of)* rat cora; *Cf.* sosroć; *(blotch on skin caused by)* sǫsrǫć khoda.

GRATE, TO—phaṭar (2).

GRATIFICATION—sõk, sonk.

GRATIFIED, TO BE—rijhuạ.

GRATING, A—siaṛa.

GRATING SOUND—cagae cagoe; cagoe (2), hadar (2), phaṭar (2).

GRATIS—dan, magni, mạnnite, mọphọt, mọstẹ, muphut, ọmnẹte, phạuti.

GRATITUDE—nungun; *(to shew)* gun manao.

GRATUITOUSLY—pọrẹpare.

GRATUITY—bạksis; *(given to shepherd)* puchiạ.

GRAVE—kabar gaḍa, kọbọr; *(yard)* kọbọr isthan.

GRAVEL—kakọr, kañkar, kãnkar, muṭkuri, rẹḍgẹč, rogṛo dhiri, roṛa.

GRAVELLY—raḍga roḍgo, ragaṛ rogoṛ, rege cege, rigoṛ rọgọṛ, roḍga roḍgo, roḍgo, rogṛo.

GRAVEN IMAGE, A—gọṛhọn muṭhạn, kundạu murhuť.

GRAVITY—sil sọrọm.

GRAZE, TO—ạtiń; *(touch)* aṛap, bhonḍor, caṛič, cheo, khemur; *(up all)* caṛpuṭ.

GRAZING—*(sound of)* rasaǩ, rusuǩ (2); *(to destroy by)* khạdiạṛ.

GREASY—cikạ̃ṛ, thakar bakar; *(of cloth)* poret.

GREAT—ajgar, anḍela, ạsrạ̃ṭ, atha, baṛiạu, bhal (2), bhale (2), hapraǩ, jọbọr, maha, marañ, napraǩ, sạmạni, talebor; *(in number)* amela, ạmilạ, chạu (2); *(& small)* darač duruč; *(man, a)* lobab, nobab.

GREATLY *(of swellings)*—dạrumdhaǩ, dhạrumdhaǩ.

GREATER PART, THE—abga.

GREEDILY, TO EAT—ạhum tạhum, habadiạ, kudhạ, lẹpẹkọpẹ, sọgọr; *(after satisfaction)* uruč supuč.

GREEDY—akaliạ, aklaha, alkhạniạ, ạsur, bhọjpuriạ, bhuskạ(M), bhuski (F), cuṭ cuṭ, khãk, khạuạ khawi, khạukhạu, kudhạ, lacañ locañ, lalca lạlci, lalca (M), lạlci (F), lebṛa (M), libṛi (F), lobhi, locṛa (M), lucṛi (F), lubhi, lubhiạ, olañ mocañ, peṭlaha; *(for flesh)* lẹmẹtuṛe.

GREEN—ḍemka, hạriạṛ, lahañ dọhañ, pọlhan, taj; *(& tender)* lẹgẹč labaǩ; *(shanks)* daǩ baṭṭa; *(& luxuriant)* labaǩ.

GREENHORN, A—ạluạ.

GREY—*(as hair)* pạnḍu; *(mixed with)* pạlku; *(dawn)* palaǩ poloǩ; *(eyed)* pẹnḍra (M), pinḍri (F); *(dark)* kajra (M), kạjri (F), sãoṛã (M), sạ̃uṛĩ (F); *(hound)* ḍhẹmọn phuciạ sadọm.

GREYISH—molso, pạnḍra (M), pạnḍri (F); *(of buffaloes)* pạnḍri (F), pạnḍuạ (M).

GRIEF—bedna, bẹdọn, bhabna, hirdạni; *(exclm. of)* durhạǩ, durre; *(to restrain one's)* jiwi tẹn.

GRIEVE, TO—bhabi, bhabna, guni bhạbiǩ, bikoł, bintirič, gunḍ, hae hiạtiń, hirdan, mọnẹ khạṭo, pachtao, titik.

GRIMY—bajrạhi.

GRIN, TO—isiṛ, isiṛ siṭkoč.

GRIND, TO—ḍiglạu, gunḍạ, rič; *(fine)* rič gunḍạ, rič lạhuť; *(into flour)* họlọń; *(teeth)* keṭer (2), kẹṭreč (2), maṭmaṭ, mẹṭrẹč, tọgọč; *(on a whetstone)* san.

GRINDING—rẹṭẹč (2); *(sound)* khayar khuyur; *(mill, a hand)* jante; *(stone, a)* gurgu.

GRIP, TO—khablao; *(repeatedly)* khabla khạbli.

GRIPE, TO—mocṛa mucṛi, mocṛao.

GRIPES—bạrẹṭ duk.

GRITTY—ragae, ragae (2), rege cege, saga roṛe.

GROAN, TO—ẽ ẽ, gerañ, gerañ huruñ, kũhṛạ kũhri, kũhṛạu, kuṅkṛạu.

GROANING—hae phoe, rẹṅgọs.

GROIN, A SWELLING IN THE—gilthi.

GROPE, TO—hatṛao, ṭạmḍa ṭạmḍi, ṭamḍao; *(with feet)* thukṛạu.

GROPING—hatṛa hạtṛi, hutṛạ huṭṛi; *(as with stick)* tahao.

GROUND—*(the)* ọt; *(on the)* ọrtọgọrẽ; *(level)* bel ọt; *(rising)* ghuṭu, ṭilhạ, ṭonḍañ; *(broken)* khanḍlaǩ; *(surrounded by ditch)* hata; *(before reaching the)* kaloǩ (2), kaloǩ marṭẹ; *(reason given)* arsa; *(level, on bank)* beḍa; *(plain & rising)* ṭạnḍi ṭikur; *(to be)* ganḍa gunḍạ.

GROUNDLESSLY—hak nahak, merayaḱ, pạthauṛi, udạcal.

GROUP, A—ạda, dọl, dọṅgọl, duṅgel, khata ; (*in*) jamka jumki.

GROUPS, BY—khaṭa khạṭi.

GROVE, A—(*sacred*) jaher than ; (*of planted trees*) bagan, bạgica.

GROW, TO—badhao, baṛhao, baṛhiao, bọcọḱ, dare, hara, họr hara, họr harta ; (*begin to*) biṛhạu ; (*luxuriantly*) candheṛ, ḍagḍagao, daldalao, ḍạṇḍhao, ḍọgḍogao, jhaṅgṛao, laglag, laklak, laṭao ; (*larger*) charao ; (*well*) dare, supṭạu ; (*to maturity*) hara buruḱ ; (*together*) jọpọreć, jọreć ; (*to stem & leaves*) ḍubuạ.

GROWING—(*crops*) cas ; (*from seed fallen in ground*) lambe.

GROWL, TO—arṛa ạṛṛi, garjao, gondrao, huṇḍrạu, taras ; (*of tiger*) guńjṛạu, huduṛ (2).

GROWLING, LOW—gọndọr (2).

GROWN—(*up*) baṛhọn, ḍaṭha ḍuṭhu, dhaṭha duṭhu, eṅga jọpọr, goṭa guṭi, hara kańjela, jhaka (F), jharkaṇḍ, lekman, muṭhu, rata, sẽra ; (*together*) jamke ; (*more than half*) kaeṇḍe ; (*well*) baṛhọntar, bolgariạ, bolman, chakmạkiạ, sean ; (*half*) bachṛa ; (*ill*) jerka.

GROWTH—baṛhọnta ; (*at full*) hara rata, hara sat, hara thul, pataṛaḱ ; (*second*) doja.

GRUDGE, TO BEAR A—bạdọṛ.

GRUFF—mọṭa ; (*sigh, a*) khọr.

GRUMBLE, TO—karać kuruć, kạruć bạruć, kẹńkẹń, pheńpheń.

GRUMBLING, ALWAYS—khẹdẹć (2).

GRUNT—khụṭọ (2) ; (*to*) họndroḱ, huṇḍruḱ ; (*of buffaloes*) ã ã, õć õć, oṇḍroć. *Cf.* PIGS.

GUARANTEE, TO—hạk.

GUARD—(*a*) pahara, pahra, pahradar, rakhwal ; (*military*) sọntọri ; (*bracelet*) ṭaghọn sakọm ; (*ring*) ṭhesa, ṭhisi ; (*to*) hebajọt, họrhọ, pahara, pahra ; (*off one's*) gạphil.

GUARDIAN—(*to act as*) tạlik ; (*without a*) nisạrthi, tala ṭạṇḍi.

GUAVA, THE—amrud, ạńjir, sạphri am, ṭẹmbros.

GUESS, TO—amdaj, annan, bad, orad ; (*to give a*) kudum ; (*to answer a*) kudum ńum ; (*by*) nindạn.

GUEST CHAMBER, A—khola oṛaḱ, mela oṛaḱ.

GUFFAW, TO—haḱhaḱ.

GUIDE—(*to*) calao ; (*a village*) dạuṛaha.

GUIDANCE—bọs, girhạṛ.

GUILE—ulbul ; (*without*) modhu, soṛa.

GUILTLESS—miridọs, nirdọs.

GUILTY—dusi, oprạdi.

GUINEA FOWL—chin sim, sẹṅgẹl ṭiṭi.

GUITAR, A KIND OF—sitạr.

GULL, TO—andha, labhae lubhai, laboṛ.

GULLY, A—khandhaṛ, khaṇḍlaḱ, khọṇḍlaḱ.

GULP, WITH A—sarpaṭ marte, sọkọṛ marte.

GULPING SOUND—ḍhọk (2), họḍọṛ (2), kadrać kọḍrọć, kiḍroć kọḍrọć, sarpaṭ, sọkọṛ.

GUM—cĩṭ, jọr ; (*arabic tree*) gabla ; (*boil*) mạskuṛa.

GUMMY—lathaḱ, lẹpẹ pẹjẹ, lọdhọr (2).

GUMS, THE—mạskuṛa ; (*bleeding from*) dãtrisạ.

GUN, A—bạnduk ; (*barrel*) nạli, nuli ; (*stock*) kundạ ; (*trigger*) lablạbi ; (*prop*) ṭhesa ; (*breech-loading*) ṭọṭa b. ; (*flint & steel*) pathor kala b. ; (*fired by fuse*) aglagwa b., jạmki b. ; (*double barrelled*) barnạli ; (*wad*) jạmin ; (*shot for*) charṛa, chiṭṭạ ; (*powder*) bạrud, dạru ; (*ramrod*) gạj, gaḱdaoaḱ, kharcạṛi ; (*spring in lock of*) kamạni ; (*report of*) ḍhae ; (*& bayonet*) barcha b. ; (*person with*) bạndkiạ ; (*to cock*) caṛhao ; (*to load*) kasao ; (*to shoot with*) ṭhu ; (*priming pan of*) rońjok.

GUNNY CLOTH—ṭạṭ.

GURGLE, TO—bhọk (2), bhọkbhọkao, sakor.

GURGLING SOUND—ḍhọḱ (2), gargaṛ, gaṛgaṛao, kọḍọć, kọḍrọć (2) ; (*in throat*) sọkọr.

GUSH—(*to*) phere (2), pọlọć ; (*out, to*) bhulkạu ; (*with a*) pọlọć marte, pọlọc marte.

GUST, WITH A—seyaṛ marte ; (*sudden*) hud marte.

GUSTO, WITH—tokop.

GUZZLE, WITH A—sorpaṭ marte, sorpoṭ marte.

GUZZLING SOUND—cak (2), cakop (2), chak (2) sarpaṭ.

GYPSIES, A TRIBE OF THIEVING,—cãecor.

H

HABIT—bhasi, laker, naṭhi, rit; *(in comp.)* bara; *(force of)* ṭhonk; *(to be in the)* laghar.

HABITATION—boskot; *(without settled)* culur bulur.

HABITS—calcolon, takrokom; *(bad)* lochon. *Cf.* DIRTY, SOLITARY.

HABITUATE, TO—hewa, rigdau, sadhao, tinjau.

HABITUATED, TO BECOME—parkau.

HACK, TO—kobak, mak, samak; *(to pieces)* mak kuṭra; *(through)* mak pasir.

HACKED—khando.

HAD......WOULD NOT—bań......honeć.

HAEMATURIA—arak jhar.

HAG, A SHRIVELLED OLD—juknuć mara budhi.

HAGGARD, TO LOOK—torlo morlo.

HAIL—arel; *(white silt mixed with water of)* arel hasa.

HAIR—up; *(a head of)* gũrchi; *(to dress)* cerkoć, suṭ; *(to tie up)* roṭ, toke; *(method's of tying up)* dhaca, Cf. suṭ; *(to smooth)* gereyom; *(to rinse)* jiań; *(to comb)* nakić; *(to seize by)* jhuṭiau, kapcao; *(to pull each other's)* contha cunthi; *(to singe)* dhursau; *(thin)* ḍhendra, kendroń, khadra (M) khadri (F); *(curly)* kircoṭ korcoṭ; *(bushy)* dadurham, damdam, dhalgum, dhapra (M), dhapri (F), hadui (2); *(short & stiff)* karcap (M), karcup (F); *(in disorder)* dalae (2), dalcań (M) dulcuń (F), dandle, dhadra (M), dhadri (F), dharkul markul, dharuk dhacuk, dindir siṭ, jaṭa, jhapri, jhupri (F); *(parted in middle)* horase; *(hanging over brow)* dhaeri, jhapri, jhapru (M); *(cropped short)* ḍundga, mundla (M), mundli (F), mundra (M), mundri (F), ṭhandga, ṭhandgaṭ; *(tied in knot at side)* lara (M) lari (F); *(a lock of on crown)* ṭuila (M), ṭuili (F); *(on end)* ciĩrau, dharkul markul, dundun; *(long matted)* jaṭla (M), jaṭli (F); *(short strip on forehead)* phera; *(on back of neck)* lopotiań up; *(on upper lip)* misi, moca goco; *(none on upper lip)* mãera, moidoń, mońdoń; *(on chin)* kewa goco; *(on pubes)* haṭa; *(on part of head which some shave)* hopyo; *(fallen off)* hendra (M), hindri (F); *(band for)* bheṭuak, phiṭa; *(rope of)* sili; *(against the)* sirgaṭ; *(a handful of)* miṭ lacha up; *(lip)* siro luṭi; *(pin)* alpin, sulak; *(without)* ṭhundga (M), ṭhundgi (F); *(a swirl on)* gheora; *(an ornament of)* huju duria, ṭoya dhaca. *Cf.* WASH, CUT, BRAID, GREY.

HAIRS—*(on body)* lopotiań up; *(on tail, white)* cãora (M), cãura (M), cãuri (F).

HAIRY—cãwãr, dagumcak, gadrum, hodgo, ragumcak, sodo bodgo, sodo (2), sodo rodo, sodro bodro, sudro budro; *(very)* darum sarum; *(faced)* badgocak.

HALE—rehlam sehlam.

HALF—adha, adkar, adnakha, atra, atrom (2), tala, tara, tarantar, tatla; *(prefix meaning)* adh; *(ripe)* demba, dembe; *(done)* khecra, khecre; *(heartedly)* biṭhiabi, licań picań, lirwa sarwe; *(more)* didhi, sarhe; *(& half)* adha adhi, alak choṭak, sogor bogor, soroboro, tara tapra; *(do a thing, to)* atra matra, laṭku paṭku.

HALT—*(lame)* khorda; *(to)* daba mara; *(without)* bharar, poyor.

HALVE, TO—sora.

HAMLET, A—di, dih, dihali; *(outlying)* gonda, ṭola; *(& villages)* gão gonda; *(& boundaries)* dih dandi, dihe dandi.

HAMMER—*(a)* hataori, hathaori, kuṭasi, martul; *(to)* kuṭam, piṭau, ṭhokao; *(in threats)* hulsiń; *(noise of)* ṭhak ṭhok, ṭhak ṭhuk.

HAMPER—*(to)* bajhua, kacal, kacar, nejbãr; *(a large bamboo)* harka.

HAND, THE—ti; (*right*) dahin; (*palm of*) talka; (*back of*) lulha; (*from the wrist*) thopnak; (*with fingers*) ti thopa; (*to put in*) cal; (*to lay or lean on*) capo; (*to take off with*) kadhao, kadhiau; (*to life with*) kutuṅ, loca; (*to thrust in*) sok; (*to lead by*) tiak; (*to take in*) egar, osrao, parsao, pasante, taltul, utjog; (*to carry in*) teweṅ; (*ready at*) mahjud; (*to bring down*) uyuk; (*at first*) nijgut; (*cuffs*) hatkari; (*a friendly*) hat bai.

HAND, TO—cal; (*over*) alae; (*round*) bilhau.

HANDFUL, A—añjle, cuput, khabol, khamcao, lapet, lot, soba, tohop; (*to take*) bokcao, loca.

HANDFULS—(*taking by*) mambra mambri; (*to come away in*) bosok.

HANDLE, A—dandit, dandom, hatwa, muth, muthi, tir; (*of box*) karu; (*protuberance on a*) dimbi; (*to*) larcar, lorcor.

HANDS—(*to catch in*) loka; (*to tie*) manjur guda; (*to lay on*) capo, hat, hatiau, ti calao; (*to join together*) añjle; (*& feet, large*) kaṅkar. *Cf* TO CLAP.

HANDSOME—mahit, rengled; (*figure*) jabrahi.

HANDY—nipun, sargharia; (*of young people*) sarpharia.

HANG, TO—aka, jabrao, jhabrao, phasi; (*on hook*) bak; (*up*) taṅgao; (*over*) atur, jhaluṅ, jhalur, lakud, lamka lakud, lapur (2), lawer; (*down*) atur, ladur, ladwir, lamka lakud, lapur (2), lawaṅ, lawak, toṅkor; (*as tongue of bell*) laraṅ (2); (*as broken wrist*) lorkod; (*down loosely*) tamkur, toṅkor; (*the head*) katbud, kirdhum, kokorbok, kondoṅ, kudbur, kuluṅ dubuṅ, kurbur, kutbur, kuyuṅ, labraṅ, laruṅ, larbuṅ, tirup, tumbut; (*about*) haja hojo, heper hende, hindo, otor ombak, ragrao; (*-through shame*) garpud gurpud; (*-in hope of getting food*) ale jañje, jalat japat, lalejañje, ñele (2); (*loosely*) ghañjloṅ, labraṅ, labruṅ, larbuṅ, larkud, laruṅ; (*by a noose*) pasi; (*& swing*) tawar (2); (*on to life*) teweṅ jiwet; (*as bats*) dhilwaṅ.

HANGING—dawaṅ (2), gawar (2), jharguak, jharpa; (*down*) diaṅ (2), gãhjur, giroe gorge, ladbur, ladgur, tikor tukur; (*in sherds*) garui tapui, gayur tapur; (*in a tangle*) gawar (2), giwar gawar; (*as dogs' ears*) jhapru; (*unevenly*) jhargoeak; (*& flapping*) jhiloṅ jholoṅ; (*far down, as clothes*) johok (2); (*as string of sticky substance*) tiro toro; (*to kill by*) phasi god.

HANK OF THREAD, A—luti; (*to wind into*) burhu.

HANKERING—hirohi, lacaṅ locaṅ, sene dewer.

HANKERINGLY—orom (2), merel.

HANSEL—baena.

HAPPEN, TO—gudrau, hoe, laga.

HAPPINESS—raska, suk.

HAPPY—bahal; (*to be*) hulas, keco bedro, raska; (*to make*) bahalao; (*looking*) kharsala.

HARASS, TO—biraj, birij (2), dabri maṅgal, dolmolao, hacpacao, khackhacao, khockhoc, paniau.

HARASSED—halua haron.

HARBOUR—(*a*) bondor; (*ill-feeling to*) eper hende, kanakani, kunkunau.

HARD—aröt, atwar, badhor, bedhor, behor, bokro, cãe, cemor, cerda (2), cetãr, coj, cond kopot, kacur (2), karkar, kathor, kecer, kekercaṅ, keted, khac, khara, kharas (2), kharus (2), kheres, kutud, pakot, pakro, patka, pokta, ratko, sokto, sokot, teptepe; (*niggardly*) kakad kukud, kuthia, som; (*as a master*) khacraha; (*of pot-herbs*) padga, rata pata, ratko patko; (*of stomach*) teptep; (*of work*) urum surum; (*in the centre*) pobo; (*& insipid*) sit siti; (*hearted*) amot; (*up*) tiraṅ; (*nor soft, neither*) keted tabud; (*to become*) degen, kerker, thela. *Cf.* WORKING, PRESSED.

HARDEN, TO—karkarao, patao; (*the body*) teñjao.

HARDSHIP—harkhet, upan jhapan; (*to cause*) cipa; (*a great*) mund moron; (*with great*) kosto mosto.

HARE, A—kulai, saphon kulai, (*fence to snare*) pacan; (*rope of net*) surka baber.

HARK !—ate, ete, heho, henda, iyo ; (*to females*) hena.

HARLOT—bạckạr, chinạr.

HARM—hạn, hạne, hạni ; (*to meet with*) huṅjaṅ, khetra ; (*to threaten*) dhirạu.

HARM, TO—bistur, jae bejae, pọr mọnda ; (*oneself*) ḍhiṅku.

HARMLESS—ugur sunduć.

HARMONIOUS—sọnọt ; (*to be*) sapaonja.

HARMONY—bọnọt, haobhao, mel, mil, milạp̣, milimisi, salsāt, sapaonja, sapo, sol suluk, sọnmọt, suluk ; (*to be in*) banao, salha, solha, suluk ; (*to bring about*) mili jili.

HARNESS—sajbaj ; (*to*) sajao.

HARRIER, THE—(*eagle*) kuhi besra ; (*Pale*) rici cẽrẽ ; (*marsh*) jola pajhar.

HARROW, A—(*without teeth*) ārgọm ; (*drawn by 2 oxen*) hạriạ.

HARSH—āṭwar, harrap̣, irạ, irsạ, khara, saegać, sọć bọdrẹć.

HARSHLY—karrạ, sidwạk̓ badwạk̓ ; (*to speak*) sirog, tạrgum.

HARVEST—abad, irok̓ din, phọsọl ; (*to*) ir samṭao ; (*mid*) dhurpạu ; (*a good*) sāwāe ; (*to obtain a good*) arjao ; (*before ripe, to*) ḍemba.

HASTE—(*to*) caṇḍạki, dharpharao ; (*to cause to*) taltalao, toltolao, tultulạu ; (*to make*) usạra ; (*to be in*) calcalua ; (*in*) daurạ dauri, umdhum.

HASTEN, TO—calao, turburạu, usạra, usrạu.

HASTILY—calcalua, caṭapaṭ, ḍarae dhampae, demer (2), dhakar pakar, dharae dhapae, dharpar, dhatar patar, dhọkọr pọkọr, ẹk tariạ, harañ huruñ, harmar, harum tarum, lolopoto, mar, mardhar, udur dhupur ; (*of tall persons*) harun pạṭun ; (*& inefficiently*) loro (2), loro thoro, loto thoro ; (*to cook a little food*) ṭuku (2).

HASTY (*of temper*)—kāiā, kāyā.

HAT, A—ṭupri ; (*leaf*) chupi, guṅgu.

HATCH, TO—busak̓ ; (*of insects & reptiles*) barkao.

HATCHET, A SMALL—tabla.

HATE—kuskusi, sikir ; (*to*) hirkhạ, kurud.

HATRED—badāo, dusṭạma, khones, khọnọs, khunes, kun.

HAUGHTY—dhọmọk, dhọmọkiạ ; (*to be*) bhades.

HAUNCHES, TO SIT ON THE—dundureuć.

HAUNTED BY A SPIRIT—bhutạha.

HAVE IT OVER !—dorok̓.

HAVEN, A—bọndọr.

HAVOC—loksan ; (*to make*) bhaṇḍañ bhuṇḍuñ, huạn, mulạhan, murạhan.

HAWK, A SPECIES OF—jalo ; (*small*) kạuḍi ḍiañ cẽrẽ ; (*large*) lọyọṅ jalo ; (*Cuckoo*) galọć cẽrẽ, galuạ cẽrẽ.

HAZE—khuạs, kuhạs, kuhrạ, rọn ; (*a thick*) rọn khurạ.

HAZY—dondho, garsilon.

HE—ini, uni ; (*& I*) ạliṅ.

HEAD—bọhọk̓, kapar, muṇḍ, muṇḍạ ; (*chief*) marañ, matha ; (*to bob*) kayar ; (*to jerk up*) dhunạu ; (*to set conceitedly*) kẹnẹkote ; (*to draw in*) kọkọrbọk̓ ; (*to hold up*) kọrkọr, saṅgil ; (*to hold at an a angle*) kece dore, kọcẹdọrẹ, kọele, kokombe, kọkrẹ ; (*to pop under water*) dubuć ; (*pressed down on shoulders*) kere (2), keren doren, kirokọrọ ; (*shaved*) ḍọṇḍgoć, ḍuṇḍge (M), ḍuṇḍgi (F), ḍuṇḍi, kolo, kọṇḍlọṅ, muṇḍlạ (M), muṇḍli (F), muṇḍrạ (M), muṇḍri (F), ṭhaṇḍgać ṭhuṇḍguć ; (*swimming*) cạkri ghum, thaṅgal thuṅgul ; (*down*) birbuñ ; (*towards, to*) muhạr ; (*front ? art of*) luṭkuri ; (*for head*) muṇḍạ muṇḍi, muṇḍhạ muṇḍhi ; (*flat at back*) khonta bọhọk̓ ; (*gear*) ṭupri ; (*horns*) siṅ muṇḍ ; (*of cattle*) muṇḍ, siṅ muṇḍ ; (*man of village*) mandar, mañjhi, mọṇḍọl ; (*of family*) morubi, murubi. *Cf.* TO BOW, HANG, SHAKE, SHAVE, NOD.

HEADED, BIG OR BULLET—ḍạṭhu.

HEADLONG—ạruć pạṭuć, ạruć tạruć, tupuć ; (*to carry*) dhọtpọt.

HEADS—(*in opp. directions*) sate ; (*& tails*) biliạ bitić, gẹjẹ pate, sobasate.

HEADSTRONG—hadrap̣, hardund, haṭhi, hurmuṭ, jahbaj, ṭiḍwi ; (*desire*) bhuc bhuci.

HEADY—tethọr, thẹṭham, thethọr.

HEAL, TO—bes, boge.

HEALTH—bega juḍa, mọtlọb.

HEALTHY—barhamtar, bẹlkẹć, nirogi, pohlan, rehlam sehlam; (*looking*) cehra, cẹṭha; (*of child*) chalchaḷia.

HEAP, A—bạḍhi, baha bạhi, bạhi, ḍań, gada, kuṭhauri, puńji, thọk, torphan; (*of firewood*) koṭhauri, kuṭhauri; (*dung*) mande; (*to make*) bạḍhi, ḍań, dumhe, gada, puńji; (*food on plate, to*) kudhạ; (*up, to*) cuṛu. *Cf.* RUBBISH.

HEAPED—baha bạhi; (*up*) bẽṛẽ (2), domdom.

HEAPS—ḍhapa ḍhopo; (*in*) biliạ bitić, thake thak, thọke thọk, thọk thak; (*in little*) curkạk bhurkạk.

HEAR, TO—ańjọm, jọm, sunạn; (*but not reply*) gampatak.

HEAR—ate, hate, ọtẹ.

HEARSAY—lại ceť katha.

HEART, THE— bọrọ, ọntọr; (*to burst*) chạti jarao; (*to take*) jọr bandhao; (*a hard*) kẹṭẹć mọnẹ; (*& soul, with*) diṛạ muṇḍte, jidajid, jiwijante, kẹṛẹć mẹṭẹć, lahkao, miť murukte, miť mọnte, goṭa mọnte, tanman, ṭhankao, ṭhonkao; (*to be of one*) jukti.

HEARTILY—cehor behor, culuń, diṛa muṇḍte, habhab, rapet, rumbuć cumbuć; (*of laughter*) haha (2).

HEART-WOOD—maoj, mańjal, mańjela, sisgạr; (*hard*) maj.

HEAT—ãc, dãk, dhãk, elań, udgar; (*sun's*) jhala; (*from flame*) jharak; (*scorching*) jhańj; (*to*) tao, tatao, tawao; (*over fire*) susum; (*anything damp*) gumạuk; (*water, to*) basań; (*solids, to*) dhipạu; (*a pot to dry it*) sondhao; (*to apply*) sekao; (*to be in*) ọtọń, ritiạu.

HEATED—lọlọ; (*to become*) garma garmi, garmao, kumblạu; (*to be*) tao, tao tạwi.

HEATH—arar pot.

HEATHEN—bedin.

HEAVE, TO—sọkọć, ṭalmal, ṭọlmọl; (*of water*) habak ḍabak; (*when walking*) ḍhakar ḍhọkọr.

HEAVEN—serma; (*to go to*) akasok.

HEAVILY—barat, bẹbaṛić, ẹṭẹć pọṭẹć, garte, rabać rubuć, rahaṕ ruhuṕ, ribić, ribọć rọbọć; (*of rain*) jhamar jhọmọr; (*as under a big load*) kẹrẹć doreć, keren doren, ṭimbạ ṭambe. *Cf.* TO BREATHE.

HEAVING—ḍọyọl (2), sọbọk kọyọk; (*as a boat*) ḍọmbọl (2).

HEAVY—ajar, bhạri, dọgdọgọ, gadha godho, gọrọb, hamal, jãk, jọbdọ, lajak lujuk, lạjuń (2); (*very*) rọhọć (2); (*as writing*) jẹbrẹ; (*of clouds*) kạridań, ńãṛadań; (*of sleep*) ọsọć (2), ọ̃sọ̃s; (*as one gorged*) robrobo; (*in fore-quarters*) ạgil, dhamọnphuciạ; (*in front, as cart*) ạgạr; (*with child*) bharti họrmọ, gạbḍulań; (*featured*) badgok (2); (*sound*) duhuṕ (2); (*& clumsy*) jọrdhe. *Cf.* RAIN.

HEDDLES OF LOOM—bade.

HEED, TO—ańjọm, batao, ceton, ganao, hetao, jogas, sọntọr.

HEEDLESS—bhulạ bhạtuạ, nicind.

HEEL, THE—idi.

HEELS—(*to take to one's*) picom podroć; (*uppermost*) birtuń; (*of on the*) daradạri, dhawa dhạwi, gọḍọe gọḍae, hẹḍẹ gọḍẹ, ragda rạgdi, rogda rugdi. *Cf.* TO SIT, TO WALK.

HEIFER, A—daṇṛi, phẽṭar, sạṇḍhin.

HEIGHT—lạuchar, usul; (*of great*) họt họtọ; (*of varying*) kadgaṫ kodgoṫ; (*to be at its*) dhurpạu, ladbad, salgao, sạrdi, sulgạu; (*of man*) unum sumuń; (*of man with arms stretched*) purus.

HEIR, AN—awạsi, oaris; (*without*) aṭkuṛạ, bẹmar, bẹmurad.

HELL—narak kuṇḍ, nọrọk kuṇḍ.

HELP—bah, modod, sạhaita, upgar, upkạr; (*a shout for*) guhar.

HELP, TO—dạhin, le calao, loe, gọṛọ, modod, sạhai, sahas, sambrao, serọm, sohga, sọhọť, tala, torao, upgạr, upkạr, usas; (*by giving*) em calao, em sọhọť; (*oneself to*) gabre, hatiạu; (*to food*) harta, parsao; (*a 2nd. time to food*) ãrti; (*when following*) sotok; (*in this & that*) jabar jubạr.

HELPER, A—oaris, sohoda.

HELPING OF FOOD, A—paras.

HELPLESS—alacar, nacar, nacariạ; (*from hunger*) ạukhạu, jaṛao; (*to be*) lacar; (*to render*) jạbṛi.

HEM IN, TO—gherao.

HEMIPLEGIA—ardhaṅgi, mit́ kar goć.

HEMP—(*drug*) bhaṅ; (*plant*) gańja; (*Deccani*) paṭ son.

HEN, A—sim eṅga; (*young*) kaloṭ; (*that has hatched first brood*) kaloṭ eṅga; (*sitting*) bubrum sim; (*brown*) heraḱ sim; (*note of laying*) kakarat́; (*coop*) ṭapa; (*nest*) sim bursi, sim pakha.

HER— —e, ini, uni.

HERBS—(*coarse*) paḍga; (*teacher of virtues of*) kambru guru. *Cf.* MEDICINAL.

HERD, A—aḍa, gahaṇḍi, gahṇḍi, jhunḍ, khar, pal; (*boy*) gupi kora; (*boy pice given to*) caṇḍkilom.

HERE—inde, nende, nete, nhate, nhende, nhonde, nhote, nonde; (*about*) neman, noman; (*belonging to*) neten, nhenden, nhonden, nonden; (*& there*) abuḱ cabuḱ, ajaḱ bujaḱ, androḱ sandroḱ, aruḱ dharuḱ, barać buruć, birla, cardaḱ burdaḱ, cindka cilaḱ, ende pende, hande nhande, jaha kahā, jande mande, jane tane, jarmaḱ jormoḱ, kabaḱ koboḱ, nande, neman, tahār bihār, taraḱ biraḱ, taral basal, ṭhanṭaratin, ṭhonṭaratin; (*to run*) baraé buruć.

HEREDITARY—(*of tenures*) maurasi, morasi; (*of qualities*) ḍhaṭhi.

HERITAGE—bapoti dhon.

HERMAPHRODITE GOAT, A—ram khasi merom.

HERMIT-LIKE—banua.

HERNIA, UMBILICAL—buka bharūr.

HERO, A TRADITIONAL—Gajilal, Liṭa.

HESITATING—dem khem, dhowa bhowa, dhuwa bhua.

HESITATION—dokha.

HEW, TO—maḱ; (*down*) maḱ gur; (*roughly*) pahṭao.

HEY!—ehe, ehere, hēho, heho, henda, hoeja, hoja.

HIBISCUS, THE—joba baha; (*edible*) ram jhiṅga.

HICCUP—hicki; (*to*) ńūraḱ; (*convulsions with*) hicki bai.

HIDDEN MEANING—morom.

HIDE, TO—adon, aelo gaelo, coko, dabrao, danań, gop, gupat́, gupti, hombo, lendeć, od, oko; (*to shirk work*) ghusau; (*inside*) bulo gonjao; (*by covering*) lotom; (*from fear*) picpic; (*head in grass*) solgat́; (*in the armpit*) bokcao; (*& seek-game*) oko eneć.

HIDE, A—harta; (*curers*) ghasi; (*strap of raw*) camaoṭa, campṭa, camṭa.

HIDEOUS—bartań

HIDING—husuć; (*place*) aotan.

HIGGLEDY-PIGGLEDY—lhimsi punsī, galoć saloć, garbar, ukaṭ pakaṭ.

HIGH—coṭ, ḍakḍaka, hucbucu, huḍhuḍu, huṭhuṭu, karja (M), karji (F), kayoḱ (2) kayur (2), khārgo, kharku, laphaṅ, lenboń, pilhoe, raeka, raela, rakḍaṅ, rakḍuṅ, rakṭaṅ, rampar, raṅkar, raṭbaṅ, riyol royol, roela, roṭboń, usul; (*very*) karūḱ (2) ṭoṅṭoṅ, ṭuiṭui; (*of rates*) mahṅga; (*priced*) akra, andhoṅ, mahaṅga, maharog, mahrog; (*spirits, in*) cakmakao, hāsi kusi, umjha umjhi, uńjha uńjhi; (*note in music*) nanha; (*key, in a*) ṭērēć (2); (*& low*) copoṭ londoć, kadga kodgo, coṭ phed; (*pressure, at*) taha tahi, urum surum.

HIGHEST—(*point*) chatna, chip; (*point of tree*) dhoj; (*point of hill*) mundhni; (*pitch, at the*) dhurpau, sardi; (*in degree*) utar.

HIGHWAYMAN, A—baṭ para, ḍakū, ghaṭamar.

HILL, A—hara; (*small*) boṭkoć, duńri; (*saddle of*) rindir; (*a sacred*) mandburu; (*end of*) buru dandom; (*& dale*) kaṭka koṭko. rodoḱ, sodoḱ rodoḱ, sopoḱ roduḱ; (*level at base of*) lodam. *Cf* SLOPE.

HILLOCK, A—damgi, dhopko, dhopo, domge, dopo; (*full of*) dhapa dhopo.

HILSA FISH, THE—ilsa.

HIM—e, ini, uni; (*self*) ać, nije; (*self, each for*) jona joti.

HIND OF RAVINE DEER, THE—ghoṭreć jel, merom jel.

HINDER, TO—akoṭ, arjhau, aṭkao, aujhar, bajhua, bidhaura, eseṭ, hatkao, nejhar, nenjhar, okoṭ, oṭkao, rok, tek, thakthakao, ṭokṭoko; (*by an obstacle*) ṭekao.

HINDERED, TO BE—abjor, takić.

HINDQUARTERS, THE—ṭiki.

HINDRANCE—badha, bidia, daga, dora daga, dordag, laṭak, leṭok, loṭok, ṭhek; (*supe natural*) ber; (*to meet with*) takić; (*without*) ṭahaka.

HINDU, A—deko, diku hopon; (*courteous*) deko pera; (*in contempt*) deko pusi; (*sacred books*) bed; (*priest*) deasi. *Cf.* CASTE.

HINDUSTAN—bharotborso.

HINGE, A—hãskol, kabja.

HINT, A—isara; (*to give*) bargao; (*with*) ṭhare ṭhore.

HIP, THE—deke, duke, pheca; (*joint*) dubhi; (*to carry astride*) heo.

HIPPOPOTAMUS, THE—dak sadom.

HIRE—ban; (*to*) acu, bhara, nacu; (*sarcastic*) hur; (*bullocks*) bãhca, urić utiń.

HIRED—(*worker*) bankar; (*house*) bhara orak.

HIRSUTE—cãwãr, gadrum sadrum, ragumcak, sodo bodgo, sodo (2).

HISS, TO—gadgadao, kha; (*of snakes*) phuphuau; (*of cobra*) khakha, khokho, usić; (*of oil in hot vessel*) gargarao; (*through teeth*) suyur.

HISSING—cheń (2), choń godo (2), sũisũi; (*of green wood burning*) soro (2); (*of hot iron in water*) gadgad; (*of steam*) chãe (2).

HIST!—ehe.

HISTORY—itihas.

HIT, TO—bajao, dhatir, jos, mukau, thapa, ṭhaṭe; (*slightly*) dadup; (*as hail*) ṭuṭi; (*with soft thing*) lapak marao; (*with elbow*) ucuń; (*with horns*) uṭić.

HITCH, A—bandhi, beora, cak bandhi; (*without*) bharar.

HITCH UP, TO—sokoć.

HITHER—note; (*& thither*) aeur bihur, androk sandrok, onte note, tarak birak.

HO TRIBE, A SECTION OF THE—larka munda.

HO! (TO GIRLS)—eke.

HOAR FROST—pala, ratań.

HOARD, TO—doho gońjao, gońjao, sãitau.

HOARDER, A—cempoṭ.

HOARSE—bukṭan, gańghar, gońgrot, kharań khuruń, moṭa, ronkhoń; (*from fear*) garra gorro.

HOARSELY—gahẽt (2), kereć (2).

HOARY—pandu.

HOAX, TO—labhae lubhai, lai puṭi

HOBBLE—(*a*) chanda baber; (*to*) chanda; (*limp*) jaret (2), kodok (2), laoak lucuk.

HOBBLEDEHOY, A—bachra kora, cenda kora.

HOBBLING—cima caṭe, tharat thorot.

HOE, A—(*large*) kudi; (*broad*) dhabru k.; (*pronged*) kaṭa k.; (*double-handed*) guji k; (*ill shaped*) dabla k.; (*handle*) k. dandom.

HOG, A—badhia; (*plum, the*) amra.

HOLD!—haha.

HOLD, TO—capar, hatwa, sahop, sap; (*together*) sambrao; (*to take*) rem; (*& carry in hand*) teweń; (*under arm*) hermet; (*as much as it will*) bẽrẽ (2); (*out hand*) atań; (*tightly*) karmaṭao; (*in lap*) gabla, gocha.

HOLDING,—(*an agricultural*) jot; (*each other by hand*) gadea gudia.

HOLE, A—bhugak, dodhor, dondher, gada, gadlak, garha, gonghor, ṭherak; (*pit*) dongada; (*muddy*) led (*in harness*) dão; (*in ground*) ghonghor; (*in a bank*) kondha, lopak; (*through & through*) phukar; (*in wall, to make*) sind, sind muhãni; (*in centre*) phońke; (*to make*) bhoskao, bogoć; (*to scratch*) geleć bhugak; (*to close up*) paṭai.

HOLES—(*in*) gadlak godlok, jhanga jhuṭa, pioń poyoń; (*full of*) gańghar gonghor, garha gorho, ubar khabar; (*pierced with*) jińjri; (*an instrument to dig*) khanta, khonta; (*emerging from many*) piopoyo; (*in, to pick*) dhusau.

HOLIDAY, A—chuṭi din.

HOLLOW—copot, dodhio, dodhor, dopot, dorpot, khaepak khoepok, khaplok, khapua, khol, khoyak, kokhrao, londoć, phuki; (*as a pipe*) dhodyo; (*of timber*) phophra; (*as eyes*) horok, ṭhoerak; (*in centre*) khońja, phora; (*concave*) khupa; (*of nose*) celpeń;

(*sound*) dham, ḍuḍuṅ, ṭhoe ; (*out, to*) khoelak, khokrao, kholao, suṫ.

HOLLOW, A—ḍhab, ḍoḍhor, ḍoṇḍhor, gaḍa, garha, handruṅ, khana, khupur khuyāk, koṇḍha, ṭhoerak ; (*on surface*) khoepak ; (*in an upright object*) lopak ; (*at back of head*) totka gaḍa ; (*in a tree*) ḍhoḍra, ḍoṇḍhor ; (*to scratch a*) geleć gaḍa.

HOLLOWED OUT TO A SHELL—ṭhoṭheo, ṭhoyo.

HOLLOWS—(*& ravines*) gadha sot ; (*on surface of fruit*) khara khōrā.

HOLY—dhorom, sonot.

HOLY BASIL—tulsi dare.

HOME—orak ; (*stead*) acir pacir, bakher ; (*to leave*) atit ; (*without a*) antharī ; (*in, to be at*) parkau.

HONE, A—kuṅj dhiri, sil dhiri ; (*to rub on*) sil.

HONEST—sora, sotea, uju.

HONEY—rasa ; (*bee, spec. of*) dumur ; (*comb*) chata ; (*forest*) modhubon.

HONOUR—mahatom, man, murad, murwad, thap ; (*your*) aprug.

HONOUR, TO—con, dahnao, gadhnao, ganao, man, manao, manot, morjad.

HONOURABLE—khara khari, manotan, manotia, matbor.

HOOF, A—khura.

HOOFS—(*sound of*) kadap (2), karap, kardap ; (*disease of*) mukhura.

HOOK, A—aṅkus, banak, kāṭa ; (*fish*) bāṛsi ; (*on rafters*) bha carać ; (*on, to*) hak.

HOOKA, THE—*Cf.* HUBBLE BUBBLE.

HOOPOE BIRD, THE—ḍabla kuṭam.

HOOTING OF AN OWL—hūhū, phercoṫ (2).

HOP, TO—kocor, ṭerok ; (*in childrens' game*) gudau.

HOPE—as, barsa, bharosa, bharsa, bhorosa ; (*in, to*) darsau ; (*of, in*) labre ; (*without*) andak tawak, beas, bebhorsa, dharma korma, hae nisas, jilwa thalwa, sithal mithal ; (*to be without*) jiwi oloṅ, niras ; (*to lose*) as chuṭau, dhil, lorao ; (*of getting*) jethe.

HORIZONTALLY—(*to fix*) bindhar; (*to interlace*) gaban.

HORN, A—dereṅ ; (*musical*) sal sakwa ; (*crumpled*) merha d. ; (*of brass or copper*) dhorori ; (*to blow*) oroṅ, tutu (2) ; (*a ram's*) siṅga.

HORNBILL, THE—boela cēṛē, dhorsa ; (*black & white*) cama.

HORNS—(*large*) ḍabe ; (*wide-spreading*) ḍaeka, laea ; (*drooping*) lara (M), lari (F) ; (*without*) muṇḍguć ; (*projecting in front*) siṅghin ; (*like callipers*) cimṭa d. ; (*to hit with*) uṭić ; (*projecting*) catra (M), catri (F).

HORRID—nepran, nichan.

HORSE, A—andia sadom, sadom ; (*kept in stable*) bandhar s. ; (*pack*) ladhna s. ; (*disease of*) kurkuri. *Cf.* NEIGH.

HORSE-RADISH TREE, THE—muṅga ; (*leaves*) m. arak ; (*fruit*) m. suṭi.

HOSPITALITY, TO SHEW—atan daram, chaklachak, daram, man, marjad, morji, pera.

HOST, A (*army*)—phad.

HOSTILE, TO BE—khaṭpaṭ, retha rithi.

HOSTILITY—badi, badisti, bairi.

HOT—chuć, ḍahḍahao, gorom, lag, lolo, udgar ; (*white*) daraṅ ; (*oppressively*) khulkhul ; (*& perspiring*) odoe balbal ; (*& steamy*) gijgij ; (*& painful*) ṭihka ṭihki, ṭihkau ; (*of sun*) jhala ; (*water*) basaṅ dak ; (*to be*) ḍahao, dhipau, dhuka, jolon. *Cf.* TASTE, TEMPER, WEATHER.

HOTTER, TO GET (*as quarrel*)—badha badhi.

HOUND—(*a large*) ḍahal seta ; (*to*) hurum durum, khackhacao.

HOUND ON, TO—carhiau, cariau, liliau ; (*a dog, cry*) lebhać, lubhai.

HOUR, AN—ghaṇṭa, lalae ; (*a clock that strikes*) dhorom ghari.

HOUSE, A—bari, orak, mahal, sal ; (*to erect*) orak ; (*empty*) mela o. ; (*hired*) bhara o ; (*large*) dolan, doṅgol, mahal, mohol ; (*site of*) diṇḍa ; (*small*) hopon o. ; (*brick*) dolan o. ; (*guest*) mela o. ; (*king's*) raj mohol ; (*pavilion roofed*) catom o., gudi o. ; (*tiled*) kaprol o., khapar ghara ; (*with low verendah roof*) ath cala ; (*with timber & earth roof*) kotha o. ; (*thatched with grass*) sauri o. ; (*lead-

ing to street) du.ra ; *(back of)* kuḍam ; *(platform round)* pinḍa ; *(one who stays in)* ghor cuṭiā ; *(parents')* naihar ; *(& possessions)* daija, oraḱ duar ; *(to house, going from)* bomboń, dhosma dhusmi, nagar bhuli (F). *Cf.* TO OCCUPY.

HOUSEHOLD—bari, eka gharia, garosṭi, gharana, ghar gusṭi, gharońj, grostali ; *(of one)* gharaia ; *(head of)* khamid ; *(members of)* palua.

HOUSES, TO OCCUPY TWO—ḍolita, pod.

HOW—cekate, cetame, ceťleka, ceťlekate, okaleka, oka tora, timin, tin ; *(is it !)* oka bate ; *(often)* ko baji ; *(far)* oka dhabić ; *(much)* timinaḱ, tin, tiriť, ṭukin ; *(—of small quantities)* tin udi ; *(long)* tin dhabić ; *(much soever)* jahãtinaḱ ; *(stupid of me !)* bhatić ; *(provoking !)* dhokran ; *(foolish)* dur karahaḱ, duṭhaḱ.

HOWL, TO—arra arri, garja garji, garjao, kirkirau.

HUB OF WHEEL—pai.

HUBBLE-BUBBLE, THE—huka ; *(with long stem)* gargaraḱ, gurguri ; *(bowl of)* cilim ; *(rod for cleaning)* gaj, siṭka ; *(packing in bowl of)* jalim ; *(part of)* bota ; *(sound of)* khodo (2), khoro (2), padraḱ, podo, podroḱ.

HUDDLE, TO—tombre, kokoso ; *(up)* surusuć, ṭunkau ; *(up & shiver)* ṭunṭunau ; *(together)* dhumbaḱ.

HUDDLED UP—kurbuń, kurcań, kuṭbur, kuṭu, murculu, romcoloḱ, sumurguć ; *(to lie)* kosmbaṭ.

HUE & CRY—huli.

HUGE—asin darin, asintara, bhunda (M), bhundi (F), dama domo, darońja, dhaṭha duṭhu, dharṅga, huduraḱ, huṭuk, jahbaj, legesaḱ, marań, silodha ; *(of things on ground)* tẽrẽjhaḱ ; *(& full-grown)* jharkarẽť.

HUKA—*Cf.* HUBBLE-BUBBLE.

HULKY—dhomsol (F).

HUM, TO—bhan, ranran ; *(of a crowd)* rãorão ; *(& haw)* hẽhũ.

HUMAN—manwa janam ; *(being)* hor, manwa ; *(beings)* manwa jaṭ, hor manwa, manoti manwa ; *(sacrifices, one who offers)* ondga.

HUMANITY—sil.

HUMBLE—nandan, nic, nindhan ; *(to be)* naraj.

HUMBLY, TO ENTER—ghusiau.

HUMID—gila, sebeć.

HUMILIATE, TO—mũ geṭ ; *(to be)* lajao.

HUMMOCKY—uṭ uṭu.

HUMORIST, A—phokṭia, phukṭia, phulania.

HUMOROUS—daṅgoḱ, galbajoria, kasia, khasia, lambhua, lamkambari, laphua, nabhua, pagal, phokṭi, phukṭi, phulania ; *(conversation)* kap, phalu ; *(to be)* isir siṭkoć.

HUMOUR—phula khasia ; *(to be in a bad)* adra, aruń paruń.

HUMOURS OF THE BODY, THE—ros ; *(derangement of)* ros amol.

HUMP, A—domcoḱ, kodgo, kumdhuć ; *(of bull)* ocoť.

HUNCH-BACKED—kaṭbuć, kaṭwić (F), kodgo, koṭbo, kuṭbuć ; *(abusive)* kabnũć.

HUNDRED, A—sae, so ; *(thousand)* lak, lakh.

HUNDREDS OF THOUSANDS—lakelak.

HUNGER—reṅgeć ; *(to bear)* sahao ; *(faint from)* hapaḱ (2), jańje, jarao ; *(parched with)* aṭap jarap ; *(& thirst)* upasa tirasa ; *(through stress of)* lać jalate ; *(for, to)* lalao, lala lali ; *(with)* miruḱ (2).

HUNGRY—aṭwasi paṭwasi, khaḱ, khańkhaila, marae (2), reṅgeć ; *(very)* kãokão, khańkha khańkhi ; *(to keep one)* kharkharao ; *(& thirsty)* upasa tirasa.

HUNKER, TO—cocoṅgoť, cucumguć, cucuṅguť.

HUNT, A—karka, sendra ; *(annual)* disom s., lo bir s. ; *(one-day)* por s. ; *(to fix date of)* dahur bulau ; *(superintendent of annual)* dihri.

HUNT, TO—jarpa ; *(up)* pakre.

HUNTER, A—sendra herel, sikari, sikaria ; *(share given to)* capo joro.

HUNTING—*(calls)* hari jui ; *(terms)* huhi, hunda, janam data, landha galoć, mandal ; *(expert in)* jalim sar, jarnaha.

HURL A DART, TO—sohor.

HURRICANE, A—birbao.

HURRIEDLY—ahaṗ cahaṗ, ahrem pahrom, ampa ompo, andaṅ tawaṅ, andhi caṇdhi, cacur macur, cahal (2), cahar (2) calcaluạ, camcam, caṇḍ, caṇḍaki, caṇḍuć, catapat, dhaar pakar, dhaper, dharne dhapae, dharpar, dhatpat, dhatar patar, dhokor pokor, hacar (2), hoele hoe, hud marte, lolopoto, tahka bahka, (& *inefficiently*) jhoto poto.

HURRY, TO—caṇḍa caṇḍi, dhaper, dharpharao, hacpacao, halhalao, hudhudạu, tạlbi, taltalao, tara tạri, tạri ghạri, tultulạu, utu dhutu; (*as work*) thotho motho; (*to be in a*) aktạu, akut, calcaluạ, caṇḍaki, loro (2), loro thoro, loto thoro; (*to cause to*) toltolao, turburạu; (*& scurry*) udur dhupur, umdhum.

HURT—lokre, lotoć; (*a*) bubu; (*to*) hahas, haso, rokor; (*to meet with*) honjaṅ, huṅjaṅ; (*feelings, to*) chorwaṅ.

HURTFUL, ANYTHING—kal.

HUSBAND, A—herel, jãwãe, purus; (*who serves for his wife*) ghạrdi jãwãe; (*private address to*) tiri; (*& wife*) tiri purus; (*& wife, to separate*) bapag, chada chạdi; (*separated from wife*) chạduạ; (*relatives of*) norha jorha; (*of sisters*) sadge, sạdhu; (*of elder sister*) teṅat.

HUSBANDMAN, A—casa.

HUSHED—gatagam, sansun; (*to be*) hapeṅ, hapo.

HUSK, TO—(*grain*) caole; (*by pounding*) huruṅ; (*dhan 1st time*) setoć; (*dhan 2nd. time*) tala; (*with teeth*) hadaṗ; (*by grinding*) darrao; (*without boiling*) adwa; (*a machine to*) ḍhiṅki.

HUSK, AFTER REMOVAL OF GRAIN—here.

HUSKED GRAIN—caole; (*broken*) khode, mạrkhu; (*partly*) beṇḍer.

HUT, A—chapri, kumbạ; (*small*) kuṛiạ oraṅ, tuṭ kuṛiạ.

HYDROCELE—aṇḍraṅ, ekasirạ, sirạ.

HYENA, THE STRIPED—hadgar.

HYPNOTISE, TO—muhni.

HYPOCRITICAL—kopoṭ, phạsiạra.

I

I—apiñ, iń; (*am told*) ote; (*have heard*) kathae; (*presume*) cele.

IBIS—(*the black*) tarjuạ; (*the shell*) suṅkhạl.

ICE—borop; (*cold as*) kankan.

ICHNEUMON, A SPECIES OF—saram babea.

IDIOTIC—kõka (M) kũki (F), koṅka (M), kuṅki (F); (*to be*) khepao.

IDLE—alnõ, awaṅsacuạ, bhacam bhucum, bhaṅguạ, bhat mara, bhuạ, boḍboḍo (F), dhemạli, dhuraha, dimak, kuṛhiạ (M), kuṛhni (F), lamkamạriạ, lamkambạri, laṅlaṅ, luruṅ buruṅ, obobo, susti; (*to be*) duruṗ, heholoṅ.

IDLER, AN—bhat dhunạ, ghor cuṭiạ.

IDLING—cerka bherka, ḍemḍem (F), demkhem (F), huluk (2); (*to go*) kabaṅ (2), kabkabao. *Cf.* TO STAND.

IDLY—oloṅ pholoṅ (M), uliń phuliń (F). *Cf.* TO TALK.

IDOL, AN—deb, murhuṭ, murut; (*Hindu*) bhạdu, dibi; (*to set up*) than bạisạu, thapna; (*house*) than oraṅ.

IF—judi, khać, khạjuk, khan, menkhan, pale, rema; (*only*) khạjuk; (*ever*) pale; (*so be*) rema; (*not*) baṅkhać, baṅkhan.

IGNORAMUS, AN—ạluạ, bemblaha, bhuc.

IGNORANCE—bhuc; (*to pretend*) erka, kothe, kuthni, peṅgha; (*through*) andha.

IGNORANT—abod, ajan, albudạha, ạlhuạ, baura, bhembha (M), bhembhi (F), bhoco, bhoto, bhuc, bhucuṅ, boka, bombo, dhundhạ (M), dhundhi (F), dundhạ (M), dundhi (F), beṅgia, hohaṅ, jambhuạ, kõka (M), kũki (F), koṅka (M), kuṅki (F), lelha (M), lilhi (F), mukhu, murkho, nirbaṅ, nirbodh, olkobaha, olo, onḍioṭ, orlo, urbhuṅ, urbudaha.

IGNORANTLY—bejan.

IGNORE, TO—pichol, rod.

ILL—dodoroso, dormad, dormoć, lạbruṅ, rugi; (*very, of fever*) para jara; (*to be*) bejar, pirit, ruạ; (*to be very*) japao, jobdao, laṅga; (*looking*) coroṅṭo, dhoṅ, orloporlo, robojholo; (*fortune*) abjos; (*at ease*) aksak, naraj; (*clad*) kaṇṭa koṇṭo; (*name*) ọpjọs; (*conditioned*) coaṛ, coṭhra, dhuraha, khecṛaha (M), kheeṛahi (F), khokṇḍo, kurmuṭaha, lẹṭrọk̃, lẹṭwẹt̃, lur na bhas, mọrgọt̃, murguć, nekṛaha, ọbọsta; (*favoured*) baṛṭaṅ; (*feeling*) khunus, laeloṭha, lag, lajbaj, laụa lagṭa; (*feeling, to harbour*) badọt, eperheṇḍe, kana kaṇi; (*fortune, from supernatural influence*) laṭu bhaṇḍu; (*grown*) jerka; (*of sores*) galak̃ (2); (*formed*) dabla (M), dabli (F), katha kothe; (*starred*) chae; (*will*) adwati, badão, badi, badisṭi, baiṛi, bibad, ḍah, kaḍha kaḍhi, kan, khones, khọnọs, khunes, lajbaj; (*wisher*) dusman. *Cf.* FITTING, NATURE, OMEN, TEMPER, &c.

ILLEGALLY—andher, binhọk.

ILLITERATE—mukhu.

ILLNESS—rọg; (*any unknown*) bẹrõṭ duk; (*to sham*) nọkọl; (*causing*) bataṛ.

IMAGE, AN—murhut̃, murut, puturạ; (*likeness*) urgan; (*reflected*) caher; (*graven*) gọṛhọn muṭhan, kundau murhut̃; (*maker of*) raj mistri.

IMAGINE, TO—kheal.

IMBECILE—olkobaha, oṇḍiot̃, urbhuṅ.

IMITATE, TO—caṭiau.

IMITATING—(*as child*) ye, yi; (*having power of*) laphuạ.

IMMACULATE—miridọs.

IMMATURE—aṇḍu, bacṛa, balok, bataṛić, chaọṛa, kãca, kaci, kacri, khica, nabalọk.

IMMEASURABLE—anbid.

IMMEDIATELY—caṭ marte, chọṭ, cọṭ, cọṭọk, daradaṛ, dhak, haṭọk, huṅ mẹnte, jaṛak̃ marte, jaṛap̃ marte, jaṭak̃, jhap mẹnte, kalak̃, kalok̃ marte, laṭ marte, phus marte, saṭ marte, taṛak marte, ṭaṭka mạr, turạt, turte; (*after*) bithag, tora.

IMMENSE NUMBER, AN—dedar, guṭek utar.

IMMERSE, TO—caḍo, topo, um; (*to be*) uḍu ḍubu.

IMMODERATELY—andha dhund.

IMMODEST—lajkhauka (M), lajkhauki (F), nilaj.

IMMODESTLY—hagaeak̃, hoehoe, họṅhọṅ, lẹslẹsẹ, pọṅpọṅ; (*clothed*) lọrọć (2).

IMMORAL—luca (M), luci (F).

IMMORTAL—omor.

IMP, AN—chae mara gidra, ḍuć mara g., jelpeć, jọć, juć.

IMPAIR, TO—ọbọsta.

IMPALED THROUGH THE FUNDAMENT, TO BE—cigi.

IMPART KNOWLEDGE, TO—ṭalim.

IMPARTIALITY—susṭob; (*with*) soloman.

IMPATIENCE—surma.

IMPATIENT—aṅkha aṅkhi, caṅmaṅgao, cọṅcọl, cuṭcuṭ, khuṭ (2), ulkhania; (*to be*) akta akti, akṭau, akut, bitla bitli, bitlau, kuput, lala lali, lọlọ, rẹṅkao, tarka irki, ukta ukti, uṛut̃ (2), uṭu puṭu; (*to begin, to be*) loṛo (2), loṛo thoṛo, loto thoṛo.

IMPEDE, TO—akọṭ, bajhua, biḍhaura, kacal, kacar, leṭaṅ, letaṛ, nejhaṛ, neṅjhaṛ, okoṭ, thakthakao.

IMPEDED, TO BE—abjoṛ, ḍhaṅ, ṭhamae ṭhukai.

IMPEDIMENT—rọkṭọk, ṭhẹk; (*of speech, having*) gaṅguṅ.

IMPEDIMENTA—ḍadha ḍumbaṛ, jhoṭra moṭra, ṭhamae ṭhukai.

IMPEL, TO—calao.

IMPELLED—kakhante; (*by strong desire*) lale.

IMPERFECT—adhkhẹcra, adpura, phi, phiṭ; (*of fruit*) kọṇḍẹ kọsẹ; (*vision*) andhet̃ dundhet̃, popolhet̃, ṭesra (M), ṭisri (F); (*work*) atra matra.

IMPERFECTION, ABSENCE OF—napae, sajọntar.

IMPERFECTLY—alak choṭak, atra matra, cacur macur, cinḍal, cinḍel, heraṅ petaṅ, kaṭać kuṭuć, raya royo; (*of sweeping*) phidga phidgi; (*executed*) idoṛ bidoṛ.

IMPERTINENT—ajgar, bahali, behoea, ektaraha.

IMPERVIOUS—daria.

IMPETUOUS—tapis; (*to be*) jhũk.

IMPETUOUSLY—aruć paṭuć, aruć taruć, paṭuć, sursur.

IMPETUS, UNABLE TO STOP FROM—sọrọṛ.

IMPINGE, TO—bajao.

IMPLEMENT—hạtiạr, khaṇḍa ; (*agricultural*) baksa, karha ; (*for digging weeds*) khurpạ ; (*to make hole in wall*) sind kạṭhi ; (*digging*) ṭamna.

IMPLEMENTS—sajbaj, sanaphana, sapạḍ.

IMPLICATE, TO—leṭha.

IMPLORE, TO—ạjij, ạri, jacao, joṛhat, kãoari, nọhõr.

IMPLORINGLY—jãore (2).

IMPORT (*meaning*)—tar, targhar.

IMPORTANCE, OF NO—aṛẹć gaṛẹć, bẹć bẹḍrẹć, merayak̕.

IMPORTANT—niṅjam.

IMPORTUNATE—ḍạṭhi, dawahi, hạṭhi, jhiki, sirṛi ; (*to be*) jạri.

IMPORTUNATELY—rẹgẹt̕, tiruṅ miruṅ ; (*& whiningly*) ṅuruṅ (2) ; (*to ask for*) khodao.

IMPORTUNE, TO—ajak̕, bestok̕, ḍẹḍhẹt̕, ḍhar ḍhur, ghigyạ, hạṭi, huṛso, jạri, jeṅjle, jhiki, jigir, juṅgi, khodrao, ṅaraṅ (2) ṅuruṅ (2), rẹgẹt̕, sirṛi.

IMPOSE, TO—(*upon*) daga, hạhi dudi, hordodo ; (*a contribution*) bab ; (*a fine*) ḍać ḍuć, ḍạṇḍ, ḍạṇḍọm, daṛ, phurạn.

IMPOSING—daroṅja.

IMPOSITION—ulbul.

IMPOSSIBLE—bẹlẹṭẹć, ọsad.

IMPREGNATE SUFFICIENTLY, TO—ada.

IMPRESS, TO—bhijạu ; (*upon*) bajao ; (*one*) aṭkar, bijạu, henat ; (*into service*) dhạrkạu.

IMPRESSION—(*to make*) gadao, uput̕ ; (*produced*) dhamas ; (*thumb*) ṭip.

IMPRINTED, TO BE—ukhṛạu.

IMPRISON, TO—kabhaṛ, kạd, kaidạu, najer bọnd ; (*pending trial*) hajọt.

IMPROPER—ajgar, dhẹj dhọṅ ; (*manner, in a*) aṭ nạ saṭ.

IMPROPRIETY—baṅ ganok̕ak̕, jusi.

IMPROVE, TO—bes ; (*of one ill*) susto.

IMPRUDENT—gạphil.

IMPUDENT—ḍhiṭ.

IMPULSE—tap ; (*to feel an*) sarbharao, uriạu.

IMPURE—adhọrọm, bagaṛ, loṅgra (M), luṅgri (F) ; (*of water*) gạrsilom.

IMPURITY, WITHOUT—rik̕ phili.

IMPUTE FALSELY, TO—phond, phorphond.

IN—re, te ; (*all*) mọṭhe ; (*a very little*) nẹ nāhak̕ ; (*vain*) ạuṛi ; (*the matter of*) babọtre ; (*order*) atom ; (*order that*) jẹmnẹ, jẹmnẹć, jẹmọn, jẹnọ ; (*place of*) bọdọl, chạḍić ; (*case it be*) rema ; (*doors*) bhitạr ; (*to put or bring*) ader ; (*& out, to go*) baṛać buṛuć.

INABSTINENT—umạs, umrạ (M), umri (F).

INACCURACIES, TO CORRECT—sudhrạu.

INACCURATE—ankatha anbetha, apa bạrịạ, ulṭi.

INACTIVE—jaba jobo, lạjuṅ (2), lạṇḍhia, lạṇḍhuạ, lapṛe (F), lijṛạha, thalpe (F).

INADEQUATE—ạkulan, ọkulạn.

INADVERTENCY—cuk, gaphlat.

INARTICULATELY—ẽć õć.

INARTISTIC—bẹḍhọb.

INCANTATION, AN—mantar, tit mantar ; (*for snake-bite*) biṅ m. ; (*to recite*) paṛhao ; (*one who cures by*) jhạrni, kambru guru, mạtri ojha ; (*to introduce spirits by*) thapna thạpni.

INCAPABLE—ạsṭạṅ, badhọr, bọsẹrṭạk, urbhuṅ.

INCARCERATE, TO—bọnd.

INCENSE—dhup, luban ; (*to offer*) dhup, dhudhup, dhup dhumạn ; (*holder*) dhup dan.

INCENSED, TO BE—kạhur mạhur ; (*& attack*) mũhạ̃.

INCEPTION—oṛ, oṛphẹḍ ; (*of putrefaction in vegetables*) kumblạu.

INCESSANTLY—barabar, gorok̕, (2), harghaṛi.

INCH—inci.

INCISION—(*to make an*) pac ; (*to make a deep*) sigi, soḍa.

INCITE, TO—arjan, aṭ, bãh, cạṛhiau, cạriạu, jhulkạu, udgạu, ulạr, uṛal, uskur ; (*used to*) sẹ ; (*one who*) uṛạliạ.

INCLINATION—dạris, gorji, sad, sadh.

INCLINE, AN—anãrgo, dhaṛdhaṛi, ranakạḍ ; (*steep*) ghaṛ ghaṛiạ.

INCLINE, TO—lawer ; (*upwards*) ạpir ; (*to one side*) leṛwak̕.

INCLUDE, TO—bhitạr, leṭha, salaḱ, sẹlẹt́; (*in number*) lekha mit́, lekha joṛao.

INCLUDING—lagaete, sạhit.

INCOHERENT—lẹcẹpẹcẹ, pharhaṛ.

INCOME—amdạni; (*an uncertain, let for fixed sum*) ijạra.

INCOMMODE, TO—andhkup, bạjhuạ; (*by projecting anything*) ṭọkṭọkọ.

INCOMPARABLE—ạprùg.

INCOMPETENT—akoḍa, aldhundhạ.

INCOMPLETE—adpurạ, akulạn, khẹcra, khecre, leñjbar, tara tapra; (*of narrative*) bạṭur sạṭur; (*to be*) lesrao.

INCOMPLETELY—atrom (2), nase sạri.

INCOMPREHENSIBLE—hạri bhọñ, nirbhuj.

INCONSIDERATELY—dẹmạriạ, pạthạuṛi.

INCONSISTENT—ọsọmbhag.

INCONTINENT—loṅgra (M), luṅgri (F), umạs, umrạ (M), umri (F).

INCONTROVERTIBLE—paka.

INCONVENIENCE, TO—andhkup, ạsiạr.

INCORRECT—bẽṛbaḱ, bẹthik, makṛe; (*of time*) bẹ̃ṛẹ̃ (2).

INCREASE—baḍ birit, baḍhaona, borket, phẹlẹn; (*of crops*) sahar.

INCREASE, TO—agad, bạḍ, baḍha baḍhi, baḍhao, bambkao, baṛhao, baṛhiao, bisi, bọcọḱ, cabhao, capao, cạṛhi, charao, coṛanti, curti, dãhgao, dahṅgao, ḍambrao, ḍẹć, ḍher, hara, juṭuć, parcao, pasar, phar, porgol, sarhe; (*of a sore*) palpalao, phadgao, phadphadao; (*in length*) goṭoć; (*in intensity*) bamka bạmki; (*by being blessed*) barket; (*in family or estate*) hoṛ hara, hoṛ barta; (*at another's expense*) cakrao; (*of fever*) dundiḱ.

INCREASING—caṛha cạṛhi, chiṛhạ chiṛhi.

INCRIMINATE, TO—ọjọḱ jalaṫ.

INCUBATED, AS AN EGG—ghorao, ghurni.

INCULPATE, TO—khoca.

INDECENTLY—soesoe (F).

INDEED!—eh, iyo.

INDEFINITE—(*article*) miṫṭẹć, miṫṭạñ, miṫṭen; (*number, an*) barọphẹṭ.

INDEFINITELY—apalheṫ, ạuṛi.

INDENTURE, AN—ikraṛ nama.

INDEPENDENT—ạnhũṭ, babbạhiạ, bẹtabe, chutṛari, hạrdund, hũṭ, masdar, maswar, matbọr, mọstọram, sạdhin, swạdhin; (*of*) bẹgọr.

INDEPENDENTLY—jạni jạti.

INDEX FINGER—uduḱ kạṭuṗ.

INDIA—Bharọtbọrsọ.

INDIAN FILE, IN—gọntọ gọtọ, ọtọñ taenọm, ọtọr gọtọr.

INDIAN CORN—joṇḍra; (*kinds of*) *Cf.* joṇḍra; (*boiled*) j. daka; (*cob*) phọṭ; (*porridge*) j. lẹṭọ; (*cobs plaited together*) jhọṭọr; (*receptacle for*) badaṛ; (*pistils of*) goco.

INDIFFERENCE, PARTICLE SIGNIFYING—dapoṛ, napoṛ.

INDIFFERENT—(*to be*) ọgọrọj; (*way, in a*) ẹmọn sẹmọn, jẹmọn tẹmọn, raya royo.

INDIGENT—ḍhạndhạniạ, heme, tasañ.

INDIGESTIBLE—gọrọb.

INDIGESTION—ạgni manda; (*to suffer from*) bhirsạha, bhirsạu, birsạha, birsạu.

INDIGO PLANT, THE—lil.

INDISCRIMINATELY—ghaser, hạrghaser.

INDISPENSIBLE—jarur.

INDISPOSED—bẹrọs, dhọrọñ pọrọñ, dodoroso, dondho mondho, dọrọñ sọrọñ, dọrọsọrọ, masmas, ọsuk, ropropo; (*from catarrh*) uru suru; (*to be*) diḍhi, pirit; (*to seem*) robojholo; (*to move*) dọgdọgọ; (*at beginning of fever*) rasras.

INDISTINCTLY—alam galam, apalheṫ, dhund, ẽć õć, ẹdẹbẹdẹ, galam, gãre, garsilom, habaḱ cubạḱ, halaṫ (2), hayam, hẹjẹ bẹjẹ, hoyam, lodo dhoroḱ, ṅalaḱ, ṅalaḱ marte, ṅaloḱ (2), palaḱ poloḱ, payaḱ poyoḱ, poloḱ. *Cf.* SPEAKING.

INDIVIDUALLY—jạ i ạti, jona joti.

INDOLENT—asket, asketiạ, gạphil, lesraha (M), lesrahi (F), maswa, maṭha.

INDUCE, TO—bhabrao, ghãose, ulạr, uṛal; (*by pormises*) lulwạu; (*illness*) batạṛ; (*one who*) uṛạliạ.

INDULGE ILLICIT LOVE, TO—lọṭpọṭ.

INDUSTRIOUS—caṭkan, chaṭkan, hunạr (F), hunạriạ (F), jạkir, jhũkel, khaṭoca, khạṭwạia, mẹhnotiạ.

INDUSTRIOUSLY—chalak (2), cham (2), hạrmạṛ, huṛum suṛum, tahatạhi, ugur sunduć.

INEFFECTIVE—ạuṛi ; (*to render*) bhạṇḍur ; (*to be rendered*) ḍigạu.

INEFFICIENT—aekom, akoḍa, bẹkam, bọsẹrṭāk, hẹndẹć.

INEFFICIENTLY—chiṇḍel, hirañ petañ, kāca, kạci, kạcuṛ mạcuṛ, keceṭ meceṭ, lẹḍẹr bẹḍẹr, lẹṇḍẹr bẹṇḍẹr, liṛwạ saṛwe, lọḍọr bọḍọr, loro boto, loṛo (2), lọṛọṅ phọcọṅ, loṛo thoṛo, luḍur buḍur, luṛuṅ buṛuṅ, oṛgo poṛgo, phanda phondo, sidi bidi, sio soyo, tara mara ; (*of ploughing*) siyoṛ (2) ; (*of music*) ruru (2).

INELEGANT—bhaskar, katha kothe.

INEPT—albakaha.

INERT—dọgdọg, robrobo.

INEXPLICABLE—hạri bhọṅ.

INEXORABLE—ḍhạṭhi.

INEXPERIENCED—aekom, ạnạri, kāca, kạci.

INFAMY—apjọs.

INFANT—balẹ bẹṭkẹć, bẹlkẹñ ; (*tender*) balẹ belteñ ; (*3 or 4 months*) ehel bẹṭkẹć, ẹlẹñ bẹkẹć ; (*cry of*) ẽhõ, koā (2), kohā (2) ; (*marasmus of*) puni ; (*disease of*) khala.

INFECTIOUS, TO BE—ucạṛ.

INFER, TO—ohman, orad, undkuṗ, unkuṗ.

INFERENCE—anman.

INFERIOR—nirọs, ọsnẹ, picọpọcọ ; (*quality*) ạu, lerañ petañ, lereć peṭeć ; (*to, to be*) sọrọs *with negative*.

INFESTED WITH WILD BEASTS—bagahi, bagher, camke, cañke.

INFILTRATED MOISTURE—sabsab, sobsob.

INFIRMITY—ghuṛại phiṛại, nijọjọr, rọg ; (*having*) roga, rugi ; (*without*) nirogi.

INFLAME, TO—salgao, sulgạu.

INFLAMED—dar ; (*to be*) isin, jaljalao, jhũkạu, jọlọn, rọkọt muhā̃, sarngao ; (*tumour of eyelid*) ṭọkẹ.

INFLAMMATION—(*area of*) dar ; (*of lungs*) betha ; (*of eye*) mẽẽ, mẹndoṅ, tirsul.

INFLUENCE—dhamas, dhọmọs ; (*of a spirit, under*) chaṭa ; (*occult adverse*) badha, bẹd, bẹṛ, bidiạ, lạṭu bạṇḍu ; (*occult, unaffected by*) obidhan ; (*by importunity, to*) ḍhar ḍhur ; (*to be under*) dhamsao.

INFLUENTIAL—madhā̃s, mandhas.

INFORM, TO—cugli, darsao, jạhir, janao, jana jạni, jangại, jạnti, khabar, khecao, lại, suć, sunạn ; (*privately*) phuski ; (*against*) cugli capạṭi, naṭ ; (*the police*) cạṇḍiạu.

INFORMATION—khabar, khọbọr, sọmbad ; (*to give*) khuṇṭạu, khuṭạu ; (*to send here & there*) huli ; (*giver of*) cugliạ, cuṅgliić, jạsu.

INFRINGE, TO—agar ḍigạr, rọd.

INFURIATED, TO BE—kisiạu.

INGREDIENT—johṛa.

INHABIT, TO—bọskọṭ.

INHABITANT—baskitiạ, nibạsi.

INHARMONIOUS—akhṛa ạkhṛi, aiṭbasaṛe.

INHERITANCE—ạidạri ; (*part of*) bāṭ bakhra ; (*paternal*) bapọti dhọn.

INIQUITY—phasad.

INJURE, TO—bosto, gāowāo, hondwañ, huañ, huloṛ, hurwañ, jae bejae, kaser, khenhao, loksan, noksan, nọstọ, pọr mọnda, sọṇḍa, tin topor khana, uper khaper ; (*by overeating*) abgun ; (*desire to, with*) badalte ; (*through envy*) hẽsaliạ.

INJURED—huṛa, lọkṛe, lọṭọć, lukṛe ; (*to be*) abọsta, borborao, khatra, kucạ.

INJURY—hạn, hạne, hạni, harakat, khatra, loksan ; (*to meet with*) hā̃si hanao, họñjañ, huñjañ ; (*susceptible to*) batọl, sohan, sohna ; (*to cause*) hanao ; (*causing*) bataṛ ; (*absence of*) napae.

INJUSTICE—aneāo ; (*to do*) andher.

INK—kạli, siạhi, sihại, siyạhi ; (*bottle*) dawat, doat.

IN-LAW—erwel.

INN, A NATIVE—sạrại.

INNOCENT—miridọs, nirdọs, sone sod.

INNUMERABLE—alekha, ạṭis kuṭis, lekha khon bahre.

INNUTRITIOUS (*of food*)—ṭanuạ.

INOCULATION—bod khoda; (*mark*) bodh ṭikạ; (*mark, having*) usnạ.

INOCULATOR, AN—bodh.

INQUIRE FOR, TO—surạg.

INS & OUTS—tak rọkọm, targhar.

INSANE—bạulạ bạuli, bạulạha (M), bạulạhi (F), bạul (M), bạulạu, bạuṛau, bạwil (F); (*to speak as one*) alok̓ bakok̓.

INSANITARY—kacar.

INSANITY—bại.

INSECT, A KIND OF—dak̓ sọsrọć, gẹgẹ tẹrẹń, ghugri, hạṭ suṅgạ, lạhiạ, maraṛ tejo, tejo; (*water*) aṅgur birhi, ghurni, icạk̓ kạkiṭteť, mahra; (*sand*) gitil gāṛī; (*which burrows under skin*) gitil; (*lac*) lahī, lạihạ; (*causing decay of teeth*) koscoya; (*crawling, sensation of*) gayam (2); (*rice pest*) bạki; (*on silk-worms*) họṛẹć gadar.

INSECTS IN GENERAL—ciũṭi pipṛi.

INSECURELY—bhọjgọć, bijgọć bọjgọć.

INSENSIBLE—ẹgher.

INSEPARABLE COMPANIONS—jọpọrjole.

INSERT, TO—goja, gotao, gutu, rẹbẹť, sọgẹ, suṛuć; (*in flesh*) pạṭi.

INSIDE—bhitạr, bhitri.

INSIGNIFICANT—bẹć bẹdrẹć, bẹdrẹć, bendreť, beń ak̓, beńjlań, bẹtreť, jelpeć, jhińji jhuri, jō̃ć, juć, kạṭić, morsitruć, sutruć, ṭum; (*creature*) bele botke; (*person*) bhạṛuạ, meraić.

INSINCERE—kọpọṭ, phạsiạra.

INSIPID—lamjak̓, paṅgať (2), pẹsẹť (2), sabak̓, sạbrạ, usạṭ, usṭạha; (*& hard*) siṭ siṭi.

INSIST, TO—ạkta ạkti, aṭ, dawa, dharamara; (*on getting*) hạkuṕ cạkuṕ; (*on immediate action*) tagaja.

INSOLENT—ektaraha.

INSPECTOR—nispeṭar.

INSPIRE, TO—bakao; (*breathe*) sahẹť ader; (*to be*) bharao, ẹsẹr.

INSPIRIT, TO—jhulkạu, puchlạu.

INSTALMENT, AN—kạndhi, kist; (*failure to pay*) kisti khilạpi; (*agreement to pay by*) kisti bạndi.

INSTANT, AN—ghạṛi, polok; (*on the*) bidnạk̓, kalak̓, phucnć marte, pucuć m., sanak̓ m., saṭ m., taṛak m., turāt, turte.

INSTANTLY—cạbhruk̓, cạṇḍuć, caṭak marte, caṭ m., chọṭ, cọṭ, culuń, cuṇḍuń, daradạr, dhak̓, ẹkkalte, ẹkdam, miť ghạṛite, iti ghạṛi, gọť, hoele hoe, họť, hugui m., kalak̓, khaṭ, laṭ m., mar, sanak̓, sanak̓ m., taṛak m., turāt, turte.

INSTEAD OF—bạdli, bọdọl, chạḍić.

INSTEP, THE—suptić.

INSTIGATE, TO—bhabrao, cạṛhiạu, cạriạu, ulạr, urạl.

INSTITUTE, TO—car, soro, sorwa; (*legal proceedings*) lọmbọr.

INSTITUTION—ạri; (*belonging to*) sarkari.

INSTRUCT, TO—batlao, ceť, samjhao, tạlim.

INSTRUMENT—hạthiạr, khanḍa; (*pl.*) sapaṕ; (*for cutting cocoons*) bakhọṛ; (*punching*) bhalwa; (*boring*) bhāora, gharra; (*for beating down earth*) dharmus; (*for digging roots*) khurpạ; (*multiple*) naharni. *Cf.* MUSICAL.

INSUFFICIENT—akulạn, odgel, ọkulạn; (*to be*) khaṭọ, ṭan, ṭanaṭạni; (*to have*) ṭọnṭa.

INSULT BY PULLING BEARD &c., TO—cọkọć.

INSULTING—ajgar, carcapaṛ, cokak̓, cokak̓ baklak̓, ektaraha, rọṛ siṭhạ, rọṛ sīṛić.

INTEGRITY—khulạsa.

INTELLIGENCE—(*news*) birtant, hạkigọṭ, halcal, hukigọt, khọbhẹr, sọmbad, sug batra; (*want of*) albạsuạ, galta golať, khepa, laṛbạṛiạ.

INTELLIGENT—husiạr, kheas, kheạsi, uạkep, wakhẹp; (*to be*) ucit.

INTELLIGIBLE—pharphạriạ, purchạ.

INTEND, TO—aoda, lagať, lạgiť, pontha.

INTENSE—āṭ; (*of clouds*) gọrọńj (2); (*to become more*) porgol.

INTENSELY—heṛan.

INTENSITY—tap; (*adj. or adv. signifying*) ạdi karte, baṛić, bẹbaṛić, bẹdhaṛak, bejāe, bẹporloe, bhagete, bogete, ẹkdhara, gaṇḍe muṇḍe, guṭek, iṭọċ pọṭọċ, kane kapar, khaclakhac, kusyã̄, kuṭnaṭ, sạmạni, tạtbiċ, utạr.

INTENT ON, TO BE—cahak manak, ṭhanṭhanao, tharthararao.

INTENTION—gorji, gọrọj, mọt, mọtlọb, murạd, murwạd.

INTENTLY—morol (2), tanman ; (*to look*) ạriċ kuriċ.

INTERCEDE, TO—kath oḍe.

INTERCEPT, TO—gurgur ; (*by straining*) chạni.

INTERCHANGE, TO—orpher.

INTERCOSTAL NEURALGIA—boṅga betha.

INTERDICT, TO—ḍaboṭ, dob ; (*a sign*) coṇḍka.

INTEREST—(*concern*) dhak, garaj, gorji, gọrọj ; (%) bẹaj, sod, sud ; (50%) deṛhi sud ; (*together with*) sud samet ; (*in kind*) ạghi. *Cf.* TO LEND.

INTERFERE WITH, TO—bolao.

INTERJECTION, AN—*Cf.* EXCLAMATION.

INTERLACE, TO—baj, bata, paṭẹċ ; (*horizontally*) gaban.

INTERMARRY, TO—jọrnaṛ.

INTERMEDIARY, TO ACT AS AN—suċ.

INTERMEDIATE—mańjla ras (M), mạńjli ras (F), modhom.

INTERMINABLE—pọhọṭ.

INTERMINGLE, TO—gaḍẹe saḍẹe, khijạu.

INTERMISSION, WITHOUT—bhọdọr (2), jamar, miċ talao, miċ rọgọr, talao, taletal.

INTERMITTENT FEVER—pạli ruạ, pạri ruạ.

INTERMIX, TO—gaḍẹe saḍẹe, laṭghaṭ.

INTERNALLY—ghus (2).

INTERPRET, TO—bhed, bhọń.

INTERROGATE, TO—kuli, ṭokao ; (*repeatedly*) tekhrao.

INTERROGATIVE, AN—ceṭ, ki.

INTERRUPT, TO—rokao.

INTERRUPTION—letań, letar, lẹṭọk ; (*supernatural*) badha ; (*with many an*) ṭhakẹṭ (2).

INTERSPACE—phāk ; (*having large*) phandṛa.

INTERVAL—phāk, talbhań ; (*without*) bhọdọr (2), bidlạị ; (*with short*) dara dạri, lagle, laglemạr, ṭaohẽ ; (*of day or two*) otahole, utạhuli.

INTERVALS, AT—baras bạris, bạris (2), riṅgọṛ rọṅgọṛ.

INTERVENTION—laṭak, lọṭọk.

INTERVIEW, AN—bhẽṭ.

INTIMATE, TO BE—hẹra ghesa.

INTIMATION—kaha kạhi.

INTIMIDATE, TO—humdhum, jhọk jhokao.

INTO—te.

INTOXICANTS—mạhur, nisạ ; (*fish*) haṛ.

INTOXICATED—kalobalo, matal, matla, mạtuạ ; (*to be*) bul, sur, ṭeremere, ṭermerao, umtạu ; (*slightly*) ńũ teṅgar, ribribạu, taṅgar mạtuạ ; (*to unconsciousness*) tuwel.

INTREPID—jạlmi, jhũkel, jọlọnịạ, nirbhọe ; (*to be*) jhũk.

INTRICATE—ẹdẹbẹdẹ, ẹdhẹ bẹdhẹ, enbend.

INTRODUCE, TO—ader ; (*spirit by incantation*) thapna, thapna thạpni ; (*extraneous matters in discussion*) gọrtọrọċ.

INUNDATE, TO—chạpilman, chạplạu.

INURE, TO—bhãwār, hewa, teńjao.

INURED—ajmao ; (*to be*) bhańjao ; (*to work*) bọhọn.

INVARIABLY—barabar.

INVEIGLE, TO—bajhao, lalkar.

INVEIGLED—ora uri ; (*to be*) lajbajhi.

INVENT, TO—jorao, turtạ.

INVENTORY—tạlikạ.

INVEST, TO—lagan bagan.

INVESTIGATE, TO—carcao, dạriạp, sutrạu, tadarat, tagada, todarot, tondehi, tondori ; (*& decide*) nolao.

INVESTMENT, AN—lagna.

INVETERATE—lạtkuṭạ ; (*to be*) hewa gịḍi.

INVIGORATED, TO BE—dọm.

INVITATION, AN—bolahaṭ, bulahaṭ.

INVITE, TO—doaṭ, nẽota ; (*personally*) bạnij ; (*to accompany*) dela, ḍoḍe.

INVOICE, AN—calan.

INVOKE, TO—bakhẽṛ, ḍakao, ḍakrao, hakrao.

INVOLVE, TO—bạjhuạ.

INVOLVED—ajbajhao, anakup, bajhar, ędębędę, ędhę będhę, phąsi.

IRASCIBLE—ankąrwa.

IRON—mẽ̃rhẽṭ ; (*cast*) dul m. ; (*sulphate*) hirąkųs, kąsis ; (*ore*) bąli, bhoṭ bąli ; (*pig*) paghal ; (*stone sand*) bąli, luhui ; (*earth contaning*) bąli hasa ; (*stone mine*) bąli gaḍa ; (*smelters*) kol ; (*thin sheet of*) patar ; (*utensils*) loha luti, m. khaṇḍa ; (*a branding*) dągni ; (*to*) istri ; (*striking iron, sound of*) ṭhaṅ ṭhuṅ; (*being hammered, sound of*) ṭhiń, ṭhiń ṭhop̣.

IRREGULAR—ajak̓ bująk̓, apa baria, dojnap, kanda kondo, kaṭbać kuṭbuć, sąṇḍ mąṇḍ ; (*surface*) cõrdań.

IRREGULARLY—cącur mącur, khedar bedar, khęję bęję, kherbejer, rikǫć rǫkǫć, sęgeć pęṭęć.

IRRELEVANT—phąlti.

IRREVERENTLY—ąuri pąthąuri.

IRREVERSIBLE—olsit̓ aṭet̓ sit̓.

IRRIGATE, TO—jhĩṭ, pąṭao.

IRRIGATED—pąṭan.

IRRIGATION—(*to condnct water for*) baelao ; (*basket for*) ḍobka, sẽrẽ.

IRRITABLE, TO BE—birghą.

IRRITATE, TO—carhao, chǫrchǫrao, ciṛhąu, harkha hąrkhi, hęṭęt̓, khijąu, khijlą khijli, khǫckhǫc, pąniąu.

IRRITAED—(*to be*) berosta, isbis, jhũkąu, kąhur mąhur, ką̃ucą ką̃uci, khą̃isą khą̃isĩ, khĩs, kickicąu, rońkhoń ; (*to become*) khą̃isą.

IRRITATING—cokak̓, cokak̓ baklak̓, isbis, kuṭkuṭ ; (*sensation*) gitgit ; (*in throat*) gargat̓, gatae, gayam (2), lęmlęm.

IS IT—(*so*) cele ; (*not so*) bańsę.

ISLAND, AN—ḍhip, ṭapu ; (*belonging to*) ṭikurią.

ISOLATED,—haeta hoeto.

ISSUE, TO—(*forth*) bhak, oḍok ; (*in puffs*) bhak ; (*continuously*) bhar (2) ; (*as water*) bhakh bhakao, bhumbuk, ḍubhąu, jhar (2) ; (*in small quantity*) pǫlǫć ; (*with a gush*) pǫlǫc, puyu (2), ṭuṇṭi ; (*with violence*) phere (2) ; (*an order*) ḍalao.

IT CAN'T BE HELPED—dapoṛ, dorok̓, napoṛ.

IT HAS BEEN SAID—kathae.

IT MATTERS LITTLE—bhala.

IT WAS THOUGHT, SAID, OR UNDERSTOOD—ęndęrege.

ITCH—kasra, khąs, khasra, khos ; (*to*) babat.

ITCHY—gargat̓, gitgit, kuṭkuṭ, sikir ; (*throat*) gatae ; (*& painful*) gumur (2).

IVORY—hathi soṇḍa.

J

JAB, TO—guṭą, guṭą guṭi, sǫbǫk̓.

JABBER, TO—bakat̓ bǫkǫt̓, bakhna bąkhni, bhęjęr (2), bhǫc (2), bokao, bǫkǫt̓ (2), phǫdǫr (2), ṭẽoṭẽo ; (*continually*) bhede (2).

JACK-FRUIT—(*tree*) kąṇṭhar ; (*seeds*) kosa ; (*wedge driven into*) guji.

JACKAL, A—karaj, toyo.

JACKET, A—kurtą ; (*long-sleeved*) ańgrǫp.

JADE, A—mara, radin ; (*hunch-backed*) kąṭwić mara ąimąi.

JAGGED—khadrak̓ khodrok̓, lacań locoń, regra, sǫṭsǫṭǫ.

JAIL—jahal.

JAM, TO—rętęt̓, ridet̓.

JAM OR JAMUN TREE—kod.

JANGLE, TO—takrar.

JANUARY—FEBRUARY—dinmas, mag, magh.

JAR—(*round*) bąhni ; (*earthen*) haṇḍha, hąthuą.

JAW—(*bone*)—jambe ; (*to*) bakhnao ; (*to move*) larǫe cakǫe, saṇḍap̣.

JAY, THE BLUE—ṭoya cẽṛẽ ; (*ornament made from*) ṭoya dhaca.

JEALOUSLY—hara hąri.

JEOPARDY—dąb.

JERK, TO—bidnąk̓, dhąrkuć, hutmą, ląkuć (2), phęt̓ ; (*the hand*) irci ; (*to oneself*) jargo ; (*up & down*) hico hoco, lawak̓, lawań, lewak̓, likić (2) ; (*head up*) dhunąu ; (*the body*) humcąk̓, humcąu, hupcąk̓ ; (*a haṭak̓*, tapseć.

JERKS, IN—dagak̓ (2), digak̓, digąk̓ (2).

JEST—(*to*) hą̃si ṭhaṭha, phukṭi, phulsi, ṭhaṭha ; (*in*) cąmpur, cąmpurte, gal bajorią, hą̃si, phukṭi.

JESUITICAL—phańga.

JESUS—Jisu.

JEWELRY—abhran, gohnapaṭi; (*a piece of*) khaga; (*loaded with*) jhane jhapane, jhanek jhapar, jhunuk jhupur.

JINGLE, TO—hanhan, tekeć, tekeḱ, ṭoḳoṛ.

JOB'S TEARS (*grass*)—gargaḍi, jargaḍi.

JOCULAR—daṅgoḱ, lambhua, lamkambaṛi, laphua, nabhua, phokṭi.

JOG-TROT OF POST-RUNNER—jhuluṅ (2).

JOGGLE, TO—ikoć sokoć.

JOGI, A—utit.

JOIN, TO—gabaḍ, joṛao, laga, milan, miṫ, toṅge; (*closely*) haṛop, sapṭa; (*end to end*) toṅge; (*hands together*) añjle; (*by splicing*) badhi.

JOINED—(*together*) jeṃthe; (*neatly*) jepeṫ; (*with wooden pin*) khila.

JOINER—*Cf.* CARPENTER.

JOINT—uṭi; (*of body*) joneṛao; (*to make a*) milan, milat; (*out of*) poṭoć.

JOINTS, TO CRACK THE—ṭhoć; (*sound of*) ciṭeṫ caṭeṫ.

JOKE—(*a*) landa katha; (*to*) hapsi, hãsna, hasnua, isiṛ siṭkoć, khelod, phalu, phukṭi, phulai, roṛ land, ṭhaṭha.

JOKER, A—phokṭia, phukṭia.

JOKING—campur, gal bajoria, hasi, hasi tamasa, hasi ṭhaṭha, irić cikić, itrau, phokṭi, phula khasia.

JOLT, TO—ḍakaṛ ḍukuṛ, daṛkaḱ doṛkoḱ, dhamcul, dhampol, dhaṛguḱ, dhaṛkaḱ dhoṛkoḱ, dhaṛkuć, tarko.

JOSTLE, TO—dhaka dhaki, dhaka dhoko, ḍhakla ḍhakli, jhaka jhaki, lepen tepen.

JOURNEY—(*a*) saphor; (*to*) daṛan; (*preparing for a*) cala cula, calcalwa; (*to go a long*) jatra; (*a day's*) jojon, muñjil; (*provision for a*) satu sambar.

JOY—has, hulas, raska; (*with*) riri (2), ritia ritii; (*without*) uchan.

JUBILANT—digi migi, hasi kusi, umjha umjhi; (*to be*) tilki bilki, ṭiṅgi.

JUDGE—(*a*) joj; (*to*) acar bicar, bicar, chiṇḍau, danai, imtan, mondot, neae, phaṇḍao, tajbij, undkup, unkup; (*to act as*) misil.

JUDGED OUT OF ONE'S MOUTH—roṛ ḍhiṅku.

JUDGMENT—uphad.

JUDICIOUS—in gan.

JUGGLER—ṭaṭak.

JUICE—ras, rasa, ros; (*without*) sitha.

JUICY—lasgar, rasanaḱ, roboć, rosgaria; (*of flesh*) reseṫ.

JUJUBE TREE—ḍedhaoṛe, ḍiḍhauṛi.

JULY-AUGUST—san, sorabon.

JUMBLE—(*a*) beńjaṅ biṅjiṅ; (*to*) arjhau, phidli; (*in a*) bilia bitić.

JUMP, TO—don, kamsa kamsi, padaḱ, phenṭoṛ; (*of footless creatures*) peresaṅ; (*or horse*) kharpaṭao; (*about*) kickicau, kuhup kudup, uć; (*over parts*) kabaḱ koboḱ.

JUMP, WITH A—padaḱ marte, padgaḱ marte, pidgić marte.

JUNCTION—(*of roads*) dobaṭia; (*of rivers*) domuhani, dul midoḱ, dunul.

JUNCTURE—tap; (*at that*) uprand.

JUNE-JULY—asaṛ; (*belonging to*) asaria.

JUNGLE—bir, jholaṇḍ, muṇḍu; (*thick*) aṭuḱ jharuḱ, badaṛ, jolaṇḍ, jhoṇḍ; (*large thick*) urni bir; (*a patch of*) cindka, ḍupka; (*patches of*) ḍapka ḍupka; (*scrub*) jhopo toṛo, pataṛ potoṛ, thopro bir; (*a track in*) chur; (*to relapse into*) banwaṭ, bonwaṭ; (*man*) bir hoṛ; (*fowl*) bir sim; (*products, edible*) jaejupaṭiń, jopatiń.

JUNIPER TREE—rothem.

JUNKETTING, FOND OF—irić cikić, itrau.

JUPITER, THE PLANET—cor kheda, rat calawa.

JURISDICTION—adol, elaka, ilaka, mahel.

JUST—(*true*) ajbi, ajib, ayã, hak, heke, hike, hok, sotea; (*before*) dela dili; (*so*) eroṅ, hẽ tho; (*as*) jaesan; (*beginning*) mereć; (*enough*) samuṅ, sumuṅ; (*then*) khange tho, uprand.

JUSTICE—dhorom, hok; (*to claim*) darsau; (*to cry for*) dohae, rae dohae; (*to deal retributive*) sajai. *Cf.* COURT.

JUSTLY—khap (2), soloman, solo sońjoḱ, somojos.

JUVENILE APPEARANCE, OF—bagar gaṭhia, bajar gaṭhia.

K

KAYASTHA (*a Hindu caste*)—kạithạ, kạt; (*a division of*) lala.

KEEN—(*eager*) khacar, khackhạciạ, khạrkhạṛi; (*sharp*) khar, lasẹr.

KEEP, TO—añgao, dọhọ, hameṭ, jakao; (*as a dog*) ḍabao; (*out of way*) aḍe, aḍger, aelo gaelo, bhac bhuc, dulkạu, gaoṛe, gerṣañ giṛsiñ, kakṛa kokṛo, lẹnḍẹć; (*to the side*) cudi; (*under*) dabao, ḍaboṭ, dạbṛi; (*at a distance*) durmar; (*shut up*) bae; (*to oneself*) añge, bạṭiạu, gabọć, guṭiạu, hameṭ; (*fingers bent till stiff*) lọklọkọ; (*at it*) rigdạu, ṭor; (*together*) sambṛao; (*in training*) teñjao; (*alive*) bañcao, teweñ jiwẹt; (*back part of evidence*) jibkạ; (*in good condition*) jogaṛsan; (*back nothing*) hiạ khalas, toṛphaṛ. *Cf.* SECRET.

KERNEL—(*of half-ripe fruits*) bhạti; (*of mangoes*) koyo.

KESTREL, A SPECIES OF—ṭikmiń cẽṛẽ, tirmuti cẽṛẽ.

KETTLE—(*singing of*) chae (2); (*drum*) dhak, ṭamak.

KEY—(*a*) chạbi, kạṭhi, kuñji; (*in the same*) sọṛọñ (2); (*on a low*) gạhlạ; (*on a high*) ṭẽṛẽć (2).

KICK, TO—phadgal, phanda; (*with hind feet*) phanda; (*out, of infants*) phada phodo; (*over*) kolsa pasir; (*back or sideways*) meṛsa; (*with sole of foot*) thạiyạ, thạyạ; (*forward*) kolsa.

KID, A—mẹrọm họpọn, pạṭhi (F)

KILL, TO—benḍao, gọć, jiwi ạgu, marao, mạutạ, ńẽṭ; (*for sacrifice*) tẹngẹn; (*by striking, &c.*) *Cf.* gọć; (*chrysalis in cocoon*) jiạu.

KILLED, EASILY (*of some plants*)—sohan, sohna.

KILN, A—bhaṭa, bhaṭha; (*potter's*) awa; (*to burn in*) rapaḱ.

KIND (*sort*)—jạt, jinis, kisim, prokar, rọkọm; (*of every*) iṛci guṛci, iṛtić gaṛtić, laṭbalań; (*a good*) jạtgar. *Cf.* WHAT.

KINDLE, TO—jẹrẹṭ, salgao, sulgạu.

KINDNESS—bũihạr, mãyã, susṭob; (*to shew*) mãyã, sostop.

KINDRED—ạpus.

KINDS—bhẫt, porkar. *Cf.* ALL, MANY.

KING, A—raj, raja; (*great*) despạti raj, maharaj; (*manager to*) dewan; (*son of*) raj kumạr; (*fisher*) kikir, ḍuć kikir.

KINGDOM—raj, rajoe, rajosti; (*of heaven*) serma raj.

KINGS—raj rapajko; (*a race of traditional*) koenḍa ṙapaj.

KINSHIP—sạgai, sọmpọk; (*by birth*) janam sạgai.

KINSMAN, A—pẹṛa.

KISS, TO—cọḱ.

KITCHEN—datka oṛaḱ, daḱka oṛaḱ.

KITE, A—gudi; (*Bengal*) kuṛiṭ; (*cry of*) ci hõ hõ; (*kind of*) ganga kuṛiṭ.

KITTEN—pusi họpọn.

KNAVERY—calạki, chọl; (*by*) pherkạṭite; (*given to*) dagabaj.

KNEAD, TO—kacṭao, paenḍao, sipi; (*while moist*) sipi; (*& mix*) thasao.

KNEE, THE—gunṭhi; (*cap*) cạki; (*having a stiff*) huṛjạ (M), huṛji (F).

KNEEL, TO—ikṛum; (*& bend forwards*) ombaḱ.

KNIFE, A—churi; (*large stabbing*) bhujạli, bogda; (*clasp*) cạku; (*to pare mango*) kato; (*curved*) binṭhi, kạidạ; (*used in basket-making*) kato; (*to cut Areca nut*) sarota; (*grinder*) sakildar.

KNIT, WELL—kuṭeṭ pañjar.

KNOB, A—ḍopṭho, gạṭ; (*having*) ḍạnṭha ḍonṭho, ḍomba ḍombe.

KNOCK, TO—bajao, bhonḍor, ḍhọp (2); (*forehead against*) tụpiń; (*against*) ṭhuḱ, thukṛau; (*foot against*) tọrọṭ; (*down*) bhindạr, bhindṛañ, dal gur, labda; (*down fruit with pole*) hunḍa; (*off*) jọṭ, kota, phaṭkao; (*together*) hạduć ṭhakuć.

KNOCKED UP—ḍoyọṭ.

KNOCKING, SOUND OF—dhọp (2), hạdbad; (*on ground*) ḍhap ḍhup; (*against several things*) thukṛạ thukṛi; (*to produce*) ṭẹć (2).

KNOCK-KNEED—bhaḍeṭ (2), bhaḍiạl.

KNOLL, A—ḍuñri.

KNOT, A—ḍhompo, ḍhoṇṭho, ḍombe, ḍoṇṭho, gāṭ ; *(on string)* ghẽṭ, giṛa ; *(in timber)* uṭi ; *(running)* asiť ; *(marriage)* bapla giṛa, lagan.

KNOTTY—badhoṛ, bedhoṛ, ḍāhā ḍẽhẽ, daṇṭha ḍoṇṭho, ḍhampa ḍhompo, ḍomba ḍombe, gāṭhia, geṇṭhe.

KNOW, TO—baḍae, baṛae, bheao, gãwao, baḍae orom, ńel orom, taphim, ṭhoḥor, toḥor, tuphim ; *(for certain)* baṛae siť, tuhkiť ; *(one's whereabouts)* khoṛo ; *(carnally)* pap.

KNOWING—uakep, wakhep ; *(without)* bejan, haeta coń joeta coń.

KNOWINGLY—baṛkać, dikbitte.

KNOWLEDGE—bhas, bidia, bidya, gian, ḥikmat, ilam, nam cinta ; *(to impart)* talim ; *(to have)* baḍae ; *(without)* ajan.

KNOWN—heto, hitu, jana suna ; *(to be)* lakhao ; *(to be well)* namḍak, namjaḍi ; *(to become)* soḍoṛ, sudri, unan, utlau ; *(to make)* jaḥir, jana jani, utlau.

KNUCKLE, TO *(as in marbles)*—ṭhep.

KOLES, THE—karmali, ke ; *(a tribe of)* muṇḍa

KUDALI, THE—kuḍi ; *(2-handed)* gují k. ; *(narrow-bladed)* ṭamni k. ; *(English pattern)* saheb k. ; *(blade of)* k. sakam.

L

LABOUR—ghamaoṭa, khaṭali, mehnoṭ ; *(forced)* begar, beṭh begar, biṭhi.

LABOUR, TO—dandha, dhamrokoṭ. ghamrokoṭ, khaṭao, kaṭwar ; *(hard)* daṛ dhup ; *(heavily)* bhondol.

LABOURER—*(daily)* majur, mojur ; *(general)* kuli.

LABURNUM, THE INDIAN—mirju baha

LAC—*(crude)* laḥi ; *(insect)* laḥi ; *(after straining)* laḥṭi ; *(insect, clour produced from)* hingu ; *(bracelet of)* laḥṭi.

LACERATING FEELING—kankan.

LACK—ṭan, ṭana ṭaṇi ; *(to)* okulan, ṭonṭa.

LACKING—*(nothing)* hamrau ; *(vitality of plants)* sohan, sohna.

LACQUER, A KIND OF—kharen.

LAD, A—bachṛa koṛa, juan ; *(12 to 14)* sisu juan ; *(about 14)* laṇḍur dhiń ; *(14 to 16)* cenḍa koṛa, choṇḍro.

LADDER—caini, siṛhi ; *(steps on)* hudra.

LADEN WITH CHILDREN & PACKAGES—jiṛo koṭe.

LADLE, A—*(pumpkin)* bokak ; *(wood)* cunḍuć ; *(oil)* dasaona ; *(iron)* kãṛchu.

LADLE OUR RICE &c., TO—le.

LADY'S FINGER, THE—jhińga.

LADYSHIP, YOUR—aprug.

LAGGING BEHIND—aṭur, jhapaṭ, ľejoṛ (2), lipaṭ lapaṭ.

LAID—*(waste)* berbad ; *(aside as useless)* giḍi ore.

LAIR—aotan ; *(of some animals)* gaḍi.

LAKE, A SHALLOW—jola.

LAMB, A—bhiḍi hopon, bakra (M), bakru (M), bakri (F).

LAME—dhoṛok, huḍuć (2), huṛuć (2), kaḍwa (M), kaḍwi (F), kaḍuć (2), khordo, khorda, khordeť, khoṛha, khurda (M), khurdi (F), leḍha (M), liḍhi (F) ; *(to go)* dhencok ; *(to be)* kaḍak kodok, leḍhak, leḍho, leṛhok ; *(in hind quarter)* kordheť ; *(in one leg, from injury to thigh)* lenca (M), linci (F).

LAMENT, TO—bhakur, ḥaecok, hae hiatiń, hae ḍhae, hiatiń, hińjrau, jare (2), tapiń.

LAMENTATION—bhẽṭra, hāhākar.

LAMP, A—diḥhe, mosal ; *(European)* baṭi ; *(wick)* baṭi, phiṭo, sulta ; *(oil-holder)* diuhe mali ; *(stand)* diaṛa ; *(black)* aenom, kajar ; *(black, receptacle for)* kajraoṭi.

LANCE—*(to, in surgery)* pac ; *(a 3-pronged)* tirsul.

LAND—bhumi, has, hasa, jaega, jagah ; *(settlement)* bondobos ; *(formed by silt)* celcekeć ; *(held by zemindar)* raj hasa ; *(all kinds of)* jami jaega ; *(tenure, a kind of)* jol sason ; *(given instead of food)* khanki ; *(held rent-free)* *Cf.* man ; *(newly reclaimed)* nãwā oṭ khet ; *(long cultivated)* nal ; *(high)* biṭha, ḍanga, ḍangal, goda, ṭikur ; *(price paid for)* pon. *Cf.* MEASURE, RICE-LAND.

LANDHOLDER—jamindar, talukdar ; *(present given to)* salami.

LANDLESS—becas ; *(to be)* bejaega.

LANGUAGE—bhaka, bhakha, bhasa, boli, buli, parsi, ror; (*the Santal*) hor ror; (*English*) angreji; (*of Hindus*) diku parsi; (*of villages*) gãowari buli.

LANGUID—dogdog, harur, ropropo, rubrubu; (*after exertion*) asket.

LANGUIDLY—sitoć sotoć.

LANKY—coeta, lamka (M), lamki (F), lapar loṅgat, larlaria, larpa, lorea, loryo, rakrić, raktaṅ, reṅta (M), riṅti (F), rikrić (F), roeda, rohda, rohra (M), ruhri (F), ṭaṭarbaṅ, ṭaṭiaha, ṭuila (M), ṭuili (F).

LAP, TO HOLD IN THE—gabla, gocha.

LAPPING, SOUND OF—caṭok (2).

LAPWING, THE—kuri ṭukuć, ṭeṭeṭeṅgoć cẽrẽ, ṭiṭirhić cẽrẽ, ṭukuć; (*method of snaring*) or dak.

LARGE—araṅga, asin darin, asintara, awal, bhõda, bhonda, bhuger, bhundu, bosti, dagor, dapthu, dargu(2), darhap, daroṅja, daru, dharahara, dhargu (2), dhargu sargu, dharṅga, dobo, dundun, haprak, hudurak, hutuk, jobor, khabela, laṭu, maraṅ, naprak, osno (2), rampar, sẽrã, ṭhabu; (*very*) ased maraṅ, habela, kabruṅ, ṭhabu; (*to become*) lagak (2), maraṅ; (*as tear in cloth*) paṅpandraṅ; (*to make*) laṭu; (*of some fish*) rindo rondo; (*of fruit*) dhambo, lokomduri; (*of a house*) darabara; (*of F. breasts*) kenel (2); (*in area*) jagesar; (*so*) ehe talaṅ, eto boro; (*& flat*) cakta; (*& small*) khaṭo badho, phucka phucki; (*lobed*) lorpe; (*& heavy-bodied*) dhabuskak; (*of corn-cobs*) riṭo roṭo. *Cf.* NUMBERS, QUANTITY.

LARGESSE—dan.

LARK, TO—makmak.

LARK, THE ASHY-CROWNED FINCH—gõeṭha lipi, lipi cẽrẽ, sirloć cẽrẽ; (*warble of*) surruć (2).

LARVAE—tejo; (*of some beetles*) gandar; (*which bore in timber*) huti; (*of mosquitoe*) kikir biṅ.

LASCIVIOUS—alak jhalak, umṭa (M), umti (F); (*woman, a*) chalak chandori.

LASCIVIOUSNESS—luca lamoṭ.

LASH, TO—carnao.

LAST—ar, ses; (*to*) ṭikau; (*year*) diṅ kalom; (*of all*) sotok sumuṅ; (*extremity, to be reduced to*) thalhalao.

LATE—aber, adin, nami; (*in day*) dhinaṅ, kubela; (*in season*) kuber; (*to be*) dera diri, diri; (*& early, as plants*) mama bhagna.

LATELY—sor dinre.

LATH, A BAMBOO—bata; (*for fastening thatch*) cipa bata.

LATHE, TO TURN ON A—kundau.

LATTICE WORK—bata, jhaṅjra, jiṅjri, piṅjra.

LAUGH, TO—gadgudao, hak (2), hiṭhiṭau, hiṭi (2), landa, khaṭkhaṭao.

LAUGHING—(*& joking*) meleć meçoṅ; (*& speaking with men*) hihi koko.

LAUGHTER—(*hearty*) haha (2), khadkhadao, khak (2); (*suppressed*) khić (2).

LAUNCH, TO—bhasan.

LAVISH—sadasuk; (*to*) sidrak badrak.

LAW, A—an, ari; (*suit*) mali mambla, mambla, mokodoma, mombla; (*suit, parties in*) kadi badi; (*without*) an dhidrik, bean.

LAY, TO—(*by*) amanot, jogao, jogar, juktau, sãitau; (*an embargo on*) rokao; (*aside as useless*) gidi toṭ; (*hold of*) hatwa; (*past*) bae, goṅjao, kenha, khenha, ret ciput, saṅcao, saṅgrau, sõc, soṅcao; (*an egg*) bele. *Cf.* HANDS, WASTE.

LAYER, A—aṭal; (*upon layer*) daria dapat, dophãr, remet (2).

LAZILY—asat osoṭ, jahpuṅ, sitoć sotoć.

LAZY—aṅsasua, asania, asaṅ poda, asan mandao, asketia, aṣtaṅ, aṭruṅ, awaṅsacua, bhacam bhucum, bhaṅgra, bhaṅgua, bhat mara, biggbogo, bodbodo (F), dare dhaṭuak, dhapka, dhemali, dhilisili, digodogo, dingar, gadut, gandhet, gandhia, gunduć gusuć, jhiṅga phulia, jodo, kurhia (M), kurhni (F), landha phucia, landhia, landhua, lapre (F), laṭea, laṭhea, lender (2), lerosia, lerwa larwe, lesoria, londhea, luruṅ buruṅ, maswa, matha, mund moroṅ, padhua, susti, tojahi; (*& dissolute*) lamoṭ, lampoṭ, lompoṭia; (*from overeating*) dhere (2); (*young woman*) bhundin; (*fellow*) bhat dhuna; (*to be*) asket. *Cf.* FAT.

Lead, to—ayur; (*by hand, &c.*) tiaḱ; (*away by false pretences*) bhabrao; (*about*) asen, ṭahlao; (*to*) upcan. *Cf.* astray.

Lead—sisa; (*red*) sindur.

Lead, to take the—lahar cahar, luhu cuhu.

Leader, a—aglaha, akyurić, gahi, guru, matha, mukhia, suba.

Leading—sira.

Leaf, a—palha, pat, pata, patta, sakam; (*petiole of*) bhekua, bhiṭuaḱ, daṭhi, khaḍi; (*midrib of*) sakam rir; (*bud*) ḍog; (*unfolding of*) gereć (2); (*of Piper Betle*) pan; (*of Laurus cassia*) tejpat; (*receptacle made from*) ṭoṭorbaḱ; (*without*) khadga. *Cf.* cup, plate, spoon.

League with, to be in—sajot.

Leak, to—joro, sudrau; (*as bellows*) posoṅ; (*in small quantity*) siḍor soḍor, siḍo soḍo, sio soyo.

Lean—coeta, copia, dẽrẽt ḍẽpẽt, ḍhadra (M), ḍhadri (F), dhandri (F), ḍhẽrẽ ḍhepe, ḍhẽrẽpete, ḍolao, jaknuć, jalpa, jalpaḱ, jalpha, japua, jiṅjri, kabaṅ (2), khad, khikrī (F), kiboṅ koboṅ, koboṅ (2), larpa, laṭlaha, leṭroḱ, leṭweṭ, liṭpiṭia, mordha, morgoṭ, patraṅga, patraṅgi (F), rakrić, reṅṭa (M), riṅṭi (F), rikrić (F), roeda, rohḍa, rohḍoć, rohor naṅjom, rohra (M), ruhri (F), ṭaṭiaha, ṭhoekoḱ; (*of children*) ṅuruć; (*& big-bllied*) jhoṭea; (*though well-fed*) laraha, laraṅ (2), rohra (M), ruhri (F); (*& weak*) leraṅ peṭaṅ, mora muri, mora jora, moroṭ; (*to be*) ḍola; (*to become*) kakra jambe, jhunki, osmao, osoḱ, pajhrao.

Lean, to—(*forward*). tirup; (*to one side*) laḍe; (*on*) beg, gaḍea guḍia, more, oṭhṅgao, ṭaḍe, ṭehaḍ; (*against*) aṭhrẽ, japaḱ, more, ṭaḍe, ṭaghen, ṭenḍar; (*against each other*) tirup; (*on hand*) capo.

Lean,—to roof, a—cari.

Leap, to—don, phenṭor.

Leaps & bounds, to move by—coroḱ (2), pardaḱ.

Learn, to—ceṭ, henḍeć, kheas, sikhnot, siknat.

Learned—biddan; (*man, a*) panḍet.

Learning—bidia, bidya.

Lease, a—paṭa, ṭhika; (*cultivating*) har paṭa; (*of land*) bonḍobos, ijara; (*document of*) ijara paṭṭa; (*hereditary*) morasi paṭṭa; (*in perpetuity*) ṭaluk; (*counterpart of*) ḳabuliat.

Leather—harta; (*workers, a caste of*) muci.

Leave—char, chuṭi.

Leave, to—alse, bagi, chonṭal, chuṭau, teag; (*over*) ubor subor; (*untouched*) baḍra, chinḍel; (*out part*) alak choṭak, atra matra; (*out nothing*) bac; (*off*) mahkup, mosoṭ; (*abruptly*) ṅirphor; (*a temporary resting place*) uṭhau; (*home, as jogi*) atit; (*some food*) itaṭ.

Leaven—tari.

Leaves—palha; (*young*) belkeṅ; (*fallen*) paṭaulaḱ; (*& branches*) patpala; (*sheath-like*) sari; (*which cattle won't eat*) pala; (*a bundle of*) guchi sakam; (*edible*) kacan araḱ; (*& firewood*) kaṭpat.

Leavings of food—aiṭha, aiṭha jũiṭha, baske, baṭur saṭur, itaṭ, jhuṭa muṭha, jom sareć; (*of a spiritual guide*) porsad. [paṭwa.

Lecherous—alak jhalak, loṅgor coṅgor,

Ledger, a—bahi, buhi.

Leech, a—jõk, keola.

Left—(*the*) kõṅye, leṅga, makre; (*to be*) sareć; (*what is*) sareć bareć; (*handed*) leṅgra (M), liṅgri (F); (*over from meal*) baske.

Leg, the—jaṅga; (*calf of*) coṭo jel, ṭhiṭraḱ; (*between knee & ankle*) narhaḍa, nas; (*from knee down*) kaṭa; (*stiff*) huḍuć (2); (*injured in one*) hurjeṭ, lecoḱ; (*of bed or chair*) kuṭhe.

Legal—(*instrument*) dalil, dolel; (*warrant, arrest by*) giripdar.

Legion—phad.

Legislate, to—acar bicar.

Legs, the—(*to draw up*) kuć kuć, kukuć, kuca, kurcaṅ; (*to cross*) paṭeṭ; (*to stretch out*) telṅjo, teṅjlo; (*weak on*) asor tambor, labas lubus; (*shaky on, as child*) ledlede, liloloko; (*strong on, as child*) ṅir keṭeć; (*with long*) ḍhaṅga (M), ḍhaṅgi (F), dheṅka, ṭampa ṭure, ṭampur.

LEGUMINOUS—*(crops, refuse of)* kuşṭạ; *(fruits, to boil)* puṭhuć.

LEISURE—aphsor, ọphsọr, ọpsọr, phursạt; *(without)* bhiṛ.

LEISURELY—asam usum, asaṫ osoṫ, jahat johot, japa jopo, jhahat jhohot, jhọhọt mọhọt, jipạ jape, jọhọt mọhọt, labhaṅ lubhuṅ, lagae logoe, (F), lambać lumbuć, lambhać lumbhuć, lọhọk, lubhuṅ (2), lubuṅ (2), rabać rubuć, rahạm rohom, rahap̣ ruhup̣, rase (2), rẹbẹ (2), ribić, rokme (2), rose (2), rosme, rọsọm; *(of wild animals)* labaṅ lubuṅ; *(of crabs, &c.)* ragabaga.

LEMON, A—lẹmbọ.

LEND, TO—bạisạu, ẹm dọhọ, ẹm hatạr, pańca; *(on interest)* bilat, lagan bagan; *(& borrow)* ẹm capal, pạlike pasa.

LENGTH—*(the)* jhạltẹṫ; *(as opp. to breadth)* jeteleń; *(of unequal)* ḍiṛhi baṛhi; *(of cloth)* lunḍ; *(at)* sesantire; *(to grow in)* gotoć.

LENGTHEN, TO—baḍhao.

LENGTHS, TO CUT INTO—ṭona, ṭona ṭuni.

LEOPARD, THE—kursạ baha kul, lekre tạrup̣, leṭea tạrup̣, sona citạ tạrup̣; *(a small)* poṭea tạrup̣; *(to become a)* aṇḍkul.

LEPROSY—murhuć jọm.

LESS—kọm, nirọs; *(to become)* dambṛao, domkao, ghaṭao, khentọ, kọm, komao, kumti, nińjhạu, norma, ṭhankao; *(than enough)* kaṭā̃ṛ; *(than ordinary length)* kọṭọṅ.

LESSER, A—ṭhikạdar, ṭhikedar.

LESSEN, TO—ạdhi, hatkao, kumti, ohra; *(by death)* gọć ạdhi.

LESSON, A—paṭ, paṭh.

LEST—bọṭẹć.

LET, TO—*(alone)* ikạ; *(go)* arak̇, chaḍao; *(loose, to be)* chuṭạu; *(off part of price)* khesarot; *(go anything tight)* phẹṫ; *(out cattle after noon)* uḍạr; *(out on hire)* bạisạu; *(out a secret)* bayaṫ buyuṫ.

LET—*(it alone)* jaede; *(me see)* bhala, dekhense; *(it take its way)* dorok̇.

LETHARGIC—diṛidaṅ, ropropo, rubrubu.

LETTER, A—ciṭhi; *(of alphabet)* akhọr, harọp; *(post)* ḍak.

LEUCORRHOEA—poṇḍ pọrdhọl, siṭkạ.

LEVEL—barabar, bel, cạuthol, miṫ sao, sạr, soman, sotel; *(on the same)* soka suki; *(not)* kaṭka koṭko; *(& broad)* camphel; *(to)* bhatao, chaṭao, sạriạu.

LEVER—*(for raising water)* ṭena ḍaṅ; *(balance)* kạsi tulạ; *(for trough)* duni; *(to tighten rope)* kạrkạri; *(to)* paṭẹṫ; *(to throw down by)* pạṭuć; *(to raise with)* uṭkạu.

LEVERET, A—kulại họpọn.

LEWD—lamọṭ, lampọṭ.

LIABILITY—dạhi, lạg, lạgti.

LIABLE TO—dạyik; *(dry up)* ṭanus.

LIBATION, TO POUR OUT A—cọḍọr, cuḍruć.

LIBEL, TO—khoca, phond.

LIBERAL—dạni, denadar, dini, diwạya, lahe cahe.

LIBERALLY—bhọcbhọcao; *(to give)* ogor, umā̃ṛ.

LIBERATION—rihại.

LIBERTY—*(at)* bahbah; *(to allow too much)* bahbạhię; *(to deprive of)* kạd, phaṭọk.

LIBIDINOUS—baṅgaṭ, umạs, umrạ (M), umri (F).

LICE, YOUNG—se tele.

LICENSE—chaṛ.

LICENTIOUS—bhanḍ (M), bhạnḍin (F), candal, candoro, lọṅgọr cọṅgọr, loṅgra (M), luṅgri (F), patit.

LICK, TO—caṭao, jal; *(as flames)* jharka jharki; *(the lips)* caṭak̇ cuṭuk̇, mẹlọṫ.

LICKER OF PLATES, A—patar caṭa.

LID, A—bẹnẹṫ, ḍabri, dhipni; *(earthen)* ḍhakna, ḍhakni; *(to put on)* bẹṫ; *(to remove)* uṭak̇.

LIE, TO—*(falsify)* ẹrẹ; *(down)* asan mạṇḍao, gitić, koṇḍel, kuṇḍel, kuṇḍlaṅ, ọbọr, ol, payar, saṇḍaṅ, sayaṛ; *(down, of animals)* burum; *(on bare ground)* oldhao, tolsaṅ; *(in wait)* aher, camke, dabkao, dabṛao, dapkao, latao, lokao, lotao, oḍao, ograo, ọtọr ombak̇, taṛā̃k̇; *(still)* gitić thir, kọsmbaṫ; *(with arms round)* hambuṫ; *(down for night)* họrmọ ol; *(with legs drawn up)* huṛbaṅ; *(down in water)* jọbẹ;

(*on side*) **pañjar bhorte gitić** ; (*on back*) **sạmbir** ; (*down in dust*) **gholṭa.**

LIEU OF, IN—**bọdọlte, satate.**

LIEUTENANT-GOVERNOR, THE—**hudiñ laṭ saheb.**

LIFE—**cola, jib, jibạ, jib dan, jiọn, jitạ, jiwẹt́, jiwi, poran** ; (*the giver of*) **janam data** ; (*way of*) **caecọlọn, cal, calcọlọn** ; (*to depart this*) **beṇdao, nọstọ** ; (*retentive of*) **jiạṛ** ; (*term of*) **jiwẹt́ bhor, jiwẹt́ janam, jao jiwẹt́, jọnọm kal, kal bhag, pormae** ; (*all one's*) **ṭuṇḍañ bhor, tire juge** ; (*a long*) **mahakal** ; (*to take*) **jiwi ạgu** ; (*to risk*) **jiwi alae, jiwi kọṭọk̕** ; (*to retain*) **jiwi rẹhẹt́** ; (*to give signs of*) **ukus pukus** ; (*to spend*) **jojao** ; (*again, to come to*) **jiwẹt́ beret́, jiwẹt́ ruạṛ** ; (*the chances of*) **khẹn** ; (*to hang onto*) **teweñ jiwẹt́.**

LIFT, TO—**rem, tul** ; (*up*) **halañ** ; (*with hand*) **kuṭuñ, loca** ; (*to strike*) **epel** ; (*& take away*) **hạr** ; (*up & throw down*) **kacao** ; (*the head*) **dhunạu** ; (*with a swoop*) **halo.**

LIGATURE, TO—**bạdhi.**

LIGHT—**marsal** ; (*to*) **jẹrẹt́, jol, salgao, sulgạu, tiṅgi** ; (*to bring to*) **sọdọr, sudri** ; (*opening to admit*) **bhāora** ; (*a temporary*) **arsal.**

LIGHT—(*not heavy*) **alga, halka, rawal, sahaj, sohij, sọhọj** ; (*of wind*) **hugni** ; (*of, to make*) **khọṭ, nihāt** ; (*tapping sound*) **ṭhopor, ṭipṭap** ; (*coloured*) **ẹsẹl** ; (*footed*) **perel** ; (*hearted*) **bahal, rijhwạr, rijhwạriạ** ; (*sleeping*) **torkal.** [**rawal.**

LIGHTEN, TO—**alga, aosan, bahalao,**

LIGHTLY—**perel marte, ruyul, ruyu (2)** ; (*of women*) **cimki ciṭiñ.**

LIGHTNING—**bijli.**

LIKE—**barag, barak, cond, ẹmọn, leka, lekan, lekate, macha, mạphik, mạpik, mohṇḍa, mọtọ, mọtọñ, nạpit́, soman, surik, tulni** ; (*the*) **sehoe** ; (*what*) **ceka leka, cekan lekan, oka lekan** ; (*this*) **ehe, inkạ, nenka, nenkan** ; (*that*) **enka, ona leka, onka, onkan** ; (*such*) **tanak̕, tanić** ; (*to die*) **mọrọn soman** ; (*myself*) **nẹ** ; (*with like*) **kitạ kẹ kitạ** ; (*to*) **bạsut, parpạsind, pạsind** ; (*to be*) **tić.**

LIKELIHOOD—**ḍọgọr.**

LIKENESS, A—**chạbi, chin, chọnd, ḍhạṭ, dol, muṭhạn, urgạn** ; (*exact*) **chanban, chonbon.**

LIKING—**hia.**

LILT, TO—**regha, regha righi.**

LILY, A LARGE—**sikiom baha.**

LIMB—(*to be flexed*) **kucạ** ; (*to move as*) **lạṛkuć, lạṛkać luṛkuć.**

LIMBS—**ti jaṅga** ; (*to lose control of*) **lẹrwak̕.**

LIME—**cun** ; (*box*) **cunạiṭi, cun ṭhoṅga, cun ṭhuiạk̕** ; (*made from shells*) **jhinuk cun** ; (*from nodular stone*) **gạṭi cun** ; (*stone*) **gaṅgiṭ, gạṭi.**

LIMIT—**simạ** ; (*boundary, the*) **simạtbạṛ.**

LIMP—**ḍolao** ; (*to be*) **ḍola** ; (*to*) **bit́ dũrũć, dhạruk̕ (2), ḍhẹcọk̕, ḍhẹñcọk̕, dhọṛọk̕, hạluć bạkuć, hoṛjañ, kaḍak̕ koḍok̕, khọrdet́, kuḍạ, lacak̕ lucuk̕, lẹcok̕, leḍha (M), liḍhi (F), ledhak̕, leḍhọk̕, lẹñcọk̕, lẹrhok̕, thọrọt́ (2)** ; (*from sore on foot*) **lacak̕ lucuk̕ (M), lạcuk̕ (F).**

LIMPING—**ḍhẹcọk̕ (2), ḍhẹñcak̕ (2), ḍorok̕ (2), kạbuć (2), koḍok̕ (2), kubuć (2), licạ lace, tharat́ thorot́** ; (*owing to short leg*) **kaḍwa (M), kạḍwi (F), kạḍuć (2), khõṛẽt́** ; (*from injury to leg*) **lẹñcọk̕.**

LINE, A—**ḍạṇḍit́, dhar, hora, len, panta, pante, pata, pạṭi, rada, thạr** ; (*a long*) **bọntọbọtọć** ; (*stock*) **jaro** ; (*in hoeing*) **pạhi** ; (*out of*) **apa bạriạ, ẹprẹ, gote** ; (*in*) **bonto boyol, gẹṭgẹṭẹ, rẹtrẹtẹ** ; (*in a long*) **mander** ; (*following in*) **giroe gọrọe** ; (*to move in a straight*) **hạrbañ hạrbuñ.**

LINES—**khạñjri** ; (*cooly*) **len** ; (*in*) **thạr, thạr kẹ thạr, tharathạr, tharethạr.**

LINGER, TO—**jama, tẹhẹ mẽhẽ.**

LINK, TO—**makạrgạti.**

LINSEED PLANT, THE—**ṭhisi, ṭisi.**

LION, A—**dhạcri kul, siḍ** ; (*old*) **siṅghọ.**

LIP—**luṭi** ; (*to bite the under*) **hạp̕ ikrum** ; (*a long under*) **lọclọcọ.**

LIPS, THE—**luṭi** ; (*to move*) **badak̕ buduk̕** ; (*to lick*) **mẹlọt́, caṭak̕ cuṭuk̕** ; (*smacking*) **cakạp̕ (2), chakọp̕** ; (*thick*) **hạpuk̕ hara** ; (*movement of when smoking*) **poyot́.**

LIQUID—(*too much*) sadar sudur, sadgur badgur, subur (2), sudur; (*to mix with*) leoha; (*semi*) leher.

LIQUIDATE, TO (*of a debt*)—sod, sud.

LIQUIFY, TO—karkarao, sabsab, sobsob.

LIQUOR—(*made from rice*) arika, bodea sodea, bodoć handi, bodoć mela, handi, lag handi, nahel gada dak, pocoe handi, tagri handi, tapandak; (*spirituous*) mahur; (*from matkom*) bhati, daru, duhli, mod, paura; (*from toddy-palm*) tari; (*oozing from malted grain*) jhar; (*from the still*) ekhan; (*first drawn off*) tań handi; (*2nd*) doja handi; (*3rd.*) bodoć handi; (*still, a*) bhathi; (*shop*) paura gadi, handi sal; (*to throw off effects of*) sarao; (*brought by visitor*) sandes; (*drunk at marriage*) sener lekha handi; (*given to village officials*) jan handi; (*given by bride's brothers*) koke handi; *given by bridegroom*) cadi; (*given to men who errect booth*) mandwa handi; (*under influence of*) teremere. *Cf.* ADDICTED.

LIQUOR AMNII—kasa dak.

LIQUORICE ROOT—kaweť.

LISP, TO—kẽrẽć dõrẽć.

LIST OF ARTICLES—talika.

LISTEN, TO—añjom, aten, kandher, lutur; (*to*) sunan; (*intently*) lutur biť, lutur odao.

LISTEN !—ate, ete, hate, ote, ote torae.

LISTLESS—gandhua, gayo gapo, godhra, gunduć gusuć, gundur musak, musak.

LITIGATE, TO—bibad; (*given to*) kuteť.

LITTER—abjor, aptar, gadrum sadrum, jobra, turutuka; (*in courtyard*) badgarak, judha, kadar kapar; (*blown by wind*) dhum dapot; (*smallest in a*) lenda, lendaturia.

LITTERED—dhum dharkar, tagatusa, udam; (*to be*) abjor, aptar.

LITTLE—bhetra (M), bhitri (F), deble, dereť, deť, geda (M), gidi (F), ghitli (F), gidri (F), gutra (M), gutri (F), letreť (M, litriť (F), pilcu, pilcuń, rega, remetele, rimsić, tembroť, temel, temreť, tepa tepe, thẽrbok (F), thõrbok (M), tura (M), turi (F); (*of living creatures*) hupţić; (*very' of children*) delem (2); (*term of endearment*) khere; (*ones*) cencuria, kapţićko; (*by little*) kurme (2); (*& big*) sele toke.

LITTLE, A—adharia, alop, as, enka (2), hãrať hũrũť, herep, inka, kheť khotor, kichu, kincit, nase, nase sari, suthni, thora, thora thuri, thora bahut, tuń; (*in comp.*) ńok; (*of leaking*) sidoť sodor, sido sodo; (*too*) okulan; (*at a time*) khucur mucur; (*here & there*) cindal; (*not*) thoren. *Cf.* WHILE.

LITTLES, TO COLLECT BY—juhrau, jumau, jurau, korpa, nare jore.

LIVE, TO—bahao, bhuńjau, jib dan, jiweť, jojao, khatao, khemao. tek, thathao, tikau; (*long in one place*) jom her; (*in forest*) banwas.

LIVE STOCK—carapia, lachmi, lukhi, mowasi.

LIVELIHOOD—dojok, gujar, rojgar.

LIVER, THE—im.

LIVING—jiweť; (*to be*) tek, tikau; (*to obtain a*) uteť; (*at expense of others*) catna (M), catni (F), catua, por cata, porchati. *Cf.* CREATURES.

LIZARD, A—cercetec, cete, ghigriń, gigriń, ginghri, hathia kakra, kajra kakra, kakra, kul seren, torhoť.

LOAD, A—bhar, bhari, boj, bojh, jhak, jhapat, jhapot; (*heavy*) kerec dorec.

LOAD, TO—bhari, bojao, bojhao, lade; (*a gun*) bojao, kasao; (*heavily in front*) agil.

LOADED—(*tree with fruit*) jhabrao; (*too heavily at back*) kere (2), pachil.

LOAF ABOUT, TO—andur mandur, andur pandur, berkeń, bhucuń, dedher, dhedre, gersań girsiń, haja hojo, harea garea, huluk (2), tamae tomoe, tambae tomboe.

LOAN, A—haulat, pańca, ; (*of seed grain*) bada; (*secirity for*) thit.

LOATHE, TO—acbic; (*food*) doyok; (*interjection indicating*) chia.

LOATHSOME—bhirik, dhirik.

LOCALITY—sarjamin.

LOCATE, TO—khoro.

LOCK, A—kulup, tala; (*of hair on crown*) tuila (M), tuili (F); (*elfin*) dhandri.

Locust—poho.

Lodge, to—thạwi ; (*a complaint*) cạṇdiạu.

Lodging, a—basa, chạuni, ḍera.

Lofty—huchucu, hudhuḍu, huṭhuṭu, khạ̃rgo, raṭbaṅ, roṭboṅ, ṭoṅṭoṅ, ṭuiṭui, usul.

Log, a—gaṇḍke, muṇḍhạ, muṇḍhak̓, muṇḍhaṭ̓, muṇḍheṭ̓ ; (*fastened to neck of cow, &c*) kurṇḍạ, muṅreṭ̓.

Loggerheads—lag ; (*to be at*) irạ iri, ṭanaṭạni, ṭhona ṭhuni.

Loins, the—ḍaṇḍa, kọmọr ; (*pain in*) ḍạḍa haso, hũk ; (*weak in*) liloloko ; (*string round*) ḍora, jạmki ḍora ; (*to bind round*) bande (F), paṭhẹ (M).

Loiter, to—bilom, ḍehẽṭ̓ ḍuṇḍuṅ, harea garea, hemkhem.

Lonely—haeta hoeto, nicol, nisun, ulạg.

Long—baela, bayul, biyol boyol, boela, boṅboṅ, bọntọ bọtọc̓, bọtbọtọ, cindạr candar, ḍakḍaka, ḍọkḍọkọ, gaboc̓ (2), gudui (2), jeleṅ, jhal, laphaṅ, laṛga (M), lạṛgi (F), layõk̓, leṅloṅ, limạṅ lamaṅ, loetoṛ, lohok̓ (2), pọr, raeka, rampaṛ, riyol royol, roela, saela boela, saṅgiṅ, sọksọkọ, ṭọhọc̓ (2) ; (*as tree-trunk*) hiṛhiṅjaṅ ; (*very*) boẽto bọyọl, hoṭhoṭo, loetoṛ, lọyọṛ ; (*as a robe*) tilpaṅ talpaṅ ; (*as beard*) gọḍọr ; (*as a road*) lẹṭ̓ lẹṭ̓ ; (*as timber*) sarhaṛ ; (*as horns*) daeka, daela ; (*way, the*) jeteleṅ ; (*& short*) baris (2), dojnap, rayal ruyul, tuluc̓ tupuc̓ ; (*& straight*) dọrdọr, sohela ; (*& sharp*) soela (M), suili (F), suilạ (M) ; (*& shaking*) lindạr lapar, lindlạpur, lọbọe ; (*& nearly horizontal*) liwer lawar ; (*& narrow*) lọṛọ ; (*& reaching feet*) cindạr cọndọr ; (*way off*) ạki laṅka, saṅgiṅ ; (*ago*) asãe sawãe, sedae ; (*suffering*) sọmbhori, suboria ; (*haired*) dhạlgum. *Cf.* TIME, LINE, LEGS.

Long for, to—arkha, bãṭ cahao, hadiạu, halkhao, harhao, haya, hurso, lalao, lala lạli, lalkao, lilkạ lilki, lolao, sasnao, uihạr, uṛuṭ̓ (2) ; (*as food*) hirohi, laklakao ; (*to cause to*) lilkạu.

Longing—hiạ, ṭhonk ; (*for*) cuṭcuṭ, ẹrẹm (2), miruk̓ (2) ; (*to have a*) thartharao, thurthurạu.

Look, to—ạriṭ̓, bẹṅgẹṭ̓, dọrsọn, najar, naṅjer, ṅẹ̃, nọjọr ; (*intently*) takao ; (*down*) oyoṅ ; (*down on*) bhades, posra ; (*up*) kọyọk̓, saṅgil ; (*to*) dạrsạu ; (*out for*) birlạṅ, cạriṭ, dhạndrạu, lạgiạ parao, lạgi bohao, sại, siri ; (*for*) baṭ ṅẹl ; (*at*) takao ; (*after*) tạtbir ; (*steadfastly*) rolo ; (*at covetingly*) celhe ; (*for anxiously*) dandrạu ; (*round*) ạhir kuhir ; (*carefully*) ạri bạndhi, ạriṭ̓ kuriṭ̓ ; (*for protection*) hirlạ ; (*to one side*) hoṇḍeal ; (*about furtively*) kayak̓ koyok̓ ; (*& then draw back*) hulkạu ; (*round proudly*) kẹṇẹkote ; (*out for opportunity*) laglagao ; (*back when fleeing*) birampaṭ.

Look—(*here*) ehe, hẽho ; (*out*) hãhãk̓, henda, khaberda, mẹn, mẹnya ; (*out, to keep a*) birlạṅ.

Looking—(*daggers*) kurkuṇḍuc̓ ; (*round about*) biṭ̓bikoc̓ ; (*glass*) ạrsi.

Loom, a—(*part of*) bade, boesar, jhap, kabhạṇḍ, nar khuṇṭi ; (*upper levers of*) jẹnẹreṭ̓ ; (*comb of*) rac.

Looming large in darkness.—dundun.

Loop, a—gạli, phạsi.

Loose—alga, bhaṛ (2), ḍhil ḍhọkọc̓, ḍikạ ḍake, gudui (2), liṛkọc̓ lọṛkọc̓, pharphariạ, pisạr pasaṛ ; (*to*) arak̓, rara ; (*to be*) lewe ; (*to get*) chuṭạu, phasuṛ ; (*to let*) chuṭạu ; (*of earth*) bhara bhuru ; (*of bowels*) cidrạ ; (*rattle, with a*) soṅkoṛ marte ; (*& shaking, as a tooth*) lọṛoṅ posọṅ ; (*by shaking, to*) ḍẹkẹṭ̓.

Loosely—bhoelo, bhọjgọc̓, bhondlo, bijgọc̓ bọjgọc̓, ḍhiloṅ ḍhọloṅ, liṛo loṛo, pisạr pasaṛ, siṅkoṛ soṅkoṛ, soṅkoṛ ; (*twisted*) bhoelo ; (*fitting, as a garment*) dhọdlọ.

Lop—(*to*) chạṭ, ḍulạu, kaman, paṅgao ; (*eared*) lạprạ (M), lạpri (F).

Loquacious—bẹjẹ (2), bhacbhacao, bhadra, bhajra (M), bhajri (F), bhọc (2), galbajri, kạhwạiyạ, khar, kuṭnạsiṭ, lạbuk̓ cạbuk̓, lahra (M), lạhri (F), lapco, lạpuk̓ cạbuk̓, lasra (M), lạsri (F), ragaṛ cagaṛ, thuthi kuṭạ ; (*of women*) caego, labar (2) lasar (2), lạsri.

Loranthus, a species of—kaṭkọm jaṅga.

LORD—bạbu rae, laṭ, mạlik, Prọbhu; (*like a*) mọstọram.

LORE—*Cf.* TRADITIONAL.

LOSE, TO—aṫ, bagdao, gạḍao, gãowão, gãwao, goão, josao, khowao, khuạu, khuwạu, pandol, pạsuṛ. Cf. FRESHNESS, FLESH, WEALTH, &c.

LOSS—ghạṭi, gunạgar, hạn, hạne, hạni, harakat, khatra, khotra, khuti, mara, ṭuṭ, ṭuṭi; (*to suffer*) hãsi hanao, ṭuṭ, ṭuṭi; (*to cause*) hanao; (*at a*) ạlmạl, andmand, ayaḱ oyoḱ, jalẹ thalẹ, jilwạ thạlwạ.

LOST—bidạraha; (*to be*) bagdao, banwas, bayaban, bhaonḍao, bilṭạu, chingạu, chuṭạu, gadha soṫ, kheanat, lop, pheṅkao; (*as unpaid debt*) ḍubạu; (*sight of*) bebilọnḍ, bọnwaṭ.

LOT, A—thak, thọk.

LOTS, TO CAST—gulibãṭ.

LOTUS, THE—upạl baha, upel baha; (*white, of Nile*) poraeni.

LOUD—andakul, aṭ, huḍuk (2); (*deep sound*) sarsar; (*& distinct*) ṭraṅ (2); (*& harsh*) cagae daṛae; (*murmuring*) galgal. *Cf.* VOICE.

LOUDLY—ajhãṭ, andakul, ạriṛ kuriṛ, cagae daṛae, daṛau, garte, kạṛau (2), kạruṛ bạruṛ, kher (2), kiriṛ, raru, sagae daṛae, taraj garaj; (*very*) kaku; (*of weeping*) kahãr kạhũr.

LOUNGE ABOUT, TO—ale jaṅje, ḍẹdhẹr, ḍhẹḍrẽ, haja hojo, japaḱ jẹrẹṫ.

LOUNGING—beṛkeń, henḍo, huluk (2), ọlọm jhọlọm, ọlọṅ phọlọṅ (M), uliń phuliń (F).

LOUSE, A—se.

LOVE—bhab, dulạria, hia, hiṫ, rij, sohag; (*to*) dulạr; (*to give rein to*) laṭpaṭ, lọṭpọṭ; (*with*) koṅkoreboṫ.

LOW—chaporae, chepko, chiạḱ, cọpọṫ, hẹṭ, hin, jahãe kãhãe, kaḍayuṫ kuḍuyuṫ, nic, nico, pedle (M), phọd, pidli (F); (*as field*) tapọl; (*as a ridge*) cepel; (*as fire*) hạrsuṛ; (*mean*) achọk, ḍiṅgar, kuṭnạ (M), kuṭni (F), nichok; (*of speaking*) gahãṛ gũhũṛ, gandar gundur, gọnḍọr (2), pasar pusur, phasar phusur, phasphus; (*of sound*) apalheṫ, bạibại, ńẹrẽ (2); (*pitched*) gạhlạ, guṅgwạoḱ, moṭa; (*of fever*) rapa ropo; (*of prices*) anḍhoṅ, oḍhoṅ, sahta, sasta; (*moist place*) sọṫ; (*& short-branched*) tulpạ; (*down, too*) phuekạ; (*spirited*) ahluṅ; (*to lay*) lạnḍhu; (*to*) bhokrao.

LOWER—hẽṭ; (*to*) ạrgo; (*to become*) khasao.

LOWING—(*of cattle*) homba (2); (*of a cow*) huduṛ(2); (*of buffalo*) onḍroć.

LOYALTY—neṫ.

LUCK—dasa, jọs, kapar, khạriạt, larbhad, nạsib, rạs, siri; (*good*) khạriạt, mahabhạg, sahar; (*bad*) abjọs, chae, sagaṛ jhagaṛ,.

LUCKY—bhạgan, lạkhi (M), lukhi (F), nạsiban, rạsṭana.

LULLABY, A—doldol, horlo lolo, lolo (2).

LULLED—cap cup.

LUMBAGO—ḍãḍa haso, hũk.

LUMP, A—bhinḍ, bhinḍa, ḍẽhẽ, ḍhimbạ, ḍhompo, kạndhi; (*to fold into*) koṭeam; (*of sugar*) bhili guṛ; (*of meat*) dholma, dhoma.

LUMPISH—bạndha (M), bạndhi (F).

LUMPS—(*in*) ḍanṭha ḍonṭho; (*with*) kanda kondo; (*to collect in*) ḍhumbạḱ; (*to form*) jimṭạu.

LUMPY—ḍambaḱ ḍomboḱ, ganḍać gunḍuć, kharạs (2), khạrus (2), kherẹs, kọṭrẽ, rambaṛ romboṛ, rombṛo; (*to become, as flour*) lẹmṭọḱ.

LUNAR MONTH, A—boṅga.

LUNCHEON—jọlpan, upạr mańjan.

LUNGS, THE—bọkọ; (*inflammation of*) betha.

LURE, TO—cạcki, muhni.

LURED—ora uri.

LURK, TO—dabkao.

LUSCIOUS—roboć.

LUST—hichạ; (*to*) jol, mẽṫ jọm, sana; (*full of*) chandgar (F), jhalka (M) jhạlki (F), matao, sạndgar (M), umạs.

LUSTY—bẹlkẹć, pakṭa; (*of bulls*) rạsiạu.

LUXURIANT—kacra kạcri, mocra mucri, labaḱ, laglag; (*& tender*) lẹgẹć (2).

LUXURIANTLY—candhẹr, ḍagdag. *Cf.* TO GROW.

LYING—(*down*) sayaṛ; (*loose*) gandra gundrạ; (*about*) aseń taseń, sadga bidiṛ, tahãṛ bihạṛ, udạm; (*apart*) setseto; *(in wait for)* canke, dapkao, lagibohao; *(on ground all night)* niyar; *(falsifying)* bat badohi.

M

MACHINE, A—kal, kol, sajbaj; *(for twisting twine)* gharri; *(for separating cotton seeds)* carkhi; *(husking)* dhinki; *(for expressing sugarcane)* raksi. *Cf.* INSTRUMENT.

MAD—bai, baul (M), baulaha (M), baulahi (F), baulau, bauran, bawil (F), khepa, konka (M), kunki (F), pagal, pagla (M), pagli (F), pagol; *(to be)* khepao; *(dog, a)* bhalok seta.

MADE UP—campur.

MAENA, THE—kare, kisni.

MAGGOT, A—tejo; *(eggs of)* asãe; *(motion of)* bukut (2).

MAGIC POWER—gun.

MAGISTRATE, A—hakim; *(to act as)* misil.

MAGNIFICENCE—thonok.

MAGNIFY, TO—aga.

MAHADEO—mahadeb; *(festival in honour of)* pata.

MAHAJON, A—deko pusi, sau.

MAHOMMEDAN, A—musla.

MAHOUT, A—mahut.

MAHRATTAS, THE—marhatha, bargi, burgi.

MAID-SERVANT—dasi, dhamri.

MAIDAN—caukan.

MAIDEN—juwan, misi juan.

MAIMED— kuda, thutha (M), thuthi (F), tuntha (M), tunthi (F); *(in feet)* kondha; *(in limbs)* thunta (M), thunti (F), thuntha (M), thunthi (F); *(to be)* nason.

MAINTAIN, TO—asul.

MAJORITY, THE—dher.

MAKE, TO—banao, benao, garhao, sirjau, sirjon; *(way)* arak, dahalao; *(over to)* dalao, gatao, hajur, saprot, soprot, sumjhau; *(light of)* gareć; *(out)* porok.

MALADY, A—karon, kasur, rog; *(having)* karni, nason, roga, rugi; *(without)* nirogi.

MALE—bhãora, herel hopon, kora hopon; *(Santal)* manjhi; *(of animals &c.)* andia; *(lamb)* bakra; *(organ)* end. *Cf.* MEMBRUM VIRILE.

MALES—herel jat,; *(in addressing)* meya, ya; *(of bride's village)* sariat.

MALEVOLENCE—badi, badisti, dahok.

MALICIOUS—cauchalia.

MALIGN, TO—phond, phorphond.

MALIGNANT SPIRIT—duarsini, kador bonga.

MALIGNITY—dhutai.

MALINGER, TO—nangos, noklahi, nokol; *(given to)* nangosia.

MALLET, A—mungar, salmungar, thupi; *(to give blow with)* kutam.

MALLOW, A—rehda arak.

MALODOROUS—bekar.

MALTED GRAIN—mera.

MALTREAT, TO—kandao, kandi kandao.

MAN, A—hepel, herel, hor; *(each)* horo (2); *(little)* thurka; *(great)* joj, lobab, mahajan, nawab, nobab; *(the first)* pilchu haram; *(of valour)* birbanta; *(who has lost several wives)* jomhem. *Cf.* OLD, YOUNG.

MANACLES—biri, hari, hatkari.

MANAGE, TO—calao.

MANAGER—dewan, karbari, rajkaj oaklaoić.

MANAGING *(of females)*—hunar, hunaria.

MANDRAKE—dudai jo.

MANE, A—carhi.

MANES OF FATHER, THE—porodhol.

MANGE, TO SUFFER FROM—khakra.

MANGO—ul; *(tree* ul dare, ule sin; *(kernel of stone)* koyo; *(grove)* bagica, ul bagwan; *(young tree)* ul kadlak; *(drink from unripe)* ul kanji; *(relish)* ul rase; *(method of preserving)* amsi, amtha.

MANIFEST—dondkoro, phanka phayar; *(to make)* sodor, sudri.

MANIFESTATION—sakhiyat.

MANKIND—manwa hopon.

MANNA—man.

MANNER—bhat, bidha, kader, rokom, surik; *(of all)* liti birsi; *(in like)* se, se ka se. *Cf.* WHAT.

MANSION, A SPLENDID—darahara orak, dharahara.

MANTIS, A GREEN—katruạ, nạu.

MANURE—khọt ; (*to*) gobrao ; (*full of*) sargạt.

MANY—ạdi, aema, ạrić, ạtụt, bẹbạrić, bẹporloe, bistọr, buruć (2), chạu (2), dạdur, dher, gadgad, guṭek, sạmạni, sange ; (*of small creatures*) gasgas ; (*of people*) ghạudạ ; (*at a time*) burbudluk ; (*kinds of*) emanteak, emanten, nana hunạr, tẹgẹć masek, unu unu ; (*kinds*) ạnu ạnu ; (*times round*) uṛhu buṛhu ; (*as*) jatna ; (*so*) hunạk, in, nhanak, nin, ninạk, numin, nun, nunak, nunan, tirit. *Cf.* COLOUR, SORTS, VERY.

MAR, TO—bhanga ; (*in trying to improve*) tegar.

MARASMUS—nanjom duk.

MARBLE—mọrmọr ; (*red*) ạbiaj.

MARCH-APRIL—cạt.

MARE, A—enga sadọm ; (*not allowed to breed*) sạdhin sadọm.

MARGIN—are ; (*on the*) dhare dhure.

MARIONETTE, A—putli, katputli, putri.

MARK— (*a*) cikhnạ, dag, nisạn ; (*to*) ãk, dag, ọl ; (*cut in wood*) ank ọrak ; (*not up to the*) ọsnẹ, picọpọcọ, raya royo ; (*to—note*) carit, tuphim ; (*nearest to the*) jilu ; (*to adhibit one's*) dọskhọt ; (*on cattle*) kạndhailạ ; (*made by goad*) topọnd ; (*with tip of finger*) ṭikak ; (*on forehead*) ṭikạ, tilạk ; (*of one unable to write*) kạndhạilạ ; (*having a*) dạgi ; (*of anything dragged*) radrad ; (*burnt on arm*) sikhạ. *Cf.* BOUNDARY, FOOT.

MARKET, A—bajar, piṭhiạ ; (*moveable*) hạṭ, hạṭea, hạṭiạ ; (*to buy at*) hạṭ bạṭ ; (*to go to*) hạṭok ; (*seller at*) hạṭwek ; (*dues*) tulạni ; (*day, next*) ghuri hạṭ ; (*& bazaar*)) hạṭbajar ; (*place or town*) sahar bajar.

MARKING-NUT TREE, THE—sọsọ dare.

MARRIAGE—bapla, bapla bihạ, bihạ ; (*a run-away*) mundu bapla ; (*to negotiate a*) sạhi juhi ; (*to give in*) gọn, jaega, ṭehad, ṭhãi, ṭhão ; (*form of*) *Cf.* bapla ; (*ceremony*) *at a*) baha saoha, bãihã, daram dak, jharaoni, katkọm, pạrchạu adẹr, sin duạr, tere ; (*knotted string intimating a*) lagan, lọgọn ; (*procession*) bariạt ; (*one who negotiates a*) raebar goco, raebarić ; (*to unite families by*) ghargharạia, jọrnạr ; (*booth*) mandha, mandhwa ; (*requirements for*) sanjok, solo sanjok, sonjọk ; (*contracted during S. rebellion*) hạulạ bapla, hul bapla ; (*pigment applied at*) arta ; (*best man at*) babrẽić ; (*party, to be one of*) baretok ; (*exchange of daughters in*) golạt ; (*a shout at*) haribol ; (*grass used at*) tasak.

MARRIED—bihạl era (F), bạhuanić (M), sindur bundi (F) ; (*to a husband, to be*) jãwão ; (*when it is raining*) badoli.

MARROW—tumul.

MARRY, TO—bapla, jọrnạr, nạrjor ; (*a 2nd. time*) sangha, saoha.

MARSH, A—dalahi, daldalahi, dạlhi, hạr, jạrhi, jola, lẹd ; (*shallow*) jhil.

MARTIN, THE SAND—bhạluạ.

MASH—gạlid.

MASHER, A DAL—ghuṭai.

MASS, A—bhind, bhindạ, dondha ; (*in*) hẹdẹ gọdẹ.

MASSAGE—iskir, malan ; (*to*) mardao, paendao.

MASSES, IN LARGE—cera (2), cerda (2).

MASTER—(*a*) gola, kirsand, khạmid, kisạr, mạlik, malkar, munib, ninjam ; (*of a*) sarkari ; (*one's own*) sạdhin, swadhin ; (*to*) cemat, kobjao, kọbọj, laker, ṭhạsiạu.

MASTERFUL—ektaraha.

MASTICATE, TO—tọgọć.

MASTOID PROCESS, THE—lutur hupạ.

MASTURBATE, TO—hejer, pisir.

MAT, A—pạṭiạ ; (*bamboo*)caṭa, jạṭi, mas pạṭiạ, ṭạṭhra, ṭhạtra ; (*palmleaf*) khi ur pạṭiạ, tale pạṭiạ ; (*reed*) surạ pạṭiạ ; (*to spread*) bel.

MATCH, A—bạnki, batarić, jorha, jọṭ, joṭić, jukur, juri ; (*lucifer*) diạ sạlai ; (*to make*) leao.

MATCHED—(*well*) juluṭhur, ọpọr jọpọr ; (*badly*) apa bạriạ.

MATE—jorha, joṭić, juri, juridar, juri jola, sọtason ; (*without a*) ekaha, ekạrha ; (*to*) juri ; (*without usual proprieties, to*) laskal.

MATERIALS—sajbaj, samagiri, sanaphana, sarajan ; (*for offering to deity*) bonga samagiri, bonga saranjam ; (*for marriage*) sanjok.

MATKOM—(*young tree*) matkom kạḍlak̕ ; (*flower*) jara, phulạ ; (*bunches of buds*) pusi jaṅga ; (*stamens of flower*) sọhọe ; (*to glean*) kọṇḍẹl, kọṇḍol ; (*fruit*) kuiṇḍi ; (*method of cooking*) laṭhẹ, phoka matkọm ; (*rind of fruit*) bakṛe ; (*refuse of*) gora ; (*pure spirit of*) phuli pạurạ.

MATRIX, A—sãnc.

MATTER—(*pus*) bele ; (*subject*) katha ; (*serious, a*) hamal katha ; (*requiring consideration*) mạli mambla.

MATTOCK, A—dạt.

MATTRESS, A DIVISION OF THREADS IN—sãk.

MATURE—bhar juạn, hapamun (F), pakoṭ, pakṛo, pakṭa ; (*to become*) hara buruk̕ ; (*to be*) jowao ; (*of herbs*) paḍga, pạṭu ; (*timber*) mañjai, mañjela ; (*to, of cooked rice*) ropam ; (*to be sexually*) ritiạu.

MAUND, A—man, mũṛĩ ; (*of grain*) kaṭ ; (*half*) khạṇḍi.

MAXIMUM, TO BE AT THE—dhurpạu, sạrdi.

MAY—baṛe ; (*hap*) cọñ cet̕ cọñ, jạnič, pasẹ.

MAY-JUNE—jeṭh ; (*a period of 13 days in*) rohni.

ME—iñ ; (*of*) tiñ.

MEAL—aṭa, họlọñ, lobok̕, sạtu ; (*coarse*) sege (2) ; (*to grind into*) họlọñ ; (*a*) sañj ; (*the noon*) mañjan ; (*the evening*) kedok̕ ; (*left from previous*) baske ; (*in return for a meal, to give*) jọm hala ; (*time*) daka jọm pọhọr ; (*time, after*) mañ he, sañjhe mañjhe ; (*provision for one*) sẹr sidhạ.

MEALY—lẹmẹñ.

MEAN—bokṛo, chiạk̕, chucạ, jãhãe kahãe, kador, kuṭnạ (M), kuṭni (F), nic, nichok, pạji ; (*to*) khaṭao.

MEANDERING—khĩṛjõñ khõṛjõñ.

MEANING—arot, bhẹd, man, mane, mọtlọb, ẹrthọ, pariạu, tar ; (*hidden*) mọrọm ; (*without*) bakbak, bhọdọr (2).

MEANS—bandheč, ukti ; (*of subsistence*) gujạr, roṭi ; (*beyond one's*) ẽč kõč ; (*not to have*) tirañ ; (*by no*) bañteť ; (*of, by*) họtẹte, niyẽ, parsadte ; (*by any*) kọkhọnọ, nirọt.

MEANWHILE—anman, hataṛ ; (*in the*) soedom, tan kurte.

MEASLES—milmiliạ, talsa.

MEASURE—(*a*) ae, amdaj, anman, ạri, kaṭha, mọn, muṇḍrạ, mũṛĩ, paemana, pạl, pạilạ, pạl mana, sọsọñak̕, suli ; (*to*) ãk, jokha, jokha jukhi, kut, map, nap, nap jok, nạpti, sọñ ; (*without*) bọae ; (*short*) bokṛo ; (*full*) ḍaṭọp ; (*beyond*) asambheṛ ; (*larger than standard*) bursạ pạl, pursạpai ; (*of 2 seers*) kạthi ; (*an honest*) bes cọlọn pạl ; (*a dry*) ḍheo, kaṭ ; (*a liquid & dry*) caṭak, chaṭak, sẹr ; (*an oil*) ḍuki ; (*a land*) bighạ, kaṭha, mũṛĩ, rẹk ; (*to use a short*) pạimara ; (*by spanning, to*) bitạ ; (*land, to*) jạrib, jurip ; (*exactly, to*) jokha sit̕, moka ḍaṭọp ; (*with forearm, to*) moka ; (*musical*) tạl.

MEASURED—kutạ ; (*rhythmical*) gọḍọp (2).

MEASURER, A—sọsọñič ; (*of land*) ạmin.

MEASURING-ROD—aṛani ḍañ ; (*of 2 cubits*) gaj.

MEAT—(*flesh*) jel ; (*roast*) rapak̕ jel ; (*boiled*) teke jel ; (*raw*) bẹrẹl jel ; (*cooked with rice*) suṛe jel ; (*lump of*) dholma, dhoma ; (*shoulder of*) phạri ; (*method of cooking*) kohra, korhe.

MECHANIC, A—mistri.

MECHANICAL CONTRIVANCE, ANY—kal, kẹl.

MEDDLE, TO—alae phulạe.

MEDDLESOME—haṭya.

MEDIATE, TO—pontha, sạlis.

MEDICAL PRACTITIONER—ḍagdọr, ḍakṭar.

MEDICALLY, TO TREAT—ran.

MEDICINAL—(*powder*) phạki, phạkni ; (*plant*) citạr kạṭhi, jạnum ḍhompa, kambraj, oponom, orsọriñ, sạru, sondhaeni ; (*roots*) jạri buṭi, ran rẹhẹt̕, rẹhẹt̕ sindhẹt̕ ; (*ointment*) ọjọn ; (*herb*) bandor jhuṭi, bañsiñ, deko sindur ; (*root, a*) bhegjira, bọc ; (*burnt clay*) eṭko hasa ; (*fruit*) pipol.

MEDICINE—murgạn, ọjọn, ran, rẹhẹt̕ sindhẹt̕ ; (*godlet of*) kambru buru ; (*a powerful*) lạg ran ; (*external application of*) bokram, kukạr, mohlon ; (*man, a*) ojha, dasãe kora.

MEDITATE, TO—bundis.
MEEK—mormor, nandan, nemor, nindhạn.
MEET, TO—dapram, daram, ńapam; (*with*) jokha.
MEETING, A—bạisi, bhẽṭ, caṭạI, darbar, dọrbar, pańc.
MELA, A—parab; (*held yearly at Budhai*) loban.
MELANCHOLY—gundur musạk̕, musạk̕.
MELLIFLUOUS—liṭhur.
MELLOWING (*of fruit*)—araraok̕.
MELODIOUSLY—ńahãṛ ńọhọ̃ṛ.
MELON—khiṛuạ, phuṭ; (*sweet*) tạrbhuj; (*wate*) khergunjạ.
MELT, TO—chẹr, galao, garao, lẹ, torlao.
MEMBERS—(*of house*) gharana, ghar gusṭi; (*of body*) họrmọ hạṭiń.
MEMBRUM VIRILE, THE—ẹṇḍ, juju, laṛ, laṭ, leoṛa, lọć.
MEMENTO, A—cikhnạ.
MEMORY—thuthi; (*to commit to*) ead, eyad, mọkọstọ, mukọstọ, yad; (*to repeat from*) mọkọstọ, mukọstọ.
MEM SAHEB, A—bibi era.
MEN—hopel.
MEND, TO—jaba jubạ, jhala jhạli, jujut, maramat, meramọt, moramot, sudhạr, sudhrạu.
MENDICANT, A HINDU RELIGIOUS—phạkir, sạdhu.
MENSES, THE—baha, sotra; (*a disorder of*) pọrdhọl, siṭkạ.
MENTALLY—mọnẹ mọnẹte.
MERCHANDISE—mal, maljal, saoda; (*a dealer in*) bepariạ.
MERCILESS—kaṭhor, kaṭ jibạ, kumaya.
MERCURY—para.
MERCY—daya, mãyã; (*to shew*) daya, mayã; (*by force of*) mãyã jalate.
MERIDIAN, THE—tikin; (*past*) ńõṛak̕; (*a little past*) nẽṛak̕, tikin eṛak̕.
MERIT—gun, gunạk̕, pun; (*religious*) pun; (*to acquire*) danpun.
MERRIMENT—rọń rij.
MERRY—rijhwạr, rijhwạriạ; (*to be*) hẹsẹć sẹkrẹć, mọgọn, mọńgọn, sẹkrẹć; (*go-round*) hinḍol.
MESSAGES, TO GO—aṭhaona paṭhaona.
MESSENGER, A—caprasi, sipạhi; (*foot*) paekan, peada; (*village*) dạuṛaha, goḍet.
MESSY—dhoro dhoso.
METAL—(*excluding iron*) darap, dorob, dorop̕; (*a*) dhat, dhạtu; (*used to make ornaments*) khapar; (*to cast*) dul; (*sound of contact of*) ṭapań.
METAPHOR, A—phẹn, phende.
METHOD—dhara, kader, mọrọm, mọt, mọtlọb, rọkọm, sik, tak rọkọm, targhar.
METTLESOME—jạlim, jọlọniạ.
MEW, TO (*of a cat*)—keõmeõ, mão, meoń, meyoń, miyuń.
MICA—abrak, lipindić.
MICTURITION, PAINFUL—karṛa.
MID-DAY—tikin; (*to-day*) dhinạń tikin; (*a little past*) eṛak̕, nẽṛak̕, tikin loṛak̕; (*meal*) mańjan; (*rest of cattle*) aḍa, gọṭ, gọṭh.
MIDDEN, A—gurić mande, mande.
MIDDLE—bhọg, gabha, madhe, mandhe, mańjla rạs (M), mạńjli rạs (F), modhom, tala; (*in the*) mańja mạńjhi, mańjha mạńjhi, tala mala; (*finger*) tala kạṭup̕; (*age, past*) bạskhapao (F); (*aged & single*) lambo; (*sized*) ghuṭ (2); (*sized & stout*) ghuṭ muṭiạ.
MIDDLING—jhaporae, mẹlcọ.
MIDGE, A—bạsṇḍi, busṇḍi.
MID-HARVEST—dhurpạu.
MIDRIB OF LEAF—sakam riṛ.
MIDST, IN THE—talare; (*of*) ghasen.
MID-WIFE, A—dạgrin, dak̕ dulić, dhại, koslaeni, kosraeni, kuslạnera, kusrạnera; (*fee of*) narkaṭaoni.
MIGHT—bọl, daṛe; (*with all one's*) jiwi lae poran, jiwi jãkte, oṛseõ, umạr samar, uduṛ dhupuṛ, utu dhutu.
MIGHTY—balgar; (*man of valour*) birbanṭa.
MILD—dhimạ, khinur, sopoṭ, ṭaṇḍha
MILDEWED—mạdhuạ, muhũṭ; (*to become*) mạndhuạ, mõde, monde, phuphuṇḍa.
MILE, A—mail.
MILES, TWO—kọs.
MILITARY—(*guard*) sọntọri; (*leader*) subạ.

MILK—toa; (*curdled*) dahe; (*sour*) gijṛi; (*to*) duhạu; (*to hold back*) kupṇạu; (*to let down*) panhao; (*not having enough*) camptạhi, coãṭiạ; (*butter*) ghoṛ; (*white*) phĩk leka; (*adhering to vessel*) ḍạdhiť; (*not reared on mother's*) dud kạṭuạ.

MILKING—(*pot*) bhanḍ, jạluạ; (*sound of*) cãe cũi, gaḍar guḍur, gad gud.

MILKY—(*plant, a wild*) nanha pusi toa, pusi toa; (*juice of plants*) lore; (*way, the*) hạṭ ḍahar, pańjar ḍahar.

MILL, A HAND GRINDING—jante.

MILLET, A CULTIVATED—gundli, layo gundli, iṛi, janhe, kode, kokor jańga, layo, leṇḍha, leńjha, moṭa gundli.

MILLIONS, IN TENS OF—karoṛ (2).

MIMIC, TO—besao, bhesao; (*each other*) bhesa bhisi.

MIMOSA TREE, A COMMON—gạbur.

MINCE, TO—ciri biri, khidir (2); (*vegetables unequally*) paṭku naṛu.

MIND—ań, bibik, mon, mone, ontor; (*of one*) banọt, ekamoe, ek saṭh, miť monte, moner moton, saṭ, saṭop; (*not of one*) bersa; (*bent of*) ḍhae, jontor; (*firmness of*) ḍharos; (*with all one's*) miť monte; (*unable to make up*) khuńju muńju; (*vacancy of*) galta golať; (*a stubborn*) keṭeč mone; (*not long of one*) keṭeč tạhuč; (*& body*) jiwi jạti; (*to turn over in the*) bundis, gundi, khańj; (*to have in*) disạ; (*to impress the*) gạdao; (*to make up one's*) onman, saniạu; (*to bring to proper state of*) sudhrạu; (*to be out of one's*) kalobalo; (*to be of feeble*) utuť tumbuť; (*to apply the*) jor bandhao, ṭesṭa; (*taken up (with, to have the*) raktao, rosao; (*set on, to have*) hader; (*to have presence of*) sarbharao, uriạu; (*what you are about!*) mon.

MINDFUL, TO BE—ucit.

MINE—ińren, ińak, tiń; (*a*) khaḍ, khạn, khõedak, sum; (*iron-stone*) bạli gaḍa; (*open coal*) koela gaḍa; (*opening or shaft of*) sum.

MINER, A COAL—malkaṭa.

MINERAL, A—dhat, dhạtu.

MINES, A SUCCESSION OF—khãedak khõedak.

MINGLE, TO—bheńjan, gadge sadge, ghorao miť, mesa misi.

MINISTER—(*a prime*) dewan, montri, raj caklaoič; (*to*) bạho, susạr, usạs.

MINIVET, THE SMALL—salui lundui cẽṛẽ.

MINNOW, A—jhõea; (*species of*) sisiń hako.

MINOR, A—nabalok gidrạ.

MINT (*plant*)—podina, pudina.

MINUTELY—bhage sạhiṭṭe.

MIRACLE, A—hahaṛa kạmi.

MIRE—bot; (*to roll in*) jobḍhao; (*to sink in*) khala; (*a pit of*) khala.

MIRROR, A—ạrsi.

MIRTH—rạsik, rạska; (*full of*) meleč mecoń.

MIRY—gaḍgaḍ, kacar, kaekao, kacor, kacpac, khadbad; (*very*) khad (2); (*to cause to become*) khadbadao.

MISCELLANEOUS—ehae balae.

MISCHANCE—ạrgạṛha.

MISCHIEF—(*always in*) chaṭpaṭiạ, ekel sekel; (*making*) londphondia, sinḍań.

MISCHIEVOUS—bạnḍhej, canḍal, cechoṛ, chae, chechoṛ, halbal, halbạliạ, hisạliạ, nakạṭiạ, saṭsuṭ, ṭenṭha, ṭhenṭa, utpat.

MISCONDUCT—tuskil.

MISCREANT—mara.

MISER, A—cempoṭ.

MISERABLE—bapuṛič, dińgar, harkhetiạ, kuṭbur, miluk jiluk; (*to make life*) gańjan, gańjon; (*looking*) jeber (2), jeṭlok (M), jiṭluk (F), mańga murạ, merlań mirliń, mirluń.

MISERLY—cae cẽṭ, cẽṭar, cimpoṭ, ciṭar, coj, cond kopoṭ, coroč mokoč, keṭeč, kikoč, konṭeť, panṭeť, pạpi, som, sum.

MISERY—harkhet.

MISFORTUNE—apjos, bipod, dạb, dae, daga, dora daga, dordag, durdesa, sonkoṭ; (*to bring*) eč.

MISGIVE, TO—digič.

MISGIVING, WITHOUT—khulạsa.

MISHAP—beoṛa, dạb, daga; (*without*) napae.

MISLAID—ať toť; (*to be*) bilṭạu.

MISLEAD, TO—ạrgońgaṛ, bakao, baṭ kaṭao, beda.

MISLEADING—ankatha anbetha, bhulạnia̤, bhulạuni.

MISPRONOUNCED—bĕr̥baḱ.

MISREPRESENT, TO—phond, phorphond, ulbul.

MISS, TO—atra, atrom, bagdao, e̤to̤m, pandol, pa̤sur̥, pha̤sur̥; (*on road*) apa ba̤r̥ia̤; (*by a hair's breadth*) ar̥ap.

MIS-SHAPEN—ḍa̤bla̤ (M), ḍa̤bli (F).

MIST—khua̤s, kuha̤s, kuhr̥a̤; (*to clear away as*) phahak.

MISTAKE—(*a*) bhisor, bhosor, bisor, cuk; (*to make a*) be̤ḍo̤ć, bhul; (*by*) ajante, andha, baglotte; (*without*) ayā.

MISTAKES—bhul bisor, bhul cuk.

MISTIFY BY SPEAKING MUCH, TO—bat kaṭao.

MISTRESS OF THE HOUSE—gharna, ghir̥ni, girni, go̤mke̤, or̥aḱ go̤mke̤, or̥aḱ bonga, or̥aḱ ho̤r̥.

MISUNDERSTAND—(*to*) ar̥gon̥gar̥; (*to cause to*) bigr̥a̤ bigr̥i.

MISUSE, TO—bĕr̥baḱ, uḍa̤i paḍao, uper khaper.

MIX, TO—bheń an, gaḍo̤e saḍo̤e, gar̥barao, ghĕj me̤j, khija̤u, laṭghaṭ, mesal, mesa misi, mesao, mila̤n, mila̤u, miť, pheṭ; (*up*) aula̤u, gabuć sa̤buć, gańja gańji, gańjao, ghãuńja̤ ghãuńji, ghe̤ńj me̤ńj, heoḍa, laṭku pa̤ṭku; (*by trampling*) le̤be̤ť gasmanḍao; (*by stirring*) ghoṅrao, ghorao, heola; (*by kneading*) thasao; (*with liquid*) leoha.

MIXED—andhe pa̤tha̤uri, bagar̥, bajhar̥, baḱ bheṅkor̥, dorsala, dorasa, gabar̥, gaḍbaḍ, hara̤ hura̤, khiear̥i, lere bere, le̤ser be̤der, milua̤, or̥ na pathan, sal mesal; (*as herds of cattle*) misrić; (*up with, to get*) gabaḍ, laptao; (*into soft mass*) bo̤ho̤r (2); (*with chaff*) khaḍa bhusa̤; (*up*) anakup; (*as oil*) saja̤n.

MIXTURE—goja, khicr̥i, mili jili; (*of rice & dal*) khicr̥i daka.

MOAN, TO—gerań huruń, kūhra̤ kūhri, kūhra̤u, kuṅkra̤u; (*& weep*) haruń.

MOCK, TO—besao, bhesao, binḍuć sa̤ṭoḱ, cigr̥i, cir̥ha̤u, ľinḍiḱ, sir̥og, ṭhaṭa̤.

MOCKING, SAID WHEN—yi; (*a child*) ye̤.

MODE—biḍha̤, dhara, kader, mo̤ṭ, mo̤tlo̤b, sik, surik, ṭak ro̤ko̤m.

MODERATELY—in gan; (*good*) me̤lco̤; (*of fatness*) udguć.

MODERN—ha̤li.

MODES, IN VARIOUS—nana bond, nana hunar.

MODEST—ba̤puṛić, soromia̤.

MODESTY—laja luka̤, so̤ro̤m; (*outraged*) be̤abron. *Cf.* OUTRAGE.

MODUS OPERANDI—kader.

MOGUL, A—mogol.

MOIST—burui (2), cabcab, gajgaj, ge̤je̤ć (2), gila, hemal, jabḍahi, jabjab, jebe (2), je̤ge̤ć ja̤gum, je̤ge̤ć (2), jo̤bo̤ (2), le̤se̤ pe̤se̤, le̤ṭe̤ (2), mehao, oda, oda moda, olahĕť, olhan, rosar̥, rosgar, roskar, sirpiṭiaḱ, ṭa̤buć; (*to be*) galgalao, lo̤ho̤ṭ; (*to become*) sabja, sarsa; (*always*) jiar̥, jiol, jior̥, jobho, jo̤bjo̤b; (*body*) gijgij; (*low place*) so̤ṭ.

MOISTEN, TO—dahlao, ḍiń ḍa̤bur, meao, purmu; (*lips with tongue*) me̤lo̤ť.

MOISTENED, WELL—cho̤b (2), co̤bco̤b; (*as food*) soroboro.

MOISTURE,—hal, ras, ro̤s; (*too much*) sadar sudur, sa̤dgur ba̤dgur, suḍur; (*always enough*) omor; (*without*) niso̤ṭ; (*infiltrated*) sabsab, sobsob.

MOLASSES—gur̥.

MOLEST, TO—khackhacao.

MOLTEN METAL, OF THE CONSISTENCY OF—lo̤po̤r.

MOMENT, A—abher̥, miť ghar̥i, miť ghur̥i; (*in*) ṭuń ghur̥ite, huć marte; (*this*) iti ghar̥i; (*at that*) ina̤ ghur̥i; (*at the right*) jokha bajao, jokha juma̤u; (*favourable*) ãrgat.

MOMENTUM, WITH GREAT—badr̥aḱ, bardak.

MONASTERY, A—mat, math.

MONDAY—so̤m, sombar.

MONEY—ka̤uḍi, ṭaka, ṭaka ka̤uḍi, ṭaka poesa; (*bag. a*) tor̥a; (*small piece of*) khucr̥a̤; (*ready*) nogda; (*to advance*) bilat; (*not paying*) udhar; (*lender*) deko pusi, mahajan, sadgal, sa̤u; (*lending*) ma̤hajani; (*lender, to act as*) lanban; (*order*) ma̤niadar; (*an advance of*) baena, da̤dni. *Cf.* SHELL, TO CHANGE, READY.

MONGOOSE, A—cemeń; (*species of*) saram babea.

MONKEY, A—gāṛī; (*spec of*) birsindić, orlo; (*the Langur*) hāṛū.

MONSTROUS—baṛtañ.

MONTH, A—boṅga, cando, mahina, mas; (*in the*) candoṭa, masṭa.

MONTHS, THE HINDU SOLAR—(*1st*) baisak; (*2nd*) jeṭh; (*3rd*) asaṛ; (*4th*) sañ, sorabon; (*5th*) bhadoṛ; (*6th*) asin, dasāe; (*7th*) kartik; (*8th*) aghāṛ; (*9th*) pus; (*10th*) mag, magh; (*11th*) phagun; (*12th*) caṭ.

MOON, THE—ṅinda cando; (*full*) buru kunami, kunami; (*waning of*) kunami kecak; (*new*) balo molok, molok cando; (*1st day of 1st quarter*) ambas; (*at meridian at sunset*) molok tikin; (*1st day of waning*) ot kunami; (*last few days of 4th puarter*) ṅirjao; (*to disappear, as*) ṅir; (*light*) terdeć; (*light, very bright*) ḍigdig terdeć.

MORASS, A—jhil, jola.

MORE—ar, arhō, artet, barti, bisi, carha, carhi, jada, jasti; (*to become*) phar; (*to give*) juṭić, juṭuć; (*to do*) barti; (*or less*) ghaṭal barhal, ghaṭi barhi, komi besi, kumi bisi; (*than likely*) hena; (*than enough*) ajhal pajhal, ṭilṭilau; (*than is right*) akardhak, jauri; (*-over*) ado.

MORIBUND—leṭep (2).

MORNING—argat, setak; (*first blush of*) piaṅ payaṅ; (*early in*) hadam hudum; (*to break as*) pahpahao; (*star*) bhurka; (*10 o'c*) basiam, khara basiam.

MORRIS BELLS—ghugra.

MORTAR, A—ukhuṛ; (*of ḍhinki*) kaṇḍi; (*clay used as*) gara; (*to set stones in*) gatao.

MORTGAGE—(*a*) bandki, ol bandhi; (*to*) bandhe, bandhok; (*property given in*) bandhoki, jaejat.

MORTIFY, TO—bele, ghalghalao.

MORTISE, A—khap

MOSQUE, A—mahjid.

MOSQUITO—sikṛīć; (*larvae of*) kikiṛ biń.

MOTE IN THE EYE, TO HAVE—cubak.

MOTH, A SILK—paṭni (F), ṭira (M).

MOTHER—ayo, budhia, budhia hoṛ, eṅga, go, toa dare; (*used by children*) aia; (*grand*) aji; (*& child*) eṅga hopon, eṅgahon; (*grown to size of*) eṅga jopor; (*of 2 children*) bar gelo gidra eṅgat; (*wife's*) hanhar; (*-in-law & daughter-in-law*) hanhares; (*relatives of*) mamkuṛ; (*milk, not reared on*) dud kaṭua; (*tongue*) jonom parsi.

MOTION—ahla; (*to set in*) calao; (*of anything small*) guḍur (2).

MOTIONLESS—dadahut, dadahut duduhut, duduhup.

MOTIVE—lochon, sabab.

MOTTLED—khanḍ (2).

MOULD, A—pharma, phorma, sāc, sānc; (*to pour into*) ḍharao; (*to cast in*) dul.

MOULDY—muhūt; (*of food*) liṭi; (*to become*) mōde, monde, muhūt, phuphunḍa.

MOUND, A—damgi, ḍhompo, ḍhopko, domcok, ghuṭu, koṭko, ṭilha; (*large*) boṭkoć; (*small*) domge; (*very small*) ḍopo.

MOUNDS—ḍhapa ḍhopo; (*in*) dumcak.

MOUNT, TO—coghe, deć.

MOUNTAIN, A—buru; (*& hills*) buru boṭkoć; (*immovable*) dondoṛcot buru.

MOURN, TO—bhakur, haecok, hae ḍhae, haelać (2), haesoe, hiatiń, hińjrau, hirdan, homoṛ, tapiń; (*over*) gunan, hae hiatiń; (*& speak*) homoṛ.

MOURNING—bhētra, hirdani; (*to be in continuous*) hae phoe

MOUSE, A—cuṭia; (*small*) coṭo; (*spec. of*) cerceṭa; (*squeal of*) cāć cūć.

MOUSTACHE, A—moca goco; (*twirled up at ends*) maṅgri goco.

MOUTH—moca, mukha, thotna; (*of animal*) mocoń; (*to open*) cahap; (*to throw into*) kaṭok, koṭok, tapak; (*to stuff into or hold in*) kopet; (*to make a noise with*) ṅaṭak ṅuṭuk; (*to put a little food into*) larum; (*slime from*) kharak; (*not to be depended on for truth*) harta moca; (*a small*) bomboryot. *Cf.* TO PUT INTO.

MOUTHFUL, A—cakop, lapet, latum; (*big*) lakop; (*to take—of dogs*) losak.

MOUTHFULS, TO TAKE—lasok, tagum, tahuṛ.

MOVE, TO—calak̇, ḍahrao, hilau, laṛao, laṛcaṛ, lọṛcọṛ, lọṛọṅ cọṛọṅ, ragbag, ṭasak, ṭaskao, tawar (2), ṭẹwẹṫ, ṭhasak, ṭhaskao, uskau, uṭuṗ (2); *(to begin to)* calcul; *(as snake)* haṛbaṅ huṛbaṅ, kiṛia paṭe; *(jaws)* laṛọe cakọe, saṇḍaṗ; *(as tired animals)* ogor (2); *(on)* helao; *(stealthily)* cagam cugum; *(with hands as support)* capo (2); *(by leaps & bounds)* coṛok̇ (2); *(quickly)* gidgidau, girgirau, hojo (2), pehlaṅ, rayul, riṅgau, rọyọl, ruyul, sarkao, sursur; *(slowly)* jipo jopo, jọpọ (2), lapa lopo, lẹdẹċ bẹdẹċ (F), lẹdẹ (2M); *(as animals tracking)* lẹgẹm (2); *(in straight line)* haṛbaṅ haṛbuṅ; *(about)* bakaṫ, phacak phucuk, usku pusku; *(aside)* bhoṅcok̇; *(from place to place)* ujil jhambil; *(forward)* sọhọr; *(uneasily in sleep)* as us; *(from side to side)* meṛsa, meṛsa meṛsi; *(by bounds, as footless insects)* phaṇṭil; *(up & down)* lewer (2); *(head & body)* lewere kodore; *(body)* dakal (2), likiṫ domok̇, laṭiċ laḍar; *(lips when grazing)* lomor (2); *(as hand at wrist)* luṛkuċ; *(limbs spasmodically)* phaḍruk̇, piṛiak̇; *(along anything narrow & raised)* ṭuṇḍaṅ; *(always on the)* bhacaṅ bhucuṅ, kadae (2). *Cf.* SITTING.

MOVEABLE PROPERTY—jalmal, sọmpọt; *(given in pledge)* jaejat.

MOVEMENT—ragbag; *(with one rapid)* rayul marte, rọyọl m., ruyul m., sor m., sorr m.; *(short sudden)* lakuċ (2); *(to make a)* calcul, usku pusku; *(of centipedes &c)* gẹnẹċ (2); *(in water, to make)* gheola, humṭak̇; *(of big men or animals)* kabuṅ (2); *(of long-legged creatures)* kadam kuḍum; *(to lose power of)* lawak̇ laṭiṅ; *(of bellies of animals who have eaten to repletion)* lida lodo; *(of body, rhythmical)* dọmọk̇ (2). *Cf.* SLOW.

MOVING—*(rapidly)* sorr; *(from side to side)* ruirui, ruyu; *(without)* rọmrọm; *(as anything in distance)* rabak̇ rubuk̇; *(about)* olocolo.

MUCH—aḍi, amda, aṛiċ, bẹbaṛiċ, bẹhaj, bistọr, chau (2), curti, ḍaduṛ, ḍher, jada, sạmạni, tẹgẹċ masak̇; *(so)* ehe talaṅ, eto, hunak̇, in, inak̇, nhanak̇, nimin, ninak̇, numin titiṫ, nin titiṫ, nunak̇, nun titiṫ, unak̇, un titiṫ; *(too)* aṛwaidha, jada, jasti, sadasuk. *Cf.* VERY.

MUCILAGINOUS—jiwer jewer, lẹṅjẹr, liṛoċ tọṛọċ, tiṛoċ toṛoċ.

MUCUS DISCHARGED FROM NOSE—suluċ.

MUD—lọsọṫ; *(to be covered with)* jobḍao, jọbẹ, jọdọ bọdọ, leṭa, lọsọṫ; *(deep)* bot, dal.

MUDDLE, TO—aulau, gaḍbẹ saḍbẹ, ghauṅja ghauṅji.

MUDDLED—oṛna saṭ, oṛna soṛ; *(of a statement)* ghauṅja ghauṅji.

MUDDY—bode, bọdọr (2), bọhọr (2), bọkọl (2), gadla, gẹṅgẹṅ, hewel bekel, jebe (2), kackac, kacpac, khadbad, khidor, kickic, laspas, lẹdhẹr bẹdhẹr, lẹjẹr (2), lẹsẹ pẹsẹ, lẹsẹr bẹdẹr, lẹṭẹ (2), sẹdgẹ bẹdgẹ; *(to)* sẹdẹ bẹdẹ, sẹdẹr bẹdẹr; *(slightly)* lẹjẹk pẹjẹk.

MUFF, A—bembha.

MUFFLED UP—gaelo (2).

MULBERRY TREE, THE—tut dare.

MULCT, TO—phuṛan.

MULE,—khacar, khọcọr: *(-like)* pephṛa, phephṛa.

MULTIPLICITY OF THINGS TO ATTEND TO—ghamaṇḍ, leṭaṅ, letaṛ.

MULTIPLY, TO—baḍ, baḍhao, baṛhiao, gunau.

MULTITUDE—họr gaḍ, maṇḍer.

MULTITUDES, IN—karoṛ (2), khaṛ kẹ khaṛ, lọcọṫ (2).

MUMBLE, TO—alam galam, lagui pagui, lakuk̇ phakuk̇, lẹgọe pẹgọe, maṅgaṛ mọṅgọṛ, pagae pugui, phakak̇ phukuk̇, pugui, that thot.

MUNCH, TO—laṛọe cakọe, maṭar muṭur, mukur (2).

MURDER—khũn; *(guilty of)* gọgọċ họṛ, khũniahi.

MURMUR, TO—kadra kadri, karaċ kuruċ, karuċ baruċ, uruṅ (2), galgal.

MUSCLES—*(spasmodic contraction of)* bandor bai; *(pain in)* markao.

MUSHROOMS—oṫ; *(stem of)* oṫ ḍaṇḍiṫ; *(poisonous)* biṅ oṫ; *(species of)* *Cf.* oṫ; *(method of cooking)* bharta, hondak̇.

MUSHY—galid, gila.

MUSIC—(*a flourish in*) laboj; (*at marriage*) sandes bajna; (*& pomp*) rajan bajan; (*time in*) tạl.

MUSICAL INSTRUMENT, A—baja, bajna, baṭa, buaṅ; (*stringed*) kabkub; (*one stringed*) peṛesaṅ; (*like buffaloe's horn*) ramsiṅga, siṅga; (*of bamboo*) sogoe; (*of bell-metal*) baṭa; (*of 2 pieces of wood*) sarpa.

MUSICIAN—bajui, bajnia, bajondar.

MUSJID, A—mahjid.

MUSK RAT—cund.

MUSSULMAN—musla; (*woman*) musla era; (*cavalry*) tuṛuk.

MUSTARD—(*plant*) lutni, man tuṛi, rai, tuṛi; (*oil*) kaṛua sunum, utiń sunum; (*seed, to recite incantation over*) tuṛi paṛhao.

MUTE—mayaṅ muyuṅ.

MUTINY—hulmal, phasad; (*to*) hul.

MUTTER, TO—gamgondar, gandar gundur, gondor (2), kaekũi, phedar (2).

MUTTON—bhidi jel; (*a shoulder of*) phaṛi jel.

MUTUALLY—apan apin.

MUZZLE—(*the*) mocoṅ; (*to*) jalkhar; (*having a black*) kuia.

MY—iṅić, iṅren, iṅak, tiṅ; (*self*) apṛẽ; (*precious one*) dhona.

MYRRH—gondhoros.

MYTHICAL HERO, A—liṭa, mun.

N

NAG, TO—baro bakhan, keṅkeṅ, khec-khecao, khijau, tergeṅ, terges.

NAGGING—regeṅ (2); (*continual*) khec-khecao; (*to keep*) khoṭ (2).

NAIK, A—nak.

NAIL, A—kaṛti, kati, parek, perek; (*finger*) rama; (*iron*) jalai; (*wooden*) bind, khil; (*to drive to head*) janjanao; (*to drive*) parek kuṭam.

NAILS—(*finger*) ti rama; (*toe*) jaṅga rama.

NAKED—bhandal bhundul, bhaṭaṅ bhuṭuṅ, bhundla (M), bhundli (F), bhuṭuṅ (2), bondo, eken hormo, gandheṭ mundheṭ, koṭo, lamṭa, laṅgaṭ, laṅṭa (M), laṅṭi (F), naṅga, odroṅ, sandoraṅ, uluṅ; (*of a child*) laṛuć baṛuć; (*in upper part of body*) banduć (2). *Cf.* FAT.

NALA, A—s doḱ.

NAME—ṅutum; (*to*) bid, bahna, gokhna, kahlao, ṅum, ṅutum dohoe; (*to call by* ṅum; (*to mention the*) ṅutum ṅum; (*to give a bad*) bodnam; (*upper*) cetan n; (*real*) mul n., latar n.; (*nick*) bahna n.; (*ill*) opjos; (*after grandfather, to*) ṅum ceṅgeṭ; (*sake, a*) gorom; (*& home*) naogao. *Cf.* GOOD.

NAMED, TO BE—bikau, kahao.

NAMELY—ać kathae, baṅma, enkathae, metaḱme.

NAMES, TO CALL—baro bakhan.

NAPE OF THE NECK—totka; (*to hit with fist on*) kilau.

NARCOTIC, A—nisa; (*under*) ṭeremere, ṭermerao; (*to recover from*) sarao.

NARRATE, TO—bean; (*fully*) khulau.

NARROW—aṭgaṭe, ciriṭ, cuṛcuria, kuciṭ, pẽnc, sakṛa, sakṛa sakṛi, sakyar, siniṭ, siyaṅ, suṛsuria, suruć; (*in hind-quarters*) phucia; (*below waist*) phucka (M), phucki (F); (*& short*) ṭepeṅ; (*& pointed*) lecoṅ.

NASAL—gãgũ, ghenne; (*twang*) gene (2), gene phene, ghaṅ ghuṅ; (*polypus*) nãk risa.

NATIVE—disi, janam dara; (*land*) des, janam disom.

NATTY—geneć (2).

NATURAL—janam dara; (*quality*) jati.

NATURE—bhasi, jati, sil, subhab, swabhab; (*in state of*) arda, arna; (*of a like*) ek jontor; (*by*) bhasite; (*of ill*) coenda, cumdiṅ (F), ira iri, khecṛaha (M), khecṛahi (F); (*to feel call of*) tolob. *Cf.* GOOD.

NAUGHT, TO SET AT—agar digar, khoṭ, nihãṭ.

NAUGHTY—nakaṭia, naṭkhaṭ.

NAUSEA—(*indicating*) chia; (*causing*) bhirik, dhirik.

NAVEL, THE—buka; (*ulcerated*) buka seresere.

NAVVY, A—beldar.

NEAR—adepase, aṛepase, cae, dhare dhure, kaele, laga lagi, logbhog, pas, phed, sor, ṭhaḱ; (*to be*) hoclo; (*to make*) sor; (*to each other*) sopor, ṭhãi (2), ṭhaohe; (*to the mark*) jilu. *Cf.* TO COME, RELATIVES.

NEARLY—gan, leha lihi, prae.

NEAT—genṩć (2), jut, mahit; (*& tidy*) cunu munu; (*to make*) jhaljhalao.

NEATLY—reṅgleć; (*executed*) jhalmalao.

NECESSARIES OF LIFE—dogoj, dojok, dorobos, khana, porbosti; (*to be in want of*) halak; (*to have*) jom puṛauk, jom suk; (*to supply*) ạsul, goras, posao. *Cf.* TO COLLECT.

NECESSARILY—asokaete, ọbosọ.

NECESSARY—cạhi, cạhiye, caṇḍ.

NECESSITOUS—dukhạr; (*to be*) aesun, hale ḍale, kalor.

NECESSITY—dhak, dhọ̃ǹj, gagọj, garaj, garsusar, gorji, gọrọj, hucuk, loṛa; (*of*) mạruk, parọk.

NECK, THE—gardan, gola, hoṭọk, sẹrọm, thotka; (*of animal*) tarẹn; (*back of*) gardan; (*nape of*) totka; (*a sore on*) hãsli ghao; (*thick*) gọrdọn, kondo; (*short*) bador saṭok, khẽsbet, kondo, okrot; (*to put arms round*) kọkẹ; (*to stretch*) kọrkọr; (*to seize, & push*) garda gardi, gardạni; (*to seize & shake*) ghuṛmucạu; (*& neck*) eklayek, rọdbọdọl, sarasar, soka suki. *Cf.* STIFF.

NECKLACE—mala, barlaṛ mala, bhãori mala, belwạri mala, jihu m., muṅgạ m.

NEED—garaj, gorji, gọrọj, ṭan, ṭanaṭạni; (*to*) jarur, ọkulan; (*to be in*) alet, ṭonṭa; (*of, to have*) reṅgeć; (*of, not to have*) ọgọrọj; (*-ful*) cạhi; (*without*) ạuri pathạuri.

NEEDLE—chũc, sui; (*thatching*) sulạk; (*not even a*) sui parjat.

NEEDY—dukhạr; (*to be*) hale ḍale.

NEGATIVE, A—baṅ; (*scornful*) chại, dhọkọr, eṇḍre; (*emphatic*) ẽhẽk, ọhọ, ọhọtet, õhõk; (*prohibitive*) alo; (*in conditions*) ọhọ.

NEGLECT—gaphlat; (*to*) bẹhephajot, bhul, ḍhil, ḍhilạu, hela, hela hili.

NEGLECTED—ạpuc, dhirẹn dhọrẹn, dhum dharkaṭ; (*of children*) gidi ore.

NEGLECTING WORK—lesraba (M), lesrạhi (F), ọlọm jhọlọm, pidić (2F).

NEGLIGENT—bhulạ bhạtuạ, gaphlat, gạphil.

NEGLIGENTLY—gaphlạti, hela, lạḍur bạḍur.

NEIGH, TO—cĩ ghoṛa, hanhanao, hĩhĩạu, hiṅhạu, ci họ̃ họ̃.

NEIGHBOURHOOD—aḍe pase, aḍe tola, ancal, aṛe pase, aspas, dhara dhạri, dhare dhure, kaele, kalhaṭ, ọncọl, pas, tolhãṭ, ṭoṭha; (*those of this*) netenko; (*which*) oka dara.

NEIGHBOURS—aḍepaserenko, aṛosi paṛosi, paṛosi, phẹḍrenko.

NEITHER...NOR—họ̃baṅ...họ̃baṅ.

NEMATODE WORM, A LARGE—mạhur.

NEMESIS—pholao, poe.

NEPHEW—bhagnạ, bhacạ, bhạicạ, bhạtija, họmọn; (*& nieces*) deo bhạgin; (*wife of*) kimin.

NERVE—(*a*) sir; (*having*) jạlim, jọlọniạ; (*oneself, to*) ṭhukạu.

NERVOUS—(*spasms*) cibik bạị; (*shaking*) lodo dhoṛo, lucpuc.

NEST, A—tukạ; (*hen's*) sim bursi.

NESTLE, TO—hạmbut.

NET, A—cạrguḍiạ, ganạri, jal, jhạli, phand; (*cast*) lebda jal; (*drag*) ọr jal; (*fish*) hunḍạ jal, kạṭhi, maha jal, ṭhelạ jal; (*bird*) laoṭa; (*to set*) oḍao; (*to drive game into*) dal jhạli; (*guard for hares'*) pacan.

NETHER WORLD, THE—hudul raj, patal puri.

NEVER—tishọ̃ baṅ; (*prohibitive*) tishọ̃ alo; (*assuring*) tishọ̃ ọhọ.

NEVERTHELESS—ẹnhọ̃, ẹnrehọ̃.

NEW—ạnạri, ạncin, hạli, miṛạ, nãwã, salas, ṭa ka (*Testament*) nãwa niṛm.

NEWS—bege juḍạ, hạkigot, halcal, hawal, hokigot, hukigot, khabar, khọbhẹr, khọbọr, khusạl maṅgal, maṅgal, mọṅgọl, sombad, sug batṛa; (*to spread*) sarsadle; (*paper, a*) gejeṭ.

NEXT—dosar, ghuri, ghuriã; (*in order*) kur.

NIBBLE, TO—hạḍap, ricap, togọć.

NIBBLING, SOUND OF—khaṭar (2), khaṭọr (2), khaṭrok (2), khaṭur (2), saṭak suṭuk, saṭar suṭur, suṭur.

NICELY—suthrạị.

NICK—(*of time*) tak; (*to*) pac; (*off a part, to*) bucạ (M), buci (F).

NICKED, TO BE—gandra.

NICKNAME, TO—bahna.

NIECE—bhạcạ, bhagin, bhagnạ kuṛi, bhạicạ kuṛi.

NIGER SEED & OIL PLANT—surguja.

NIGGARDLY—cãe, cẽṭ, chucạ, cimpọṭ, ciṭạṛ, coj, cọnd kọpọṭ, cọṛọ́ć mọkọ́ć, kã́ć kṹć, kakać kukuć, kikić kọkọ́ć, kikọ́ć kọkọ́ć, kọṇṭeť, kọṛọ́ć mọṭọ́ć, kuṭhiạ, pạṭweť, som, sum, tojahi; (*of giving food*) chochna (M), chuchni (F); (*giver, a*) pạpi kọkọ́ć.

NIGH—sor; (*to make or come*) sor.

NIGHT—ńindạ; (*every*) jao ńindạ; (*last*) teheń ńindạ; (*during*) rạt birạt; (*feeding at*) rạtcora; (*to retire for*) họṛmọ ọl, jaega; (*time to retire for*) kedoǩ jọm saṛasạtiń; (*-mare*) biṛki; (*jar*) hạpuǩ. *Cf.* ALL, BLIND.

NIGHTFALL—ạyup̌, mạci andhar, siṅgạṛ; (*a little after*) ạyup̌ lumbạǩ, jọpọǩ, lumbạǩ, ńumbạǩ.

NILGAI, THE—murum jel; (*hind of*) sosam.

NIMBLY—buć buć, perel, perel marte.

NINE—are; (*-teen*) gẹl are, unis; (*-ty*) are gẹl.

NIP, TO—itić; (*of eyes &c*) aral koral, chẽk, pirić (2); (*off*) pạṭẹ́ć; (*sound of*) poć.

NIPPLE—cuńci.

NITS—se bele.

NO—ba, bań; (*scornful*) dhọkọṛ; (*emphatic*) ọhọ, õhõǩ; (*parley*) ekbhạkiạ; (*one to trust*) behirlạ; (*sooner than*) bhạgte; (*one knows where*) dahades.

NOCK, THE—(*of an arrow*) phõk; (*of bamboo bow-string*) poṛcha phõk.

NOCTURNAL—rạtcora.

NOD, TO—(*when drowsy*) jhumạu; (*the head*) ḍubuk, ḍubuǩ (2), kabaǩ (2), kọbọǩ (2), kodoǩ (2), kọḍọr, kọyõṛ (2), lewere kodore; (*when walking*) ḍạbuṅ (2); (*from side to side*) kidọr kọḍọr.

NODDING—doloe (2), kọbọǩ (2).

NODE, A—gãṭ, uṭi.

NODULAR LIMESTONE—gaṅgiṭ, gạṭi.

NOISE—awaj, dham, gabaṛ guńj, gajaṛ, galgul, sabad, sabod; (*to make a*) andka ạndki, andkao, andoṛ, ansa, galgalao, gul, hạuhạu, hạuṛạu, hạuạṛạuạ; (*to make a loud*) kạumạu; (*to make a slight*) kadaṛ kuduṛ, ragať rogoť, saṭpaṭ; (*a tumult of*) kạukạu; (*with a loud*) rạhṛuǩ marte, rihiṛ bidiṛ. *Cf.* SOUND.

NOISELESSLY—bạibạí, sagam sugum, sugum (2).

NOISILY—andakal, andkul, ạriṛ kuriṛ, kereń mereń, rubdạí (2).

NOLENS VOLENS—dhara bandha, mạruk, napaṛọk, paṛọk.

NONE, ABSOLUTELY—niti.

NONPLUSSED, TO BE—bud hara.

NONSENSE—badṛaǩ (2), bakbak; (*to talk*) bhackao, bhaǩ bhoǩ, bhẹcọr (2), bokao, bọkbọk.

NOON—tikin.

NOOSE, A—pạsi, phand, phạsi; (*running*) phạsi gạli; (*to*) pasi, phạsi.

NORTH—utạr, uttạr, utạr nakha, utạr mohṇḍa, utạr sẹn; (*of*) utṛaha.

NOSE, THE—mũ; (*to cut off*) mũ geṭ, nakkaṭa; (*to blow with fingers*) huri; (*to make noise through*) phorao; (*deformed*) hura (M), huri (F), hurwań; (*straight, narrow*) khemseḍ; (*septum of*) nạthu; (*discharge from*) sẹṛẹ́ć, sulúć. *Cf.* BRIDGE, NASAL.

NOSTRILS—(*to make noise through*) nạthu phoṛao; (*noise of obstruction in*) sakor.

NOT—a, ba, bań, bẹ-, chạí, dhọkọṛ, ọ-, ọhọ; (*prohibitive*) alo; (*emphatic*) bańteť, ọhọ; (*to be*) bạnu; (*in use*) chuṭạ; (*until*) aneć, eneć; (*till then*) in aneć, in utạr, un aneć, un utạr; (*too much*) inka; (*fully*) tara mara; (*equal to*) ạsṭaṅ; (*yet*) ạuri; (*at one time*) rikọ́ć rọkọ́ć; (*enough*) ọkulạn; (*one*) niti; (*we*) bale.

NOTABLE—dondkoṛo.

NOTCH—khańj, khap, khedli, khiḍli; (*to*) kobaǩ; (*on arrow*) phõk.

NOTCHED—bandra, gaṇḍra, gaṇḍrao, khaṇḍọ, khiḍli, regra; (*wristlet*) regra sakọm.

NOTCHES—khańjri; (*full of*) gaṇḍra.

NOTE, A—(*letter*) ciṭhi; (*of hand*) tamasuk, tọmọsuk; (*of bird*) raǩ; (*currency*) loṭ, noṭ.

NOTE, TO—carit, ṭhọhọr, ṭọhọr; (*carefully*) ạri bandhi; (*to take no*) pichol.

NOTED—lọhani.

NOTHING—bạnu, orop̌ koṭop̌; (*at all*) ceť hõ bań, sui parjat; (*for*) bẹphao, ọmnẹte, pọrẹpare; (*remaining*) siť; (*more than*) ṭukin.

NOTICE, A—istihar ; (*written*) parwana ; (*to take*) jigas, khoj puchar, puchau ; (*to take particular*) anman, tuphim.
NOTORIOUS—namjadi ; (*to be*) damdahe.
NOURISH, TO—asul, palao, pokhao, porbosti, pos, posao.
NOVEMBER DECEMBER—aghar.
NOW—ene, hali, lit, marge, nit ; (*& again*) baras baris, baris (2), chada mela, chadbid, ghane (2), jali khali, pake sake, ringor rongor, solo sanjok ; (*& quickly*) marge ; (*-a-days*) tehen gapa, nebetar, netar ; (*that I remember*) se bhatic.
NUDE—*Cf.* NAKED.
NUDGE, TO—gawic godak, thukri, tukuc, utkut ; (*with elbow*) ucun.
NULL & VOID, TO RENDER—nasti.
NUMB—tukun ; (*to be*) ranran, runrunau, tatao ; (*from cold*) sitlo.
NUMBED—kath, kathnau ; (*to be*) kathnao, kathua ; (*to become*) rahao. *Cf.* FEAR.
NUMBER—lombor, namor, talika ; (*to*) guni, lekha, talika, tankhi ; (*without*) alekha ; (*a great*) amela, beporloe, gutek utar ; (*indefinite*) barophet.
NUMBERS, IN LARGE—andel mandel, dhae, dungel, durum (2), gada gud, gadal pital, jhamela, jhar (2), tanak busak.
NUMERAL, A—ak ; (*used with*) gotan, gotec, goten, tan, tec, ten.
NUMEROUS—ada umar, bujuk (2), buruc (2), chau (2), gadagad, gadel, gaja guju, henjet (2), jhamela, kalkal, kanbol, laskar, locot (2), mele (2), palpal, palua, sagal (2), sange, segebege, sobot (2), tanak busak ; (*very*) atut, adi baric ; (*to be*) ganganao ; (*prosperous*) gangania ; (*of children*) genec (2) ; (*small bodies*) saga rore ; (*as leaflets*) sirric birric.
NURSE, A—hebeoic, joktonic, susaria, tapos ; (*to*) hepajot, jogao, joton, sostop, susar, ughar samhar.
NURSING, CAREFUL—chikisa, cikisa.
NUTS—pesta jo.

O

O !—eh, iyo.
OAK TREE, THE—allon dare, balut dare.
OAR, AN—dadu, lauri ; (*to pull*) dadu ghanta ; (*one who pulls*) lauria.
OATH, AN—halap, holop, kasam, kiria ; (*mild*) hader katha, mairi ; (*to take*) dib, holop jom, kasam, kasat, kiria ; (*to give*) dib oco, holop em.
OBDURACY—bhuc bhuci.
OBDURATE—gojra, khara, tidwi.
OBEDIENT—behut ; (*to be*) rohom dohoe.
OBEISANCE, TO BOW THE HEAD IN—dubuk (2).
OBESE—lodhor (2) ; (*& flesh quivering*) lobhok.
OBEY, TO—basut, batao, con, ganao, hetao, manao, tewet ; (*not at once*) letho.
OBFUSCATE, TO—argongar.
OBJECTIONS—(*to raise*) aphoti, roktok ; (*having*) tegec tagum.
OBJURGATE, TO—tergen.
OBLIGATION—tamasuk, tomosuk ; (*to pay*) lag, lagti ; (*to discharge*) puranti.
OBLIGATORY—jhakmar, maruk.
OBLIQUE—ayar, gotle, koce, terha ; (*eyed*) pelka (M), pilki (F), tera (M), tiri (F).
OBLIQUELY—apir, chalkao, cholkao, colkhao, ghatra, giria, horsec, korse, tarcha.
OBLITERATE, TO—mohor marao, mohor metao ; (*by smearing with dung*) gobor mati.
OBLOQUY—kalak, kali ; (*fear of*) kalak.
OBSCENELY, TO TALK—bhacka bhacki.
OBSCURE—gohlao, khandri ; (*to*) dalop, dambrao, dhakao, gohlao ; (*to be made*) dabao.
OBSERVANT, TO BE—ucit.
OBSTACLE, AN—badha, cak bandhi, thek ; (*to meet with*) dhan, takic ; (*to place*) bidhaura, tekao.
OBSTINATE—batkati, beporbhae, daria, darmot, dhit, digor, digrali, dundur, ek sirri, ektiar, gador, gadut, hadrap, haora, jahbaj, kathin, latkuta, letho, liloj, matha, pephra, phephra, tethor, thetham, thethor, thethramu, tidwi ; (*to be*) agdhao.
OBSTREPEROUS—ecepece, ecpec.
OBSTRUCT, TO—akot, atkao, nejhar, nenjhar, patet, roktok, tek, tekao.
OBSTRUCTED, TO BE—dhan ; (*when floating downstream*) jhaua.

OBSTRUCTION—letaṅ. letar, lạṭuk̇, ruk-ṭuk ; (*without*) nirola.

OBTAIN, TO—jurta, juṭau, kurạu, ṅam ; (*with trouble*) bạnij ; (*goods on credit*) ḍhal.

OCCASION—dhak, garaj, gọrji, gọrọj, lora, susi ; (*to have*) jarur.

OCCIPUT, THE HOLLOW BELOW—totka gaḍa.

OCCULT ADVERSE INFLUENCE—badha, bəd, ber, bidia, lạtu bhaṇḍu ; (*unaffected by*) obidhan ; (*danger from*) lạṭu bhaṇḍu.

OCCUPANCY—lọkhọl.

OCCUPATION (*work*)—bhed.

OCCUPIED—ạujhar, calcalwa ; (*fully*) bhir, lajhar ; (*to be*) laga.

OCCUPY, TO—lọkhọl, laga ; (*a new house*) maṇḍao, maṇḍiạu, mariạu, uḍhạu.

OCCUR TO ONE ON SPUR OF MOMENT, TO—sarbharao, uriạu.

OCCURRENCE, AN—ghoṭna ; (*unexpected*) hũya.

OCEAN, THE—dariạu, doreão.

OCTOBER—akṭobar ; (*-November*) kạrtik.

ODD—bejuri, ekaha, ekarha ; (*to become*) phuṭ ; (*jobbs, to do*) badha ; (*player, an*) luṭhu kuṇḍạ ; (*cultivated corners*) ạrthi pạrthi, ạ̃uṇṭhi pạ̃uṇṭhi.

ODIOUS—nepran, nichan, nichnaha (M), nichnahi (F).

ODORIFEROUS—mahkao.

ODOUR—bas, sọ ; (*pleasant*) mahak, mọ̃họ̃k.

OF—ak̇, aṅ, reak̇, reaṅ, ren ; (*that or this*) takar ; (*course*) baṅchan, bhatić, dhora, sə bhatić ; (*many kinds*) unu unu ; (*all kinds*) chatik.

OFF—(*one's guard*) gạphil ; (*one's head*) bạulạ bạuli ; (*with you*) dhur (2). *Cf.* STRAIGHT.

OFFENCE—tuskil ; (*to take*) khis, roṅ khoṅ ; (*to give*) digić.

OFFENDED, TO BE—kalrao, raṅgao, tạkić, uprak̇ ; (*easily*) kudraha, kuṭil ; (*& waiting revenge*) kuskusạu.

OFFENSIVE—nakara, nekra ; (*from dirt*) hagal gạṇḍiạ.

OFFER, TO—em lega, em gelak̇, habak̇, nə, ni ; (*incense*) dhup dhumạu ; (*sacrifice*) dạrẽ samaṅ, samaṅ ; (*first-fruits*) loban, nạuwãi ; (*prayer*) oḍe.

OFFERING—*Cf.* SACRIFICE.

OFFICE—ạmali, bahali, haedae, hudạ, tọndạri ; (*to appoint to*) bahal.

OFFICIAL, A ZEMINDARY—ḍihdar, ohdar.

OFFICIOUS—araraok̇, lahar cahar, lahe cahe ; (*to be*) lẹhẹ (2), luṭhu.

OFFSPRING—họpọn, janmal, jonmol ; (*to bring forth dead*) gabḍhao.

OFTEN—bare (2), darak̇ (2), hiḍir (2), huluk (2), siṅ sạṭup, tatle, tatle mar ; (*very*) ạṭis kuṭis, ạḍi dhao ; (*& quickly*) huć huć.

OH !—ih, ish ; (*dear !*) hae hae ; (*that !*) bare.

OIL—sunum ; (*kinds of*) *Cf.* sunum ; (*to rub on*) ọjọk̇ ; (*to put in ear*) arjo ; (*cess paid in*) telhan ; (*sweet smelling*) sọ sunum ; (*cakes fried in*) sunum piṭhạ ; (*vessel*) cukak̇, ḍhudhuạ, kupa, kupi, mali ; (*cup*) kạṭhli, kạṭli ; (*& wick*) diuhe ; (*to express*) lẹn ; (*cake*) kare, khari ; (*measures*) ḍuki ; (*ladle*) dasaona ; (*to daub on*) kalgat, kalhat̃ ; (*& turmeric, to anoint with*) tere ; (*amount from one press*) ạṛkuć ; (*wrapper used in pressing*) gaske. *Cf.* PRESS.

OILMEN, A CASTE OF—kulhu, teli, tili.

OILY—cik̃ạr, poret ; (*feeling, to have*) bọrọr.

OINTMENT—makhan ; (*medicinal*) ọjọn ; (*applied to eyes*) anjan ; (*to apply*) ilet̃, lep, ọjọk̇, makhan ; (*to smear with*) kukạr.

OLD—adharo budharo, budi (F), burhạ (M), burhi (F), dhadra, doḍhio, doḍo (M), ḍhạdri (F), haram, jhadgọć, kokhrao, mare, mare purnạ, maren, mari, ore, sei, ṭhaekok̇ ; (*to become*) haram, jomhẹr ; (*of cloth*) korga, mare ore ; (*very*) adharo budharo, juiuṅ (2), rot pạṇḍu (M) ; (*getting*) adhẹr, cipoć cupoć ; (*age*) haram jọkhẹć, budhi pariare, haram pariare ; (*men*) haramko ; (*maid*) arharo barharo ; (*man & wife*) arharo barharo, haram budhi ; (*man*) budhạ, haram, morubi, murubi ; (*woman*) budhi, budi era, burhia, jukni; *(& large)* ạsrā̃ṭ; *(& huge, as tree)* jharkaṛē̃ṭ; *(& untidy)* bodre; *(& weak)* dhopyo, tukuṗ (2); *(Testament)* mare niạm; *(matter, to bring up an)* ṭhakrao; *(times)* sedae.

OLEANDER, THE SWEET—raj baha, arak̓ raj baha, poṇḍ raj baha.

OLIVE TREE, THE—jạitun dare, jalpại.

OMEN, AN—jatra, sạgun, sar sạgun; *(good)* jatra, joe, paetara, sar sạgun; *(bad)* asaha dusaha, bẹsạgun, coṭaha; *(a bird studied as)* uṛić; *(water-pot as)* sạgun ṭhili; *(to foretell by)* paetar.

OMISSION—bhul cuk; *(of duty)* bhisor, bhosor.

OMIT, TO—bad, ikạ.

OMITTING—chaḍa, chaḍakate, choṛkate.

ON—cetan, re, upạr.

ONCE—eka hạriạ, mit̓ chọṭ, mit̓ dhao; *(round)* hạriạ, khiạ, lar. *Cf.* AT ONCE.

ONE—eka, eka chinạ, ekam, ekam dukạm, mit̓, mit̓ṭaṅ, mit̓ṭẹć, mit̓ṭẹn; *(in comp.)* ṭak̓; *(in arithmetic)* koḍa; *(alike)* saman; *(of wristlets)* phạṛa; *(a whole)* gọṭanak̓; *(each)* koḍa ke koḍa; *(not)* niti; *(that)* onaṭak̓; *(this)* noaṭak̓; *(by one)* ạmiṅ, eka eki, ẹkẹ ẹkẹ, parti; *(side)* ẹkdhar; *(after the other)* atom, bhasaṅ bhusuṅ, dorpha (2), gayar guyur, gọntọ gọtọ, gujur (2), hạḍẹ gọḍạ, hẹrẹć tureć, ladlad, ladlud, lega ligi, ludlud, tayọm maraṅ, otahole, ọtọṅ taenọm, ọtọr gọtọr, pacha pache, tarae toroe, utạhuli; *(above another)* biliạ bitić, corda pore, gaḍea guḍiạ, lada upar, uphrạ uphri, uprạ paṛi; *(& a half)* ḍeṛh, ḍirhi; *(half more)* ḍiḍhi, sarhe; *(fourth more)* sawa; *(or two)* eka dukạ, ekam dukạm, eskar toskar; *(fold)* hạriạ; *(beyond another)* haṭạhuṭ; *(side, to)* hõ̃rsẹć, paṭhe; *(& all)* jọtọ; *(thing on another, to put)* lade; *(p. m.)* tikin ṅõ̃rā̃k̓; *(of, to be)* sọhga; *(of a series)* choha.

ONESELF—apnar, nij, nije; *(by)* nijut.

ONION, THE—peaj, piạj; *(kinds of)* *Cf.* peaj.

ONLY—ạika, chuchạ, ẹkẹn, eskar, khạli, mọṭọ, nạri ṭhuri, sadhẹr, sirip, sudhe, sukhle, ṭukin; *(child)* ekaput; *(one word)* ẹkbhạkiạ; *(a little left)* leha lihi; *(then)* un utạr.

ONYX—bẹlạur.

OOZE OUT, TO—biriṅ (2), jọrọk̓, sabsab, sarsa, sẹrẹ, seteṅ, sobsob.

OOZY—labar lobur.

OPEN—khulạ, khulạsa, phada, sandoraṅ; *(countenance)* khạsa; *(space)* phāk; *(woven bag)* khuṅgi; *(mouthed)* caehaṗ (M), caehiṗ (F); *(in the)* sọdgọrọ.

OPEN, TO—bhirobhoro, bhoskao, bọgọć, jhić, khulạu, pasar, saṇḍaṗ; *(mouth)* cahaṗ; *(of ripe pods)* caṭić, ọṭẹć; *(as book)* oṭak̓; *(as flower)* saṛ; *(eyes)* bẹṅgẹt̓; *(up)* bhaṅgao; *(out)* bhạruṛ; *(as a pair of compasses)* cag caga; *(out anything adherent)* phidli.

OPENING, AN—nikạs, phā̃k, phukạr; *(chance)* ạt; *(window)* bhạora, bhugạk̓; *(for ingress & egress)* duạr; *(covering)* ẹnẹsẹt̓; *(with wide)* phandra.

OPENLY—hakao, khulạ khuli, sahạsae, sọdọrte, sọhọka, sọhọsae, ṭhaṅka ṭhoraṅ.

OPERATE, TO—bhijạu; *(surgically)* hẹyọ.

OPHTHALMIA, CHRONIC—penḍra mẽ̃t̓.

OPINION—rae, rại, mọt; *(to form)* ọnman; *(to take)* taḍbir.

OPINIONATIVE—ạnhũ̃ṭ, ṭiḍwi.

OPISTHOTONUS—dhạnuk bại.

OPIUM—aphim; *(plant)* posta; *(seed)* p. dana; *(a prep. of)* sidhi; *(pill for smoking)* phuṭuk.

OPPORTUNE—subita; *(to be)* saṅjok parao; *(moment)* asãe sawãe.

OPPORTUNITY—aphsor, asãe sawãe, ạt, bāh, ber, dão, dao ghao, ghại, ghaṭ, joh, lisi, ọphsọr, ọpsọr, phā̃k, phursạt, saṅjok, sinić, sonjok, subita, tak, uphaṅ; *(without)* bẹat; *(to watch for an)* elem celem, elhe celhe, laglagao, lokao, lotao.

OPPOSE, TO—ạnhũ̃ṭ, birud, daram, ṭhag, ṭhọk; *(obstinately)* ṭheṭnamũ̃.

OPPOSITE—sạnmuk, sọnmuk, ulṭạ; *(to what is right)* ulṭạ, ulṭau.

OPPRESS, TO—cipa̤, da̤bri, durduri, ga̤rib mara, ha̤hi duhi, hane mar, hã̤un̤d̤i, huja̤t, hujut, jae ejae, jaejulum, jo̤bo̤rjo̤s, jobrau, jobra̤ni, jo̤r julum, julum, kuckuca̤n, mara.

OPPRESSIVE—bo̤hũt̤, dharkat̤, gajgaj, ghul (2), ha̤rdund, hut́ (2), olkopolko, ulkhu pulkhu.

OPTICAL INSTRUMENT, ANY—durbin.

OR—ba, bha̤i, ki, se̤; (*else*) bakhać, bańkhan, bo̤tə́ć; (*something*) jahan; (*not*) ki bań; (*such*) tanak̕, ta̤nić.

ORACLE, TO ENQUIRE AT AN—rumjhum.

ORANGE—nara̤ṅgi.

ORAONS, THE—urão.

ORATOR—kahba̤jia̤.

ORCHID—dare ba̤ṅki; (*growing on rocks*) dhiri banda.

ORDAIN, TO—soro, sorwa.

ORDEAL, A TRIAL BY—d̤a̤li d̤ha̤ura̤k̕, d̤a̤li phuli.

ORDER—rae, ra̤i; (*an*) hukum; (*written*) cit̤ha̤, parwana; (*to issue an*) d̤alao, ja̤ri; (*to—sarcastic*) hur̤; (*in*) atom; (*that, in*) je̤mne̤, jemo̤n; (*to put in*) dursut; (*without*) a̤lma̤l, a̤lma̤lao, pasa̤r, sadgaeak̕, sa̤guć ba̤guć, sigić bigić; (*next in*) kur; (*something to be made, to*) pharmas, phorman.

ORDERS—(*without*) thare mare; (*to pass stringent*) jãk.

ORDINARY—a̤uri, ca̤lit; (*people*) ne̤ ho̤rko.

ORGAN—(*the female*) buya̤, cocko, coko, cucṳ, cucuk̕, mãi; (*part of F*) coe, t̤oe; (*the male*) *Cf.* MEMBRUM VIRILE.

ORGANIZE, TO—bo̤ndo̤bo̤s.

ORIGIN—bunia̤d, but̤a̤

ORIGINAL—buniadi, ja̤r, mare, mul, nij, ora̤t́, sa̤bik; (*state, in*) a̤n̤d̤u; (*Santal septs*) nij.

ORIGINATE, TO—janam, soro, sorwa.

ORIOLE, THE GOLDEN—pio cẽr̤ẽ, sasań pio.

ORISSA, THE PEOPLE OF—ud̤ia̤, ur̤ia̤.

ORNAMENT—abhran, saj; (*to*) husna̤k, saj; (*a kind of*) kakna; (*forehead*) t̤ikli; (*toe*) ba̤t̤ri; (*ankle*) bãk, ba̤ṅki, kha̤ru, lipur, pa̤iṅga̤n; (*neck*) hã̤s, hã̤sli, mala, mandoli, sili; (*arm*) bã̤ihã̤, baju, la̤ht̤i, phudna̤, ta̤bij, t̤a̤d̤; (*wrist*) ra̤sunia̤, regra sako̤m, sako̤m, sańkha, pit̤na sako̤m; (*hair*) huju d̤uria̤; (*worn by men*) ko̤mo̤r kat̤hi; (*silver*) t̤hel; (*a silver chain*) gunsi; (*ear*) jhim jhimi, jhiṅgur, jhur jhuri, kanphul, nara; (*nose*) put̤ki; (*feather*) t̤oya dhaca; (*without, as ears*) pit̤u. *Cf.* RING.

ORNAMENTS—ahran paharand, co̤ndro̤har, gohna pa̤ti; (*to put on*) jabrao; (*hollow*) jhunka̤; (*covered with*) seke doke, seke meke, se̤kse̤ke̤, sit̤a̤r pa̤t̤ar; (*a maker of*) sonhar.

ORNATE—t̤ho̤no̤k.

ORPHAN, AN—t̤apar, t̤ua̤r; (*to become*) t̤ua̤r.

OSCILLATING—d̤e̤ke̤t́ (2).

OSTENTATION—d̤had̤nas.

OSTRICH, THE—ũt̤ cẽr̤ẽ.

OSTRACISED—bit̤la̤ha.

OTHER—ar, e̤t̤ak̕, hana; (*the*) e̤t̤ak̕ak̕, e̤t̤agić; (*side*) o̤n paro̤m, hanasa; (*world*) hanapuri; (*side, to put to*) paro̤m.

OTHERS—ara̤min, baje̤.

OTHERWISE—bakhać, bańkhan.

OTTER, THE INDIAN—lodam, odam.

OUGH!—chia̤.

OUR—tabon, talań, tale, talin̕; (*selves*) aprẽ; (*selves, like*) ne̤; (*selves, within*) gãye gho̤re, gho̤re (2).

OUT—(*to put*) bahre; (*to put, go, or come*) o̤d̤ok, o̤d̤o̤n̕; (*in some games*) thukum; (*of season*) a̤din, be̤batar; (*of sight*) ańkher; (*of place*) antha̤ri, uda̤m; (*of time*) be̤ra̤r, be̤r̤ẽ (2); (*of temper*) berod; (*of sorts*) darań duruń, dholomolo, dho̤ro̤ń po̤ro̤ń, dodoroso, dondho mondho, dondorkole, do̤rmo̤ć, do̤ro̤ń so̤ro̤ń, do̤ro̤so̤ro̤, masmas, orloporlo, o̤suk, robojholo, uru suru; (*on the plain*) tala ta̤n̤d̤i; (*of breath*) do̤me̤do̤m, se̤ṅge̤t́; (*of the way*) e̤k sirta̤l; (*of way, to get*) ho̤se̤ć; (*of line*) e̤pre̤, gote.

OUT-CASTE, TO—bit̤la̤ha, ca̤uda̤l, d̤o̤ṅka, e̤k sirta̤l, oja̤t; (*to have been*) nija̤t.

OUTER COVERING, TO REMOVE—po̤t̤ak̕, ur.

OUTGROW, TO—hara latar.

OUTLET—nika̤s.

OUTLINE—(*dim*) bõhõk; (*irregular in*) lacań locoń.

OUTLYING—baher, bahre; (*country*) pọhọṭ; (*hamlets of village*) gọṇḍa, ṭola.

OUTRAGE MODESTY, TO—bẹbhọrọm, bẹhurmat, bẹmarwạd, bibhọrọm.

OUTRIGHT—(*in comp.*) atạr, dapoṛ, napoṛ; (*to do anything*) sumạr.

OUTSIDE—bahar, baher, bahre; (*on the*) dhar dhur, huruṛ (2); (*those*) arạmin; (*beautiful on*) camraṅga.

OUTSTANDINGS—damkam; (*to collect*) dhạra.

OVER—(*to go*) parọm; (*to be*) hoe; (*again*) sạni; (*& above*) amdạni, bihri baṭạ, phadel, phajil, phạuti, uprạnd; (*there*) ẹntere, hẹntẹ, hẹntẹre, hụntẹ, ọntẹ; (*from past years*) mare purnạ; (*against*) muhạ̃ muhĩ; (*head & ears*) ụrhu buṛhu; (*& over again*) ạcur bihur, ghurại ulṭai, rigiṛ, teret̕ boret̕; (*ride, to*) jaejulum; (*bearing*) calak, hạrdund, harrap̕; (*cloud, to*) unạu.

OVERCOME—aṅkha ạṅkhi, ayak̕ oyok̕, bhạgui; (*with faintness*) kạrigham; (*to*) bhagao, daṛe, dombṛao, hạl kạhil, hạlkạl, hạr, hãrop̕, haṭao, hẽṭ, hẽṭao, jạbin, jạbri, jạbun, jitạu, kạbu, lahao, lẹṭẹć, liṭhi, ńẽṭ, hoṭak̕ pạsir, pelao, pesṛao, sẹṭẹć, ṭasak, ṭhasak, ṭhasiạu; (*displeasure, to*) rijhạu; (*a difficulty, to*) torao.

OVERFLOW—(*to*) chạpilman, chạplạu, coṛań, ḍublạu, sareṛ, ṭapu; (*channel, an*) pãerẽ.

OVERFLOWING—cehel (2), cehel cepel, cohol bohol; (*full to*) dorobotolo.

OVERGROWN—adaṛ odoṛ, badak̕.

OVERLAY WITH PRECIOUS METALS, TO—ạńu.

OVERLOOK, TO—at̕ tot̕, bacol, bẹdọć, bhul, cindạl, kacokam, map, maph; (*to be*) phạsuṛ.

OVERMUCH—bạtil, bhuceṛ, bhuteṛ, buceṛ, phadel, phạjil, phạlti, sadasuk.

OVERPOWER, TO—jabdo, jạbin, jạbun, kạhil, ṭhasiạu.

OVERPOWERED, TO BE—armarao.

OVERREACH, TO—hạhi dudi, họrdodo.

OVERRUN, TO—jhapṭao, taloi.

OVERSIGHT OF—(*to take*) tạhkiạt; (*one who takes*) tạgidar.

OVERSPREAD, TO—cabhao, cão marao.

OVERTAKE, TO—pańja tiok̕, tebak̕, tiok̕.

OVERTHROWN, TO BE—dhaṅdhaser.

OVERTOP, TO—hara latar, talom, tạri.

OVERWEENING, TO BE—phulạu.

OVERWEIGHTED—(*to be*) ṭebẹ (2); (*with care*) dhãe khãe.

OVERWHELM, TO—cape; (*to be*) uḍu ḍubu.

OWE, TO—dharao, laga; (*nothing*) nidhạruạ.

OWING TO—badat, dhọrọs, iạte, khạtir, lasãṛhẽ, niạ, niyẽ, tạraste, tese, uthum; (*work*) kajẹ kajẹte.

OWL, AN—dundu, kọkọr; (*spec. of*) dereń k., lat̕ k., ńindạ rakas, pheca cẽrẽ, pọṭọm d, dọndọr k.; (*a small*) peca; (*cry of*) hõć (2), hũhũ, peco, phercot̕ (2) sorkoṭ.

OWN—apnar, khas, nij, nije; (*brothers or sisters*) mit̕ lać boeha.

OWNER—gola, kisãṛ, maldar, mạlik, malkar, nińjam, oaris; (*without an*) phạuti.

OX, AN—dạṅgra; (*polled*) muṇḍrạ ḍ.; (*red*) rạṅgiạ ḍ.; (*small*) geḍa ḍ.

OXEN—(*a yoke of*) eka hariạ; (*a row of, treading grain*) dạhin.

P

PACE—(*unable to keep*) jẹpẹ thope, jhapaṭ, jope thope, lạmbri; (*at a fair*) ṭimbok̕ ṭombok̕.

PACIFIC—sapot̕, sopot̕, supotia, supud.

PACIFY, TO—bod, bodhao, ẹnẹć, ẹrẹ mọńj, ẹrẹ suk, ropha, ṭạndha, samjhao; (*for a time*) thap thop.

PACK—(*to*) kasao; (*close, to*) khacao. *Cf.* BULLOCK, HORSE.

PACKAGES—mọṭ jhọṭ, moṭra jhoṭra.

PACKED CLOSELY—rẹnṭẹ pẹnṭe, rẹpẹ cirit̕, rẹṭẹpẹṭẹ, rẹt̕ tẹpẹt̕, saṭasaṭ, sẹgẹ begẹ; (*to be*) rẹpẹ cirit̕.

PACKET, A—rẹt̕; (*small*) puriạ; (*to wrap up*) rẹt̕.

PAD, A—(*for eliphant's back*) hạti sạr, sạr; (*for head*) kạṇḍhum.

PADDY BIRD, THE—kõk̕; (*white*) bak, bitkil kõk̕, lọbọe bak; (*brown*) lobok̕ kõk̕; (*poetical name for white*) bakoli; (*a kind of*) cãuriạ bak.

PADLOCK, A—kulup, tala ; (*& key*) kulup kaṭhi, tala kuṅji, tala cabhi.

PAGE, A (*of book*)—sakam.

PAHARIAS, THE—munḍa.

PAIN—bedna, bedon, betha, haso, kalkal, saset ; (*to*) buyuṫ (2), hahas, chorwaṅ, rudi, tarwa ; (*to cause, or be in*) saset ; (*exclm. of*) aege, ahh uhh, ayuguh, hae, haehae, ih, is, isb, oh, ohae, ohae hae, uh ; (*burning*) chan (2), jolon ; (*gnawing*) khal (2) ; (*throbbing*) kankan, kankanao, tugum (2) ; (*spasm of*) hiṙiṅ ; (*in loins*) ḍaḍa haso ; (*internal*) doḍ ; (*in bones*) haḍ hamus ; (*in side of head*) khapar jaḍi ; (*in muscles*) maṛkao ; (*of side & chest*) pachiaṛi ; (*in stomach*) ṣuṭa ṣuṭi, paṭhok ; (*in neck*) haḍi ; (*sharp*) badgak.

PAINFUL—daṛun, dormoc, hanas, kaḍaṅ kuḍuṅ, kaskas ; (*to be*) mackao ; (*excessively*) kiṛiṫ (2) ; (*& itchy*) gumur (2) ; (*of a boil*) ṭihka ṭihki, ṭihkau.

PAINS (*trouble*)—dandagiri ; (*to take*) jahiṫ ; (*taking*) mehnotia.

PAINT, TO—roṅ.

PAIR—(*a*) joṛ, joṛa, joṭ ; (*to*) joṛ ; (*well-matched*) jhomoke jhomok, jomoke jomok ; (*broken by death of one*) joṛ bhaṅga.

PALACE, A—doṅgol, gaṛ, mahal, raj mahal.

PALANKIN, A—palki ; (*kind of*) caudal, caupala, cir caudal, kharkhari.

PALATABLE—sebel.

PALATE, THE HARD—taru ; (*perforation of*) sursa.

PALE—*Cf.* FAIR.

PALKI, A—aswaria ; (*kind of*) ḍola, ḍuli, khuṛkhuṛi, rahi, sowar, sowari ; (*bearer*) kahar.

PALLIATE, TO—anduṅ.

PALM—(*tree, a*) khijur ; (*of hand*) talka ; (*to yield the* pandol.

PALMYRA PALM—tale, tale siṅ ; (*leaf*) ḍemka, ḍemkok ; (*green fruit*) ḍemkok ; (*fibre*) bagṛa ; (*seeds*) kosa ; (*kernel*) tarkur ; (*withered leaf*) ḍhoḍia.

PALPITATE, TO—dhak (2), dhuk (2), lir giṫ, lukuṫ.

PALTRY—mersitur, mer sitruc, situr.

PAN, A—(*fire*) seṅgel bursi ; (*iron*) kara, luhi, luhia, luiha.

PANCHAYAT, A—baisi, catak, dorbar, dos, kulhi durup, more hoṛ, sobha ; (*a matter for*) mambla.

PANDER, A—kuṭna (M), kuṭni (F).

PANDIT, A—paṇḍet.

PANIC-STRICKEN—bilbilau, chilbilau, daldalao, liki phiki.

PANNIER—chala, gore ; (*& saddle-cloth*) gunpalan ; (*a small*) bania potole.

PANT, TO—dhuk (2), hāphai, hapho, hāsrao, phōphā, phās (2), sōphō, upardom ; (*from thirst*) ahka ahki, ahkaok.

PANTHER, THE—kursa baha kul, saṭhdag kul, kurse baha tarup.

PAP—cunck.

PAPER—kagaj, kagoj ; (*a quire of*) dista, jista.

PAPERS—poter ; (*a bundle of*) nathi.

PAPPY—labar lobur.

PAR—(*below*) picupocu, raya reyo ; (*on a*) eklayek, soka suki.

PARABLE, A—lolok ror, phen, phende.

PARADE— pareṫ enec.

PARAKEET, A—miru ; (*Spec. of*) doe m., dodhari m., kuiṇḍi m.

PARALLELL, NOT—terga.

PARALLELLOGRAM, THE SHORT SIDES OF—ganade.

PARALYSED—boroc ; (*by fear*) dhakcakao, haemoekaṭ ; (*on one side*) miṫ kaṛ goc.

PARALYSIS AGITANS—ṅokor.

PARASITIC PLANT, A—alagjari, banda, icak bando, petcamra banda, turi sim, ul banda.

PARCHED—chat (2) ; (*of lips*) catcat ; (*of soil*) khangot ; (*with thirst*) ataph jarap ; (*to be*) kharṅgao ; (*to become*) sokhao ; (*rice*) khajari, khoi, taben.

PARDON, TO—ika.

PARE, TO—chalkao, chāṭ, chaṭao, cholkao, cokhlao, colkhao, husiṫ, jharao ; (*with axe or hoe*) lak.

PARENTS—eṅga apa, eṅgat apat ; (*house of*) naihar.

PARESNATH—maraṅ buru.

PARLEY, WITHOUT—cuṇḍuṅ, ẹkbhạkiạ.

PAROQUET, A—miru ; (*spec. of*) bheladạgiạ m , bhọṇḍa m.

PARRY, TO—eran, ẹrẹr.

PARSIMONIOUS—sum ; (*in giving food*) chechna (M), chuchni (F).

PART, A—hĩs, hisạ, kitạ, tarantar ; (*the greater*) abga ; (*with the hands, to*) piskić ; (*in*) kọṭek.

PARTAKE OF FOOD OR WARM RICE-WATER, TO—bukạ lọlọ, ọnjọlok.

PARTIAL—bẹhọk, sajọk, ṭọrọpdạri.

PARTIALLY—halaṫ (2), hayam, hoyam, tara tapra.

PARTICIPATING IN—bakhradạri.

PARTICLE—(*a*) khudri, rukhi ; (*every*) gẹć gạyum, ralak masak.

PARTICLE, A—(*emphatic*) cọ, cọṅ, dọ, do, ẹe, teć, thoya, thọ, thọr, tọ ; (*vocative*) ẹ ; (*intensive*) tạthić ; (*plural*) tora ; (*of doubt*) cọ, cọṅ, na ; (*of indifference*) dapor, dorok, napọr ; (*of entreaty*) dẹ, dẹu, dẹnya, dẹse, dini ; (*optative*) ma ; (*conjunctive*) menkhan, mẹnte ; (*when offering*) nẹ, ni ; (*like the speake*) nẹ ; (*a little*) ńik ; (*quickly*) gọṫ, họṫ ; (*going away*) tora ; (*at once*) tora ; (*encouragaing*) sẹ.

PARTICLES—(*non-cohesive*) phoska ; (*separated into small*) bĩjir (2).

PARTICULAR—(*fastidious*) badạriạ, bạdgạriạ ; (*a*) phalna, phạlni ; (*thing, this*) nhẽkẹ ; (*one, this*) nhĩkĩ, ni ; (*one, that*) onaṭak.

PARTICULARISING, WITHOUT—mela.

PARTICULARLY—asokaete.

PARTIES—(*in*) phacphuc ; (*to gather in*) hẹć jaora, sẹn jaora ; (*both*) duyokul.

PARTISAN, A—sajọk, sọṅ, ṭọrọpdar, tulni.

PARTITION, A—ẹnẹteẽ ; (*across middle*) tala ẹneteẽ.

PARTNER, A—bhagiari, juri jola, rasiạ, sạrik ; (*with*) sajha.

PARTRIDGE, A—sukri ; (*grey*) citri, ṭipoṅ ṭọrọṅ ; (*black*) muṇḍhaṫ citri.

PARTS—(*equal*) sọgọr bọgọr, sọmọjọs ; (*rough & smooth*) hender (2) ; (*peeled off*) odra udri ; (*thick & thin*) khaṛa khõṛã.

PARTURITION—bian ; (*to be near*) thalbalao ; (*near, of animals*) thalbạli.

PARTY, A—dọl, dọṅgọl, duṅgel, pal bhiṅjan, thọk ; (*large*) phạd ; (*in*) jamka jumki.

PASS—(*a permit*) calan, pas ; (*through hills, a*) ghaṭ ; (*at each*) ghaṭe ghaṭ.

PASS, TO—(*of time*) bitạu, ghusạu, gudrạu, gujar, gujrạu, kal kaṭao, khapao, khemao, ṭalao ; (*by*) ẹtọm ; (*wind*) gasić ; (*through*) tap ; (*away*) calak ; (*over*) atra matra, atrom, bạdra, chiṇḍel, ciṇḍel, dahin, ẹndel, ẹrgejak, ẹtọm, ika, parọm, phạsuṛ, phoṭao ; (*over nothing*) bac ; (*off stolen good*) sọlọm lọṭọm ; (*on*) ḍakedak ; (*round, as in tying*) merhao ; (*through an opening*) piyol poyol.

PASSING WORLD, THE—mọṅcọpuri.

PASSION—cọrcọṭaṅ ; (*to be in a*) siki (2), tiriṅ ; (*to take life, to be seized with*) bhuṭạu ; (*to give rein to*) laṭpaṭ, lọṭpọṭ.

PASSIONATE—ankạrwạ, coenda, cọṅ bạị, cọrcọṭa, kạdrai, kạiạ̃, khanṭaha (M), khanṭahi (F), khanṭạr.

PASSIVELY—sanegumane.

PASSOVER, THE JEWISH—sẹn parọm pọrọb.

PAST—gọṭọ ; (*in the*) nindara ; (*meridian*) ñẽrak, ñọrak ; (*child-bearing*) ṭhoekok ; (*its best*) jhạkaṇḍ, jharkaṇḍ ; (*middle-age*) bạskhapao (F) ; (*to go*) parọm ; (*to lay*) bae, kehna, sõc.

PASTE—cĩṭ, le ; (*of consistency of*) lẹpẹć, lẹpẹr (2), lọpọr.

PASTURE—cauõṭ, cạrõṭ.

PAT, TO—ṭhapa ṭhopo, thapo (2), thapṛe.

PATA FESTIVAL—(*after 1st baisak*) amal gaṅjal ; (*2nd day of*) polhar.

PATCH—(*a*) pend ; (*of jungle*) ciṇḍkạ, ḍupkạ, jhọṇḍ ; (*work*) kantha ; (*up, to*) jaba jubạ.

PATCHES, IN—cardak burdak, ciṇḍka cilak, hidaṅ ṭhapaṅ, patar potor, puṭur (2).

PATELLA, THE—caki.

PATERNAL ESTATE—bapọti dhọn ; (*to divide the*) begar

PATH, A—họr ; (*without*) bẹhọr.

PATHAN, A—paeṭhan; *(belonging to)* paeṭhạni.

PATIENCE—dhirjạ; *(to have)* sạbur, sọmbhori, upuť.

PATIENT—mạ̃hīr, sạburi, sobori, suboria; *(to be)* jiwi, jiwi hataṛ, sahao.

PATRIARCH, A—ạgil hapṛam, purkhạ.

PATRIMONY—bapọti dhọn.

PATRONAGE, TO BE UNDER—ṭehaḍ.

PATTER, TO—bhad, bhọṭ (2), cọrọć (2), dhaṛdhuṛ, khaṛkhaṛao, kuduṛ (2), paṭpaṭ, paṭpaṭao, bhadbhadao.

PATTERN—chand, chọnd, cọnd, ḍhạṭhi, ḍhọb, nạmunạ; *(to draw)* ọl; *(parts of)* koṭha.

PAUNCH OF RUMINATING ANIMALS—poṭa.

PAUNCHY—poṭra (M), puṭri (F).

PAUPER, A—papoṛ.

PAUSE—talbhaṅ; *(to, in song or dance)* toṛao.

PAVEMENT—bạisạu dhiri.

PAVILION ROOF—*(ends of)* khupi; *(corner rafters of)* kọlkaṇḍ.

PAW, TO—jadgo; *(the earth)* paska.

PAWN—*(to)* bandhe, bandhọk; *(in)* bandhọki.

PAY—bẹtọn, darmaha, tọlọb, tọlọp; *(advance of)* agotar, khoraki, khuṛạg, khuṛạki, pesgi, peski; *(of a shepherd)* carwạhi; *(obligation)* lạg, lạgti.

PAY, TO—calao, dạkhil, posan; *(up)* phujạu; *(gradually)* ọm jaora; *(to fail to)* kilạp; *(in full)* bhuktạn, bhuktạu; *(off)* sọd, sud; *(what is due)* khara khạri; *(up)* usul.

PAYMENT—*(without)* mạgni, mọphọt; *(acknowledgment of)* roka, uslạt; *(method of extorting)* dharna, muisil; *(to give property in)* hạri bhạri, harna bharna; *(a customary)* lẹg, ligi; *(in kind)* bạni; *(in advance, to force)* cacao.

PEA, A—baṭra, mọṭọr; *(unsplit)* goṭaṛ; *(split)* b. dạl; *(stakes)* jhaṭa.

PEACE—bạnọt, nirại, sạnti, sapo, sol suluk, sọnmọt, suluk; *(to live in)* sapọonja; *(without)* uchạn; *(a disturber of)* pilhoe

PEACABLE—gaemae, same game, sapoť, sopoť, supotia, supud.

PEACH, TO—bayaṫ buyuť.

PEACOCK, A—maraǩ, piṅcạr m.; *(tail)* pinc; *(disc on tail)* pinc, maraǩ ṭikli; *(short-tailed)* ḍẹṇḍẹ piṅcạr m.; *(crow)* m. raǩ.

PEAFOWL—maraǩ; *(call to)* curu (2); *(hen)* mạrtu m., mạtu m.

PEAK, A—domcoǩ, mundhni, muthni; *(having a)* bucbucu.

PEAL, TO *(of thunder)*—ṭher; *(with a)* ṭher marte.

PEAR, THE PRICKLY—sạpin dare.

PEARL, A—mạnik, moti, muti; *(necklace)* muti mala.

PEBBLE, A WHITE TRANSPARENT—hisir.

PECK, TO—conthao, sogaǩ, ṭhoṭhkao, tobaǩ, toť, ṭoṭkhao; *(each other)* topoť.

PECULIAR—ẹkdhara, khas.

PEDAL, A—lẹnẹbẹť.

PEDICLE OF A COCOON, THE—bọ̃k.

PEDLAR OF SALT, TOBACCO, &C., A—bạ̃ṛiạ̃, bhaoriạ.

PEEL OFF, TO—codaǩ, coṭaǩ, coṭaǩ ur; *(of skin)* rọrọť, rọť; *(part)* poṭaǩ.

PEELED OFF—*(to be)* bọnḍor; *(parts here & there)* odra udri.

PEEP, TO—hulkạu.

PEER, TO—rolo; *(stooping)* ayaṅ oyoṅ.

PEEVISH—askandni (F), askạndnu (M), bẹṅbẹṅ; *(to be)* abaṛ, birạsạli; *(whine of a child)* ebeǩ.

PEG, A—ṭaṅgna; *(in each end of yoke)* paṭsamle.

PELT, TO *(of rain)*—barat, jhar (2), nijhor.

PEN, A *(writing)*—kọlọm; *(reed)* kọlọm kạṭhi; *(& ink)* kọlọm sihại.

PENALTY—gunạgar; *(to impose a)* ḍạćḍuć; *(of crime)* gunạgar, poe.

PENCIL, A—pilsin.

PENDULOUS—gạ̃hjur. *Cf.* BELLY.

PENETRATE, TO—gabcao, gaj, sẹṭẹć.

PENIS, THE—*Cf.* MEMBRUM VIRILE.

PENNILESS—ḍhaṇḍhạniạ.

PENSION—pilsin.

PEON—caprasi, peada, sipạhi.

PEOPLE—*(poor)* gane gạrib, gạni gurib, guni gurib; *(say)* bọlẹ, ọtẹ; *(ordinary)* nẹ họrko.

PEPPER—maric; (*round*) gol maric, gulki maric; (*long*) ḍinḍi maric; (*a kind of*) caole m., sãci m., santhi m.

PER CENT—saekara, sotkora.

PERCEIVE, TO—aikau, ńel ńam, pachan.

PERCOLATION, TO CARRY AWAY BY—led-lede.

PERCUSSION CAP—ṭupi.

PERENNIAL—omor.

PERFECT—cikãṛ, pura, purau, sabit, sid, sidho, utaṛ; (*to*) kamal, sid em.

PERFIDIOUS—nimak haram.

PERFORATE, TO—roḱ.

PERFORCE—jhakmaṛ, maruk, naparok, parok.

PERFORMER—(*as at dance*) khelwaṛ; (*troupe of children*) kuṛum.

PERFUME, TO EMIT A—mahkao.

PERFUNCTORILY—herań petań, keceṭ meceṭ, ladur badur, loro boto; (*of sweeping*) phidga phidgi.

PERHAPS—arki, botec̆, cahe, cele, co, coń, dandha mandha, hoeto, janič, kajak, kajap̆, mena, pacek, pale, palek, pase, pasere pase, tanaḱ.

PERILOUS—khatra khotra.

PERINEAL ABSCESS—andhãrgãnḍ.

PERIOD—ãṭre, miad; (*short*) arsiń barsiń, ursiń barsiń; (*long*) mahakal.

PERISH, TO—kheanat, loksan, noksan.

PERMANENT, TO BE—ṭahrao, thambhao.

PERMANENTLY, TO SETTLE—bas, basgaḍi.

PERMEATED, TO BE—andkao.

PERMISSABLE—chaḍ.

PERMISSION—chuṭi; (*without asking*) hurmuṭ; (*to depart, to give*) bida.

PERMIT, A—chaṛ, pas.

PERPENDICULAR—khãidu, sidup̆; (*almost*) ekalte sidup̆ daṛań; (*off the*) lade; (*to cause to lose the*) sãrgom; (*to assume the*) teńgo.

PERPETUALLY—khane (2), kobot̆ (2), kombet̆ (2), kombot̆ (2), mokoror.

PERPLEX, TO—ãodão, aulau.

PERPLEXED—abhu cabhu, aka baka, akham dukham, akul bakul, anḍa manḍa, andmand, anduḱ manduḱ, aral koral, asbas, asbasao, aṭpaṭ, aula auli, beakul, budhara, calcalwa, cońcol, haran, haron, eńgel peńgel, jilwa thalwa, koḱ kodro, uduṛ dhupuṛ; (*to be*) almalao, esto besto, hale dale, kaula kauli, khondoḱ lopoḱ, khuńju muńju, mondoḱ (2), thukit, titikhak, ulmal; (*in mind*) khadbad, khadbadao.

PERPLEXITY—phanḍo.

PERQUISITES—(*to collect*) arpa, korpa; (*of servants at harvest*) korpa; (*of daughters at marriage*) korpa, kuṛpa; (*customary*) leg, ligi; (*of panchayat at irregular marriage*) jhuli bhaṭi; (*of bride's relatives*) itat̆; (*at last rites of dead*) kand-kaṭhi daka.

PERSECUTE, TO—aṛič, kandi kandao, khed, phidu, santao.

PERSEVERE, TO—jakir, jid, jidhi, markaṭ, rigiṛ, tokraṛ.

PERSEVERENCE—muruk; (*wanting in*) ulkhania.

PERSEVERING—jidahi, jidajid, jiddhi, johol, mit̆ murukte.

PERSIST, TO—akta akti, ãṭ, jidhi, rigiṛ, siṛi; (*in difficulties*) marhaṭha.

PERSISTENCY—jidaṭ, jum.

PERSISTENT—dhaṭhi, haṭhi. jarnaha, jid, jidahi, jiddhi, johol, jutań, siṛi; (*under difficulties*) jiwer jewer; (*person, a*) rogoria.

PERSISTENTLY—jidajid, ragra ragri, reget̆, rogor, rogot̆ (2), rogra rugri.

PERSON, A—jon, jona; (*which*) okoe-taḱ; (*insignificant*) bharua, meraič; (*good only for eating*) jomer ańgra; (*diseased*) karni; (*in company with*) teko; (*to put on the*) bande, horoḱ, pahrau; (*put on*) pahraua.

PERSONAL—(*effects*) ḍadha ḍumbaṛ; (*recognisance*) macalka, mocolka, mucalka.

PERSONS—(*of little importance*) sič soč; (*to be supported*) palua.

PERSPIRATION—balbal, halbal daḱ; (*bathed in*) jhaḱ jhaḍur, jhaḱ (2).

PERSPIRE, TO—balbalao, garmao; (*from exertion*) garma garmi.

PERSPIRING—ghama ghami; (*& dirty*) gajgaj, gijgij.

PERSUADE, TO—bãosão, bhãosão, bujhau, cacki, dahalao, ere libuḱ, ghãose, lol, manta, mosokusi, nehra jehra, ramjau, rijhau, samjhao, sãorao, ular, ural.

PERSUADED, TO BE—ạṅkus, ramuč.

PERT—galbaṛi ; (*of little girls*) oaego.

PERVADE, TO—bambkao, ḍambrao.

PERVERSE—ghạnia, hạrur, koṭbẹ, maṭha, pạtit, pạṭweť, pendla, perta, phepṛa (M), phipṛi (F), tẽrga, thetha.

PERVERT, TO—bhaṅḍao, bhaṅga, bhaṅgao, bhaṅṭao, bhiṅgrau, bigṛa bigṛi.

PEST, A RICE—bạki.

PESTER, TO—dikiạu, jhãora jhãuri, khijlạ khijli.

PESTERED, TO BE—dọgụdhọa, kạulạ kạuli, kickic.

PESTLE—(*of ḍhinki*) dhusra ; (*for husking grain*) tok.

PET BY STROKING OR RUBBING, TO—sudhạ.

PETIOLE—bhekuạ, bhiṭuak̕, ḍạṭhi, khaḍi ; (*of tobacco leaf*) khaḍạ.

PETITION—(*a*) arja, ạrji, aroj, darkhas, ọrọj, ujur ; (*to*) bakhẽr, soal, ujur mujur ; (*to present a*) pes ; (*official who presents*) peskar.

PETTED, TO WISH TO BE—alaṛok̕.

PETTY—mer sitruč.

PETULANT—uḍi ; (*to be*) adra.

PETULANTLY—tiruṅ miruṅ. *Cf.* TO SPEAK.

PEWTER—raṅ, raṅga ; (*wristlet*) ṛaṅ ṭoḍọr.

PHAKIR, A—jugi.

PHEASANT, A—korkoṭ marak̕ ; (*crow*) mạhkạl ; (*cry of*) kuhuť (2).

PHIAL, A—sisi.

PHILTER, A—muhni.

PHLEGM—kharak̕, kop.

PHTHISIS—dhõk, kạsi dhõk, raj rọg.

PHYSICAL STRENGTH—kaya.

PICE, A—anaphana, ḍhibuạ, kaca, kaudi, khaṅca, paesa, poesa ; (*half*) adhela ; (*fourth*) chedam, dokra ; (*eighth*) dạmbṛi, dạmṛi ; (*double*) dabal poesa, ḍụbọl poesa ; (*dumpy*) golokpuri poesa, jọjọ jaṅ kạuḍi.

PICK, A—dãt.

PICK, TO—họṭọr, ricap̕, toť ; (*without appetite*) hap̕ ; (*up*) halaṅ ; (*off*) codak̕ ; (*off stamens*) suč ; (*out*) bac, bachao, họṭọr ; (*out of many*) bachao toť ; (*up, as hawk*) kamṭao ; (*up leaving*) bạdha ; (*holes in*) dhạusạu ; (*up a little*) ladap̕, latap̕ ; (*up anything ownerless*) rimi ; (*out impurities*) sala ; (*grains of maize from cob*) ur ; (*a quarrel, seeking to*) ḍhĩṭão ; (*vermin from head*) gọseč.

PICKLES, TO GIVE IN—curuč.

PICTURE, A—chạbi, ḍol, naksa.

PIEBALD—kabra (M), kạbri (F).

PIECE, A—bhuṅgạr, giṇḍṛa, kạndhi, kitạ, kuṭi, kuṭṛa, pahat, pahṭa, ṭukṛa ; (*large*) dhọlma, dhoma ; (*small*) beṅjak̕, culuṅ, cuṭki, kạṭič culuṅ, talaṅ, thoṛa gạn ; (*very small*) ḍuknač, huḍu huḍuč, khuḍri ; (*of ornaments*) phạṛa ; (*cut off*) bhuṅgạr ; (*broken off*) cowak̕ ; (*broken out, to have a*) khẹcọ, khendo, khendwaṅ ; (*together, to*) milạṭ.

PIECES—ṭukṛa ṭukṛa, ṭukṛa ṭukri, ṭuṭạ bhaṅga ; (*to make into*) bhagao, kiṭṛa, kuṭṛa, kuṭṛa kuṭri, ṭukṛa ; (*to make into small*) ciri biri, guṇḍạ, guṇḍạ guṇḍi, kaṭra kuṭṛa, khiḍi (2), khiḍi biḍi, khuḍṛa, khuṭri ; (*in*) chinci punci ; (*in small*) chiri biri, dhiṅgal saṅgal ; (*large*) lapa dhopa, lapha dopha ; (*detached*) odra udri. *Cf.* TO BREAK &c.

PIER, A (*of bridge &c.*)—tham.

PIERCE, TO—bhosa, gạbcao, gaj, khacak̕, kirbič, rok̕, sẹṭẹč, so ; (*by something thicker than needle*) sob ; (*as nail*) janjanao ; (*as thorn*) kuca, sorlok̕ ; (*as arrow*) haraṛ, sar, tuṅ janjanao ; (*suddenly*) khacak̕ marte ; (*deeply*) gajlak̕ marte, pạṭi janjanao.

PIERCED ALL OVER—cacak̕.

PIG, A—sukri ; (*veiled name*) ọt uk̕ṭauič ; (*grunt of*) hokao, hokhok, hoṇḍrok̕, huṇḍruk̕ ; (*squeaking of*) kẽkẽ ; (*call to*) drudru, ḍurḍur, heḍok̕ ; (*snout of*) cilim, harta pal, jaṅ nahel ; (*method of tying feet of*) sukri gạli ; (*headed*) thetṛamu ; (*iron*) paghal.

PIGEON—(*Rock or domestic*) parwa ; (*wood*) potam ; (*Imperial*) gudur ghum ; (*Green*) huhaṛ ; (*with feathered legs*) jhaṅga parwa ; (*spec. of wild*) bhosko potam, kudbur p., kuṛbur p., pẹṭẹr p., pondhar p., toyo hodgor p. ; (*cry of*) bakbakur, kubũṛ (2), kuku ku, sas ghaṭi ; (*a call to*) ṭai ṭai ; (*trap, part of*) kal, kal jeṭha.

PIGMENT, A RED—alta, arta.

PILE, A—bạdhi, baha bạhi, bạhi, ḍañ, kuṭhauri, thak, torphan ; (*of cloth*) kicrié gada.

PILE UP, TO—bojhao, capao, conda, ḍañ ; (*one above another*) cake, condo.

PILED UP—baha bạhi ; (*to be*) dundun.

PILGRIM, A—jatri hor.

PILL—(*a*) buṛi, guli ran ; (*to*) khãpḍ.

PILLAGE, TO—luṭ, luṭpaṭ ; (*given to*) luṭia.

PILLAR, A—khunṭi ; (*boundary*) tehara, thum.

PILLOW, A—balis, ṭakia.

PIMP, A—kuṭnạ (M), kuṭni (F).

PIMPLE,—pusri ; (*kind of*) topoć ; (*small*) bhumbri.

PIMPLY—aṭpa eṭpe, ḍhampa ḍhompo, khadrak khodrok.

PIN—(*wooden*) bhañj khunṭi, bind, cargć, khil ; (*fixing shafts of cart*) karlạ ; (*on which cotton rolled*) khuili ; (*joined with a wooden*) khilạ ; (*to*) rok ; (*a projecting*) ṭhuni.

PINCERS—cimṭa, sandasi sarasi, sãrsi ; (*to seize with*) cimṭa ; (*crab*) diṭom.

PINCH—(*strait*) ajgar, somsom ; (*small*) duknũć, suthni ; (*at a*) dukharok jokheć ; (*to*) itić ; (*off the top, to*) roco ; (*above weight, a*) cunka.

PINCHED—dukhar ; (*to be*) hale dale.

PINE TREE, THE—saru dare.

PINEAPPLE, THE—ananas.

PINNACLE—chatna, chip, cura.

PINS & NEEDLES, ON—cañmañgao.

PIOUS—bhakti.

PIPAL TREE, THE—hesak ; (*variety of*) jamro hesak.

PIPE, A—bulan, nal, nol ; (*bamboo*) conga ; (*drain*) mogra, mongra ; (*wooden water*) gandbhur, gandhbhur.

PIQUED, TO BE—khis.

PISS-BED, A—jorea ponda.

PISTIL—(*of matkom flower*) khõc ; (*of flowers of maize*) goco.

PIT, A—dungada, gada, gadlak, garha, khad, khãiyuk, khana, khapur khãyũk, khãyuk, khõedak, khondlak, kund, sum, sund ; (*small*) khupur khuyãk ; (*deep & narrow*) kupur khũñak ; (*of water*) ḍhabuñ, khãiduk, khũidaha ; (*of mire*) khala ; (*of filth*) narak kund ; (*from which earth is dug*) has gadlak, kadha gada, khanta gada, la gada ; (*fire*) gambhra gada ; (*fall*) khãiduk, khãiyuk, khapur khãyũk, khãrĩ khãyuk, kund ; (*falls, full of*) khãedak khõedak.

PITAPAT—ṭipṭap ; (*to go*) dhak (2), dhuk (2), dukduk.

PITCH—ral ; (*fork a*) akhaini ; (*on low key, to*) gahla, guñgwaok ; (*a tent, to*) bereć.

PITEOUSLY—awapapa, daya, gerañ huruñ, hathea, hatiare.

PITHLESS—alaklandi, aṭho siṭho, siṭha ; (*& slovenly*) thosoć morgoć, tosot morgot.

PITIABLE—becara, haṭiar chucha, merlañ mirliñ, mirluñ.

PITIFULLY—hathea, hatiare, ñarak (2), ñerek (2).

PITS—(*a succession of*) khãedak khõedak ; (*& ravines, full of*) garha gorho, khoñja khuñji, sadga badga.

PITTA, THE INDIAN—huć bir.

PITY—daya, mãyã, moh ; (*to shew*) daya, jeb doho, mãyã, rahai sahai ; (*by force of*) mãya jolate ; (*& sympathy*) daya mãyã ; (*oneself, to*) baesoe

PLACE, A—jaega, jagah, pakar, sõc, ṭhãi, than, thani, thanit, ṭhão, ṭhec, ṭhen, thol ; (*as for dancing*) sal ; (*out of*) antharı, sadga bidir, sadgaeak, sarsadle, sodgoro, udam ; (*in that*) ende, entere, unde, tãhã ; (*in this*) nende, nete, neten, nhate, nonde, nenden ; (*in which*) okare, oka then, oka utar ; (*distant*) biran ; (*convenient*) ghai ; (*lonely*) nicel jaega ; (*low moist*) sot ; (*where cattle collect at noon*) got ; (*to live long in one*) jom hor ; (*to fix*) nenda ; (*to place, from*) barać buruć, jarmak jormok, thanṭaratiñ.

PLACE, TO—bas, doho, jaega, ṭhãi, ṭhão, ṭhekan, ṭhikan ; (*under*) athrẽ ; (*a bed &c.*) hel ; (*one thing above*

another) conda, capao; (*at right angles*) gaṇḍe; (*anywhere*) gaṇja guṅji; (*on fork*) hāṛop̣; (*in front of*) samaṅ.

PLACENTA, THE—baha; (*of animals*) ãowãr, ganthar.

PLACES—(*in many*) hiḍo hoḍo; (*from many*) joṛo joṭo; (*in some*) bajek birla, tãhã, ṭhãi ṭhãire, ṭhão ku ṭhão.

PLACID—ṭaṇḍha.

PLAGUE—(*the*) maha maṛi; (*to*) aṛis, asiaṛ.

PLAID, A LARGE COTTON—pichauṛi.

PLAIN—(*ugly*) behusnak; (*level*) mit́ são; (*white*) sada; (*a*) bilan, bilaṇd, caukan, ṭaṇḍi; (*to make*) ṭaṇḍi; (*a wide*) melan ṭaṇḍi; (*& rising ground*) ṭaṇḍi ṭikur; (*seen from above*) otet; (*manner, in a*) ṭhak̃ ṭhok̃.

PLAINT—arja arji, aroj, darkhas, dohae.

PLAINTIFF—baḍi, mudoe, phiriaḍi; (*& defendant*) dae mudoe.

PLAINTIVELY—daya, ṅerek̃ (2).

PLAISTER, TO—thopram, thorothopo.

PLAISTERED—soroṅ potoṅ.

PLAIT—(*to*) baj, galaṅ, gatao, kaso, paṭet́; (*of hairs, a*) cãurić.

PLAITED—(*band, a*) jamki; (*loinstring*) jamki ḍora.

PLAN, WITHOUT—khedar bedar.

PLANE—mit́ são, sotel; (*to*) chaṭao; (*a*) raunda, ronda; (*tree*) tidhar dare.

PLANET JUPITER, THE—cor kheda, rat calawa.

PLANK, A—takta.

PLANT, A—dare; (*young*) cara; (*common*) agyo, bana etka, baraṅgom, bariaṛ, barsa pakor, bhador jhapni, gitil ran, haṇḍi kuṇḍi, huṭer, karla, saparatiń, ṭhoć; (*climbing*) asaria, aser, babu janga nãṛĩ, bayaṅ, beṅgo nãṛĩ, bidhanta, bir malhan, bodlaṛ nãṛĩ, cihṛi lamak̃, cihũṭ laṛ, coṭo lutur, dare japak̃, dudhi loṭa, etka, god, kapu, kawet́, kitauri, kundri, lamak̃, lat, lota, maraṅ koṅgat, nanha dudhi loṭa, nãṛĩ murup̣, piska, serwaṅ, tejo mala, tihon, tirra, utri dudhi; (*found in moist places*) akaṛ baha, dak̃ icak̃, dak̃ kudur, gukhla janum, kalha baha, pansiṅgha, sunsuni; (*common in rains*) bir kana arak̃, dare orsa, dhãi, gundli arak̃, hatkan, masuṛdaṅ, kalmeg; (*leguminous*) buru raheṛ, disom horeć, gasua rambṛa, ghaṅgra, ghaṅgri, guṇḍri kurse, horeć, jhaṭa korkoṭa kesaṛi, khesari, kulsa, malhaṅ, muṅ, ot kondro, ot murup̣, rambṛa, raheṛ; (*jungle*) bir buṭ, bir ghaṅgra, bir horeć, birsaṅ, bir miru baha, bir sãuraj, boṅga ṭaeni, capot́, hẽbẽl, ghiu chimbṛi, ghora lidi, ićer, jaṅ tirṛa, jhimbria, jom laṛ, kedar nãṛi, kolo, koṇḍeń, koṅgak̃, merom mẽt́, nanha bir jhunjhuni, orop̣, ṭaini; (*small*) baephol, bahu ṭuṭuri, iliń ciń, janhe hirom, janhe nańjom, jhawa jhara, jhãwar khaṇḍera, lilkaṭhi, lopoṅ arak̃, nirbis, parwa jhaṛa, paṭwa ghãs, seta kaṭa arak̃; (*annual*) bagluca, baṛa pathol, bereń phul, boṅga barchi, cakaoḍa, cipcirip̣, dare dhompo, jhurjhuri, ot dhompo, ṭaṇḍi catom arak̃; (*bulbous*) ot ṭipoć, ukurit́; (*small trailing*) joka sakam; (*flowering*) baṛe baha, bonkapsi, caulia, cuṭia candbol, dhiri japak̃, ḍora bohok̃, gaḍa pacwani, gulańj baha, jugi topa baha, kaṇṭa phul, kharbaṛi, khode baha, raila baha, raniphul, saram lutur, selep̣ samanom, sinić samanom baha, sogot́ baha, sunsuni, surgi baha; (*with edible root*) jhiṅgur, kanda saru, kunam, ol, pedgo, piṇḍe, saṅg, suthni; (*cultivated*) jhiṅga, kaita jhiṅga, khirwa, man kanda, ram jhiṅga; (*wild*) beṅgaṛ beṭahet́, bir jhunka, bir kubet́, kantha arak̃, karmbi arak̃, kaskom ran, kaṭić jhunka, moṭa bir jhunka, pańjot, petṛa da, san karla; (*in rice-fields*) kedar; (*with red flower*) man baha; (*village*) moṭa bhidi janaṭet́; (*tank*) ulḍha; (*with spines*) gokhla janum; (*egg*) beṅgaṛ; (*hedge*) bereńjo, bherṇda, kahu botke, puṭki malla; (*thorny*) kaṇṭa saru, raṅgaini; (*sensitive*) lajao baha, ṭaṇḍi jhapni; (*stingnig*) seṅgel siń; (*a kind of*) ajua, bhaisa, bharbhari, bhedwa, bhiḍi achim, bhiḍi janaṭet́, bir narcha, bir surguja, boṅga ghaṇṭi, buḍhi ghasić, buru ekasira nãṛĩ, buru kaṭkom careć, ḍaṅgra janum, dare huṭer, dare kudrum, daṭra, ḍimbu baha, eṭkeć, gaḍa kalha, gai ghura, gaṅga tulsi, jargaḍi, jhapni, jhãwar, kaḍa mẽt́, kanṭa kuca, maraṅ jhunka, merom mẽt́, miru baha, nanha jhunka, naṅjom rehet́, orsõr, paṛo, parwa cipcirip̀, picki, piṭua ghãs, rali, saoraj, seta pan, son jhunka, ṭanḍi bhiḍi janeṭet́, ṭanḍi khode baha, ṭanḍi meral, ṭanḍi sol, tayar baha, ṭipoć, ṭuṭuri, urić alaṅ. *Cf.* POT-HERB, SHRUB, BUSH, PARASITIC, MEDICINAL.

PLANT, TO—bit́, rohoe ; (*rice in spaces*) gaban ; (*begin to*) pacaṭi, puhna.

PLANTAIN—kaera ; (*kinds of*) jahaj k., mohan basi, mortoman, rana, sauri ; (*seeds*) kosa.

PLANTED (*opp. to self-propagated*)—ropa.

PLANTS—(*used as pot-herbs*) aṛaḱ sakam ; (*air*) banda.

PLASTER, TO—chõc, jereṛ, lasrao, lesrao, leṭa ; (*up a hole*) ilet́ ; (*roughly*) thorothopo ; (*with clay*) jolom ; (*straw & clay*) baja ; (*with cow-dung*) lunḍa.

PLATE—bartan, ḍhalwa ; (*stone*) pathra ; (*leaf*) paṭra, paṭri, sartal ; (*brass*) chipi, thara, thari ; (*flat like*) sartalaḱ ; (*one who licks*) patar caṭa.

PLATFORM—pinḍa, maṛom ; (*for altar*) pinḍ ; (*raised*) macan, manḍom ; (*shooting*) aṭa ; (*for storing straw*) parãoca.

PLAUSIBLE—phaṅga.

PLAY, TO—eneć, khel, kheldu, khelekhel, khildu ; (*as cat with mouse*) loka ; (*false*) phaki, ṭhar ; (*cards*) jua eneć, tas eneć ; (*a flute well*) baskari ; (*wind instrument*) oroṅ ; (*harp &c.,*) phet́ ; (*thing, a*) khilauna.

PLAYFUL—khela bhaṭua, ikil sikil ; (*& touching each other*) gawić godaḱ.

PLEA, A—arsa.

PLEAD, TO—deḍhet́, nehõr, soal, sowal. *Cf.* EXCUSE.

PLEADER, A—ukil,, wakil.

PLEASANT—curba, jut, liṭhur, ṅorom (2), sobha, sohan, sohbod ; (*looking*) cohõk ; (*sensation*) gumur ; (*of smell of rice*) muhur (2) ; (*of smell of roasted grain*) sondhaṛ.

PLEASE—baṛe ; (*to*) mon gaḍiau ; (*a child, to*) labhae lubhai.

PLEASED, TO BE—dahin, khusi, kusi, raji, rasik, rijhua, rit, ritiau, rumuć ; (*very*) riṅgi ṭiṅgi ; (*to cause*) rijhau ; (*with*) suktau.

PLEASING—rij roṅ, sohan ; (*to the senses*) jeṅget́ (2).

PLEASURE—hãs, hĩt, hub, khema, khusi, kusal, kusi, marji, morji, murji, rij, roṅ rij, sahnas, sõk, sonk ; (*interj. of*) ah ; (*to feel*) bhog ; (*with*) hesec sekreć, khos, sekreć ; (*to give*) khemondoḱ.

PLEAT, A—kanaso.

PLEDGE—(*to*) bandhe, bandhok, sahi, suhi ; (*property given in*) bandhoki, jaejat ; (*oneself, to*) ikraṛ, karaṛ.

PLEIADES, THE—sorenko.

PLENTIFUL—bhocbhocao, retekote, sasta, udhiã.

PLENTY—borket, puran, purun, ranebane ; (*a year of*) hamram sãwãe serma.

PLETHORA, A (*sarcastic*)—kokoaḱ.

PLEURISY—koṛam haso.

PLIANT—lewa, libhra, licaṛ, naram, narma ; (*too*) labus (2), lipsa, lubus (2).

PLIES—(*in*) remet́ (2) ; (*two*) duhri.

PLOT—(*to*) mis ; (*of land surrounded by water*) ṭikur.

PLOUGH, A—nahel ; (*to*) jot, si, ṭhoṭho ; (*handle*) kãrba, ṭir ; (*& handle in one piece*) kãrba nahel ; (*point of*) ṭoḍa ; (*staple of*) pasi ; (*partially, to*) laṭku paṭku ; (*deeply, to*) gargarao ; (*to yoke a*) nahel jorao ; (*to break up with*) lehe (2) ; (*a field in sections, to*) atre ; (*to carry suspended*) sok ; (*beam*) isi ; (*sown rice-plants, to*) kaḍhau ; (*to sink unevenly*) khaḍar khuḍur ; (*a 2nd. time, to*) si lahut́.

PLOUGHING—(*1st.*) paṛaḱ ; (*2nd*) deć ; (*3rd*) uṭhau ; (*3rd rice-field*) jaboḍ ; (*4th*) calao : (*inefficient*) siyoṛ soyoṛ.

PLOUGHMAN—halboha, harwaha, siokić.

PLOUGHSHARE—pal, nahel pal ; (*broad*) dhalpa pal.

PLUCK—dil ; (*to*) sit, tot ; (*up, to*) ukhrau ; (*off, to*) potor ; (*leaves, to*) hoé, hejer ; (*fruit, to*) got.

PLUCKY—dhados, dilgar, dilman, jalim, jhũkel, jolonia ; (*to be*) dil, jhũk.

PLUG, TO—tubet, tuwet ; (*up a hole or crack*) ilet.

PLUM, THE HOG—amra.

PLUMB-LINE, A—sahul.

PLUME MADE FROM FEATHERS OF BLUE JAY—toya dhaca.

PLUMP—badgae bodgoe, bhuger, bigaboge, chik chok, dhabar dhubur, ehel (2), lendker, lusku lundur, mandhak, mangar, odor (2), susurtak ; (*of children*) bhundla, (M), bhundli (F), chalchalia, ledgeé, ludgup ; (*of infants*) lesker, luskur ; (*with a*) hudur marte, lesrok marte.

PLUMPING INTO WATER—cabhur, cadak cuduk, caduk (2), caruk (2), hudur marte.

PLUNDER, TO—lut, lutpat, metoé ; (*one who*) lutia.

PLUNGE, TO—cado ; (*into*) khadke, khanjo ; (*suddenly into*) khab.

PLUNGING SOUND—dhabos, dhabos marte, hudrak, hudrak m., khub marte.

PLURAL, SIGN OF—ko.

PNEUMONIA—koram haso.

POCKET, A—dukhri, jeb.

POCK-PITTED—bandra, khadrak khedrok ; (*face*) mari mõtãhã.

POD, A—(*of cotton*) dindi ; (*unripe*) chimbri ; (*to take out of, with teeth*) hadap ; (*to remove covering of*) jan.

POET, A—kobi, seren jokraoić.

POINT—combe, kasi, muthni ; (*tapering to a*) cuicui, kcoń ; (*of, on the*) dela dili, lega ligi, mara ; (*highest*) chip, mundhni ; (*to touch with sharp*) gayuk, kabak, thotkao, tũda ; (*out, to*) batlao, uduk ; (*on, to put a*) cuibor ; (*to twist to a*) pungi.

POINTED—cocko, cuicui, cuila, locoń, rocrocu ; (*sharp*) bucbucu, khoca ; (*piece of wood*) haiar.

POISON—bis, jahar, kal, mahur ; (*for arrows*) dakra, jahar mahra ; (*fish, to*) rup ; (*without*) nirbis ; (*having*) bisal ; (*of snakes, method of treating*) dhuriau ; (*fish*) har.

POISONOUS—bisaha, bisan ; (*words*) bisbakhan ; (*mushrooms*) bis ot.

POKE, TO—larga, lurga ; (*out*) hotor ; (*at*) tunda, tundu ; (*in hand or snout*) sondra sundri.

POLE, A—dań ; (*to propel boat*) cihiri dań ; (*long*) laktha, larga dań ; (*on which things slung to carry*) sabri, sangra, tada ; (*on which umbrella hoisted*) chata dań ; (*on which things press*) katri ; (*fastened to cart*) banki ; (*on top of sheaves*) aras.

POLICE—(*man*) kanastabal ; (*rural*) digwar ; (*to inform*) candiau ; (*station*) phundi, thana ; (*station, person in charge of*) thanadar ; (*in plain clothes*) goenda ; (*man, head*) doroga, jamadar, jamedar.

POLISH, TO—molao, sikil.

POLISHED—cikãr, jhere (2), jhile mile, jhuru (2).

POLITENESS—sil.

POLLED—dondo, mundguć, mundla (M), mundli (F), mundruć.

POLLUTE CEREMONIALLY, TO—bhõnda.

POLLUTED—bhõnda, nakara, nokra ; (*to be*) hedge hesak.

POLO, THE GAME OF—pati eneć.

POLYPUS OF NOSE—nãk risa, simbra.

POMEGRANATE, THE—anar ; (*fruit of*) dalim.

POMP—digi migi ; (*& music*) rajam bajan.

POND, A—(*natural*) ablra ; (*small*) ahar.

PONDER, TO—biear, gandon, guman, gumun, gund, hudis, khanj, khańjao, khondrond, nandi gandi, uakep.

PONDEROUS—hamal.

POOL, A—aghorni, dabra, dobhak, khala dabha ; (*deep*) daha, khãiduk, khãiyuk, khal ; (*deep river*) paya ; (*in river*) darha ; (*miry*) led.

POOR—alatoka, bapurić, becara, dingar, dolao, garib, gayur gapur, gurib, home, henla, jhińji jhuri, jonje, jenjroć, jorpoć, kangla, kańla, lamta, landha, katlaha, lenda turia, lerań petań, lereć peteć, nandan, nindhan, phakir, rengeć, tasań, tewelgat ; (*abjectly*) rengeć oreć ; (*people*) gane garib, gani gurib, guni gurib, thut langat, tut langat ;

(*& wasted*) miluk jiluk; (*to become*) bẹhal, bhaṅga suli, lạbṛuk, lạrbạr-ao, libṛuk, nataj; (*to be*) dola; (*to be very*) tirañ; (*to kill the*) gạrib mara.

POP, TO—(*into mouth*) kaṭok, kọṭọk; (*head under water*) ḍubuć.

POPLAR TREE, THE—libne.

POPULOUS—barjao, bạsti, bosti, gạdi, gạhagạd, rạsi; (*very*) rạsi bạsti; (*village, a*) bạsti ato, gadel ato; (*& prosperous*) gangan.

PORCUPINE, THE INDIAN—jhik.

PORK—sakri jel.

PORRIDGE—(*of consistency of*) lọdọr bọdọr, lọhọr bọhọr, lọpọr; (*corn*) jondra lạṭọ.

PORTION—bakhra, bāṭ, bhag, bhag bāṭ, his, hisạ, tarantar; (*of inheritance*) bāṭ bakhra.

PORTMANTEAU, A—bẹg.

PORTRAIT—bọhọk.

POSITION—ṭẹp; (*a*) bahạli; (*to lose*) bhaṅga suli; (*in*) ragraga, rẹgrẹgẹ.

POSITIVELY—ṭhae.

POSSESSED—(*by a spirit*) boṅga capaṛ, capaṛ; (*to be*) bharao, ẹsẹr, rum; (*one*) cauraha.

POSSESSION—adọl, aidari, amda, amọl, dọkhọl; (*to be in*) amda, dọkhọl; (*of, to take*) aoda, cakrao, moṭiao, muṭiau, tạmil; (*affix indicating*) an; (*to come into*) hạsil.

POSSESSIONS, ALL ONE'S—sạnṭi umṭi, uṭhai paṭhae.

POSSIBILITY—sọmbhọb; (*implying a future*) dina.

POSSIBLY—bạrić, bọtọć, cele, idu, kajak, kajạp, marpase.

POST—(*a*) khunṭi; (*to tie to a*) khunṭau; (*letter*) ḍak; (*office*) ḍak oṛak; (*runner*) ḍakwala; (*up, to*) khuṭau; (*notched on top for beam*) khap khunṭi; (*king*) kham khunṭi, tham khunṭi; (*at corner of funeral pyre*) toṛe khunṭi; (*with wooden cushion on top*) piṛhi khunṭi; (*forked*) caṅga khunṭi; (*to which bullocks tied when threshing*) mehkhunṭi; (*to which bullock tied for breaking in*) rẽnca; (*boundary*) thum.

POSTAGE—mạhsul, ḍak mạhsul.

POSTERIORS, THE—bituć.

POSTERITY—ãosa bãosa, họṛren họpọn.

POSTPONE, TO—agdhao.

POSTPONED, TO BE—mạhkup, mạkup, mukup.

POSTURE—(*to*) lạtić ladar; (*of one's affairs*) hal, halat.

POT, A—bhajan; (*earthen*) celañ, cukạk, hạṭhua, nandwa, paya, ṭukuć, ṭumạñ; (*small earthen*) chabha, ḍhuḍhua; (*for palm-juice*) lạbui; (*milking*) bhanḍ, jạlua; (*lower part of water*) lohta; (*water*) ghaṛa, ṭhili; (*cooking*) luiha; (*straw stand for*) binḍi; (*colouring*) gạbis.

POTATO, THE SWEET—sakarkenda.

POT-BELLIED—diridañ, hahadañ, robea, rodea.

POTENCY—partap; (*having*) lag.

POTHERBS—aṛak, aṛak sakam, ḍurvạ aṛak, garũnḍi a., jạnum aṛak, sirgiṭ a.; (*fresh*) kanḍer; (*too mature*) palo; (*eaten by caterpillars*) tejo a.; (*cultivated*) gandhạri a., piriń, ponḍ gandhạri a.; (*wild*) anḍia dhurup a., apaṅgir a., aṭkura a., bir lọpọñ a., gitil a., ioạk a., jẹreń a., kana a., kạri gandhạri, kulai lutur, lọpọñ a., lopotiañ a., matkọm a., mọrọn a., moṭa gundli a., moṭa hemca a., moṭa uṛić alañ, muć a., nanha hemca a., orsa a., sauri a., tagoć a., thuiạk a., toa a., togoć a., uṛić alañ; (*a kind of*) bạhu jãwãe a., bhatuạ a., bheḍa dereń, cạndni, catọm a., cãurić a., coromokoć, datrọm a., dhurup a., hạpuk a., jãwãe lạḍu a., kedok a., ọhọć a., sukri lutur a., tabẹn a., udri dudhi a.

POTS & PANS—ṭukuć celañ.

POTSHERD, A—jinṭhi, kelhać.

POTTERS—(*Hindu caste*) kuṅkạl; (*wheel of*) kuṅkạl cak.

POTTERY—kuṅkạl bhajan; (*piece of broken*) kelhać; (*underbaked*) bhiro-bhoro.

POUNCE ON, TO—jhapṭao; (*from all sides*) jhapṭa jhapṭi; (*& press down*) ota; (*suddenly & close egress*) jạpuć; (*with a*) khap mẹnte.

POUND, TO—huruñ; (*fine*) h. gunḍạ, h. lahuć; (*grain*) sọk; (*sound of*) cọbhọr (2), khud (2), ṭhaṛak ṭhuṛuk.

POUNDS, A WEIGHT OF ABOUT TWO—sẹr.

POUR, TO—bubhạu, ḍharao, dul; (*of rain*) achal gañjal, um arẹć; (*out*) ujhlạu, uṗ; (*out a little*) cuḍruć, cuḍur; (*away*) uṗ giḍi; (*into mould*) ḍharao; (*out libation*) cọḍọr, cuḍruć; (*off liquid*) arẹć hiñjiť, aṛić.

POUT, TO—binḍuć saṭok, lọclọcọ, mọcmọc, sui.

POVERTY—(*to meet with*) jarkhar; (*to be reduced to*) ṭuṭạu; (*always complaining of*) hae phoe, ninyā̃u; (*to cry*) ninyā̃ ninyī.

POWDER—(*gun-*) bạrud, dạru; (*a medicinal*) phạki, phạkni, puria ran; (*a red*) ạbir; (*for blackening teeth*) misi; (*for eyelids*) ajan; (*an aromatic*) nokhi; (*to reduce to*) chakachun, bọlọṅ, họlọṅ lọpọṅ, lọṭọk, lọṭọr, podor; (*to be ground to*) gaṇḍa guṇḍa; (*to*) lạhuť.

POWDERED—lẹmẹń, lọṭọr; (*easily*) bhara bhuru, bhaṛ (2).

POWER—bọs, butel, butlạk, daṛe, iktiar, khẹmọta, mạgdur, sạd, sạddi, sạdhi, sạkti, sukti; (*of comprehension*) suj; (*over men or things*) dhamas; (*having*) baṛiạu.

POWERLESS, TO RENDER—jạbin, jạbun.

PRACTICE—bẹbọhar, beohar, pas; (*to*) bhāõar, hewa.

PRACTISED—kabel, kạbil; (*to be*) linḍar, linḍor.

PRAISE—jọs, sabasi; (*to*) gun manao, ńum, õṛhẽ, sarhao, suhu; (*in song, to*) duraṅ, õṛhẽ.

PRANCE, TO (*as a horse*)—kẹcmecao, kharpaṭao.

PRANKS, GIVEN TO—sihạn, sihạnia.

PRATE, TO—bakbakaok, bakhna bạkhni, bakhnao, bhac (2), bhacbhacao, bhackao, bheder (2), bhẹjẹr (2), bhọc (2), bhọcọr (2), bokao, phedaṛ (2), thuthi kuṭa.

PRATTLE—gọlpọ; (*to*) bhẹjẹr (2).

PRAWN, A—icạk, nicạk, raṇdo icạk, sọlẹ icạk.

PRAY, TO—bakhẽr, dạhnao, dẹhẹť ḍunḍheť, kọe; (*of Moslems*) nemaj paṛhao.

PRAYING-BEADS—udrạð mala.

PREACH, TO—binti, manadi, monadi, porcar, pracar, procar.

PREACHER, A—porcarok, pracarak procarok.

PREARRANGED—aṭẹť siť, ọlsiť aṭẹť siť.

PRECEDENCE—(*to concede*) apạj, henda hindi; (*to take*) liṭhi, luhu cuhu.

PRECEDING—sabik; (*& following each other in birth*) soptok.

PRECIOUS—dhạni; (*stone, a*) boidurjọ, cuni, dạmạnạk dhiri, gomedak, guggul, jismọ, koṭahela, lal, lalkanṭọ, lilmạni, losuniọ. mạni, morọkọt, nilkanṭọ, peroj, pitmạni, pọdmarọg, sọrnọkanṭọ, surjọkanṭọ, tamrọ.

PRECIPICE, A—dạrga.

PRECIPITOUS—daṛaṅ, khạidu, khọndọr khọcak.

PRECISELY—sinạm, taman, taṅgaṭ, tanman.

PREFER, TO—parpasind, pạsind; (*a complaint*) pes.

PREFERABLY—sẹ bhal, sẹ samta, sẹ bickọm, sẹ bọrọm.

PREFIX, A PREVITATIVE—a-, an-, bẹ-, ọ-.

PREGNANT—asapaṭi họrmọ, bar jiwi, bhạrti họrmọ, gạbḍuyạk, gọrọb họrmọ, porọati; (*of animals*) gạbhin, poạti; (*to be*) họrmọ, lajok; (*woman, ghost of*) curin.

PREJUDICED—sajọk, tọrọpdạri.

PREMATURE BIRTH, OF—adpakolia.

PREMIUM ON LOAN, A—dhoraṭ.

PREPARATIONS—lagan; (*to make*) sarsor, taltul, tanabhana; (*for cooking, to make*) saṭka suṭku.

PREPARE, TO—banao, benao, johṛao, juṛạu, jutṛạu, karao kuṛạu, mohjut, sapṛao, sirjạu. sọmọl, tear, toenat, torajut; (*& take on journey*) sọmọl; (*food*) aro.

PREPARED—jujhạu, tear; (*to be*) aodhan, khaṛa, mạhjud, sạniạu, ṭhak (2).

PREPOSSESSING—cẹmkẹć (F), chakmạkia, cikon cokon, cọhõk.

PREPUCE—*Cf.* FORESKIN.

PRESAGE OF SUCCESS, A—joe.

PRESENCE—ạblạ; (*of, in*) samańre, sạmuk.

PRESENT—hạli; (*to be*) hạjir, hajur, mõhjam, mohńjam; (*at*) ṭuṅ ghuṛī, nahak, nẹbẹtar, nit, soedom; (*for *the*) anman, bạrsiń ursiń, hatar; (*need exceeding*) bạtil; (*a petition, to*) pes.

Present, a—dan, ilạm, nońjor; (*from a visitor*) sandes; (*of meat*) mạrjạdi; (*to landlord*) salami; (*to a superior*) salami, suniạ. *Cf.* cloth.

Presently—nahak̕, nẹ, nẹ nahak̕; (*when scolding*) nẹ nẹroń.

Presents—(*given at marriage*) banda pọn, culhạ ǰaraoni, gọnọń tọraoni, itạt̕, jạituk, jhanạuri, jiạ itạt̕, jọm itạt̕, jọra jạituk, kaka salaka, mạṇḍlạ, net puri.

Preserve, to—baclao, dok̕, hebajọt, jakao; (*as forest, game, &c.*) rakha; (*alive*) jiạu.

Press—(*for oil &c.*) ghạni, kulhu, iẹlẹnak̕, paṭa; (*a wine*) had; (*of business*) beoṛa, gạhul, jala.

Press, to—bhẹrọsta, halhalao, lẹn, robot̕; (*against*) jalat̕; (*down to ground*) ota gur; (*down*) cipạ, dabao, gadao, kasao, ota; (*together*) khacao; (*in*) kocao; (*with hands*) lin; (*clay into crack*) thasao; (*close to*) bhiṛạu, koclao; (*upon*) ghaṭ ghaṭao.

Pressed—(*together*) rẹnṭẹ pẹnṭẹ, rẹṭẹpẹṭẹ; (*to be hard*) hạluạ harọn, jalẹ thalẹ, kọstọ mọstọ, kuckucạu, tiṛanicạ; (*down to be*) tẹn.

Pressing—cahat̕, cọhọ̃ṭ; (*as agricultural work*) halhal.

Pressure—pẽc, pẽnc; (*of business*) dhọ̃nj; (*of, by*) kakhante; (*to bear, to bring*) aĩṇṭhao, pẽc lagao, ucạṭ.

Prestige—dhọmọs.

Presume, I—cele.

Presumptuous—bahali.

Pretence—arsa, barkac̕, dhaḍnas, lisi, sinic̕; (*to lead by false*) bhabrao.

Pretend, to—bạuli, beda, eńgol, ẹrẹ, họr beda, ińgul, jhuṭa muṭhạ, jhuṭh pus, jhuṭọ puso, nańgọs, phẽs phãs; (*to eat*) hap̕ ińgul; (*not to possess*) ninyạ̃ ninyĩ. *Cf.* ignorance.

Pretender, a—bhiduk, ḍhaḍnạsiạ.

Pretending—ḍhọrḍhosaba, ẹrẹ ẹrẹte, jhuṭa muṭhạ; (*not to understand*) pephṛa, phephṛa.

Pretext—susi; (*on some*) paṛagaṛe; (*of, on the*) lasãṛhẽ.

Pretty—kẹnẹkẹc̕, mọńj, nạnuạr, sundạr; (*& little*) gẹnẹc̕ (2).

Prevail upon by entreaty, to—bhão-são.

Prevaricate, to—dudrạu.

Prevent, to—akọṭ, aṭkao, dombṛao, rok, rokao, ṭekao, ṭokao.

Prey—aher.

Price—bhao, bhao baṭa, dam, dọr, dọrdam; (*a stiff*) khạra dam; (*a cheap*) kọm dọr; (*current*) nirik; (*for a bride*) conda ṭaka; (*to*) mol; (*to fix*) dam dạri, dọr marao; (*to fix without weighing*) mulạiyạ; (*to agree to*) dọrdar; (*to fall in*) monda; (*to let off part of*) khesarot; (*to rise as*) coranti; (*paid for rented land*) pọn. *Cf.* low, high.

Prick, to—badgak̕, buyut̕ (2), cubuc̕, kabak̕, khacak̕, paṭi, sagak̕, so; (*in tattooing*) khoda; (*up the ears*) birlạń.

Pricking sensation—cabac̕ cubuc̕, chuc̕ marte.

Prickly heat—balbal bhumbri.

Pride—adọr, bhuc bhuci, dhọmọk, mit̕ saṭha.

Priest—(*sacrificing*) pujhạr; (*Santal village*) kuḍam naeke, naeke; (*a Hindu*) deasi; (*officiating at Jatra*) susạri; (*land of*) naiyạli mạn.

Prime—(*just reached one's*) nawatur; (*past*) adher, khapao. *Cf.* minister.

Primeval—akaṭ, arna; (*forest*) ạkuṭ bir, ạṭuṭ bir, arna bir, urni bir.

Priming pan of gun—rońjok.

Prince—kuạr, lobab, nobab, raj kumạr.

Principal—aol, goṭa guṭi, marań, matha, mukhiạ, mul, pordhan, sirạ; (*money*) mul; (*& interest*) mule sude, sude mule.

Print, to—chaba, chap.

Prison—garad, kabhar, kạd, phaṭọk; (*house*) jahal khana; (*to put in*) hajọt, kocao, leglao; (*to send to*) calan; (*one in*) hari biri họr, kaidi.

Private—khas, mọphọsọl.

Privately—ạde, bhorma, ekan, ekãt, ekõt, eskarre, gape gupe, gãye ghọre, okote; (*to talk*) gampis.

Privative prefix, a—a-, an-, bẹ-, ọ-.

Privelege, a—ijạra.

PRIZE—(*a*) baksis, ilam ; (*to lever*) utkau.

PROBABILITY—dogor, sombhob ; (*implying future*) dima.

PROBABLY—mena.

PROCESSION, A MARRIAGE—bariat.

PROCLAIM, TO—binti, dae dae, damdahe, donkao, lai sade, manadi, monadi, lai sodor ; (*a decree by beat of drum*) digri pitau.

PROCLAMATION, A—istihar, manadi, monadi.

PROCLIVITY—dhae.

PROCRASTINATE, TO—adorok ; (*given to*) asania.

PROCURE, TO—(*for another*) tela ; (*by means of another*) barmangao.

PROD, TO—guta, guta guti, hurau, kucau, tunda, tundu ; (*in a hole*) khocok ; (*with thumb*) ghusa, ghusa ghusi ; (*sound of*) khocor (2).

PRODUCE, AGRICULTURAL—arjon, cij, durib, hasil, lukhi, oncun, orjon, upja, upjan.

PRODUCER, A—arjonia.

PRODUCTIVE—bian.

PROFANE, TO—bhosto, bosto.

PROFESS, TO—angrau, anrau.

PROFESSION (*calling*)—birit, bitti, udam.

PROFICIENCY—caher.

PROFICIENT—gakhur, gansud, khand, khand akhar, kharkahi, pagol ; (*to be*) cemat, laker.

PROFIT—barphai, bhalai, lab, labhe, lapha, mulapha, napha, phaeda, porho ; (*promising*) aedhon ; (*to*) lapha, posau, torao ; (*without*) bephaeda.

PROFLIGATE—luca (M), luci (F).

PROFUSION—ranebane, targal.

PROGNOSTICATE BY DIVINATION, TO—paetar.

PROGRESSION, CONTINUED—poyor.

PROHIBIT, TO—dob, rok, rokao.

PROHIBITION—(*not, in*) alo ; (*sign of*) condka ; (*exclm. of*) haha.

PROJECT, TO—kotkoto, kutkutu.

PROJECTING—dakdaka, dokdoko, ododo, rakraka, seksek, sokosoko.

PROLAPSUS—(*ani*) bhandar algao ; (*uteri*) hormo algao.

PROLIXITY—gap.

PROLONG, TO—laphan.

PROMINENT—daedae, potpoto, ut utu.

PROMISCUOUSLY—latae ghotae, leser beder.

PROMISE—(*to*) ekrar, gacao, gok, ikrar, joban, karar, sahi, suhi ; (*a written*) ekrar nama ; (*to break*) arkhao, harkhao ; (*to make false*) labori.

PROMONTORY, A—locon.

PROMPT, TO BE—tagaja, talbi.

PROMULGATE AN ORDER, TO—jari.

PRONUNCIATION—ucaran, ucran ; (*difference in*) garmak.

PROOF—cinha munda, nisana ; (*documentary*) dalel, dalil, dolel ; (*to put to the*) pacha ; (*over*) ekhan.

PROP, A—taghen, teghan, tekhadak, tham, thegan, thek, thesa ; (*for a cart*) sirpa ; (*with V head*) tibhi.

PROP, TO—athre, othngao, tesa ; (*under*) othngao.

PROPER—cahiye, khas, majbut, manjgut, sãoha ; (*to be*) saja ; (*way*) tar, targhar ; (*state*) batar ; (*place, out of*) sadgaeak, thaprok. *Cf.* TIME.

PROPERLY—gan, sahitte, suthrai ; (*ripe*) bele jaru.

PROPERTY—amda, basut, darja, daulat, dhon, durib, ghorkorna, jinis, tij ; (*moveable*) jalmal, sompot ; (*inherited from wife's relatives*) jarapi ; (*made over to creditor*) jãt ; (*to steal*) cokcanda ; (*having*) daulatan ; (*of a semi liquid*) tokor (2) ; (*to give in debt payment*) hari bhari, harna bharna ; (*given in pledge*) jaega ; (*of family, to give away secretly*) pãere.

PROPHESY, TO—bhao, nabi.

PROPHET, A—nabi, nabi era (F) ; (*true*) sat sokha.

PROPITIATE, TO—dahnao, kudrau, puruchun.

PROPORTIONS—(*in equal*) munda mundi, mundha mundhi ; (*of ill*) bartan, bhond bogla, sand mand.

PROPPED UP—(*to be*) tehad ; (*that which is*) tehadak.

PROPRIETOR—maldar, malkar.

PROPRIETY, CARELESS OF—garsa gale.

PROSECUTE, TO—calao ; (*a search*) pacha, pecha.

PROSPERITY—borket, khaṭa baṛha, lukhi, partap; (*having*) gangan, gangania.

PROSTITUTE, A—baçkaṛ, bosṛi, chinaṛ, daṛi.

PROSTRATE, TO—saṛgom; (*oneself*) ti jaṅgare giḍi; (*to lie*) kunḍel.

PROTECT, TO—aḍ, dok, hebajoṭ, kapok, oḍ, sambṛao; (*oneself*) ghao jogao.

PROTECTION—porbosti; (*to claim*) darsau; (*without*) nisarthi; (*to look for*) hirla.

PROTRACT, TO—laphaṅ.

PROTRACTED—pohoṭ.

PROTRUDE, TO—puipui; (*tongue*) lakar (2), meloṭ; (*so as to be seen*) ṭayal ṭuyul.

PROTRUDING—rocroco; (*as horns*) rap-rapa.

PROTUBERANCE ON A HANDLE, A—ḍimbi.

PROTUBERANT—daedae, laṭkum, uṭ uṭu. *Cf.* STOMACH.

PROUD—aḍai baḍai, baḍai, badaria, badgaria, condok, dhecor, dhomokia, gorob, gorobia, matbor, phulau; (*flesh*) toloke.

PROVE, TO—baca, barkać, bidau, dahao, darao, dorao, goṭa, jaj, jojao, nisṭa, ohjao, oj, parikha, porman, sabud, suhi.

PROVED, TO BE—ghoṭao.

PROVERB, A—kahtuk, lohok roṛ.

PROVIDE, TO—johrao, juhrau, jumau, jurau, karao kurau, kulau, kurau, sap sor; (*with food & drink*) khilau pilau.

PROVIDED—(*that*) khajuk; (*with, not*) okulan.

PROVIDENCE—bhidata.

PROVINCE—(*a*) elaka, ilaka; (*within one's*) amda.

PROVISION—(*for travellers*) rosod, sambar, saṭu sambar; (*for one meal*) ser sidha, sidha.

PROVISO, WITH THIS—aika.

PROVOKE, TO—cirhau, corcoṭaṅ, heṭeć.

PROVOKED—(*to be*) berosta, isbis, kahur mahur; (*easily*) khac.

PROVOKING—isbis, nepran, nichan, nichnaha (M), nichnahi (F).

PROWL, TO—laghar.

PRUDENT—gangante, husiar; (*to be*) sentor.

PRUNE, TO—chaṭao, ḍulau, her, hese, kaman, kolom

PRY INTO, TO—bhidi.

PSALTERY—bina banam.

PUBES, THE—kuṭhi; (*region over*) panḍe.

PUBESCENT—nijuan.

PUBLIC—sarsadle; (*the*) aramin; (*in*) sodorte; (*to make*) daeḍae, lai sade, lai sodor, phuṭau, sodor, sudri; (*to become*) unan; (*works, cess*) pabli.

PUBLISH, TO—ḍoṅkao, jahir, lai pasnao, sodor; (*slanders*) ḍoṅka, ḍuḍa.

PUDDLE, A—dobhak; (*wet as*) jabḍahi.

PUERILE—albudaha, urbudaha.

PUFF, TO—loko phoko, phak (2), phok (2), phokphoko; (*of cobra*) khakha, khokho, usić; (*as bear*) lokphokao; (*out*) bhara, bharao; (*with a*) podoe marte.

PUFF-BALL, A—puṭka; (*edible*) hor p., roṭe oṭ, roṭe p., seta p., erok p., tumba oṭ.

PUFFED—(*up*) beker bendaṅ, ruṭruṭu; (*out, to be*) pokpoko.

PUFFING—doṅgoe, podoe; (*out smoke*) odoe padoe; (*sound*) soyoṭ (2).

PUFFS, IN—doṅgoe; (*to issue*) bhak.

PUFFY—pokos.

PUG-NOSED—cepe mũ, cepre, cepreć, ceprot mũ.

PULINGLY—tiriṅ goriṅ

PULL, TO—dhara dhari, or, ṭanao, tege nere, tege (2); (*as noose*) or asit; (*at*) tegtege; (*out, of elastic*) tegtege; (*to, a door*) laḍak; (*off*) boć; (*tight*) kaskasao; (*through*) nimbhau; (*out of*) oar; (*out*) racak, toć; (*down*) otor, upar khapar; (*the beard*) c.koć; (*an oar*) dadu ghanṭa; (*one unwilling to go*) ghece (2), ghiro goco; (*out with stick*) hoṭkor; (*each other*) khamca khamci, ṭanaṭani; (*each other's hair*) contha cunthi, kapcao, topoć; (*ear of straw*) ṭũć; (*to pieces*) khinḍi hunḍi.

PULLED—(*down to be*) bhodor, dodoroso, jhaṭkao, jhunki; (*out, to be*) bikor bokor.

PULLET, A—sim kaloṭ.

PULLEY WHEEL, A—ghaṛ ghaṛi.

PULP OF FRUIT—gabe.

PULPY—labar lobur, lapos.

PULSE, A CULTIVATED—masri, mõc, sutri; *(a preparation of)* adauri.

PULSE—*(at wrist)* dhat, nala, nari, natika, natka; *(in throat)* lokoť; *(at child's fontanelle)* lenetep; *(to feel the)* ti tunum.

PULVERISE, TO—chakachun, chiti chaṅ, khijau, lemeń.

PULVERISED—lemeń; *(of soil)* phodlo; *(not)* ḍambak ḍombok.

PUMMELO, TO—ḍabha.

PUMP—*(a)* bambkol; *(up, to)* surkau.

PUMPKIN, A—bãria kohnda, hotoť, kadu, kohnda, kondha; *(dish from shell)* laua.

PUN, A—tulau phen katha.

PUNCH, A—antil, bhalwa.

PUNCTURE WITH HOT IRON, TO—bal.

PUNGENT—karua, khara, lag, tasil, tej, titi, tito.

PUNISH, TO—ead, eyad, ilaj, oṛ, sajai, sorad; *(by beating)* karai.

PUNISHMENT BY MOVING FROM PLACE TO PLACE—daura soproť.

PUNY—copa, coroetho, corońto, cothra, dhuruč, letweť.

PUPIL, A—catia, cela; *(of eye)* kharen, rajas.

PUPPET, A—cador bador, putli, putri, putura.

PUPPY, A—kutru, seta hopon; *(fit to be taken from mother)* gutruť; *(call to)* kurkur, kurkutu, kutu (2).

PURCHASE, TO—kharid, kiriń.

PURCHASER, A—gaharak, gahki, kharid-dar; *(would-be)* gahãk.

PURE—arik parik, nichora, nińjam, nira, nirola, sudh; *(of water)* jiri (2), pharia phati, phini phik, phĩrĩ-phič.

PURGATIVE, A—julap.

PURGING—cidir.

PURIFIED, TO BE—solthonok.

PURIFY, TO—sudh; *(ceremonially)* amiń, um amiń.

PURLOIN, TO—gob.

PURPLE—kurse baha roń.

PURPOSE—joh, mot, motlob; *(to)* noda, menjoń, mone, mon suba; *(for no)* banahak, bertha, jhuth pus, phẽs phãs; *(without)* ajlatia, alak didi, alaklandi, kulań, lirok lorok, lorok (2); *(to effect one's)* jos; *(hidden)* moroni; *(serving no)* auri pathauri, pathauri; *(without disclosing)* para-gare; *(of, for the)* ńutumte; *(of set)* barkač.

PURRING SOUND—gargor, kharkhor; *(of tiger)* khadar khodor.

PURSE, A—bugli; *(tied round loins)* gańjia; *(long narrow)* tora.

PURSUE, TO—khuda khudi, khudau, laga; *(closely)* ragdao; *(& overtake)* khudau tiok; *(an enquiry)* pacha; *(& seize)* hapca.

PUS—bele.

PUSH, TO—dhaka, dhaklau, dhunau, pelao, thela, thelao; *(in a crowd)* daka daki, dhakla dhakli, thela thili, thele paese; *(with head &c.)* thukrau; *(again & again)* dhaka dhaki, dhaka dhaki; *(from or to)* gari; *(along ground)* gasrao, ghas-kao, gharao; *(one along)* gurda; *(& cause to fall)* dhaka gur; *(oneself in)* gusuč, hureť; *(in)* gutu; *(in between)* soge; *(in head first)* sund-nč; *(into fire)* thekao; *(back)* hatao; *(out)* hotor; *(& pull)* jhilo jholo; *(aside)* mambrao; *(to front)* thare mare; *(one unwilling to go)* ghiro ghoco; *(a point with force)* sobok.

PUSHING & PULLING—dhaka dhoko, hura huri, jhaka jhaki, mambra mambri.

PUSTULES OF SMALL-POX—guti.

PUT, TO—*(in)* bhorao, bojhao, sajao; *(down)* doho; *(down-snub)* dabri mańgal, dabruč, dhapkao, dhuńg-rau, dhurmar, durmar, hantao; *(on fuel)* tingi; *(under arm)* hermeť; *(into hand)* cal; *(on fire)* conda; *(into water)* cado; *(down in small quantity)* churuč, curuč; *(past)* bae, bae gońao, kenha; *(from one)* dur; *(in order)* dursut; *(off with a pro-mise)* ere suk; *(upon)* ergejak; *(one's hand to)* eteč; *(out of sight)* gupať; *(on the person)* arao, bande *(F)*, denga *(M)*, horok, huraṛ, jabrao, jhabrao, oyo, pahrau, por-hao; (*into*) gotao, sambao; (*together*) leothe; (*oneself forward*) luthu; (*another forward*) bejha; (*off*) manta; (*out*) akbakao, odok, odoñ, toč; (*aside*) kehna, sa, sah; (*out of way*) bargao, borkas, gob, otak; (*out, as fire*) ĩrĩč; (*up to*) puski; (*up with*) sahao; (*into, as mouth*) ajo, lakum, lapeč, latum, soloñ; (*to a distance*) sahar; (*to usury*) baisau; (*at rest for present*) thap thop; (*close to*) tomboñ, tumbuč; (*away a vessel dirty*) dhabao; (*on lid*) tok. *Cf.* TIME.

PUTRIFY, TO—sea gajwak; (*to begin to, of vegetables*) kumblau.

PYRE, A FUNERAL—sara; (*corner-post of*) torre khunti.

PYTHON, A—buru dañgra, jambro, jamro; (*species of*) man baha.

Q

QUAGMIRE, A—dal, dalahi, daldalahi, dalhi.

QUAIL—(*to*) pucpuc; (*a*) bata, ghura (F), gundri, ore, tira (M); (*decoy*) gundri gahi; (*kind of*) huker gundri, huter gundri, kasi jera, kasi gundri; (*way of catching*) ser bata; (*patch on throat of*) dumil.

QUAKE, TO—lukur, pilpilau, saksak; (*with fear*) sirsirau, sisirau.

QUALITY—gun, mahatom, sil; (*of inferior*) au; (*impaired*) khidor.

QUANDARY, TO BE IN A—dhuku cuku, khuñju muñju.

QUANTITY—(*proper*) as; (*very small*) duknũč, hudu huduč, phusphas; (*a small*) culuñ, thora gan, katič culuñ, peseč (2), riñji, talañ; (*a large*) amela, bahi, cohol bohol, dadur, remhe regoč, thauka, titič; (*an immence*) dedar; (*so large a*) ehe ehe; (*in large*) hujlak, huluč (2), teretese; (*of grain threshed*) manda.

QUARREL, A—conda cundi, jhagra, kajia, khõc, lajbaj, lag, laua lagta, neao jhogra, ragar jhagar, thaica; (*to make up a*) samge.

QUARREL, TO—atã ãti, beke (2), bibad, contha cunthi, dhuna dhuni, jhogor, jigra jigri, kajia, kala jhagra, keñmeñ, kharhiau, laelaktha, laga, lage lore, laktha, laolokta, larhai, lektha, lokta, regeñ tegeñ, rego peto, repeč, ropor, ropor ropok, takrar, tegeñ; (*& strike each other*) kapta kapti; (*fiercely*) dhuñgra dhuñgri; (*with each other*) kharhia kharhi.

QUARRELER, A PERSISTENT—rograha (M), rograhi (F).

QUARRELING—bakhera, harka harki, khanda khandi, raga ragi; (*fiercely*) rañga rañgi; (*& threatening*) dhira dhiri.

QUARRELSOME—akhra akhri, cãe, cumdiñ (F), dharkat, dhĩtão, duraha, huteč, jhagraitha (F), jhagrahi, jhograhi, kadraha (M), kadrahi (F), kuteč, larañkar, londphondia, rograha (M), rograhi (F), suia, suipak, turphi.

QUARRY, A—dhiri gada, pokhoria khad.

QUARTER, A—pao; (*more*) sawa; (*direction*) seč, sen; (*seer*) pao.

QUARTERS, TO TAKE UP ONE'S—dirheč.

QUARTZ (*gravel*)—kañkar.

QUEEN, A—rani; (*great*) moharani; (*white ant*) bunum eñga.

QUELL, TO—kobjao, koboj.

QUESTION—(*a*) sawal, sowal; (*to*) khuriau, kuli, sawal; (*subject*) katha; (*to cross-*) jera, sowal; (*to repeat a*) tekhrao, thetha; (*to strictly*) kablau; (*to examine by*) kabla kabli; (*to settle a*) mimañsa.

QUEY, A—sandhin.

QUIBBLE, TO—phẽkphãk.

QUICK—catkan, chatkan, kharañ khacañ, taji; (*to be*) phurti; (*in movement*) hat chut, hath chuti; (*tempered*) kãiã, kãya, khacar, kharañ khacañ; (*to wound to the*) chorchorao; (*to be torn to the*) sirba.

QUICKLY—ahap cahap, ahrom pahrom, akardhak, andak tawak, andhi candhi, aruč patuč, bhac marte, bhoc marte, buč (2), cagae, cahal (2), cahar (2), camcam, cand, candaki, canduč, cão marte, catak mente, catapat, catpat, cemer (2), chae (2), chalak (2), cham (2), chat, chatpat, cogor, cotok, cunduñ, curamar, cure mare, curmar, dacañ (2), dahar (2), dandanao, daruk daćuk, daura dauri, demer (2), dhak, dhamdhaser, dhaora dhauri, dhaper, dhara dhari, dharae dhapae, dhardhur, dharpar, dhatpat, dhatar patar, digir (2), digladig, dirdir, dir dirau, doro (2), durmar, ekep sekep, ek taria, geser (2), ghusuṅ, gisir (2), got, hacar (2), hakophare, hakopako, hakup cakup, hala, haraṅ huruṅ, harephare, harmar, harum tarum, hatok, hatpat, hidić dikir, hojore, hot, huć (2), huć marte, hugui marte, huń mente, hupcak mente, hura huri, hurgus marte, hurmur, jãusa jãusi, jhak (2), jhap mente, jhatpat, jhãusa jhãusi, kacur macur, kalak, kharekhar, khuda khudi, kobor (2), kuyur (2), lacar (2), lećeć (2), mar, mardhar, marmar, ńire hojor, oryo potyo, pedel (2F), phat (2), phucuć, phurti, phus marte, pucuć, remhe regot, riat (2), ribir (2), satpat, taha tahi, tahbi, tahkabahka, talbi, tarak marte, tatka mar, torko morko, usara; (*very*) akabaka; (*of tall persons*) haruń patuń; (*of small persons*) tebeć (2M), tibić (2F); (*of small creatures*) pidil (2); (*of walking*) cemel (2), tambuć (2); (*of one impatient*) surma surmi, tarka irki; (*& indistinctly*) hodo dodo, lador bador; (*& easily*) lubur marte; (*& forcibly*) dagar, hujlak marte; (*& badly*) soto poto; (*to go*) daurau; (*to do*) satsut; (*to cause to do*) tagaja. *Cf.* TO MOVE.

QUICKSILVER—para.

QUICK WITTED (*of young persons*)—sarpharia.

QUID, A—khili.

QUIET—cãć cũć, capcup, dundur musak, gaemae, gambhir, gam gundur, gohle, isthir, mãhĩr, mesa, nijhum, sapot, supotia, supud; (*to*) dabruć, labhae lubhai, ropha; (*to become*) suman, thir; (*perfect*) gamgum.

QUIETLY—bhorma bhormate, capecupe, ghusuń (2), hać huć, hapać hupuć, jute (2), kalebale, phusuć (2), raste, rigam cagam, riṅgam ciṅgam, ruyu (2), same game, sanegumane, ugur sunduć; (*& meekly*) mormor.

QUILL FEATHERS ON A WING, THE FIRST THREE—kanso ik.

QUILTED CLOTH WORN BY WOMEN—dalpuń.

QUIRE OF PAPER—dista, jista.

QUIT, TO—bagi, teag.

QUITTANCE, A—pharkati.

QUIVER, TO—daldalao, dalkao, lipir (2), liplip, lukur, saksak, talmal, tolmol; (*as bog*) dalmal.

QUIVERING—dihil (2), juluć (2), lodo dhoro, lukur, saksak; (*of bog*) thalthal; (*as fat*) thaluk (2).

R

RABID—bhalok.

RACE—(*stock*) bõs, dahgi, jaro, jat; (*human*) manwa jat; (*to run a*) ńir haparao; (*with a*) khirir mente.

RACK & RUIN, TO GO TO—jarkhar.

RADIANCE FROM SUN BEFORE IT RISES—jholphol.

RADIATION—ahla.

RADISH, THE—mula arak.

RAFT, A—gharnai, suli.

RAFTER—borga; (*sapling as*) habka, rola, ruli, sener; *corner*) kolkand; (*strengthening*) sota; (*hook on*) baha carec; (*a support under*) pela; (*with thick end*) pacla sener; (*framework laid on*) chatãr.

RAG, A—cethra, cethreć, gendrak, gendreć, kethreć.

RAGE—tapis; (*to*) bekaeda, kisiau, kunkunau, seke (2), siki (2), tamtamao, targum; (*to, of fire*) bamka bamki.

RAGGED—gadrum, hedreć, jorpoć, khekre; (*& dirty*) gadroć sadroć.

RAGS—gendrak cethrak, gendrak cetrak; (*clad in*) gayur gapur, leder peder (F).

RAIL—(*a*) rel; (*wooden, a*) bindhar; (*at, to*) hengsta, tara tura.

RAILWAY—rel sorok; (*train*) rel gadi; (*fare*) rel bhara, rel masul; (*sleeper*) silpat.

RAIMENT, A CHANGE OF—palat.

RAIN—dak, serma dak; (*to*) dak, jeri; (*of rainy season*) japut; (*slight*) puhi; (*fairly heavy*) achar, chapar chupur, rajak (2); (*large drops of*) lacak pacak, ṭapać ṭipić; (*heavy continuous*) bor̤ok (2), jhamar jhomor, jhomor (2), nijhor, satahi; (*light continuous*) jhuṭuć; (*7 days'*) satahi; (*seasonable*) haṭhia japut; (*with E. wind*) halae (2); (*driven by wind*) jhaṭas; (*which falls with sun in sign Leo*) singh japut; (*to collect in clouds*) paghrao; (*a full supply of*) sawãe; (*heavily, to*) achal gańjal, jomkao; (*gently, to*) phuhi, puhi; (*sparks, to*) bhurbhuri; (*hat, a leaf*) chupi; (*bow*) liṭa ak; (*fine*) podor (2), rabać ribić, ribić, rubuć.

RAINY SEASON—japut, japut din, jarge japut, jarge, nadi nala din, nandi nala; (*beginning of*) adra.

RAISE, TO—alga, carhao, rem, tul, uṭhau; (*as dust*) loṭok, udiau; (*to upright position*) beret, teńgo; (*up*) ukhrau, uskau; (*up earth*) bhurkak; (*a matter*) ukti, upusti; (*with lever*) uṭkau; (*anew*) ghurpak, jhalao, utlau; (*the arm*) awil; (*corner of mat*) kuku; (*a dam*) bhokar; (*lever of dhinki*) rim; (*to strike*) epel; (*body to jump, &c.*) pidgić.

RAISED—(*as blister*) luṭluṭu; (*ground*) koṭko; (*up, to be*) aṭap uṭup; (*above surface*) laṭa luṭu.

RAKE UP OLD MATTERS, TO—khoṭa, uṭka paṭka, uṭkau paṭkau.

RAKISH—longor congor.

RAM, A—bheda, boda; (*with sprouting horns*) soso dereń bheda; (*horn of*) ramsinga, singa.

RAM DOWN, TO—gadao.

RAMPANT—matao.

RAMROD, A—gakdaoak, banduk gaj, kharcari.

RANCOROUS—dahgoria.

RANDOM, AT—akhar bakhar, alak balak, alam galam, andare pandare, andhe mandhe, andhe pathauri, angom, angot bangot, aṭ saṭ, at tot, badrak (2), baru soṭro, bhasa bharṭa, dhãk jiba, dhok jiba, jahã man tahã, jande mande, jundemunde, jane tane, pathauri; (*to talk*) bakbakaok, bhac bhacao, bheder (2), bhocbhocao.

RANGE, TO—dhankao, dhawa.

RANK—(*station*) darja; (*luxuriant*) toḥoć (2).

RANSOM, A—chakdao dam.

RAP, TO—koṭap, ṭhop (2); (*with stick on ground*) ṭhak ṭhok.

RAPID MOVEMENT, WITH ONE—rayul marte, sur marte.

RAPIDLY—akabaka, bhac marte, bhoc marte, candaki, canduć, caṭapaṭ, chão, curamar, dhatpat, digir (2), digla dig, dir dirau, geser (2), harephare, harmar, haṭpaṭ, kacur macur, khirkhirau, kuyur (2), mar, mardhar, ńire hojor, pedel (2F), phurti, riaṭ (2), taha tahi; (*of small creatures*) pidil (2); (*of walking*) ṭambuć (2).

RAPIER, A—dhup; (*long*) khenjer.

RAPPING SOUND—dhop (2), dhup marte, karap kurup, phidrak (2); (*loud*) ṭhańka ṭhorań; (*on ground*) dhap dhup; (*to make*) koṭap.

RARE—aprug, salas.

RASCAL, A—bodmas, dhurbaj, mara, nakaṭia.

RASCALLY—coar, copa kuṭa, corpoṭ, dhurbaj, harmad, luca (M), luci (F), nakaṭia.

RASH—(*of prickly heat*) balbal bhumbri; (*over body*) milmilia.

RASPING SOUND—sarak (2); (*with a*) sarak marte.

RAT, A—hon, musa; (*spec. of*) godo, murup godo; (*tree*) banwar; (*musk*) cund; (*bandicoot*) bhus; (*water*) gada godo; (*field*) cãuria hon, ergo; (*large*) sarnga hon, urić hon; (*opening of hole*) siniń, topoṭ; (*roof of hole*) phuṭ; (*track of*) goyon; (*squeal of*) cać cũć *Cf.* SQUEAKING.

RATE—bhao, bhao baṭa, dam, dor, dondam, nirik; (*to fix*) dor marao, nirik; (*to*) tara tura.

RATHER—bickom, borоń; (*than that*) samta, so bhal, so samta, so bickom, so borom.

RATIFY, TO—suhi.

RATTAN, A—bet.

RATTLE—(*to*) badar budur, hadar ṭhapar, hadbad, jham, jhanaṭ, rakrok, rekreć, rokor, rokroć; (*with a*) jhanar (2), rakrok marte, rekreć m., rodoe m., rogoe m., rokor m., rọkṛọċ m., ṭọpọr m.; (*inside, to*) rakar rokoṛ; (*in throat, to*) sakor; (*in throat, with a*) sọkọr marte.

RATTLING SOUND—bạdar buḍur, ḍhakọṛ (2), jhanar (2), jhumur (2), khaṛ khọṛ, paṛpaṛ, rodoe, rogoe; (*loose*) siṅkoṛ soṅkoṛ; (*of wood bell*) ṭọpọr.

RATTAT ON DRUM—beḍo (2), ḍọbẹ (2), ḍẹhẽk̀ (2), dhạtiṅtiṅ, dhundhạṛbheṭ, dhurumjak̀, ḍoḍom (2), kuṛuḍubu, kuṛum ḍubu ḍubu; (*at hunt*) ḍubu (2); (*to give alarm*) guhriạ.

RAVAGE, TO—mũhạ̃.

RAVAGED BY, TO BE—thalhalao.

RAVE, TO—bhasa bharṛa, bokao, kalobalo, kuṭnạsiṭ.

RAVEL, TO—ạrjhạu, ạujhạr.

RAVELLED—ajbuj, aṛjha ạṛjhi, baj; (*to be*) lạujhạ.

RAVEN—(*the*) bhọṇḍa kạhu: (*to*) caṅke, kaṭaha.

RAVENOUS—caṅke, cuṭ cuṭ, khãk, khaṅkhạilạ, rọkọṭ muhạ̃.

RAVINE, A—gaḍlak̀, khandhaṛ, khoṅja, nala, nạli, sọḍgọk̀, sọḍọk̀.

RAVINES & HOLLOWS—gaḍha sot.

RAW—(*unripe*) bẹrẹl, kãca, kạci, taj; (*stupid*) aẽ, albakaha, ạnaṛĩ, boka, gãowãr; (*of a sore*) bẹrẹl, garal (2); (*meat*) bẹrẹl jel.

RAYS OF SUN—rãt; (*direct*) setoṅ, tala setoṅ; (*indirect*) jẹḍẹr; (*level*) jhik jhikạ.

RAZOR, A—holaṭ.

RE-, AS IN RE-CALL—sạni.

REACH, TO—habṛao, tiok̀; (*cause to*) ṭesao, ṭhesao; (*unto*) ṭuṅgạu; (*up & pull down*) tiok̀.

REACHING EAR DOWN (*of clothes*)—jọbọk̀ (2), jọhọr, limạṅ lamaṅ.

READ, TO—paṛhao; (*& write, able to*) kagjia.

READILY—lẹcẹċ (2).

READINESS—(*in*) moteam; (*to be in*) johjohao, mohjam, mohṅjam, motaen, ṭhanṭhanao; (*to get in*) mohjut, sọmọl.

READY—tear, usṛau; (*to be*) aodhan, ghatghatao, khaṛa, mạhjud, ṭhak (2); (*to stand*) jujhạu; (*to get*) karao kuṛạu, sapṛao, taltul, tear, thul, thur, toenat; (*money*) nogda, nogda nogdi, roka; (—*not paying*) udhạr.

REAL—asọl, mul; (*fact, the*) mul katha

REALLY—ayã, ayã, baṅsẹ; (*exclm.*) eh, iyo; (*not*) jhuṭo puso.

REANIMATE, TO—jinạu.

REAP, TO—hahar, hatar, ir, irok̀; (*for immediate use*) ṭạmuṭi.

REAPPEAR, TO (*as disease*)—uswạu.

REAR—(*the*) kuḍạm; (*to be in the*) tayọm; (*bringing up the*) jhapaṭ; (*to*) pokhao, posao.

REASON—(*cause*) kaha kạhi, karne, karọn, mọtlọb, sabab; (*to*) gundi, khẹṅjẹr mẹṅjẹr; (*with, to*) samjhao; (*to accept a*) kar manao; (*for what*) kahe khạtir, kạhite; (*for that*) inạte, khạtir; (*for this*) khạtir, lasạṛhẽ; (*of, by*) kakhante, sabab; (*powers of*) suj; (*without*) ajlạtia, akha makha, alaṅ pholaṅ, andak, andap̀, bẹphokọṭ, bẹsabab, binhọk, dẹmạrịa, ḍhọrdhosaha, haknahak, họknak, khanakha, khanọkha, khomọkha, lọrọk (2).

REASONABLE—in gan, ọj mạphik; (*amount*) ọj.

REBEL, TO—haṅgam, hul; (*given to*) haoṛa.

REBELLION—(*the Santal*) hul; (*an exciter to*) huhuliċ; (*of the S.*) hạulạ; (*leaders of the S.*) subạ.

REBOUND, TO—chonṭal, phạnṭil, ṭhikrạ ṭhikri, ṭhikrạu.

REBUKE, TO—ḍạnṭao, dhamka dhạmkĩ, dhamkao, dhomkao, dhuṅgrạu, domkao, haba dubạ, hama homo, hantao, jobdao, kandhao, ram rọr, ruheṭ (M); (*both parties*) ḍaṭa ḍạṭi; (*used to*) ea.

RECALCITRANT—adọpiạ; (*to be*) adọp, ther.

RECEDE, TO—pạc; (*& carry along*) gheola.

RECEIPT, A—rạsid, uslạt; (*to give*) rạsid kaṭao; (*for money*) dạkhila; (*in full*) pharkạti.

RECEIVE, TO—ataṅ, hatao, milan, milạu, tela; (*not*) phus caṭao; (*& give necessaries to*) goras.

RECENT—hạli, nãwã, ṭạṭka, upriạ.

RECENTLY—sor dinre ; (*very*) ne.

RECEPTACLE, A—anatan ; (*for rice to be husked*) gad ; (*for storing rice*) kuṭhi ; (*of twisted leaf*) ṭoṭōrbaḱ ; (*for corn*) badaṛ ; (*for a charm*) madoli.

RECESS IN A WALL—kundhi, pakha.

RECITE, TO—bornon, paṛhao ; (*incantation over mustard seed*) tuṛi paṛhao.

RECKLESSLY—bhos (2).

RECKON, TO—joṛao.

RECOGNIZE, TO—baḍae, barnao, bheao, bichnau, cinhau, gamao, ńel orom, orom, pachan, pacnao, pharmao, phohom, phormao, pohom, poṛok, ṭaphim, ṭhohor, ṭohor, tuhkiḱ, tuphim ; (*each other*) ńepel ṭhipik, ńepel oprom, pacna pacni ; (*force of an argument*) bijau.

RECOIL, TO—laṭić.

RECOMPENSE—badla, hala hali, labhe, phaeda, phal ; (*to*) bodla, hala hali ; (*without*) jhuṭho.

RECONCILE, TO—manta, milaṕ, milau, milijili, ropha, samge, samjhao ; (*privately*) rapdhap.

RECONNOITRE, TO—bhidi.

RECORDS OF A COURT—misil, nathi, saristha ; (*place where kept*) saristha ; (*officer who keeps*) saristhadar.

RECOVER, TO—bancao ; (*from illness*) bes, bharuṛ, pharia, pharia phaṭi, pharnao, sarao, susto, taja, ṭamak ṭumak, ṭonko ; (*from serious illness*) jiweṭ bereḱ ; (*cause to*) jinau ; (*from season of distress*) jat jut ; (*flesh*) pheṭ ; (*one's senses*) nijau.

RECOVERED (*from illness*)—nikarkhar, pharia.

RECOVERY, TO BE PAST HOPE OF—japao, jobdao.

RECRIMINATE, TO (*of women*)—epeger.

RECRUIT, TO—bharti ; (*recover*) ṭonko.

RECRUITER, A COOLY—aṛkaṭhia.

RECUR, TO—acur soṛta.

RECUSANT—adopia, dundur ; (*to be*) adop.

RED—araḱ, rangia ; (*raw*) garal (2) ; (*to dye*) ńoḱ ; (*tinged with*) lopotian araḱ ; (*bright*) jengeḱ (2), joroń (2), ńenget ; (*slightly*) polso ; (*pigment for feet*) alta ; (*powder*) abir ; (*lead*) sindur ; (*lead, applying*) sindra dan ; (*ochre*) giru ; (*thread*) posta ; (*bordered cloth*) posta padlaḱ. *Cf.* SINDUR.

REDDISH—lopotian araḱ, polso araḱ, ranran ; (*brown*) gola (M), guli (F).

REDUCE, TO—adhi, jharao ; (*to subjection*) sad ; (*to ashes*) bhasam. *Cf.* POWDER.

REDUCED—jaro, jerbar ; (*to be*) jere (2), khasao ; (*in circumstances, to be*) alatoka, harsuṛ ; (*to last extremity*) ala mara, hapu hara.

REED, A—chuci ; (*kind of*) nanrata ; (*tall*) paṭio!

REELING—kandeḱ mandeḱ.

REFLECT, TO—(*think*) bicar, nandi gandi.

REFLECTED—(*image*) caher ; (*to be, as sound*) tapiń.

REFLECTION—(*shadow*) umul ; (*suspicion*) kalak ; (*thought*) phikir.

REFRACTORY—haruṛ.

REFRESH, TO—ṭhanḍha, tinjau.

REFRESHED, TO BE—cerṭha, judasi, ṭankao, ṭonko ; (*after fatigue*) jiwi ṭhanḍha, jiwi judasi.

REFUGE—aotan, asrae, par ; (*to take*) ad, mariau, od ; (*without*) bead.

REFULGENT—baran (2).

REFUND, TO—adai.

REFUSE—badra ; (*food*) baṭur saṭur ; (*from oil press*) kaṛe ; (*cotton*) makṭha ; (*after threshing*) kusṭa ; (*matkom*) gora.

REFUSE, TO—bac, bacao, badra, bań, mahrau, mohrao ; (*assent*) nakabul ; (*anything offered*) agra ; (*with disdain*) agra ; (*from ill-temper*) gajha gajhi.

REFUTE—loṭom.

REFUTED, TO BE—bhodor.

REGARD—mil, milua, rohom ; (*to*) hetao, kahlao, ucit ; (*of consequences, without*) aroṭ.

REGARDING—babotre, bisoe, reaḱ, reań, sombondre.

REGIMENT, A—khata, palṭon, phad.

REGISTER—(*a*) bahi, buhi ; (*an attendance*) hajri bahi ; (*to*) rejisṭari.

REGRET, TO—kasta kasti, kastao ; (*exclm. of*) ũhũḱ, uhu uhu.

REGULAR—barabar.

REGULATE, TO—bọndọbọs.

REIGN, TO—raj.

REINS—ras.

REINVIGORATE, TO—tiñjau; (*to be*) ṭọnkọ.

REITERATE, TO—tokraṛ.

REJECT, TO—bac, bacao, bad, bẹbạsut, bhọstọ, bostọ, duṛ, giḍi, phi, phiṭ; (*a complaint*) khạrij.

REJECTED—bhọdọr, bhọṭ, giḍi ore, rạdi, rudi.

REJOICE, TO—cakmakao, hulasok, khusi, kusi, rạskạ.

REJOICING—hạsi kusi, kusi, rạsik, rạskạ, sạhnạs; (*with*) rumbuć cumbuć, umjhạ umjhi, uṅjhạ uṅjhi.

RELAPSE, TO—(*of illness*) damsao, dohlao, uswạu; (*into jungle*) banwaṭ, bọnwaṭ.

RELATE, TO—barnan, bayan, bean, bean, binti, bọrnọn.

RELATED—(*by marriage*) larjar, loṛjor, naṛha joṛha, naṛjoṛ; (*remotey*) dak dak peṛa.

RELATION—sombond.

RELATIONS—ạpus, pạrbhạ, pạriba, peṛa pạrbhạ; (*near*) asọl peṛa, bhạiạdi; (*on father's side*) hadkuṛ; (*on mother's side*) mạmkuṛ; (*by marriage*) naṛhạ joṛha; (*sarcastic*) sodaram; (*not*) aramin; (*without*) bẹmar, bẹmurạd, eka jiba, ẹk jibạ.

RELATIONSHIP—nata sutạ, sạgai, sampak, sọmpọk; (*by marriage*) naṛjoṛ, bapla tọpọl sạgai; (*to assume*) nata; (*to establish*) cinparco; (*to elder brother's wife*) hilia; (*between children of sisters*) mamạsi; (*of wives of brothers or cousins*) natea; (*of parents-in-law*) bala, saka; (*of wife's father & husband's uncles*) kaka bala; (*of in-laws*) landa sạgai; (*of brother & sister-in-law*) ḍhạuliạ; (*to husband of elder sister*) teṅa, teṅaea, teṅa era; (*assumed*) ato sạgại peṛa; (*of husbands of sisters*) sadge, sạdhu; (*between grandfather & child*) tataea.

RELATIVE, A—kuṭum, peṛa; (*near*) boeha; (*distant*) dak dak peṛa; (*blood*) nij peṛa.

RELATIVES—*Cf.* RELATIONS.

RELAY, A (*of horses or palki-bearers*)—ḍak.

RELENTLESS—kaṭhor, kaṭ jibạ, kumaya.

RELIANCE—bharsa.

RELIEF—aosan, par, rạkhia, rihại, rukhiạ, salsat; (*to get*) usạs; (*to give*) aosan, usạs.

RELIEVE, TO—rạkhia, rukhiạ; (*one of property*) cokcanda.

RELIEVED, TO BE—khalsa, ṭankao; (*from encumberance in stomach*) khạlis.

RELIGION—dhọrọm, din.

RELIGIOUS—bhakti; (*merit*) pun; (*rite, to perform*) puruchun; (*service, to join in or conduct*) girjạ.

RELINQUISH, TO—istopa.

RELINQUISHED, TO BE—mạhkup, mạkup, mukup.

RELISH—(*to*) tarkao; (*of meat, a*) jel utu; (*for, to lose*) kọsẹć, mọkọṅ; (*without*) licaṅ picaṅ, paṅgat (2), pasak; (*for, having no*) ọgọroj.

RELUCTANTLY—ẹskõs, kọrọć mọṭọć, lạriạ pạriạ, licaṅ picaṅ.

RELY ON, TO—as, hirlạ.

REMAIN, TO—(*be over*) bacọl, lẹoṭhẹ, sarẹć; (*stay*) tahẹn, ṭahrao, ṭarhao, thambhao, ṭhaṭhao, ṭikạu.

REMAINDER—bạki bọkọea, kasar, sarẹć barẹć, satarẹć.

REMAINING—(*very little*) leha lihi, lihạ lahe; (*what is*) sarẹć barẹć.

REMEMBER, TO—bundis, disạ, ead, eyad, gamao, kheas; (*with affection*) uihạr.

REMEMBRANCE—naenam, nam cintạ; (*a*) cikhnạ.

REMISS, TO BE—hela hili.

REMIT, TO—(*of rent &c.*) minạ.

REMITTANCE—calan.

REMNANT—kasar, res, sarẹć barẹć; (*of beast's kill*) harbhaṅj, siṅ muṇḍ.

REMONSTRATE, TO—mana, ram roṛ.

REMOTE—taphat, tophad; (*relative*) dak dak peṛa.

REMOVE, TO—chadạo, họsẹć, kaṭao, kaṭić, ọcok, odhrao, odrao, oṭak, sorao; (*by stick*) hoṭak; (*outer covering*) sala; (*by pushing or pulling*) ṭarao; (*from place to place*) ncar; (*as water falling on earth*) sidgir; (*silk-worms from tree to tree*) capan; (*a lid*) oṭak.

RENAL DISEASE—karṛa, koṛṛa, ṭan korṛa.

REND, TO—charchar, ciṛa, ciṛi çunṭhi, ciro, ụrẹć, tarar; (*sound of*) ceṭ ceṭ; (*the heart*) chạti jarao.

RENEGADES—pạcko.

RENOUNCE, TO—istopa; (*all claim*) dạbinas.

RENT—agotar, bhaṛa, jama, jọma, keraya, khajna, mạhsul, malgujari, masul; (*to*) bhaṛa; (*yearly amount of*) jama, jọma; (*house*) oṛak masul; (*paying*) mal; (*free*) ulphạ; (*& cesses*) khajna bajna; (*additional assessment on*) bhẹja.

RENT, A (*tear*)—bañ bañ, dar; (*to make a big*) pañpaṇḍrañ.

REPAIR, TO—jaba juba, jate jute, jutjat, maramat, meramọt, moramot, sudhar, sudhrau, torajut; (*thatch*) oriao.

REPAST, A SLIGHT—jọlpan.

REPAY, TO—ạdai, ẹm hála, hala, phujạu, usul; (*a debt*) torao; (*borrowed things, not to*) hajam.

REPEAT, TO—ghuri phiri, rigdạu, tokrar; (*in comp.*) aro; (*tell*) lai; (*a question*) tekhraọ. *Cf.* MEMORY.

REPEATEDLY—dẹmẹdọm, ghane (2), hole (2), holo (2), jaoge (2), kane (2), tatle mar, tereṭ boreṭ; (*to do*) idor bidor.

REPENT, TO—kastao, pachtao.

REPERCUSS, TO—tạpiń.

REPLETION, TO (*of children*)—ruṭyuṭ.

REPLY—jabab, jobab dạhi, juạb, utar; (*to*) jobab, kakale, rọr ruar; (*to a call, a*) oi; (*sullenly, to*) as us; (*testily, to*) baṭañ (2), beṭeñ (2), carap (2).

REPORT, A—(*rumour*) bakhara, bhakara; (*sound*) awaj; (*of gun*) dhae; (*false*) bhakara; (*of good*) lohạni; (*well known by*) jana suna; (*to cause a*) ṭhu; (*to spread as*) unạn.

REPOSE, TO—thọl.

REPRESENTATION, A—(*likeness*) bọ̃họk, chand, chond, chin, naksa; (*to make*) ọrọj, ujur; (*of trees &c. on walls*) likhọn gọrhọn.

REPRESS, TO—kabja, kabọj, kạbu; (*one's desires*) jiwi hatar.

REPRIMAND, TO—ram rọr.

REPROACH—kalak, khọṭ; (*to*) bẹman, kạdhao, khạdao, tara tura.

REPROOF—nisrauna.

REPROVE, TO—haba duba, mana.

REPUDIATE, TO—dhatka, dodao.

REPULSED, TO BE—haṭkao.

REPULSIVE—barṭañ.

REPUTATION—dhọrọm kọrọm, jọs, man; (*to make*) ńutum harjọñ; (*of no*) jọ̃ć.

REQUEST—arja ạrji, arọj; (*to*) bab.

REQUIRE, TO—jarur.

REQUIREMENTS FOR A CEREMONY—sańjok, solo sańjok, sonjok.

REQUITE, TO—badla, badla bạdli, gun manao, nun gun manao.

RESCUE, TO—dak, oar, rạhạu; (*one who*) okwarić.

RESEMBLANCE—ḍhạṭ, mohṇḍa, muṭhạn, urgạn; (*close*) chanban, chonbon.

RESEMBLE, TO—tić.

RESEMBLING—barag, barak, macha, mạphik, mạpik.

RESENTMENT, TO HARBOUR—kunkunạu.

RESERVE, WITHOUT—ṭhak ṭhọk, ṭhañka ṭhorañ.

RESERVED—(*taciturn*) bukṭan, dundur musạk, gạdia, gamgundur, gasać gusuć, gọhle, mesa

RESERVIOR, A—ahra, band; (*small*) gạdia.

RESIDE, TO—ḍharao, kạmbhir, tahẹn, thạwi.

RESIDENCE—basa, girạbas, mokam, nao ṭhikạn, thamgạdi, thạnit; (*to take up*) basgạdi, bọskọt, girạbas, bẹrẹl japak, mạṇḍao, thamgạdi; (*to change*) dar, gẹndher; (*to fix one's*) gạdiạu; (*to be in*) thawi; (*of zemindar*) garh; (*particulars of*) nao ṭhikạn; (*those in original*) buniạdi hoṛko; (*to change often*) ucar nacar.

RESIDUE—bạdra, res.

RESIGN A SITUATION, TO—istopa.

RESILIENT—ṭhikra ṭhikri.

RESOLUTE, TO BE—bhuc bhuci, muruk, ṭhanaọ, ṭhukạu.

RESOLVE, TO—goṭa.

RESOURCE—bāh, kut; (*to be without*) asusar, hapu hara, osusar, lacar; (*without*) aṭpaṭ, ayak oyok, jale thale, nacar, nacaria; (*full of, of females*) hunar, hunaria.

RESPECT—man, murad, murwad, tamai, thap; (*to*) basut, batao, con, ganao; (*to shew*) manot, marjad, morjad, pucau; (*a term of*) baba, hujur; (*to, to pay*) gadhnao, manao, maswar.

RESPECTABLE—bhal, bhale (2), bhodran, bhodro, darmal, khamid, madhās, mandhas, manotan, manotia, pordhan; (*to become*) manus man.

RESPECTING—babotre.

RESPITE—aosan, bacol, koljol, talbhaṅ, uphaṅ; (*to give or get*) usas.

RESPLENDENT—bilik balaṅ, ḍigḍig, jhalmal, jhikimiki, jikimiki, pirit, ṭhonok.

RESPOND, TO—ragbag.

RESPONSIBILITY—bhar, dae, dahi, gara, hae dae, jabab dahi, jobab dahi; (*to accept*) arār, gae makhao; (*to take*) aṅgikar, aoda, dipil, jabab dahi emok, teṅgo; (*on, to throw*) bohok; (*of giving account*) jawab dahi; (*free from*) elak chada; (*to transfer to another*) henda hindi.

RESPONSIBLE—dayik; (*to be*) sen hamalok; (*not*) ilak chada.

REST—bacol; (*to*) ḍaba mara, dom, jirau, dhōk marao, ṭahrao, ṭarhao; (*on, to*) athrẽ; (*on each other, to*) tepen; (*during heat of day*) kharaori; (*on journey, place of*) chauni.

RESTIVE—dhacrar, erce perce, kharnaha, kharu paṭu; (*to be*)kacmacao, kecmecao, khaṭpaṭ, kicmic, mecka micki.

RESTLESS—akal sakal, aṭpaṭ, bethir, bhacaṅ bhucuṅ, bonwaṭ, caṅmaṅgao, chaṭpaṭ, chaṭpaṭia, concol, culuṅ bhuṭuṅ, cunḍul bhuṭul, cuṅgur muṅgur, gayaṅ guyuṅ, ghuṭ (2), halbal, halbalia, haṭya, hucku cukur, ikil sikil, kharu paṭu, khaṭ khuṭ, khaṭpaṭ, olocolo, pidić (2), utpat; (*to be*) bikla bikli, bikol, caṭpaṭao, chaṭpaṭao, kharbarao, phaṭak phuṭuk, phirphir; (*of hungry infant*) pakas pukus; (*from anger*) siki (2); (*from cold*) ukur sukur; (*from heat*) aka baka; (*& mischievous*) saṭsuṭ, utpaṭia; (*& staring about*) cuṅgur muṅgur.

RESTLESSNESS—bandor bai.

RESTORE, TO—phirau.

RESTRAIN, TO—dabao, ḍaboṭ, dabruć, dobnao, gurgur, jabdo, jabid, jabed, kabej, kabu, sambrao, tambhao; (*grief*) jiwi ten.

RESTRAINT—rohom; (*self*) dhirja; (*without*) bahbah, khaji, nirdhok.

RESULT—ae upai, gunak, jo, phal, phol; (*without*) lorkaeni.

RESURRECTION, THE—jiwet beredok.

RETAIN, TO—doho; (*what is for others*) ameṭ, hameṭ; (*food*) jirau.

RETARD, TO—leṭaṅ, letar; (*as recovery from illness*) uswau.

RETCH, TO—doyok, okok, uchlau.

RETREAT—aotan; (*to*) haṭkao.

RETRIBUTE, TO—pholao.

RETRIBUTION—hala hali.

RETURN—(*a*) bapha, ras; (*full*) rasi puṅji; (*to yield or obtain a*) posan; (*to give nothing in*) jom unum; (*for, in*) kar; (*of seed sown, not to give*) bic mara; (*after deductions*) phirot.

RETURN, TO—acur, hala, em hala, nacur, phirau, phirot, ruar; (*go back*) lauṭau; (*cause to*) ruar; (*of a loan*) hala, phujau; (*as illness*) uswau.

RETURNING—ghuri.

REVEAL, TO—lai sodor; (*as much as is convenient*) jetho.

REVELRY, FOND OF—irić cikić.

REVENGE—badla, ken; (*to take*) badla badli, badla hala, kasur jharao, sadhao; (*full of*) dahgoria, hisalia.

REVERBERATE, TO—dalmal, dildilau, duldul, rāoāo, tapiṅ.

REVERBERATION—dildil; (*loud*) ribir.

REVERENCE—tamai.

REVERSE—ulta; (*to*) ultau; (*of what is right*) lur na bhas, ulta, ultau, ulti.

REVILE, TO—bhades, dhuṅgra dhuṅgri, nindau.

REVIVE, TO—cetha, jinau, jiwet, jiwet ruar, tiṅjau.

REVOLVE, TO—ạcur, bharbharao, bhẹrbhẹr, bhẹrbhẹrao, bihur, gaṛgaṛao, ghaṛghaṛao, ghuṛghuṛạu, nạcur.

REVOLVING—(*swing, a*) hiṇḍol; (*easily*) kalgar.

REWARD—kuṛại. [luban.

REZIN—dhũṛã; (*of Boswellia seratta*)

RHEUM FROM THE EYES—beṅjak̓.

RHEUMATISM—bat; (*of joints*) gạṭhiạ bat; (*muscular*) sir bat.

RHINOCEROS, THE—gaṇḍ garuṛ.

RHYTHMICAL—gọḍọp̓ (2).

RIB, A—pañjar, pạñjri; (*the 5th*) ibil pañjar.

RIBS—pạñjri; (*under the*) kokha; (*side below*) pạni kokha, pokha; (*of umbrella*) catọm pạñjri.

RICE—an, hoṛo, khorca; (*to sift*) ãiṭạu; (*to cook*) daka; (*husked*) caole; (*boiled*) daka, hoṛo daka, kak̓; (*cooked*) daka, mạṇḍi; (*well cooked*) biḍiṛ (2); (*uncooked*) kharca; (*insufficiently cooked*) mañja; (*parched*) khạjạṛi, khoi, tabẹn; (*unhusked*) hoṛo, huṛu; (*not well husked*) beṇḍer; (*stale cooked*) jọjọ jhara; (*an ear of*) gẹlẹ; (*water*) dak̓ mạṇḍi, daka mạṇḍi; (*to cook along with*) sure; (*cooked in milk*) khir; (*cooked with flour*) dạtri; (*boiled before husking*) usnạ; (*broken in husking*) caole khode, mạrkhu; (*given by bridegroom*) cạḍi caole; (*pest, a*) bạki; (*to thin out*) gạchiạu. *Cf.* LIQUOR.

RICE-FIELD, A—khẹt; (*high*) bhetṛa bhiṭri; (*always moist*) buhi khẹt, ḍabar, ḍaber, ḍabra, ḍhab, gahḍa, jạṛhi khẹt; (*wood used to level*) rakhsa; (*a valley of*) sokṛa, soṅgha; (*3rd. ploughing of*) jabọḍ; (*ridge round*) aṛe; (*on a slope*) karnạli.

RICE-LAND—ahar, jạmi, jạmin, jumi; (*high*) bhetṛa bhiṭri, goḍa hoṛo; (*large area of rich*) jumi sagọr; (*reclaimed by dam*) hiṛ; (*reclaimed at own expense*) khạṇḍet, khạṇḍit, khãṛti, khũṭ kaṭa; (*newly reclaimed*) loeya khạṇḍit; (*with plenty water*) bohal, jubhi; (*dependant on rain*) sate sote; (*small plot of*) ṭopra; (*3rd. class*) bad; (*1st. class*) bạihaṛ; (*to divide*) rekhja.

RICE-PLANT—hoṛo, huṛu; (*an ear of*) sisi; (*wild*) dal, uṛi h.; (*black*) heṇḍẹ koeya, murchi h.; (*varieties of*) ạgnisạr, ạrhạiạ, bạd kolma, bạdrạs, bag aenom, bag pañjar, bajal, bana koṛam, basmạti, benaphul, bhạdoe, bhasa, bhuṇḍi kolma, boaṛdạl, boaṛi, boro h., candar gạhi, ciṅgul, ciṅgul, ḍahar, dhusri, dubrạj, dudhkạni, ghisạli, gitạ, gọẹṭhasar, gopal, gopal bhog, guhmạ, guiphạ rạṅgi, gurpạ, hemca, jagarnath, jạli h., jaṭa h., jãwãe lạḍu, jhagṛa h., jhagṛi h., jhaṛa, jhiṅgạ sạl, kadolia, kạjri, kạmạni, kanakcur, karhạni, kạribạṅki, kạrimsạl, kạsi phul, kele, khetorni, kọdọm sạr, koeya h., kolma h., koya h., lachman, lachman bhog, loton, macnothor, mahadeb, mahadeb jaṭa, maloti, mohan mala, mohipal, moticur, mugdi, musur, nạgi, nanha, narda, nona, parmonosạl, pasa, patnại, puṭki, raebundi, raemundi, raja muni, rajmohal, rajpol, ramsạl, rạṅgi, rạnki h., rạtuạ kaṇḍa, rọkọt cọndọn, rudhin, sal muṅgạr, sạmundar phen, sạṭhi h., sitạsạl, sundor mukhi, suruj muni, ṭaṅgabeṭ, tilạ sạr, til kancan, tulsi phul, tarsi phul, uṛi h.; (*a blight of*) ṭạku.

RICH—aṇḍela, ạṇḍiạ, anẹć dhanẹć, asẹć tasẹć, bạrião, bạriạu, bhal bhal, bhale (2), bhogdo, bhuṭela, dhanghar, dhanghara, ḍheke, dhunin, ganganea, itil, jọbọr, khabela, moṭa, rạsiãu, talebor, tạliạu, telgar, thakaman, tuli; (*of soil*) sargat, ṭạsil; (*to become*) kisãṛ, umbrạu; (*man, a*) kisãṛ, nabab, nawab; (*men*) kipisãṛ. [paloe.

RICK, A—cake, paloe; (*to make into*)

RICOCHET, TO—phạṇṭil.

RIDDLE, A—kudum.

RIDE ROUGHSHOD, TO—ãrgọm, laga.

RIDER, A—aswạriạ, sowar, sowari.

RIDGE, A—rindiṛ, riṛ, sindiṛ; (*dry*) ṭonḍañ; (*of rice-field*) aṛe, pindhạ; (*of earth*) pãuchi; (*to dam water*) mande; (*break in*) khạṇḍọ; (*of roof*) mạrkoca; (*tiles*) magra, mogra, moṅgra; (*pole*) mundhạn, muri khuṇṭi, mutul pạṛ; (*formed by back-bone*) bisi riṛ.

RIDICULE, TO—hapsi, monj, nisrau.

RIDING, ACT OF—aswar, aswari, sowari.

RIFT, A—phāk.

RIGHT—(*correct*) cahiye, dhorom, hak, heke, hike, hok, jothat, majbut, manjgut, sombhob, thik, thik thak; (*claim*) adol, hak, sat, sot; (*opp. to left*) etom, jojom; (*to be*) jutrau; (*to have the*) amda; (*to make*) sudhrau, thik thak; (*more than is*) jauri; (*hand, the*) dahin, dahna, etom ti, jojom ti; (*hand, to leave on*) dahinau; (*to turn to*) gengahi; (*& left*) etom kõnye; (*angles, at*) gand (2); (*angles, to place at*) gande; (*angle, not a*) ayar, toe.

RIGHTS, TO PUT TO—jatejute, jatjut, jhala jhali, jutjat, jutrau, sudhar, sudhrau.

RIGID—kekercan, kerker, ketkete; (*to become*) kikircit, tarkhao, tenten.

RILE, TO—chorchorao.

RIM, A—kankha, kankhi, khankha; (*of a net*) kundli; (*having a piece out of*) kheco, khecro, kherco; (*without*) mirũ, moidon, mondon; (*round bottom a vessel*) bindi.

RIND—coklak; (*of fruit*) baklak, cokak; (*to break the*) cokhlao; (*of kũindi*) bakre.

RING—(*to*) thok; (*with a*) taran marte, thae m., thin m., thoe m., thun m., tun m.; (*a finger*) mundam; (*marriage*) bapla mundam; (*a finger or toe*) thikari; (*a toe*) ãotha, bichia; (*an ear*) cepre, makori, pagra; (*on birds' neck*) gerwel; (*an iron, to yolk cattle*) halka; (*a nose*) nat, nath, nathni, not.

RINGING SOUND—dhun (2), ririn, taran, thae, thin, thoe; (*of different tones*) thae thui; (*of small bell*) timpi tirin.

RINGWORM—sukri bãrã, dad.

RINSE, TO—bohoe; (*out*) budoc; (*off*) bohoe gidi; (*the mouth*) budruc, hutum; (*mouth & wash face*) acak; (*the hair*) jian.

RIOT—hulmal, kando; (*to*) hangam, hul.

RIP, TO—(*up*) bhoskao; (*with tusks*) hotak.

RIPE—bele, pakr, pakot, pakta; (*to be*) jowao; (*half*) demba, dembe; (*nearly*) gadar, parpande; (*fully*), bele har, bele jara, bele jaru, jarum; (*over*) bele liduena, bele lahaena, boram, har, jhurãt, lambo, lasak pasak, lemtok.

RIPEN, TO—bele, gele belek, lidu; (*after plucking*) goso bele, borea bele; (*within sheath*) kope; (*beginning to, of grain*) lendet moca; (*beginning to, as fruit*) pendko.

RIPENING—araraok; (*just before*) patarak.

RIPPING, SOUND OF—satak sutuk.

RIPPLING—bohor (2), hewel bekel, lipir (2).

RISE, TO—beret, lutlutu, rakap, uskau; (*up*) bhulkau, phurkau; (*as prices*) coranti; (*in bubbles*) bidic (2), buruc (2); (*& fall, as water*) capel, dulup (2), dundun, habak dabak; (*straight up*) kutla; (*to surface*) phinau, uplau, utlau; (*to surface at a distance*) putak; (*into sight*) tayal tuyul; (*to surface & float*) uphlau, uphla uphli; (*in social position*) tuli; (*& descend*) dap dup; (*to, to give*) upcan.

RISING—(*& falling*) dombal dombol, doyol (2); (*above surrounding surface*) domdom, latkum, ut utu. *Cf.* GROUND.

RISK LIFE, TO—jiwi kotok, jiwi alae.

RITES—acar; (*burial*) bidhan, ganga gaya, kaj korom, kandkathi, kathoria.

RIVALRY—bada badi, hara hari, hata [badi.

RIVER, A—gada, nai; (*large*) dariau; (*small tributary*) saba; (*deep place in*) darha; (*bend in*) kucel; (*true course of*) ret; (*traditional*) sora nai; (*the Damuda*) nai; (*& forest*) gada mundu; (*junction*) domuhani, dul midok.

ROAD, A—bat, hor, rah, rasta, sorok; (*a difficult*) behor; (*made by use*) dahar; (*rough*) dharkak dhorkok, gadha godho; (*macadamised*) paki sorok; (*earth*) kaci sorok; (*to take the*) dahrao; (*cess*) rod ses.

ROAM, TO—cundul bhutul, dhankao, dhawa.

ROAR, TO—(*of wild beast*) guṅjrau, gurgur, hadur (2), handrao, hudhudau, taras; (*as tempest*) harhar; (*of fire or flood*) gudur (2), hudhud, hudhudau, phorphor.

ROAST, TO—andak, rapak; (*beans &c.*) odo; (*grain*) ata; (*peas, to half*) ala.

ROB, TO—lut, lutpat, metoc; (*one who*) daku, lutia.

ROBUST—datmot, rehlam sehlam, susurtak.

ROCK—(*large flat*) catani; (*very large*) hutuk; (*in river bed*) raro; (*about, to*) dildal.

ROCKET, A—saragbati.

ROCKY (*as river-bed*)—rogor.

ROD, A MEASURING—arani daṅ, gaj.

ROGUE, A—natkhat; (*little*) kherwec mara gidra; (*buffalo*) bayar.

ROLL, TO—darrao, dardarao, gargarao, ghargharao, gurgau, khirkhirau, peresaṅ; (*in walking*) dhakar dhokor, ladak luduk, ladhar lodhor; (*down*) dhardhar; (*on ground*) ersen torsec, gholtao, girgirau, gudrau, gurgurau, gurkau, uru kundel; (*over one another*) garda gurda, lapta lapti; (*up*) garha gurhe, gurhe, merhao, peprẽt, totro; (*in dust*) gholta, gholta ghulti; (*of thunder*) harhar; (*into small compass*) korea motea; (*into ball*) gulu mulu; (*food into ball*) lakop; (*about*) bidbidau, latpat; (*from side to side*) lebda libdi, ulta ulti; (*about in globules*) thal (2), thol (2); (*a muster*) hajri bahi; (*to make into a*) peprẽt; (*of drums, with a*) taraṅ marte.

ROLLED UP—cuikup; (*as a scroll*) totro.

ROLLER, A CLOTH—tur.

ROLLING—ghar gharia, tiha tahe; (*along*) halak dalak; (*of thunder*) hudur (2); (*of drums*) taraṅ; (*to break to pieces by*) gasmandao.

ROMP, TO—makmak.

ROOF—cal, chapri, chat, chauni, sarim; (*to*) sarim; (*projecting*) sate; (*ridge of*) markoca; (*tax*) chapar bandhi; (*tile*) khapra, khaprol; (*a lean-to*) cari; (*centre post of*) kham khunti. *Cf.* BEAM.

ROOFED—(*shed, a*) duara orak; (*steep*) dharshi.

ROOM—(*a*) hudra, kuthri; (*not enough*) sakra, sakra sakri; (*& stead, in*) bodol; (*in verandah, a small*) khundri.

ROOMY—phael, phaela, samil.

ROOT—buda, buta, da, phedat, rehet, tali; (*aerial*) joro; (*to take*) birhau, rehet; (*to, of swine*) uta; (*the tap*) mul rehet; (*an edible*) ahra, at, dura saṅ, kalo; (*tuber, a*) da, jhal da. *Cf.* MEDICINAL.

ROOTED—(*up, to be*) ukhrau; (*as if*) jekre, jerpẽret, jerpet, jopjopo.

ROOTS—(*to tear up by*) tarao; (*used for food*) jar mar; (*digging instrument for*) khurpa.

ROPE, A—(*thick*) barahi; (*straw*) bor; (*thin straw*) sikol; (*to plait straw in*) bor galaṅ; (*for tying animal in stall*) jora; (*hair*) sili; (*to lead by*) tiak; (*like*) tiroc toroc; (*to twist 3rd strand into*) carhi; (*to tighten*) jhik; (*yoke*) jote; (*to twist a*) merao; (*wound round bandi*) ojha.

ROSARY, A—udraṅ mala.

ROSELLE PLANT, THE—ambaro, arak kudrum.

ROSY—joroṅ (2).

ROT, TO—sea; (*off*) budur, gandrao ṅurok, garao; (*to begin to*) lambao.

ROTATE, TO—bherbher.

ROTATION, IN—pali pasari.

ROTTEN—gandrao, phophra, phoska, poca, poch, podra, sarlaha, sea; (*inside*) ponda; (*ness*) jaṅruli.

ROTUND—soroc; (*as stomach*) rata rutu; (*not, of goats & swine*) sõrga; (*equally*) sondmond.

ROUGH—apa baria, bandra, cacarhat, cardak burdak, cedro, cocraha, gadlak godlok, gadrum sadrum, ghat ghut, harcat horcot, hatap hutup, jhador pador, jharhoehak, jharoeak, jobodhon, kãca, kanda kondo, katha kothe, khadrak khodrok, ragae, ragṛe (2), ragat, ragda rogdo, ragha rogho, ragha roṅgho, rape, rege cege, rodga, rodgo, rodot, rogda, rogda rogdo, sadga badga, saegat, sirgat, sodo bodgo, sodo rodo, sodo (2), sodro bodro, sudro budro, ubar khabar; *(as sheep)* gadrum; *(of speech)* ragat cogat; *(of hair)* raguisak, ragumcak, ramcam, rudrudu; *(to become, of skin)* rorot; *(as sculpture)* badgok (2); *(skin)* atpa etpe; *(& uneven)* darkak dorkok, dharkak dhorkok, dumdumi, gadha godho; *(surface)* jhargoeak, sardum bardum, seder beder; *(& stony)* ragar rogor, rigor rogor, rogro; *(feeling)* har; *(voiced)* kharan khurun, ronkhon; *(hew, to)* pahtao; *(headed)* dhapra (M), dhapri (F), riskit; *(from things sticking up)* sadgum badgum, saga rore, sege rore.

ROUGHLY—kharan khurun, sidi bidi, sithasare; *(harshly)* karra, regen (2); *(as plaster)* thorothopo; *(executed)* jhador pador, jharoeak, sede bede, sedge bedge; *(speaking)* angom, regen (2F).

ROUND—dumdumdhukak, dumka, gol, gudmuc (2), guland, gulu mulu, gurmuria; *(to turn)* acur; *(about)* anacur, bera biri, berhae, bilhau, gota tandi, laphan, pakar; *(small bodies, a lot of)* sege rore; *(shouldered)* katbuc, kojo, kutbuc. *Cf.* ONCE.

ROUSE, TO—busku, siklau cariau, uskur; *(anger)* saniau; *(to be)* jhũkau.

ROUT, TO—bagdao, thasiau.

ROW, A—*(line)* panta, pante, pata, pati, rada, thar; *(noise)* bakhera, galgul; *(in a)* ret rete; *(of thatch, a)* ager; *(to make a noise)* andka andki, andor, galgalao; *(to, with an oar)* ghanta.

ROWS, IN—atal, dorpha (2), pante, thar, thar ke thar, thara thar, thare thar.

ROYALTIES—mahsul; *(at ghat, one who receives)* ghatwek.

RUB, TO—gasao, ghasao, ghasar, ragdao, ragrao, rogdao; *(on, as oil)* ojok; *(between finger & thumb)* tirmit; *(of clothes)* har; *(off the skin)* bhongar, bhondor, khal; *(body or limbs)* iskir, malan, mardao, paendao; *(off a bit)* potak; *(in hands)* tirhol; *(the eyes)* itkit, tirhol; *(on a stone)* urut; *(against anything)* gasrao; *(against one another)* ghasa ghasi; *(teeth with fingers)* hurtir.

RUBBED, OFF, TO BE—bondor, cotak.

RUBBING BODY WITH HANDS, SOUND OF—rahat pahat, rohot pohot.

RUBBISH—gadrum sadrum, gandaura, garda, jabra, jaejumdha, judha, kadar kapar, katua, ladauri, rata pata, sambhaora, turutuka; *(heap of)* dangaura, gandaura, lenjhar; *(lying about house, &c.)* abjor, hur, jaejumdha, jobra, kata katua.

RUDE—tethor, thethor; *(to be)* badagiri.

RUDDER OF BOAT—cupi.

RUE—arud.

RUFFLED—dhunsi punsi, jhargoeak, latae ghotae, risrisi; *(feathers)* bomborket.

RUFOUS—podgoe.

RUG, A—satrangi; *(sleeping)* dari.

RUIN—halak, sorbonas; *(to)* baric, bosto, dhandhaser, josao, kankhar, khankhar, landur bhandur, mulehabad, murahan, nas, nosto, obosta, uchad, ujar, upar khapar, uran; *(crops by grazing, to)* haler; *(to go to)* bhangor; *(to meet with)* jarkhar, landbhandao.

RUINED—baric, bemal, berbad, dhangladhas, kharap; *(to be)* babilond, bebilond, behal, bhosto, dhargoc, halak, kheanat, tutau.

RULE—ari, niam, rai; *(as a)* bastobik, dherkaete; *(a foot)* gaj; *(to make for oneself)* acarok, acar bicar.

RUMBLE, TO—duldul, gargarao, gudgud, harhar; *(of stomach)* bhat bhut.

RUMBLING SOUND—atap utup, hadhud, haras; *(in stomach)* karkur; *(a succession of)* ladlad.

RUMOUR—bhakara, birtant, gap, udacal, udau, uphar; *(to spread a)* goga; *(to spread as a)* unan.

RUMPLE, TO—phidli, dharpilak.

RUN, TO—atu, dar, gender, nir; *(of a sore)* birin (2), galgalao, piric (2); *(as king's writ)* bohao; *(away with)* atkir; *(here & there)* barac buruc, bid bidau, dar dhup; *(out)* bikor bukor, hoshesao; *(up a bill)* dhar; *(fast)* digdig; *(gently, of liquid)* lingi; *(at moderate pace)* lujhuk (2); *(a race)* nir haparao; *(over)* hiric;

(*& jump about*) kuhup kudup ; (*away*) pạnduć ; (*into as thorn*) sorlok ; (*down, to be*) ala ạli.

RUNNER—(*a village*) dạuṛaha ; (*a postal*) ḍakwalla.

RUNNING—bạhi ; (*over*) baha bạhi ; (*water*) bohi dak, buhi dak ; (*noose*) phạsi gạli, pạsi ; (*sound of animal*) haṛpaṭ ; (*out, as coil of rope*) bokor (2) ; (*of fat animal*) bhanḍal bhunḍul, bhanḍul ; (*getting quickly into position for*) oṛyo poṭyo.

RUPEE, A—poṇḍ poesa, ṭaka.

RUPTURE SEMINAL DUCTS, TO—kọṭẹć.

RUSH, TO—(*at*) ghisghisạu ; (*through, of work*) thotho motho ; (*headlong*) sọhọr ; (*in, of wind*) pogoe ; (*here & there*) chilbilạu ; (*with a*) geser mẹnte, ghusuń, hud marte, jhama jhum, jhumạ jhum, jhunạ jhun, pọdrọć marte, pogoe m., pọlọc m., puyul m., sayań m., sayaṛ m., sur m. ; (*like plant, a*) pathor orot.

RUSHING—dir dir ; (*angrily*) dandanao ; (*of water*) cạbhur (2), gadgadao, hadhad, họdọṛ (2), sọhọe (2) ; (*footsteps*) dhaṛ dhuṛ ; (*sound, with a*) kiriṛ mẹnte ; (*of wind*) sayań, sọyọń.

RUST—ić ; (*to*) ić, murcạ.

RUSTLE—(*to*) rọgọs, rọskọt, sarsoṛ, sọṛsọṛ ; (*with a*) hud marte, rodoe m., rogoe m., rọgọs m., rọskọt m., ṭhopor m.

RUSTLING SOUND—hadar (2), hadar ṭhapar, hadhud, hadui (2), hagae hugui, haṭpaṭ, khaṛ khọṛ, racap rucup, radabada, radbad, radgo badgo, radobado, radrad, ragabaga, ricot rọcọt, rodo bodo, rodoe, rogoe, rọgọt cọgọt, rọgọt (2), sạnsan; (*slight*) ṭhapa (2), ṭhapar, ṭhopor ; (*of clothes*) hadae hudui, hagae hugui.

RUT, TO—bayar, matao.

RUTTY (*of a road*)—cọpọt lọndọć.

RYOT, A—porja, porja pạni, praja, raeot.

S

SACK, A—bora, bosta ; (*cloth*) ṭaṭ.

SACRED—sọnọt ; (*books*) sastọr, sọstọr ; (*to males of household*) abge.

SACRIFICE—(*a*) bolidan, dāṛẽ, samańak ; (*to offer*) caṛhao, dāṛẽ, samań ; (*of human blood*) bul māyām ; (*materials for*) bonga saranjam ; (*animal for*) pạhuṛ ; (*fowl for*) tiạk ; (*bullock for*) kuṭạm ḍangra ; (*offered*) samańić ; (*not yet offered*) samańokić ; (*to the dead*) poṛha dāṛẽ ; (*& worship, to offer*) pujạ ; (*to kill for*) tẹngẹn ; (*to sell at a*) ādhoń mādhoń ; (*at end of year*) maghi pujạ ; (*for silk-worms*) ahạri ; (*after restoration to health*) saket ; (*to sun*) joṛa samań ; (*one who offers human*) oṇḍga ; (*priest who offers*) pujhar.

SAD—ahluń, anduk canduk, ahjhluń, ạtruń, cirmok, heholok, hẹmẹṛyõk, jeṭlok (M), jiṭluk (F), jiṛmok, kolok (2), merlań mirlių, mirluń, mọćmọć, momoyoć, mulin ; (*to be*) marak morok, mayak moyok, mulin, ọlọń ; (*looking*) dolomolo, jiput, jirlun, kolok (2), mańga murạ, orloporlo.

SADDLE—(*native*) palan ; (*girth*) beṛband ; (*of hill*) rindiṛ.

SAFE & SOUND—nirọpọn, sonesod.

SAFETY—salsāt ; (*place of*) aotan.

SAG, TO—jhạlur, khońja.

SAGO—sạgudana.

SAIL, A—badọm.

SAKE OF, FOR THE—iạte, lạgit, ńutumte.

SALARY—tọlọp, tonkha ; (*monthly receipts of*) masṛa.

SALE OF DAY, THE FIRST—buhni ; (*to make*) pạhnạ.

SALINE—rabraba, raham ; (*of soil*) kharna, khorna, rehḍa ; (*water*) chapar dak, khorna dak, nunchaha.

SALIVA—uli dak ; (*dried at corners of mouth*) patahań, patohań.

SALT—buluń ; (*to*) adạ, buluń ; (*a kind of*) korca b. ; (*having taste of*) rabraba, raham ; (*-petre*) sora.

SALTED—(*under*) alnõ, hayam ; (*over*) cẹncẹń, hewer, rabraba, raocao.

SALUTATION—*Cf.* ADDRESS.

SALUTE—(*the common*) johar, sọ johar ; (*by bowing, to*) ḍọbọk, ḍọnḍọbọt ; (*to return, of an inferior*) jiạ, jio ; (*said by F. when returning*) cipcirуоp, leoń ; (*mutual*) jopohar ; (*kinds of*) *Cf.* johar.

SALVATION—bañcaoḱ, bacǫl.
SALVE FOR EYES—ajan.
SAME, THE—inạ, saman, sehoe.
SAMPLE—chand, chǫnd, cǫnd, ḍhạṭhi.
SANCTIFY, TO—dhǫrǫm, nem; *(as officiating priest)* nẽo.
SAND—gitil; *(river)* gaḍa gitil; *(fine)* lǫmǫń g., *(carried by water)* balgada; *(in food)* rege cege; *(to scour with)* gitil; *(iron stone)* bạli, luhui; *(to hollow out cavity in)* suť.
SANDAL—*(a kind of)* cạṭki, kharpa; *(wooden)* badha, muṇḍrạ badha; *(wood)* candan, rǫkǫt cǫndǫn; *(toe peg of)* bạulạ; *(sound of)* ciṭeť caṭeť.
SANDY—gitlạha, saedañ.
SANTAL, A—hǫṛ, hǫṛ hǫpǫn, mạńjhi (M), mạńjhian (F), santal (M), santalni (F), sãotal (M), sãotalni (F); *(language)* hǫṛ rǫṛ; *(village officials)* godet, jǫg mạńjhi, jǫg paranik, mạńjhi; *(rebellion)* hul; *(over chief)* binṭikạ raj, pargana; *(original septs)* *Cf.* nij; *(septs & sub septs)* *Cf.* pạris; *(of countryside)* disom hǫṛ; *(old name of)* kharwar, kherwar; *(who broke from tirbe)* bedea. *Cf.* TRADITIONAL.
SAP,—hal, ras, rǫs; *(without)* nisoṭ, rạḍhuạ, roroć; *(wood)* aṇḍu kaṭ.
SAPLING—bachṛa dare, lodhra, opať; *(of 1 year)* kacrať; *(used as rafter)* rola, ruli, sǫnǫr.
SAPPY—rosaṛ, rosgar, rosgạriạ, roskar.
SARI, A—khaṇḍa; *(kind of)* doal, halań sạṛi; *(method of wearing)* bentar; *(striped)* sạṭki sạṛi.
SATAN—sǫetan.
SATIATED—ṭui ṭui; *(to be)* aghaḱ, bi, kǫsǫť, tobo, toreť; *(& stomach distended)* ṭǫbṭǫbǫ.
SATIETY—subita; *(to)* chǫć bǫć, ruṭyuť; *(over)* bǫrǫdań.
SATISFIED—poṭpoṭo, riṇḍiol; *(self)* ṭhulạu; *(to be)* adhar, aghaḱ, ale, bhurti, bi, dhirpur, khusi, rạji, upuť.
SATISFY, TO—bujhạu, purạn, rij, rijhạu, tirpit; *(a demand)* purạnti.
SATURATE, TO—bhijạu, dahadạhi, dahalao, ḍiń ḍabur.
SATURATED,—sabsab, sobsob; *(to be)* bijạu; *(to be, of soil)* jarkao.
SATURDAY—sạnichar, sunibar.
SAUNTER, TO—bilǫm, dera diri.
SAVE, TO—baclao, bańcao, doḱ, rạhạu, rạkhi jogao, rạkhiạ, rukhiạ; *(of money)* sańcao, sońcao; *(from borrowing)* upạr; *(except)* bin; *(to be)* bacǫl.
SAVINGS OF YEAR—mare.
SAVIOUR, A—dhatkaha.
SAVOUR—mahatom; *(without)* lamjaḱ.
SAVOURY—lasgar, mahka mạhki, sebel, sirạḱ baraḱ, sǫrǫm, sǫsṭǫḱ; *(of food)* tạṛibos; *(of flesh)* sereť bereť.
SAW—*(a hand)* ạri; *(to)* khǫṭǫ (2), reta; *(a pit)* ara, kạṭa, korot; *(sound of)* kharkharao, reto (2).
SAY—*(to)* kakale, lại, mǫn, rǫṛ; *(to have nothing to)* kokloso; *(as they)* ać kathae, ako kathae, mǫnako.
SAYING, A—kahạni, kạhni.
SCAB, A—ceto, sondor, sondro; *(to suffer from)* khakṛa.
SCABIES—khas, khasra.
SCAFFOLD, A RAISED—macan, maṇḍom, marǫm; *(for straw)* parãoca.
SCALD—*(to)* arae oroe, lǫ; *(so as to blister)* lǫ poṭaḱ; *(head)* uru ghao.
SCALE—*(a)* cokaḱ; *(off, to)* caṭić, ciṭić (2).
SCALES—*(weighing)* ḍaḱwaḱ, pasnga, toraju, tulạ; *(for weighing gold)* nikti tulạ; *(of fish)* ạs, cũiṭḱ.
SCALP, AN ABSCESS OF—uru eṅga.
SCALY—cacarhať, rǫrǫć.
SCAMP—*(a)* nakạṭiạ; *(to)* adha padha, adhkhǫcra, atra matra, chiṇḍel, ciṇḍel, kaṭać kuṭuć, lǫḍǫr bǫḍǫr.
SCANDAL—kalak; *(indicating)* chi; *(full of)* nico.
SCANTILY—bijǫ bǫjǫ, bokro. *Cf.* CLAD.
SCAPULA, THE—dạbi; *(ridge of)* bale dạbi.
SCAR—dag; *(of burning)* ḍạhni dag.
SCARCE—etań; *(& dear)* maharog, mahrǫg; *(to be)* khaṭǫ, ṭau, ṭanaṭạni, ṭǫṇṭa; *(to make oneself)* lǫṇḍǫć.
SCARCITY—akal, dorloe, haora, kańḍoṛ, lukhi palon, palon, ṭan, ṭanaṭạni.

SCARED, TO BE—bhiṛkạ bhiṛki, bhiṛkạu, bidṛạu, biṛkạu, biṛki.

SCARLET—arak̓ ; (*to dye*) ńeš.

SCARRED—khadrak̓ khodrok̓.

SCATHE—loksan ; (*to cause*) huạń.

SCATTER, TO—asẹć tasẹć, barać buṛuć, birbitban, cḥikican, chirchạtur, chiriạ chit, chiriạu, chitiạ bitiạ, chitiạu, ẹr, pasante, tamtase ; (*as rain*) bijir (2) ; (*& destroy*) birbithan ; (*& spill*) hirić pạrić.

SCATTERED—alẹć tasẹć, ciribiri, hirak̓ (2), hiṭań jharań, jhiṅgor (2), tamtase, taral basal ; (*to be*) bebilọṇḍ, bidlạị, bhiṅgạu, bikhạṛ, chitir bitir, dahades, ẹr, tarak̓ biṛạk̓ ; (*to the winds, to be*) bạbilọṇḍ ; (*by falling*), *to be*) tarse.

SCENT—bas, sọ ; (*sweet*) mahak ; (*to have a*) andkao ; (*to*) bas.

SCHEME—(*a*) kạrkhana ; (*to*) mili guṭi, mili misi, mis, pontha.

SCHEMING—cạtur, ghagọr ; (*with much*) nana bond.

SCHISM, A—khũṭ.

SCHOOL, A—iskul, paṭsal, paṭh sal ; (*head boy of*) paṭh cela.

SCIATICA—ṭan bat, jaṅghi.

SCINTILLATE, TO—jalat̓ julut̓.

SCISSORS—kạpci.

SCOFF AT, TO—ciṛhạu, hẹnọsta.

SCOLD, TO—alẹć, bakat̓ bọkọt̓, bọkọt̓ (2), cheń cheńaok̓ (F), dạbri, dhuṅgrạu, dundrạu, ẹgẹr (F), hutmạ, kẹńkẹń, kuṭạu, lese, pọkọt̓ (2), ram rọr, ruhet̓ (M), soda, sọṇḍa, tạrgum, ṭhanka ṭhanki ; (*continually*) kimbot̓ kọrọt̓ ; (*in return*) ruhet̓ hala ; (*& wave arms*) hutmạ hutmi ; (*whiningly*) pheń (2).

SCOLDING—dhodya (M), dhodyo (F) ; (*always*) khẹḍẹć (2) ; (*used in*) bedot rasa, darya dapak̓, dạtri, dondor puli ; (*to go*) tul.

SCOOP OUT WITH HAND &C., TO—halo.

SCORCH, TO—ḍahao, ẹṛẹć (2), jalao, jhā̃usạu, kharao.

SCORCHED—(*to be*) khaṅgao ; (*& withered, to be*) jhāorāo ; (*by fire*) jharkao.

SCORCHING—caraṭ (2), jharla jhạrli ; (*of sun*) cereń, jhańj, uṛuć puṭuć.

SCORE—(*a*) isi, mit̓ isi ; (*a full*) isiạ gan ; (*out or off, to*) kaṭao.

SCORN—(*indicating*) chi ; (*to feel*) chi tho ; (*to meet with*) ạpuc.

SCORPION, A—kediń kaṭkọm, kidiń kaṭkọm ; (*small*) kamar kidiń.

SCOTCH, TO—chẹo.

SCOUNDREL, A—bodmas, condho, cọrpọṭ mara, mara, nakạṭiạ, pạji, rạdin(F) ; (*by Fs.*) tenae gaṇḍke ; (*great*) cọrpọṭ.

SCOUNDRELLY—copa kuṭạ, cọrpọṭ, harmad, lucạ (M), luci (F), pạji, raḍ (M), rạdin (F) ; (*by Fs.*) tenae gaṇḍke.

SCOUR, TO—mājao, ragdao ; (*with sand &c.*) gitil, mańjao.

SCOURGE—(*a*) cạmuk, carcạri, karṛa, koḍra, korra ; (*to*) cạmkạu, karṛa, koḍra.

SCOURING IN CATTLE—ạṛhạiạ.

SCOUT, TO (*scoff*)—hẹnọsta.

SCOWL, TO—biṇḍuć saṭok̓, mọkmọkọr ; (*with a*) kosle.

SCRAGGY—jhadọr padọr, jharọeak̓, ruńruń.

SCRAMBLE, TO—ciri cunthi, garda gurdạ, gurdạ gurdi, ragọr pagọr ; (*for*) jhapṭa jhạpṭi.

SCRAP—(*a*) beńjak̓ ; (*not a*) rukrạbon.

SCRAPE, TO—ghasao, ghasar, khadrao, khayọt̓, khoḍrao, khokrao, khoṭrao ; (*with feet*) ragọr pagọr ; (*out*) gẹć, kodrao ; (*off*) gẹć, hurit̓ ; (*to oneself*) gạduć ; (*with claws*) gạdur ; (*the tongue*) hatar.

SCRAPING—(*to cut by*) khoṭrao ; (*sound of*) hạdur (2), kharok̓ (2).

SCRAPINGS—hoṭak̓ khoḍrak̓ ; (*& all*) gẹć gayum.

SCRATCH, TO—bhoṇḍor, gạdur, gaegam, gạigum, jadgo, khal, phadgal ; (*with nails*) gạdur, rabọr ; (*a*) bubu, hudrit̓ ; (*a deep*) bhoṅgar ; (*of bear &c.*) gạduć ; (*in earth*) gẹlẹć ; (*a hole*) gẹlẹć bhugak̓ ; (*out. a hollow*) gẹlẹć gaḍa.

SCRATCHING, NOISE OF—carcar, hadar (2), hạdur (2), kharok̓ (2), khẹrẹć (2), khọrọk̓, phadruk̓.

SCREAM, TO—khaṭkhaṭao, khẹrkher, kikiạu ; (*loudly*) kirkirạu.

SCREEN—(*a*) ṭaṭi ; (*to*) aḍ, oḍ, aḍon ; (*from sight, to*) oḍ.

SCREW—(*a*) kaṭi, pẽc, pẽnc ; (*to*) peṭer ; (*to put on the*) ecepẽce, ẽcpẽc ; (*driver, a*) pẽckas.

SCRIMPLY CLAD—gaṇḍheť muṇḍheť, gaṇdur gapur.

SCRIMPY—cãe.

SCRIPTURES—sastor, sostor.

SCROLL, A—totro ; (*to roll up as a*) totro.

SCROTUM—(*of a boar*) duṛe ; (*swelling of*) siṛa ; (*of bull, dried*) ḍhuḍhua.

SCRUB—(*to*) gasao, ragda ragdi, rogdao, rogdo rugdi ; (*with hand, to*) ragdao ; (*jungle*) jhopo toṛo, jhopṛo, paṭaṛ potoṛ, thopro bir.

SCRUBBER FOR BUFFALOES, A—gaske.

SCRUPULOUS—iman.

SCUM—chale, garsilom ; (*red*) nagi gaṇḍo, naṅgi gaṇḍo ; (*on cane juice*) gad, haṛam gad, mahut.

SCURF (*on head*)—upiãs.

SCUTTLE, TO (*of birds*) geṇḍher.

SEA, THE—dariau, doreão, jala, jalakhar, jalaphi, jalapuri, kalapani, puri, samud, samudar.

SEAL—(*a*) mohor ; (*to*) chap, mohor.

SEAM, A—rotoǩ.

SEARCH, TO—cesṭa, luṭuć suṭuć, ṭesṭa, surag ; (*for*) banij, cia, dandha, dhandrau, dhans, dhãs, ḍuṇḍhau, jigas, ńam gelaǩ, ńam baṛa, pakre, sai, sendra, siṛi, ṭewan ; (*for a clue*) bhidi ; (*to prosecute a*) dhans, dhãs, khoj pańj, pacha, pecha, tolas ; (*out*) tuhkiť ; (*for, with hands*) hatṛa haṭri, hatṛao, hutṛa hutṛi, sandṛa sondṛe, suṭuć, ṭamḍao ; (*everywhere*) dhandṛa dhundṛa, soǩ sutruć ; (*eagerly*) dhãosa dhãusi ; (*diligently*) dharuǩ dhacuǩ ; (*in dark*) ṭamḍao ; (*here & there*) dhundṛa dhundṛi, dhuṅṛa dhuṅṛi, khoj pańj ; (*for roots in jungle*) hunar ; (*under a warrant*) ḍuṇḍha.

SEASON—batar, din mas, okte, rewaj, rit, ritu, rosa, tak ; (*to*) hewa, tińjau ; (*to, of food*) ada, chanka chanki, chankao ; (*to, of wood*) ropam ; (*in*) sale (2) ; (*in, of animals*) bauha, bauhari, ritiau ; (*out of*) aber, adin, bebatar, kubela ; (*proper*) ghai, okte macha, tak batar ; (*busy*) ahibahi, dhurpau ; (*late in the*) nami ; (*merchandise*) amdani.

SEASONABLE—batar, tak batar ; (*of rain*) hathia japuť.

SEASONED—(*well*) pokta ; (*not*) beroṅ.

SEASONS—(*fixed*) niṭ oktekо ; (*to come round as*) bihur.

SECOND—dosar, dosra ; (*hand*) bohon ; (*growth or brew*) doja.

SECRET—chapit, mophosol ; (*a*) luka chapa ; (*to keep*) bhidi, gape gupe, gop, gupti, luka chapa ; (*to divulge a*) bakať (2), bayať buyuť, buyuť mente ; (*unable to keep*) labaǩ cabaǩ, lapuǩ capuǩ, ukuť bukuť.

SECRETE, TO—oko.

SECRETLY—ade, bhorma, bhorma bhormate, cape cupe, chapkaote, gupti mar, okote ; (*to act*) bhidi, ; (*to go off*) bilṭau ; (*to give away*) paeṛẽ.

SECT—dol, dola doli, doṅgol, khũṭ, thok.

SECTION, A—dhara, hora, khanḍ.

SECURE—nidandi, niṛai, pharia phaṭi ; (*to make*) raṭpaṭ.

SECURELY—akjak, rakjak, raṭpaṭ, ruć ruć ; (*in comps.*) raṭpaṭao.

SECURITY—japti, salsãt ; (*bail*) hãǩ ; (*pledge*) bandhe, bandhok, thit.

SEDAN CHAIR—caudal ; (*with tassels*) cir caudal.

SEDATE—gambhir.

SEDENTARY—sukhwar, sukwar.

SEDGE, A COMMON—nakić ghãs, nanha bindi mutha, suṛa, ṭanḍi suṛa.

SEDITION—phasad.

SEDUCE, TO—bajhao ; (*to be*) lajbajhi.

SEDULOUSLY—dhamkau, dhampa dhure.

SEE—iyo ; (*to*) ariť, dorson, najar, ńel, sujhau ; (*a vision*) dorson ; (*particularly*) sujhau ; (*distinctly*) phohom, pohom ; (*& hear*) sakhi sabha ; (*that all is right*) tankhi ; (*in the act*) tebaǩ ; (*through*) ńel tapaṗ.

SEED—ita ; (*bed, a*) aphor gadi ; (*grain*) ita ranu ; (*sown in mud*) lewa aphor ; (*sown in beds*) aphor ; (*sown on first auspicious day*) muṭ ; (*loan of*) bada ; (*cotton*) baṅgaura ; (*of jack-fruit &c.*) kosa.

SEEDLING, A—cara ; (*ready for transplantation*) gachi ; (*of a tree*) poha.

Seedy—daraṅ duruṅ, dholomolo.
Seeing—(*faculty of*) nañjer, nọjọr; (*indistinctly*) jipạ.
Seek, to—cesṭa, dhạndrau, ḍuṇḍhau, khọj, khọj puchar, ńam, surạg, utjog; (*for*) ńam bara, ṭesṭa; (*to do*) rina; (*out each one*) sok sutruc.
Seem, to—nẹl.
Seemly—sãohã; (*to be*) saja.
Seen—(*to be*) dekhaok; (*through, that can be*) phirphoṅ, phoṅke.
Seer, a—sẹr; (*of 20 gandas*) pạki sẹr; (*of 12 or 18 gandas*) kạci sẹr; (*wooden measure*) kaṭ sẹr; (*brass*) pitạr sẹr; (*stone weight*) sẹr dhiri; (*1/16th*) choṭak; (¼) pawa; (2) kạṭhi; (2½) ara, ạrhaiạ; (5) paseri; (10) dhara, suli; (20) bisa.
Segregated—pharhaṛ.
Seize, to—capaṛ, dharao, dhawa, dhorao, jhuṭiau, kamṭao, kapṭao, khamca khạmci, pakaṛ, pakṛao, saṗ; (*by hair*) kapcao, jhuṭiạu; (*prey*) capot; (*& devour*) capot; (*goods for debt*) beṛhand, ḍoelao; (*& shake*) hutina; (*suddenly*) khap marao; (*& take away*) jhaṭiạu: (*with pincers*) cimṭạ; (*with hands*) karmaṭao; (*with hand*) khamcao; (*& close fist on*) muṭhiau; (*top with fingers*) roco; (*with both arms & throw down*) tam; (*the neck & push*) gardani; (*by neck & shake*) ghurmucạu; (*after pursuing*) hapca; (*& throw down*) kacṛao.
Seized, to be—(*with panic*) bilbilạu; (*by a fit*) bại, bạị c pãṛ, bayok, bhẹn (2), ucrạu.
Select, to—bacao, bachao, hat bacha, leao, ńam cet, uolao, nọljọl, parpa-ind, pạsind; (*carefully*) bachao sit.
Self—apnar, khud; (*of*) apan ạpin; (*control, lacking*) ulkhạniạ; (*sown*) lambe; (*restraint*) dhirtạ; (*abuse*) hejer, pisiṛ; (*willed*) ạnhũṭ, banḍhej, batkạṭi, bẹporbhase, bẹsrọm, bherọṭ, budrạg, dhacraṛ, dhọcọr, ḍigor, ḍigrạli, ḍiṭhạu, dundur, ẹk sirṛi, ẹktiạr, gạdut, hardand, hạruṛ, hạṭhi, hurmaṭ, hũṭ, kuput, leṭho.
Selfish—abge.
Sell, to—ạkriń, besaha, khardạu, kheja; (*at under value*) ãdhoṅ mãdhoṅ, ạndhoṅ mandhoṅ.
Seller, a (*mainly of live-stock*)—pherwek.
Semblance—ch.in.
Semen—leṛ, les.
Send, to—bheja, bhejao, kol, paṭhãona, rawana; (*away by artifice*) ṭarkao; (*for*) barmaṅgao, mańgao.
Senile decay—ṭan paṅgla.
Sensation—(*pleasant*) gumur; (*irritating*) git git; (*of touching skin*) gaegam, gạigum; (*of over-eating or dropsy*) ạrseń toṛseń; (*of grit in food*) cagae cagoe, cagoe (2), (*after a full meal*) ḍọbḍọbọ, ḍọgḍọg, ẹṭ ẹṭẹ; (*of itching in throat or mouth*) gatãe; (*of insect crawling*) gayam (2); (*of dry skin*) kuṭkaṭao. *Cf.* CREEPING, PAIN, TINGLING.
Sense—buj, hos, hus, lor, lordhej, lur, suj; (*of decency*) sil sọrọm; (*without*) albudạha, họtọ budhi, urbudaha.
Senses—(*pleasing to*) jẹṅgeṭ (2); (*to bring to one's*) kas marao, sãorao; (*to recover one's*) nijạu.
Sensible—uạkẹp, wakhep; (*of, to be*) ạikạu.
Sensitive to touch—aṅ.
Sensual—umra (M), umri (F).
Sentence, a—ayat.
Separate—begar, bẹlọk, bises, bitoṅ (2), pharak, taphat, tophad; (*to be*) aparek; (*as husband & wife*) bidrạ bidri.
Separate, to—amba phara, ạmiń, apa barịa, apan ạpin, bac, baḍ, begar, bẹlọk, bhina, bhiṅgạu, bichṛi, chadao, chãṭ, chaṭa, chenghao, chingạu, codak, juda judi, phuṭ, phuṭa phuṭi, phuṭ phaṭ; (*of husband & wife*) bapag, chaḍa chạḍi; (*disperse*) phaṭ phuṭ; (*by straining*) chakao; (*by brushing with hand*) urlạu; (*into small globules*) bijir (2); (*threads of warp*) bhitara.
Separated—alag, chuṭạ chuṭi, hirak (2); (*to be*) bhiṅgạu; (*easily*) bọsok, (*by death, to be*) gọc haṭiń; (*from family*) banwas; (*into small bits*) bijir (2).
Separately—ạmiń.
Separating—(*as an assembly*) calcul; (*with the hand*) urlạ urli.

SEPT, A—paris; (*Santal*) *Cf.* paris; (*of same*) gutia pera.

SEPTEMBER-OCTOBER—asin, dasãe; (*belonging to*) asintara.

SEPTUM OF NOSE—nathu.

SEQUESTRATE, TO—jabid, jabod, jobod, jobot, kurki, kuruk.

SERENADING OF CATTLE AT SOHRAE—jagao.

SERIES, ONE OF A—choba.

SERIOUS—gambhir, kathin.

SERIOUSLY—andak tawak; (*ill*) jabri.

SERPENT, A—lar; (*tail of*) mund; (*goddess of Hindus*) monsa; (*a note emitted by*) kakarat. *Cf.* SNAKE.

SERPENTINE—karban kurban, khĩrjõñ khõrjõñ, kirboñ korboñ, kiria pate, liyor loyor, pitua patwe.

SERVANT, A—cakor, dasi (F), naokar, nokor, sebok; (*agricultural*) guti (M), kamia (M), kamin (F), kamini (F), kamrĩ (F), karmi kuri (F), munis (M).

SERVANTS—gutiko dasiko, nokor cakor; (*agricultural*) jon kamia, jon munis; (*land given to*) nankar; (*belonging to*) munsali.

SERVE, TO—bãho, dewa, sapdap, sewa; (*out*) bilhau, bilo; (*out food*) bimas, harta; (*rice from pot*) lo.

SERVICE—aũgra, bhalai, naokari, nankri; (*non-agricultural*) cakri; (*a religious*) girja.

SERVING—(*at a feast*) sap dap; (*no purpose*) auri pathauri, pathauri.

SESAME OIL PLANT, THE—til, tilmiñ; (*wild*) kat tilmiñ.

SET, TO—(*of sun &c.*) hasur; (*a trap &c.*) odao; (*on*) bargao, carhiau, cariau, liliau; (*down-snub*) dapkao, dhamkao, dhapkao, dhomkao, dhurmar, dombrao, durmar, jabdo, jobdao, jobdy; (*on end*) dorom; (*to*) dhorao, dhurau; (*upon*) jhũkau; (*up*) khara; (*out*) rawana; (*aside*) amangt, añgao, pandol; (*one's heart on*) barmañgao; (*one's hand to*) oram, utjog; (*agoing*) parsao; (*oneself to*) porton; (*fire to*) atar, jalao, jeret, jol, jundi, sengel lagao; (*on from all sides*) kacta kacti; (*up an idol*) than baisau, thapna; (*bricks in mortar*) gatao; (*in a hole*) bit; (*a fish-trap*) baj; (*the head, as horned animal*) atañ.

SET—(*of four, a*) ganda, gonda; (*off*) mojra.

SETTLE, TO—(*fix*) baisau, bondobas, chĩudau, gota, ikot, ja, khanj, mahkup, metao, metmat, mimansa, mohor marao, niptau, nirnk, nit, rahai sahai, rikit, ropha, tahrao, tarhao, thambhao, thanao, thekau, thikan; (*live*) girabas, thamgadi; (*of dregs*) tapuk; (*a dispute*) mondot, neae, parcha, phandao, phariau, saphai; (*down*) birhau, gadiau, gira basi, kambhir; (*privately*) rap dhap, rop dhop; (*permanently*) bas, basgadi, baskitia.

SETTLED—isthir, paka, sidbid.

SETTLEMENT, A—bondobos; (*to make an amicable*) jat jut, jut jat.

SEVEN—eae, sat; (*-teen*) gel eae, gel khon eae; (*-ty*) eae gel.

SEVERALLY—apan apin, jani jati, jona joti, parti, picha, piche, proti.

SEVERE—jaejulum, patpat; (*of fever*) gahri.

SEVERELY—andha dhund, bebarić, etoć potoć.

SEW, TO—rok, silãi; (*with long stitches*) jalai.

SEXUAL INTERCOURSE—(*to have*) der, dhakuć, loro; (*unlawful*) latghat, lotghuti.

SHADE—umul; (*to be thrown into the*) pandol; (*of dead father*) porodhol.

SHADOW—caber, umul; (*worn to a*) dhẽrẽpeta.

SHAFT—dandit dandom; (*of cart*) hudar; (*union of cart*) tundi; (*of carriage*) bam, bom; (*of mine*) sum.

SHAGGY—dagumcak, darum sarum, dhalgum, gadle, gadrum sadrum, gudui (2), hadui (2), hodgo, raguisak, sodo rodo, sodo (2), sodro bodro, sudro budro.

SHAKE, TO—dagmagao, dakar dokor, dakar dukur, daldalao, dalkao, dalmal, damsao, dewañ, dhacal dhucul, dhalui (2) dildil, dolmolao, dupai, eser, hilau, ikoć sokoć, jhalui (2), larao, larcar, lewak, lewe, lewere kodore, liplip, locoe (2), lokoe (2), lorcor, loroñ coroñ, lukur, ribi (2), ruku, rukum tukum, sakoć,

saksak, ṭalmal, tarko, ṭasak, ṭaskao, ṭawar (2), tharthar, tharṭharao, ṭhaskao, ṭhirṭhirau, ṭhurṭhurau, ṭiwić, ṭolmol; *(in ague)* **lakaṛ lukuṛ, rukum (2)**; *(from weakness)* **ḍalak ḍubuk, dhuluć dhupuć**; *(up)* **bhusku, sokoć, tagatusa**; *(out)* **dundlau**; *(the head)* **dhuluć dhupuć, ḍubuń (2), kodor, kodok (2), koyõr (2)**; *(ears, tail &c.)* **ṭhepe, ṭhere-ṭhepe**; *(up & down)* **lewer (2)**; *(off)* **koṭa, phaṭkao**; *(head when walking)* **ḍa ... (2)**; *(while holding in mouth)* **ici**; *(of one possessed)* **ṣser**; *(as in fast train)* **dakal (2)**.

SHAKING—**dalae (2), dhandcul, dulop (2), halak dalak, hilak dalak, lodo dhoro, lodop, lucpucia, lukur**; *(to sparkle on)* **jipir (2)**; *(of mud)* **thalthal**; *(of old person)* **thaluk thapuk**; *(of tattered clothes)* **lindar lapar, lindlapur**; *(of dog's tail)* **ṭiyal (2)**; *(the body)* **dhucul (2), demok (2)**; *(gently)* **dole (2)**; *(the head)* **ḍubuń (2)**; *(of fat)* **ludhur (2), pedor (2M), pidur (2F), thaluk (2)**; *(to loosen by)* **deket**.

SHAKINGS—*(of grain)* **hotak khodrak, jhala jhula, jhara jhera, jhuru (2), rap kotap**; *(not even the)* **oṭop koṭop**.

SHAKY—**digo dogo, dika ḍake, lida lade, lidwa ladwe, liṛwa sarwe**. *Cf.* LEGS.

SHALLOW—**celcekeć, chap chap, teljeń, ṭemeć**.

SHAM, TO—**naṅgos**; *(ilness)* **nokol**; *(apt to)* **naṅgosia**.

SHAME—**bhorom, laj, laja luka, sil sorom, sorom**; *(exclm.)* **chi**; *(to cause)* **bebhar, behurmat, bidot**; *(sense of)* **lajao**; *(to feel)* **lajao, lajbij**; *(to put to)* **serma surmi**; *(faced)* **harea garea, soromia**; *(full of)* **nilaj, sorom**.

SHAMELESS—**behoea, besormi, lajkhauka (M), lajkhauki (F), laṭkuṭa, nilaj, paṭis, sormi**; *(in dress)* **bojge**; *(person, a)* **sandgar (M), sandgaria (M), chandgar (F), chandgaria (F)**.

SHAMPOO, TO—**paendao**.

SHAPE—**bõhõk, chin, chond, ḍhob**; *(to put out of)* **leore** *(to get out of)* **cokro**; *(to beat into)* **daṭ bhaoar**; *(uncomely in)* **sondmond**; *(without)* **bedhob, berup, sandmand**; *(of good)* **reṅgleć**.

SHARE—*(a)* **bakhra, bāṭ, bhag, bhag bāṭ, hīs, hisa, joro**; *(to)* **bakhra, bāṭ, behosa, bhag, haṭiń, joro, laowao, lawao**; *(to, of cooked food)* **bimas**; *(iron staple fastening to plough)* **pasi**; *(holder)* **sarik**; *(holders, of two)* **ejmali**; *(an extra, given to killer of game)* **capo joro**.

SHARER, A—**bakhradaṛi, bhagiari, rasia**.

SHARES, TO DIVIDE INTO—**bhagao, laowao**.

SHARK, A—**haṅger hal o, hoṅgor hako**.

SHARP—**coclo, cuila, khar, laser, ṭasil**; *(taste)* **lag, tej**; *(of tone)* **nanha**; *(clever)* **bujhantar, sean**; *(edged)* **rodga**; *(pointed)* **bucbucu, khoca**; *(angrily)* **karra**.

SHARPEN, TO—**cuihor, molaṭ, san, silau**; *(by heating & hammering)* **hulsiń**.

SHATTER TO PIECES, TO—**chakacun**.

SHAVE, TO—**hoyo, hoyo hutur**; *(graze)* **arap, carić**; *(the head)* **dondlon, dundguṭ, dundu**; *(each other)* **hopoyo**.

SHAVED HEAD—**dond oṭ, dundge (M), dundgi (F), dundu kolo, kendloń, ṭhandgaṭ, ṭhanggaṭ ṭhundguṭ**.

SHAVING—*(a wood)* **chailak**; *(with razor, sound of)* **kharkharao**.

SHAWL, A—**barki, sal**; *(large cotton)* **pichauri**; *(cloth)* **cador, cadra**.

SHEAF, A—**binda**; *(small)* **ahla, aṭi**; *(band to bind)* **chonṭ, chõṭ**; *(daily perquisite of servant)* **aloi, ir arpa**.

SHEAR, TO *(as sheep)*—**kaṭop, kaṭrop**.

SHEATH—*(of sword &c.)* **bokhar**; *(to draw from)* **boć**.

SHEAVES—*(to make into)* **binda**; *(to spread on threshing floor)* **chitau**.

SHED—*(a marriage)* **mandha, mandhwa**; *(a cattle)* **char, gora**; *(to)* **aṭu**.

SHEEP, A—**bhidi**; *(up-country)* **gador b.**; *(a call to)* **druheṭ (2), durheṭ (2)**; *(fold)* **bathan, char, gudri, gujhi**; *(whose wool has fallen off)* **khedra b.**; *(contents of stomach of)* **gubri**; *(a breed of)* **lurka**.

SHEER—*(down)* **khaidu**; *(despair, in)* **dhok jiba**.

SHEET, A—cadọr, cadra ; *(corrugated iron)* cadra ; *(iron, thin)* patar.

SHELF, A—*(hanging)* jhaba ; *(recess in wall)* pakha.

SHELL—cokak, coklak ; *(used as money)* kạrạ kạudi, kạudi, kạuri phuṭia kạudi ; *(conch)* kạudi enga, sak ghonga, sak rọkọć ; *(of water-snail)* gongha ; *(snail's)* rọkọć ; *(hollowed out to a)* ṭhoṭheo ; *(to)* jan, sala.

SHELLAC—lạhṭi.

SHELLALAH—lạuri ; *(one who can twirl)* lạuria ; *(the monkey's-fruit)* bandor lạuri.

SHELTER—aotan, asrae, umul ; *(to)* ad, adon, danan, dok, od ; *(to take)* mạndiau, soro ; *(without)* bead ; *(a temporary)* capchanda, cari ; *(of branches, a)* jhupri ; *(in a thicket, to)* jhurgusia.

SHEPHERD, A—bhidi gupiić ; *(pay of)* carwahi.

SHERBET—sarbat, sorbot.

SHIELD—*(a)* dhal, dhalwa ; *(to)* dok ; *(oneself, to)* ghao jogao ; *(a metal)* phiri ; *(of, to be under)* ṭehad ; *(oneself at another's expense, to)* bejha, dudrạu.

SHIFT—*(a)* jota, pạli ; *(to)* ucạr ; *(from place to place, to)* ucạr nacạr ; *(by)* para pạrite, pạri pạrite.

SHIMMERING—jaral (2).

SHIN—ṭhiṭrāk ; *(bone, the)* ṭhõrẽ ; *(up a tree, to)* aple.

SHINE, TO—cakmakao, camkao, dig digauk, jhalkao ; *(of moon)* tẹdẹć ; *(of sun after clouds)* pahak, pohok, uphạn ; *(brightly)* liplip.

SHINING—barat borot, borot (2), cakmak, jhak (2), jhile mile, piṛit ; *(with tinsel)* jhala mala.

SHINY—cikan, cikạr, jhẹrẹ (2).

SHIP, A—jahaj, nao ; *(steam)* dhuạkọs ; *(crew of)* jahaj cakl oko.

SHIRK, TO—harur ; *(work)* dhapka, lanlan, lạruć bạruć, lẹndẹr pẹndẹr, lurun burun.

SHIRT, A—kamis.

SHIVER, TO—lukluk, rukum tukum, sisirạu, susua, ṭhak (2), ṭhuk (2), ṭhuk ṭhukạu ; *(in fever)* dẹrẹć (2), jarjar, rukum (2) ; *(to atoms)* chaka cun, chiti chan.

SHIVERING—ṭhak (2), ṭhuk (2); *(ill clad &)* kanṭa konṭo ; *(noise of)* susu (2).

SHOCK—*(exclm, of)* chi ; *(causing)* aris ; *(headed)* dhapra (M), dhapri (F).

SHOE, A—panahi ; *(English)* mundla p. ; *(horse or bullock)* nal ; *(heel-plate of)* panahi nal ; *(flower)* joba baha ; *(maker)* panhaiya ; *(makers, a caste of)* ghasi, muci ; *(sole of)* tala ; *(kinds of) Cf.* panahi ; *(to take off)* hoć ; *(noise made by old)* thẹrẹt (2).

SHOG, TO—sọkọć.

SHOOGLY—lida lade.

SHOOT, A *(plant)*—kani, oponom, ṭusa ; *(bamboo)* helta ; *(small)* opak ; *(from tree)* patạrak ; *(from ground)* ọt oponom, poha ; *(from root)* gạra.

SHOOT, TO *(with gun)* ṭhu ; *(with bow)* tun ; *(at a mark)* bejha ; *(arrow straight up)* kuṭla ; *(arrow to allow for trajection)* teran ; *(blunt arrow)* ṭuṭi ; *(2nd. time)* ṭọṭa ; *(at each other)* tupun ; *(of pain)* hīṛić ; *(forward)* sọrọr.

SHOOTS—*(from stump)* kacrat ; *(sprouting)* perepere ; *(tobacco)* dugi.

SHOP, A—dokan, gadi ; *(liquor)* handi sal, paura gadi ; *(work, &c.)* sal ; *(keeper)* bạria, dokani, dokandar, dokkanić, mudi.

SHORE—dhip ; *(to)* ṭesa, ṭhẹk, ṭhesa.

SHORT—banda bandi, dẹbẹ (2), duda, duluć dupuć, geda (M), gidi (F), gedok, gidri (F), gudri (F), hau, jerka, keṭen, ledgo (M), pidgi (F), pedle (M), pidli (F), reme ṭele, ṭhepo, ṭhuṭha (M), ṭhuṭhi (F), ṭhuṭkuk ; *(in stature)* bãorã (M), bạurī (F), bhuṭka, buṭra (M), buṭri (F), dheba (M), dhebra (M), dhiba (M), dhibi (F), dhibri (F), gedra (M), gheṭma (M), ghitli (F), gheṭmi (F), ghuṭla (M), ghuṭli (F), gidri (F), gudra (M), gudri (F), guṭhla (M), guṭhli (F), guṭra (M), guṭri (F), jorma (M), jurmi (F), kendle (F), kendra (M), ledma (M), ledmi (F), lidmi (F), reṭhma (M), reṭhmi (F), ṭebra (M), ṭibri (F), ṭemso, ṭhemka (M), ṭhimki (F), ṭhemsok (F), ṭhepca (M), ṭhikri (F), ṭhipci (F), ṭhomsok (F), ṭhurka (M), ṭhuṭka (M), ṭhuṭki (F), *(ears of grain)* butuć ; *(clothes)* ṭepen, ṭipin

(2); (*measure*) bokro, thepo; (*of hair*) dundga, tope (2), tulkup, tulpa (M), tulpi (F); (*necked*) bhakum, bomborket, khesbet, kubdha, tombrot; (*bodied*) kumdhuc; (*to be*) khato, kumti; (*to fall*) atra; (*of breath*) upardom; (*& youthful looking*) gathia; (*sighted*) pelka (M), pilki (F); (*of*) han, odgel; (*cut, a*) khato hor; (*& long*) khato badho; (*too*) phucka; (*of destination*) thaprok, (*handed, to be*) tiranica; (*song, a*) akhar; (*to make*) adhi; (*comings*) ghat guna, ghati; (*tempered*) alkhania, ankarwa, arra arri, bispitaha, cun bai, corcota, khaisaha, khaisa khaisi, khantaha (M), khantahi (F), khantar, kudraha, kurmutaha, ulkhania. *Cf.* TIME, STEPS.

SHORTER THAN CUSTOMARY—lipan lapan, thutha, tutha.

SHORTLY—(*soon*) nahak; (*briefly*) sanchep.

SHOT (*for gun*)—charra, chitta.

SHOULDER—phari, taren; (*to carry on*) bharia, gok; (*blade, the*) dabi, phakrak, phari jan; (*to shoulder*) khacakhac; (*of meat*) phari.

SHOUT, TO—gadra godro, hoho, karur barur, kikia kikiyi, kirir, taraj garaj; (*in answer to shout*) tokar; (*when watching crops*) hakar phukar; (*out*) hakao; (*for help*) guhar; (*at & threaten*) haka hasi; (*to dog*) hari; (*to buffalo*) hariak; (*to cattle*) hum; (*together*) rugdai, rugdai marte; (*at marriage*) haribol; (*in boys' game*) hoja (2).

SHOVE, TO—dhaka, kucau, pelao, thela, thelao; (*in a crowd*) dhaka dhaki, thela thili, thele paese.

SHOW—digi migi; (*a*) lila, tamasa; (*to*) batlao, uduk; (*to make a*) ete cete; (*of, to make a*) engol, ingul; (*decked out for*) jhalak malak; (*off, to*) cahak mahak, chamak, chamak damak, ete cete, jelep (2), jhil jhol, jilip (2), lalak, liplep, lolok, malkao.

SHOWER OF RAIN, A HEAVY—achar.

SHRED—(*a*) rukhi; (*to*) khutri; (*torn to*) khuri.

SHREWD—catur, ghagor.

SHRIKE, THE—bagha kerketa.

SHRILL—bere (2), ceren, terec (2); (*to sound*) raran; (*sound, with a*) raran marte, ririn marte; (*sound of some insects*) ranran.

SHRIMP, A—icak, nicak; (*spec. of*) rando icak; (*large*) sule icak.

SHRINE—(*to visit a*) dorson; (*of Jatra festival*) jatra m uda.

SHRINK, TO—pac, run; (*as stomach*) jilpat; (*back*) latic.

SHRIVEL, TO—cacalkat, run, run tukun; (*of fruit*) cupuikut, jolkhot, jolkot.

SHRIVELLED—caekop, copa, copa cupi, coroetho, cothra, cuikup, jalpa, jalpak, jalpha, karcan latiaha; (*of old people*) jaknuc, japua, jhukmuc, joknot, jukni (F).

SHRUB, A—akaona, baghin janum, barni, bonga sariom, budhi tilai, campa baha, icak, kia baha, sij; (*scandent*) had jora, kari, kujri, nari; (*small flowering*) pichari baha; (*small garden*) toa baha.

SHRUNK—cuikup.

SHUDDER, TO—c hik bai, cihrau.

SHUFFLE, TO—(*cards*) phet; (*feet*) carhat corhot, cirhot, corhot.

SHUFFLING—cirhot corhot, thisot thorsot; (*sound of*) carhat corhot, thoyot (2).

SHUT, TO—lidak, sandap; (*up* bond, sin potom, sikup; (*of door &c.*) japak, ladak, sin; (*partly*) ladep; (*in*) phatok, sin potom; (*out*) sin bahre; (*almost*) lidak; (*suddenly*) sitap; (*up, to keep*) bae.

SHUTTER, A MATTING—tati.

SHUTTLE—maku; (*thread wound for*) nari.

SHY—cakla coklo, kakra kokro, kokro; (*to*) bhercak.

SICK—(*to be*) bec, phatkar, ula; (*to feel as if about to be*) serer.

SICKENING—bhirik, dhirik; (*of smells*) ghara ghari.

SICKLE—(*small*) datre; (*big*) kaidą; (*toothed*) datrom; (*without handle*) laṅt datrom; (*with ferrule*) samble datrom.

SICKLY—mandhua; (*to look*) dholomolo, orososo; (*to cause to be*) jhur.

SICKNESS—bighin, rua; (*& disease*) rog bighin; (*to feel*) serer.

SIDE—are, kar, pahat, pahta, pas, sa, sah, seć, sen, torp; (*division*) torphan; (*the*) dhara, kokha, pani kokha, sorta; (*one*) ek dhar; (*at the*) ek sirtal; (*on this*) ne parom, ne parom; (*on that*) enparom, enparom; (*the other*) hnasa, parom; (*this*) noasa, nhasa; (*which*) oka seć; (*from the*) ghatra, giria; (*to one*) ghatra, hõrseć, koce, pathe; (*on the out*) hurur (2); (*to incline to one*) lerwak; (*to lie on the*) panjar bhorte gitić; (*to put on the other*) parom; (*to side, from*) dakar dosor, horjań hurjań; (*to side, to move from*) bit bidya, lebda libdi, ulta ulti; (*on which animal falls*) gur leteń.

SIDES—(*on all*) bi hau, gobla gubli, tirkot; (*from all*) amin, bujuk (2); (*both*) duyokul.

SIDEWAYS—apir, ghatra, horseć, koce, kõrse.

SIEVE, A—cala, jhańjri; (*like*) jhańjra, jheńjre; (*winnowing*) hatak.

SIFT, TO—amiń, cala, hoseć; (*flour &c.*) kecel; (*with a hatak*) ãitau, gum, gum begar, kodor, phatkao.

SIFTING—(*a method of*) lapuk; (*sound of*) ceher bedeć, pheteć (2).

SIGH—(*to*) barań buruń, pheknok, phũ; (*with a*) sõ marte; (*with a long*) khor marte, phukur m. pukus m.; (*a heavy*) khor; (*for, to*) hadiau, hiatiń; (*for, to-of food*) hirohi.

SIGHT—(*a*) lila; (*vision*) najar, nańjer, nojor; (*out of, to be*) ańkher; (*to keep out of*) ade, chapkao, husuć; (*to put out of*) gupat; (*pleasant to the*) ńorom (2); (*to go out of*) ayak, sen ayak.

SIGN—(*a*) cikhna, isara, jatra, nisana, nistan; (*to*) sahi, suhi; (*to make a*) isara; (*of prohibition, a*) condka.

SIGNATURE—sahi, suhi; (*to adhibit one's*) doskhot.

SIGNIFY, TO—khatao.

SILENCE—(*dead*) sirik taham; (*to*) tewet; (*in*) saċ suċ.

SILENT—gasać gusuć, ghania, gundur musak, gurum, masać musuć, mayań muyuń, mosmoso, musak, romcom, sansun, tomtom; (*to be*) hape, hapo, kirdhum, ńomor; (*& sullen*) ṭarią bus ą, tomtom; (*as the grave*) saċ suċ; (*through stupidity*) loryo; (*& dejected*) mosmoso; (*& alone*) gusuń (2).

SILK WORMS—*Cf.* TASSAR.

SILKY—cikãr.

SILLY—alak bakak, loryo.

SILT—pãk; (*of*) pãkuha; (*land formed by*) celcekeć; (*on a field*) jolan.

SILVER—rupa, taka; (*coin, a small*) suki; (*smith, a*) sonhar.

SIMILAR—saman, soman, somasom, tulni; (*to be*) tić; (*something*) tanak, tanić.

SIMPLE—albudaha, alga, areć goreć, beboj, loryo, lur na bhas, medhu, mukhu, olkobaha, sojha, sora, thuṅgla (M), thuṅgli (F), urbudaha; (*medicinal herbs*) jari buti.

SIMPLETON, A—alup, bemhha, thuṅgla (M), thuṅgli (F).

SIMULTANEOUS—burbudluk; (*not*) rikoć rukuć.

SIN—apai, ghat, guna, gunha, kai, pap; (*to*) ghati, kai; (*to receive recompense for*) pap pholao.

SINCE—khoć, khon; (*then*) un khon.

SINCERE—khulasa, niskapat, pharia, pharia phati, sora.

SINDUR—(*receptacle for*) dharapkia, kia; (*marked with*) sindur bundi; (*lawful application of*) ituk s., sindra dhan; (*irregular application*) ituk; (*long straight mark of*) dordor; (*to apply*) te.

SINEW, A—pat, patsir, pawa.

SINFUL—kaidar, papi, papista.

SING, TO—durań, regha, serek; (*praises*) õrhẽ; (*well, one who*) gaenaha.

SINGE, TO—dhursau, jharkao, jhãnsau, rụ; (*hair off carcase*) dhursau.

SINGING—regha righi; (*as a kettle*) chae (2).

SINGLE—eka china, mit, sadher; (*out, to*) bachao; (*file in*) ọtọn tayọm; (*thing, a*) ṭẹć, ṭen.

SINGLY—eka china, ẹkẹ ẹkẹ, mit, mimit, phac phuc, rikọć rọkọć.

SINGULAR—bises.

SINK, TO—gạdiạu; (*in water*) unum; (*as eyes*) horok; (*as in bog*) thạli; (*deeply*) aogar, gabgab; (*at once*) ḍabḍub; (*& rise again*) ḍabać dubuc, uḍuć ḍubuć; (*once for all*) ḍub.

SINUS, A—ghugri ghao.

SIR—hạjur, hujur.

SISTER—boehạ, misera; (*young*) bọkọt kuṛi; (*elder*) ạji, ạjiạ (*pl*), dại, sạwasin; (*husband of elder*) teńat; (*in-law*) ajhnar, erwel kuṛi; (*children of*) deo bhạgin; (*relationship of children of*) mamạsi.

SIT, TO—beṭhār, durup; (*with knees on chest*) ẹdhẹ, ẹhẹr; (*long in one position*) as mạnḍao, herpat; (*able to, of child*) sidup kẹṭẹć; (*huddled up*) lọplọpọ; (*on heels*) cocongot, cucumguć, cucungut, dundurcut, huchucu; (*on hind legs*) comcorok; (*tailorwise*) asan manḍao, patganḍo; (*on eggs*) burum, ụbụr; (*till prayer granted*) dharna.

SITE OF A HOUSE—diṇḍa.

SITTING—(*on eggs*) bubrum; (*to break by*) gasmanḍao; (*huddled up*) romcọlọk; (*close to ground*) dondkoro; (*to move while*) gẹndher, ghasghassao, ghesọk (2), hosọt, jiki.

SIX—turui; (*each*) tutur; (*-ty*) turui gẹl, pẹ isi; (*-teen*) gẹl turui, solo, sulo.

SIZE—(*to change the*) agad; (*increasing in, of a sore*) lagak (2), phadgao; (*of equal*) ọpọr jọpọr; (*inferior in*) nirgs; (*of different*) dhalać dhaluć, dhuluć dhupuć, lẹḍẹć thẹkrẹć. *Cf.* UNDER.

SKEIN, A—lạti, phola; (*of thread*) lạti sutạm, phiṭi.

SKELETON, A—dhạdra. *Cf.* WORN.

SKID, TO (*of wheels*)—ghasghasao.

SKILFUL—hat chut, hath chuṭi, kabel, kạbil, nipun; (*to make*) lewa.

SKILL—caher, hẽt, hikmat, hunar, lor, lordhej, lur, lurbhas; (*to gain*) hewa jaora.

SKILLED—bhaoar, bhawār, kharkhaha, kharkhạri, pakṭa; (*in black arts*) kaṭkuṭ.

SKIM, TO—(*as cream*) oar; (*along surface*) chalchalao, chalkao, cholkao, kabak kobok, khẹncẹr.

SKIN—chal, harta; (*to*) chal, khal, khalkhalao; (*to cast*) ur; (*to break the*) cokhlao, hadra hạdri, hadrao; (*dryness of*) kaṭkaṭao; (*blotches on*) surhi; (*disease, a*) agyo, cạnrią, dad, kạrghao, khạs, khasra; (*rough*) aṭpa eṭpe; (*tender*) beleń (2); (*sensation of touching*) gaegam; (*uncomfortable feeling of*) lasak pasak; (*of fruit*) cokak, ganthar; (*vessel for oil*) kum, kupạ; (*blotch on*) sọsrọć khoda. *Cf.* RUB, THIN, THICK.

SKINNY—liṭpiṭiạ, rakrić, reńṭa (M), riṇṭi (F), roeda; (*very*) ruhuń rupuń.

SKIP, TO—lep, uć.

SKIRT, A—kạcni; (*worn by little girls*) ghańgri.

SKITTISH, TO BE—phirphir.

SKULK, TO—dabkao, lota luti; (*off*) ghaskao.

SKULL, THE—kapar, khapri; (*hollow bellow*) totka gạḍa; (*half*) adh khạpri.

SKY, THE—serma.

SLABBER, TO—sẹmbẹ suruć, siluń pituń.

SLACK—hhiso bhoso, dhil, dhil dhọkọć, dhiloń dhọluń, lirkọć lọrkọć, lirọć lọrọć, liroń lọroń, lirwa sạ we, pisạr pasar; (*attention to*) dhilạu.

SLAG (*from smelting furnace*)—ić.

SLAKE, TO (*as lime*)—barao.

SLAMMING, SOUND OF—darae (2).

SLANDER—(*to*) dohmot, phecań, phond, porphond; (*to publish*) dońka, ḍuḍa.

SLANTING—gholkạo, colkhao, gapuć, ghatra, lạde, tarcha, ṭerha, tircha, tircha tirchi, toe.

SLAP—(*to*) cetak̕, dhatir, thapa; (*sound of a*) carat, paras, patas; (*with a huk marte*, paras m, patas m; (*each other, to*) thapa thopo; (*dash, to go*) tahap tatup.

SLASH, TO—hubag, mak̕, mań.

SLATE, A—silat, silot; (*wooden*) pata.

SLATTERNLY—bajrahi, bhosudo, dalsiń talsiń, dhadra (M), dhadri (F), dhejraha (M), dhejrahi (F), dindirsić (F), dindirsić, ganduk̕ sanduk̕, hejleć pejleć, hidra gisra, lesraha (M), lesrahi (F), pandrahi.

SLAVE,—(*a*) golam, gulam; (*to*) khatao.

SLAVERING—loro boto, sembe suruć, sere sibuć; (*& perspiring*) sembe suruć.

SLAY, TO—goć, mauta.

SLEEK—jhere (2), jhuru (2); (*of hair*) celkot, cendkot̕; (*to become*) umbrau.

SLEEP—(*to*) gitić, janapit̕, japit̕; (*to be in a deep*) ghumghor; (*to wake from*) ebhen; (*to rise from*) gitić beret̕; (*to be heavy with*) lithi; (*to move in*) as us; (*food to cause child to*) janapit̕ak̕; (*to, as foot*) katkatao, rahao; (*in company with, to*) gitić goro; (*without*) lutuk̕ (2); (*a rug for*) dari; (*lightly*) torkal; (*feeling of one wakened from*) andha ondho.

SLEEPER, A RAILWAY—silpat.

SLEEPY—asam usum, dudrum; (*very*) jhap (2); (*to be very*) umdhi; (*headed*) gojra; (*looking*) orloporlo.

SLEEVE—astin.

SLEIGHT—thakai.

SLENDER—jalpa, jalpak̕, jalpha, nenheć, siwiń (2), siyań; (*very*) larlaria.

SLICE—(*to*) cheo, katrao; (*deeply, to*) laher, lahur; (*thinly, to*) caki, katrao; (*a thin*) cakti.

SLIDE, TO—lenjer, pichol; (*down*) dhardhar; (*sitting*) ghasghasao.

SLIGHT—etań, halka, nakwal, nanha; (*sound*) satapata; (*& frequent, of diarrhœa*) siroć soroć; (*of fever*) dărã sõrẽ; (*to*) batul, dhat dhut, ergejak̕, gańjon, khot, lende, nandan, nehat, nemor, nihăt, ninda, nindhan.

SLIGHTED—apuc.

SLIGHTLY—alpalua, arap, dara soro, dorasa, doyo, halat̕ (2), khet̕ khotor, laplonde, phusphas; (*very*) phusphas; (*opp of tight*) dhimsi, dhiusi; (*of fever*) roproro, resom, rosoposo.

SLIM—jalpa, jalpak̕, jońje, jońjroć, khad, khadea, lorea, loryo, nanha, rakrić rańgap, renta (M), rinti (F), rikrić (F), siyań, tatiaha, tuila (M), tuili (F); (*& tall*) laklakia, lorea, loryo, tatarbań; (*as a stick*) sisiar; (*& feeble*) lapar longat̕.

SLIME FROM MOUTH &c.—kharak̕.

SLIMY—cikăr, tioć toroć.

SLING, A—(*for carrying*) sikuar; (*for throwing stones*) genduar, gindwar.

SLINKING HERE & THERE—gayań guyuń.

SLIP—(*fault*) galti, khoc; (*to*) darrao, lenjer, phuskut̕, pichlau, pichol, piclau; (*off, to*) buć, buruć; (*out, to*) buruć, phuskuć; (*from under, to*) buruć; (*through fingers*) buruć; (*out of hole*) buryuń; (*down*) dhasao, hoshosao; (*gradually*) hosur; (*through*) paskao; (*away*) phasur; (*to make a*) bedoć; (*to let*) phuskut̕; (*on, to*) harar.

SLIPPERS—catki panahi; (*without heel*) silpat; (*hitting heel, noise of*) catać cetuć, citat̕ catet̕.

SLIPPERY—barać buruć, lenjer; (*deceitful*) endə pende; (*& wet*) lejek pejek.

SLIPPING—ghar gharia; (*a pin to prevent anything*) thuni.

SLIPS, TO SPLIT INTO THIN—chiri biri.

SLIT—(*a*) khanj; (*to*) boguć.

SLOBBERING—sere sibuć, siluń pituń.

SLOPE—(*a*) dhalu, dhardhari, tarcha; (*to*) dhalu; (*not having enough*) mandhal; (*of hill*) dangi, darsăr, dasna, dhasna; (*having a*) dharkalha.

SLOPPY—labar lobur.

SLOTHFUL—ańsasua, asania, asketia, awańsacua, bhańgra, bhańgua, dare dhatuak̕, digo dogo.

SLOUGH—(*to*) ur; (*of snake*) biń kańcur.

SLOVENLY—bajrahi, bhasudań, bhosdoń, bhondo, bijo bojo, bojge, bojra (M), bujri (F), dalcań (M), dulcuń (F), dhadra (M), dhadri (F), dhẹjraha (M), dhẹjrạhi (F), gạnduk sạnduk, gesoṭiạ, gesṭạhi, gọsọc, gọsrẹ, hẹjlẹc pẹjlẹc, heńjlań peńjlań, hirań petań, jhadga, jhadge, jhadọc (2), kador, lejraha (M), lejrạhi (F), leńjraha (M), leńjrạhi (F), lesraha (M), lesrạhi (F), lijrạha, mạdhuạ, mạndhuạ, mańga murạ, mọrgọt, pandrạhi, thosot morgot, tosot morgot; (*& lean*) mọrgọt.

SLOW—bẹhọd, dapadopo, gạṇḍhiạ, jaba jobo, jaha joho, japa jopo, jape tope, jipạ jape, jọbọdhọń, lạmbri, lapre (F), libạ labe (F), libọc lọbọc (M), libo lobo, modhu, sotyot, susti, thalpe (F); (*speaking*) gahãt gẹhẽt, thothra (M), thuthri (F); (*in movement*) gahat gẹhẽt, kobon (2), lajak lujuk, lạjuń (2), laṭea; (*& dull*) joḍo.

SLOWLY—baibai, chio choko, dhire suste, dholo (2), dhoyot dhopot, dolodolo, galań guluń, jahat johot, jhahat jhohot, jhọhọt mọhọt, jọhọt mọhọt, kạḍań kuḍuń, kale, kale (2), kẹrmẹ kẹrmẹte, kiḍạ kaḍe, labań lubuń, labhań lubhuń, lagae logoe (F), lọhọk, lubhuń (2), lubuń (2), mẹhẽt (2), mẹsẹt (2), ọstẹ (2), phanda phondo, rabac rubuc, raham rohom, rahan rohon, rahap ruhup, rase (2), rẹbẹ (2), ribic, riboc rọbọc, ribon kobon, rigạm cagam, rimbạ rambe, riṅgạm ciṅgạm, rimkạ ṭamke, rinji, rose (2), rosme, rọsọm, sitoc sọtọc ṭahari, ṭahri, ṭhạhri, tharsat thorsot, thirsot thorsot; (*of eating*) ruput (2); (*& hesitatingly*) lubus (2); (*& painfully*) japań jupuń, jipạń japań; (*& feeling with feet*) tharsat thorsot. *Cf.* TO MOVE.

SLUGGISH—amoṭ, asket, asketiạ, ḍariạ, digo dọgọ, gạndhet, gạndhiạ, goda, gọsrẹ, haja hojo, jaba jobo, jodo, kobon (2), lạndha phuciạ, lạndhiạ, lạndhuạ, lapre (F), laṭea, laṭhea, lejraha (M), lejrạhi (F), leńjraha (M), leńjrạhi (F), lijrạha, mạdhuạ, mạndhuạ, modhu, robrobo, thalpe (F); (*in movement*) dapadopo, jaha joho, jọbọdhọń, joho (2), libạ labe (F), libọc lọbọc (M), libo lobo.

SLUR—(*over, to*) hela hili; (*on, to cast a*) khọṭ.

SLUSHY—cabcab, cọbcọb, hẹjẹ pẹjẹ, jọbọc (2); (*to be*) cahla.

SLUT, A (*dog*)—eṅga seta.

SLY—husiạr.

SMACKING—(*of lips*) cakap (2), chakọp; (*sound*) liṭhum, paṭapaṭ; (*sound, with a*) huk marte, liṭhun m., paras m., paṭas m.

SMALL—bẹc bẹdrẹc, bẹdrẹc, bendret, beńjak, beńjlań, bẹṭret, bheṭra (M), bhiṭri (F), bhuṭkạ (M), bhuṭki (F), ceńcuriạ, cerca, cuni, ḍac ḍuc, ḍẹbẹ (2), ḍẹblẹ, ḍẹrẹt, ḍẹt, ḍẹt (2), ḍhena, ḍuc, duluc dupuc, ḍumkạ, ḍumkuc (2), galae, gendlań, gẹńjlań, gẹńjọr, guḍ guḍạu, huḍiń, jẹlpẹc, jenec, jõc, juc, jurạ, jurgạ, jurmi (F), kaḍayut kuḍuyut, kạpṭic, kạṭic, khedra, kherra, lenda, leṭret (M), liṭrit (F), lẹṭwẹt, mer sitruc, nic, pilcu, pilcuń, puṭuryut, regaṭhiạ, rembre, reṭhạ, reṭhma (M), reṭhmi (F), rimsic, royo, royo ropo, ruiạ, salpot, semec, siṭkạ, sutruc, ṭebra (M), ṭibri (F), ṭembec ṭuruc, ṭembrot, ṭemret, ṭeṇṭhạ, ṭepa ṭepe, ṭhemka (M), ṭhimki (F), ṭhepca (M), ṭhipci (F), ṭhikri (F), ṭirạ (M), ṭum, ṭunạ (M), ṭuni (F), ṭurạ (M), ṭuri (F), ṭuryut; (*too*) phuckạ; (*of stature*) baorã (M), bhãuri (F), berga, chepko, ḍhebra (M), ḍhibri (F), gedra (M), gidri (F), jorma (M), jurmi (F); (*of children*) gadar gudur, pedec (2), poṭyot, ṭembe ṭurạ (M), ṭembe ṭuri (F); (*of dwarfs*) gadar gudur; (*of creatures*) hupṭic; (*of ears*) piṭu; (*of leaves*) sidric bidric; (*of fields*) ṭapra ṭopra; (*of piece of wood*) ṭhuṭkut; (*in space*) atgạṭe; (*fine*) digir; (*to become, through use*) ṭhuṭki; (*to make*) guṇḍạ, guṇḍạ guṇḍi, guṇḍrạ; (*& great*) hupṭic hapṛak, ṭurạ ṭuri; (*& lean*) cerca bayar, lẹṭra (M), liṭri (F); (*& round, as hole*) ruru (2); (*& flat*) cạkti; (*& dirty*) silmoc; (*& shrivelled*) copa cupi; (*talk*) gọlpọ; (*& ill-looking*) jarac juruc; (*mouthed*) homboryot; (*pox*) guṭi, mari guṭi. *Cf.* PIECE, PIECES, QUANTITY.

SMART—(*clever*) bhãoar, bhãwãr, celko melko (F), ghagọr, hat chuṭ, hath chuṭi, husiạr; (*to*) chuc, ẹrẹc (2), parpạrao, sidic marte.

SMARTING—*carat* (2), *carenpar*, chan (2), chak, grec (2), ragam (2), sidic.

SMASH, TO—kecet, khaia i aeru, posak, poset, talga tauak; (*up*) chitra phutau; (*to atoms*) gejer; (*dash*) aruc taruc; (*sound of a*) hadbad.

SMEAR, TO—choc. jodbodao, lasrao, lesrao, leta, thopram; (*with dung*) choc gobor, gec garic, guric kukar, landa; (*with ointment*) kukar; (*soft clay*) paliau.

SMEARED—(*roughly, as floor*) jede bede; (*with mud, to be*) jodo bodo.

SMELL—bas, so; (*to*) bas, ji, so; (*strong*) andka andki, lag so; (*sweet*) mohok, bes so; (*sweetly, to*) mahkao; (*a bad*) ais, baric so; (*a rotten*) morot, sea so; (*unpleasant*) ankhaila; (*sickening*) ghara ghari; (*to rise, as a*) bhak, phutau; (*badly, to*) sitic; (*danger, to*) birlan; (*urinous*) thothot, tothot.

SMELTING IRON—kuthi; (*slag from it*); (*amount produced*) muha.

SMILE—(*to*) landa. malac muluc, muskoc, muluc; (*with a*) muckok marte.

SMIRCHED—(*to become*) garsa gale; (*with black*) koya, kuya; (*with soot*) nolhat.

SMITHY, A—pasra, kamar pasra, kamar sal.

SMOKE—dhua, dhuagia, jharak, jhol motha; (*to*) dhua; (*to, as hams*) dhua rata, gk; (*blowing out*) edoe padoe; (*uncomfortable from*) kokkodro, okkodro.

SMOKED—jhulainda; (*in cooking, to be*) okkodor, okkodro.

SMOKING A PIPE, &c., SOUND OF—soyot (2).

SMOOTH—chuk (2), cikan, cikar, ciknar, gereyom, hender, hendra, jhere (2), jhuru (2), lenjer, lumun, ser; (*to*) mathao; (*to make*) sariau; (*of water*) camphel, phiriphic; (*down, to*) gereyom; (*of hair*) celkot, cendkot, galgaeatin; (*in parts*) hender (2).

SMOULDER, TO—mondok (2).

SMUTTED WITH SOOT—jhol, jhol motka, jhulainda, koya, kaia, kuya.

SNAIL—(*a*) rekoc; (*an edible*) jom r.; (*a water*) gongha, seta r.; (*a land*) tandi gongha, tandi r.; (*like*) jahat johot, jhahat jhohot, johot mohot.

SNAKE, A—bin, kal; (*river*) gada b.; jola b.; (*water*) gada citi; (*grass*) dolodan, horhoran; (*cobra*) ayan bin, babra ayan; (*hill*) lar b.; (*tree*) sakam ret b., patarhan b.; (*R rye*) bitkil dhond, buka sebek b.; (*spotted*) bandphora b., citi b; (*poisonous*) ambaitar b., gandet b.; (*burrowing*) sunum b.; (*rock*) boda b., jambro, jamro, kod jambro, man baha; (*slough of*) bin kancur; (*to move as*) biryon boryon; (*charmer*) bin ekenecic, sapaharia; (*moving quickly, sound of*) sae sae; (*bite, charms for*) bin mantar; (*bite, cure by charms*) jhar; (*bite curer*) jharni.

SNAKES—(*& scorpions*) bin kidin; (*basket for keeping*) piri; (*spec. of*) dak cita, dhond, dudhia ayan, dudhia boda, duludan, hawal murum, jergn ayan, kari nangin, man baha, murum, nagnagin, potolia, soc gada b., thutri b., tutri b.; (*method of treating poison*) dhuriau.

SNAP, TO—cywec, coak, cowak, ratpat, satok, topak; (*at, in speech*) hatan (2), beten (2), regen (2F); (*the fingers*) cutki; (*of anything brittle*) thas; (*at*) lese; (*with a*) tergen marte, thas m., thes m., thus m., tun m.

SNAPPING, SOUND OF—carat, tes, thas, thes, thus.

SNARE—(*a*) jhali; (*to*) jhali, pasi, phasi; (*to set a*) jhali odao; (*a bird*) kombet, kubet, kumbet phasi, kur, laota, tapok, tepok; (*lapwing sitting on eggs*) or dak.

SNARL, TO—ghai (2), ghao (2), gondrao.

SNATCH, TO—jhapta jhapti; (*away*) atkir; (*of several people*) hura huri.

SNEAK ABOUT, TO—hulkau.

SNEER, TO—binduc; (*at*) lende.

SNEEZE, TO—achim; (*said to child who*) nak badho.

SNIFF, TO—ji, surkau, susu; (*of dog*) kayan kuyun.

SNIGGER, TO—hithitau, isir sitkoc.

SNIP OFF, TO—hese, hucak, hucec, hulak, petec, ricot; (*with fingers*) holec, hulec, tungau; (*end*) helec.

SNIPE, THE—dak batta, caha, dhanuk batta; (*painted*) dok sere; (*jack*) gindu̧ar bata.

SNIVEL, TO—sergeć, surué.

SNORE, TO—khadar khodor, kharkhor, sosq, udur.

SNORT, TO—nathu phopao, phopao, phaphuau, phur, phurgu, susu; (*of bull*) huka, su; (*& paw the ground*) tawić.

SNOT—sulué; (*like*) sere sibuć.

SNOUT—mocoń, nathu, thotna, tothna; (*a pig's*) cilim, harta pai, jań nahel; (*to turn up with the*) ute.

SNOW—him, pala; (*white*) phik leka; (*water*) itiń dak.

SNUB—(*to*) dabao, jabdo, jobdao, jobdo; (*nosed*) nakta (M), nakti (F).

SNUFF, TO—phur.

SO—ado, ene to, emon, eto, ieke, iyo, nun, nunak; (*that*) jemne, jemnać, jemon, jano; (*& so*) emon semon, ia, phalna (M), phalni (F), tuske; (*long as*) dhabić, dharić; (*they say*) bole. *Cf.* MUCH, MANY, &c.

SOAK, TO—diń dabur, sembe surué; (*in*) bhijau; (*through*) soro.

SOAP—sabun; (*stone, a kind of*) mungia pathra.

SOB, TO—barań buruń, bharań bharuń, heke (2), hakuć (2), kahar kohur, kasać kusuć, khusuć (2), kuhur (2), kusuć (2), surué; (*& weep*) asać usuć, biriń (2).

SOBER—sote.

SOCIAL—(*priveleges, to deny*) joi ghuti baron; (*customs, fine for transgressing*) kutum dand; (*customs, to transgress*) londbhond; (*position, to rise in*) tuli.

SOCIETY, A—khut.

SOCKET—khanj; (*of door*) bhurni.

SODOMY—jogna.

SOFT—alga, bhar (2), bhud bhudia, bhusur (2), burui (2), busur (2), gudgudau, labić, lablabi, labar (2), leher, lebreć, lejar (2), lenjraha (M), lenjrahi (F), lepes, late (2), liblib, libuk, licar, lobhor, ledor bodor, logoć (2), loher bohor, lotoe, lubur, lublubu, lumuń, luyum (2), mogoe (2), molam, naram, narma, norma, nogom, phoksaha, phoska, pokye, sarlaha, toget, tolgoyum; (*of quick-sand*) bugur (2); (*of fruit*) bilbilau, labus (2), lapos, libir (2), lidu; (*as roasted grain*) bhara bhura; (*of mud*) labar lobur, ledher bodher, lewa; (*as wool*) layam luyum; (*as pillow*) lomoń; (*of grass &c.*) lopioń; (*of iron*) maskuta; (*to be*) liblib; (*to become*) bangam, borborao, jau, labić, ladbad, lebreć, norma, noryum; (*feeling of eating anything*) lepe; (*mass, mixed into a*) buhor (2); (*& sticky*) leje peje, lebjer bobor, lepe pepe; (*& beautiful*) lerem (2); (*to mouth*) mongre (2); (*& clear, of music*) sahar hohor; (*& insipid*) phoksaha; (*to make*) dahalao, jau, manta.

SOFTLY—gemeń (2), phusur (2).

SOGGY—sembe surué.

SOHRAE FESTIVAL, THE—got sohrae porob; (*custom at*) jale; (*rice given at*) sisir daka; (*liquor at*) sisir handi; (*serenading cattle at*) jagao.

SOIL—has, hasa, ot; (*moist*) jabdabi ot; (*exhausted*) hirhat; (*saline*) kharna, khorna; (*dry*) kuthar; (*soft*) labić h.; (*fertile*) lag h.; (*unproductive*) cothra, khangot ot, malot; (*stiff*) maruć hende h.; (*mica schist*) lipindić h.; (*good*) sebel h., hasawan ot; (*hill*) buru ot, kotko ot; (*gravelly*) kankar h., mutturi ot, rodge dhiri ot; (*stiff clay*) rehda h.; (*a friable*) tirom h.; (*used to dye cloth*) mancha h.; (*manured with cattle dung*) gurić h.; (*displacing the*) padgak; (*to turn over the*) paska.

SOILED—margaitha, ritha; (*to become*) garsa gale; (*by liquid dripping*) hirar garer.

SOLATIUM—(*on divorce*) chadaodi; (*to elder sister*) taram gande.

SOLD FOR A PRICE, TO BE—bikau.

SOLDER, TO—jorao, rasao.

SOLDIER, A—palton, sipahi; (*European*) gora.

SOLE—(*of foot*) talka; (*of boot or shoe*) tala.

SOLICITOUS, TO BE—ande sale, nẹhŏr, thurthurạu.

SOLICITUDE—hadọs, hią, jala, jogas, phikir, porbhae, sẹnẹ dewer, ṭhonk; (*without*) khulạsa, phạrią phạṭi, rehăr.

SOLID—kaṭhor, nimon, nisạnḍ; (*to become*) sạkiť.

SOLITARY—bạnua, ekan, ekŏt, gasaċ gusuċ, nisun, sadhẹr; (*habits, of*) birnạha, gasaċ gusuċ, mesa.

SOLVE, TO—hudis ńam.

SOME—adhan, adọm, bajẹ, birlą, jahan, kichu; (*one*) jăhăe, jahanić; (*thing*) cetaṫ, jahanak; (*times*) bajẹ, bajẹkhanẹ, bajẹk, chaḍa mela, chaḍbiḍ, jạli khạli, khanẹ, pake sake, solo sańjok; (*where*) nạhi nindhạn.

SOMERSAULT, TO TURN A—bidią, sunbajik.

SON—(*a*) bạbu, họn, kora họpọn; (*1st*) marań kora; (*2nd*) tala kora; (*wife of 2nd*) tala bahu; (*3rd*) sańjlạ kora; (*4th*) mańjlą k., hudiń sańjlą; (*of young brother or sister*) goṅgo k.; (*affectionate*) beṭa; (*& daughter-in-law*) họn kimin; (*-in-law*) jăwăe gọ, jăwăe gọmkẹt; (*-in-law, living with father-in-law*) ghardi jăwăe; (*of man, the*) mańwa họpọn.

SONG, A—sereń; (*to compose*) sereń jorao; (*short*) akhor; (*verse of*) akhor; (*chorus*) corań; (*to praise in*) durạń; (*preliminary to*) lahoj, taha reta, yore; (*dancing, &c.*) *Cf.* sereń.

SOON—coṭok, halą.

SOOT—ńolhaṫ; (*smirched with*) gẹyak, jhọl mọṭka, jhulạinda, ńolhaṫ.

SOOTHE, TO—bahalao, boḍ, boḍhao; (*by st. oking*) sudhạ.

SOPHISTICATED—phạṅga.

SORCERY—ban, guni; (*a practiser of*) gunidar, ṭọṭọk.

SORE, A—ghao; (*of throat*) gańghar; (*of neck*) hạsli ghao; (*kind of*) boṅga khoda, pạchiạri, rọkọċ ghao; (*specific*) chuchandạr; (*malignant*) nargi; (*of feet*) dhọrọṫ (2), lipcċ lọpọċ, paeṭhan, paiṭhanī ghao, ras; (*at angle of mouth*) mẹrọm ghao; (*between the eyes*) doemoń; (*with sinus*) ghugri ghao; (*raw*) bẹrẹl ghao; (*to spread as*) ạtiń, ghalghalao; (*to be*) hanas, haso; (*to run as*) biriń (2); (*large dirty*) galak (2); (*discharge from*) garań dak; (*of armpit*) kakh bilạr ghao; (*inside nose*) poca nargī.

SOREL, THE INDIAN—arak kudrum.

SORES—(*gathering*) copsa; (*a means of curing*) dhuṛiạu.

SORROW—bhab, bhabna, bhuk, duk, duk, dukh, hadọs, hirdani; (*to*) bhạbi, bhabna, hirdạn; (*to cause*) santao, santap; (*exclm. of*) ạyuguh, hae, haehae, haere, jare (2), eh, ohae, ohae hae, uh; (*over, to*) guni bhạbik, hińjrạu.

SORROWFUL—kolok (2), momoyoṫ, ńarak (2), ńẹrẹk (2); (*to be*) haemoe, mọnẹ khaṭọ, udạs.

SORRY—(*to be*) kasta kạsti, kastao, khaekhabrọk, pachtao; (*plight, to be in*) haruń.

SORT—jinis, kisim, porkar, prokar, rọkọm; (*every*) bạrghaser.

SORTS—(*two*) bar rọkọm; (*many*) ligiṛ sigiṛ, lere bere, liṭi birsi, parkar, nana parkar; (*out of, to appear*) robojholo. *Cf.* ALL, OUT OF.

SOTTISH—anta.

SOUL—atma, jib, jiwi.

SOUND—(*noise*) awaj, sabad, sabod, saḍ; (*flawless*) nimon, niphuṭ, nisạnḍ; (*healthy*) nirogi; (*without a*) saċ suċ, sansun, siṛiċ soboṫ, siṛik taham; (*a deep*) huḍur (2), huduṛ (2); (*non-resonant*) phadar phọdọr; (*of striking hollow object*) ḍhuń (2), raṛań; (*volume of*) raru; (*of anything dry when disturbed*) ragam cagam; (*of striking flawless vessel*) rão rão; (*of knocking several objects*) thukṛạ thukṛi; (*of soft body falling*) laṛbhad; (*of elephant walking*) dahap duhup; (*of animal running on wet soil*) badṛak (2); (*of taut string*) bhạṫkur; (*of ḍhiṅki*) dampol (2), dhạmpuṛ (2) (*of light objects falling*) ḍap ḍup; (*of rotten egg when shaken*) ḍhọkọk (2); (*of wood dragging on ground*) họḍọr (2); (*of branches shaken*) jhaṛọe (2); (*of driving thread home in weaving*) ṭhakṛok; (*of stringed instrument*) turuṅ (2); (*a long-drawn*) rāoāo. *Cf.* DRUM, WATER, CRASHING, CREAKING, &c.

SOUND, TO—baja, bajia, sade; (*as bell*) ririṅ; (*shrilly*) iiraṅ raraṅ; (*loudly*) dildil; (*empty*) raṅruṅ; (*in succession*) ṭharaṅ ṭhuruṅ.

SOUP—rase, sirwa; (*from bones*) jaṅ rase; (*a thick*) ariyan.

SOUR—hilweť, hirhať, jojo, kasať, titi; (*of milk*) giri; (*of food*) liṭi; (*to become*) muhũť, phaṭao.

SOUTH, THE—dakhin, dakhna, mora muhã; (*from the*) dakhnahi.

SOW—(*to*) er; (*for transplantation, to*) achra, aphor; (*after one ploughing, to*) camaeṭa; (*to begin to*) puhna; (*discord, one who*) bajhani, batar; (*a*) sukri eṅga; (*a young*) sukri paṭhi.

SOWN, SELF—lambe.

SPACE—(*small in*) aṭgaṭe, eṭke ṭorẽ; (*to take up*) gabao; (*open*) phãk; (*occupying much*) laclaca, lapickak (F), lapǝkak (M), lapondaṅ, laslasa, leclece; (*after a short*) lagle, ṭaohẽ; (*of time*) ghari; (*with much*) phael.

SPACES BETWEEN, HAVING—siṭar paṭar, siṭo soṭo.

SPADE, A—(*Cf.*) khudali.

SPAN, A—ber, bita; (*between thumb & fore-finger*) dhingur.

SPANGLE, A—ṭikli.

SPARE—(*slim*) jalpa; (*to*) bacol.

SPARINGLY, TO USE—romoč koṭoč.

SPARKLE, TO—barač buruč, bilik balaṅ, biliť, jalať juluť, jirip (2); (*when shaken*) jhipir (2), jipir (2).

SPARKS—ceṭe; (*to rain*) bhurbhuri.

SPARROW, THE—gharwa; (*chirp of*) ciric (2).

SPARSE—etaṅ, hidaṅ ṭhapaṅ, hiṭaṅ jharaṅ, patar satar, satar patar, taral basal; (*& not well-grown*) rayam rayum.

SPASM OF PAIN, A—hiric.

SPASMS—bai, camek bai; (*nervous*) cihik bai; (*of muscles*) bandor bai, tarkha tarkhi; (*to be seized with*) ṭarkha ṭarkhi; (*to move limbs in*) phadruk, piriak.

SPATCH, WITH A—pacak marte.

SPATTER, TO—chidgai, chiric (2), pasir; (*from side to side*) chidga chidgi.

SPEAK, TO—gal, galmarao, galsal, kakale, men, phedrao, ror; (*eager to*) kharkhar; (*at random*) bhacbhacao, bhackao, bhocbhocao; (*much & loudly*) bhekbhekao, boktaok, eren beteń; (*nonsensically*) akhaṭ bakhaṭ, alok bakok, bakao, bhak bhok; (*back*) carap (2), dundrau; (*softly*) gandar gundur; (*loudly*) cancan, ṭarkhi; (*angrily*) corcoṭaṅ, etraṅ, keńkeń, ruheť (M), taraṅ tiriń tiriń taraṅ; (*harshly*) sirog, targum; (*distinctly*) pusṭau; (*distinctly, unable to*) bodo; (*quickly & indistinctly*) lese (2); (*together*) lapai, mepen; (*evil of*) cugli capaṭi; (*kindly*) chuchkar; (*against one*) gokhla; (*petulantly*) keoṅ meoṅ, tiriń goriń; (*as one learning language*) kẽrẽč dõrẽč.

SPEAKER—(*a*) sawalia; (*the*) aprẽ.

SPEAKING—galgul; (*without*) ghusuṅ (2), kokleso; (*to help by*) ror sohoť; (*from the throat*) buktan, gehẽť (2); (*through the nose*) gãgũ, ghenne; (*terms, not to be on*) ada adi, bikhar, rusa rusi; (*continually*) bikoť (2), geheť gundur, khodor (2); (*seldom*) dundur musak, gahãť geheť, masač musuč; (*& weeping*) hene phene; (*indistinctly*) hodo dodo, thať thoť. *Cf.* LOW. SLOW.

SPEAR, A—barchi, bolom, borlom; (*fish*) kahli, ṭenṭa.

SPECIAL—nij.

SPECIES—jinis, tur; (*a good*) jaṭgar.

SPECIFIC SORE—cuchundar ghao.

SPECTACLE, A—khilod, lila, tamasa.

SPEECH—bhaka, bhakha, bhasa, boli, buli ror; (*having defect in*) gaṅguṅ, gitak, ladar bador, thotha, thothia, thothra (M) thothri (F), thotra (M), thutri (F), totha, totra; (*indistinct*) gaela (2), ghaṅ ghuṅ, lodro; (*slow of*) gehẽť, thotha, thothra (M), thothri (F), thotra (M), thutri (F); (*to falter in*) thať thoť. *Cf.* FLUENT.

SPEECHLESS—haemoekaṭ, haimuikaṭ, thothoť; (*to become*) cokao; (*to render*) sursunduč.

SPELL—(*to*) banan; (*a*) lagu; (*to be under a*) lagu lagaok; (*on, to cast a*) aha, pathri, paṭihar; (*of evil eye*) hoe hisiṫ; (*for crying children*) aṭasi paṭasi; (*for choking*) chuchukuṫ.

SPELLS—jhinṭhi pathri, jinṭhi pathri.

SPEND, TO—bhangao, bharabhat, bistur, buḍau, buṛau, oherkot, khelao, khorea, nipat; (*life*) jojao. (*Cf.*) TIME.

SPHERICAL—gol, guṇḍ, gulu mulu, guṛmuria; (*& small*) guḍnuc (2).

SPICE—masola; (*a*) jauan, mithi; (*tamarind*) palwa; (*like ginger*) nirbis.

SPICES—mar masala; (*stone for grinding*) paṭi dhiri; (*cooked in certain way*) roṅ; (*to add to cooked food*) chanka chanki, chankao.

SPIDER, A—bindi; (*spec. of*) kul b., kuṛanḍum; (*thread spun by*) b. sutam; (*web of*) b. gaṇaḳ.

SPIKENARD—joṭamasi.

SPIKEY—ranga oonga, rangha rongho.

SPILL, TO—aleč taseč, bhubhau, bubhau, chilkau, hirič, leceč; (*of grain*) bujur; (*of water*) ciwaḳ cawaḳ; (*& scatter*) hirič pasir; (*when pouring out*) cidor codor; (*when carrying*) ciwaḳ cawaḳ, loroḳ toroḳ.

SPIN, TO—(*thread &c*) tahos; (*round*) bharbharao, bheu (2); (*round, to cause to*) uruṫ; (*out*) ramoč koteč.

SPINACH, A KIND OF—palak araḳ.

SPINDLE, A HAND—dhera; (*winder for*) naṭwa.

SPINE, THE—bisi jaṅ; (*depression on side of*) bisi gaḍa.

SPINNING—(*top, a*) bhuncampa; (*wheel*) carkha; (*wheel, band of*) mal; (*wheel, part of*) awa, malkaṭhi; (*wheel, axle of*) ṭaku; (*noise of*) daedão, hedor (2), hendor (2), ṭekos.

SPINSTERHOOD—ḍangua, dingi ḍangua.

SPINY—singhin; (*caterpillars*) singhin bharua.

SPIRE—(*a*) cura, muthai; (*to*) sui.

SPIRIT—atma, jiwi, mon, mone; (*anger*) rag; (*a*) bonga, buru, gosae, jin; (*pure distilled*) mahuar, phuli paura; (*a malignant*) acraeli bonga, duarsini, ghurni dano bonga, kadu bonga; (*the chief*) maraṅ buru; (*to come out*) suman; (*without*) alno; (*to introduce*) thapna thapni; (*of deceased father*) porodhol. *Cf.* POSSESSED.

SPIRITED—khāc, khackhacia, khanṭaha (M), khanṭahi (F), ragi, ragragia, taji, tej; (*low*) ahluṅ; (*away, to be*) angen, bakao, banwas.

SPIRITS—(*in high*) riri (2), ritia riti, ritiau; (*depressed in*) hulas bhanga; (*dangerous from*) kotaha.

SPIRITUAL PRECEPTOR, A—purhut.

SPIT, TO—tho; (*out*) ula.

SPITE—dahoḳ, edre, kan, khunus, kun; (*to harbour*) kana kani; (*full of*) hesalia, ira, iraa, pur hesalia.

SPLASH, TO—bhubhau, chilkau, ḍabra, hudraḳ, phicir, picir, ṭabač ṭubuč, ṭabaḳ ṭubuḳ; (*up*) humṭaḳ; (*with a*) cabur marte, chabur m., cabhor m., cobor m., kabur m., phec m., phicir m., ṭabaḳ m., ṭubuḳ m.

SPLASHING SOUND—cabhar cabhur, cabhur, cabur, capur (2), chabur, dhaba dhubu, gudu (2), kabar kubur, kabhar kabhur, kabuḳ; (*to cause a*) ṭabač ṭubač, ṭabaḳ ṭabuḳ.

SPLEEN, THE—pila; (*enlarged*) ḍhobea, pila; (*a very large*) khapra pila.

SPLENDOUR—acel, partap, ṭhonok, ṭhosok.

SPLICE, TO—badhi.

SPLINTER—(*a wood*) sarlaḳ; (*to*) caṭkao, caṭaḳ, khidi bidi; (*to pierce hand*) sirba.

SPLIT, TO—amba phara, bichri, cagaṫ, cira, cirkau, ciro, dardarao, paraḳ, sira, sora, taraṛ; (*into pieces*) bichri, dal; (*into thin slips*) chiri biri, ciri biri; (*fruit, peas &c*) dal; (*sound of a*) phaṭ m.

SPOIL, TO—bemel, bhanga, dhun, durgathan, ghand guhend, josao, monda.

SPOILED, TO BE—bagḍao.

SPOKES OF WHEEL—ora.

SPONGE—(*a*) ispanj; (*like, of wet soil*) bilbilau.

SPOON, A—camac; (*small wooden*) cunduč; (*flat wooden*) ḍadu; (*iron*) ḍabu; (*leaf*) cukruč.

SPORT—*(to)* khamda, khamdi khamdi; *(to make)* kheldu, khildu, thatha.

SPOT—dag; *(on the)* surjumin, thar, thor; *(without)* sirik perik.

SPOTTED—ablakia, cerka bhorka, chit, citar kabar, dagi, kabar, kabra kotha, kabrak kobrok, tiklak tiklak; *(with white)* kabra dharra.

SPOUT—*(to)* sudrau; *(a)* tontorot; *(up or out, to)* pirurkau.

SPRAINED, TO BE—bickau, bielau, lotoc, mackao, meckao.

SPRAWL, TO—phada phodo, taptapa.

SPRAY—*(to)* piopoyo; *(to fall in)* phec; *(with a)* phec m., phicir m., picir m.

SPREAD, TO—atet, bambkao, charao, chirbitir, chiria, chit, chitiau, cirbitir, dabao, dundlau, gohlao, khaya khutri, parcao, pasante, pasar, pasnao, phaela; *(of a sore)* atin; *(of fire)* gotor; *(out)* asen tasen, ciri biri, laslasa, pacak, sartalak; *(out to dry)* mandrao, melao, tase rghor, tase; *(out to receive)* atan; *(sheaves for threshing)* chitau; *(as water falling)* pasir; *(a mat)* bel; *(soft clay)* paliau; *(as rumour)* carcao, goga, ungn; *(as news)* sarsadle; *(abroad)* dahadahi, damdahe; *(over)* jabrao, jhabrao; *(with the hands)* phidgil; *(here & there)* pasna pasni; *(from one to another)* duda; *(quickly)* caomarao. *Cf.* WIDE.

SPRIG—cikon cokon.

SPRING, A—*(water)* cua, dadi, jharna, ukhur dadi; *(hot)* kund; *(traditional)* kere dadi; *(of gun-lock)* kamani; *(without)* rabuc rubuc; *(with)* dhamcuk marte; *(to issue from)* bhak, bhukur (2), jhar (2).

SPRING, TO—*(of plants)* janam, omon, patarak, phutau; *(of water)* bhakh bhakao, bhulkau, bhumkau, dubhau; *(of elastic force)* dhamcuk, lawan, lewak; *(upon)* jhaptao; *(back)* chontal, phantil; *(up)* uptan; *(up suddenly)* kutla; *(up & down)* lawak, likic (2), likir, loeoe (2).

SPRINGY—lahuc (2); *(to be)* lawar (2), locoe (2); *(at ends, to be)* lawic, liwic.

SPRINKLE, TO—chitkau, irci, jhatiau, phicir, picir, tirri.

SPROUT, TO—ankur, omon, pataragok, pote; *(from root, a)* p jhar; *(up pyramidically, to)* sui.

SPRUCE—chakmakia, cikon cokon.

SPUE, TO—uchlau.

SPUR—*(of fowl &c)* suba; *(of fighting-cock, steel)* kat.

SPURIOUS—phit, phosol.

SPURN, TO—bhades, phadgal; *(with hands)* phidgil.

SPURT—*(to)* bhak, chirchir, tirlik, tanti; *(with a)* bhokor marte, poloe m., tuyul (2).

SPY—*(a)* bat para, bhidia, bhiduk; *(to)* bhidi, ciu, jasu.

SQUAB—matku.

SQUABBLE, TO—beke (2), regen tegen, tegen, tekhra tikhri, tekra tikri.

SQUALID, TO LOOK—torlo morlo.

SQUANDER, TO—asec tasec, berbad, bharabhat, budau, burau, charkat, chorkot, dulau, nahas, naba kharba, obosta, riai khiai, riyai khiyai, tahas, ubla dubla, udai padae, udau, uper khaper.

SQUARE—*(a)* khond; *(four)* pon sira; *(off the)* toe; *(to, as a log)* pohol; *(roughly, to)* pahtao.

SQUASH, TO—lapak capak, locke, lecre, reset, seret; *(as fruit)* ladbad.

SQUASHY—labar lobur.

SQUAT—matku, thomsok (F); *(to)* asmandao, dondkoro, obor; *(to reside)* berel japak.

SQUEAKING—cece, ceco, rec, receo; *(of rats, &c.)* cac cuc, coc (2), coco, cuc (2), cui (2), kohor (2) satasutu; *(of pigs)* keke; *(of boots)* macmac.

SQUEAL—*(of animals)* cec, cek; *(of wooden axle)* cao.

SQUEEZE TO—kuca, lin, retet, ridet cirit, robot; *(in)* kasao; *(out)* bodoc, rodoc; *(out, as stone of fruit)* toloc; *(in the hand)* sipot; *(between finger & thumb)* tirmit.

SQUINT—*(to)* apir; *(eyed)* pelka (M), pilki (F), perla (M), pirli (F), tera (M), tiri (F), thesra (M), thisri (F).

SQUIRM, TO—gewel, kawal (2), kewel (2), kiwil (2).

SQUIRREL, A—(*striped*) toṛ; (*spec. of*) sega; (*large*) sisiaṛiñ; (*call of*) cuḍrué (2).

SQUIRT, TO—phickaṛi, phooṛ; (*out of mouth*) budrué.

ST. VITUS DANCE—bandor bạị, ṅokor.

STAB, TO—bhosa, sọbọk; (*a knife to*) bogda.

STABLE—(*a*) astabal, sadọm oṛak; (*to be*) ṭikạu.

STAFF, A—ṭheṅga; (*light*) hapa; (*blow with*) ṭheṅga; (*& gun*) ṭheṅga banduk.

STAG, A—boda jel; (*Sambar*) saram.

STAGE ON ROAD,—caṭṭi, ḍak cauki; (*to stage, to pass from*) ḍakeḍak.

STAGGERING—bajṛa bạjṛi, bić bidyạ, ḍẹbẹ (2), ḍhanman, ḍika ḍake, ḍoya ḍape, jambak jombok, jañje, kanḍeć manḍeć, kinḍeć manḍeć, konḍa manḍe, lẹcẹlẹcẹ, liṛwạ saṛwe, sọbọk koyọk.

STAIN—(*a*) gab, khọṭ; (*to*) dag, gabao, jọdbodao, rañ, roñ; (*to wash off*) ạruḅ.

STAINED—chīṭ, dagi; (*travel*) dạruk dạcuk; (*with oil &c*) poret.

STAIR—siṛhi.

STALE—bạsi, baske; (*of cooked rice*) mare ore.

STALK, A—budạ, ḍanḍi, ḍhanḍkạ; (*of sugarcane*) ạk ḍanḍi, ḍọg; (*having only one*) niphoṛ; (*of some plants*) ḍaṭhi.

STALLION,—ạnḍiạ sadọm.

STALWART—jahbaj, muṭhu.

STAMENS OF MATKOM FLOWER—sọhọe; (*to remove*) jhiliạu, sué.

STAMINA—dhẹj; (*lacking in*) laṛbaṛiạ, thosoć morgoć, tosot morgot.

STAMMER—bherruba; (*to*) bobe, bodṛo, lador bador, laṛbaṛao, laṛkhaṛao; (*with a*) thać thoć, that thot.

STAMP—(*a*) ṭikạs, ṭikis; (*to print*) chaba, chap, ukhṛạu; (*the foot, to*) dhạḅ (2); (*on with foot, to*) thạiyạ.

STANCHED, TO BE—ṭhamkao.

STAND, TO—bereć, teṅgon; (*of boys*) ḍiḍạ; (*of girls*) ḍiḍi; (*still*) tambhao, teṅgo; (*on tiptoe*) conḍok; (*ready*) jujhạu, tạhṭhao; (*in the way*) manḍmanḍe; (*idling*) anḍur manḍur, anḍur panḍur, ḍẹmḍẹm, heholok; (*with feet apart*) hẹjhẹjẹ (M), hidhidi, hijhiji (F); (*for pots a*) gārsande; (*for tame parokeet, a*) ṭena; (*on hind legs*) japaṛ, kargo.

STANDING—(*up, as hair*) rape, riskić, risrisi, rudrudu, rusrusu; (*to seize & throw down when*) kacṛao; (*to fall from*) gur; (*of no*) jhiñji jhuri.

STANZA, A—akhaṛ, akhoṛ.

STAPLE ON PLOUGH, AN IRON—pạsi.

STAR, A—ipil; (*morning*) bhurkạ; (*evening*) sukạṛ; (*4 in Great Bear*) budhi parkọm.

STARE, TO—ahirkuhir, anḍar onḍor, anḍir kunḍir, aril kuril, bẹṅgẹć, dhoro (2), lanḍa lonḍo, ripripi; (*round*) arić kurić; (*vacantly*) arak orok, marak morok.

STARING—ḍhẹrẹ (2), jaral jurul, korwak, muṭur (2), ripripi, takonia; (*eyes*) lonḍkoć, lonḍo (2).

STARLING, THE—kare, kisni; (*large*) bhonḍa kisni; (*pied*) care kisni, ẹrẹ kisni; (*chatter of*) kẹcọ bẹdṛọ.

STARVATION—teṅgo rụạ; (*to suffer from*) awañ ewer.

START, TO—(*begin*) calcul, dhundhaṛbheć, ẹhọḅ, gatao, gotao, upusti; (*jump*) camkao, cihik, cihirạu, cihkạu, cihrạu, kẹṭel, lẹṅgẹć, lukuć, luyuć, pạdgak, pehlañ, phirphir, sirsirạu, sisirạu, tharthar, tharthạrao; (*with a*) lukur marte, luyuć m., padgak m., pẹhlañ m., pidgić m., puyul m.

STARTLE, TO—boṛkao.

STARTLED, TO BE—bharao, bhilki, bidrạu, bilbilạu, birkạu, camkao, caṭo, cihirạn, cihkạu, comkao, dhakar pakar, koṭel, lẹṅgẹć, liṅgić; (*& unable to move*) ṭakṭạki.

STARVED—ẹṅgẹć; (*half*) cothra.

STATE—(*condition*) dasa, dob, dosa, gutik, hal, halat, hal hawal, hawal, tẹḅ; (*pomp*) ḍigi migi; (*in this*) hale; (*in its first*) tẹsnẹk; (*the proper*) batar; (*belonging to the*) sarkari.

STATEMENT—katha; (*a true*) hak katha; (*a false*) labar katha; (*to make a*) janao; (*in introducing*) kathae; (*in court &c*) ejahar, ijahar.

STATION (*rank*)—darja.

STATUE, A—murut; (*to become*) sidho.

STATURE—lauchar. *Cf.* SHORT, LARGE, &C.

STAY, TO—tahẽ, tahen, tahrao, tek; (*for a little*) tahẽ ńõgok.

STEADFAST—kajak, kirkir (F), korkor (M), muruk, mutur (2), romrom, urić; (*to remain*) tahẽ urić.

STEADILY—gomeń (2).

STEAL, TO—atkir, gob, kombro, komro, kumbru; (*from*) cokcanda; (*eatables, given to*) locra (M), lucri (F).

STEALTHILY—cagam cugum, chapkaote, hapać hupuć, paragare, rigam cagam, ringam cingam, sagam sugum, sanegumane, sugum (2), (*in comp.*) rawić; (*of wild beast*) chapka chapki; (*to take*) gabre.

STEAM—bhaph; (*to*) bapha, bhaphao; (*hissing of*) chãe (2); (*ship*) uhuãkos.

STEEL—ispat, ispat mẽrbẽt.

STEEP—darań, darnga, dhardhari, dharsãr, gharghariа, hirhir, ranakap; (*roofed*) dharahi.

STEEP, TO—bhijau, bijau; (*till germination begins*) jawa; (*before roasting*) bulkau.

STEER—(*a*) damra; (*to*) mohlao, mohada.

STEM, A—dandit.

STENTORIAN—cagae.

STEP—(*a*) kadam, kodom, taram; (*of dance*) khod; (*to take a false*) pichlau, piclau; (*by step*) khode khod; (*father*) kaka baba, ńam apat; (*mother*) kaki enga.

STEP, TO—taram; (*short*) lebet hań; (*gingerly*) dharak dhorok; (*lightly*) corhot.

STEPS—(*with long*) ribir (2), tahuć (2); (*with short*) debe (2), dugur (2), guduć, kede (2), ledeć bedeć (F), lede lede (M), tebeć (2), turuk (2); (*of ladder*) hudra.

STERN—khão, khackhacia; (*of a boat, the*) pachla.

STERNUM, THE—kondoram.

STEWARD, A—landbandić, lonbon, londbond; (*house*) bhandari; (*to act as*) lanban, lonbon.

STICK A—thenga; (*thick*) danta, munga mutak, mutak; (*sharp*) goja, khuci; (*sword*) gupti t.; (*forked*) guti t.; (*with iron rings*) taini; (*used to throw at small game*) talha; (*used for carrying*) bharia; (*walking*) hapa; (*to twirl round fingers*) lauri; (*to lead by*) tiak; (*to strike on ground*) taktaki; (*to beat with*) tathe.

STICK, TO—dhań, jalat, laskao, lat, latkao, thekom; (*to*) jatak, jatak (2), jilet, latha, leothe, letkom, thokre, tokre, thubre; (*together*) cepthe, jeperet, jeret, jerka, jemthe, jimtau, leothe, sapta, satao; (*in*) kirbit, rebet, thema; (*up or out*) kotkoto, kutkutu, toktoko; (*into*) rebet gońjao; (*in throat*) kantet.

STICKING—(*out*) rakraka, raprapa, rokroko, seksekе, ; (*out, of teeth*) sota, sotmal; (*up*) rocroco, rokroko, sotsoto.

STICKY—bohor (2), jatak (2), jeber (2), jekre, jemthe, jenthe, jerjer, jetke, jewen, jewer, jiwer jewer, lasak pasak, lat, latak, latak (2), latak patak, latha, latlat, latlatia, latpatia, lejepeje, letko.

STIFF—kekercań, kerker, ketkete, khara, teptepe; (*of neck*) keskese, kerker, kirkir; (*necked*) bherot, phephra; (*of a breeze*) seyar; (*to be*) luńkar, tatao; (*to become*) karkarao, kerker, rahao, sir tatao; (*to become, of exposed clay*) satkao; (*thigh or knee, having*) herca (M), hirci (F), hurja (M), hurji (F); (*kneed, gait of one*) hercań; (*& bent*) luńkar.

STIFLING—ukbuk, ukhu pukhu, ulkhu pulkhu; (*heat*) ãc; (*from smoke*) okkodro.

STIGMA—dag, khot.

STILL—(*quiet*) cać cũć, camdarak, capcup, dadahut, dadahut duduhut, dondorcot, duduhuṕ, guṛum, isthir, kiṛkiṛ (F), koṛkoṛ (M), mirot, rumrum, ṭak, thir; (*nevertheless*) gureho; (*to*) suc; (*to be*) domkao; (*to become*) thir; (*perfectly*) gutagam; (*a liquor*) bhaṭhi, paura bhaṭhi; (*liquor from a*) ekhan; (*-ness*) gamgum; (*unable to remain*) bhacaṅ bhueuṅ, ukuṛ sukuṛ, *Cf.* TO LIE, TO STAND.

STILTS, TO WALK ON—kiḍoṅ koḍoṅ.

STIMULATE, TO—puchlau, uskur,

STING—(*a*) suṅga; (*to*) chorchorao, toṛ.

STINGILY—curkuć bhurkuć, kikoć, koroć moṭoć.

STINGING—(*of speech*) ragaṫ cegaṫ; (*of pain*) caṛeṅpaṛ, chan (2), gargaṫ.

STINGY—abge, bokro, churca, conḍ koṗeṭ, coroć mokoć, kāć kūć, kakać kukuć, kikić kokoć, kuthia, panṭeś, papi, paṭweś, tojahi.

STINK—(*to*) moroṫ, sīṛić; (*a*) ankhaila.

STINT—(*to*) mara; (*without*) beae, bidić (2), behisab, nirdhok,

STIR, TO—ghanṭa, ghur ghurau, hoḍa, hudgar; (*up*) bhusku, bolao, hoṭaḱ, hudgar, koḍa, puchlau, siklau cariau; (*up-incite*) carhao, ghamao, tatao, udgau, uskur; (*about*) ghanṭa ghanṭi; (*rapidly*) handkur; (*when cooking*) hondaḱ; (*to cause to*) ṭasak, ṭaskao, thasak, thaskao.

STIRRING—(*always*) kharu paṭu, khaṭkhuṭ; (*in pot, sound of*) hadgur, handruṅ (2), ṭoke (2). *Cf.* TO MIX.

STIRRUP, A—lenabeṫ.

STITCH, TO—silai.

STOCK—(*family*) boṅ, buḍa, dahgi, gusṭi, gutri, jaro, khūṭ; (*of gun*) kunḍa; (*goods*) punji, punji paṭa. *Cf.* LIVE.

STOCKS, WOODEN—turuṅ.

STOCKSTILL—biḍbiḍi, camdaraḱ, ḍekḍel, ḍemḍem (F), ṭak, ṭakṭaki.

STOLEN PROPERTY, PART OR WHOLE OF—bomal, loṭ, momal.

STOLIDITY—galta golaṫ.

STOMACH, THE—lać, peṭ, poṭa, seṅgel bugli; (*1st*) bhosam, poṭa; (*1st., of birds*) okoṫ; (*2nd.*) remeṫ; (*of sheep, contents of*) gubri; (*to contract the*) lać orsec; (*full*) poṭpoṭo, ṭebṭebe; (*cramp in*) beroṭi; (*swelling in*) kachma bai, puṭi; (*wind on*) aṭaṗ uṭuṗ, ḍeṗ (2); (*commotion in*) ḍunṭauḱ; (*tight feeling in*) ḍubḍubi, reṗ (2); (*shrunken*) hahal-pat, hapaḱ (2), laparkaḱ, larpa, larpaṅ; (*protuberant*) jahurae, juru (2), ledhra (M), lidhri (F), lohta, lublubu, poṭea, poṭma (M), puṭmi (F), poṭreć, raboskaḱ; (*uncomfortable feeling in*) akul bakul, kaṭać kuṭuć, khan (2); (*with an empty*) laparkaḱ, leperkaṫ; (*acidity of*) amol; (*to turn*) doyoḱ, sereṛ; (*ache*) ḍuṭa ḍuṭi, lać hase, masmas, paṭhok; (*rumbling in*) karkur.

STONE—(*a*) dhiri; (*to*) tiṅ; (*to rub on a*) uruṫ; (*large flat*) caṭani, dhiri cakta; (*very small*) hopon (2) dhiri; (*hard*) jīweṫ dhiri; (*hewn*) kunḍau dhiri; (*soft slatey*) maṭia pathra; (*an athlete's*) bhanj dhiri; (*to roll as a*) dardarao; (*fruit*) jaṅ; (*in bladder*) karra, bharagmut, korra; (*a round*) gurgu; (*on which spices ground*) paṭi dhiri; (*for grinding turmeric*) sasaṅ rit dhiri; (*& all*) raṭi kuṭi. *Cf.* PRECIOUS, PLATE.

STONES—(*small*) kakor, moṭkuri, muṭkuri, rodgoṫ, roṛa; (*full of*) retekote.

STONY—radga rodgo, ragar rogoṛ, rege cege, rigoṛ rogoṛ, rodga, rodga rodgo, rodgo, rogoṛ, rogṛo; (*very*) retekote; (*ground*) dhiri oṭ.

STOOL, A—maci; (*with back*) ṭendar maci; (*to place*) bel; (*piece of wood used as*) ganḍe; (*to go to*) ić joṅ, phirau, ṭanḍi seć; (*to strain at*) kutha.

STOOP, TO—dabṛao, engoṫ, inguṫ, kaba kobo, kaya koyo, kiba kabe, kijo kojo, koḍo, kojo, kubkubu, kuluṅ ḍubuṅ; (*as an old person*) keḍe; (*repeatedly*) kaba kobo, kabuṅ (2); (*& peer*) ayaṅ oyoṅ.

STOOPING—kayaṅ kuyuṅ, kiḍa kaḍe, kiḍma kaḍme, kodo; (*under a load*) koro (2); (*of old person*) koṭbo; (*& rising*) kabuć kubuć, kubuć (2);

(*to avoid being seen*) koye (2); (*tall &c*) kaṛbun.

STOP—(*exclm.*) hāhā; (*shout to cattle*) hum; (*in some games*) thukum; (*to*) akoṭ, aṭok, bond, rokao, ṭahrao, tambhao, ṭarhao, ṭok, tham, thir; (*up a hole, to*) paṭaṛ, ṭepeṭ.

STOPPER, A—bonṭ, dhipni, ṇnoṭ, ṭhipi.

STORE—(*a*) bhanḍar; (*to*) bae, roṭ ciput, soc; (*to have in*) roṭ ciput; (*up, to*) gonjao, sṭitau; (*carefully, to*) jogaṛ; (*house a*) bhanḍar, gola, gola oraṅ, hamar, hamer, hamor, ṭhek; (*grain, to*) bandi, thutwa; (*a grain*) ḍhula, muṛai.

STORK, A SPECIES OF—ḍheṅka garuṛ.

STORM OF WIND & RAIN—andhi daṅ, hoe daṅ; (*darkness before*) guṇj.

STORY, A—gam, gap, golpo, kahani, kahni, khesa; (*partly sung*) gam sereṅ; (*strange*) had katha; (*old & true*) jaṛ jaṛ katha; (*to bring up old*) jojogna; (*of house*) aṭal, mahla; (*an upper*) kotha.

STOUNDING (*of pain*)—hiric.

STOUT—badgae bodgoe (F), bhosoṅga (M), bhosoṅgi (F), darmoṭ, daṭmoṭ, ḍhulki (F), dhuma (M), dhumi (F), dhumṛa (M), dhumṛi (F), dumerae, gabduyaṅ, huṭeṭ panjar, ibil panjar, kuṭeṭ panjar, kuṭmel, lodga (M), ludgi (F), lodhea, lokomdoroṅ, lothro (M), luthri (F), luṭkum, moṭa, moṭa muṭi, musra (M) musri (F) pikopoko, ramdhu, raṭko, rotho, thutma (M), thutmi (F), thutwa; (*very*) dhomsol (F), jobodhoṅ, lapir jadir (F), udur dhuma; (*& coarse*) badaṅ, badgae bodgoe (F), (*& short-necked*) bhakum; (*& vigorous*) daṭmoṭ; (*& well-grown*) dohara, laraṅka; (*but effeminate*) goboria; (*& heavily clad*) lidgoe lodgoe; (*of children*) pedgor (M), pidgur (F), phodle (M), phudli (F). *Cf.* FAT.

STRADDLE, TO—cagcaga, caṅcaṅ, ciga cage, hejheje (M), hijhiji (F), hida hade, hidhidi, higa hage, hija haje, kija kaje, ṭanda.

STRAGGLING—alag balag; (*as branches*) rakraka, rape, raprapa.

STRAIGHT—miṭ mohnḍate, sarhaṛ, sidha, sojhe; (*of instruments which should be curved*) ayaṛ; (*off the*) ghoca, hoyaṅ kanḍeṭ, konḍeṭ, lade, perta, tarcha, tircha tirchi; (*away*) kalaṅ, sojhe mojhe; (*across country*) sopoṅ rodoṅ; (*& of uniform thickness*) sāoār, sāwār; (*grained*) sāoār, sāwār. *Cf.* FORWARD.

STRAIN, TO—(*out*) chani; (*by squeezing*) rodoc; (*at stool*) kutha.

STRAINED, TO BE—mecka micki, meckao.

STRAINING, TO SEPARATE BY—chakao, chani.

STRAIT—(*difficulty*) ajgaṛ, gaṛ, gara jala, garkugar, ghar, gor, janjal, jonjal, kugar, muskil, pec, peno, siniṭ, somsom, sonkoṭ; (*narrow*) aṭgaṭe, ciriṭ, kuciṭ, sakra, sakra sakri, sakyaṛ, siniṭ; (*very*) koroc; (*to be in a*) acsun, asusaṛ, chaḍ chuḍ, dolmolao, hale dale, kacar, khondoṅ lopoṅ, laṭpaṭ, osusaṛ, sakra sakri; (*to put in a*) ocepoc.

STRANGE—algei, anaṛi, ancin, birnaha, had, aptia.

STRANGER, A—pordesi, uni; (*belonging to*) uni.

STRANGLE, TO—lin goc, phasi; (*sound of*) kedroc kodroc.

STRANGURY—karra, kodra, korra.

STRAP, A—(*of raw hide*) camaoṭa, campṭa.

STRATAGEM—bandhec, phirka, porkar, prokar; (*by*) pherkaṭite.

STRAW—auri, aṛ, busuṅ, chani; (*from which grain trodden out*) guchi, ocha; (*mixed with clay*) baja; (*scaffold for*) parāoca; (*shakings*) jhuṛe (2). *Cf.* ROPE.

STRAY, TO—bahka bahki, bahkao, bhakanḍao, bhanḍao, bhanṭao, bidaraha, bilṭau, caukau, chingau, gabad, pheṅkao; (*to cause to*) bahkao.

STREAKED—kabraṅ kobroṅ.

STREAM, A—don gada, gada, nala, nali; (*small*) gaṭa; (*bend in*) kucel; (*down, to*) din dabur.

STREAMING—dhar (2), ladlad; (*gaily along*) bidra bidri.

STREET—mahal ; (*village*) kulhi ; (*lower end of*) hẹ̃ṭ kulhi ; (*upper end*) upar kulhi ; (*entrance*) kulhi muṇḍạ.

STRENGTH—aṅ, aṭha saṭha, bọl, daṛe, jor, kut, mạgdur, muruk, sạddi, sạdhi, sạkti, soaṅ, sukti, tagoj ; (*physical*) kaya ; (*without*) abol, nirbos ; (*with all one's,*) daṛe bhor, bhorsak, lać orseć ; (*to recover*) saṇṭhao ; (*to lose*) tirmirạu, usạṭ ; (*to bring to bear*) jọr bandhao.

STRENGTHENED, TO BE—diṛho, saṇṭhao, ṭankao.

STRENUOUSLY—ajhãṭ.

STRETCH, TO—bọkbọkọ, ṭanao, tege (2), tiạr, tić, tiriạu ; (*the arm*) ạwil, bẹg, laphao ; (*the legs*) telńjo, teńjlo ; (*out the hand*) ti tiạr ; (*to stiffness*) ṭaṇṭanao (*oneself*) der, kuṛkuṛ ; (*from point to point*) gak̕ ; (*forward the body*) bẹg.

STRETCHED OUT—tọć tọć.

STREW, TO—chikican, chitiạ bitiạ, chitiạu, chitir bitir.

STRICKEN, TO BE—thal̕halao.

STRICTLY—kajak, khacṛaha. *Cf.* TO CHARGE.

STRIFE—badão, khaṇḍa khaṇḍi ; (*to be at*) ṭanaṭani ; (*a causer of*) naṭer guru, rogṛaha (M), rogṛahi (F).

STRIKE, TO—dal, dhạtiṛ, domao, humạk̕, kehnao, mukạu, ṭhaṭe, ti calao, uyuk̕ ; (*of clock*) baja ; (*to raise*) epel̕ ; (*with something soft*) lapak̕ marao ; (*head against*) tạkić, tạpiń ; (*foot against*) tạkić, tọhọṭ ; (*each other*) daṅga, dapal, kapṭa kạpṭi, ṭhapa (2) ; (*against*) bajao, tạpiń, ṭhapa ṭhuk̕ ; (*with stick*) ṭhẹṭhe, thegṛao ; (*with heel of fist*) guḍạu, kedra kidri, kilạu, kuhạu, kudṛạu, thegṛao ; (*end of stick on ground*) ṭakṭaki ; (*mouth, as insult*) cọkọć ; (*between the shoulders*) hẹ̃k ; (*a ball in the air*) phoṭao ; (*the ground*) khemur.

STRING—baber ; (*of beads*) lar ; (*fiddle*) tãt ; (*brass fiddle*) tar ; (*round waist*) ḍaṇḍoli, ḍora ; (*knot on*) ghẹ̃ṭ ; (*to*) gotao, gutu, huraṛ ; (*to, of a bow*) dak̕ ; (*on spokes of spinning-wheel*) awa.

STRINGY—tọkọr (2) ; (*of fruit*) baja.

STRIP, A—cirạ, pahaṭ, pahṭa, pạṭi, sirạ ; (*of home-made cloth*) pạṭkạ ; (*of raw hide*) comaoṭa, campṭa, camṭa.

STRIP, TO—jhaṛao, siboṛ ; (*off*) poṭor, surkạ ; (*off clothes*) bhũṛũć (M), lańṭa (M), lạṅṭi (F) ; (*off outer cover*) poṭak̕ ; (*off by running hand up stalk*) hadra hạdri, hadrao, họṭ ; (*as fibre*) sala ; (*as locusts*) murhuć ; (*flesh from bone*) huruṛ.

STRIPE, A—ọnọl.

STRIPED—analonol̕, gorla (M), gurli (F), ọnọl bọnọl.

STRIPLING, A—chọṇḍrọ, lạṇdur dhiń.

STRIPPED—bẹabron ; (*as a tree*) jhaṛ jhuṛ, khaḍ, khaḍea, khaḍra.

STRIVE, TO—jhọgọṛ, keṛe, kuṛpaṛ, oḍabaḍ, reṭha riṭhi, upại, uphrạ uphri, uprạ paṛi ; (*with*) ṭhọk ; (*together*) haparao, rapṭa rạpṭi.

STROKE, A—(*with board sword &c*) ghao ; (*difficult*) bẹhọṛ ghao.

STRONG—ãṭ, balgar, bẹlkẹć, bolgariạ, bọlman, ḍaṭmọṭ, diṛho, dọṛhọ, jọbọr, jorgar, jorwar, kajak, kẹṭẹć, lạg, lọgnọ, majbut, mańjgut, muṭhu, pakṭa, pokṭa, ṭasil, tej ; (*of a smell*) gandha gạndhi, sọndgọnd ; (*as wind*) sayaṛ ; (*& well-proportioned*) jabrạhi, lọgnọ ; (*& healthy*) bolgariạ, bọlman, chalchạliạ ; (*to be*) saṇṭhao ; (*& offensive, of smell*) ghạ̃ṛa ghạ̃ṛi ; (*headed*) dundur, hũṭ ; (*voiced*) ghogo ; (*but useless*) asaṅ poḍa ; (*youth, a*) chaela juạn.

STRONGLY—andakal̕ ; (*of breathing &c*) phaphu.

STROW, TO—pasnao.

STRUGGLE, TO—jid, phẹṇṭẹ phẹre, sugubugu ; (*in death-throes*) armarao ; (*to get free*) khẹnṭe pere, khẹrẹpẹṭe.

STRUGGLING—gaḍea guḍia, kẹremẹṭẹ, khaṛu paṭu, rẹpẹć ipicak̕, uphrạ uphri, uprạ paṛi, uprạ upri ; (*to grab*) luṭa luṭi.

STRUMPET, A—kusmbi.

STRUTTING—ọlọm jhọlọm.

STUBBLE—ḍhaṇḍka, ḍhaṭhi, karcap̣, laṇḍha.

STUBBORN—batkaṭi, besrom, bherot, diṭhāu, harur, keṭeć, paṭweť, tenḍos, ṭiḍwi; (*to be*) agdhao.

STUCK TOGETHER—jemṭhe.

STUDY, TO—parhao.

STUFF, TO—tubeť, tuweť; (*in*) kocao; (*in to mouth*) kopeť; (*the belly*) lai puṭi. *Cf.* FOOD.

STUFFY—ukhu pukhu, ulkhu pulkhu.

STULTIFY ONESELF, TO—labori.

STUMBLE, TO—darṛao, dhargut, haraķ, sobok koyok, taham tukuć, tahap̣ ṭaṭup̣, takić, tawak ṭaṭuk, tohoť, toroť, tukuć.

STUMP, A—(*tree*) huruť, khunṭuť, munḍha, munḍhak, munḍhaṭ, munḍheť; (*& rump*) gayum.

STUMPY—banḍa (M), banḍi (F), banḍa banḍi, kherṛa.

STUNNED, TO BE—caṭo.

STUNTED—bhuṭka, cerca, cerca bayar, coroeṭho, corońṭo, cuni, curcuṭuć, damcak, dhuruć, duluć dupuć, ḍumka, geḍa (M), giḍi (F), jere bedhe, jerka, jorgel, rega, regaṭhia, reme ṭele, reṭha, ṭhōrbok (F), ṭhōrbok (M); (*of trees &c*) thoro thopo; (*of a breed of cattle*) jura, jurga; (*to be*) jere (2); (*of some plants*) luṭa.

STUPID—aẽ, akil gawar, alać oloć, alap̣ bakap̣, albakaha, aldhundha, alhua, alua, baura, bekup, bhakcu, bhembha (M), bhembhi (F), bhoco, bhuc, bhucuń, bodo, boka, bombo, bonḍo, galak salak, galať solať, gāowar, gāwar, haora, hari bhoń, lelha (M), lelha melha, lilhi (F), lordho, salaṭ, urbhuń; (*of me, how*) bhaṭić; (*& ignorant*) bhoto.

STUPIFIED—anbhul; (*to be*) aral koral; (*by narcotic &c*) bul.

STURDY—darmoṭ, dhaḍos, dilgar, huṭeť pańjar, ibil pańjar, kuṭeť pańjar.

STUTTER, TO—bobe, bodro.

STY, A—(*on eyelid*) ṭoke; (*pig*) sukri bāra.

SUBDUE, TO—dapkao, dobon, dombrao, ghal, hal kahil, halkal, jobḍao, jobdo, kabja, kaboj, kabu, kahil, kaidau, kal, kas marao, khenhao, kobjao, koboj, loṭom.

SUBDUED, TO BE—kirdhum.

SUBJECT—(*topic*) katha, tal; (*dependant*) porja, porja pani, praja, prajapaṭi, tabe, tabedar; (*to another*) par adhin; (*to*) gobol, tabere.

SUBJECTION—rohom, tabeteť, udhin; (*to bring into*) kabja, kaboj, kabu, or, sad, sakuć; (*to keep in*) kaidau.

SUBJUGATE, TO—kas marao, sakuć.

SUBMERGE, TO—unum.

SUBMISSION—udhin; (*to reduce to*) kuć kuć; (*to take attitude of*) gola gamcha.

SUBMISSIVE—bapurić, behūṭ; (*to be*) jańga latar.

SUBORN, TO—bargao, kan phuka, sikau, sikhau.

SUBSCRIPTION—canda; (*to collect*) canda uṭhau.

SUB-SEPT—*Cf.* paris; (*of the same*) gutia, gutia pera, gutia naya.

SUBSEQUENT—kur.

SUBSIDE, TO—calpać, ohra; (*of water*) jhakao, or; (*of swellings*) maskao.

SUBSISTENCE—(*means of*) gujar, roṭi, ruṭi, udkhud; (*allowance*) nankar.

SUBSTANTIAL—darahara, dharahara, dirho, jama juṭa, kajak, majbut, mańjgut, moṭa muṭi, pokta.

SUBSTANTIATE, TO—jaj, jojao, nireṭ, porman.

SUBSTITUTE—(*a*) badli, oja, uji; (*to*) badli, bodol.

SUBTERFUGE—chol; (*without*) niskapaṭ; (*to employ*) phekphāk.

SUBTRACT, TO—lad, mina.

SUBURBS OF A TOWN—gonḍa.

SUCCEED, TO—dhaṭ, jinau, jojao, jos, jowao, lahao, laṭeć, seṭeć, usrau; (*by blessing*) barket.

SUCCESS—khaṭa barha, ras; (*-ful*) usrau.

SUCCESSION, IN—kur, ladlad, ladlud, otor gotor, tarae toroe; (*close*) lagle mar, paṭpaṭ, tatle, tatlemar.

SUCCOURER—sohoda.

SUCCULENT—labak.

SUCH—ạsọn, ẹtẹ, lekan, nenkan ; (*like*) eman, ẹmọn, ẹmọn sẹmọn, nenkan ; (*as this*) ebe, nenke, nonkan ; (*as that*) onkan ; (*a great*) ẹtọ bọṛọ.

SUCK, TO—cẹpẹć, cọpọć, cusạu, jẹmbẹt́, nunu ; (*in*) sirup̣, surkạu ; (*soft food*) *noisily*) hạbruḱ.

SUCKING SOUND—chọp (2), sirpuṭ, sọrkọṭ, sorpọṭ ; (*to make a*) sạruḱ.

SUCKLE, TO—nunu.

SUDDEN—(*on the*) marte, mẹnte, phucuć m., puc m., pucuć m. ; (*start, with a*) lukuṭ m., pehlaṅ m.

SUDDENLY—acka, acọk, ancọṭ, bhas bhus, bhus, char, chaṭ, gọt́, haṛas, haṭọk, họt́, huć marte, hud m., hugui m., lọyọṅ m., lọyọṛ m., mer-mer, paṭ m., paṭpaṭ, phucuć m., phuṭ m., pucuć m., ṭaṭak, ṭaṭka mar ; (*of fear*) puc m. ; (*to move*) pehlaṅ.

SUE, TO (*in court*)—mọkọdọma.

SUFFER, TO—bhọg, bhuṅjạu, bidot, jọm, lahao, sahao, sombhrao, sumbhrạu ; (*for wrong-doing*) pholao.

SUFFERING—bidot, bipod, dukhạli, kọsṭọ, mar muhim, muhim, saset ; (*to cause*) bidot, kosola, santao, santap, saset, tin topor khana ; (*to be in*) saset ; (*with much*) kọsṭọ mọsṭọ ; (*people*) dukhi ; (*greatly*) chaṭ (2). *Cf.* LONG.

SUFFICE, TO—ada, aṇṭao, hoe.

SUFFICIENT—purạn, purun ; (*to have barely*) ńũ lọlọ ; (*to be*) aṇṭao, ku-lạu ; (*more than*) biḍić (2), ebe tebe, thele (2) ; (*less than*) kaṭạṛ.

SUFFOCATING—ukbuk, ulkhu pulkhu.

SUGAR—(*lump of raw*) bạli guṛ, bhili guṛ, cạkti guṛ ; (*refined*) cini ; (*partly refined*) sakar ; (*candy*) mis-ri ; (*crystalised raw*) gitil guṛ.

SUGARCANE—ạk ; (*stalk of*) ạk ṭạṇḍi, dọg, khoca ; (*cutting*) ḍoga ; (*a kind of*) kajri ; (*shoot of*) kạni ; (*press*) mahasal, rạksi ; (*to express*) ạk lẹn ; (*juice, 1st. product*) guṛ ; (*juice, 2nd. scum of*) phulgad ; (*juice, pan for boiling*) kara ; (*juice, vessel for*) khora ; (*juice to boil down*) ranjao ; (*enclosure for press-ing*) kulsạr ; (*juice mixed with water*) gurpạna ; (*scum of juice*) haṛam gad, mạhut ; (*beam of press*) kạtri.

SUGGEST ITSELF TO, TO—sarbharao, uriạu.

SUIT—(*to*) laga ; (*a law*) makordama, mọkọdọma ; (*law, to bring a*) namor ; (*to follow*) bẹsao.

SUITABLE—gan, jut ; (*to be*) jowao ; (*time or season*) ghạt.

SUITOR, A—bạḍi, mudoe.

SULK, TO—adọr, adra, ạruń pạruń, beńcoḱ, beṛńcok, bheńcoḱ, birạsạli, deona diuni, gajha gạjhi, gajhao, gampatao, gote gore, kãucạ kãuci, khanaḱ khonoḱ, khanas khonos, komkom, kọsọt́, lerwe, lọcloco, mọkmọko, mọkmọkọr, pencoḱ, pherkoṭ, rusạu, rusrusu, urun (2), usạt́ ; (*& refuse to eat*) lọṭlọṭọ ; (*& refuse to speak*) họmọń gọrọń ; (*to cause to*) bãocao.

SULKY—ạruń pạruń, ạtruń, berod, bi-rod, irạ iri, khãs khũs, kosle, uḍi ; (*to be*) pọkpọkọ ; (*to look*) kọskọsọ.

SULLEN—khãskhũs ; (*to be*) komkom, kope baorẽ, mọkmọkọr, rusạ rusi, rusạu, rusrusu ; (*way, in a*) kosle, phirphir.

SULLY, TO—khọṭ.

SULPHATE—(*copper*) tutiyạ ; (*iron*) hi-rạkọs, kasis.

SULPHUR—gandhak, gọndhọk.

SULTRY, TO BE—gamgam.

SUM UP, TO—ikọṭ.

SUMMERSAULT, TO TURN A—bạji.

SUMMON, TO—ḍakao, saman, tọlọb.

SUMMONS, A—bolahaṭ, bulahaṭ, ḍak, pukạr, saman ; (*to serve*) jạri.

SUN, THE—bela, ber, siń bọṅga, cando, siń cando, suraj ; (*well-risen*) jẹḍẹr kẹṭẹć ; (*obscured by clouds*) gholao ; (*oneself, to*) jẹḍẹr ; (*shine*) dhup, jẹḍẹr, ṭhikạri ; (*shine, fierce*) setoń ; (*rise*) ber rakap̣ ; (*rise, before*) hadam hudum, payaṅ ; (*set, after*) lumbạḱ, lupạḱ, ńuhum, ńumbạḱ ; (*stroke*) suruj bạt ; (*god*) surjạhi bọṅga. *Cf.* RAYS.

SUNDAY—aṭhwar, etwar, khara din, kharạli, khora din, rọbibar, saṇḍe.

SUNDRY—eman.
SUNK—celpeń, khaplok, khupua.
SUP, TO—sirup.
SUPERABUNDANT—algé tasgé, sadasuk ; (*to be*) țilțilau.
SUPERCILIOUS, TO BE—bhades.
SUPERFLUOUS—algasi, chuța, chuțalia, phalti.
SUPERIMPOSED, TO BE—tepen.
SUPERINTEND, TO—bețhaura.
SUPERIOR—osno (2), sir, sorgs, upor ; (*to be*) sorgs.
SUPERNATURAL.—*Cf.* OCCULT.
SUPERSTITIOUS FEAR—bhae, lacpuc.
SUPPER—kedok ; (*time*) kedok jom harop, pohor, jokhoé.
SUPPLICATE, TO—jorhat.
SUPPLY THE NECESSITIES OF LIFE, TO—asul, goras, posao.
SUPPORT—dogoj ; (*to*) asul, sangarhe, tambhao, țehad ; (*by post &c., to*) țesa, țhesa ; (*under rafters, a*) pela.
SUPPORTER, A—sota ; (*of a family*) orjonia.
SUPPRESS, TO—gapegupe, gop ; (*information*) jhurgusia ; (*truth*) aldhom.
SUPPURATE, TO—belo.
SUPREME BEING, THE—țhakur.
SURE—paka, paki ; (*to make*) nisța ; (*to be-exclm.*) bhatić, dhora, sake, sarige, sa bhatić.
SURETY—hak, jamani, jamin, jamindar; (*to become*) darmal, deao, jamani, jamin, tela ; (*for goods*) deaoki.
SURFACE—(*uneven*) cõrdań, lacań locoń, sadga badga ; (*rough*) jhargoeak ; (*to skim along*) chalchalao ; (*to float on*) camdhul, caple ; (*to glide over*) horiõr ; (*to break the*) khaida baida, padgak ; (*to break a smooth*) khaeda khuidi ; (*to make smooth*) sariau.
SURFEIT, TO—chaklachak, sarua, tobo.
SURLY—aitaha.
SURMOUNT, TO—sarao ; (*a difficulty*) torao.
SURPLUS—batil, phadel, phajil, phalti, phauti ; (*for year*) mare.
SURPRISE—(*exclm. of*) aoge, ajgut, au, ayo, ayuguh, bapo, bohaj, dekja, dhani, dure, eh, heran, hobae, hore, iyo, mor, morhak, ohae, ohae hae, oka bate ; (*by*) gupti mar ; (*causing*) bulai, heran ; (*to take by*) hatma.
SURPRISED, TO BE—haka caka.
SURREPTITIOUSLY (*in comp*)—rawié.
SURROUND, TO—saçé acur, gherao.
SURVEY, TO—jarib ; (*land, one who*) amin.
SURVIVE, TO—goé sargé, sargé, țek, țikau.
SUSCEPTIBLE TO INJURY FROM EATING CERTAIN FOODS—batol.
SUSPECT, TO—bad, dighi, digić, indik, sondho, subha.
SUSPEND, TO (*hang*)—aka, dińdawak, tańgao.
SUSPENDED—dawań (2), diań (2) ; (*in hand, to carry*) teweń.
SUSPICION—digdha, dighi, kalak, subha; (*absence of*) khulasa, pharia phați ; (*to be relieved from*) ikoț ; (*on*) badalte ; (*given to*) durukia.
SUSTAIN, TO—sambrao.
SUSTENANCE—dak daka, dana pani.
SWAGGER, TO—badagiri, bilik balań, bilić, cahak mahak, jhil jhol, olom jholom ; (*in a grand dhoti*) jhitor jhotor.
SWALLOW, A—bhalua, dak dakram cẽrẽ ; (*spec. of*) buru bhalua.
SWALLOW, TO—cabhao, kodoć, uć ; (*with difficulty*) kion doyon ; (*whole*) kuryuć (2) ; (*liquor*) hongor.
SWALLOWING, SOUND OF—kadraé kodroé, kidroé kodruć, kodoć.
SWAMP, A—dol doli, jarhi.
SWARMS, IN—bujuk (2), dão (2), duńguć (2), hujuk (2), soboć (2).
SWARTHY—ńangal ńițe.
SWAY, TO—darã durũ, dildal, hilau, kodor, liko loko ; (*of a crowd*) dalmal ; (*to & fro*) bajra bajri, dhanman, dole, lawak lutić, lebda libdi ; (*the body*) horlo lolo ; (*back & forwards*) larań pațań, laruń (2), luruń (2) ; (*up & down*) ikoć sokoć ; (*when dancing*) likić domok, lohok.
SWAYING—doloe (2), dolop (2), domok (2), halak dalak, hidić dikir, hilak dalak, konda mande, lodop ;

(& *nodding*) **lewa saṛē**; (*gently*) rayal ruyul.

SWEAR, TO—dib; (*eternal friendship*) phul patao, saika.

SWEAT—balbal, balbal dak; (*to*) balbalao, ghama ghami; (*pouring*) jhak (2).

SWEEP, TO—jok; (*clean*) jok ṭaṇḍi, jok sapha; (*on*) chalchalao; (*in circles*) manḍrao; (*taking in one*) jhaṇṭe jhaṛe; (*away*) khiri muṇḍia.

SWEEPING (*long*)—bayul, biyol boyol, cindar candar.

SWEEPINGS—hoṭak khodrak, jhaṛa; (*of a goat's house*) laḍauṛi.

SWEET—heṇem, herem, liṭhur, miṭha, sebel, sosṭok; (*very*) ṅuṭuk (2); (*of smell*) mahka mahki, songdgond; (& *juicy*) ṅorom (2); (*of sound*) ṅahāṛ ṅōhoṛ, ṅōhōṛ (2).

SWEETMEAT, A—jili laḍu, laḍu, miṭhai, peṛa; (*seller*) halwae.

SWELL, TO—bhara, bharao, domo, mo, phulau, pokpoko, puipui, raṭa ruṭu; (*as sea*) habak ḍabak, ; (*as stomach*) puṭi.

SWELLING, A—ḍēbē, jo; (*dropsical*) bharao; (*in groin or armpit*) gaṇḍ; (*of lower jaw*) sonpat; (*out*) od odo.

SWELTERING—gijgij.

SWERVE, TO—aere.

SWIFTLY—khiṛkhiṛau; (*to run*) ḍigḍig.

SWILL CLOTHES IN WATER, TO—bohoe.

SWIM—(*to*) paera, payar; (*of fish, the*) ḍulḍul.

SWIMMING—(*expert in*) paeraha (M), paerahi (F), satral; (*noise of*) ḍaba ḍubu, habka dubka; (*of one fatigued*), ḍobe (2), habuk ḍabuk

SWINDLE, TO—ṭhag, ṭhok.

SWING—(*a child's*) jhilo; (*a revolving*) hinḍol; (*in full*) bharkhar, dhurpau, dhurup, umdhum; (*round the head, one*) ek ghaṭia.

SWING, TO—jhilo; (*round*) ghiria, ghur ghurau, ghurpāk, hurla; (*arms*) bit bikoc, hurla.

SWINGING FESTIVAL, CONTRIVANCE FOR—radha coṛok.

SWIRL, TO—gurla gurli, gurlau; (*as water*) ghaṇṭa ghaṇṭi; (*in hair, a*) gheora.

SWISH—(*to*) phoṅ, phuṅ; (*with a*) khaṭ (2), phoṅ marte, phuṅ m., phuk m.; (*sound of*) cabhar cabhur, ḍhabuskuc.

SWITCH, A—chiṭkiric.

SWOLLEN—beker beṇḍaṅ, goda, laṭa luṭu, leṇḍker, mo, ruṭruṭu; (*of belly*) poṭpoto; (*body*) ḍhopsa (M), ḍhupsi (F); (*as a corpse*) diṛidaṅ; (*to be*) pokpoko; (*face*) komkom; (*gland, feeling of*) laṛkac luṛkuc; (*very*) dama domo; (*to become*) puṭric.

SWOON, TO—kikiṛciṭ, taṛkhao.

SWOOP, WITH A—jhup marte, khap mente; (*to lift*) halo.

SWOP, TO—dolbadol.

SWORD, A—paṇḍu biṅ, tarware, horec gadar; (*2-edged*) dhup; (*stick*) gupti ṭheṅga; (*straight*) kheṅjer; (*to use*) tarware calao; (*to carry*) gaḍiau, t. ṭhema; (*to touch with point of*) gayuk; (*to perform with*) khelod.

SYMMETRICAL—jhabrali; (*non*) gheje bajā.

SYMPATHY—māyā; (*to feel*) sir ṭaṭao.

SYMPHYSIS PUBIS, THE—paṇḍe

SYRINGE, A—phickaṛi, phecoṛ; (*to draw up by*) surkau.

SYSTEM, WITHOUT—ajak bujak.

T

TABLE, A—mec, mej.

TABOO, TO—baron.

TACITURN—masac musuc, mayaṅ muyuṅ; (*to be*) ṅorṅor.

TACKED ON—ḍhiusi.

TAIL—caṇḍbol, caṇḍlom; (*of pig or goat*) caṇḍkilom; (*of bird or fish*) cupi; (*of snake*) moṇḍ; (*of peacock*) pinc; (*part cut off*) baṇḍa (M), baṇḍi (F); (*like a*) botoc; (*to turn*) picom podroc; (*to wag the*) ṭhepe; (*to twist a bullock's*) puchla puchli, puchlau; (*of horse or cow, long hairs in*) cāoar, cāowār; (*without, of a fowl*) ḍeṇḍe, ḍeṇḍkec.

TAILOR—*(a)* dạrji; *(wise, to sit)* asan maṇḍao; *(bird)* jiạm, jion, ghar-didi, malhan cẽṛẽ; *(bird, cry of)* phecań (2), ṭipi (2).

TAKE, TO—aṅge, atań, gatao, haṅge, hatao, hạtiạu, moṭeam, tela; *(up)* ambaṛ omboṛ; *(out of)* oar, rọl; *(out of pod &c)* hadap̣; *(hold of)* pakaṛ, pakṛao, rem, sap̣; *(back)* hatao ruạṛ; *(off or out)* siboṛ; *(off garment)* bọć; *(to do with)* tagada; *(note of)* carić, ṭọhọr; *(place)* uptạn; *(possession of)* moṭiao; *(along with)* ḍuriạu; *(one in)* ẹrẹ lipuk̕, ẹrẹ mọńj, ẹrẹ suk, ẹrẹ suruć, luṭuć; *(up space)* gabao; *(upon oneself)* gae makhao; *(shape)* gaṛhao; *(all)* hameṭ; *(out of fire)* họṭkọr; *(for oneself)* gabọć; *(stealthily)* gabṛe; *(by force or fraud)* rẹć; *(out improperly)* puṭuć; *(away)* gẹmẹr, idi, jhotrao, siboṛ; *(away one's land)* bẹjaega; *(to)* bạsut, pohncao, sebel; *(away gradually)* idi jaora; *(out a little)* kaḍhao, kạḍhiạu, khańjao; *(a little from each)* kaḍha kạḍhi; *(money & give nothing in return)* mosao; *(a great deal)* baḍhi. *Cf.* CARE, HAND.

TAKING—lekate; *(favourably)* mạrji.

TALC—abṛak.

TALES—*(bearer of)* bajhạni, bạjnia, cuk̕gliić, durạha, naṭer guru; *(bearing)* cugliạ; *(to tell)* bajhao, cạuwạj, cokhna, cugli, cugli capạṭi, jojna, jojogna, khocao, lọndphọnd, nundni, sulạ.

TALIPES EQUINUS, TO WALK AS ONE HAVING—herca (M), hiṛci (F).

TALK—bhakara, gap; *(humorous)* kap; *(small)* gọlpọ; *(obscene)* bhakhna bhạkhni.

TALK, TO—rọṛ; *(idly)* bakhna bạkhni, bakhnao, bhacka bhạcki, bheder (2), bhẹk (2); *(privately)* gampis; *(big)* khuṭlạ, ṭher, uć, usić; *(continuously)* kiroť kọrọť; *(over)* ẹrẹ libuk̕, rạmjạu, ridkhid, rọndkhọnd, rọnkhọn, sãorao; *(glibly)* pharphar, ṭẽoṭẽo. *Cf.* NONSENSE, AT RANDOM.

TALKATIVE—bat baḍohi, batkạṭi, beṭeń (2), bhacko, bhadra, bhajra (M), bhạjri (F), bhọcbhọc, caego (F), cẹṭẹ (2), gal bajoṛiạ, galbajṛi, gạpi, kạhwạiyạ, kharkhar, labak̕ cabak̕, labar labar (F), lacar, lahra (M), lạhri (F), lapco, lasar (2F), lasra (M), lạsri (F), lece cẹre (F), lẹsẹr (2).

TALL—baela, biyol boyol, boeboe, boela, daela, ḍakḍaka, ḍhaṅga (M), ḍhạṅgi (F) ḍheṅka, hahadań, hinrihić (F), hiṛhińjań (M), họthọtọ, huḍhuḍu, jeleń, jhạl, kạbṛuń, kaṛja (M), kạṛji (F), kạyõk̕ (2), khãrgo, khạrku, lahaṅga (M), lahạṅgi (F), lamka (M), lạmki (F), laṛga (M), lạṛgi (F), lẹńbọń, raela, rakḍań, rạkḍuń, rak̕ṭań, rańkaṛ, riyol royol, roela (M), ruili (F), ruilạ (M), saela boela, soela (M), suili (F), soela boela, suilạ (M), ṭuiṭui, usul; *(very)* kaṛũk̕ (2), raṭbań, roṭboń, ruirui (F); *(& slim)* kakaṛcań, kạkuṛcuń, kańkaṛ, kạyuṛ (2), laklạkiạ, lamka (M), lạmki (F), loṛea, loṛyo, rạkḍuń, ruilạ (M), ruili (F), ṭampa ṭuṛa, ṭaṭaṛbań; *(& bent)* kạṛbuń; *(& stout)* laṛańka.

TAMARIND TREE, THE—jọjọ dare; *(spice from leaves of)* palwạ.

TAMARISK BUSH, A SMALL—jhãwar.

TAMASHA, A—dhum, kheloḍ, khiloḍ, lilạ.

TAMBOURINE, A KIND OF—ghera.

TAME, TO—kabja, kabọj, kạbu, kas marao.

TAMPER WITH, TO—bhaṅga, bhaṅgao.

TAN—*(a)* kas; *(leather, to)* kọs.

TANG OF ARROW HEAD—baraṅgi.

TANGLED—gawar (2), giwạr gawar; *(branches)* jhaṛ jhuṛ.

TANK, A—abhra, band, pokhoṛ, pukhri; *(traditional)* pokhori, toṛe pokhori; *(part of)* ḍaṇḍ; *(overflow channel of)* paeṛẽ.

TANTALISE—*(to)* harkha hạrkhi, iṛu; *(with food, to)* eṛo; *(to be)* harhao, lalao, lolao.

TAP—*(to)* ru, ṭhọp̣ (2); *(with a)* ṭhopor marte; *(root)* mul rẹhẹť; *(a piece of burning firewood, to)* koṭop̣; *(& cause to sound, to)* ṭhokiã bạjiã.

TAPE—phitạ

TAPERING TO A POINT—cuicui.

TAPPING SOUND—kaḍap̃ (2), phidrak̃ (2), ṭap̃ (2); *(of hoofs)* karap̃; *(to make a)* koṭap̃, ṭeć ṭeć; *(a series of)* phạdruk̃, phidrak̃ (2), ṭap̃ (2); *(to make a loud)* ṭhap̃; *(a light)* ṭhapar, ṭhapa (2), ṭhopor.

TAR—*(gas or coal)* kuila sunum; *(wood or coal)* alkatra sunum.

TARDY—lạmbri, riboć rọboć, ribon̄ koboń.

TARGET, A—bejha; *(to shoot at)* bejha.

TARIFF—nirik; *(to fix a)* nirik.

TARJUA BIRD, CALL OF—kẫyũr (2).

TARNISH—*(to)* khọṭ; *(to become)* garsa gale.

TARO PLANT, THE—sạru.

TARRY, TO—bilọm; *(for)* taṅgi.

TASK, ALLOTTED—nirik; *(to fix)* nirik.

TASSAR SILK WORM—ạḍa; *(& moth)* dhuṛiạli lumạm, lumạm; *(rearing place of)* ạḍa bạri; *(cocoon)* ḍhaba lumạm, lumạm; *(1st. moult)* sagee; *(2nd.)* dejra; *(3rd.)* ṭeka; *(4th.)* koela; *(rites connected with)* bhaṅga pujạ, lumạm peṭeć pujạ; *(to transfer)* capan; *(bag for hatching eggs)* khuli; *(F. moth)* lumạń pạtni; *(bag for moths)* khuṅgi; *(one who tends)* pạiha; *(cess on rearing)* patkar; *(to fasten to tree)* ṭipạn; *(a stick used for)* guṭi ṭheṅga; *(a disease of)* aṅgạri; *(univoltine moths)* dhuṛiạ; *(branch for transferring)* tạli; *(sacrifice for)* ahạri; *(tree for rearing)* guṭi.

TASSEL, A—durịạ.

TASTE, TO—cakha; *(by eating)* jọm gelak̃; *(by drinking)* nũ gelak̃; *(a sharp)* lạg, tej; *(pleasant)* ńọrọm (2), sebel, sọsṭọk, torọp; *(disagreeable)* harań, helem; *(without)* lamjak̃, sabra, sithạ; *(to lose)* hedgẹ hesak̃; *(hot)* jhal, karua; *(of animals which have died naturally)* liṛoć ṭoṛoć.

TATTERED—cacak̃, gadlo, gadṛoć, gadrum, garui ṭapui, gayur ṭapur, jhạrgeeak̃, jọrpọć, khẹkre, khendreć; *(& holed)* hẹdrẹć; *(clothes)* gendrak̃ cethrak̃, gendrak̃ cetrak̃.

TATTLE—gọlpọ; *(to)* gal gọppọ, gọppọ; *(one who)* lạṛu caberi.

TATTOOING—khoda; *(without)* adwa; *(tribe who live by)* khodua (M), khudni (F); *(to prick, as in)* khoda.

TAUGHT, NOT FULLY—hẹndẹć.

TAUNT, TO—hẹj, siṛog.

TAURUS, SEVEN STARS OF—sọrẹnko.

TAUT—ṭạnṭan; *(to become)* ṭẹnṭẹn; *(to make)* dak̃.

TAX—*(a house or roof)* chapar bạndhi; *(to)* telao.

TAZIA OF THE MOHAMEDANS, THE—tajia.

TEA—ca, cha; *(for drinking)* ca dak̃; *(plant)* ca dare; *(garden)* bagiea, ca bagan.

TEACH, TO—binti, ceť, parhao, puski, sikat, sikạu, sikhnạt, siknạt, tạlim.

TEACHER, A—guru; *(of village school)* sarkar; *(of charms)* kambru guru.

TEACHING—sikhạt, sikhạuna, sikhnạt, siknạt.

TEAK TREE, THE—leṭpoṭe dare, sạgun.

TEAR, TO—chachak̃, charchar, ciru, ciro, conthao, ọrẹć, pańpạṇḍrań, pharpharao, siṛo, tarar, ṭẹgẹ nẹrẹ; *(up by roots)* tarao; *(of beast of prey)* cạblạu, ciri cunthi, ṭahur; *(off)* cagar, cagat; *(to shreds)* chachak̃, ṭana ṭukrạ; *(up or out)* racak̃. *Cf.* FRAGMENTS.

TEARING, SOUND OF—carcar, pharphar; *(with a)* phạṭ marte.

TEARS—jạrum dak̃, mẹt dak̃; *(to flow as)* hidir (2); *(eyes to fill with)* birin̄ (2), ḍabḍabao, ḍhar (2), pẹpẹrkat.

TEASE, TO—*(torment)* dikiạu, iṛu; *(card or comb)* dundlạu, phidli, piteť.

TEDIOUS—bẹdhọr, dayak̃ (2); *(of a road)* bẹhọr.

TEEMING—gahagaḍ.

TEETH—dạṭa; *(grinder)* jambe d.; *(of comb)* bakhọr; *(to fix into)* cạblạu; *(to gnash)* tọgọć dạṭa, maṭmaṭ; *(to clean)* daṭạni; *(to take firm hold with)* gẹr urić; *(to bite with front)* hạmbur; *(to rub with finger)* hurtir; *(to shew the)* isir; *(having gaps in)* khạnḍọ bodgak̃, khạnḍwań; *(having lost front)* phogra (M), phugri (F); *(sticking out)* soṭa; *(to be set on edge)* khoro; *(to whistle* *through the*) suyur; (*to extract*) boć; (*lips fallen in from loss of*) khando khapua; (*of cattle, a worm which destroys*) kasai; (*powder to blacken*) misi. *Cf.* TO GRIND.

TELEGRAPH, THE—tar.

TELL, TO—janao, janti, jetho, lai, latić, men, sunan; (*all*) khulau; (*& go away*) lai oto; (*as one goes away*) lai tora; (*& spread*) lai pasnao. *Cf.* TALES.

TEMPER—mejaj; (*out of*) berod, birod, coenda; (*uncontrolled*) ankarwa, kāyā; (*able to control*) subod, suboria; (*to shew*) adra, agra agri; (*ill*) corcotań. *Cf.* QUICK, SHORT.

TEMPERAMENT—jat, jati, jontor, mejaj, rawā, subhab.

TEMPERANCE—dhirja.

TEMPERED—(*short*) ankarwa, bispitaha; (*bad*) coenda, khecraha (M), khecrahi (F); (*hot*) jhāk, kadraha (M), kadrahi (F), kutil, surpil (F); (*good*) subod, suboria; (*ill*) birgha, jhagrahi, kadrai, suia, suipak.

TEMPEST, ROARING OF A—gudgud.

TEMPLE, A—mandil, mandir, mat, math, mondil, mundil, mundir, than orak; (*Brahman resident in*) panda; (*right or left*) kapar jadi.

TEMPORARY—amnam; (*erection for guests*) camda, capchamda, chamda; (*relationship*) nata.

TEMPORISE, TO—agdhao.

TEMPT, TO—bahkao, bidau.

TEN—gel; (*seers*) dhara; (*o'clock a. m.*) basiam.

TENACIOUS—tokor (2), torter; (*of purpose*) johol, muruk.

TENANT, A—asami, proja, porja pani, praja, prajapati; (*cultivating*) jotadar, raeot; (*without*) nisun.

TEND, TO—asen; (*cattle, &c.*) gupi.

TENDER—ali, bale, balebās, botkoć, kakosia; (*of pot-herbs*) kander; (*of fleshmeat*) resot, sirak barak; (*to become*) tarwa; (*in feet*) dharak dhorok; (*age*) licar; (*of cattle, a*) gupiić, gupi kuri (F).

TENDON, A—pawa.

TENON, TO—sula.

TENSE—tan tan, tantan; (*to be*) tenten, tiltilau.

TENT, A—chauni, tambu; (*small one-ply*) chaldari.

TENURE—(*a rent-free*) jaigir, naeke man, aśiyali man; (*kind of*) jol sason.

TERM (*period*)—miad; (*having a*) miadi. *Cf.* LIFE.

TERMINATION—mucat, ses.

TERMITE, A SPECIES OF—bhuku, bhuska, buska, ńindir.

TERMS, TO BE ON GOOD—hera ghesa, hilmil.

TERRIBLE—botor.

TERRIFIED—kokloset, lucpucia, luyut cuput; (*to be*) bhirka bhirki; (*off*) caukau.

TERROR—bhorok, dhoros; (*to be in*) bilbilau, camal comol, luyut; (*stricken*) pucpuc, tharbasao; (*to cause*) durduri.

TEST, TO—ajmao, barkać, bidau, dahao, lega, parikha; (*by comparison*) bhear.

TESTICLE—andga, andge, bele, pante bele, peska; (*having only one*) ekasira, sira; (*tumour of*) andrak.

TESTIFY, TO—goha em, goha gujrau, sakhi em, sakhi purau.

TESTILY, TO REPLY—batań (2), beteń (2).

TESTIMONY—suhi.

TETANUS, TO SUFFER FROM—katkatao.

TETHER, TO—candiau.

THAN—khoć, khon.

THANK, TO—gun manao, sarhao.

THANNA, A—phandi.

THAT—bańma, en, hana, hina, hona, hone, ina, iti, lona, ona, one, se, tahā, uni; (*in introducing oblique narration*) je; (*one, animate*) hani, huni; (*one, inanimate*) hina, hona, hone; (*same*) se, taha; (*at any rate*) se getho; (*much*) inag, inak; (*present*) iti; (*which*) one; (*so*) jaha lekate; (*is to say*) ać kathae, bańma, enkathae, metakme.

THATCH, TO—dap, dalop, urien; (*the finishing*) bhindia; (*to repair*) oriao; (*one row of*) ager; (*framework for*) chatār; (*lath for*) cipa bata.

THATCHING—(*grass*) daƙ daƙramaƙ, ḍhoḍhia sauri, sauri ghās; (*needle*) sulak.

THEIR (*in comp.*)—(*pl.*) tako; (*dual*) takin.

THEME—tal.

THEMSELVES—nije.

THEN—ado, enbetar, eṇḍe, eṇḍe eneć, eṇḍekhan, eṇḍe nahĩ, eṇḍe nahĩ to, eṇḍerema, eṇḍe reseṭ, eṇḍete, enkhać, inre, kate, khan, khange, khange tho, kir, reseṭ, tobe, tobe khać, un, un jokha, unimre; (*only*) eṇḍe bapo, eṇḍete eneć, in aneć, in utar, tobe nahĩ, un aneć, un utar; (*since*) un khon; (*not till*) eneć; (*till*) un habić.

THERE—eṇḍe, entere, ete, haṇḍe, hane, hante, hente, hentere, honte, nhaṇḍe, oṇḍe, tãhã, ṭhar, ṭhor; (*of*) nhaṇḍen, oṇḍen; (*one*) one onage; (*is an end of it*) atar, dapor, napor; (*upon*) kur; (*about*) nahi nindhan.

THEREFORE—inate, onate, tobe eroñ.

THESE—(*anim.*) enko, nhoko, noko, noƙõeko; (*inan.*) noako; (*2, anim.*) nhukin, nikin, noƙõekin, nukin; (*2, inan.*) noakin; (*particular*) noƙoeko; (*two, which or there*) onekin.

THEY—onko, ko; (*themselves*) ako; (*two*) akin; (*& I*) ale.

THICK—boḍe, cerdha, daria, daria dapaṭ, edebede, garha, godbra, ladlad, later, leper (2), lodhor (2), mandhak, mosto, moṭa, thutba, thutwa; (*as water*) bohor (2); (*dense*) athe athoñ, atuƙ jharuƙ, damdam, delop (2), gahagaḍ, gañjer, gargadlaƙ, ghacpac, ibil, jhopro, saṅge; (*of liquid*) gadhra, gadra, geñgeñ, lathaƙ; (*of stick &c*) mutak; (*of clouds*) karidañ; (*so*) ehe talañ; (*not*) royo, royo ropo; (*& muddy*) gadla, hewel bekel; (*& frothy*) lodhor (2); (*of hair or leaves*) paṭa, paṭo; (*as fruit on tree*) ghauda, ghauñja ghãuñji; (*headed*) behod, bhoda, bhonda; (*necked*) gordon; (*skinned*) amoṭ, daria, darmoṭ.

THICKER—(*than usual*) therethepe; (*at one end*) dhamon phucia, phucka.

THICKET, A—badar, jhar, jhar jhur, jholaṇḍ, jhuṇḍ, jhur, jolaṇḍ; (*to shelter in*) jhurgusia; (*in a ravine*) kandor; (*in a marsh*) khalar.

THICKLY—gargadlaƙ, jabre.

THIEF, A—kombro, kombro bokro, kumbru.

THIGH, THE—bulu; (*under side of*) dhara.

THIN—ciri biri, curcuria, etañ, hadgẽra, hidañ ṭhapañ, joñje, joñjroć, lapar (2), mĩhĩ, nakwal, nanha, patar satar, patla, phinphinia, piliñ, raṅgap, ruñruñ, satar patar, siwiñ (2), siyañ; (*to become*) dublau; (*of cloth*) ghaṅgri; (*of hair*) henra (M), hinri (F); (*of liquid*) leber (2), leher, tiñṭiñ; (*of grass &c*) lubui; (*as mango-skin*) amchola; (*as a stick*) nenheć, sisiar; (*of semi-liquids*) sadar sudur, sadgur badgur, sudur; (*very*) mĩhĩ (2), piliñ; (*& flapping*) lapar (2); (*strips split into*) ciri biri; (*out dhan, to*) bakra, gachiau, ; (*skinned*) khantar.

THINE—amren, amaƙ, amañ; (*in comp.*) tam.

THING, A—cij, jinis, podartho, tij.

THINGS—(*all*) sanamaƙko; (*in general*) cij.

THINK, TO—atkar, bundis, dandha, gaṇḍon, hudis, kheal, mone; (*over*) gunan, gunan, guṇḍ, khañj, sõc; (*deeply over*) gundi; (*lightly of*) alga, halka; (*out*) hudis bundis; (*about*) oman; (*well of*) basut, parpasind, pasind; (*affectionately of*) uihar.

THIRD, THE—tesar, tesra; (*of children*) sañjla (M), sañjli (F).

THIRST—tetañ, tiras; (*to*) tetañ, tetoas; (*to be faint from*) lakar (2); (*parched with*) atap jarap; (*distressed from*) ahal (2), ahka ahki, ahkaoƙ, potoṭ; (*& hunger*) upasa tirasa.

THIRTEEN—gelpea.

THIRTY—pe gel, miṭ isi gel, tis.

THIS—ina, isko, iti, iyo, na, nha, nhanaƙ, nhoa, nhui, nia, no, noa, noƙõe; (*anim.*) nãi, nui; (*one, anim.*) ini, nhãi, nhãitaƙ, nhaić, nikĩ, nui;

(*one, inan.*) nhaṭak̇, niạṭak̇, noaṭak̇; (*particular one*) ẹkẹ̃, nhẹ̃kẹ, nhĩkĩ, nikĩ, ni, nuiṭak, nukũi; (*present*) iti; (*& that*) hana nha.

THONG BINDING YOLK TO PLOUGH-BEAM—naṅgle, umadha.

THORN, A—carẹċ.

THORNS—jạnum, kạr; (*armed with*) raṅga coṅga; (*to block with*) ram, rampha.

THORNY—raṅga coṅga, raṅgha roṅgho; (*tree or bush, a*) jạnum.

THOROUGHLY—bes ọkọċte, paka, paka pạki.

THOSE—enko, nhoko, onko; (*inan.*) onako; (*2, anim.*) unkin; (*2, inan.*) onakin; (*which*) ọnẹko; (*of*) renkin, renko; (*over there*) hanko.

THOU—am; (*weak form of*) em.

THOUGH—rehõ, ẹnrehõ.

THOUGHT—cintạ, dandagiri, nam cintạ, phikir, porbhae, sõc; (*to take*) dand, guni bhabik̇; (*to bestow much*) nạndi gạndi; (*with much*) dandra dạndri, nana bond; (*without*) akhaṛ bakhaṛ, bhasa bharṛa, bhulạ bhạtuạ, gạphil, nicind, phạriạbaj.

THOUGHTLESSLY—andhe pạthạuṛi, ankatha anbetha, ạri ḍhạri, ạurạ, ạuri pạthạuri, badrak̇ (2), barọ sọtrọ, bẹhudis, bhọs (2), hurạ huṛi, lạḍur bạḍur, pạthạuṛi.

THOUSAND—(*a*) hajar; (*a hundred*) lakh; (*hundreds of*) lakelak.

THREAD—sutạm; (*to*) gatao, gutu, huraṛ; (*the sacred*) jạnu, jạnạu, poeta; (*red*) arak̇ sutạm, kasta, kosta, posta; (*silk*) lumạm s.; (*a reel of*) ril s.; (*to make 3 strands from single*) sim lać; (*spun by spider*) bindi s.; (*length spun at once*) eora; (*not raised in weaving*) tạpuk̇; (*of a screw*) righi; (*bare*) hẹndra.

THREADS, HAVING INTERVALS BETWEEN THE—jaljạliạ, jeljelia, jhiljhiliạ.

THREAT, A—dhọmọk cọmọk; (*used in*) iạ ạikạ; (*with a*) dhora dhori.

THREATEN, TO—dạbṛi, dhamae dhurạ̣i, dhum, dundrạu, haba dubạ, hagao, kandhao, taṛkhạ, ṭhakrao, ṭhokrao, ṭhukrạu, ṭokrao; (*future harm or loss*) dhirạu; (*to assault each other*) dapa dạpi; (*exclm.*) bedot rasa.

THREE—pẹ. pea, pẹnẹ, tin; (*collectively*) pẹnẹ; (*sided*) tin pohol; (*times*) tebọṛ, tebṛa; (*each*) pẹpẹ goṭạn; (*at a time*) pẹpẹ

THRESH, TO—(*of grain*) dal, ẹn, ẹn lạhuṫ; (*with flail or stick*) dal, dal lạhuṫ; (*in small quantities*) ṭamuṭi; (*half*) carmanḍọ, ẹncar manḍo.

THRESHING-FLOOR—khạrại; (*a place beside*) ḍegha.

THRESHHOLD, ON THE—dạkhil.

THRICE—pẹ choṭ, pẹ dhao, tẹboṛ, tebṛa.

THRIFTLESSLY—bhọsbhọs.

THRIFTY, TO BE—rạkhi jogao, rukhi jogao.

THRIVING—gangan.

THROAT, THE—gola, kanṭa; (*sore*) gaṅghar; (*swollen, of cattle*) gola kanṭa; (*to cut*) jaba, jabe, jạbu; (*to stick in*) kanṭeṫ; (*to speak from*) bukṭan, gẹhẽṫ (2); (*itching in*) gargaṫ, gatae, gạyam (2), lẹmlẹm; (*to clear*) kharak̇; (*pulsation in*) lokoṫ.

THROB, TO—buṭuń (2), buyuṫ (2), dhak (2), dhuk (2), ḍuk (2), pidgạk̇.

THROBBING—kankanao, ṭihkạu, tugum (2), uhui (2); (*in head*) uṭhul (2).

THRONE, A—raj gạdi, siṅghạsọn.

THRONG, TO—hader.

THROTTLE, TO—họṭọk̇ limbọṫ, limbọṫ; (*sound of*) kẹdrọċ kọdrọċ.

THROUGH—dara, họtẹte, iạte, lasãṛhẽ, lọcna, niạte, parsadte, tese.

THROW, TO—capaṫ, lebda, lebda libdi, pelao; (*as a javelin*) sọhọr; (*about*) chitiạ bitiạ; (*away*) gidi; (*into*) khadle; (*at*) labda; (*on ground*) tasrao; (*to one side*) mạnḍwa mạnḍwi; (*up—vomit*) uchlạu; (*at & break*) tiń gẹjẹr; (*into water*) bhasan, caḍo, ḍoelao; (*a stick in air & hit it with another*) lapka; (*anything sticky at a wall*) lạthiạu; (*forward with force*) chidgai; (*from side to side*) chidgạ chidgi, lebda libdi; (*off effects*) nijạu, sarao; (*oneself down*) oldhao, thasṛao; (*oneself at another's feet*) ti jangare gidik, god pari ; *(away as useless)* gidi tot ; *(animals)* har ; *(dust in eyes)* er tepet, hor beda ; *(oneself on another's pity)* hendkok, herkok ; *(water at)* arec ; *(one side forward when walking)* hondeal. *Cf.* MOUTH.

THROW DOWN, TO—kacrao, landur, lesrok, lethec, mandwa mandwi, tasrao, tawak, thasrao ; *(often)* tasra tasri ; *(of wall &c)* lendur ; *(at random)* ganja gunji ; *(by a lever)* patuc.

THROWING A STICK INTO A TREE, NOISE OF —jhargoe (2).

THROWN, TO BE—capat ; *(away)* berbad.

THRUST, TO—dhaka, dhaklau ; *(at)* kucau ; *(forward)* sohor ; *(a point)* sobok ; *(in)* gotao, sok ; *(suddenly into fluid)* khab ; *(out lip)* binduc.

THUD—*(to)* bhadbhud, bhud, rokroc ; *(to fall with a)* bhadbhud ; *(a)* luthum, phatphut ; *(with a)* bhud marte, dhakur m., dhui m., khabkhub, khat (2), lithum m., ludgup, ludgup m., luthum m., rihrak m., rokroc m., sarpat m., thok m., thugul m. ; *(sound of)* dahap (2), dhankur (2), dharae, dirim, harhur, lapak (2), lithum, lopok, ludgup, rihrak, sarpat ; *(a succession of)* ladlad, ladlud, ludlud, luthum.

THUMB, THE—enga katup, budha katup ; *(to flip with)* thep ; *(impression)* tip ; *(to prod with)* ghusa, ghusa ghusi ; *(to shew in defiance)* endre, katup uduk, thepo ; *(to remove with)* piskic.

THUMP—*(to)* gudau, parat ; *(with a)* dhui marte, kuhut m., lithum m., luthum m., sarpat m. ; *(sound of)* darae (2), dhae, dharae, dhikur, dhinkur, duhup (2), gadap gudup, gudup, kuhut (2), lithum, luthum, patapat.

THUNDER—*(to)* rimil sade ; *(to rumble, as distant)* duldul, gudgud, hadhud, hudur (2), rahruk ; *(bolt, a)* ceter.

THURSDAY—biraspat, lokhibar, lukhibar.

THUS—ehe to, enka, enka enkate, hale, nhanka, nhenka, nhenka leka, nonka ; *(emphatic)* se ge thor.

THWACK, TO—parat ; *(with a)* parat marte.

THWART, TO—hanao.

TICK, A—tik ; *(the cow)* camki ; *(sound)* tot tot.

TICKET, A—tikas, tikis.

TICKLE, TO—bokro, gutlu ; *(the fancy)* laboj.

TIDE, EBB & FLOW OF—gheola.

TIDINGS—birtant, hakige.

TIDY—barat borot, borot (2), camkec, mahit ; *(oneself, to)* singar.

TIE, TO—bandhon, candiau, tol ; *(equal)* rodbodol ; *(up)* galot ; *(to a post)* khuntau ; *(into a bundle)* kop (2) ; *(running knot)* asit ; *(2 ends together)* tonge ; *(with, what is used to)* tonol ; *(up a cloth)* ghet ; *(up hair)* rot, sut, toke ; *(hands together)* manjur guda ; *(small articles in cloth)* gopea.

TIED—lat ; *(loosely)* bhiso bhoso, dhiusi ; *(up)* bandhar.

TIGER, A—mundra dangra, rangia dangra, enga kul, kul, maran tarup ; *(like animal)* tarup ; *(very large)* ardu ; *(to become)* andkul ; *(to growl as)* gunjrau, gurgur, hudur (2) ; *(a big-headed)* boak, maran datkap kul ; *(den of)* kul dander.

TIGHT—kaskas, keskese, koskos, ratratao, sokot, sokto, tantan, tuntun, uric ; *(very)* koruc ; *(to become)* tenten ; *(place, to be in a)* khonja.

TIGHTEN, TO—dak, karkarao, kasao, kaskasao, koskos ; *(by pulling)* tantanao ; *(by twisting with a lever)* jhik.

TIGHTLY—akjak, rakjak, ratratao, ruc (2) ; *(in comp.)* ratpatao ; *(to hold)* karmatao ; *(not fitting)* sonkor.

TILE, A—*(roof)* khapra ; *(broad flat)* tali ita ; *(having)* khaprol ; *(on ridge)* magra, mongra.

TILL—dhabic, dharic, habic ; *(then, not)* enec.

TILT, TO—*(up)* dap dup, dhinku, dorsec, tarkuc, ular ; *(vessel to pour out liquid)* tan ; *(full)* umdhum.

TIMBER—kat ; *(mature)* manjal, manjela ; *(supporting roof-beams, a)* sordol.

TIME—amol, bat̤, bela, ber, bidal̤, car, chot̤, dhao, garte, ghor̤i, ghur̤i, bel, jǫhẽt, jokha, jokhan, jǫkhǫé, jug, kal, kar, lahe, ǫktǫ, par̤ia, payar, pǫhǫr, rosa, sat̤, samǫe, tak, tap; (*the 1st.*) sakas; (*at proper*) argat, at̤, batar, ghai̤, jokha bajao, jokha jumaṳ, ǫktǫ macha, sale (2), sańjok, sońjok, tak, tak batar, targhar; (*not at proper*) bǫtak; (*out of*) bǫrar̤; (*to spend*) bhańjao, bhuńjau, kal kat̤ao, khemao, khepao, t̤alao, t̤hat̤hao; (*to put off*) adǫrok, agdhao, ahil mahil, bilom, dǫhẽt dunduń, dera diri, diri, hemkhem, lǫhǫr pǫhǫr, tǫhǫ mǫhǫ̃; (*putting off*) hǫndǫ pǫndǫ, jape tope, nemor; (*to lose*) kǫmhai̤; (*a long*) ad̤i ghar̤i, jǫt̤hǫr pǫt̤hǫr, mahakal, rǫńgǫs; (*a short*) ar̤siń bar̤siń, mit ghar̤i, mursiń bar̤siń, musiń, ursiń bar̤siń; (*in a short*) cão marte, hatepate, laga lagi, nǫ, phus marte; (*at the present*) t̤uń ghur̤i, nǫbǫtar, nitok; (*this*) nia̤ dhao; (*without loss of*) dhãora dhãur̤i, t̤uń ghur̤i; (*behind*) diri, kubela; (*at that*) ǫnbetar, inre, khange thǫ, unre; (*another*) et̤ak garte, ghurikaete; (*of, just at the*) abe tabe; (*convenient*) ghai̤; (*a space of*) ghar̤i; (*a point of*) khan; (*at any*) jadhio, sobbo kal, tishǫ̃; (*for a long*) jǫt̤hǫr pǫt̤hǫr, jiki jaran, jot̤hor pot̤hor; (*appointed*) lagan, lǫgǫn; (*at no*) tishǫ̃ bań, tishǫ̃ alo, tishǫ̃ ǫhǫ; (*a point of*) tap; (*in my*) iń par̤iare; (*in music*) tal̤; (*at what*) tis, tin jǫkhǫn, tinreman; (*after time*) bare (2), garak (2), ghane (2), ghuriã (2), ghur̤i (2), here phere, hid̤ir (2), huluk (2) khane (2), pǫhrǫk (2), ter̤et bor̤et; (*past*) sa̤bik; (*from sunset to midnight*) harǫp; (*with short interval of*) laga lagi, lagle; (*between night fall & moonrise*) ńũtat̤; (*of day, at this*) nia̤ pǫhǫr; (*ago, a short*) hal̤i sal̤i; (*next year, this*) ghuriã din; (*piece, a*) ghar̤i. *Cf.* TO PASS, TO FIX.

TIMES—tekhar; (*all*) sobbo kal; (*fixed*) nit̤ ǫktǫko; (*round, many*) ur̤hu bur̤hu; (*in past*) nindara, sedae; (*many*) ad̤i dhao; (*fold*) d̤abǫl; (3) tebor̤. *Cf.* SOME.

TIMID—cirgal, d̤orokia̤, d̤urukia̤, halso, poera (M), pueri (F).

TEN—khapar, t̤in; (*a*) t̤im.

TINGLE, TO—(*of ears*) cão, cão marao, tińgit; (*of pain*) ranran.

TINGLING SENSATION—cabué cubué, rumuń (2).

TINKLE, TO—chań (2), jhan jhanao, t̤ipiń (2), t̤ipi (2), t̤iriń; (*of a bell*) kurun (2), t̤hir̤iń, t̤impi t̤iriń; (*with a*) t̤hir̤iń m., t̤ir̤iń m., t̤ir̤iń t̤ipiń.

TINKLING—chamak, chań (2), jhamar jhumur, jhan (2), jhuluń (2), jhumur (2) t̤arań t̤urań, t̤ipi (2).

TINY—d̤ǫbǫ (2); (*& neat*) d̤ǫblǫ.

TIP—(*the*) t̤usa̤; (*out, to*) up; (*toe, to stand on*) cond̤ok; (*water from one vessel to another, to*) dhar̤kao; (*up a fan, to*) lǫcǫc.

TIRE—(*of a wheel, the*) hal̤; (*to*) mǫkǫń; (*out, to*) harao.

TIRED—ala al̤i, alao, ałapala, asbas, asbasao, d̤oya d̤ape, et̤her pot̤her, lakar phakar, lakar̤ thakar̤, lǫcǫpǫcǫ, lǫcǫr pǫcǫr, lǫrǫ thǫrǫ, lǫkǫr phǫkǫr, thakar bakar, thaka tha̤ki, tharrao, thorrao, thukit; (*by sitting*) lǫt̤hǫr pǫt̤hǫr, ot̤hor pot̤hor; (*to become*) torlad; (*to be*) elao, lańga, lar̤buk, thakao; (*looking*) jabpuń.

TITLARK, THE—cańcir.

TITLE, A—amali, hae dae, huda̤, pod; (*to, to have*) amda; (*of eldest son of rajah*) t̤iket; (*of 2nd son of rajah*) kuar; (*of some landlords*) raja, t̤hakur; (*given to Brahmans*) t̤hakur.

TITTLE TATTLE—gal golpa.

TOAD, A—rǫtǫ; (*stool*) loyom, loyoń.

TOBACCO—tamakhur, thamakhur, thamar; (*kind of*) sada; (*young shoots of*) d̤ugi; (*strong*) lǫg t.; (*to chew*) t. jǫm; (*to smoke*) t. ńũi; (*addicted to chewing*) khadkia̤; (*addicted to smoking*) pust̤i; (*raw*) kharsan, surti, moera; (*mixed with gur̤*) gurakhul; (*plant, a kind of*) mogra t.; (*local*) ka̤cri t.; (*petiole of leaf of*) khad̤a.

TO-DAY—roka, teheń.

TODDLE, TO—caco, ḍagar ḍugur, ḍalaṅ ḍuluṅ, ḍuluṅ (2), iubus (2).

TODDY—taṛi; *(measure, a)* lạbni; *(drawer, a)* pạsi. *Cf.* PALMYRA.

TOE—*(a)* kạṭup̣, jaṅga k.; *(big)* eṅga k.; *(little)* sić k.; *(nails)* jaṅga rama; *(ring)* ãoṭha, bichiạ; *(rings, sound of)* chamak, cham (2); *(walking on the)* licạ lace.

TOGETHER—goṛ, hẹdẹ gọdẹ, jomka jumki, jọmọk, juma jumi, loe, pal bhiṅjan, sajha, sạmil, são, sạṭ, sạṭọp̣, sọlgọl, sọṅgẹ lọṅgẹ; *(to put close)* sạṭao; *(with)* gudiạ gudyi, salak̕, samet, sạmit, satalak̕, sẹlẹt̕. *Cf.* ALL.

TOIL—ghamaoṭa; *(to)* dhamrọkọt; *(& trouble)* daṛ dhup.

TOKEN—nisạna, nisṭạn, sạkhi.

TOLA, ONE—bhori.

TOLD—*(off, to be)* badao; *(as soon as)* lại tora.

TOLERABLE—jhaporae, mẹlcọ.

TOLERATE, TO—uput̕.

TOLL—mạhsul; *(person in charge of a)* ghaṭdar.

TO-MORROW—gapa, gapanok̕.

TONE—*(in the same)* sọṛọṅ (2); *(to speak in a low)* gahãṛ gũhũṛ, pasar pusur.

TONGS—saṇḍạsi, saṛạsi, sãṛsi.

TONGUE, THE—alaṅ, cạu; *(of bell)* laṛu; *(to scrape)* hatar; *(to protrude)* lakar (2), mẹlọt̕; *(to make a slip of)* pichol; *(unhealthy)* alaṅ poṭak̕; *(tied)* alaṅ ọbọr, lat̕; *(a thin film on)* gitạk̕.

TONSILS—kaṇṭa; *(disease of)* gola kaṇṭa.

TOO—hõ; *(much)* arwạidha, jạsti.

TOOLS—hạtiạr, sajbaj, sanaphana, sapap̣.

TOOT, TO—*(on a horn)* tutu (2); *(sound of)* thoro thoto, thoto thoro.

TOOTH, A—dãt, daṭa; *(pick)* carẹć, daṭa họk̕ṭọrak̕; *(brush)* datạni, ṭuṭki jọnọk̕; *(on a karha)* kạkwạ; *(ache)* reṅgot̕, sitoṛ; *(having)* regṛa, righi; *(without)* lạkuk̕ phạkuk̕, phogra (M), phugṛi (F).

TOP—chip; *(a spinning)* bhuṅcampa, buṅcampa; *(of a tree)* chatna, cọṭ dhọj; *(to pinch off the)* roco; *(on the)* sọdgọrọ.

TOPIC—tal.

TOPPING—*(of bird)* duci.

TOPSY-TURVY—ajbuj, gẹjẹ pẹtẹ, ulạṭ palaṭ, ulṭạ palṭa, ulṭau palṭao, ulṭi pulṭi; *(to)* uṭkạ paṭka; *(to be)* pasaṛ.

TORCH, A—bamber, cecha, checha, mosal.

TORMENT, TO—dikiạu, kạndi kandao; *(by fault-finding)* khijạu, khijlạ khijli, khọckhọc.

TORN—gadrọć, gạdrum, jhaṅga jhuṭạ, jharọć jhapọć, khẹkre; *(to shreds)* khendreć, khucri; *(to be)* bhoṅgar; *(to the quick)* sirbạ.

TORPID THROUGH OVER-EATING—bọrọḍaṅ.

TORRENT, ROARING OF A—guḍguḍ.

TORTOISE—họrọ, kạchim, kaṭ họrọ, kumḍhiạ h.; *(swelling of stomach from)* kacma bại.

TORTUOUS—anacur.

TOSS, TO—ḍikạ ḍake, sọkọć; *(with horns)* uṭić; *(about)* chaṭpạṭao, kuṭlạ kuṭli, laṭpaṭ; *(up)* họṭak̕.

TOTAL—guṭ, moṭ, moṭhe, purạ, purạu, ṭhaukạ; *(to)* lekha guṭ, moṭ, muṅjrạ, thur.

TOTTER, TO—dhanman, lakaṛ lukuṛ, likọ lọkọ, tharam thurum.

TOTTERING—asoṛ tamboṛ, hiḍaṅ ṭhapaṅ, hiṇḍaṅ ṭhapaṅ, japaṅ jupuṅ, jipaṅ jạpaṅ, kẹdmẹr, kiṇḍet̕ maṇḍet̕, lẹcẹlẹcẹ, lẹcẹr pẹcẹr, liṅwạ sarwe, thạluk̕ thapuk̕; *(of an old person)* keḍbak̕; *(of a child)* liḍạ laḍe.

TOUCH, TO—capo, jak̕ jọṭẹt̕, jọṭẹt̕, laga, thukṛi; *(close)* jọpọk̕; *(slightly)* ḍaḍup̣, jọhọt, thukṛi, tukuć; *(another)* gạwić godak̕; *(each other, playfully)* gạwić godak̕; *(to call attention)* cukuć, gạḍuć, godak̕; *(everything)* halobalo; *(with sharp point)* gạyuk̕, kabak̕, ṭhoṭkao, ṭũḍạ.

TOUCHING—*(sensation of)* gaigum; *(each other)* ludgup̣, rọpọk̕, ṭesaṭes, ṭhesaṭhes.

Tough—paṭka.

Tour, a—saphar, saphor.

Tout, a—dalal.

Towards—sẹć, sẹn, tọrọp.

Tower—buruj, buruńj.

Town—nagar, nagraha, naṅgar, naṅgraha, sahar, saher, sọhọr; *(part of)* paṛa; *(market)* sahar bajar; *(suburbs of)* goṇḍa.

Towzled—dhạrpilạk̕, dhunsi punsi, laṭae ghoṭae; *(to make)* phidli.

Toy, a—khilạuna.

Trace—*(a)* surạg; *(to)* gohnao, pacha, pańja, pańja suhi, pecha, ṭhekan, ṭhikạn.

Track—*(a)* gọyọn, surạg; *(to)* gohnao pacha, pańja, pańja suhi, pecha; *(a jungle)* chur; *(a rat)* gọyọn; *(by blood, to)* mãyãm pańja.

Trade—birit, bitti, saoda, udạm; *(to)* bạnij, bạnij bepar, bepar, lanban, lọnbọn, pạikạr, phor bepar, saoda.

Trader, a—bepari, landbandić, lọndbọnd, mistri, pạikạr.

Tradition—lại calak̕, paltuṛ; *(recited during karam festival)* karam binti.

Traditional—*(lore)* kạhtuk, kạhtur, paltuṛ; *(lore, versed in)* budhạ kohna, kạhtukiạ, kọhna; *(place names)* bạhi duạr, cae, cae campa, campa, chae, haradata, hihiṛi pipiṛi, kẹrẹ ḍạḍi, khạira, khaṇḍerae bir, khọjkaman, koẹṇḍa gaṛ, pokhori, sasaṅ beḍa, sãt disom, sun gaṛ, somae sokṛa, soṛa nại, soṛa sạmud, toṛe pokhori; *(person, a)* gạjilal, gujạ, kãrã, madhosiṅ, mạlin budhi, mando siṅ, pilchu haṛam, pilchu budhi; *(tree, a)* labaṛ atnak̕, soho doho, tope sarjọm, ule sarjọm; *(birds)* hãs hạsil; *(earthworm)* gicho rạni; *(horse, a)* siń sadọm.

Traduce, to—cugli capạṭi, phond.

Traffic—bheja bheja, saoda; *(to)* bepar, besaha, saoda.

Trail—*(to)* ạtur; *(of, on the)* lạgiạ paṛao, lạgibohao.

Trailing—gawar (2), giroe gọṛọe, giwạr gawar.

Train—*(to)* bhãoar, bhãwãr, bolao, rigdạu, rigṛạu, sạd, sadhao, tińjạu; *(a railway)* rẹl gạḍi.

Trained, well—gạkhuṛ, soghoṛ.

Training—*(without)* hoe hoe; *(to keep in)* tẹńjao.

Traitorous—dagabaj, uphạdiạ.

Tramp—*(a)* ḍhanḍhanao, ḍhanman; *(sound of)* dhap̣ (2).

Trample, to—khaeda khạidi, khạidạ baidạ, lẹbẹt̕; *(under foot)* lẹbẹt̕ gasmaṇḍao, lẹsẹn; *(to pieces)* gasmaṇḍao, lẹbẹt̕ gẹjẹr, lẹbẹt̕ lạhut̕; *(over)* pelao; *(on)* ẹrgejak̕, rạunda rạundi; *(sound)* harpaṭ; *(& mix)* lẹbẹt̕ gańjao.

Trampled—ganjha gạnjhi.

Tranquil—khạtiran, suk; *(to be)* khạtir.

Transact business, to—lanban.

Transfer, to—ucạṛ; *(dust to cloth)* ẹn, enẽlngol; *(responsibility)* henda hindi.

Transfix, to—haraṛ.

Transgress, to—lạṇḍhu, nẹhọ̃t, neṅghao, rọd, sạrgọm, ṭalao; *(social customs)* lọṇḍbhọṇḍ.

Transgression, a—ạpại.

Translate, to—tạrjumạ, utrạu.

Transparent—riṛim (2), ruńruń, ruruń (2); *(as water)* ṭińṭiń; *(semi—)* phiń phiniạ.

Transplant from where plants are thick to thin, to—gạchiạu, phoṛao.

Transplantation, to sow seeds for—aphọr.

Transport, to—*(of convicts)* ḍamul, kalapani.

Transverse—gaṇḍe, gạṇḍgaṇḍ.

Trap—*(a)* baj, dharap̣, jhali, kal; *(to)* jhali, oḍao, phand; *(to be caught in)* dharap̣: *(a fish)* jheńjra, jhimbri, jińjri, saera, tọrọdań; *(fish, part of)* ghạṭi, mukhạr; *(a rat)* hạndruk̕, tunuń; *(a bird)* kubet̕, kuṛ, laoṭa, ṭapok̕, ṭepok̕; *(bird part of)* jheṭha; *(fish, to set)* baj.

Trapper of game, a—sikạri.

Trappings, to put on—jabrao.

Travail in birth, to—bedan, bijhạuk̕.

Travel—*(to)* daṛan; *(stained)* dạruk̕ dạcuk̕.

Travellers—musaphir, rạhi; *(giving*

charity to) rahdani; *(provision for)* rosod.

TRAVERSE, TO—*(disprove)* ḍarao; *(cross)* rãodão, raundau.

TREACLE—guṛ.

TREAD, TO—lebeť; *(in another's foot-steps)* lebeť lotom.

TREASURE UP, TO—jogao.

TREASURY, A—khajanci, khajanti; *(clerk in charge of)* khajanci babu.

TREAT, TO—*(hospitably)* man marjad; *(ill)* gañjon, hacpaca, kondoli.

TREATMENT, ILL—koelon, kondol; *(exasperated by)* kondolia.

TREE, A—dare; *(top of)* coṭ ḍhoj; *(upper part of)* mutul dar; *(up till half-grown)* kaḍlak; *(crooked)* ladea dare; *(a kind of)* amber, babla, babur, bana haṭak, baru, bhorkond, boi bindi, bekom baha, chaili, dedhaore, ḍidhauri domkodokoč, gada pañjon, gada terel, haṭ, jarge terel, kambla, kamla, kadru pala, mar baha, ratama dare, sari sarjom, sakri phol, tarop; *(timber)* arma, chaṭni, kauha, kome; *(small)* marãr, meral, nim, saparom, sekra, siñ arak; *(small thorny)* karkaṭ, kãrwat, loṭo; *(large deciduous)* kadam dare; *(forest)* aṭkura, atnak, bhadu, bhandu, birnju, buc, buru mackunda, capoť siris, coreo, ḍaha, dhela, doka, dundukiť, gõrẽ, hesel, hope, hoṛ podo, kargali, lopoñ, pañjon, pitonj, pojo, pusi pan, roṭ, sal, salga, sarjom, satsayar, sekreč, udal; *(large)* car sira, ganjher, hiñjor, jañ siris, jugia, kandwer, kanṭa siris, karam, karke janum, kasmar, kome, korkoṭ, korouj, kumbir, kuruñj, kusum, mackunda, makarkenda, matkom, ome, pader, popro, rol, ruhen, sahar, telhec, terhec; *(small)* garbha gojha, gua guli, jañ olat, jhiñjhir, jhiñjiṭ, jinjir, kanjia, lodam, merleč, murga, murup niuri, ñũrũč, olať, phoska olať, pinde, poska olať, riḍe, sahra; *(traditional)* labar atnak, tope sarjom, ule sarjom; *(climber)* nãrĩ murup; *(fruit)* cuduk kod, sarpha, so, soh, tarop, totonopak; *(silk-worm)* guṭi dare; *(banyan)* bare dare; *(young, cut as rafter)* habka.

TREE-PIE, THE—borqriñ.

TREES—ruk birit; *(a clump of)* cumkak dare.

TREMBLE, TO—dupai, haḍuč ṭhakuč, hilau, lakar lukur, lewe, liplip, lokoe (2), lukluk, lukur, runrunau, saksak, ṭalmal, thar (2), tharthararo, ṭhirṭhirau, tirmirau, ṭolmol; *(as one weak)* lawak latiñ; *(to be all in a)* luyuť.

TREMBLING—dekeť (2), dihil (2), hipir (2), lucpuc, lucpucia, lukur, saksak; *(from fear)* luyuť cuputť.

TREMOR IN THE EARTH, A—bhui cal.

TREMULOUS—hipir (2).

TRENCH, A—dar, gaḍa, kaṭin, khana; *(to cut)* soda; *(a fire)* jhili gaḍa, khandha; *(hollowed out by water)* sodgok, sodok.

TREPIDATION—*(in a state of)* comol; *(extreme)* luyuť cuputť.

TRIAL—jala; *(to send up for)* calan. *Cf.* ORDEAL.

TRIBE—ḍahgi, gusṭi; *(Santal)* paris; *(a small Dravidian)* bir hoṛ; *(of gypsies)* caecor; *(wandering)* gul gulia; *(of tattooers)* khedna (M), khudni (F).

TRIBUTARY OF RIVER, A SMALL—saba.

TRICE, IN A—bhac marte, bhoc marte.

TRICK—calaki; *(a deceit)* chol kopoṭ; *(to)* phaki, phareb.

TRICKLE, TO—jharao, jhiri (2), jiri hiri, jiro joro, joro, lingi; *(of tears)* hidir (2); *(as grain from hole in bag)* hujur; *(down)* horiõr, jhiri hiri.

TRICKLING—ḍhar (2), sidor sodor, sio soyo, siro soro.

TRICKY—cechor, chae, chechor, kopoṭ, naṭkhaṭ, phakua, phanga, phasiara.

TRIDENT, A—tirsul.

TRIFLE, TO—alae phalae; *(with)* gareč.

TRIFLING— enka (2), micha michi; *(matter, a)* ṭuṅ katha.

TRIG—cunu munu.

TRIGGER OF GUN—lablabi.

TRILLING SOUND, TO MAKE A—ranran.

TRIM—comkeč, geneč (2); *(to)* her;

(*to make*) jhal jhalao ; (*to be*) jhalmalao ; (*with a hoe, to*) lak.

TRIP—(*excursion*) hupka, jhāk, jhapat, jhapot, khep ; (*to*) harak, kedekede ; (*to, of child*) ghutghat, torok.

TRIPE, A PREPARATION OF—laċ leto.

TRIPPINGLY—debe (2), dugur (2), guduċ, pidga pidgi, temel, turuk (2) ; (*of small Fs.*) cimkicitiń, tibiċ (2) ; (*on the tongue*) pharphar.

TRIUMPH OVER, TO—kahil.

TRIVIAL—mer sitruċ, mersitar, mersitur, phus, phusphas, situr.

TROOP, A—phad ; (*in a*) juńgur (2), pidga pidgi.

TROT, TO (*of a horse*)—kondoń, lujhuk (2).

TROTTERS (*of sheep &c*)—kata.

TROUBLE—ajar, bipod, dik, duk, dukdukuas, dukh, dusko, gańjan, gara, haran, harkhet, haron, jańjal, jońjal, khirri, koclos, kondol, kugar, mehnot, pajet, phajhet, saset, sondhe ; (*to*) ansa, aris, dik, diksik, hudgu dugur, hujat, pajet, phajhet, tamardak ; (*to be in*) dhak (2), saset ; (*to cause*) eċ, khirri, kosola, saset, tin topor khana, torlad ; (*to take*) jahit ; (*meaning to cause*) halwani, harwani ; (*water, to*) humtak.

TROUBLED—akbakao, akham dukham, andak tawak, at pat, harkhetia, kutla kutli, titik ; (*in mind*) akar kukar ; (*to be*) bikol, dugodhon, haka caka, kaisau, titikhak, toras, ulmal.

TROUBLESOME—bhojokoto, harwani, kackac.

TROUGH, A—(*wooden*) dakadak, dhońga, don, tagar ; (*stone*) duńgi dhiri, nandwa ; (*lever for*) duni.

TROUSERS—jańghia, jańre ; (*down to ankles*) jhańga.

TRUANT, TO PLAY—ańkher.

TRUE—ajib, asol, ayā, bote, hak, hẽ, hoe ke bote, hok, jar, jothat, khati, saca, sari, sarinak, sat, sot, sotea, suca (M), suci (F), uju ; (*perfectly*) sari utar ; (*statement, a*) sari katha.

TRULY—arse tāhā, ayā, khati, niscae, nitsahi, sarige, sarinak.

TRUMP UP, TO—turta.

TRUMPET, A—bakea, dhurri, dhururi, karnal, peprit, torre ; (*large*) mandanbhed ; (*horn*) sakwa ; (*sound of*) bhõbhõ, hõ, pẽpẽ ; (*sound of 2*) pẽpõ ; (*to blow*) oroń ; (*to, of elephant*) kirkirau.

TRUNDLE, TO—gargarao, khirkhirau.

TRUNK—(*elephant's*) sund ; (*body*) gund ; (*of tree*) buta ; (*of tree above bole*) mul dar ; (*of high tree*) herhińjań, hirhińjań.

TRUST—barsa, bhorosa, girhar, jima ; (*to*) as, danań, patiar, patiau ; (*to betray*) amet ; (*to give in*) amanot, jima ; (*in or to, to*) birla ; (*worthy of*) iman, patiar, sotea.

TRUSTWORTHINESS—etbar, itbar, thap.

TRUTH—dhorom, sacai, sat, sot ; (*of a*) arse tāhā, ayā, sarige ; (*to suppress*) aldhom.

TRUTHFUL—ajbi, saca, suca (M), suci (F).

TRY, TO—eteċ, gela, lega ; (*to find, in dark or water*) tamdao.

TUB, A LARGE EARTHEN—paya.

TUBE, A—nal, nol ; (*bamboo*) cońga.

TUBER—da, jar mar ; (*an edible*) patal kohnda.

TUCK—(*a*) kanaso ; (*up dress, to form bag, to*) gabla.

TUESDAY—mańgal, mańgar, mońgol, mońgor.

TUFT, A—jhar ; (*on bird's head*) duci ; (*to become*) mōrā.

TUFTS, IN—cedro, dumcak.

TUG, TO—dagar, tege nere ; (*at each other*) khamca khamci.

TUITION—talim.

TUMBLE, TO—(*down*) dhaskao ; (*down backwards*) bindrań ; (*& toss*) lotpot ; (*about on ground*) akar okor, ersen torseċ, gholtao, gurda gurdi, lapta lapti, sara, uru kundel.

TUMBLER, A—(*glass*) gilas.

TUMOUR, A—doho ; (*cystic*) batori, baturi ; (*of testicle*) andrak.

TUMTUM, A—bagi.

TUMULT—dham, dhum, gajar, galgal, golmal, gondogol, gulmal, ragau (2); (*of noise*) kaukau; (*to make a*) andor, galgalao, golmal, gul, gulmal, kaurau; (*with a*) gadra godro, keren meren, rubdai (2).

TUNE—(*a*) kahni rar, khod, rar; (*an accompaniment to a*) labgj; (*out of*) berar, bẽrẽ (2).

TURBAN, A—dahri; (*large*) cak dahri; (*end of*) botoć; (*cloth as*) patka.

TURBID—bode.

TURF, A PIECE OF—cepa.

TURKEY COCK—thuthukur; (*gills of*) lapoć.

TURMERIC—sasań; (*colour of*) sasań dak; (*branchings from root of*) gãt; (*stone to grind*) sasań rić dhiri.

TURMOIL—gajar.

TURN—(*rotation*) pali, pari; (*once round*) pãk, pher; (*about*) olapalite, orapalite, pari; (*coat, a*) beńparsi, ispat.

TURN, TO—acur, nacur, pãk, pherao; (*round*) acur, nacur, phirphir; (*round, as shuttlecock*) bherwań; (*up*) cedre, utka patka; (*back*) cikić, lautau; (*the back*) dea, thot; (*aside*) eran, erer, ghajer, tarao; (*half round*) kerõt; (*over*) otak, paska; (*away head*) konde kose, kose (2), phentoć; (*tail*) picom podroć; (*on back*) sara; (*up with snout*) uta; (*over soil*) utkau patkau; (*out—become*) utrau; (*round without moving*) caorao, thão gurgur; (*sharp round*) bhertań; (*a summersault*) baji; (*from side to side*) bakać (2); (*to right*) gengahi; (*over in mind*) khańj; (*on a lathe*) kundau.

TURNED ASIDE, TO BE—corań.

TURNING—(*of stomach*) serer marte; (*over everything*) lutuć sutuć, sok sutruć.

TURNIP, A—salgam.

TURNS, BY—bodla budli, olapalite, orapalite, para parite, pari (2).

TURPENTINE—tarpin sunum.

TUSK, A—sonda; (*to rip with*) hotak.

TUTOR, TO—puski, sikau, sikhau.

TUTORED—sajok.

TWANG—(*to*) pheń (2), phoń, phuń; (*with a*) phuń m.; (*nasal*) gene (2), ghań ghuń.

TWELVE—gelbarea.

TWENTY—bar gel, bis, mić isĩ.

TWICE—bar chot, bar dhao, bar guna; (*over*) dobor dand; (*round*) bar khia.

TWIG, A—kadeć, kadgeć, kahle, kargeć; (*point of*) dog; (*of sarjom*) dharwak.

TWILIGHT—ńamba ńumba, ńuhum, pirton porton, ńaham ńahum; (*after*) singar.

TWINE—baber; (*machine for twisting*) gharri; (*at foot of bed*) uphãnd; (*a large ball of*) lundi; (*a piece of knotted*) ojha.

TWINKLE, TO—bilić, jalać juluć, jirić (2), juluć (2), liplip.

TWINS—jawa.

TWIRLING IN THE AIR—hoyań.

TWIST, TO—aĩnthao, ghurpãk, mocrao, peter; (*a rope*) baber galań, merao, pãk, uń; (*a*) pãk; (*& turn*) ecepẽce, ẽcpẽc, erce perce, kacra kacri; (*between finger & thumb*) tirmić; (*between palms*) tirhol; (*bullock's tail*) puchla puchli, puchlau; (*to a point*) pungi; (*a rope backwards*) rańjao; (*edge of cloth to point*) sulta; (*mouth & turn away head*) gote gore; (*in ear*) gũrtuć; (*from side to side*) mocra mocri; (*3rd strand into rope*) carhi; (*the ankle*) huroć..

TWISTED—baka, kandeć, kondeć, kukurbań, merha (M), mirhi (F), perta, tẽrga; (*to be*) mackao; (*loosely*) bhoolo.

TWIT, TO—thakrao, thokrao, thukrau, tokrao.

TWITCHING—cihik bai, dagak (2); (*of pain*) kankanao; (*of muscles, involuntary*) bai mara, tarkha tarkhi; (*of eyelids*) pidgak.

TWITTER, TO (*of birds*) cerobero.

TWO—bar, barea, do; (*plies*) duhri; (*fold*) duna, bar guna; (*each*) babar gotań; (*without intervening birth*) sonotoḱ ; (*& a half*) ạḍhạiạ, ạṛhạiạ ; (*joined together*) jamka ; (*edged*) dẹnẹ banar dharana.

TWOS OR THRESS, IN—phao phuc.

TYING, A METHOD OF—gạli.

TYRANNY—jaejulum.

U

UBIQUITOUS—dacaṅ (2).

UDDER—ạṇḍwạr, thanel ; (*large*) dudhạri ; (*small*) camptạhi, coãṭiạ.

UGH !—chiạ.

UGLY—bạdor saṭoḱ, bẹḍhọb, bẹhusnạk, bẹsajọn, bhaskar, bhọṇḍ bogla, dạblạ (M), dạbli (F), ḍhọṅ, dhorsoṫ morsoṫ, doemoṅ, kạbḍuċ, kenderpeċ (F), kubdhạ, okhulạn, sạṇḍ mạṇḍ, tamboṛ ; (*& lumpish*) lạbhuạ.

ULCER, AN—ghao ; (*on front of leg*) gạḍi g. ; (*large*) kherkhone ; (*deep*) cukạḱ g. *Cf.* SORE.

ULIGINOUS—labar lobur.

UMBILICUS—bukạ ; (*cord*) nạr ; (*hernia at*) bukạ bhạṛũṛ.

UMBRAGE—(*to take*) kạhur mạhur, roṅkhoṅ ; (*to cause*) kandao ; (*giving*) jhabrạli.

UMBRELLA, AN—catọm, chatar ; (*bamboo*) catọm, maṫ catọm ; (*cloth*) chọtọr ; (*shank of*) c. ḍạṇḍiṫ ; (*ribs of*) kamạni, c. pạṅjri.

UNABLE TO—(*do better*) naparọk ; (*work or earn*) nehạli ; (*remain still*) bhaoaṅ bhucuṅ.

UNACCUSTOMED—aẽ, albakaha.

UNADORNED—bẹhusnạk, bẹsajọn.

UNADULTERATED—nichora, niṅjam, nirạ, nirola.

UNANIMOUSLY—jomka jumki.

UNANNOUNCED—ancọṭ.

UNANTICIPATED—kalbhag.

UNAPPETISING—pẹsẹṫ (2).

UNASSERTIVE—behũṭ.

UNASSUMING—soromiạ.

UNAVAILINGLY—merahiṫ.

UNAWARES—gupti mar, kalbhag.

UNBECOMING—nico.

UNBEFITTING—tẹgẹċ tạgum.

UNBELIEVING—obiswạs.

UNBEROTHED—chuṭạ, chuṭaliạ.

UNBIND, TO—raṛa.

UNBROKEN—rambaṛ romboṛ, rombṛo ; (*to work*) aboṭ, arda, arna, auṛaha.

UNCARED FOR—bạhephajot.

UNCEASINGLY—ragra ragri, rọḍọḱ (2).

UNCERTAIN—ạlmạl, dandha mandha, dhọa bhọa, dhowa bhowa, dhuwạ bhuạ, digạḱ, kẹcẹṫ (2) ; (*to be*) dhuku cuku, dighi, sọndhọ ; (*to make*) dhokha.

UNCERTAINTY—digdhạ, dighi, dokha ; (*signifies*) cọ, cọṅ, idu, marpase, na.

UNCHASTE—bạṭuạ (M), bạṭwi (F), loṅgra (M), luṅgri (F).

UNCIVILISED—arna, bẹsọbbọk.

UNCLE—ka, kaka, kaka khuṛạ, kakat, khuṛạ ; (*maternal*) mama, mamọ ; (*& nephew or neice*) kakaea ; (*wife of maternal*) mạmi ; (*father's sister's husband*) kumạ ; (*& nephew or niece*) mama bhạgnạ, mamoea.

UNCLEAN—gesṭaha (M), gesṭahi (F) ; (*ceremonially*) bhọ̃ṇḍa, chut ; (*feeding*) achọk ; (*of grain*) khada bhusạ.

UNCOIL, TO—bhuṛi.

UNCOMELY—bhaskar, tamboṛ ; (*in shape*) sọndmọnḍ.

UNCOMFORTABLE—akṣak, ạsuk, bekar, ẹther pọther, bẹṭhik, kaskas ; (*of sitting*) oṭhor poṭhor ; (*from smoke*) kọḱ kọḍṛọ ; (*to make*) ucạṭ.

UNCOMMON—ọsọmbhag.

UNCOMPLIMENTARY TERM, A—kãhãka ; (*of step-mother*) kạki gọṛhọn ; (*by women to girls*) kadhạl.

UNCONNECTED—barọ sọtrọ.

UNCONSCIOUS—acet, ạnbhul, anhos, bẹhos, galasaṅ, khem, nicind, ogher, tewelgaṫ, tuwel ; (*state*) bại.

UNCONSENTING—bẹraji.

UNCOOKED—berẹl ; (*victuals*) sidhạ ; (*part*) tapra, tara tapra ; (*food*) kharca.

UNCOVER, TO—oṭaḱ, ughrau.

UNCOVERED—odroṅ, phaṅka phayaṛ, sandoraṅ, ughaṛ.

UNCULTIVATED—aṛthi paṛthi, khil, khil khũṇṭ, khil khũṭ, okoḍa, paṛti, patit.

UNCULTURED—auṛaha.

UNDECEIVE, TO—samjhao.

UNDER—latar, niros, taṛi; *(to put)* latar; *(tone, in an)* ṅeṛẽ (2); *(part the)* penda; *(sized)* bagar gaṭhia, bajar gaṭhia, berga, cerca, curcuṭuć, damcaḱ, ḍemḍa, dhuruć, geḍa (M), giḍi (F), geḍoḱ, gheṭma (M), gheṭmi (F), kherṛa, regaṭhia, reme ṭele, reṭha; *(sized in scolding)* khemṭoḱ; *(sized, with protuberant stomach)* ledhra (M), lidhri (F).

UNDERMINE, TO—kholao.

UNDERNEATH—latar, tali, taṛi; *(to put)* latar.

UNDERSTAND, TO—buj, bujhau, ḍhakwa, samjhao.

UNDERSTANDING—aṅ, bibik, budakil, buj, suj; *(of feeble)* utuṭ tumbuṭ; *(without)* bebuj; *(beyond)* buj khon bahre.

UNDERSTOOD, IT WAS—ṇḍerege.

UNDERTAKE, TO—aṅgrau, aṅrau, egar, karaṛ.

UNDETACHED—ragraga, regrege.

UNDIMINISHED—samthul, thul.

UNDISTURBED—*(as soil)* akoḍa.

UNDO, TO—bhaṅga, raṛa.

UNDOMESTICATED—bir, birnaha.

UNDRILLED—auṛaha.

UNDYING—omor.

UNEASY, TO BE—bikla bikli, bikol.

UNEMPLOYED—ajauṛi, chuṭa, chuṭalia, paṛti, phada, phauti, udhma, ulpha.

UNENCLOSED—phada.

UNENCUMBERED—ulpha.

UNEQUAL—bejuri, ḍamka ḍumka, ḍamka ḍura, ḍiḍhi baḍhi, khaṭo baḍho, liruaṅ; *(to)* boserṭak; *(in height)* darać duruć; *(in thickness)* badgoḱ (2); *(in length)* dirhi barhi; *(in balance)* jhiṅka jhakur, jhiṅka taṛe, jhiṅko jhokor, jhiṅko toro.

UNEQUALLED—aprug.

UNEVEN—caṛdaḱ burdaḱ, cedro, cõrdaṅ, ḍhapa ḍhopo, dharkaha, ḍomba ḍombe, duluć dupuć, epre, gadlaḱ godloḱ, harcaṭ horcoṭ, haṭaṕ huṭuṕ, hidić dikiṛ, kadga kodgo, kaṭać kuṭuć, khanḍ (2), khẽrẽ khõrẽ, koṭrẽ, locoṅ, sadga badga; *(of road)* dumdumi, gaḍha goḍho.

UNEVENLY—rikoć rokoć, tuluć tupuć.

UNEXPECTED—algel, osombhag.

UNEXPECTEDLY—bhasbhus, bhus, guyuṅ marte, kalbhag.

UNEXPENDED, TO REMAIN—baṅcao.

UNFATHOMABLE—atha.

UNFEELINGLY, TO ACT—hane mar.

UNFENCED—phada.

UNFERTILE *(of soil)*—cothra, kharkhanḍ, khokndo, narca; *(to become)* marca.

UNFERTILIZED—paṛti; *(as Indian corn)* ḍaṅgua.

UNFILLED *(of ears of grain)*—copa.

UNFINISHED—adha padha, baske, besajon, leṅjhar, sadgayaḱ, sodgoro; *(to be)* lesrao.

UNFIT—*(for work)* adãt; *(for use, as water)* bikol bokol.

UNFIXED—auṛi.

UNFLEDGED—belteṅ.

UNFOLD, TO—pasar; *(as leaf from bud)* gereć (2).

UNFORTUNATE—abhagia, abjos, astaṅ, bebhagan, becara; *(to be)* behal.

UNFRIENDLY—kurmuṭaha.

UNGENEROUS—kikić kokoć.

UNGRATEFUL—nimak haram.

UNHAPPY—uchan.

UNHEALTHY—*(took)* orososo; *(to cause to be)* jhur; *(& stunted)* luṭa.

UNHOLY—adhorom, odhorom.

UNIDIOMATIC—bõrbaḱ; *(& mispronounced)* makre.

UNIFORM—saman; *(not)* apa baṛia, rayal ruyul.

UNIMPORTANT—beṅjaḱ, beṅjlaṅ, mersitruć, mersitur, mirsitaṛ, situr.

UNIMPREGNATED *(of silk moth)*—basia.

UNINITIATED—sobgar.

UNINJURED—sone sod.

UNINTELLIGENT—ajbuj, albakaha, aṭnaṣaṭ, nirbhuj, nirbodh, olkobaha, thotho.

UNINTELLIGIBLE—anakup, andhe paṭhauri, ankatha anbetha, aṭnaṣaṭ, bakbheṅkor, galak salak, hod, iriṅ biriṅ, ornaṣaṭ, ornasor, orna pathan, paṭhauri.

UNINTENTIONALLY—baglote, bajan.

UNINTERESTING—liṅgiṭ (2).

UNINURED—aṅ, albakaha, arda.

UNION—milijili; (*to form an illicit*) milwa milwi.

UNIQUE—aprug.

UNISON, IN—soroṅ (2); (*not*) bajuri.

UNITE, TO—jorao, milan, milau, mit, seleṭ, toṅge; (*with*) johra, solgaṭ; (*2 families by marriage*) ghargharaia.

UNITED—ekamoe, ek sath, jamke, juma jumi, ṭhekom; (*to be*) jereṭ, jerka.

UNIVERSE, THE—dharti.

UNJUST—andher, aneão, behok, obicar, oneae, oneao; (*to, to be*) dhusau.

UNKEMPT—damcak (M), damci (F), ḍhiso ḍhoro, dhosodhoro.

UNKIND—beraji, kaṭhin.

UNKNOWN—anari, ancin, mira, upria.

UNLAWFUL—manahi; (*carnal knowledge*) loṭ ghuṭi.

UNLEARNED—hohak.

UNLESS—anec.

UNLIKELY—osombhag.

UNLIMITED—ajhal pajhal, amela, amila, asambher, bethikan, besumar.

UNLUCKY—abhagia, abjos, bebhagan, chae, coṭaha, kharao; (*day, an*) khara din, kharali, khora din, khorali.

UNMARRIED—behor, daṅgua, diṅga daṅgua, kuar, kuari; (*& of full age*) phel (F); (*woman, forcible marking of*) te.

UNMATCHED—ḍiḍhi baḍhi, dojnap.

UNMIXED—nichora.

UNNERVED—haemoekaṭ, haimuikaṭ.

UNOBTRUSIVE—soromia.

UNOCCUPIED—ajauri, phauti.

UNPAIRED, TO BE—phuṭ.

UNPALATABLE—capos (2), copsaha, haraṅ, heben, hemhem, hilwet, paṅgaṭ (2), pasak, peseṭ (2), siṭ na sawad, sitik sabak.

UNPLEASANT (*to sight*)—bejelgak.

UNPOLLUTED—sudh.

UNPRACTISED—aṅ.

UNPREMEDITATEDLY—paragare.

UNPREPOSSESSING— dabla (M), dabli (F), dhorsoṭ morsoṭ, kabḍuc, kubdha, okhulan, siṭkoc.

UNPRESENTABLE—dhiroṅ dhoroṅ.

UNPRINCIPLED—luca (M), luci (F).

UNPRODUCTIVE—kaṅkhar, khaṅkhar, maloṭ, rayam rayum; (*of saline soil*) jerṅgaha; (*to become*) marca.

UNPROFITABLE—bephaeda, bertha.

UNPROPITIOUS—jere (2).

UNPROTECTED—phada.

UNQUALIFIED—auri.

UNRAVEL, TO—chiṇḍau.

UNREASONABLE—becol, bephokoṭ, demaria.

UNRELIABLE—asathi, ende pende, konṭeṭ, locor pocor, pend, pendla.

UNRELISHABLE—peseṭ (2).

UNREMITTING—bisi suṭuc, jõhoṭ.

UNRESERVEDLY—hia khalas, goṭa monte, torphar.

UNREST—bethir.

UNRESTRAINED—bahbahia, budrag, elak chaḍa, ilak chaḍa, udhma.

UNRIGHTEOUS—adhorom, odhorom, oneao.

UNRIPE—berel, ciṭo, ḍemka, kãca, kaci, kacri, khica.

UNRUFFLED (*of water*)—camphel.

UNRULY—cechor, chechor.

UNSATISFIED, TO BE—adorok.

UNSAY, TO—dhatka, dodao.

UNSCRUPULOUS—pephra, phephra.

UNSEASONABLE—bebatar, beṭak.

UNSEASONED—(*of food*) beroṅ.

UNSEEMLY—baḍak̇ (2), tẹgẹċ tạgum ; *(of rubbish)* turu dhum, turutukạ ; *(condition, to be in a)* lọṭpọṭ.

UNSERVICABLE—bẹhal, dạlsiṅ tạlsiṅ, ḍopca, jhan̈ jhạuak̇, lamjak̇, poca ; *(to make)* hurwaṅ.

UNSHAPELY—bhaskar, dhapuạ ; *(in waist)* bojra (M), bujri (F).

UNSHEATH, TO—bọċ.

UNSIGHTLY—jọbọḍhọn̈ ; *(of rubbish)* turu dhum, turutukạ.

UNSOCIAL—bạnua, bẹdhọṛ, mesa, perta.

UNSOILED—ạrik pạrik.

UNSOLICITOUS—nidạndi.

UNSOPHISTICATED—bombo, soṛa.

UNSOUND—rugi.

UNSPECIFIED—ạuri.

UNSPENT—amanọt.

UNSPLIT *(of a pea &c)*—goṭạṛ.

UNSTABLE—ḍikạ ḍake.

UNSTAMPED *(of a lẹtter)*,—biriṅ.

UNSTEADY—darã durũ, lẹcẹ (2), lẹcẹ pẹcẹ, lẹcẹr pẹcẹr ; *(of child)* thalak̇ thuluk̇ ; *(to be)* dakaṛ dokoṛ, daṛadoṛo.

UNSTINTING—lahe cahe.

UNSTRETCHED—bẹtiạr.

UNSTRING A BOW, TO—ạsiṫ.

UNSUBMISSIVE—adọpia, ạn dhidrik, dundur.

UNSUBSTANTIAL—kãca, kạci ; *(to be)* bhọdọr.

UNSUCCESSFUL—orgo porgo, siṭhal miṭhạl ; *(to be)* pesrao.

UNSUITABLE—bẹsajọn, khoyak̇, phi ; *(to be)* diṅgiċ.

UNSULLIED—phĩk leka, phĩṛiphiċ.

UNSYMMETRICAL—khẽṛẽ khõṛẽ, saṇḍ maṇḍ.

UNSYMPATHETIC—arõṭ, bẹdhọṛ, ẹk jibạ.

UNTAINTED—nirogi.

UNTAMED—abuṭ, arna.

UNTENANTED—sunạ, sunsạn.

UNTIDY—bhosḍoṅ, cọrọñṭo, dạlsiṅ tạlsiṅ, damcak̇ (M), dạmci (F), dạruk̇ dạcuk̇, dhimsi punsi, dhorodhoso, dhum dharkaṭ, dhum dharkaṛ, dindirsiċ (F), dindirsiṫ, dolomolo, gạrlaṅ gurlun, gesṭaha (M), gesṭahi (F), ghesṭaha (M), ghesṭahi (F), hẹjlẹċ, hẹjlẹċ pẹjlẹċ, hidrạ gisrạ, hiraṅ petan̈, pandrạhi, pẹjlẹċ, sadgạyak̇, solok̇ bokok̇ ; *(to be)* aptar.

UNTIL—ạuri, dhạbiċ, dhạriċ, hạbiċ, hạriċ ; *(not)* eneċ.

UNTRAINED—aõ, ạuṛaha.

UNTRIMMED—jhadọr padọr, jhargoeak̇, jharhoeak̇, jharoeak̇.

UNTRUE—asạrthi, asat, asathi, nase, nisạrthi, ọsọṭ.

UNTRUSTWORTHY—pend, pendla.

UNTRUTHFUL—labṛa (M), lạbṛi (F).

UNTUTORED—ạuṛaha.

UNTWIST, TO—bhạruṛ, bhuṛi ; *(as end of rope)* phodlo.

UNUSED—amanọt.

UNUSUAL—ẹkdhara, had, salas.

UNVARNISHED—jạṛ.

UNWARNED—kalbhag.

UNWARY—nicind.

UNWASHED—ḍhiso ḍhoro, kadrok̇, kãṭh, khariaṭ, kharkhaṇḍ.

UNWEANED CHILD, A—nunu gidrạ.

UNWEARIED—nirdhõk.

UNWELL—ọsuk.

UNWHOLESOME—bataṛ, batọl ; *(of water)* gadhṛa, gadṛa.

UNWIELDY—adaṛ odoṛ, amoṭ, asãt osõt, bhõḍa, bhogao, bhoṇḍa, biḍgoe boḍgoe (F), lạjuṅ (2). *Cf.* FAT.

UNWILLING—dimạk, licạn̈ picạn̈.

UNWIND, TO—ạsiṫ, bokor (2) ; *(easily)* bhạṛ (2).

UNWONTED—salas.

UP—*(to)* bhor, dhạbiċ, dhạriċ, hạbiċ, hạriċ, jọhọk̇, pọrjọṛt ; *(side down)* ulạṭ palạṭ, ulṭạ palṭa, ulṭi pulṭi ; *(side down, to turn)* ulṭạu, ulṭạu palṭao ; *(& down)* kạbuċ kubuċ, kubuċ (2), usul cọpọṫ.

UPBRAID, TO—cokhna, kaḍhao, khaḍao, nisṛau, tẹrgẹṅ, ṭhakrao, ṭhokrao, ṭhukrạu, ṭokrao.

UPON—upạr.
UPPER—cetan ; (*side down*) tabẹr.
UPRIGHT—sojha, soṛa, subod, uju ; (*position, to assume*) teṅgon.
UPROAR—kạukạu ; (*to make*) andoṛ, kạuṛạu ; (*making an*) andakul, rubdại (2).
UPS & DOWNS—harcať horcoť, hidić dikiṛ, kaṭka koṭko, upạn jhapan.
UPSET, TO—dọ̃ṛsẹć ; (*& spill contents*) duṛuć.
UPSTRARTS—sić soć.
URETHRAL DISCHARGE, ANY—gạrmi, gurmi.
URGE, TO—bhẹrọsta, calao, udgạr, uskur ; (*each other*) henda hindi, hẽsã hĩsi.
URGENCY—ạkut, dhọ̃nj, jọ̃bọt.
URGENT—cahãṭ, caṇḍ, cọhọ̃ṭ, halhal, jaoṛe (2), jạri jạnti, jạruṛ ; (*to be*) halhaolao.
URINATE, TO—aḍo, racasẹć ; (*M. child*) jorea ; (*F. child*) jurni ; (*of children*) ṭuilạ ; (*to feel a call to*) panpanao.
URINE—(*white*) poṇḍ jhar ; (*smell of*) thọthọť, tothoť ; (*deposit in*) jhar ; (*to hold back*) kupnạu.
USAGE—acar, acar beohar, bebohar, beohar, bidhạ, cạli, dạstur, nạthi, rewaj.
USE—aṅgra, colit, kaj, kam ; (*& wont*) car ; (*to*) bebohar, beohar, laṛcaṛ, lọṛcọṛ ; (*of no*) nehạli ; (*up, to*) nipạt ; (*not in*) chuṭạliạ, phạuti ; (*worn small with*) ṭuṭki ; (*lavishly, to*) sidraǩ badraǩ ; (*a new article for first time, to*) uḍhạu.
USED—(*of plates &c*) sạkhṛi ; (*up*) bẹhal, ḍọyọť, rạdi.
USELESS—akaj, badhọṛ, bẹkam, bẹmal, bẹnahak, bẹphaeda, merahiť, nahak, ọkaj, ṭoseạ.
USUAL—culti.
USURY—sud ; (*to put out to*) bạisạu.
UTENSILS, IRON—loha luti, mẽṛhẽť khaṇḍa.
UTERUS—*Cf.* WOMB.
UTILITY—aṅgra.
UTMOST—(*at the very*) jọskọs ; (*height, to be at*) sạrdi.

UTTERLY—sae ; (*lost or ruined*) bạbiloṇḍ ; (*destitute, to be*) awaň ewer.
UVULA, THE—suṇḍ.

V

VACANCY OF MIND—galta golať.
VACANT—khạli.
VACANTLY, TO STARE—aṇḍar oṇḍor, araǩ oroǩ, mayaǩ moyoǩ.
VACATE A SITUATION, TO—istopa.
VACCINATION—ṭikạ ; (*marks, having*) usnạ ; (*one who performs*) bodh.
VAGABOND, A—naṅgar bhulạ (M), naṅgar bhuli (F) ; (*like a*) jarmaǩ jormoǩ, jarmaǩ tormaǩ, tormaǩ.
VAGRANT—coloe boloe, mạri poda ; (*a*) despoḍa.
VAGUE—dandha mandha, hạṛať hũṛũť, oṛna sạṭ, oṛna soṛ.
VAIN—(*to be*) bạdại, phulạu ; (*dispute*) bakheṛa ; (*in*) ạuṛi, jhuṭho, khanọkha, khomọkha, liṛok loṛok, loṛkaeni, lọṛọk (2), merayaǩ, michạ, michạ michi, pạthạuṛi, phạṛiạ baj, situr.
VAINLY—alakḍiḍi, alaklạṇḍi, aṭho siṭho, ạuṛa, ạuṛi pạthạuṛi, bẹnahak, bertha, khanakha, nahak, phẽs phãs.
VALID, TO BECOME—kayem.
VALLEY—buru nala, ḍhip ; (*of rice-fields*) sokṛa, soṅgha.
VALOUR, A MAN OF—birbanṭa.
VALUE—dam ; (*of no great*) lạdea ; (*increasing in*) aedhọn ; (*of rare*) ạprug ; (*to sell under*) aṇḍhoň maṇḍhoň ; (*equal in*) sordor.
VANISH, TO—chan.
VANQUISH, TO—daṛe, hãṛọp̌, hẹ̃ṭ, hẽṭao, lahãt, pesṛao, ṭhạsiạu.
VANQUISHED, TO BE—hạrit.
VAPOUR—bhaph.
VARIANCE—badão ; (*to be at*) birodhi, biroṭ, eper heṇḍe, haṛka haṛki, hupuṭeť, iṛạ iri, kaḍha kaḍhi, kạdi bạdi, kẹňmẹň, khaṭpaṭ, khõca khũci, laelokṭha, laga, lakṭha, laolokṭa, lekṭha, leṭha, lokṭa, neae, odabạd,

rerad, resa risi, retha rithi, simpasare, tana tani, thona thuni; (*to set at*) bigra bigri; (*at*) akhra akhri.

VARIEGATED—cand bagar, chit, citar kabar, cit kabar, kabar, rosanjon.

VARIETY—kisim.

VARIOUS—alag balag, aṅkut baṅkut, emanteak, emanten, harghaser, nana hunar, unu unu.

VARNISH, TO—roṅ.

VAST—ajgar; (*numbers, in*) duṅgel.

VAUNT, TO—teretere, uć, usić.

VEAL—mihũ jel.

VEDAS, THE—bed.

VEGETABLE, A—potol, purai nari, sāk alu; (*cutivated*) paror jhiṅga.

VEGETABLES—arak sakam, tari torkari; (*a way of cooking*) bharta, hondak, lat arak; (*cooked with rice*) arak sure; (*a caste who cultivate*) kuiri; (*unequally cut*) patku naru.

VEGETARIAN, A—bhagat, bhogot.

VEHEMENCE—āt, tapis; (*with*) awapapa, tarkha, tirit leka.

VEIL, TO—ad, od; (*the face*) tuturi.

VEILED TERM, A—soṅgar; (*to cremate*) gok sahan; (*for marriageable girl*) hira; (*for silk-worm tree*) guti; (*for a child*) amka (M), amki (F).

VEIN, A—sir; (*of leaf or water*) dak sir.

VELOCITY—tor.

VENGEANCE—khonos, kuskusi; (*harbouring*) kurmutaha, kuskusau, kutil, por hẽsalia.

VENISON—jel jel; (*a shoulder of*) jel phari.

VENOMOUS—bisan, cauchalia.

VENTURE, TO—samsao.

VENUS, THE PLANET—(*as evening star*) sukar; (*as morning star*) bhurka.

VERACIOUS—jar.

VERANDAH, A—baranda, cari, dhaba; (*lower than roof*) atań pinda.

VERBAL PARTICLE—(*conditional*) ke, kok; (*departure*) ato, oto; (*for self*) joń.

VERBALLY—mokosto, mukharat, mukosto.

VERBIAGE—gap.

VERITABLE—jar.

VERMIN, TO PICK—(*from the head*) gosoć.

VERSE, A—aet, ayat, kali; (*of song*) akhor.

VERTICALLY, TO SET UP—dorom.

VERTIGO—bhãori, karigham.

VERY—adi, atha, adi barić, barić, bebarić, bejãe, khub, okoć, utar; (*much*) ajlot, amda, aroń, behisab, curti, dedar, gutek, gutek utar, kusik, tirit, titit; (*much, of swelling*) darumdhak, dharumdhak; (*many*) ada umar, ajlot, amda, anbid, andel mandel, aroń, athe athoń, atis kutis, atut, adi barić, tanak busak, dedar, gadagud, ojut, kalkal, saṅge, tanak busak, tirit, tirkõt; (*many, of small creatures*) gasgas; (*of hunger*) phakphak, phokphok; (*of fear*) picpic, puyul; (*of height*) rakdań; (*of obesity*) dheke, thotho, thothomthorok, udur dhuma; (*of cold*) kaṅkirit, kankirit, ritit (2); (*of whiteness*) tehe (2); (*of darkness*) karań (2); (*of weight*) rohoć (2).

VESICAL CALCULUS—kharagmut.

VESSEL, A—bhajan; (*earthen*) cukak, cukri, curiak, dudumdhukak, kārwas thili, kotnak tukuć, mohor, patloe, patna, taknak, tawa, tokak, toklak, tukuć, tunma; (*receiving*) anatań; (*used*) aitha; (*milking*) bhand, jalua; (*drinking*) gilas, jam bati, jhari lota, lota, luti, tunti lota; (*skin*) kum; (*for sugar-cane juice*) khora; (*for rice sent with bride*) thili; (*for toddy juice*) labni. *Cf.* COOKING, OIL.

VESTIGE—cinha munda.

VEX, TO—carhao, kondoli, takać tukuć.

VEXATION, AN EXCLM. OF—dhat, dhidhi, dhir, dhirhak, dhirkara, dhurhak, dhurkara, dhut, dut dut, i.

VEXED—beros; (*to be*) kaĩsau; (*to look*) uruń (2).

VEXING—cokak baklak.

VIBRATE, TO—deket (2), lewak, likić (2), likir, locoe (2), phet, tawar (2).

VIBRATION—(*to be affected by*) tarko ; (*of flexible body, sound*) ricič.

VICE, WITHOUT (*as a horse*)—gambhir.

VICEROY, THE—laṭ saheb.

VICINITY—ado ṭola, ancal, are pase, dhara dhari, kalhaṭ, oncol, para, pas, tolhāṭ, ṭoṭha ; (*in the*) kaele ; (*of this*) noten.

VICIOUS—canḍal, luca (M), luci (F).

VICISSITUDE—upan jhapan.

VICTIM, A—dāṛē.

VICTIMISE, TO—andič, phaki.

VICTORY—jae, jit ; (*to gain*) bhagao.

VICTUALS—ata sata ; (*uncooked*) sidha.

VIE, TO—haṭa badi, haṭha badi, haṭha baji.

VIEW, TO COME INTO—dekhaok.

VIGILANT—gangante, sahitte ; (*to be*) sontor.

VIGOROUS—āṭ, badak (2), balgar, jhūk, jhūkel, jidahi, jorgar, jorwar, pohlan.

VIGOUR—jor, muruk ; (*to lose*) marca ; (*in prime*) nawatur.

VILE—māriā piṭia, nekra ; (*of abuse*) siṭ bhānd, siṭhbhānd.

VILIFY, TO—baro bakhan, bisbakhan, khoṭ.

VILLAGE, A—ato, basti, di, gā ; (*decayed*) bhanga sulia ato ; (*near*) para ; (*compact*) cukak ato ; (*populous*) gadel ato, gadi ; (*part of*) cok, cokkaṭi, para, ṭola ; (*area of*) dih dandi, nager caker ; (*country surrounding*) dihali ; (*lands, division of*) khicri bāṭ, misri bāṭ ; (*chief*) mandar, manjhi, mondol ; (*chiefs*) mapanji ; (*chief's wife*) manjhi era ; (*censor of morals*) jog manjhi ; (*social chief*) handi manjhi ; (*runner*) dauraha ; (*watchman*) caukidar, khamdar ; (*priest*) naeke, kudam naeke ; (*officials' land*) man ; (*festival*) erok sim ; (*belonging to*) gāoali ; (*to village, to pass from*) dakedak ; (*& hamlets*) gāo gonda ; (*official, a*) jog manjhi, jog paranik.

VILLAGERS, AMONG THE—gāye ghore.

VILLAIN—mara ; (*like*) latkuṭa.

VINDICATE ONESELF, TO—andun.

VINDICTIVE—dahgoria, por hēsalia.

VINE—angur, dak, dak nāri ; (*dresser*) dak kakmanič ; (*yard*) dak bagwan.

VIOLATE, TO—agar digar, bhōnda, rod.

VIOLENCE—ajhāṭ, joborjos, jobrani, jor julum, phasad, phesad, ṭapis ; (*to offer*) dhara dhari.

VIOLENT—bhalok, dharkaṭ, hadrap, jobori ; (*of quarrel*) jhuna jhun.

VIOLENTLY—cagae darae, chirha chirhi, cirha cirbi, durmar, huluč (2), jhumajhum, paṭuč, ṭarkha.

VIRGIN—(*a*) arda kuri ; (*state, the*) jenkete.

VIRTUE—gun, gunak, jos, pan ; (*having*) bhodran.

VISCOUS—jiwer jewer, laṭak (2), leje peje, lenjer, lenjer boror, lepe peje, lopor, tiro toro, ṭokor (2), ṭoṭor.

VISHNU, AN EPITHET OF—naran.

VISIBLE—sodgoro ; (*to be*) lakhao.

VISION—najar ; (*a*) bheona, samek ; (*in a*) dikhitte ; (*to see a*) dorson ; (*imperfect*) andheč dundheč, palak polok, popolheč ; (*having imperfect*) perla (M), pirli (F), ṭesra (M), ṭisri (F), ṭhesra (M), ṭhisri (F).

VISIT—(*to*) ajare, hiri, horok, pahna, pera, pera horok ; (*of condolence, a*) bhēṭ ; (*a shrine, to*) dorson ; (*not the first*) ghalok.

VISITOR, A—pera hor ; (*to whom uncooked food is given*) hīt mitan.

VITAL SPOT, A—ghar.

VITALITY—(*of low*) kokhndo ; (*to lose*) borao, tirmirau, usaṭ.

VITRIFIED IN BAKING—(*of pottery &c.*) jhāua.

VITUPERATE, TO—tara tura, tergen.

VOCATIVE PERTICLE—e.

VOICE—aran, gala, sabad, sabod ; (*at top of*) darau ; (*weak*) ṭereṭere ; (*loud*) cagae, darau, ghogo, karau (2).

VOICES, SOUND OF—gubur (2), gundur (2).

VOLUME—(*a*) khand ; (*in large—of smoke*) tuč tuč ; (*of sound*) rarı.

VOLUPTUOUS—umtạ (M), umti (F); *(to become)* umkạu, umtạu, umuk.

VOMIT, TO—bẹć, dọyọḱ, phaṭkar, uchlạu, ulạ; *(sound when about to)* oḱoḱ.

VORACIOUS, TO BE—khaṅkha khạṅkhi, tẹgẹć tạgum.

VOW—*(a)* kiriạ; *(to)* akhaji, gacao, manan; *(to make a)* manan dọhọ.

VOYAGE—hupkạ.

VULTURE, A—gidi; *(Indian king)* sẹṅgẹl gidi (M), rạilạ gidi (F); *(red-backed)* kẽhẽ; *(spec. of)* pajhaṛ, karse koṭaṗ, tarse koṭap cẽṛẽ; *(mythical)* soner gidi; *(& kites)* gidi kuṛiť.

VULVA—*Cf.* ORGAN.

W

WAD OF GUN—jạmin.

WADDLE, TO—asāt osōt, ḍakaṛ ḍukuṛ, ḍẹbẹ (2), dildal, hatam hutum, ladać luduć, ladak luduk, lẹbẹ (2), udhuć (2); *(of one tired)* thạluḱ (2).

WADDLING—bhạṇḍul, idhoć ọdhọć; *(of very fat person)* lisoť losoť.

WAG, TO—ṭiwić; *(of tail)* ṭhepe, ṭhẹrẹ-ṭhẹpẹ.

WAGER—*(a)* bạji, bạrjid; *(to)* apṭhao.

WAGES—bạn, bẹtọn, dam, darmaha, kuṛai, mojuri, tankha, tọlọb, tọlọp, tonkha; *(daily)* mạjur, mojuri; *(daily, in kind)* bẹrhọn; *(mouth's)* mạhinạ; *(week's)* hapta; *(grain given as)* dạhnạ; *(to work for)* nalha.

WAGGISH—nạbhuạ.

WAGTAIL, THE—gaḍa caṅcir.

WAIL, TO—họmọr. ; *(loudly)* kạuạ rạuạ.

WAIST, THE—ḍaṇḍa; *(unshapely in)* bojra (M), bujri (F); *(string round)* ḍaṇḍoli, ḍora; *(thick)* hoe hoe.

WAISTCOAT, A SLEEVELESS—phatoe.

WAIT, TO—ograo, sạbur; *(for)* bāṭ cahao, tạṅgi. *Cf.* TO LIE IN, LYING IN.

WAKE UP, TO—ẹbhẹn; *(as lazy man to work)* garmao; *(easily)* torkal.

WALK, TO—calaḱ, ḍahrao, dāṛā, daṛan, dhamsao, saṅgar, taṛam; *(of child or dwarf)* ḍuluṅ (2), ṭẹrọḱ; *(about)* dāṛā baṛae; *(gingerly)* cipạ cape, kuḍạ; *(bent)* hijạ haje; *(slowly)* kiḍọṅ kọḍọṅ, lipoć lọpọć; *(on stilts)* kiḍọṅ kọḍọṅ; *(unsteadily)* hạluć bạkuć, lẹḍẹć bẹḍẹć, lẹḍẹ (2), tharam thurum, thọrọť (2); *(lamely)* hadać huḍuć; *(on tip-toe)* camal cọmọl, caṇḍaḱ coṇḍoḱ; *(on heels)* kaḍać kuḍuć; *(to & fro, to cause to)* ṭahlao; *(heavily)* ṭigạ ṭage; *(as a camel)* dãeyoḱ; *(with legs crossing)* haṛaḱ paṭaḱ, haṛẹť paṭẹť.

WALKING—*(feebly)* dahāć duhūć; *(on toes)* licạ lace; *(heavily)* ṭihạ ṭahe; *(stick, a)* hapa; *(with stiff hip)* dhạluć dhạkuć, dhọkṛẹ, heṛca (M), hiṛci (F); *(straddled)* hiḍạ haḍe; *(of young animals)* labas lubus; *(of one feeble or tired)* ṭimpạ ṭaṛe. *Cf.* GAIT, QUICKLY.

WALL, A—bhit; *(mud or clay)* kāt; *(enclosing)* pạcri; *(wattle & daub)* onoť, ṭạṭiol bhit; *(recess in)* kundhi, pakha.

WALLET, A BEGGAR'S—dhukṛi, dukhṛi.

WALLOW, TO—laṭpaṭ, lọṭpọṭ; *(in mire)* jobḍao, jọbẹ, jọḍọ bọḍọ.

WALLPLATE, A—sordol.

WALNUT, THE—akhroṭ.

WANDER, TO—asoḱ ṭayoḱ, cạukạu, chingạu, taraḱ biraḱ; *(about)* alaṅ pholaṅ, aṇḍa maṇḍa, baelao, coloe boloe, culuṅ bhuṭuṅ, ḍhankao, ḍhaṇḍkao, ghuṛạ ghuri, hala ṅūlaḱ, tahāṛ tahāṛoḱ; *(away)* bahka bạhki, bahkao; *(under influence of a spirit &c)* chaṭa.

WANDERED—biḍaraha.

WANDERER, A—despoḍa, naṅgar bhulạ (M), naṅgar bhuli (F).

WANDERING—bạuhari, bhulạ bhạtuạ, dhanka ḍhạnki, mari poḍa.

WANING OF MOON—kunạmi kecaḱ.

WANT—garaj, gorji, gọrọj, malọṭ, ṭan, ṭanaṭani; *(to)* jạruṛ, ọkulạn; *(to be in)* halak, hale ḍale, kalor, khaṭọ, khaṭọ baḍha; *(having no)* ọgọrọj.

WANTED—cạhi.

WANTING—bin; *(in patience)* ạlkhaniạ.

WANTON—baṭuạ (M), baṭwi (F), candro (F), celko melko (F), jhalka (M), jhalki (F), longra (M), lungri (F), paṭwa; (*pleasure*) rij rọṅ.

WAR—laṛhai; (*of words*) bakheṛa.

WARBLE OF FINCH-LARK—surṛuć (2).

WARD, TO—tạlik.

WARES—saoda.

WARLOCK, A—boksa (M), boksi (F).

WARM—golop (2), gorom, lolo, urgum; (*to*) tatao; (*as pepper*) jhal; (*up, to*) ṭhankao, ṭhonkao; (*oneself at fire, to*) jadwahi, jorok; (*to work, to*) garmao; (*manner, in a*) cehor behor.

WARN, TO—cehao, cetao, jobdao, kandhao, mana, sạkti, samjhao, talao; (*off*) dur.

WARNING—cetaona; (*exclm. of*) iạ aikạ, hãhak, mọn, yoi; (*without*) acka, acok, cạbhruk, guyuṅ marte, haṭok, huć marte, huṅ m., loyoṅ m., loyor m., lubur m., mermer, paṭ m., phuṭ m.

WARP OF WEB—otor; (*to separate threads of*) bhitạra, phạriạu; (*& weft*) otor bharna.

WARPED—tẽrga.

WARRANT, A—aronṭ, waront; (*to execute*) aronṭ jari; (*to attach under a*) jarid, jobod; (*to arrest by*) giripdar.

WART, A—doho, jone; (*having*) ḍanṭha ḍonṭho.

WARY—cirgal.

WAS—tahẽkana.

WASH, TO—(*clothes*) cokoć, dhubi, sobot; (*off*) bohoe; (*over*) chilkau; (*clean*) arup sapha; (*hair*) nakṛa, naṛka; (*away*) hehel, sidgir; (*body*) um; (*hands &c.*) abuk; (*off stains*) arup; (*fibre*) sobot; (*half*) heṅjlaṅ peṅjlaṅ.

WASHERMAN, A—dhubi, dhubi mistri.

WASP, A—susurbaṅ; (*spec. of*) bana s., bunum bararin, careć s., kalsakoa, khudiạ s., kuṅkal, litạ tombṛe, sengel s., tombre.

WASTE—apco, kaṅkhar, khaṅkhar, kharaṅ, rạdi, rudi; (*to*) abosta, aleć taseć, badṛa, baṛić, bendao, bharabaṭ, bistur, budạu, buṛau, charkaṭ, chorkoṭ, nahas, narba kharba, noksan, nosṭo, obosta, riại khiại, riyại khiyại, sidrak badrak, tahas, ublạ dublạ, udại padae, udạu, uper khaper; (*to, as tissue*) ghalghalao; (*to lay*) dhun, hulạr, kaṅkhar, khane karap, khaṅkhar, mulạhạn, murạhạn, nona, ujạr, urạn; (*time, to*) hemkhem; (*by eating, to*) jom gidi; (*in using, to*) badṛa; (*away, to*) osok.

WASTED—baṛić; (*by illness*) dhobea; (*to be*) kheanat.

WASTING—(*of children*) khala, khala dabha, puni; (*of body*) naṅjom duk.

WATCH, TO—beṭhauṛa, carit, horho, jagarna, jagron, jaigir, luṭuk (2), pahara, pahra, takao; (*for*) johjohao, tãṛak; (*eagerly for*) tahtahao; (*of children*) ededẹ. *Cf.* OPPORTUNITY.

WATCH, A—ghaṛi, jeb ghaṛi.

WATCHES, THE FOUR—caupohor.

WATCHFUL—cirgal, sote; (*to be*) sontor.

WATCHMAN, A—caukidar, koṭal, pahara, pahra, pahradar, rakhwal; (*village*) khamdar; (*night*) rondar; (*call of night*) ron; (*to act as*) caukidạri.

WATER—dak, pani, roṭe marom; (*unboiled*) jiweṭ d.; (*cold*) berel d., sitol pani; (*saline*) chapar d., khorna d.; (*hot*) basaṅ d., lolo d., susum d., (*become cold*) basaṅ goć; (*muddy*) bohor (2), hewel bekel, khidor, sodor (2); (*running*) bohi d., buhi d.; (*oozing out of*) jorok; (*wide expanse of*) bilạt d., jala, jalaphi; (*deep stagnant*) khal; (*pool of*) aghorni, dabra, dobhak; (*a pit of*) dhabuṅ; (*a flood of*) dak dubạ; (*spring of*) dadi, ukhur dadi; (*reservoir*) band; (*in which plates washed*) sukri kạnji; (*rice*) mandi; (*sugary*) pana; (*full of*) joboć (2); (*to*) aṅu; (*to be carried by*) bhasao; (*to cover with*) dubạ, dubạu; (*to agitate, as fish*) hunṭak; (*to wipe off*) ohoe; (*to bale out or throw*) areć; (*course, a small*) garha, gatạ, lala, nala; (*course, to become a*) bhangaṭ; (*fall, a*) hudhudi, sonodor, sunudur; (*logged, to become*) dahalao, dahlao, jarkao; (*clearing fruit*) nirmoli; (*from one vessel to another, to tip*) dharkao;

(*which has stood overnight*) **ḍhoena daḱ.**

WATER, NOISE OF—(*falling*) **cọdọ (2),** god (2), gọdọ, (2), had (2), **sad (2)** sudur (2); (*pouring*) **sodọr (2);** (*plunging into*) dhabos; (*agitated in hole*) sodgo bodgo, ṭabuḱ; (*falling into water*) god (2), godo (2), sodo, sodsodao; (*falling on ground*) **suṭuḱ;** (*struck by feet when swimming*) ṭaba ṭubu; (*with a*) **suṭuḱ marte;** (*about to boil*) sãe (2); (*poured out of bottle*) dhọḱ (2); (*shaken in bottle*) **ḍhọkọḱ** (2); (*anything moving in*) **sedẹ bedẹ,** setẹ petẹ. *Cf.* SPLASHING, RUSHING, RIPPLING, DRIPPING.

WATERPOT, A—kanḍa; (*brass*) **gagra, ghagra, ghaṛa;** (*small earthen*) **ṭhili;** (*rim of*) kanḍa kańkha; (*lower part of*) lohta; (*stand*) gãrsande.

WATERY—bikọl bọkọl; (*of liquor*) **sajan;** (*substance oozing from mass*) **birin** (2).

WATTLE & DAUB WALL, A—**onnot, onot,** ṭaṭiol bhit; (*to plaster with clay*) jelom.

WAVE, A—ḍheo; (*movement of*) **gheola;** (*to rise & fall as*) habak **dabak.**

WAVERING—dupiṭhia, hucku **cukur,** kẹṭẹć tabuć, olocolo.

WAX—(*bees'*) siteṭ, sithaṭ; (*ear*) ẽrgoṭ.

WAY—(*road*) họr, rah; (*method*) **bhaṭ,** dhara, kader, mọt, **mọtlọb, sik;** (*of life*) calcọlọn; (*of exit*) **ghaṭ;** (*down to river &c*) ghaṭ; (*out of the*) ẹk **sirtal;** (*that*) **hanka;** (*in that*) ọntẹ, ọntẹ; (*by that*) **hanka,** hinka; (*this*) nẹtẹ, notẹ; (*in this*) nhanka; (*by this*) nhatẹ; (*in any*) jahã leka, jahã lekate, jaṭe, (*in what*) ceṭ leka, oka leka; (*in every*) **sanam** lekate; (*the long*) jeteleń; (*off, a little*) noman; (*to stand in the*) manḍmanḍe; (*each to go his own*) apan apin, phuṭạ phuṭi, phuṭ phaṭ; (*to make*) aṛaḱ, dahalao; (*to keep out of the*) aelo gaelo, gersań girsiń, lẹnḍẹc; (*to go out of the*) dulkạu, ghusạu, họsẹc; (*to force*) gusuć; (*to put out of*) bargao, oṭaḱ, pheńkao; (*to block a*) paṭẹṭ; (*to give*) **pae.**

WAYS—(*in many*) **nana bond, nana hunar;** (*& means*) **amdani.**

WAYWARD—ulbul.

WE—abo, abon, ale; (*dual*) alań, ạliń.

WEAK—**abol, adpakolia, aṭho siṭho, aṭna saṭ, bẹṭkẹć, ḍińgar, halso, haṭya, hin, japa jopo, jaro, jero, jilwa ṭhalwa, kedbaḱ, kẹdmọr, komjor, lakruć, laṭlaha,** latwaḱ, **leńjraha (M),** lenjrahi (F), lerosia, **lesoria, lẹṭẹć pẹṭẹć,** leṭep (2), lẹṭẹr **peṭẹr,** licar, lirwa sarwe, liṭir piṭir, **morjha,** morọṭ, nemor, nijhulia, **nijọr,** nirbos, nisoḱ, osad, paṛao, **picopọcọ, pocla, rẽhẽ, ruiṣ,** ruṅku **juḍuń, ruńruń, siṭha,** sotyoṭ, **tewelgaṭ;** (*of loins*) lakać lukuć, Jilo **loko;** (*as a spring*) **lipsa;** (*to be*) **hiwel hawal, kọmọr bhańga;** (*to become*) **jaṛao,** jhulạu, kọmjor, **lawaḱ laṭiń,** libruḱ, lorao; (*on legs*) **asoṛ tamboṛ;** (*from age or illness*) **ahluń, dhopyo, lakar thukur;** (*& leaning on staff*) jukan jukun; (*& tired*) hinḍań ṭhapań; (*—ness*) nijọjọr; (*from hunger*) **hapaḱ** (2). *Cf.* EMACIATED, LEAN.

WEALTH—**acol, daulaṭ, dhọn, jinis, lachmi, lukhi, maljal,** ọndhọn, **ọrjọn;** (*to lose*) **bahal, bhańga** sulị; (*of, a*) **anẹć dhanẹć, anẹć tasẹć.**

WEALTHY—**anḍela, anẹć dhanẹć, asraṭ, bahbahia, bhale** (2), **bhuṭela, darmoṭ, daulatan, dhanghar, dhanghara, dheke, dhunia, madhãs, maldar, mandhas, mosto, moṭa muṭi, napraḱ, omor, one dhone, rasiạu, taliạu, tear;** (*to become*) **sarhe.**

WEANED, FIT TO BE—**bakarna, bakorna.**

WEAPONS—**hathiar,** khanḍa; (*to keep in good condition*) **jogarsan;** (*a cutting*) **piṭi khanḍa.**

WEAR, TO—(*away*) **bhonḍra, hehel, hẹr, khiạu, khokrao;** (*away slowly*) **murca;** (*clothes*) bande, **họrọk, gọgọḱ.**

WEARIED—**ala ạli, alọć palọć, asbasao, eṭher poṭher, jẹrbar, thakar bakar, thaka thaki;** (*of sitting*) **oṭhor poṭhor;** (*to be*) **alao, alapala, bhoṭko, elao, ẹstọ bẹstọ, harit, larbuk, titạu, tọmọldaḱ;** (*to become*) **torlad.**

WEARINESS—dhọk.

WEARISOME—**dayaḱ (2), lińgiṭ (2);** (*of a road*) **lelengeṭ, lẹńgeṭ** (2).

WEARY—(*to*) **dhik, harao, pesrao, tita titi;** (*to be*) **thukit;** (*out, to*) **tamardaḱ;** (*with exertion*) **hiḍań ṭhapań.**

WEATHER—(*bright*) phiripan; (*the hot*) duka din, jhala din, jhanj din, niron, niron seton, raudari, seton din; (*the cold*) raban din; (*the wet*) japut din.

WEAVE, TO—teñ; (*garlana &c*) galań.

WEAVER, A—teteńić; (*muslim*) dhunia, jolha; (*present given to*) ninghraeni; (*bird*) hisi cẽrẽ; (*Hindu*) tãti; (*price of*) teńok bara; (*part of loom of*) kabhand, rac; (*brush of*) jotoé; (*sticks used by*) sarae.

WEB, A—(*of cloth*) lund, than, than kicrić; (*spider's*) bindi ganak.

WEDGE, A—guja, guji, pacar, pat; (*to put in*) athrẽ; (*in cart-wheel*) sal.

WEDLOCK—bapla; (*born out of*) bidhua.

WEDNESDAY—bud hilok.

WEED—(*to*) herhet; (*a common*) belãonja, bindi mutha, mutha ghãs, rondoé; (*a rice*) mandri, marndi; (*a prickly*) ujar kanta.

WEEDS—(*to pull up*) herhet; (*to gather*) kokot, korkot; (*instrucment for*) khurpa.

WEEK—(*a*) hapta; (*next*) ghuri hapta; (*wages of a*) hapta.

WEEN, TO—undkup, unkup.

WEEP, TO—asać usać, garjao, kahar kõhũr, kando, rak; (*for*) hae hiatiń; (*& sob*) birić; (2); (*& groan*) harun; (*loudly*) kaua raua; (*& laugh*) khunũ (2); (*gently*) kasat kusut, khusut (2), kuhũr (2), kuhũt (2).

WEEPING—huhu, hũkhũk, jhãora jhauri, raona jhaona; (*& speaking*) hene phene; (*gently*) kusũt (2).

WEEVIL, A—(*attacking leguminous seeds*) huti; (*attacking rice*) jarndi, surhi

WEIGH, TO—ojon, tula, tulau; (*in the mind*) khańjao.

WEIGHT—bhar; (*a*) batkara, dheo; (*short*) bokro; (*an unfair*) bań colon ojon; (*of little*) halka; (*a little over*) unka; (*of 5 seers*) pasari; (*of 40 seers*) mon; (*2 lbs.*) ser; (*½ oz.*) tola; *of fish-net*) kathi.

WELCOME, TO—atań daram.

WELFARE—dosa, khata barha, khusal mangal, kusal mangal, mangal, mongol.

WELL—bes, bhage, bhage sabitte, bhala, hoge, colhok, dagdag, dhab dhob, dhabe dhabe, khilkau, khub, khub leka, majbut, mańjgut, nirpon, phusać (2), renglee, sãohã, sostok, subita, sustok, suthrai, tosgor; (*a*, indara, kũi;) (*a natural*) dadi; (*to do*) boge; (*up, to*) bhumkau, se; (*then*) bhala; (*done!*) bah, bahware, halla; (*nigh*) hoclo; (*made*) jama juta; (*being*) dosa; (*behaved*) soghor; (*fed*) goboria; (*-to do*) barião, calti, culti, darmal, ganganea, gangania, masdar, maswar, mathor, mosto, telgar, thakaman, tuli; (*-to-do, to become*) manus man. *Cf* GROWN, KNOWN, MATCHED, &c.

WERE—tahẽkana.

WEST, THE—pachim, pochim; (*from the*) pachia, pachmahi.

WET—gejeć (2), heje peje, jabdahi, jabjab, jegeć jagum, jegeć (2), jhargo pargo, jharruk parruk, jobjob, joboć, jobo (2), joć (2), jor bodeak, lesepese, oda, oda moda, purmu, sirpitiak; (*very*) jebe jobe; (*to*) dahalao, purmu; (*to be*) lohoć; (*slightly*) mehao; (*& slippery*) lejek pejek.

WHACK, TO—parat.

WHAT—cele, celeć, cet, cetame, jage, je, oka; (*exclm.*) eh, iyo; (*to do*) ceka; (*do you call it*) ia; (*is it*) oi; (*kind*) cekan, cekan lekan, cet lekan, kon aesan, oka lekan; (*manner*) oka leka, oka lekan; (*place*) okare, oka then, oka utar; (*thing*) cetat; (*then*) kir, bab kir.

WHATEVER—jage, jãhã, jathe, je, jege, jekichu; (*way, in*) jate; (*time of day*) jãhãtinre; (*direction, in*) jãhã seć.

WHEAT—an, anaj, gohum, guhum; (*an ear of*) gele; (*flour*) maeda.

WHEEDLE, TO—bãosao, bod, labor, lalkao, lalkar, libuk, lilkau, lipuk, lol, lulwau, muhni, phusalau.

WHEEDLING—dombaj; (*by a show of friendship*) luhum suhum.

WHEEL, A—cak, gadi; (*cart*) sagar; (*potter's*) kuńkal cak; (*metal bush o*) ula; (*hub of*) pai; (*pulley*) ghar ghaṛi ; (*parts of*) bandh, kund, paṭi, putla ; (*tire of*) hal ; (*to set back on axle*) kak̄hiau ; (*round, to*) bherwaṅ ; (*a conveyance on*) gaḍi, ghoṛ bagi. *Cf.* SPINNING.

WHEEZE—(*to*) khāi (2), ṭhēs ; (*with a*) ṭhēs marte.

WHEN—jab, jobe, jokhon, khan, kobe, menkhan, timinak̄ ; (*on same day*) tin jokheć, tinre, tinrenaṅ ; (*not to-day*) tis, tisok̄ ; (*ever*) bithak, jāhātinre, jāhātisre.

WHERE—oka, okare, okor, okorić, okorkin, okorko, toka, ukurić ; (*ever*) jāhā, jāhāte, jāhā ṭhen ; (*fore*) cak̄, caṅ, cedak̄, kahe khatir, kahite.

WHERRET, TO—dabṛi maṅgal.

WHET, TO—san.

WHETHER...OR—baṅ do...baṅ do, bhai, cahe... cahe, kahi...kahi, ki bhai... ki bhai, parlek...parlek.

WHETSTONE, A—kuńj dhiri ; (*revolving*) san ; (*to grind on*) san.

WHICH—oka, okako, okoe ; (2) okakin ; (*one*) okaṭak̄, okoeṭak̄ ; (*direction*) oka seć, oka dara ; (*way, by*) oka tora ; (*ever*) jāhāṭak̄. *Cf* PLACE

WHILE—tahē̃ tuluć ; (*after a little*) mit̄ ghuṛi tayomre ; (*a little*) ghuṛiṭek, herep̄, thora ghuṛi, ṭuṅ ghuṛi ; (*ago, a little*) enaṅ.

WHIMSICAL—nabhus.

WHINE, TO—aēũi, kaǒ (2), kāe (2), kāekūi, kāskūs, keoṅ meoṅ, khāo (2), kūi (2), ńere (2), ńuruṅ (2) ; (*of child*) ar, ehek̄, gene phene, jenephene ; (*with a*) ńerek̄ (2), tiriń goriń, tiruṅ miruṅ.

WHIP—(*a*) camuk ; (*a horse*) cabuk ; (*to*) carnao ; (*up, to*) tuṛbuṛau.

WHIR, TO—ḍhere (2), ghargharao, ghurghurau, reǒreǒ, ṭekos, ṭekoskot̄ ; (*to cause to*) ghur ghurau ; (*with a*) ṭekos marte.

WHIRL—(*to*) bhar bharao, ripi (2) ; (*round, to*) bhen (2), bher (2), bherbherao, bherṭaṅ ; (*pool, a*) bahni, ghurni ; (*wind, a*) bharṇḍo.

WHISH, TO (*of sharp weapon*)—khar.

WHISKERS—kanwa goco, panwar goco.

WHISPER, TO—khae khoe, lusur, (2), lusur phusur, pasar pusur, phasar phusur, phasphus, phuski, phusur (2), pusur (2).

WHISTLE—(*a*) murli ; (*to*) gol, siso soso, siu, siyuṛ ; (*through teeth, to*) sić soć, sisi (2), siu, suyuṛ ; (*on fingers, to*) siuṛ, siyuṛ ; (*with a*) siu marte, siuṛ m., siyuṛ m., soyoṅ m., suyuṛ m.

WHITE—barat̄ borot̄, borot̄ (2), poṇḍ, sada ; (*pure*) phīk leka ; (*slightly*) polso ; (*very*) tehe (2) ; (*of hair*) paṇḍu ; (*to become*) poṇḍ ; (*not quite*) malcha, malgot̄, polso poṇḍ, poṇḍ macha ; (*skin, having a*) kaila (M), kaili (F), paṇḍra (M), paṇḍri (F) ; (*on under side of body*) dharra (M), dharri (F) ; (*eyed*) paṇḍra (M), paṇḍri (F) ; (*hot*) daraṅ ; (*heat, to heat to*) tao ; (*to make*) poṇḍ. *Cf.* FOREHEAD, ANT.

WHITES (*a F. complaint*)—siṭka.

WHITEWASH—(*to*) paṇḍrao, potao ; (*silt used as*) poṇḍ hasa.

WHITLOW, A—aṅgur biṛhi, kherkhoć.

WHITTLE A PIECE OF WOOD, TO—sula.

WHIZ, TO—harhur, hurhur, hurmarte.

WHO—cele, celeć, okoe ; (*dual*) okoekin ; (*pl.*) okoeko ; (*knows*) konṭhekan.

WHOLE—bhor, bhurti, goṭar, khilkam, rambar rombor, rombro ; (*the*) bebak, caba, car, catur, gayum, geć gayum, geṭa, hoṭak̄ picak̄, irci gurci, irtić gartić, lae, liṭi birsi, nirdae, pura, purapuri, samphola, sara, sosa gora, sudha ; (*one*) goṭanak̄ ; (*night or day*) caupohor ; (*piece, the*) ṭhauka ; (*life*) ṭunḍaṅ bhor.

WHOM—okoe ; (*dual*) okoekin ; (*pl.*) okoeko ; (*soever*) jāhāeṭak̄.

WHORL ON A HORN, A—bakuk̄.

WHY—cak̄, caṅ, cedak̄, cekate, kahe khatir, kahite.

WICK, LAMP—baṭi, phiṭa, sulta.

WICKED—baṛić, canḍal, dusṭu, kharap, niloj, nimak haram, panṭet̄, raḍ (M), raḍin (F).

WICKEDNESS—dusṭama, phesad.

WIDE—baṅbaṅ, caṅcaṅ, dabdaba, dhab dhaba, dhodlo, hondroṅ, honhoṅ, lablab, layōk̄, lohok̄ (2), mela, osar, phael, phaela, phānḍ, samil ; (*of river*) let̄ (2) ; (*of anklet*)

jhaṇḍel (2); (*as mouth*) caehar; (*to make*) osar, phaelao; (*very*) dapdapa; (*area, in a*) maṇḍer; (*hole, a*) baṅ baṅ; (*of cloth*) cindar condor; (*openings, with*) phandra; (*at one end*) dhamon phucia; (*spreading*) capcapa, carpir, ḍhalka, jhabrali, jharpa, laea, ṭalṭal. *Cf.* EXPANSE, APART.

WIDOW, A—doja kuri, penda ḍopoṭ, raṇḍi, raṇḍi era, raṇḍi maejiu, tara kecak.

WIDOWER, A—doja kora, raṇḍi, raṇḍi herel, tara kecak.

WIDOWS & POOR PEOPLE—raṇḍi dukhi, raṇḍi era heme era, peṭari.

WIDTH—onosar.

WIFE—bahu, orak boṅga, era, era uru, gharna, ghirni, girni, gomke, orak gomkeṭ, hor, orak hor, rinić, arak tekkeić, ṭoṭko; (*1st*) barki, baṭki; (*2nd*) chuṭki, mañjhi, hirom; (*3rd*) chuṭki; (*of chief, &c*) era; (*to take to oneself a*) bahu joṅ; (*without a*) behor; (*a separated*) chaḍwi; (*of father's young brother*) kaki; (*of 4th son*) mañjhli bahu; (*of nephew*) kimin; (*of maternal uncle*) mami; (*young brother or sister of*) erwel; (*elder sister of*) ajhnar; (*mother of*) hanhar; (*father of*) hoñhar; (*relatives of*) narha jorha; (*property of relatives of*) jarapi; (*grandmother of*) here jiaṭ; (*elder brother's*) hili.

WILD—arna, bir, birnaha, kharnaha, okoḍa; (*animals*) bir posu, bir janwar; (*beasts, infested with*) bagahi, camke, caṅke, koṭaha; (*fire*) bijli.

WILDERNESS—hãhakar.

WILE—porkar, prokar, ulbul; (*to*) cacki.

WILFUL—ḍhiṭ.

WILL—marji, murji; (*with a*) urum surum; (*left to one's own*) budrag; (*against one's*) dhara bandha; (*you?*) hoi.

WILLING—(*to be*) aṅkus, jujhau, khara, raji; (*to become*) rumuć; (*or no*) naparok.

WILLINGLY—khos, khusi khos, rumbuć cumbuć.

WILT, TO—kumblau, tolmoć.

WILY—ghaṭi; (*& tenacious*) pephra, phephra.

WIN, TO—jind; (*over*) rijhau, saorao.

WINCE, TO—cihirau, cihkau.

WIND—bao, hoe, hoyoṅ; (*to pass*) gasić, ghasić; (*given to passing*) padna (M), padni (F); (*sound of breaking*) poroṭ, sereṭ; (*carried by the*) oṭaṅ, udia udi, udiau; (*noise of strong*), gudgud, hadae (2), halae (2), harhar; (*& rain, sound of*) jhoroe (2); (*bag, a*) gal bajoria; (*instrument, to play a*) oroṅ; (*on stomach*) aṭap uṭup, ḍep (2); (*without*) nirot; (*pipe, the*) naṇḍri, narri.

WIND, TO—gurhe, merhao; (*into hank*) burhu, laṭi; (*thread*) bãurĩ, nari; (*bobbins*) beṭhaon; (*up a clock*) chabi.

WINDER, A (*on which thread spun*)—naṭwa.

WINDING—akuṭ bakuṭ, anacur, bak bheṅkor, piṭua paṭwe.

WINDOW—khirki, phirki; (*frame*) caukaṭha.

WINE—dak rasa; (*press, a*) had.

WING, A—phakrak, phakura; (*large feathers of*) kanso il. *Cf.* TO FLAP.

WINK, TO—ripi (2); (*with both eyes*) ripiṭ.

WINNOW, TO—lapuk, phaṭkao, rel, te; (*a sieve to*) haṭak.

WIPE, TO—joṭ haweṭ, joṭ; (*out*) meṭao; (*out entirely*) mohor meṭao; (*nose with fingers*) huri.

WIRE—tar.

WISDOM—akil, bud, budhi, buj, hikmat, ilam, rae.

WISE—akil, budan, budgaria, bujhantar, gansud, kheas, kheasi; (*to be*) ucit.

WISH—gorji, goroj, hĩcha, burso, morji, moṭ, moṭlob, murad, murji, murwad, rij, sad, sadh, sana; (*strong*) rogor; (*to*) cahao, hurso, lomosoro, mon, monjoṅ, mone, monsuba, sana; (*for, to*) anijok, ñam; (*for what another has, to*) harkhao.

WISTFULLY—merel, miruk (2); (*to look*) orom (2), mele (2).

WITCH, A—bokos, boksi, ḍan, mara, nañjom, phukrin; (*finder*) dikli, jan, jan guru, sat sokha, sokha;

(*finder's assistant*) phul dharia; (*doctor, to get answer from*) baca; (*craft*) dan, jadu; (*finder, fee to*) bunda.

WITH—salak, samet, samit, são, selet, setelak, songe, te, tuluc, uparre.

WITHDRAW, TO—bhagni, buruc, pac.

WITHER, TO—borao, borce, goso, jhāorão, larua, lerwak, telmec; (*& die*) garao; (*a house*) dhup orak.

WITHHOLD, TO—(*assent*) mahrau; (*food*) erao, pokhao.

WITHIN—bhitar; (*ourselves*) gāyeghore.

WITHOUT—a, be, begor, bin, o-; (*outside*) bahar, bahre; (*anyone to look to*) beamda. *Cf.* DELAY, REASON, WARNING, &c.

WITLESS—bhakcu, thotho.

WITNESS—(*a*) goha, goha sakhi, porman, sakhi; (*to bear*) goha, goha gujrau, sakhi em; (*to cause to bear false*) kan phuka.

WIT'S END, AT ONE'S—andmand, bud hara, jilwa thalwa.

WITTINGLY—barkae.

WIVES—(*brothers'*) ńamea, ńatat era; (*relationship between*) natea.

WIZENED—kabań (2), kiboń kobon, koboń (2).

WO (*stop*)—hum.

WOBBLE, TO—dakar dokor, daradoro, dhakar dhokor, latie ladar, lidwa ladwe.

WOE—(*begone*) miluk jiluk, nirghin; (*is me!*) haere, jare (2).

WOLF, THE INDIAN—hundar.

WOMAN, A—aimai, go, maejiu; (*Hindu*) diku era; (*little*) gidi aimai, thurki; (*fat*) bodgoe; (*lascivious*) chalak chandori; (*abusive*) cumdiń; (*ugly*) dabli mara aimai; (*divorced*) penda dopot; (*traditional*) malin budhi, pilchu budhi; (*who has lost several husbands*) jomhem; (*mark on forehead of*) kedar; (*father & brothers of*) apa bare; (*an unmarried, who enters house of man she chooses*) dhukni. *Cf.* OLD, YOUNG.

WOMB, THE—khukhi, kukhi, lac; (*blood from*) arak pordhol.

WON OVER, TO BE—le.

WONDER—(*to*) bharo, hahara, malun, mayak moyok, tharbhasao; (*exclm. of*) behaj; (*to cause to*) malun, thak.

WONDERFUL—balai, ek jontor, hahara, kathin, osombhag.

WONT—cali, colit.

WON'T YOU?—hai, hoi.

WOOD—kat; (*&c*) kat maker; (*log of*) gandke; (*chip of*) chailak; (*tar*) alkatra sunum; (*worker in*) badhi, badhoe, badohi, kat badhoe; (*expert in*) badhoria, katkut; (*to cut or pare*) lak; (*soft*) labit kat; (*heart*) maj, mańj, sisgar; (*& brake*) pakar; (*turners a caste of*) koriṅga; (*drift*) hadi; (*a pointed piece of*) haiar; (*a piece of, tied to animal's neck*) hodgor; (*pecker*) ere, gutrut, seṅgel ere.

WOOF—bharna.

WOOL—bhidi up; (*cloth of, a*) dhus.

WORD—katha, ror; (*without a*) hapac hupuc, kale bale; (*a deep*) gahir k.; (*to put in the first*) kharkhar; (*to break*) arkhao; (*with double meaning*) bhenta; (*of mouth*) mocate laiak, mokosto, mukharat; (*not dependable*) cudur budur; (*used at funerals &c, a*) sāhak.

WORK—bitti, kaj, kam, kamkaj, karsaj, khatali, udam; (*to*) kamao, kami, khatao, khatua; (*to lose time for*) kam kamahi; (*to cause to lose time for*) kam khatori; (*to shirk*) laruc baruc; (*slow at*) lendor (2); (*driven at*) jhak (2); (*imperfect*) atra matra; (*inured to*) bohon; (*press of*) gahul; (*to prepare for*) sarsor; (*inefficiently, to*) kacokam; (*for wages, to*) nalha; (*against each other, to*) kami haparao.

WORKER, A—khatwaia; (*daily*) mojur; (*in wood*) badhoe, badohi.

WORKING—khatwaia; (*order, not in*) dalsiń talsiń; (*hard*) catkan, chatkan, dar dhup, katwar, mehnotia.

WORKSHOP, A—karkhana; (*carpenter's*) kat sal.

WORLD—(*the*) dharti, dunia, mirtika, ot, pirthimi, prithimi, puri, sańsar, sansar, sońsar, sonsar; (*this*) noa puri; (*the other*) hana puri; (*the *nether)* patal puri ; *(the passing)* moṅco puri ; *(the dying)* morot bhũi ; *(to be brought into the)* busạṛ.

Worldly goods—*(all one's)* samṭi umṭi ; *(to have enough of)* jom puraułk.

Worm—*(the earth)* lendeṭ ; *(causing toothache, a)* reṅgoṭ ; *(in animals' lungs)* joka ; *(in stomach of cattle)* horec gadar, juki ; *(in teeth of cattle)* kasai ; *(intestinal)* paṭwa ; *(a nematode)* mahur ; *(a traditional)* gicho rani ; *(the glow)* kidiń ; *(in rice plant)* buki ; *(eaten)* cacak, tejo arak ; *(wood)* nag dana. *C.f.* TASSAR.

Worn—*(out)* alap (2), aloc paloc, behal, dhadra, dhedre, dhiroń dhoroń, dhodro, ḍoḍbio, ḍoḍo (M), dhaḍri (F), doya dape, doyoc, jaro, jerbar, jero, jhadgoc, jharoc jhapoc, jhedge, jirluń, kokhodo, latwak, nisoń, ore, sōrmbot ; *(out, of old)* daṅga, momomoc, monjolo ; *(out by disease &c.)* alapala, labejan, lakphak ; *(out of shape)* dabla (M), dabli (F) ; *(small)* ṭenṭha, ṭhenṭa, ṭheṭha, ṭhuṭki, ṭuṭki ; *(wide)* hinḍroń honḍroń ; *(bare)* hender, hendra ; *(into holes)* dhodro ; *(to a skeleton)* dẽrẽt dẽpẽt, dhadra (M), dhadri (F), dhẽrẽdhepe, dhẽrẽpeṭe ; *(& cracked)* dhoroṭ (2).

Worried, to be—biraj, dogodhon, kạisau, kaula kauli, khis, titau, tomoldak.

Worry—gańjan, ghamanḍ, jhakojhoko, pajhet, phajhet ; *(causing)* nepran ; *(& anxiety)* jhańjhaṭ ; *(with)* jhiko jhoko ; *(to)* ansa, aris, birij (2), dikiau, jhãora jhãuri, jhikjhikau, khackhacao, khijla khijli, pajet, phajhet, tamardak, tita titi ; *(by threats, to)* hurum durum.

Worship—puja ; *(to)* dahnao, dewa, ḍobok, sebok ; *(to perform act of)* sewa ; *(an object of)* buru ; *(& sacrifice at harvest)* janthar puja ; *(peformed during Sohrae, a)* gohal puja.

Worthily—leklekate.

Worthless—akorma, au, dhuraha, okaj ; *(to become)* bhanḍur.

Worthy—bhodran, bhodro, khamid, lek ; *(to be trusted)* sotea.

Wound—*(a)* ghao, jakham, jokhom ; *(a contused)* gań ; *(to)* cheo, ghal, jakham, jokhom ; *(slightly, to)* bhonor ; *(having a)* lokre ; *(to the quick, to)* chorohorao.

Woven—*(not closely)* ghaṅgri, jaljalia, jeljelia, jhańjra, jheńjre, jhil jhilia, lejra, lijak, lijra ; *(with a pattern)* maci kotha.

Wrangle—*(a)* kajia, ragar jhagar, ṭhaica ; *(to)* apṭha apṭhi, aṭa ãṭi, bakhar, bibad, hupuṭeṭ, jhogor, jigra jigri, kaha kahi, kajia, kala jhagra, kockoco, lekṭha, rapṭa rapṭi, regeń tegeń, rego peto, ropor, takrar, tegeń ; *(given to)* bakharia, bakhera.

Wrap—*(a)* barki ; *(up, to)* galot, garim sarim, korea moṭea, poṭom, reṭ ; *(round, to)* bedhao, korea moṭea, poṭom ; *(in leaves, to)* laṭ.

Wrapped up—gaboc (2), gaelo (2), gahagoho, golop (2) ; *(to seem big)* goho (2). [gaske.

Wrapper, a—*(woolen)* dhus ; *(inner filmy)* ganthar ; *(for pressing oil)*

Wrath—edre, pit.

Wrench, a—peter totoṭak.

Wrenching—tege nere ; *(sound)* caṭ caṭao, rasak, sarak (2) ; *(with a)* rasak marte, sarak marte.

Wrestle, to—tapam ; *(one who)* mal, pahalwan, pahlwan.

Wrestling—*(to compete in)* tapam haparao ; *(bout, a)* kusti.

Wretched—harkhetia ; *(-ness)* pajet ; *(to make)* pajet ; *(looking)* miluk jiluk.

Wriggle, to—biryoń boryoń, harbań hurbań, kawal (2), kewel (2), khiria paṭe, kiwil (2), phenṭe phere, piria paṭe, ribi (2), ribribau.

Wriggling—jambak jombok, piria paṭe ; *(mass, a)* bikir (2).

Wring, to—*(out)* bodoc, rodoc ; *(the neck & kill)* peter goc.

Wrinkle—*(to)* joṅgrao ; *(having)* joknoṭ, joko, kircoṭ korcoṭ.

Wristlet, a—amcola sakom, curi, piṭna sakom, regra sakom, sakom, thel ; *(women's)* rasunia ; *(men's)* ṭoḍor ; *(of shell)* sankha ; *(of lac)* lahṭi curi.

WRITE, TO—hende, ol.

WRITERS (*court*)—amla.

WRITHE, TO—caṭpaṭao, chaṭpaṭao, kacmacao, mocra mucri, mocrao, peṭer, phete (2); (*& twist*) khente pere, phente phere.

WRITING—likha; (*a*) likhal; (*heavy as*) jebre.

WRITTEN—(*document*) khot, nama; (*agreement*) ekrar nama, ikrar nama.

WRONGFULLY—andher.

WRONG—(*to go*) bagdao; (*way, the*) sirgaṭ.

WRY—ghoce, gote, goṭle; (*neck*) ghoce hoṭok', kocle, kokre.

Y

YAK, THE—kapil gai.

YARN—sutam; (*to*) badohi, lahna, phaph.

YAWN, TO—angop.

YE—aben, ape.

YEAR—(*a*) bochor, sal, serma; (*last*) din kalom, goto bochor, hana sal; (*before last, the*) holkalom; (*next*) kalom, darakan sal, ghuri sal; (*after next, the*) satom; (*3 hence*) mahkalom, mahsatom, phersatom; (*3 ago*) mahkalom; (*this*) halsal, nes, neskar, nia bochor, nia sal; (*the whole*) baromas, baromasia, salbhor; (*every*) soneson.

YEARLY—bachri (2), bochorke bochor, salesal, salsal, soneson; (*rent, amount of*) jama, joma.

YEARN FOR, TO—jiwi, uihar.

YEARNING—sene dewer, ṭhonk.

YEAST—ṭari.

YELLOW—sasañ dak'; (*pale*) barañ (2); (*to become, as leaves*) pandu.

YES—ã, hai, hẽ, hẽhẽ, hẽhõ, hoe ke boṭe, hoihoi, oi; (*surely*) hẽ ente, hẽ ge coñ.

YESTERDAY—hola, holanok'; (*the day before*) mahander, mahnder.

YET, NOT—auri.

YIELDING—lebreć, licar, molam.

YOKE—(*a*) arar; (*an iron*) halka; (*to*) jorao; (*beam to which attached*) isi; (*peg*) paṭsamle; (*rope*) jote; (*wood used to break in to*) ghũrã; (*an iron ring*) halka; (*centre of*) mahadeb; (*end of*) sakwa; (*thong of*) nañgle, umadha; (*unequally, to*) eknar.

YOLK OF EGG—bele botke.

YONDER—hande, hane, hante, honte, nhande, nhanden.

YORE, OF—sabik.

YOU—ape, aprug; (2) aben; (*& I*) alañ, abon; (*yourselves*) eron.

YOUNG—abod, ali, bachra, bacra, bale, balebõs, balok, bele botke, belkeñ, beṭkeć, ceñcuria, botke, dać duć, geñjor, hopon, hudiñ, juan, kapṭić, kaṭić, lahañ dohañ, lenda, nabalok, polhan; (*of any animal*) hon; (*man, a*) banda, juan kora, kora; (*woman*) bandi, juan kuri, kuri; (*child*) bale gidra; (*he-goat*) paṭha; (*hen*) kaloṭ; (*plant*) cara; (*woman address to*) biṭi; (*who have left their dam*) kalhuri; (*to be with*) argo, gabhin, hormo, poati; (*to bring forth*) busak', hopon.

YOUNGER—jokar; (*brother, address to*) ja, ya; (*brother or sister*) bokoṭ.

YOUNGEST OF FAMILY—cunda (M), cundi (F), hudiñić, lenda, lendaṭuria.

YOUR HONOUR—aprug.

YOURS—(*dual*) taben; (*pl.*) tape.

YOURSELF—aprug.

YOUTH, A—juan, juwan, misi juan; (*full grown*) hara juan; (*preserving a look of*) gaṭhia, jhaṭa kerkeṭa, kerkeṭa; (*a strong, well grown*) chaela juan.

Z

ZEALOUS—ãṭ; (*manner, in a*) rikir; (*to be*) dhipau.

ZEMINDARY—(*cess, a*) kar, sama; (*official, an*) ohdar.

ZEST, WITH—lahkao.

ZIG-ZAG—añkuṭ bañkuṭ, bak' bheñkor; (*to move in a*) harbañ hurbañ, liyor loyor.

ZINC—dosta.

INDEX TO SCIENTIFIC NAMES.

QUADRUPEDS.

AXIS MACULATUS—jhaṅkar, posta.
BOS GRUNNIENS—kapil gai.
CANIS—(*palipes*) huṇḍar ; (*aureus*) toyo.
CERVULUS AUREUS—murghos.
CUON RUTILANS—ḍahal, tan.
FELIS—(*tigris*) kul ; (*leopardus*) poṭea taruṗ, sona cita ; (*pardus*) taruṗ.
GAVAEUS GAURUS—kapil gai, sal.
GAZELLA BENNETTII—badar seleṗ, ghoṭra, ghoṭreṭ jel, kurmbi seleṗ, merom jel, meṭreć jel, seleṗ.
GERBILLUS INDICUS—cạuria hon.
HERPESTES MOTICOLUS—saram babea.
HYAENA STRIATA—haḍgar.
LUTRA NAIR—lodam, odam.
MANIS PENTADACTYLA—arba, harba, suraj mukhi.
MELLIVORA INDICA—parkom bana.
MUS MALABARICUS—bhus.
PARADOXURUS HEMAPHRODITUS—mahala, mahla, maṅgo.
PORTAX PICTUS—murum (M), sosam (F).
PRESBYTIS ENTELLUS—hạrũ.
RUSA ARISTOTELIS—saram.
SCIURUS PALMARUM—toṛ.
SOREX CAERULESCENS - cund.
SUS INDICUS—bir sukri.
URSUS LABIATUS—bana, boyo bana.
VIVERICULA MALACCENSIS—sogoć.
VULPES BENGALENSIS—khikṛī.

BIRDS.

ALCEDO ISPIDA—ḍuć kikir.
ANASTOMUS OSTICANS—suṅkhal.
ARACHNECHTHRA ASIATICA—sakwa suć, suć cẽṛẽ.
ARDEA—(*argala*) garuṛ ; (*leucocephala*) manikjoṛ.
BRACHYOTERNUS AURANTIUS—kabra ere.
CAPRIMULGUS MONTICOLUS—hapuk.
CARPOPHAGA SYLVATICA—gudur ghum, guḍru gum, kisạṛ potam.
CENTROPUS RUFIPENNIS—mahkal.
CIRCUS SWAINSONII—rici cẽṛẽ.
COCCYSTIS JACOBINUS—jhomojhoć, jhorojhoć.
COLUMBA INTERMEDIA—parwa.
CORRYDALLA RUFULA—cancir.
CORVUS LEVAILANTII—bhõḍa kahu, bhonḍa kahu.
CROCOPUS CHLORIGASTER—huhaṛ.
CRYPTOLOPHA CINEREOCAPILLA—sasaṅ cẽṛẽ.
DENDROCITTA RUFA—bororiṅ.
DICRURUS MACROCERCUS—ḍhipcui.
EPHIALTES PENNATUS—kokor.
FALCO CHEELA—kuṛić.
FRANCALINUS VULGARIS—munḍhaṭ citri.
GALLINAGO SCOLAPACINUS—dhanuk baṭṭa.
GALLUS FERUGINEUS—bir sim.
GERONTICUS PAPPILOSUS—tarjua.
GRACULA RELIGIOSA—bhõḍa kisni, bhonḍa kisni.
GRACULUS—(*javanicus*) dak sim ; (*macei*) kalaiya
HEIROCOCCYX VARIUS—galoć cẽṛẽ, galua cẽṛẽ.
HYDROCISSA CORONATA—dhorsa.
HYSTRIX LEUCURA—jhīk.
LANIUS MELANOCEPHALUS—bagha kerkeṭa.
LOBIVANELLUS GOENSIS—kuṛi ṭukuć, ṭeṭeṭeṅgoć cẽṛẽ, ṭiṭirhīć cẽṛẽ.
MALACOCERCUS TERRICOLOR—bhonḍa jihu.
MEGALAIMA CANICEPS—gutruṭ.
MENICEROS BICORNIS—dhorsa.

MEROPS VIRIDIS—ṭirom cẽṛẽ.

MOTACINLA LUZONIENSIS—gaḍa caúcir.

OLOGYPS CALVUS—seṅgel gidi (M), raila gidi (F).

ORIOLUS MELANOCEPHALUS—pio.

ORTHOTOMUS SUTORIUS—ghardiḍi, jiam, malhan cẽṛẽ.

ORTYGORNIS PONTICERRIANUS—citri, ṭipoṅ ṭoroṅ.

PALAEORNIS—*(torquatus)* doć miru; *(alexandri)* ḍoḍharia miru; *(rosa)* kulṇḍi miru.

PASSER INDICUS—gharwa.

PERICROCOTUS PEREGRINUS—sului lundui cẽṛẽ.

PHYLLORNIS JERDONI—baromasia.

PICUS MAHRATTENSIS—bhõḍa ere.

PITTA BRACHYURA—huć bir.

PLOCEUS BAYA—hisi cẽṛẽ.

PYCNONOTUS PYGAEUS—ṭićṭorok.

PYRRHULAUDA GRISEA—gõeṭha lipi, lipi cẽṛẽ, sirloć cẽṛẽ.

ROSTRATULA CAPENSIS—dok cẽṛẽ.

SARCIOPHORUS BILOBUS—kuri ṭukuć, ṭeṭeṭeṅgoć cẽṛẽ, ṭiṭirhić cẽṛẽ.

SCOPS BAKKAMOENA—dereń kokor.

SPILORNIS MELANOTIS—kuhi besra.

STURNOPASTOR CONTRA—care kisni, ere kisni.

TERPSIPHONE PARADISE—laṅtiti.

TINNUNCULUS ALANDARIUS—tirmuti cẽṛẽ.

TOTANUS GLOTTIS—dak baṭṭa.

TURNIX SYKESII—ghura, gunḍri.

TURTUR—*(cambayensis)* barge potam, sanḍi karkar potam, ṭhekro potam, ṭhikri potam; *(surattensis)* kẽṇḍrõ potam.

UPUPA EPOPS—dabla kuṭam, kuṭam dabla.

XANTHOLOEMA—*(haematocephala)* tuť cẽṛẽ; *(indica)* gutruť.

BAT.

PTEROPUS EDWARDSI—kahu barduṛũć.

MOTHS.

ANTHERAEA MYLITTA—lumam, ṭira (M), paṭni (F).

ATTACUS ATLAS & SELENE—bharua, siṅghin bharua, b. ṭira (M), b. paṭni (F).

INSECTS.

COCCUS LACCA—lahi.

GRYLLODES BERTHELLUS—soãriń.

HIERODULA TECTIFORMIS—katrua, nau.

PEDICULUS CAPITIS—se, tele.

PLATYPLEURA OCTOGUTTATA—rereń.

SCOLOPENDRA VERSICOLOR—seṅgel marmar.

STERNOCERA CHORYSIS—sansunia, sunsuni.

TYPHLOPS BRAMINUS—sunum biń.

FISH.

CYPRINUS DENTICULATUS—ruhi hako, rui.

PLANTS.

ABRUS PRECATORIUS—ponḍ kaweť.

ABUTILON INDICUM—miru baha.

ACACIA—*(arabica)* babla, babur, gabla; *(catechu)* khayar; *(intsia)* kondro janum; *(farnesiana)* gabur.

ACHYRANTHES ASPER—cipciriṗ.

ACTERNANTHERA SESSILIS—garũnḍi arak.

ADIANTUM LUNULATUM—dodhari.

ADINA CORDIFOLIA—karam dare.

AEGINETIA INDICA—pathor orot.

AEGLE MARMELOS—sińjo.

AERUA LANNATA—lopoṅ arak.

AESCHYNOMENE ASPERA—sol.

AGAVE AMERICANA—koṅga, koṅgak, koṅgať, moraba.

ALANGIUM LAMARCKII—ḍhela.

ALBIZZIA—*(odoratissima)* jań siris; *(myriophilla)* kanṭa siris; *(lebbek)* siris.

ALLIUM CEPA—peaj.

ALSTONIA SCHOLARIS—chaṭni.

AMARANTUS—*(gangeticus)* gandhari arak; *(spinosa)* janum arak; *(frumentacens)* kukrucuť baha; *(paniculatus)* larka baha; *(tristis)* ponḍ gandhari arak.

AMORPHOPHALLUS CAMPANULATUS—ol, piṇḍo.

ANANASSA SATIVA—ananas, anaṛo̦s.

ANDROGRAPHIS—*(echioides)* bir kubet; *(paniculata)* kalmeg.

ANDROPOGON—*(muricatus)* bena, sirom; *(schaenanthus)* nanha ḍuḍhi ghās; *(aciculatus)* seta sagak̕.

ANEILEMA NANA—gundli araḱ.

ANGELICA GLAUCA—oponom.

ANISOCHILUS CARNOSUS—gitil ran.

ANISOMELES OVATA—surgi baha.

ANOGEISSUS LATIFOLIA—ho̦so̦l.

ANONA—*(reticulata)* amsophori, gom, sạphri am; *(squamosa)* mandargo̦m, sạrphạ.

ANTHISTIRIA WIGHTII—lo̦bo̦e ghās, lubui ghās.

ANTHOCEPHALUS CADAMBA—kadam dare.

ANTIDESMA DIANDRUM—maṭha araḱ.

APLUDA ARISTATA—ḍhoḍhia̦ sạuṛi, ḍuḍhi ghās, ḍuṛhi ghās.

ARGYREIA SPECIOSA—kedok̕ araḱ.

ARGEMONE MEXICANA—ạṭkuṭi, ujạṛ kanṭa.

ARECA CATECHU—guạ.

ARISTIDA DEPRESSA—khaṛañ, lo̦bo̦e khaṛañ ghās.

ARTEMISIA PARVIFLORA—bañsiń.

ARTOCARPUS—*(integrifolia)* kanṭhaṛ; *(lakoocha)* ḍahu.

ARUNDINELLA—lukui ghās.

ASPARAGUS RACEMOSUS—kedar nạṛī.

ATYLLOSIA—*(scarabaedois)* bir ho̦ṛeč; *(mollis)* bir malhan.

BAMBUSA STRICTA—buru mat̕.

BARLERIA—ṛaila̦ baha; *(prionitis)* kanṭa phul.

BARRINGTONIA ACUTANGULA—hińjoṛ.

BASELLA ALBA—purạ̣i nạṛī, kạṭič purạ̣i araḱ.

BASSIA LATIFOLIA—jamṛo matko̦m, matko̦m.

BAUHINIA—*(retusa)* birnju, jhińjiṭ; *(variegata)* jhińjhir, jińjir; *(vahlii)* cihṛi lamaḱ, jo̦m laṛ, lamaḱ, lamaḱ laṛ; *(purpurea)* hoe ranakap̕ araḱ, sińaraḱ.

BEGONIA PICTA—dhiri japaḱ.

BETA VULGARIS—palak araḱ.

BIOPHETUM SENSITIVUM—bhado̦r jhạpni, jhạpni.

BLUMEA—*(lacera)* gaḍa pacwạni; *(wightiana)* rondoč.

BOMBAX MALABARICUM—edel, rui, soho doho.

BONNAYA VERONICAEFOLIA—kedar.

BORASSUS FLABELLIFORMIS—tale.

BOSWELLIA SERRATA—salga.

BRASSICA CAMPESTRIS—luṭni, rạ̣i, tuṛi, ṭhạḍia̦ tuṛi, man tuṛi.

BRIEDELIA RETUSA—kạḍru pala, karke jạnum.

BRYONIA LACINOSA—kạhu botke.

BUCHANANIA LATIFOLIA—tarop.

BUETTNERIA HERBACEA—deko sindur. kambraj.

BURSERA SERRATA—ạrmu.

BUTEA—*(frondosa)* murup̕; *(superba)* nạṛi murup̕.

CAESULIA AXILLARIS—belãońja.

CAJANUS INDICUS—raheṛ.

CALAMUS ROTANG—bõ̦t.

CALLICARPA MACROPHYLLA—buḍhi ghạsič.

CALOTROPIS GIGANTEA—akaona.

CAMELLIA THEIFERA—ca dare.

CANAVALIA ENSIFORMIS—tiho̦n.

CANNABINIS SATIVA—gańja.

CANTHIUM DIDYMUM—garbha gojha.

CAPPARIS HORRIDA—buru asạria̦.

CARDIOSPERMUM HALICAEABUM—puṭki malla.

CAREA ARBOREA—kumbiṛ.

CARISSA CARANDAS—kãṛwat̕.

CARUM—*(carni)* jira̦; *(copticum)* ạjuạ.

CASEARIA TOMENTOSA—corco, riḍe.

CASSIA—bandor lạuṛi, mirju baha, ńũṛũč; *(tora)* bheḍa dereń, cakaoḍa; *(mimosoides)* o̦t kondro, paṭwa ghās.

CASSYTHA FILIFORMIS—alag jạṛi.

CASUARINA EQUISETIFOLIA—sãe sũi dare.

CELASTRUS PANICULATUS—kujri.

CELOCASIA ANTIQUORUM—sạru.

CELOCIA ARGENTA—sirgiṭ araḱ.

CENTIFIDA ORBICULARIS—bhiḍi achim.

CHEILANTHUS TENUIFOLIA—nanha bodhari.

CHENOPODIUM ALBUM—bhaṭuạ aṛak̕.

CHLOROPHITUM ARUNDINACEUM—jọrọń aṛak̕, jọrọṭ aṛak̕.

CICER ARIETINUM—buṭ.

CINNAMONUM OBTUSIFOLIUM—tejpat.

CISSAMPELOS PAREIRA—tejo mala.

CISSUS QUADRANGULARIS—haḍ joṛa.

CITRUS MEDICA—jạmbir dare.

CLEMATIS NUTANS—boṅga ghạnṭi.

CLERODENDRON—(*infortunatum*) bạrni, kharbạri; (*phlomoides*) pańjot; (*serratum*) saram lutur.

COCHLOSPERMA GOSSYPIUM—hopo.

COIX LACHRYMA—gargạḍi, jargạḍi.

COLEBROOKIA OPPOSITIFOLIA—bhãisa.

COLOCASIA—picki.

COMBRETUM—(*decandrum*) aṭen; (*nana*) berdoṛ, bhursạ.

COMMELYNA—(*salicifolia*) bir kana aṛak̕; (*suffroticosa*) dare oṛsa; (*bengalensis*) kana aṛak̕.

CORCHORUS—bir narcha; (*capsularis*) kaskom ran.

CORDIA—(*macleodii*) jugiạ; (*myxa*) buc dare.

CORIANDRUM SATIVUM—dhạniạ.

COSTUS SPECIOSA—orop̕.

CRINUM—sikiom baha.

CROSPHORA PILCATA—parwa jhaṛa.

CROTALARIA—(*calcyna*) bir jhunkạ, moṭa bir jhunkạ; (*juncea*) sọn jạṛi, sọn kudrum, sãci sọn, san, sọn; (*prostrata*) kạṭić jhunkạ, nanha jhunkạ; (*alata*) marań jhunkạ; (*striata*) sọn jhunkạ.

CROTON OBLONGIFOLIUS—gote.

CRYPTOLEPSIS BUCHANANI—utri dudhi.

CUCUMIS—(*melo*) phuṭ, tạrbhuj, tạrmuj; (*sativus*) tahẹr.

CUCURBITA—(*lagenaria*) họtọṭ; (*moscheta*) kohṇḍa.

CURCUMA—orsoṛiń; (*longa*) gãṭ, sasań.

CUSCUTA CHINENSIS—alag jạṛi.

CYAMOPSIS PSORALIOIDES—buru raheṛ, raheṛ.

CYANOTIS AXILLARIS—moṭa gundli aṛak̕.

CYATHOCLINE LYRATA—bereń phul.

CYNODON DACTYLON—dhubi ghãs, dhubi tasak̕, dub ghãs, tasak̕.

CYPERUS—(*tegetum*) suṛạ; (*rotundus*) ṭạnḍi suṛạ.

DALBERGIA—(*latifolia*) satsayar; (*lanceolaria*) capoṭ siris; (*volubibilis*) naṛi siris.

DESMODIUM—(*polycarpum*) baephọl; (*triflorum*) sunsuni, ṭạnḍi catọm aṛak̕, ṭạnḍi sunsuni; (*gangeticum*) ṭạnḍi bhiḍi janaṭeṭ.

DHATURA—(*alba*) dạtrạ, dhạtrạ; (*fastuosa*) dạtrạ, dhạtrạ.

DIGERIA ARVENSIS—kạri gandhạri.

DILLENIA—(*indica*) korkoṭ; (*pentagyna*) sahar.

DIOSCOREA—(*bulbifera*) beṅgo nạṛi; (*daemonum*) kolo; (*oppositifolia*) piskạ; (*fasciculata*) sutbni.

DIOSPYROS—(*tomestosa*) jarge terel, terel; (*montana*) gaḍa terel; (*embrypoteris*) makaṛkenda.

DOLICHOS—(*biflorus*) họrẹć; (*lablab*) malhan.

DREGIA VOLUBILIS—koṅgak̕, marań koṅgat.

DYSOPHILLA VERTICILLATA—pansiṅgha.

ECHINOPS ECHINATUS—ḍaṅgra jạnum.

ECLIPTA ALBA—lal kesạri.

EHRETIA LAEVIS—pusi pan.

ELAEODENDRON ROXBURGHII—niuri.

ELEUSINE—(*corocana*) kọde, lạpṛa k., lapra k., lạpsi k., mạnḍwi k., bhadọr k.; (*aegyptiaca*) suntu bukuć, suntu bukuć.

EMBELIA ROBUSTA—bhạbri.

EMILIA SONCHIFOLIA—kulại lutur.

ENTADA SCANDENS—bidhạnta.

EQUISETUM DEBILE—buru kaṭkọm carẹć.

ERAGROSTIS—(*tenella*) ickoć, jebkhoć; (*bifaria*) lopotiań ghãs; (*ciliaris*) toṛ caṇḍbọl.

ERIOLOENA HOOKERIANA—guạ guli.

ERIOSEMA CHINENSIS—konḍeń.

ERVUM LENS—mạsri.

ERYCIBE PANICULATA—kạri.

ERYTHRINA—(*indica*) marãṛ; (*arborescens*) buru marãṛ baha.

EUGENIA—cuḍuk̕ kod; (*jambolana*) aṛa, kod, sọ, soh; (*operculata*) totonopak̕.

EUPHORBIA—(*antiquorum*) ọṭkẹć, sij; (*scrabrifolia*) janhe hirom; (*dracunculoides*) jhawa jhara; (*granulata*) kantha aṛak̕; (*thymifolia*) nanha pusi toa; (*pilulifera*) pusi toa.

EVOLVULUS ALSINOIDES—ṭạṇḍi khode baha.

FERONIA ELEPHANTUM—kaṭ bel, kõc bel.

FICUS—poḍo; (*bengalensis*) baṛe dare; (*tomentosa*) capakią baṛe; (*religiosus*) hesak̕, jamṛo hesak̕; (*cunia*) hoṛ poḍo, poḍo; (*glomerata*) loa; (*scandens*) mạdhur lata; (*infectoria*) pakaṛe dare; (*hispida*) seta poḍo; (*cordifolia*) sunum joṛ; (*conglomerata*) hãṛũ.

FIMBRISTYLIS—(*monostachya*) binḍi muthạ, muthạ ghãs, nanha binḍi muthạ; (*milliacea*) nạkić ghãs.

FLACOURTIA RAMONTCHI—mọrlẹć.

FLEMINGIA—(*congesta*) bir buṭ, buru ekasirạ nãṛĩ; (*nana*) ọt murup̕.

GARDENIA—(*turgida*) ḍuṇḍukić; (*latifolia*) popṛo.

GARUGA PINNATA—kaṇḍwer.

GLOBBA ORIXENSIS—saparatiń.

GLORIOSA SUPERBA—selep̕ samanom, sinić samanom baha.

GLOSSOGYNE PINNATIFIDA—barańgom.

GLYCINE SOJA—disom hoṛẹć, ponḍ disom hoṛẹć.

GMELINA ARBOREA—kasmar.

GNAPHALIUM INDICUM—tagoć aṛak̕, togoć aṛak̕.

GOMPHRENA GLOBOSA—ḍuńḍuń baha.

GOSSYPIUM—(*neglectum*) bhoga kaskom; (*herbaceum*) buḍhi kaskom; (*arboreum*) jurguḍạ kaskom, koca kaskom, dare kaskom.

GREWIA—(*campbelii*) bạrsạ pakor; (*asiatica*) jań olać; (*vestita*) olać; (*taliaefolia*) olać; (*polygama*) seta ạndir, seta ãrga, seta kaṭa; (*villosa*) tarse koṭap.

GUIZOTIA ABYSSYNICA—surguja.

GYMNEMA HIRSUTUS—mọrọn aṛak̕.

GYNANDROPSIS PENTAPHYLLA—seta kaṭa aṛak̕.

HEILANTHUS ANNUUS—surạj mukhi, suruj mukhi.

HELICTERES ISORA— peṭcamṛa.

HETEROPOGON CONTORTUS—sauṛi ghãs.

HIBISCUS—(*sabdariffa*) ambaṛo, arak̕ kudrum, coromokoć; (*cancellatus*) bheḍwa; (*cannabinus*) dare kudrum, paṭ son; (*esculentus*) ram jhiṅgạ; (*rosasinensis*) joba baha.

HIPTAGE MADABLOTA—san karla.

HOLMSKIOLDIA SANGUINEA—jhimbria.

HORDEUM VULGARE—jao.

HYGROPHILLA—(*spinosa*) gokhla jạnum, gokhulạ jạnum, gukhla jạnum; (*salicifolia*) matkom aṛak̕.

HYMENODICTION EXCELSUM—bhorkonḍ.

HYPTIS SUAVEOLENS—gaṅga tulsi.

ICHNOCARPUS FRUTESCENS—dudhi loṭa, ghiu chimbṛi, nanha dudhi loṭa.

IMPERATA ARUNDINACEA—cero.

INDIGOFERA—(*pulchella*) dare huṭer, huṭer; (*tinctoria*) lil, nil; (*linifolia*) ṭạṇḍi khode baha.

IONIDIUM SUFFRUTICOSUM—bir surạj mukhi, ṭạṇḍi sol.

IPHEGENIA INDICA—cuṭią caṇḍbol.

IPOMAEA—(*turpethum*) bana etka; (*pestigridis*) coṭo lutur; (*speciosa*) kaṛmbi aṛak̕; (*quamoclit*) kidiń baha; (*batatas*) sakarkenda.

ISCHAEMUM RUGOSUM—mạrṇḍi.

IXORA PARVIFLORA—mọrom mẽṭ.

JASMINUM ARBORESCENS—gaḍa hunḍ baha.

JATROPHA CURCUS—bherṇḍa.

JUGLANS REGIA—akhroṭ, akroṭ.

JUSSIAEA SUFFRUTICOSA—dak̕ icak̕.

JUSSIOCA SUFFRUTICOSA—petra da.

JUSTICIA BELONICA—tayar baha.

KYDIA CALYCINA—phoska olać, poska olać.

LAFFA ACUTANGULA—jhiṅgạ.

LAGENARIA VULGARIS—kạdu.

LAGGERA FLAVA—bir surguja, bir tuṛi.

LARGESTROEMIA PARVIFLORA—sekreć.

LASIA HETEROPHYLLA—kaṇṭa sạru, sạru.

LATHYRUS SATIVUS—kesạri, khasạri, khesari.

LAURUS CASSIA—tejpat.

LAWSONIA ALBA—mehni dare, mihindi dare.

LEBEDIEROPSIS ORBICULARI—kargạli.

LEEA—(*macrophylla*) hatkan; (*hirta*) duria hatkan.

LEONATES NEPETAEFOLIA—boṅga barchi, dare dhompo, janum dhompo.

LEPIDAGATHIS CRISTATA—ot dhompo.

LEPIDIUM SATIVUM—halim.

LEUCAS—(*cephalotes*) andia dhurup arak; (*clarkei*) eṅga dhurup arak; (*mollisima*) gitil arak.

LIMNOPHILLA—(*conferta*) mota hemca arak; (*gratioloides*) nanha hemca arak, nanha jubhi arak; (*roxburghiana*) akar baha, kalha baha.

LINUM USITATISSIMUM—cikno, thisi, thisia, tisi, tisia.

LOBELIA TRIGONIA—cäurič arak.

LORANTHUS BUDDEOIDES—icak bando.

LUFFA ACUTANGULA—paror jhiṅga.

LYGODIUM FLEXUOSUM—badgocak.

MALLOTUS PHILLIPINENSIS—rora.

MANGIFERA INDICA—ul.

MARSILIA QUADRIFOLIA—catom arak, dak sunsuni, sunsuni.

MARTYNIA DIANDRA—bagluca.

MELIA—(*azadarach*) bokom baha; (*azadirachta*) nim.

MELOCHIA CHORCHORIFOLIA—thuiak arak.

MEZONEURUM CUCULLATUM—baghin janum, baghin jhawa.

MILIUSA VELUTINA—kome, ome.

MILLETTIA AURICULATA—hëhël.

MIMOSA RUBICAULIS—sega janum.

MOMORDICA DIOICA—kacan arak, karla.

MONGEOTEA IMMERSA—sealom.

MONOCHORIA PLANTAGINEA—seta pan.

MORINDA TINCTORIA—chaili.

MORINGA PTERYGOSPERMA—munga, munga arak, suti.

MUCUNA PURIENS—etka.

MURRAYA EXOTICA—athel.

MUSA PARADISIACA—kaera.

NELSONIA CAMPESTRIS—jugitopa baha.

NERIUM ODORUM—pond raj baha, raj baha.

NYCANTHUS ARBOR-TRISTIS—saparom.

NYMPHOEA LOTUS—poraeni, upal baha, upel baha.

OCHNA SQUAROSA—campa baha.

OCIMUM—(*basilicum*) bharbhari, dimbu baha, kapur mali baha, mali baha, modor muli baha; (*canum*) bharbhari; (*sanctum*) tulsi dare.

ODINA WODIER—doka.

OLAX NANA—merom mẽč.

OLDENLANDIA SENEGALENSIS—ilin cin.

OPHIOGLOSSUM VULGARE—ot poraeni.

OPUNTIA DILLENII—sapin dare.

OROBANCHE INDICA—turi sim.

OROXYLON INDICUM—bana hatak.

ORYZA SATIVA—horo, uri horo.

OUGENIA DALBERGIOIDES—rot.

PANDANUS ODORATISSIMUS—kia baha.

PANICUM—(*colonum*) bare badwarak, bari badwak, sama ghas; (*stagninum*) dal, dol; (*miliare*) gundli; (*antidotale*) layo gundli; (*crusgalli*) iri, kokor jaṅga iri; (*flavidum*) jera janhe; (*helopus*) mota gundli; (*vestitum*) nari ghas; (*repens*) adagathia.

PASPALUM SCROBICULATUM—janhe.

PAVETTA INDICA—budhi ghasič, budhi tilai.

PENCILARIA SPICATA—lendha, lenjha.

PENNISETUM TYPHOIDEUM—lendha, lenjha.

PENTAPETES PHAENICIA—bare baha.

PHASEOLUS—(*aconitifolius*) alpalua, bir alpalua, mõc; (*mungo*) birsan, mun, rambra; (*calcaratus*) sutri.

PHOENIX SYLVESTRIS—khijur.

PHYLLANTHUS—(*lanceolarius*) bãriã kandhum; (*juniperinoides*) jhãwar khandera; (*emblica*) meral; (*multilocularis*) nanha bãriã kandhum; (*simplex*) tandi meral; (*urinaria*) tandi meral.

PHYSALIS MINIMA—handi kundi, thoč.

PIMPINELLA ANISUM—muhri, panmuhri.

PIPER—(*belle*) pan; (*longa*) rali; (*nigrum*) gol maric, golki maric.

PISUM—(*arvense*) mator, motor; (*sativum*) mator, motor.

PLUMBAGO ZELANICA—citar kathi, jog kathi.

PLUMERIA ACUTIFOLIA—golanj baha.

POGMATHERUM SACCHAROIDEUM—boṅga carač.

POLLINIA ERIOPODA—bạckọm.

POLYALTHIA CERASOIDES—pańjon.

POLYCARPOEA CORYMBOSA—janhe nańjọm.

POLYGALA—(*chinensis*) gại ghurạ; (*crotalarioides*) lilkạṭbi.

POLYGONUM—(*plebejum*) muć ạrak; (*indicum*) rạniphul; (*glabrum*) sạuṛi ạrak.

PONGAMIA GLABRA—kọrọńj, kuruńj.

PONZOLZIA PENTANDRA—icạk ạrak.

PORANA PANICULATA—pańjot nạṛī.

PORTULACCA—(*oleracea*) moṭa uṛić alań, uṛić alań; (*quadrifolia*) nanha uṛić alań.

PREMNA—(*latifolia*) ḍańgra sea; (*herbacea*) kaḍa meť.

PSIDIUM GUYAVA—amrud, amrut, ạńjir.

PTEROCARPUS MARSUPIUM—murgạ.

PTEROSPERMUM ACERIFOLIUM—mackundạ.

PUERARIA TUBEROSA—jań tirṛạ, patal kohṇḍa, tirṛạ da.

PUNICA GRANATUM—anar, ḍalim.

PUTRANJIVA ROXBURGHII—pitońj.

RANDIA—(*dumetorum*) boi bindi, loṭo; (*uliginosa*) piṇḍe.

RAPHANUS SATIVUS—mulạ ạrak, murạị ạrak.

RICINUS COMMUNIS—eraṇḍom dare.

ROTTBOELLIA PERFORATA—kaṭkọm carẹć.

RUELLIA SUFFRUTICOSA—cạuliạ.

SACCHARUM—(*officinarum*) ạk; (*spontaneum*) kạsi ghās, khạsi ghās; (*sara*) sar, sạri sar.

SALIX TETRASPERMA—gaḍa sigrik, sũṛũkuć.

SANTALUM—candan, cọndọn.

SCHLEICHERA TRIJUGA—bạru, kusum.

SEMICARPUS ANACARDIUM—sọsọ.

SESAMUM INDICUM—kaṭ tilmiń, til, tilmiń.

SETARIA—(*italica*) erba; (*glauca*) kukrạ.

SHOREA ROBUSTA—jahẹr, sal, sarjọm.

SIDA—(*humilis*) bạriạṛ, joka sakam; (*carpinifolia*) bir miru baha.

SMILAX OVALIFOLIA—ạṭkir.

SOLANUM—(*melongena*) beńgaṛ, hẹndẹ beńgaṛ; (*stramonifolium*) beńgaṛ beṭaheť; (*xanthocarpum*) ẹḍhẹ rạńgạini, rạńgạini.

SOPUBIA DELPHINIFOLIA—dak kudur.

SORGHUM VULGARE—bajṛa.

SOYMIDA FEBRIFUGA—ruhen.

SPATHOLOBUS ROXBURGHII—bando, cihũṭ laṛ.

SPERMACOCE HISPIDA—piṭuạ ạrak, piṭuạ ghās.

SPIDAGATHIS CRISTATA—agyo.

SPONDIAS MANGIFERA—amṛa.

STEPHEGYNE PARVIFOLIA—gõṛẽ.

STERCULIA—(*villosa*) gańjheṛ; (*urens*) telheć, terheć; (*colorata*) udạl.

STEREOSPERMUM SUAVIOLENS—paḍer.

STREBLUS ASPER—sahṛa.

STROBILANTHUS AURICULATUS—gaḍa kalha, harna pakoṛ.

STRYCHNOS POTATORUM—khucilạ, khuclạ, kucilạ, kuclạ.

SYMPLOCOS RACEMOSA—lodam.

TACCA PINNATIFIDA—bońga ṭaeni, ṭạini.

TAMARINDUS INDICUS—jọjọ dare.

TAMARIX ERICOIDES—jhāwar.

TECTONA GRANDIS—loṭpoṭo dare, sagun, sạgunạ, sagwan.

TERMINALIA—(*tomentosa*) atnak; (*arjuna*) kạuhạ; (*belerica*) lọpọń dare; (*chebula*) juńgi, rọl.

TETRANTHERA MONOPETALA—pojo.

THEMUDA GIGANTEA—kũs.

THESPASIA LAMPAS—bọnkạpsi.

THEVITIA NERIIFOLIA—bereńjọ.

THYSANOLOENA ACARIFERA—karsaṛ, kharsaṛ.

TRAGIA INVOLUCRATA—sẹńgẹl siń.

TREMA AMBOINENSIS—jhāwar.

TRITICUN SATIVUM—guhum.

TRIUMFETTA RHOMBOIDEA—nanha bhiḍi janaṭeť.

TYLOPHORA LONGIFOLIA—sondhaeni.

URARIA LAGOPOIDES—lọpọń heṛak.

URENA SINUATA—moṭa bhiḍi janaṭeť.

UTRICULARIA BIFIDA—arak jhāwar.

VANDA ROXBURGHII—dare bańki.

VENTILAGO CALYCULATA—bońga sarjọm, sarjọm.

VERNONIA—(*cinerea*) bạhu ṭuṭuri, barañgom, bir lọpọṅ arak', ḍuryạ arak', jhurjhuri, ṭuṭuri; (*anthelmintica*) sãoraj; (*divergens*) baṛa pathol; (*roxburghii*) ḍora bọhọk'.

VIGNA—(*vexillata*) bir ghañgra, seṛwañ; (*catiang*) boḍa ghañgra, cihṛi ghañgra, ḍañ ghañgra, ghañgra, ghạngri.

VISCUM—(*attenuatum*) kaṭkọm jañga; (*monoicum*) peṭcamṛa banda.

VITEX—(*alata*) bhạdu; (*negundo*) sindwạri dare.

VITIS—(*adnata*) bod nạṛi, bodlaṛ nạṛi; (*tomentosa*) ghoṛa lidi; (*latifolia*) ićer, ićewer.

WEDELIA WALLICHII—mạsuṛdañ.

WENDLANDIA—(*exserta*) pichạri baha; (*tinctoria*) tilại dare.

WOODFORDIA FLORIBUNDA—icạk'. nicạk'.

WRIGHTIA TOMENTOSA—aṭkuṛạ, aṭkuṛạ arak', buru mackunda.

YUCCA GLORIOSA—ghi kuạr.

ZEA MAYS—goco, joṇḍra.

ZEHNERIA UMBELLATA—at, kundri.

ZINGIBER OFFICINALE—ada, adhẹ.

ZIZYPHUS—(*jujuba*) ḍeḍhaoṛe, ḍiḍhauṛi, ẹdhẹ jạnum, jạnum, jọm jạnum; (*xylopyra*) karkaṭ; (*oxyphylla*) kuṛić rama, rama kuṛić; (*rugosa*) sekra.

ZORNIA DIPHYLLA—jhạpni, ṭạṇḍi jhạpni

PUFF—BALLS.

LYCOPERDON—puṭkạ.